# SMOKESTACKS

## an anthology of

Wild
Onion
Books

EDITED BY
DAVID STARKEY AND
RICHARD GUZMAN

# SKYSCRAPERS

## chicago writing

an
imprint of
loyola press
chicago

 **Wild Onion Books**

*an imprint of*
Loyola Press
3441 North Ashland Avenue
Chicago, Illinois 60657

*Wild Onion Books publishes titles on Chicago themes that offer diverse perspectives on the city and surrounding area, its history, its culture, and its religions. Wild onion is a common nickname for Chicago.*

Copyright acknowledgments appear on pages 536–38 and constitute a continuation of this copyright page.

*Interior design by Jill R. Shimabukuro*

**Library of Congress Cataloging-in-Publication Data**
Smokestacks & skyscrapers : an anthology of Chicago writing / edited
  by David Starkey and Richard Guzman.
      p.   cm.
    ISBN 0-8294-1013-9 (pbk.)
    1. American literature — Illinois — Chicago. 2. Chicago (Ill.) —
Literary collections. I. Starkey, David, 1952 – . II. Guzman, Richard.
III. Title: Smokestacks and skyscrapers.
PS572.C5S56 1999
810.8'0977311 — dc21                                     98-54708
                                                          CIP

Printed in the United States of America
99 00 01 02 03 / 10 9 8 7 6 5 4 3 2 1

# Contents

# Acknowledgments

David Starkey wishes to thank the following: Ann Durkin Keating of the North Central College history department for help, both early and late, in putting Chicago literature in historical perspective; the Faculty Development Committee of North Central College for a summer grant that enabled me to investigate more fully nineteenth- and early-twentieth-century authors; and, above all, June Sawyers of Loyola Press for her unflagging enthusiasm for the project. A widely recognized expert on all things Chicago, June could easily be listed as a third co-editor of *Smokestacks and Skyscrapers*. Without her dedication, this volume would not exist.

Richard Guzman wishes to thank Gwendolyn Brooks for her generosity, Carlos Cumpian for his forbearance, Jim McManus for his encouragement of and enthusiasm for Chicago literature, June Sawyers at Loyola Press for so firmly and graciously editing the editors, and Linda Bonifas for her extraordinary friendship.

# Introduction

*Aurora on in to Lake Michigan, from Half Day to Flossmoor, King Panic reigns in fast forward. Believe it. The Hawk has skipped town it's so hectic. While above the Sears Tower, on this crisp Tuesday morning of bright zero Indian summer, a chevron of mallards flies by, headed north by northwest toward the Arctic. It's strange. Traffic's impacted along Lake Shore Drive and the Kennedy, on the Ryan and Edens and Stevenson, and on 294 and the Daley — and out toward O'Hare it gets worse. The side streets are no picnic either. Down Cottage Grove, across 35th Street, up Halsted, it's one long gigantic stampede. The Magnificent Mile's a bad joke. Suicides bounce down the sides of the Hancock, finding the future in huge frantic gulps, while a single handheld Panasonic is catching the antics of gawkers. Looters and gropers are having a field day as well, getting trampled and crushed in the process, but still. And the Loop's a continuous frenzy. There's gunfire, bloodshed galore, and loud music, and countless premortem tableaux. Just believe it. For while in most other million-plus cities much north of the Tropic of Cancer it's already all but all over, in Chicago it's still just beginning.*

JAMES McMANUS

✦ ✦ ✦

The word *crude* has shadowed Chicago culture since at least 1892, when Stanley Waterloo accused the influential Chicago journal *The Dial* of fawning over sophisticated East Coast writers. Eugene Field lampoons another sort of philistinism in "Professor Lowell in Chicago": the young, bombastic city's unjustified pride in its own cultural life. There's Sherwood Anderson's essay "An Apology for Crudity." There's Theodore Dreiser's description of Chicago as a "poet in chaps and buckskin . . . a maundering yokel with an epic in its mouth." In *With the Procession*, Henry Blake Fuller shows us crass commerce, full of "vast and vulgar" storefronts "heaped with cheap truck cheaply ticketed." "A raw, slangy city," Albert Halper called it.

But this crudity isn't just a matter of rawness or yokeldom: it's a matter of energy. This is, as Carl Sandburg tells us in his now famous lines, a new, unprecedented powerhouse: "Flinging magnetic curses and the toil of piling job on job, here is a tall bold slugger set vivid against the little soft cities; / Fierce as a dog with tongue lapping for action, cunning as a savage pitted against the wilderness." We began with the opening page of James McManus's *Chin Music*, a page crackling with a kind of energy that has both blessed and cursed Chicago writing. In that novel the missiles of World War III have been launched, forcing, among other things, the cancellation of game three of the World Series. Yet in Chicago it *isn't* over. There's something about this city's rumbling, El-train capitalism, its taste for cutting deals, its toddling-town gangsterism that seems to emit an energy shield so strong it could keep even missiles at bay. It has certainly kept its writers and artists at bay.

In Chicago, as Saul Bellow often complained, "The pulse of culture beats thinly." And, in a 1918 speech read to the Women's Aid Organization, Frank Lloyd Wright wrote:

> To know Chicago is an experience in first principles: a despair and a great hope. A despair, not so much because Chicago is cruel and crude as because "culture" has been stuck upon its surface as a businessman's expedient or thoughtlessly bought by the rich as a luxury. Bought in blissful ignorance of the more vital, less fashionable contribution Chicago has to make to life.

To know what that hope, that contribution, is, you have to fight through layers of anticulture grime. Chicago is physical before it's intellectual, the city of broad shoulders, a working city always suspicious of the smart guy. George Ade's character Artie is typical in his mistrust of anything that smacks of dandyism: "There was too many Charley-boys ridin'. You know the kind I mean — them dubs with the long hair and the badges all over the coats. . . . I couldn't stand for nothin' like that. They was out just to make a show o' themselves." So culture is indeed second class here; but while that might make Chicago a Second City in this respect, there's always been a feeling here that being culturally First is effete — is New Yorkish. "It's robust," says Cyrus Colter, comparing New York and Chicago. "It's less academic, precious, and mandarin — less Byzantine." "New York affects a superior sophistication, and in part it is genuine," noted H. L. Mencken. "But in Chicago there is an eagerness to hear and see, to experience and experiment." New York is Broadway. If Chicago has to have culture, nothing less than the noble sweep of Greek drama will do. "I went to Chicago as a migrant from Mississippi," wrote Richard Wright in his introduction to St. Clair Drake and Horace R. Cayton's *Black Metropolis,*

> And there in that great iron city, that impersonal, mechanical city, amid the steam, the smoke, the snowy winds, the blistering suns; there in that self-conscious city,

that city so deadly dramatic and stimulating, we caught whispers of the meanings that life could have, and we were pushed and pounded by facts much too big for us. Many migrants like us were driven and pursued, in the manner of characters in a Greek play, down the paths of defeat; but luck must have been with us, for we somehow survived.

Wright had fled to Chicago, he says, "with the dumb yearning to write, to tell my story." If Chicago energy, Chicago no-nonsense impatience, has re-signed art, music, literature — the whole "culture" thing — to the sidelines, it has somehow also nourished it there as well with a constant flow of particulars so brute and extreme that writing can't help but get fat on them. It is the hard, unforgiving facts of the real world that send Nick Romano to the electric chair in Willard Motley's *Knock on Any Door*. The city defeats all challenges to its hegemony. Or as Nelson Algren writes, "Between the curved street of the El and the nearest Clark Street hockshop, between the penny arcade and the shooting gallery, between the basement ginmill and the biggest juke in Bronzeville, the prairie is caught for keeps at last." That's why "realism" or "gritty realism" are other terms most often applied to Chicago literature. Even when speaking of the fantasy and reality combined in Stuart Dybek's work, Fred Shafer says, ". . . yet the fantasy and the myth seem to come right out of the reality, and they come right out of Chicago reality." Dybek himself says:

> . . . Chicago doesn't have a Márquez. The big names that people pull out of a hat are Farrell and Dreiser, and one of the great achievements, one of the things that people love Bellow for, applaud him for, is the fact he had maintained kind of an original voice and yet has remained a realist. There's a strong stake in maintaining and sustaining realism.

Bellow owes more to Chicago's grinding materialism than he probably wants to admit. There may even be important aspects to Chicago materialism that distinguish it from the materialism now ascendant in late twentieth century America. Again, the word *crude* comes to mind, a vision of the chastising Robert Herrick appears. But perhaps we can understand it all better by pro-posing that Chicago's materialism is new and open as opposed to contempo-rary and diffused, that it is ordinary as opposed to sophisticated, and that it has somehow led to visions that are more compassionate than cynical.

To risk an ultraposh stance momentarily, we refer to Michel Foucault's idea that the greater the power, the greater it masks itself, and the greater it diffuses into a host of particulars and largely hidden networks. (Just ask nineteenth-century Native Americans like Metea and Simon Pokagon, who saw their land stolen from them through all manner of subterfuge.) Yet for all the secret corridors and smoke-filled backrooms that Chicago power travels through to create Chicago materialism, one still sees its processes and products always unmasking themselves in stunning ways — most times deploringly, virulently, sometimes with a naiveté that borders on sweetness. When Martin Luther King, Jr., called Chicago the most segregated city in America, it was certainly an indictment, but also a curious testimony to the open bluntness of its racism, the unapologetic squalor of its turf wars. For all its vaunted hidden controls, we were reminded over and over again as Chicago awaited the 1996 Democratic National Convention, of how openly the ugly workings of the Daley machine appeared in 1968. If a Byzantine diffuseness and an ultracovert insidiousness characterize materialism in contemporary America, Chicago, while claiming more than its fair share of these, still also retains an odd openness. Look at the early heroines of Chicago fiction — Hamlin Garland's Rose Dutcher, Elia Peattie's Kate Barrington, Theodore Dreiser's Carrie Meeber, Willa Cather's Thea Kornblum: they all find something of what they are looking for because so much here is so clearly exposed, even to the uninitiated eye. Even Wright, who felt pushed here and there by Greek fates, finally characterized Chicago as "the known city." Everything about it, including its materialism, is *there*, or *out there* — or will be soon.

When E. B. White wrote about New York, he tended to focus on emanations, vibrations, invisible buffers. In contrast, this *there-ness* defines Chicago, as does what Reginald Gibbons calls "a profound and appealing ordinariness in the world of people and of relationships." Chicago and Chicago writing reject urbane sophistication, placing a premium on what Stuart Dybek refers to as "a certain kind of savvy . . . more like street smarts . . . Hemingway called it having a good crap-detector." There's a certain cynicism in this, but, as Dybek notes, it's a cynicism mixed with "another trademark of Chicago writing, one that maybe distinguishes it from other urban traditions, a certain sentimental streak."

In *Notes of a Native Son* James Baldwin warns us about sentimentalists. Their ostentatious parading of feelings, their moist eyes, conceal an arid heart, an inability to feel, and, therefore, says Baldwin, "a violent inhumanity." There's some of that kind of sentimentality in Chicago writing, but not in most of what we have selected here. If it is sentimental, it's a sentimentality rising from struggling and somehow managing to survive a violent inhumanity, that "deadly dramatic" ethos Richard Wright described, an ethos that traps people between the grandest buildings in America and a poverty as extreme as any in the world. "Compassion" is a better word. We prevail, rising above a suicidal cynicism because we somehow come through the most crushing circumstances of life, amid the indifferent materialism of the city, with our capacity to feel still, miraculously, intact. That's what so much of the literature collected here seems to say and to celebrate. Jane Addams points to "the mixed goodness of Chicago . . . the simple kindness of the most wretched to each other." It shows in Karl Shapiro's blending of a detached, nearly cynical vision of human pride and folly with a tenderness toward the disasters of life, and in Maxine Chernoff's coupling of "deflationary humor" with an admiration for the difficult ways people adapt to life's unexpected turnings. It is here too in the way Sterling Plumpp says the blues "Tacks declarations / on confinement. / Mates / its words over the bonding pond of / drought."

"There is an open and raw beauty about that city," says Richard Wright, "that seems either to kill or endow one with the spirit of life." "Everything," claims Albert Halper, "comes into Chicago." Again, *there-ness*, an openness amid the crudity, and person after person, writer after writer, has taken a chance on Chicago because of that. Some — Bellow, Algren — send themselves into exile rather than face the city's monumental indifference. More — Finley Peter Dunne, Robert Herrick, Edgar Lee Masters, Ring Lardner — seem to wither when they leave, cut off from the vitality the city gives so grudgingly, but gives nonetheless. So Chicago's is an immigrant *and* an emigrant literature, like so much of its population. But whether they have stayed or left, or, as in Ana Castillo's case, stayed and left and returned, all the writers in this anthology have vital Chicago connections, and Chicago forms the backdrop of most of the pieces we have chosen. We move through the ethnic neighborhoods of Finley Peter Dunne, Willard Motley, Harry Mark Petrakis, Maxine Chernoff, and Tony Ardizzone, into the West Point Baptist Church at Thirty-sixth and Cottage Grove and into Mount Pisgah at Forty-sixth and King Drive with Leon Forrest, into a dormant Comiskey Park with Neil Tesser, into the hothouse atmosphere of the Chicago Stadium with James McManus. Sterling Plumpp celebrates the blues and Koko Taylor. Saul Bellow ranges from the city's business elite to its small-time hoods. Daniel Pinkwater tries to return to a classic greasy spoon of his childhood, and, unfortunately, succeeds, though he shows in a strange way how a lousy childhood can be redeemed simply because it was lived in Chicago. And there is a larger Chicago history, too, some of it filled with blood: Simon Pokagon's story of the Fort Dearborn Massacre, Haki R. Madhubuti's memorial to the deaths of Fred Hampton and Mark Clark, and Gwendolyn Brooks's tribute to the death of Emmett Till. These pieces illustrate and complicate the ideas of energy, materialism, and openness we have tossed around here. So much of this material, even in its most horrific moments, moves to a distinctly Chicago rhythm, a beat that leads from dire circumstances, through a near-fatal cynicism, to a miraculous survival of human feeling, even if that survival is so tenuously balanced.

There are exceptions, of course, like Richard Wright's portrayal of Bigger Thomas's growing hatred of do-good white liberals, or James T. Farrell's over-the-edge cynicism in "Studs." But it has also been Wright's comments about both despair and hope that have run through this introduction nearly from beginning to end, and, as many have commented, Farrell was driven by a pity and loathing for meanness and ugliness, for anything that destroyed human feeling. No, as bitter as some of the pieces may get, the other rhythm holds its own. Sometimes you can feel it in the smallest passages. "I finished lunch with my spring wheat man in the Wrigley Restaurant," writes Richard Stern in "Packages,"

> . . . and walked alone by the Chicago River. Immense brightness, the Sun-Times Building a cube of flame. All around, the steel-and-glass dumbness of this beautiful, cruel town. *I noticed, then noticed I noticed, the bodies of women, white and black. Thank you, Mother, for my pleasure in such sights.*

Or near the end of "Loverboys," where Ana Castillo writes:

> There's something insupportable about being pissed with the one person on this planet that sends your adrenaline flowing to remind you that you're alive. It's almost like we're mad because we've been shocked out of our usual comatose state of being by feeling something for someone, for ourselves, for just a moment.

You feel it in the total pattern of so many pieces: In the way the often cold and satiric Kate Barrington in Elia Peattie's *The Precipice* is nevertheless the recipient of so many "silent good wishes . . . that the world of pain and shame would not too soon destroy what was gallant and trustful in her." In the way Carolyn Rodgers's poem "how i got ovah II/It Is Deep II" speaks of someone returning to church "just when i thought i had gotten away" and is surprised by the touch of the Holy Ghost. Or at the end of the excerpt from Paul Hoover's *Saigon, Illinois,* in the way Mr. Grubbs calls the protagonist a "contemptible weakling" and yet the two of them realizing they are mourning the death of Grubbs' son, Terry, *together.* "Even our pretended culture is not yet vicious," wrote Frank Lloyd Wright in 1918; and it could be that for all the viciousness of the city and all the viciousness in its literature, there's something here that's kept our feelings alive. Though we are often despondent, maybe the atmosphere isn't precious or pretentious enough to sustain the supposedly higher forms of despair.

Maybe Chicago just never grew up. That is, it never listened to all those adult voices that equated maturity with cultural sophistication, or with making all the correct, responsible choices and compromises that slowly settle us into a life of quiet desperation. In the 1998 *Esquire* magazine poll of great restaurant cities, Chicago comes in second again, this time to San Francisco; and it does so not necessarily on the strength of its food, but because of an atmosphere heavy on fun and light on pretension. When David Letterman brought his show to Chicago some years back, one noticed — in contrast to the cool enthusiasm of New York laughter, the demure spaciness of L.A. laughter — a Chicago overeagerness that seemed to want to claim sophistication on the one hand, but whose porky good-heartedness revealed the persistence — the *survival* — of an openness, an ordinariness, even a sentimentality that touches its literature as well, sometimes for ill, but also for good. We wrote the first draft of this introduction just days after experiencing the Grant Park celebration of the Chicago Bulls's fourth NBA championship in six years. For all the ego, all the money involved, all the secrecy endemic to dealings with the two Jerrys (owner Reinsdorf and general manager Krause), there also shone forth in that celebration an old-fashioned faith in the virtues of family (as extolled by Michael Jordan), of community (extolled, via Zen, by Phil Jackson), of hard work (extolled by Dennis Rodman, whose dyed, tattooed *there-ness* is thin cover for his shy, teary sentimentality). Even the normally moody, diffused Scottie Pippen presumed to bypass the smoky contract negotiations sure to follow by publicly pleading for the return of Jordan, Rodman, and Jackson. It was a wonderful expression of a sweet faith in openness, and everything was embraced with an unironic goodwill that bordered on the gullible.

It's probably dangerous to end an introduction to a literary anthology this close to the posture of the Chicago Super Fans, whose obsession with the Bears and the Bulls is satirized via Second City on *Saturday Night Live*. In a way such a conclusion might be interpreted as doing what we've said Chicago always does to its artists: pushes them to the sidelines. This, however, is not our intent. Jim McManus, the author of the passage that opens the introduction, juxtaposes the Bulls and Dante in "Finalogy," also included here. Finally, our hope for this anthology is this: that it will help culture, especially literary culture, to be seen less and less as marginalized, but as standing next to, juxtaposed to, the grinding materialism and all of the other bursting concerns that have traditionally maintained literature's second-class stature. Perhaps that's the best we can hope for in Chicago — and, all in all, that's no paltry hope. In *Notes of a Native Son,* James Baldwin called America a nation "dedicated to the death of the paradox," and therefore unwilling to confront the grit, complexity, and humanity of real life. Taken as a whole, the pieces in *Smokestacks and Skyscrapers* capture and complicate the paradoxical balance of hope and despair, material crudity and spiritual aura, bitter experience and sweet innocence. They make a fair claim that Chicago and its literature are less typical of America's dedication to the death of paradox, and hence more faithful to life.

# Jacques Marquette, S.J.

## (1637-75)

JACQUES MARQUETTE, *a Jesuit priest, was born in Laon, France, in 1637 and died near present-day Ludington, Michigan, in 1675. An adventurous spirit, Father Marquette passed up the opportunity to teach in French universities so that he could evangelize in the New World. He arrived in Quebec in 1666, and by 1673 was accompanying Louis Jolliet in birch bark canoes on an expedition that eventually reached the Mississippi River. On a subsequent voyage of exploration, Marquette's party landed at the mouth of the Chicago River. All the evidence of his journal would seem to indicate that the winter Father Marquette spent in Chicago was a miserable one. Living in a tiny cabin near what is now Damen Avenue and the South Branch of the river, he suffered from dysentery and fever, relying in part on the good graces of the local Native Americans to help him make it through the brutal season. Father Marquette's prose is spare and to the point. He records important things: the game that was killed, the goods that were traded or given to the "Sauvages," how his body felt, the status of his soul. While it would be foolish to ascribe Chicago's literary ethos to a single stray traveler, there is, nevertheless, something about Jacques Marquette's plainspokenness that would reverberate through Chicago literature for centuries to come. The translation used here, by Reuben A. Thwaites, was first published in 1902.*

✦ ✦ ✦

## *from* FATHER MARQUETTE'S JOURNAL

DECEMBER 1, 1674 — We went ahead of the *Sauvages* so that I might celebrate the holy mass.

3 — After saying holy mass, we embarked, and were compelled to make for a point, so that we could land, on account of floating masses of ice.

4 — We started with a favoring wind, and reached the river of the portage, which was frozen to the depth of half a foot; there was more snow there than elsewhere, as well as more tracks of animals and Turkeys.

Navigation on the lake is fairly good from one portage to the other, for there is no crossing to be made, and one can land anywhere, unless one persist in going on when the waves are high and the wind is strong. The land bordering it is of no value, except on the prairies. There are 8 or 10 quite fine rivers. Deer-hunting is very good, as one goes away from the Poutewatamis.

12 — As we began yesterday to haul our baggage in order to approach the portage, the Ilinois who had left the Poutewatamis arrived, with great difficulty. We were unable to celebrate holy mass on the day of the Conception, owing to the bad weather and cold. During our stay at the entrance of the river, Pierre and Jacques killed 3 cattle and 4 deer, one of which ran some distance with its heart split in 2. We contented ourselves with killing 3 or 4 turkeys, out of the many that came around our cabin because they were almost dying of hunger. Jacques brought in a partridge that he had killed, exactly like those of France except that it had two ruffs, as it were, of 3 or 4 feathers as long as a finger, near the head, covering the 2 sides of the neck where there are no feathers.

14 — Having encamped near the portage, 2 leagues up the river, we resolved to winter there, as it was impossible to go farther, since we were too much hindered and my ailment did not permit me to give myself much fatigue. Several Ilinois passed yesterday, on their way to carry furs to nawaskingwe; we gave them one of the cattle and one of the deer that Jacque had killed on the previous day. I do not think that I have ever seen any *Sauvages* more eager for French tobacco than they. They came and threw beaver-skins at our feet, to get some pieces of it; but we returned these, giving them some pipefuls of the tobacco because we had not yet decided whether we would go farther.

15 — Chachagwessiou and the other Ilinois left us, to go and join their people and give them the goods that they had brought, in order to obtain their robes. In this they act like the traders, and give hardly any more than do the French. I instructed them before their departure, deferring the holding of a council until the spring, when I should be in their village. They traded us 3 fine robes of ox-skins for a cubit of tobacco; these were very useful to us during the winter. Being thus rid of them, we said the Mass of the Conception. After the 14th, my disease turned into a bloody flux.

30 — Jacque arrived from the Ilinois village, which is only six leagues from here; there they were suffering from hunger, because the cold and snow prevented them from hunting. Some of them notified la Toupine and the surgeon that we were here; and, as they could not leave their cabin, they had so frightened the *Sauvages*, believing that we would suffer from hunger if we remained here, that Jacque had much difficulty in preventing 15 young men from coming to carry away all our belongings.

JANUARY 16, 1675 —As soon as the 2 frenchmen learned that my illness prevented me from going to them the surgeon came here with a *Sauvage*, to bring us some blueberries and corn. They are only 18 leagues from here, in a fine place for hunting cattle, deer, and turkeys, which are excellent there. They had also collected provisions while waiting for us —; and had given the *Sauvages* to understand that their cabin belonged to the black gown; and it may be said that they have done and said all that could be expected from them. After the surgeon had spent some time here, in order to perform his devotions, I sent Jacque with him to tell the Ilinois near that place that my illness prevented me from going to see them; and that I would even have some difficulty in going there in the spring, if it continued.

24 —Jacque returned with a sack of corn and other delicacies, which the French had given him for me. He had also brought the tongues and flesh of two cattle, which a *Sauvage* and he had killed near here. But all the animals feel the bad weather.

26 — 3 Ilinois brought us, on behalf of the elders, 2 sacks of corn, some dried meat, pumpkins, and 12 beaver-skins; 1st, to make me a mat; 2nd, to ask me for powder; 3rd, that we might not be hungry; 4th, to obtain a few goods. I replied; 1st, that I had come to instruct them, by speaking to them of prayer, etc.; 2nd, that I would give them no powder, because we sought to restore peace everywhere, and I did not wish them to begin war with the muiamis; 3rd, that we feared not hunger; 4th, that I would encourage the french to bring them goods, and that they must give satisfaction to those who were among them for the beads which they had taken as soon as the surgeon started to come here. As they had come a distance of 20 leagues I gave them, in order to reward them for their trouble and for what they had brought me, a hatchet, 2 knives, 3 clasp-knives, 10 brasses of glass beads, and 2 double mirrors, telling them that I would endeavor to go to the village, — for a few days only, if my illness continued. They told me to take courage, and to remain and die in their country and that they had been informed that I would remain there for a long time.

FEBRUARY 9 — Since we addressed ourselves to the Blessed Virgin Immaculate, and commenced a novena with a mass, — at which Pierre and Jacque, who do everything they can to relieve me, received communion, — to ask God to restore my health, my bloody flux has left me, and all that remains is a weakness of the stomach. I am beginning to feel much better, and to regain my strength. Out of a cabin of Ilinois, who encamped near us for a month, a portion have again taken the road to the Poutewatamis, and some are still on the lake-shore, where they wait until navigation is open. They bear letters for our Fathers of st. François.

20 — We have had opportunity to observe the tides coming in from the lake, which rise and fall several times a day; and, although there seems to be no shelter in the lake, we have seen the ice going against the wind. These tides made the water good or bad, because that which flows from above come from the prairies and small streams. The deer which are plentiful near the lake-shore, are so lean that we had to abandon some of those which we had killed.

MARCH 23 — We killed several partridges, only the males of which had ruffs on the neck, the females not having any. These partridges are very good, but not like those of france.

30 — The north wind delayed the thaw until the 25th of March, when it set in with a south wind. On the very next day, game began to make its appearance. We killed 30 pigeons, which I found better than those down the great river; but they are smaller, both old and young. On the 28th, the ice broke up, and stopped above us. On the 29th, the waters rose so high that we had barely time to decamp as fast as possible, putting our goods in the trees, and trying to sleep on a hillock. The water gained on us nearly all night, but there was a slight freeze, and the water fell a little, while we were near our packages. The barrier has just broken, the ice has drifted away; and, because the water is already rising, we are about to embark to continue our journey.

The blessed Virgin Immaculate has taken such care of us during our wintering that we have not lacked provisions, and have still remaining a large sack of corn, with some meat and fat. We also lived very pleasantly, for my illness did not prevent me from saying holy mass every day. We were unable to keep Lent, except on Fridays and Saturdays.

# Metea

## (?-1827)

*A Potawatomi chief from near the Wabash River,* METEA's *birth date is unknown, although it is believed that he fought for the British during the War of 1812 and died in 1827. Metea's words come to us translated by explorer Henry Rowe Schoolcraft, who included the speech in his* Travels in the Central Portions of the Mississippi Valley *(1825); the address was later reprinted in* Pictures of Illinois One Hundred Years Ago *(1918).*

*Metea addressed the 1821 Chicago Council four times. (Note: "My Father" was a traditional Native American expression of respect to whites.) The first address, delivered on August 19, is reprinted below. Schoolcraft described Metea's oratory as follows: "His sentences have a measured flow, and he always appears to have a ready comment of language. His voice is not unpleasant, nor can his manner be considered as vehement, comparatively speaking. It is rather in his sentiments, than in his action and manner, that he is bold, fearless, and original."*

✦ ✦ ✦

## *Address at the Chicago Council*

My Father,—We meet you here to-day because we had promised it, to tell you our minds, and what we have agreed upon among ourselves. You will listen to us with a good mind, and believe what we say.

My Father,—You know that we first came to this country a long time ago, and when we sat ourselves down upon it, we met with a great many hardships and difficulties. Our country was then very large, but it has dwindled away to a small spot; and you wish to purchase that! This has caused us to reflect much upon what you have told us, and we have, therefore, brought along all the chiefs and warriors, and the young men and women and children of our tribe, that one part may not do what the other objects to, and that all may be witness of what is going forward.

My Father, — You know your children. Since you first came among them, they have listened to your words with an attentive ear, and have always hearkened to your counsels. Whenever you have had a proposal to make to us — whenever you have had a favour to ask of us, we have always lent a favourable ear, and our invariable answer has been "Yes." This you know!

My Father, — A long time has passed since we first came upon our lands; and our people [ancestors] have all sunk into their graves. They had sense [wisdom]. We are all young and foolish, and do not wish to do anything that they would not approve, were they living. We are fearful we shall offend their spirits if we sell our lands; and we are fearful we shall offend you, if we do *not* sell them. This has caused us great perplexity of thought, because we have counselled among ourselves, and do not know how we can part with the land.

My Father, — Our country was given to us by the Great Spirit, who gave it to us to hunt upon, and to make down our beds upon, when we die. And he would never forgive us, should we now bargain it away. When you first spoke to us for land at St. Mary's, [Ohio], we said we had a little, and agreed to sell you a piece of it; but we told you we could spare no more. Now, you ask us again. You are never satisfied!

My Father, — We have sold you a great tract of land already; but it is not enough! We sold it to you for the benefit of your children, to farm and to live upon. We have now but little left. We shall want it all for ourselves. We know not how long we may live, and we wish to leave some lands for our children to hunt upon. You are gradually taking away our hunting grounds. Your children are driving us before them. We are growing uneasy. What lands you have, you may retain for ever; but we shall sell no more.

My Father, — You think, perhaps, that I speak in passion; but my heart is good towards you. I speak like one of your own children. I am an Indian, a redskin, and live by hunting and fishing, but my country is already too small; and I do not know how to bring up my children, if I give it all away. We sold you a fine tract of land at St. Mary's. We said to you then, it was enough to satisfy your children, and the last we should sell; and we thought it would be the last you would ask for.

My Father, — We have now told you what we had to say. It is what was determined on, in council among ourselves; and what I have spoken is the voice of my nation. On this account, all our people have come here to listen to me; but do not think we have a bad opinion of you. Where should we get a bad opinion of you? We speak to you with a good heart, and the feelings of a friend.

My Father, — You are acquainted with this piece of land — the country we live in. Shall we give it up? Take notice it is a small piece of land, and if we give it away, what will become of us? The Great Spirit, who has provided it for our use, allows us to keep it, to bring up our young men and support our families. We should incur his anger, if we bartered it away. If we had more land, you should get more, but our land has been wasting away ever since the white people became our neighbours, and we have now hardly enough left to cover the bones of our tribe.

My Father, — You are in the midst of your red children. What is due us, in money, we wish, and will receive at this place; and we want nothing more.

My Father, — We all shake hands with you. Behold our warriors, our women and children. Take pity on us, and on our words.

# Juliette Kinzie

## (1806-70)

JULIETTE KINZIE *was born Juliette Augusta Magill to a prominent New England family in Middletown, Connecticut, in 1806. She married John H. Kinzie, an "Agent of Indian Affairs," in July 1830, and in September they came by steamboat from Detroit to the wilderness outpost of Fort Dearborn. Although much of the information and inspiration for* Wau-Bun *(named after the Kinzie's house) was provided by her mother-in-law, Eleanor Little Kinzie, it is Juliette Kinzie who ultimately assembled family and local history into a vivid chronicle of "the early day in the north-west."*

*Following the successful publication of* Wau-Bun *in 1856, Juliette Kinzie published two frontier novels in the 1860s:* Walter Ogilby *and* Mark Logan the Bourgeois. *In all three books, Kinzie's style is polite and generally sanguine. Chapter 17 of* Wau-Bun *gives a sample of her prose as well as a fairly reliable picture of Chicago in 1831, when the city was little more than a scattered collection of rough-hewn buildings.*

*Juliette Kinzie's Chicago is, of course, completely unrecognizable to us today. Indeed, the city she first knew had virtually disappeared by the time she died in 1870.*

✦ ✦ ✦

## *from* WAU-BUN: THE "EARLY DAY" IN THE NORTH-WEST

Fort Dearborn at that day consisted of the same buildings as at present. They were, of course, in a better state of preservation, though still considerably dilapidated. They had been erected in 1816, under the supervision of Captain Hezekiah Bradley, and there was a story current that, such was his patriotic regard for the interests of the government, he obliged the soldiers to fashion wooden pins, instead of spikes and nails, to fasten the timbers of the buildings, and that he even called on the junior officers to aid in their construction along with the soldiers, whose business it was. If this were true, the captain must have labored under the delusion (excusable in one who had lived long on the frontier) that the government would thank its servants for any excess of economical zeal.

The fort was inclosed by high pickets, with bastions at the alternate angles. Large gates opened to the north and south, and there were small posterns here and there for the accommodation of the inmates. The bank of the river which stretches to the west, now covered by the light-house buildings, and inclosed by docks, was then occupied by the root-houses of the garrison. Beyond the parade-ground which extended south of the pickets, were the company gardens, well filled with currant-bushes and young fruit-trees.

The fort stood at what might naturally be supposed to be the mouth of the river, yet it was not so, for in those days the latter took a turn, sweeping round the promontory on which the fort was built, towards the south, and joined the lake about half a mile below; so that these buildings, in fact, stood on the right bank of the river, the left being formed by a long spit of land extending from the northern shore, of which it formed a part. After the cutting through of this portion of the left bank in 1833 by the United States Engineers employed to construct a harbor at this point, and the throwing out of the piers, the water overflowed this long tongue of land, and continually encroaching on the southern bank, robbed it of many valuable acres; while, by the same action of the vast body of the lake, an accretion was constantly taking place on the north of the harbor.

The residence of Jean Baptiste Beaubien stood at this period between the gardens and the river-bank, and still further south was a rickety tenement, built many years before by Mr. John Dean, the sutler of the post. A short time after the commencement of the growth of Chicago, the foundations of this building were undermined by the gradual encroachment of the lake, and it tumbled backward down the bank, where it long lay, a melancholy spectacle.

On the northern bank of the river, directly facing the fort, was the family mansion of my husband. It was a long, low building, with a piazza extending along its front, a range of four or five rooms. A broad green space was inclosed between it and the river, and shaded by a row of Lombardy poplars. Two immense cotton-wood trees stood in the rear of the building, one of which still remains as an ancient landmark. A fine, well-cultivated garden extended to the north of the dwelling, and surrounding it were various buildings appertaining to the establishment — dairy, bake-house, lodging-house for the Frenchmen, and stables.

A vast range of sand-hills, covered with stunted cedars, pines, and dwarf-willow trees, intervened between the house and the lake, which was, at this time, not more than thirty rods distant.

Proceeding from this point, along the northern bank of the river, we came first to the Agency House, "Cobweb Castle," as it had been denominated while long the residence of a bachelor, and the *sobriquet* adhered to it ever after. It stood at what is now the south-west corner of Wolcott and N. Water streets. Many will still remember it, a substantial, compact little building of logs hewed and squared, with a centre, two wings, and, strictly speaking, two *tails*, since, when there was found no more room for additions at the sides, they were placed in the rear, whereon a vacant spot could be found.

These appendages did not mar the symmetry of the whole, as viewed from the front, but when, in the process of the town's improvement, a street was maliciously opened directly in the rear of the building, the whole establishment, with its comical little adjuncts, was a constant source of amusement to the passers-by. No matter. There were pleasant, happy hours passed under its odd-shaped roof, as many of Chicago's early settlers can testify.

Around the Agency House were grouped a collection of log-buildings, the residences of the different persons in the employ of Government, appertaining to that establishment — blacksmith, striker, and laborers. These were for the most part Canadians or half-breeds, with occasionally a stray Yankee, to set all things going by his activity and enterprise.

There was still another house on the north side of the river, built by a former resident of the name of Miller, but he had removed to "Rivière du Chemin," or Trail Creek, which about this time began to be called "Michigan City." This house, which stood near the forks of the river, was at this time vacant.

There was no house on the southern bank of the river, between the fort and "The Point," as the forks of the river were then called. The land was a low wet prairie, scarcely affording good walking in the dryest summer weather, while at other seasons it was absolutely impassable. A muddy streamlet, or as it is called in this country, a *slew*, after winding around from about the present site of the Tremont House, fell into the river at the foot of State street.

At the point, on the south side, stood a house just completed by Mark Beaubien, sen. It was a pretentious white two-story building, with bright blue wooden shutters, the admiration of all the little circle at Wolf Point. Here a canoe ferry was kept to transport people across the south branch of the river.

Facing down the river from the west was, first a small tavern kept by Mr. Wentworth, familiarly known as "Old Geese," not from any want of shrewdness on his part, but in compliment to one of his own cant expressions. Near him were two or three log-cabins occupied by Robinson, the Pottowattamie chief, and some of his wife's connexions. Billy Caldwell, the Sau-ga-nash, too, resided here occasionally, with his wife, who was a daughter of Nee-scot-neemeg, one of the most famous chiefs of the nation. A little remote from these residences was a small square log building, originally designed for a schoolhouse, but occasionally used as a place of worship whenever any itinerant minister presented himself.

The family of Clybourn had, previous to this time, established themselves near their present residence on the North Branch — they called their place *New Virginia*. Four miles up the South Branch was an old building which was at that time an object of great interest as having been the theatre of some stirring events during the troubles of 1812. It was denominated Lee's Place, or Hardscrabble. Here lived, at this time, a settler named Heacock.

Owing to the badness of the roads a greater part of the year, the usual mode of communication between the fort and "The Point" was by a boat rowed up the river, or by a canoe paddled by some skilful hand. By the latter means, too, an intercourse was kept up between the residents of the fort and the Agency House.

There were, at this time, two companies of soldiers in the garrison, but of the officers one, Lieutenant Furman, had died the autumn previous, and several of the others were away on furlough. In the absence of Major Fowle and Capt. Scott, the command devolved on Lieut. Hunter. Besides him, there were Lieuts. Engle and Foster — the latter unmarried. Dr. Finley, the post surgeon, was also absent, and his place was supplied by Dr. Harmon, a gentleman from Vermont.

My husband's mother, two sisters, and brother resided at the Agency House — the family residence near the lake being occupied by J. N. Bailey, the postmaster.

In the Dean House lived a Mr. and Mrs. Forbes, who kept a school. Gholson Kercheval had a small trading establishment in one of the log buildings at "Wolf Point," and John S. C. Hogan superintended the sutler's store in the garrison.

There was also a Mr. See lately come into the country, living at the Point, who sometimes held forth in the little school-house on a Sunday, less to the edification of his hearers than to the unmerciful slaughter of the "King's English."

I think this enumeration comprises all the white inhabitants of Chicago, at a period less than a quarter of a century ago. To many who may read these pages the foregoing particulars will, doubtless, appear uninteresting. But to those who visit Chicago, and still more, to those who come to make it their home, it may be not without interest to look back to its first beginnings; to contemplate the almost magical change which a few years have wrought; and from the past to augur the marvellous prosperity of the future.

# Benjamin Franklin Taylor
## (1819-87)

*Generally considered Chicago's first significant poet,* BENJAMIN FRANKLIN TAYLOR *was born in Lowville, New York, in 1819. He graduated from Hamilton Literary and Theological Institute in 1838 and moved to Michigan, where he lived until 1841. After working as a public school teacher, Taylor moved to Chicago in 1845 and served as the literary editor of the* Chicago Daily Journal *for the next twenty years. From 1865 to 1887, he lived in La Porte, Indiana (halfway between Chicago and South Bend), where he was a freelance poet and writer. Taylor died in Cleveland, Ohio, in 1887.*

*Benjamin Franklin Taylor's major works include the travel book* The World on Wheels *(1874),* Old Time Pictures and Sheaves of Rhyme *(1874),* Songs of Yesterday *(1875),* Dulce Domum *(1884), and* Complete Poetical Works *(1886). Although his work seems dated today, Taylor's poetry nevertheless reflects the early "booster" image of Chicago as a place of manifest destiny, unimpeded by catastrophes like the Fort Dearborn Massacre and the Great Fire. In "Fort Dearborn, Chicago," Taylor writes, "Her charter is no dainty thing of parchment and of pen, / But written on the prairie's page by full a million men." And in "Chicago," he personifies the city as Moses, who "rent his swaddling bands" and "beckoning to the drowsy lands / Made half the world Chicago Street."*

♦ ♦ ♦

## FORT DEARBORN, CHICAGO
*The Old — October 8th, '71.   The New — October 8th, '73.*

Born of the prairie and the wave — the blue sea and the green,
A city of the Occident, Chicago lay between;
Dim trails upon the meadow, faint wakes upon the main,
On either sea a schooner and a canvas-covered wain.

I saw a dot upon the map, and a house-fly's filmy wing —
They said 't was Dearborn's picket-flag when Wilderness was king;

I heard the reed-bird's morning song — the Indian's awkward flail —
The rice tattoo in his rude canoe like a dash of April hail —
The beaded grasses' rustling bend — the swash of the lazy tide,
Where ships shake out the salted sails and navies grandly ride!

I heard the Block-house gates unbar, the column's solemn tread,
I saw the Tree of a single leaf its splendid foliage shed
To wave awhile that August morn above the column's head;
I heard the moan of muffled drum, the woman's wail of fife,
The Dead March played for Dearborn's men just marching out of life,
The swooping of the savage cloud that burst upon the rank
And struck it with its thunderbolt in forehead and in flank,
The spatter of the musket-shot, the rifle's whistling rain —
The sand-hills drift round hope forlorn that never marched again!

I see in tasselled rank and file the regiments of corn,
Their bending sabres, millions strong, salute the summer morn;
The harvest-fields, as round and red as full-grown harvest moon;
That fill the broad horizons up with mimic gold of noon;
I count a thousand villages like flocks in pastures grand,
I hear the roar of caravans through all the blessèd land —
Chicago grasps the ripened year and holds it in her hand!
"Give us this day our daily bread!" the planet's Christian prayer;
Chicago with her open palm, makes answer everywhere!

I hear the march of multitudes who said the map was wrong —
They drew the net of Longitude and brought it right along,
And swung a great Meridian Line across the Foundling's breast,
And the city of the Occident was neither East nor West!
Her charter is no dainty thing of parchment and of pen,
But written on the prairie's page by full a million men;
They use the plowshare and the spade, and endless furrows run,
Line after line the record grows, and yet is just begun;
They rive the pines of Michigan and give them to the breeze —
The keel-drawn Charter's draft inscribes the necklace of the seas,
'Tis rudely sketched in anthracite, engraved on copper plate,
And traced across the Continent to Ophir's Golden Gate!
The Lord's Recording Angel holds the Charter in his hand —
He seals it on the sea, and he signs it on the land!
Unroll the royal Charter now! It "marches" with the West,
Embossed along its far frontier, Sierra's silver crest;

Along its hither border shines a sacred crystal chain:
God cursed of old the weedy ground, but never cursed the main,
As free to-day from earthly sin as Eden's early rain!

"I found a Rome of common clay," Imperial Caesar cried;
"I left a Rome of marble!" No other Rome beside!
The ages wrote their autographs along the sculptured stone —
The golden eagles flew abroad — Augustan splendors shone —
They made a Roman of the world! They trailed the classic robe,
And flung the Latin toga around the naked globe!

"I found Chicago wood and clay," a mightier Kaiser said,
Then flung upon the sleeping mart his royal robes of red,
And temple, dome, and colonnade, and monument and spire,
Put on the crimson livery of dreadful Kaiser Fire!
The stately piles of polished stone were shattered into sand,
And madly drove the dread simoom, and snowed them on the land!
And rained them till the sea was red, and scorched the wings of prayer!
Like thistle-down ten thousand homes went drifting through the air,
And dumb Dismay walked hand in hand with frozen-eyed Despair!
Chicago vanished in a cloud — the towers were storms of sleet,
Lo! ruins of a thousand years along the spectral street!
The night burned out between the days! The ashen hoar-frost fell,
As if some demon set ajar the bolted gates of hell,
And let the molten billows break the adamantine bars,
And roll the smoke of torment up to smother out the stars!
The low, dull growl of powder-blasts just dotted off the din,
As if they tolled for perished clocks the time that *might* have been!
The thunder of the fiery surf roared human accents dumb;
The trumpet's clangor died away with a wild bee's drowsy hum,
And breakers beat the empty world that rumbled like a drum.

O cities of the Silent Land! O Graceland and Rosehill!
No tombs without their tenantry? The pale host sleeping still?
Your marble thresholds dawning red with holocaustal glare,
As if the Waking Angel's foot were set upon the stair!
But ah, the human multitudes that marched before the flame,
As 'mid the Red Sea's wavy walls the ancient people came!
Behind, the rattling chariots! the Pharaoh of Fire!
The rallying volley of the whips — the jarring of the tire!
Looked round, and saw the homeless world as dismal as a pyre —

Looked up, and saw God's blessèd Blue a firmament so dire!
As in the days of burning Troy, when Virgil's hero fled,
So gray and trembling pilgrims found some younger feet instead,
That bore them through the wilderness with bold elastic stride,
And Ruth and Rachel, pale and brave, in silence walked beside;
Those Bible girls of Judah's day did make *that* day sublime —
Leave life but *them*, no other loss can ever bankrupt Time!
Men stood and saw their all caught up in chariots of flame —
No mantle falling from the sky they ever thought to claim,
And empty-handed as the dead, they turned away and smiled,
And bore a stranger's household gods and saved a stranger's child!
What valor brightened into shape, like statues in a hall
When on their dusky panoply the blazing torches fall,
Stood bravely out and saw the world spread wings of fiery flight,
And not a trinket of a star to crown disaster's night.
"Who runs these lines of telegraph?" A clock-tick made reply:
"'The greatest of the three' has brought this message from the sky,
The Lord will send an Angel down to work these lines to-day!"
Charge all the batteries good and strong! Give God the right of way!
And so the swift evangels ran by telegraphic time,
And brought the cheer of Christendom from every earthly clime;
Celestial fire flashed round the globe, from Norway to Japan,
Proclaimed the manhood of the race, the brotherhood of man!
Then flashed a hundred engines' arms — then flew the lightning trains;
They had that day the right of way — gave every steed the reins —
The minutes came, the minutes went — the miles fled just the same —
And flung along October night their starry flags of flame!
They all were angels in disguise, from hamlet, field, and mart,
Chicago's fire had warmed the World that had her woe by heart.
"Who is my neighbor?" One and all: "We see her signal light,
And She our *only* neighbor now, this wild October night!"

"I found Chicago wood and clay," the royal Kaiser cried,
And flung upon the sleeping mart the mantle in his pride;
It lay awhile — he lifted it, and there beneath the robe
A city done in lithograph, the wonder of the globe;
Where granite grain and marble heart, in strength and beauty wed, —
"I leave a mart of palaces," the haughty Kaiser said.

Now, thanks to God, this blessèd day, to whom all thanks belong —
The clash of silver cymbals, the rhyme of the little song —

Whose Hand did hive the golden bees that swarm the azure dome,
Whence honey-dews forever fall around this earthly home —
Did constellate the prairie sod and light it up with flowers —
That hand defend from fire and flood this Prairie Flower of ours!
This volume of the royal West we bring in grateful gage,
We open at the frontispiece and give it to the Age,
Who wrote the word "Chicago" twice upon the title-page!

## Chicago

A wide-winged bird, a schooner brown,
Swam shoreward in a lazy way,
And shook her lifted plumage down,
    Where in a wild-rice cradle lay,
      As tender as a water-cress,
      The Moses of the wilderness!
An empty Egypt lay in sight,
    No Sphinx to stare the ages out,
No Pharaoh nor Israelite,
    A painted savage lounged about,
    A paddle in his gray dug-out,
And watched the child beside the lake;
    Fort Dearborn's guns were marble mute,
The world walked in by trail and wake,
    As silent as a naked foot.
Ah, picket line beyond the law,
    Where cloudless nights were such a boon,
For half the year the sentry saw
    His nearest neighbor in the moon!

This Moses rent his swaddling bands,
    He sprang upon his youthful feet,
And beckoning to the drowsy lands
    Made half the world Chicago Street,
That found at last, where'er it went,
The gate-way of the continent.
Some Samson gave a mighty lift
And sent the ponderous gates adrift:
By dust and wave, by wheel and sail,
And glittering wake and ringing rail,
    In cloud and calm, and day and night,

In lumbering wain, and lightning train
    That flies as if its load were light,
The engines with their hot simoom
Throb redly through the midnight gloom,
The genii pant, the giants row,
The hosts are going West to grow!
The world is coming up the road!
The highway clear, the gate-way broad!

A monotone from farthest West!
    Was it a growl of heavy breath
      Through White Nevada's snowy teeth?
Or murmur from a Thunder's nest?
    Or echoes of the coming world
      From Rocky Ranges backward hurled?
Like trumpet's mouth the opening roar,
It widens, deepens more and more,
    Until, behold in lengthened line,
      With fragrant leaves and silken shine,
The train from China at the door!
And all the while the nerves of wire
Are thrilled with quick electric fire,
And East and West talk back and forth
Round the great circles of the earth
With instant words that never wait,
Like lovers at a garden gate
When roses blow and moon is late!

# Simon Pokagon

## (1830-99)

SIMON POKAGON *was born in Berrien County, Michigan, in 1830, the son of Leopold Pokagon, chief of the Potawatomies for more than forty years. He attended Oberlin College for a year and Twinsburg Institute, near Cleveland for two years, then served as chairman of the Potawatomi business committee. A controversial figure to his own people, Pokagon was criticized for, among other things, selling the tribe's interest in the Chicago lakefront by way of quitclaim, and for too readily acquiescing to the demands of whites.*

*Nevertheless, Pokagon is an important early Native American literary figure. He is usually credited with writing the first novel about Native Americans by a native,* Queen of the Woods/O-Gî-Mäw-Kwe *(1899), although some scholars believe the book was actually ghostwritten by his publisher. Pokagon's speech at the World's Columbian Exposition in 1893 is emblematic of his career. He generally praised white civilization in his address, yet he also sold his book* Red Man's Rebuke *(1893) at the fair, which paints a much less favorable portrait of native-white relations. His major works are the essays "An Indian on the Problems of His Race" (1895), "The Future of the Red Man" (1897), and "An Indian's Plea for Prohibition" (1898). Pokagon died in 1899.*

*"The Massacre of Fort Dearborn at Chicago" was published in* Harper's Monthly *in 1899. As the essay's subtitle suggests, Pokagon was not an eyewitness; the material is "gathered from the traditions of the Indian tribes engaged in the massacre." By turns angry and apologetic, the piece is a fascinating example of Pokagon's lifelong attempt to balance the competing demands of his tribe and the culture that had conquered it.*

✦ ✦ ✦

# The Massacre of Fort Dearborn at Chicago

*Gathered from the Traditions of the Indian Tribes Engaged in the Massacre, and from the Published Accounts*

My Father, Chief Leopold Pokagon, was present at the massacre of Fort Dearborn in 1812, and I have received the traditions of the massacre from our old men. Since my youth I have associated with people of the white race, and sympathize with them as well as with my own people. I am in a position to deal justly with both. Whatever I may say against the dealings of white men with the Indians, I trust no reader for a moment will think that Pokagon does not know, or does not appreciate, what is now being done for the remnant of his race. He certainly does, and with an overflowing heart of gratitude and pride he reviews the lives of those noble men and women who in the face of stubborn prejudice have boldly advocated the rights of his race in the ears of politicians and government officials. In order to present the facts as nearly as possible, I shall rely on the written history: but the earliest detailed account I have been able to find was written by a woman, who claimed the story was told her by an eye-witness twenty years after occurrence, and she did not publish it until twenty-two years later. Thus the account was traditional when first published.

In considering the real causes we must bear in mind that during the settlement of this country, up to the time of the Chicago massacre, the great Algonquin tribe, with others, were slowly but surely being pushed before the tidal wave of civilization towards the setting sun. Our rights were not respected; we saw no sympathy being shown for us, for our love of home; no respect paid to the graves of our fathers. At the close of the eighteenth century numerous tribes, numbering many thousand people, found themselves crowded into what is now known as western Ohio, northern Indiana, northern Illinois, Michigan, and Wisconsin. Our tribe, the Pottawatomies, occupied western Wisconsin, the country around Chicago, and the valley of the river St. Joseph in Michigan and Indiana. While we were being pushed westward another tidal wave of pale-faced humanity came moving against us from the south, driving before it the red man, like buffaloes before the prairie on fire. Our fathers saw it, and trembled at their fate. Anxiously they inquired of each other, If we stand still with folded arms until the two advancing columns meet, where will our country and the red man be? In our ignorance we did not comprehend the mighty ocean of humanity that lay back of the advance-waves of pioneer settlement. But being fired by as noble patriotism as ever burned in the hearts of mortals, we tried to beat back the reckless white men who dared to settle within our borders — and vast armies were sent out to punish us. We fought most heroically against overpowering numbers for home and native land; sometimes victory was ours, as when, during the last decade of the eighteenth century, after having had many warriors killed and our villages burned to the ground, our fathers arose in their might, putting to flight the alien armies of Generals Harmar and St. Clair, hurling them in disorder from the wilderness across our borders into their own ill-gotten domain. But only four years after, while yet we were rejoicing over our success, the white man, under General Wayne, with "wasplike venom," swept our land. During 1803 our jealousy was aroused almost to the war pitch by the building of Fort Dearborn, strongly garrisoned and equipped, in the very heart of our territory. We looked upon it as a dangerous enemy within our camp.

About this time Tecumseh, a great orator and hero in war, visited the different tribes, unfolding to them his plan to unite them as one nation and make a desperate effort to regain and hold their ancient lands. He sent out runners before him to announce the time he would meet each tribe at their council fires and make known his plans. He and two other chiefs went from tribe to tribe, riding spirited black ponies finely equipped, and themselves gayly dressed. When he arose in the council-house his bearing was so noble that cheer on cheer would be given before he would open his mouth to speak. My father and many others who listened to the speeches of Tecumseh many times repeated to me his words when I was a boy, but it was impossible to give an idea of their spirit and power. He generally spoke as follows:

"Before me stands the rightful owners of kwaw-notchi-we au-kee [this beautiful land]. The Great Spirit in His wisdom gave it to you and your children to defend, and placed you here. But, ä-te-wä [alas!] the incoming race, like a huge serpent, is coiling closer and closer about you. And not content with hemming you in on every side, they have built at She-gog-ong [Chicago], in the very centre of our country, a military fort, garrisoned with soldiers, ready and equipped for battle. As sure as waw-kwen-og [the heavens] are above you they are determined to destroy you and your children and occupy this goodly land themselves.

"Then they will destroy these forests whose branches were in the winds above the graves of your fathers, chanting their praises. If you doubt it, come, go with me eastward or southward a few days' journey along your ancient mi-kan-og [trails], and I will show you a land you once occupied made desolate. There the forests of untold years have been hewn down and cast into the fire! There be-sheck-kee and waw-mawsh-ka-she [the buffalo and deer], pe-nay-shen and ke-gon [the fowl and fish], are all gone. There the woodland birds, whose sweet songs once pleased your ears, have forsaken the land, never to return; and waw-bi-gon-ag [the wild flowers], which your maidens once loved to wear, have all withered and died.

"You must bear in mind these strangers are not as you are — they are devoid of natural affection, loving gold or gain better than one another, or ki-tchi-tchag [their own souls]. Some of them follow on your track as quietly as maw-in-gawn [the wolf] pursues the deer, to shoot you down, as *you* hunt and kill mé-she-bé-zhe [the panther]. But a few years since I saw with mine own eyes a young white man near the O-hi-o River who was held by our people as a prisoner of war. He won the hearts of his captors with his apparent friendship and good-will, while murder was in his heart. They trusted him as they trusted one another. But he most treacherously betrayed their confidence, and secretly killed not less than nech-to-naw [twenty] before his crimes were detected, and then he had fled. After this, when Chief Harmar [a United States general] invited some of our head men to meet him at Fort Harmar to try and settle our war spirits, that same young man lay in wait, and secretly shot down I-cme-no-au-nish-naw-by [a good Indian man] just as he reached the treaty grounds; and yet for that outrageous crime he went unpunished, and to-day is being *petted* by wau-be au-nene-eg [white men] as you pet him who kills mé-she-bé-zhe [the panther]. I speak of this case — and there are many of them within my own personal knowledge — that you may know our enemies are cunning, crafty, and cruel, without honor, without natural affection.

"When we were many and strong, and they were few and weak, they reached out their hands for wido-kaw-ké-win [help], and we filled them with wie-aus and maw-daw-min [meat and corn]; we lived wa-naw-kiwen [in peace] together; but now they are many and strong, and we are getting few and weak, they waw nen-dam [have forgotten] the deep debt of mawmo-i-wendam [gratitude] they owe us, and are now scheming to drive us towards ke-so [the setting sun], into desert places far from ke-win [home] and da-na ki aukee [our native land]. Eh [yes], they come to us with lips smoother than bi-me-da [oil], and words sweeter than amose-poma [honey], but beware of them! The venomous amo [wasp] is in their odaw [heart]! and their dealing with us when we have not tamely submitted, has ever been maw-kaw-te and ashki-koman [powder and lead]; against such mau-tchi au-nene [wicked men] our only pagos-seni-ma [hope], our only inin-ijim [safety], is in joining all our tribes, and then, and not until then, will we be able to drive the soulless invaders back! Fail in this, and awak-ani-win [slavery] and ne-baw [death] are ours!

"And lastly, do not forget that what peace you have enjoyed the past fifty years in your homes and on your hunting grounds you entirely owe to the brave Pontiac, who, at the risk of his own life, destroyed the forts of your enemies around the Great Lakes, driving the white invaders back."

Not one tribe refused to unite in the great Algonquin confederacy. While Tecumseh was at work night and day preparing for the inevitable struggle between the two races, General Harrison, quiet as the wolf, invaded our territory with a vast army, defeating Elks-wa-ta-wa, an Indian prophet and twin brother of Tecumseh, at Tippecanoe, Indiana. He slew many warriors, women, and children, burned our villages and supplies, leaving us and our little ones naked and destitute. This was the fourth time, in a few years, our country was invaded in autumn-time, near cold weather, and all our supplies for winter's use burned or destroyed, which created a feeling of revenge in the hearts of our people.

These outrages portrayed by the eloquence of Tecumseh, who was holding daily councils with the different tribes, fanned the slumbering embers of the war spirit into a blaze that could not well be quenched.

In June, 1812, war was declared by the United States against Great Britain. One year before, and during that summer, British emissaries came among our fathers, enlisted sympathy, and stirred up their prejudices against the United States by telling them it was the intention of the government to destroy them and take their lands for their own children. They said that their King, who ruled beyond the ocean and the Great Lakes, would defend them and fight for them from generation to generation. They said that his warriors outnumbered the stars in the heavens, and that when the sun rose and set red, it was but to remind them of the King's warriors. Our young men confided in these emissaries, and calling to mind the long death-roll of the warriors killed at Tippecanoe the previous autumn, many of them began to talk of driving the white men out of the Indian territory.

On August 1st of that year a white man who had formerly been a fur-buyer, and could speak our language well, came among us from northern Michigan. He appeared much excited, saying that he was a messenger sent by the British chief to inform the Pottawatomies that he had joined his forces with their brave Tecumseh to help save their native land. He also informed us that Mackinaw Island, the fort of Mackinaw and its garrison, had surrendered to the British and Indians the day before he left; that in all probability Detroit and the United States fort there had shared the same fate; and that it was necessary, in order to secure our ancient lands and liberty, Fort Dearborn, the only stronghold remaining in the Northwest, should be taken at once. He admonished us, furthermore, that if we had one spark of sa-ka-i (love) for our homes and hunting-grounds, we should consider it a duty we owed ourselves, our wives, and children to sound at once the war-whoop and besiege the fort.

A few days after this, Captain Heald, commander at Fort Dearborn, called the head men of our people together to meet him in council. To their surprise, he told them he intended to evacuate the fort the next day, August 15, 1812; that he would distribute the fire-arms, ammunition, provisions, whiskey, etc., among them; and that if they would send a band of Pottawatomies to escort them safely to Fort Wayne, he would there pay them a large sum of money. To this the Indians agreed, apparently well satisfied. Some goods were given them, but the fire-arms and ammunition were secretly destroyed, and, worst of all for some, the whiskey too, which was poured into the river. Some of the Indians, finding the whiskey was being poured into the river, rushed in, drank the water freely, declaring it was more groggy than fire-water itself. Under the influence of the strange mixture a war-dance was gotten up by the young men and some of the reckless older ones.

The day before the massacre a white man came to the fort with twenty Miami Indians to escort the garrison to Fort Wayne. This aroused the jealousy of the Pottawatomies, who took it for granted their services would not be appreciated. Furthermore, the white man was a Captain Wells, who, having been brought up with the Indians, and having fought with them several years against the white man, afterwards joined his own race and fought against the Indians most desperately; many of the Pottawatomies knew him, and regarded him as a base traitor.

I have heard it said that when the fort was evacuated the Pottawatomies pretended to be acting as escorts for the soldiers, when, in fact, they were luring them to their death. This I regard as untrue. I have many times heard old warriors say that they were led by this Captain Wells and his Miami Indians, some in front and some in the rear. This seems probable, in view of the fact that on the day before the evacuation they gave Captain Heald to understand they were dissatisfied because the whiskey, fire-arms, and ammunition were destroyed, and in view of the fact that Captain Heald was informed the night before that there was serious trouble ahead, under which circumstances Captain Heald would not have dared to trust them.

On August 13, 1812, the fort was evacuated, and the line of march commenced southward along the shore of Lake Michigan. The Indian warriors stationed themselves about two miles south of the fort, and on the right of the line, placing it between themselves and the lake. When they were discovered, a halt was made, and an order given by Captain Wells to charge them on the right of the line of march. Then, more like a herd of buffaloes at bay than trained soldiers, headlong they plunged through the Indian line on the right, which was broken. They fought most desperately, on right and left, what old warriors called a rough-and-tumble fight, until hemmed in on every side by overpowering numbers. They finally surrendered, with the proviso that their lives should be spared.

Captain Wells was forsaken by his Miamis, who fled at the sound of the first war-whoop; but he fought one hundred or more single-handed, on horseback, shooting them down on right and left, in front and rear, until his horse fell under him and he was killed. I have many times heard old warriors say that during the battle a rush was made to secure the baggage in the rear. This was guarded by several white warriors, who shot down many of the attacking Indians, and having no time to reload, used their guns as clubs until they were all killed. I have further heard that a young Indian, infuriated by drink and the death of so many of his comrades, killed several children with his tomahawk, for which he was hated by the tribe ever after. Out of nearly one hundred of the garrison, two-thirds at least were killed or badly wounded, while the Indian loss must have been twice as great.

Turning from the slaughter, where the Angel of Mercy seems to have been asleep, let us recall individual efforts made, showing that pity and mercy yet lived in some of our race. The night before the massacre, Chief Maw-kaw-be-pe-nay (Black Partridge) came into the fort, and in tears said to Captain Heald: "Great Chief, I have come here to give you this medal that I wear. It was given me by your people, as a token of good-will between us. I am sorry, but our young men declare they will shed the blood of your people. I cannot restrain them. And I will not wear this medal as a friend while I am forced to act as an enemy." As the captain reluctantly received the medal in silence and surprise, the old chief said: "As you march away from here, be on your guard. Linden-birds have been warbling whispers in my ears to-day." Captains Wells and Heald both personally knew the old chief as an honest, truthful man, and it would seem such timely and pathetic warning as that, from such a reliable source as that, couched in such heart-eloquence as that, should not have gone unheeded by any reasonable, sober men. During the fighting around the wagons, the young Indian who murdered the children, being upbraided by Mrs. Helm, the young wife of the lieutenant of the fort, he struck at with his tomahawk. She grabbed him about his neck, and tried to take his knife from his belt; in the struggle an old Indian grasped her in his arms, ran to the lake, and plunged her in. She soon saw it was the same old chief, in war-paint, that gave the warning of danger the night before to Captain Heald, and that instead of trying to drown her, he was trying to save her life. The old chief must have realized he was liable to be shot down by those he sought to save, as an enemy, or by his own people as a traitor. But he saved the woman's life, and she was restored to her friends.

My father, Leopold Pokagon, chief of the Pottawatomie Pokagon band, was not informed of the war spirit existing among his tribe around Fort Dearborn until within twenty-four hours of its evacuation. He had a great reputation among the tribe as a wise counsellor, and his influence over mi-gas ag-i-ma (the war chief) Sa-naw-waw-ne at other times had been accepted: and he felt in his heart if he could reach Chicago in time, he could prevent the conflict which he knew could only result in evil to his people. But he was then at his summer home in Michigan, one hundred miles away. He at once informed my mother's father, Saw-awk, and Chief To-pa-na-bee, an uncle of mine. The three started in great haste on horseback around the head of Lake Michigan, and by riding all night reached Chicago the next morning just before the battle began, but too late for counsel or advice.

At the close of the fight, my father and the two chiefs who were with him from Michigan were counselled regarding the terms of surrender. The lives of the survivors were all to be spared except the officer of the fort. With regard to him, Sa-naw-waw-ne, the war chief, and his warriors, most of whom were from Green Bay, Wisconsin, and many of whom were Winnebagoes, declared "that if he did not die of his wounds before a-bit a-tib-i-kad [midnight], his life should be taken." The war chief revengefully charged the officer with breaking his pledge in not turning over the provisions, fire-arms, and whiskey in the fort, which he maliciously destroyed. He protested emphatically that it had not been their intention, or even desire, to take the lives of any of the garrison, but only to take them as prisoners of war, that they might control Fort Dearborn, and Chicago as well, believing that, against such overpowering numbers, the garrison would surrender without fight, as did that at Fort Mackinaw a few days before. Others charged the wounded man with having acted on the orders of the arch-traitor Captain Wells, who rushed headlong through their lines before a bow was bent or gun was fired, shooting their warriors, who fell like leaves before the autumn blast. It was therefore through his fault that so many Indian warriors were lying dead on wad-ge (the mound) about him. My father tried in vain to persuade the war chief to spare the life of the wounded officer.

While the victorious braves were holding a powwow, my father and his two friends, under cover of darkness, quietly stole away the wounded officer, carried him down the terrace to the shore of Lake Michigan, where he and his relatives, with some other friendly Indians, put him into a boat, where they had secured some more of the unfortunates, and rowed them across Lake Michigan to St. Joseph, thence up the St. Joseph River to the old Pokagon village, near the present site of the city of Niles, to my father's wigwam, where they were kindly cared for until their wounds were nearly healed.

A few days after their arrival, an Indian came across the lake and reported that the Winnebago warriors were coming to the Pokagon village to retake the prisoners, whereupon they were taken down the lake in a boat to Mackinaw Island, three hundred miles away, and delivered over to the British as prisoners of war. This was done by the advice of the wounded officer, who told the friendly Indians that was the safest course. All the prisoners promised before their God that they would reward us richly for our kindness, but they were never heard from after.

I have read several times in history that the Indians treacherously killed several men after the terms of surrender were consummated, and in after-years my father was charged by white men with having done this. He declared to the day of his death that the accusation was false; and that the only charitable excuse he could surmise for the whole story was that the survivors of the battle who reported it thought the terms of surrender were agreed upon before they were, or else that some Indian warriors, having no knowledge of the surrender, may have pressed the fight at some point of the battle-field. This was the case of the last great battle fought between the English and Americans, at New Orleans, which was fought weeks after the two powers had signed a treaty of peace.

Nearly all the rest of the prisoners were taken north to Green Bay, Wisconsin. In order not to shield my own people from blame, I give the following account of their usage and final disposal. We must fancy ourselves at the Pottawatomie village on Green Bay, Wisconsin, two hundred miles from Chicago. Ten days have passed since the battle. There comes along the winding trails from the south a long line of dusky warriors on their return home. They have in guard several white prisoners. Among them is a fair young pale-faced mother, carrying an infant child about five months old. The inhabitants of the village have been informed they are coming, and are swarming out to meet them. They learn from them that many of their friends have been killed on the war-path. Hark! hear their wailing and cursing; and see — they now seek revenge by pulling the prisoners' hair and cuffing them. The women and children of the village come marching out of the camp with sticks and clubs. They are forming in two long single lines, facing each other a few feet apart. They have ordered the prisoners to run the gauntlet. One by one they rush down between the two lines of the women and children, while savage blows are rained down upon them thick and fast, amid laughing, yelling, and cursing. There stands near the head of the lines, apparently unmoved, the young mother with her child. Is it possible they will compel her to run the gauntlet too? Yes, see, they are ordering her forward now! She looks down between the long lines of unlifted sticks and clubs, folds her blanket close around her child, and breathes a silent prayer. There she goes, running between the lines while the blows fall thick upon her head and shoulders. The race is run; she passes the goal bruised and bleeding, but the child, thank Heaven! remains untouched. There she stands, without a sigh, without a tear, expecting no pity and asking no mercy. But look once more! An elderly Indian woman goes running towards her, puts her arms about her, and whispers in her ear. "Come, go with me." They two go into a wigwam; the Indian feeds her, binds up her wounds, kindly cares for her, and saves her life.

During the fall and winter that young mother, carrying her child, accompanied by several other prisoners and the Indian warriors, set out from the village on Green Bay with the promise of being delivered over to the Americans under the regulations of war. They went south around Lake Michigan, then north through the wilderness of Michigan to Mackinaw Island, which she found in the hands of the English and Indians. From there she was taken through deep snows, half starved and less than half clothed, still carrying her child, to Detroit. To her disappointment, that place was found in the hands of the English, the race to whom she belonged. Instead of receiving and taking care of her, they allowed her to go away with the Indians to Fort Meigs, where General Harrison was in command of the United States troops. She was delivered to him, and was finally sent home to her parents in Ohio. This young mother and the other prisoners travelled over nine hundred miles on foot, carrying her child through a wilderness of deep snows and fierce blizzards. No reasonable excuse has ever been given by the English at Mackinaw for forcing her to be dragged three hundred miles through the woods; and again no reasonable excuse has been given by those at Detroit for suffering her to be dragged to Fort Meigs. She was held as a prisoner of war by the allies of the English, and should have been rescued and taken care of at the first English military station. It does not seem possible that any woman could live through what that mother endured.

They who call themselves civilized cry out against the treachery and cruelty of savages, yet the English generals formed a league with Tecumseh and his warriors, at the beginning of the war of 1812, with a full understanding that they were to take the forts around the Great Lakes, regardless of consequences. The massacre of the Fort Dearborn garrison was but one link in the chain of civilized warfare, deliberately planned and executed. Disguise the fact as the pride of the white man may, when he joins hands with unaltered savages in warfare he is a worse savage than they.

In a book published at Chicago in 1820, entitled *The Chicago Massacre of 1812*, I find this statement: "Here was the native savage (not ignorant of other ways, for he had the thrifty white man under his eyes for four generations) still showing himself in sense a child, in strength a man, and in cruelty a fiend incarnate." The author certainly must have been ignorant of the fact that those white men with whom our fathers had to deal were generally of the basest class. All our traditions and the accounts published by the dominant race show conclusively that the white man's dealing with our fathers was of such a character that they were made much worse, instead of better; and Pokagon calls on Heaven to witness that in many battles before and after the Chicago massacre there was far less mercy and justice shown our race than our fathers exhibited towards the garrison of Fort Dearborn.

I find it recorded in history that the year after the Fort Dearborn battle, the Este-mus-ko-kee (the Creek Indians) in the State of Alabama, feeling themselves aggrieved by the white race, who were swarming into the country the government had assigned to the Indians, destroying with their superior weapons the buffalo, deer, and fur animals, arose in arms against the invaders, as they supposed they had a right to do. General Coffee was sent out by the United States with nine hundred warriors, and, like mousing cats, they sprang upon the Indian village Tal-lu-shat-che, and burned the town, leaving not a man, woman, or child alive. Then, by forced marches, surprised the Indian villages Tal-la-de-ga and Au-tos-seea, and they met a similar fate. In March following, General Jackson with a large force stormed the breastworks of their last retreat, driving the half-starved savages into a river, where, huddled together, one thousand warriors, with their women and children, were put to death. The historian adds: "These battles completely conquered and subdued the Indians — almost exterminated them." The Fort Dearborn battle has been denounced by the dominant race as a brutal massacre, regardless of its many individual acts of mercy and kindness. In this wholesale slaughter not one white man stretched out a hand to save a single soul.

Your own historians, true to their trust, have recorded the cruelty of their own race, that unborn millions might read it as a testimony against them. In the name of all that is sacred and dear to mankind, tell Pokagon, if you can, why less love, pity, or sympathy should be required of civilized and enlightened people than of untutored savages.

My father always declared, to the day of his death, if there never had been ash-con-ta-nebesh (fire-water), there never would have been a Fort Dearborn massacre. And I believe it. There was no sober, intelligent excuse for evacuating the fort under the circumstances; it was criminal recklessness. If the garrison had remained there, they could have held out against all the poorly armed Indians that could gather at such a point. Father frequently said that when shipments were received at the fort, ish-kot-e-wabo (the whiskey) was far in excess of all other goods, and traders would frequently boast that whiskey is legal tender for the red men. He often said, with a sigh, "I have seen du-zhawsk [musk-rat] hides sold for a swallow of it; waw-goosh [fox] skin for a gill of it; du-mick [beaver] skin for a pint of it." Not long since I examined the old account-books of the American Fur Company, kept for inspection as relics at the old Astor House on Mackinaw Island, Michigan — the invoice of goods received, in books dated 1816 and 1817, and so on. I found the entries of whiskey to nearly correspond with what my father said about it at Fort Dearborn. I do wish that all who visit the island would examine those books for themselves. They were well kept. I think the writing the plainest I ever saw. While examining them the Great Spirit whispered in my ear: "Pokagon, you can rest assured, if these books are required in evidence against the white man in the supreme court of the world beyond, no expert will be called for to read them."

# Eugene Field

## (1850-95)

*The son of New England parents,* EUGENE FIELD *was born in St. Louis. From the age of twenty-one until his death of heart failure in 1895 at the age of forty-five, Field was a newspaperman. He worked for the* St. Louis Evening Journal *and* Times Journal, *the* St. Joseph Gazette, *the* Kansas City Times, *and the* Denver Tribune. *In 1883 he joined the* Chicago Daily News, *where he began writing his popular "Sharps and Flats" column, a lively mixture of cultural criticism, gossip, and pure satire. Like several of the columnists who followed him — George Ade and Finley Peter Dunne among them — Field's work reached a national audience, though his poetry was probably more popular than his prose. A decidedly minor poet, Field nevertheless penned several classic children's verses, including "Wynken, Blynken, and Nod." Culture's* Garland *(1887) collects many of the "Sharps and Flats" columns and gives us Field at his sardonic best. "Professor Lowell in Chicago" lampoons the young city's pomposity and faux sophistication and points out how gauche Chicago's supposed intellectuals really are when they come in contact with a man of genuine learning.*

✦ ✦ ✦

## Professor Lowell in Chicago

### *from* CULTURE'S GARLAND

The presence of Mr. James Russell Lowell has given Chicago a tremendous boom as a literary centre. In literary circles this boom is not spoken of as a boom, but as an impetus — impetus being a word of such classic pedigree as to render it preferable to the lowly and vulgar word boom. This impetus first became apparent last Saturday afternoon, when one of the distinguished members of the Chicago Literary Club — a manufacturer of linseed-oil — happened to call at the business office of another distinguished member of the club, a wholesale dealer in hides and pelts.

"I see by the papers," said the first *littérateur,* "that James Russell Lowell is going to be in town next week."

"Lowell? Lowell?" queried the second *littérateur,* as if he were trying to place the name. "Oh, yes! I remember — the author of 'The One-Hoss Shay'!"

"Yes: he's going to read a poem in Central Music Hall next Tuesday," explained the first *littérateur,* "and it has occurred to me that we ought to elect him an honorary member of the club."

"Well," said the second *littérateur,* "we'll think about that — there's no special hurry. You know, we have to be a little careful about taking up with every stranger that comes along: however, we'll talk it over at the next meeting. Here, you Jim, go up on the back roof, and drag in them calf-pelts out of the rain!"

Since Mr. Lowell's address last Tuesday afternoon, we have taken pains to mingle pretty freely with the recognized literary folk of the town, and we have been mightily interested in the opinions that are expressed of Mr. Lowell and his work. We are told at the house of A. C. McClurg & Co., that during the last forty-eight hours there has been a terrific demand for Lowell's books. One order came from a wealthy pork-packer, and was for "Lowell's works in binding to match my 'Vues de Paris.'" Another order was for Lowell's books, provided the whole set cost more than a hundred dollars. These little incidents pleased us greatly, because they evidence that there is springing up among our people a choice, a discriminating, an exacting taste, which demands only the best works of an author.

"Last evening," said two board-of-trade men, "we had the pleasure of a long talk with Mr. Lowell. We were fully prepared to create a favorable impression; for in anticipation of meeting him, and following the example of our other fellow-townsmen, we had secured a complete line of Mr. Lowell's poems and essays, and had been feeding upon them for a fortnight. Much to our disappointment, however, Mr. Lowell appeared disinclined to traverse the poetic and misty vistas of the past with us; and when we contrived — with consummate art and ineffable subtilty, as we fondly imagined — to introduce into our introductory remarks an apt quotation from 'Hosea Biglow,' he dampened our ardor by adverting to the location of Chicago, its salubrious climate, and the immense volume of its trade. Mr. Lowell said that he had driven about the city a good deal, had been charmed with the beauty of our avenues, the extent and embellishments of our commons, the magnitude of our pond, and hospitality of our citizens. He said that he had visited the packing-houses on the South Side, and that he was convinced that the Western methods of flaying and disembowelling live-stock had its advantages over the conventional New-England way of removing the bristles of a pig with an iron candlestick. At one of the rendering-establishments the proprietor received the distinguished poet with great cordiality. After escorting him about the place, and acquainting him with the delicate details of the art, this hospitable host conducted Mr. Lowell to the private office, and insisted upon opening a case of champagne. To make the situation all the more comfortable for his guest, the host remarked pleasantly, 'We always whoop it up to you newspaper men; for, like as not, when you get back home, you'll write us up."

Another gentleman who called on Mr. Lowell was a Mr. Elisha K. Robbins, who represented that he was organizing a club which he wanted to call the James Russell Lowell Literary and Debating Lyceum. He sought Mr. Lowell's sympathy with the enterprise to the extent of a donation of twenty-five dollars. Mr. Lowell was really very much embarrassed; he sympathized heartily with the scheme suggested, and he appreciated very keenly the compliment which Mr. Robbins and his associates were ambitious to confer; but he was compelled to inform Mr. Robbins in the most delicate manner possible, that, in the hurry and excitement of starting upon his Western tour, he had carelessly left his wallet on the *escritoire* in his room at home. Mr. Robbins so heartily shared Mr. Lowell's regret at this awkward occurrence, that, at a meeting of his accomplices last evening, he formally moved that "this organization be, and hereby is, named the Julian Hawthorne Literary Club."

It were useless to deny that many of our citizens were much disappointed at the change which substituted a lecture on "Richard III" for a political address. We heard several of our most cultured fellow-townsmen say that Dick Oglesby could talk all around Lowell: one of our most influential citizens — a wholesale liquor-dealer — remarked, "I have heard 'em all now, — Lowell and Logan, and Gin'ral Palmer and all of 'em; but for real eloquence and scholarship, give me Carter H. Harrison in a spring campaign, every time!"

Austin Fisher, the well-known art-connoisseur, and dealer in leaf-lard, said, "This man Lowell is a scholar and a nice gentleman — there's no denying *that*; but, do you know, after all, I think I prefer Bill Nye."

Col. Ben Higgins, the owner of Prairie Belle, Sly Boots, and other noted flyers, thought that Mr. Lowell's address was an outrage. "The club is very indignant," he said. "We were all there in our best harness, and we expected that the race would come off as advertised. Of course, we were mad when we found that the programme had been changed. The event was billed as a mile-and-a-quarter dash; and it was, in fact, only a best-three-in-five trot, and slow at that!" Col. Higgins went on to say that Mr. Lowell had offended all the leading turfmen in Chicago by choosing to talk about Shakespeare when he had agreed to come here and make an oration on the Washington Park Club.

The theatrical people, too, are berating Mr. Lowell for having maintained that Shakespeare did not write "Richard III." "If the governor were here," said Mr. Horace McVicker yesterday, "you can just bet he'd have a card in all the papers, doing Mr. Lowell up in great shape! The governor is a great admirer of Shakespeare: when he was but four years old, he played one of the little princes in 'Richard III.'"

Manager R. M. Hooley was the only theatrical man who approved the Lowell theory. "I remember having experimented with 'Richard III' once on a time," said he. "It was about three years ago that George Edgar brought a company to my theatre, and tried to convince me that Shakespeare wrote 'Richard III.' After he had tried it for two weeks, I paid railroad-fares for the whole crowd back East. After Mr. Lowell's lecture the other afternoon, I walked up to the platform, and grasped Mr. Lowell's hand. 'You have told the truth,' said I: 'I know how it is myself, for I have been there.'"

Mr. T. Percy Bottom-Jones, one of our wealthiest and most cultured citizens, tells us that he entertained Mr. Lowell at dinner the other evening; and, from the description Mr. Bottom-Jones gives, we judge that the entertainment was in every way worthy of Chicago's reputation. "We had eighteen courses," says Mr. Bottom-Jones, "and the whole spread cost me in the neighborhood of seven thousand dollars. Lowell seemed to be particularly pleased with the sherry. 'I must compliment you,' he said, 'upon the nice discrimination you have evinced in your choice of sherries: this is simply delicious.' — 'Well, it ought to be,' says I; 'for I paid sixteen dollars a bottle for it!'"

"What did Mr. Lowell say to that?" we asked.

"Say?" echoed Mr. Bottom-Jones. "He didn't say any thing; but you never saw a more surprised-looking man in all your born days."

This brought to mind very vividly the lines of Paulinas Varro, the Latin poet: —

> Mæcenas is a model host,
>  Who, o'er his viands nice,
> Is wont to name each dish, and boast
>  Its quality and price.

We do not know how this epigram will impress others; but, taking it with the results of our daily observations, it goes a long way toward convincing us that (to indulge in a pardonable metaphor) the mantle of the most luxurious, the most fastidious, and the most refined, of grand old Roman times has fallen, so to speak, upon the shoulders of the representatives of Chicago wealth and culture.

Writing to us upon one of his bill-heads, a prominent member of the Chicago Literary Club takes us severely to task for "indulging in unseemly sarcasm and untimely levity at the expense of Mr. Lowell and those cultured Chicagoans who are seeking to create a healthy literary atmosphere in the West." Our correspondent goes on to set up a defence of Mr. Lowell's lecture last Tuesday afternoon, as if a defence were necessary! He says that we should remember that any utterance coming from Mr. Lowell is worth listening to; that to the study of the subject which he treated last Tuesday, Mr. Lowell devoted much time, and that Chicago ought to regard it as a high compliment that Mr. Lowell had prepared especially for her edification a discourse at once so scholarly and so eloquent, and necessarily involving so much time, patience, and discrimination in its preparation.

Our correspondent's burning words would have great weight with us did they not come to us written upon a sheet whose prefatory printed material informs us that the writer is the proprietor of a soap-manufactory. We decline to take kindly to that atmosphere, literary or otherwise, which a soap-factory is likely to create. As far as regards the suggestion that we have aimed sarcasms at Mr. Lowell, we will say that there is no truth in it; and touching the allegation that Mr. Lowell wrote his Shakespeare lecture especially for the edification of the Chicagoans, we will say that there is no truth in that, either.

We have before us a copy of "The Boston Evening Transcript" of last Wednesday; and in it we find a scholarly, thoughtful, and elegant editorial, entitled "Mr. Lowell in Chicago." We quote a few lines:—

"While Mr. Lowell's praises were being sounded here yesterday, Mr. Lowell himself was creating a great deal of discussion at Chicago by suddenly changing the topic of his address before the Union League Club from a political to a literary one, and talking about the authorship of 'Richard III,' instead of American politics. No doubt, it is quite natural that there should be a good deal of disappointment expressed at the change of programme, since, in lieu of a piquant and healthy political sensation, Mr. Lowell gave his audience a critical address, which had already been delivered at Edinburgh; but he had looked the ground over, and doubtless had reason to believe that he did wisely in altering his programme."

This is startling information: it gives us to understand, as distinctly as if we had been hit with a club, that, so far from serving up to us a specially prepared discourse, Mr. Lowell regaled us with a chestnut — and a Scotch one, at that! We regard it as the severest joke ever played upon our community.

Speaking of jokes reminds us of a little incident that is being told of the experience Mr. Lowell had at a dinner given in his honor the other evening. A wealthy patron of the arts and sciences wanted to entertain the distinguished poet in fine style, and he invited in all his rich neighbors to help him do the hospitable act. As soon as Mr. Lowell entered the parlors, and was presented to the company, one of the ladies, giggling and gushing, said, in those tones peculiar to giddy female idiocy, "O Mr. Lowell! we've been anticipating this pleasure *so* much; for we've all read your poetry, and we know you can be ever so funny when you try!"

Another genial imbecile, who wore about twenty thousand dollars' worth of big, vulgar diamonds, smilingly assured Mr. Lowell, that, although she had never met him before, she had always felt as if she were well acquainted with him; "for," she added, "my maiden name was Bigelow."

In its editorial discussion of Mr. Lowell's lecture, "The Boston Transcript" says that the distinguished critic has obtained his heterodox opinions touching the genuineness of "Richard III" from a study of the folio edition. This strikes us as a plausible explanation of the instigation of the melancholy heresy which Mr. Lowell has disseminated in the midst of us. From a scholarly gentleman who is regarded hereabouts as an authority in literary quotations, we learn that the so-called folio edition of Shakespeare's works is the most palpable fraud ever put upon the market. Its proof-reading alone, so says our informant, is so loose and incorrect as to render the work a bane to admirers of proper orthography and correct punctuation. Among the Chicago people, the most popular edition of Shakespeare is that sold on our trains and at all newsstands for fifty-five cents net. The folio edition costs eight dollars; and we agree with this scholarly gentleman who tells us about it, that a man must be a pitiful idiot indeed to pay eight dollars for a volume of Shakespeare when he can get a great deal better edition for fifty-five cents net. One of the beauties of the Chicago edition of Shakespeare's works is the numerous elegant engravings, made from designs of local artists. The picture of "Margaret Mather in the Tomb of the Capulets under the Management of J. M. Hill" is said by local art connoisseurs and critics to be a *chef d'oeuvre;* and one of the finest iambic tetrameter poems we ever read was inspired by a view of that superb engraving representing that distinguished member of the Citizens' Association, Col. J. H. McVicker, disguised as the first grave-digger. We have heard the pictures of Tom Keene as "Hamlet," Master Walker Whitesides as "Richard III," George C. Miln as "Romeo," and N. S. Wood, the boy-actor, as "Lear," — these portraitures we have heard spoken of as masterpieces. It is impossible, we think, that an edition embellished with such works of art should be supplanted by an edition whose typographical incorrectness is so violent as to be the surest and quickest cause of ophthalmia.

# Harriet Monroe

## (1852-1936)

HARRIET MONROE *was born in Chicago in 1852. Although she traveled widely during her life in Europe, Russia, China, and South America, Monroe was a fixture of Chicago's cultural life from her early days as an art critic for the* Chicago Tribune *through the twenty-plus years she served as editor of* Poetry *magazine, which she founded in 1912. Monroe's "Columbian Ode" was the official poem of the World's Columbian Exposition of 1893, and was reprinted as far away as New York, but she will always be better known as an editor than as a poet.* Poetry *is generally regarded as one of the two or three most important literary magazines in the country's history, and it helped promote the early work of many of the century's greatest poets, among them Ezra Pound, T. S. Eliot, Robert Frost, Carl Sandburg, and William Carlos Williams. Monroe had just completed the manuscript of her autobiography,* A Poet's Life *(1938), when she left in August 1936 for the fourteenth International P.E.N. Congress. While traveling in the high mountains of Peru she suffered a fatal cerebral hemorrhage and was buried in the village of Arequipa. In the December 1936 issue of* Poetry, *dedicated to her, Ezra Pound wrote, "Measuring by space and time, the elasticity of her perceptions and the freshness of her interest were those of a great editor, and as no one more acrimoniously differed with her in point of view than I did, so, I think, no one is better to testify to her unfailing sincerity, to the unfailing purity of her intentions. We will not see another such patience, another such kindliness, in her place."*

*"543 Cass Street," chapter 28 of* A Poet's Life, *refers to the address of the magazine's early headquarters (Cass is now Wabash Avenue). As the chapter makes clear, the offices were a lively place where poets dropped in to chat and staff members debated the strengths and weaknesses of modern poetry.*

✦ ✦ ✦

## *from* A POET'S LIFE

At this time three of our family group were making our home together in an old-fashioned apartment at Rush and Ohio streets — my widowed sister, the

Weezie of my childhood, her younger daughter, and I; while her only son, John Wellborn Root the second, was finishing his architectural course at the Beaux Arts. My relatives had been quite heroic about the magazine, my brother and his wife, and my niece Margaret Root Fetcher and her husband, cheering me on valiantly, my sister Lucy Calhoun and her beloved diplomat in faraway Peking supporting it with high hope for the best, and all three pairs signing the guarantor pledge. And Dora Louise, who could not afford financial testimony, and felt the enterprise to be a precarious adventure in a world full of magazines, yet loyally concealed her fear that not enough good poetry could be found to fill even the small sheaf of my early planning. Anxiously she watched its first six or seven numbers — was exhilarated by Ezra, thrilled by Lindsay, intrigued by the imagists, enraptured over Allen Upward's manuscript, gradually becoming convinced that something she had not expected was going on. But through that winter her vitality, always so powerful, was ebbing away. Suddenly she was ill; one May morning we saw a collapse and knew that the rich sands of her life were running out; and in a day or two she was dead. We had been very close since the death of her husband; she was no longer imperious, as in her childhood, but everyone felt her power and loved her for her penetrating sympathy and humor. An influence brave and strong, and gay for the world's diverting clash of characters, passed from my life with her.

I could not pause. The magazine became a consolation and a refuge, absorbing my interests more and more.

From the beginning there were three denizens of the office to divide the work according to necessity and temperament. The "business manager" and the associate editor were half-times, the former giving the morning to her job of opening and sifting the mail, taking care of subscriptions, typing letters, etc.; the latter coming in more irregularly, doing most of the "first reading," and developing, out of our utter ignorance, the technical details of the magazine business. Meantime it became more and more necessary for me to give all my working day to *Poetry*, except that through its first two years I was still handling the *Tribune* art criticisms.

As the stage for the poets' drama, the scene and center of all controversial action in the art, the old *Poetry* office in Cass Street began to develop "atmosphere." I had never been the actual mistress of any home which had sheltered me, but this little kingdom was mine, and I rather enjoyed dispensing its fleeting hospitalities. Not mine quite alone, however, for a succession of clever associate editors shared my work and its rewards, and most inconsiderately their agile minds kept me scrambling for precedence.

I have mentioned the first of these, Alice Corbin, the poet — Alice Henderson, the wife and mother and critic — who enlivened our office for three and a half years. Her round face with its smiling Cupid mouth, blue eyes, and impertinent little nose, set in a pretty tangle of curly blond hair, looked blandly innocent, never preparing one for the sharp wit which would flash out like a sword. She was a pitiless reader of manuscripts; nothing stodgy or imitative would get by her finely sifting intelligence, and we had many a secret laugh over the confessional "hot stuff" or the boggy word weeds which tender-minded authors apparently mistook for poetry. We had long sessions over the poems which she, as first reader, had found perhaps worth printing, discussing their qualities with searching frankness. In her province was the registration of successful contributors, she sent back rejections and typed a few letters, though most of the correspondence fell to my share. I made the final decisions and wrote the letters to poets recording acceptance, these being usually in uncopied longhand, for I have never learned to run a typewriter, or to dictate with any style. Alice and I made a strong team, and our arguments never quite brought us to blows or bloodshed.

When in the early spring of 1916, the doctors found that tuberculosis was the cause of Alice's waning strength, and exiled her to Santa Fe for a strict regimen of rest and quiet in a less rigorous climate, I felt her banishment not only as a personal grief but also as a very serious loss to the magazine. By way of grateful acknowledgment of her service I kept her name, for seven years more, on the staff list which we publish in every volume, although her work for *Poetry* ceased absolutely when she left us. This honorary listing was a mistaken policy as it has led to misapprehension, certain critics assuming that she actually worked for the magazine throughout its first decade.

Our work was often interrupted by visitors. Poets from far and near came as to a kind of headquarters of the art, hoping to find sympathy with their elusive moods, and readiness to discuss their problems. Youngsters would bring sheaves of manuscript, as eager to consult the editor as if she were an oracle. Sometimes there was promise, if not achievement, in what they showed, but more often the halting and platitudinous rhymes amazed when they did not amuse. In those days I had not laid down the necessary rule that poems submitted by new aspirants could not be read and discussed in their presence, and I made embarrassing efforts to cover refusals politely without lying about the quality of the jingles or jangles brought in with anxious hope or overweening confidence.

Then poets we had accepted would come in to get acquainted whenever they lived near enough or passed through the city. Thus I gradually developed a varied and interesting visiting list, and sharpened my wits by contact with original and creative minds. There were always new books to talk about, books sent in for review. Indeed, the place rapidly filled up with books, until the *Poetry* library became, as it still is, a problem demanding space and shelving which the carefully planned magazine budget could ill afford. Every year or two we would have to weed out and sell for little or nothing the utterly worthless discards, and each time they were carted away I trembled lest some "first edition" of a poet chosen for future fame by the muses might be on the way to a ragpile.

During those first years Alice Corbin was not only a well-nigh indispensable member of *Poetry*'s staff, but also one of the gayest and most brilliant slingers of repartee in the groups which soon began to gather in the *Poetry* office. For amid all the exciting controversy we enjoyed the chief reward of editorial labors when some of the new poets opened our office door. My brief essay in *Poetry* for June, 1913, describes the emotional effect of these "Incarnations":

> Being an editor involves a few surprises. It seems a cold enterprise at first, an adventurous reaching out into mysterious voids and distances, a groping with empty hands. But soon one's finger-tips tingle with spirit touches, psychic manifestations of life afar. Documentary evidence of this life comes rushing in white-winged messages of sympathy, messages of protest. Human eyes stare through the veil, human hands reach it through one's isolation, human souls tell their most sacred secrets, flaunt the colors of their most darkly besieged dreams.
>
> Printed books soon begin to seem unresponsive to an editor, strangely remote and cold. For manuscripts, even the modern kind beaten into type are alive; each one is charged with personality, it comes hot from the author's hand. Sometimes the queer ones are the most poignant of all — the ragged epic, the stodgy tragedy, the plodding lyric, on which some lonely but adventurous fellow-creature has staked his hope of fame. Yes, the most poignant these, for each, whatever its content, is a tragedy; the stake is lost, the midnight oil has been burned in vain.
>
> And now and then some dimly imagined figure takes shape, some half-heard voice becomes definitely audible, some signer of manuscripts becomes a poet incarnate, who walks into one's office like any beggar or king, any queen or milkmaid, of this ever various world.

One of the first of these visitors was Rabindranath Tagore, the serenely noble Laureate of Bengal. We had assumed, in printing his "Gitanjali" in our third number, that the distinguished Bengali poet was in London or India; but when the poems had made their first appearance in the English tongue, and the Chicago *Tribune* had welcomed them in an editorial, we received a letter from young Tagore, a student of chemistry in the University of Illinois, informing us that his father was his guest in Urbana and would like a few copies of the magazine containing his poems.

Here was an unexpected honor, and we rose to it by promptly inviting the distinguished Oriental poet, playwright, novelist, to visit Chicago. But when he accepted for some date in January, Alice and I found ourselves in a predicament. *Poetry* had no fund for entertainment, and neither of its editors could make room, in her contracted family quarters, for this foreigner from afar and the son and daughter-in-law who had become an element in the problem; nor could we afford the expense of a hotel. So once again Mrs. Moody, friend of poets, came to the rescue. She lived and conducted her catering business in a spacious old South Side mansion. There she graciously received the three Hindus, and entered into a lasting friendship with the poet during his three or four visits in that winter of 1912–13, nearly a year before the Nobel Prize made him famous throughout the world.

Tagore was a patriarchal figure in his gray Bengali robe, with a long gray beard fringing his chin. His features were regular and Aryan, his skin scarcely darker than a Spaniard's. The Hendersons and I—and others—used to gather around Mrs. Moody's hearth fire, listening to his chanting of his lyrics, or to his talk of Oriental creeds, which made us feel as if we were sitting at the feet of Buddha. His English was more perfect than ours, but we loved best to analyze the formal Bengali rhythms and rhymes as his high tenor voice sang them. And we were interested in his satirical-humorous observations of Western civilization, his surprise over its utter separation of religion from life. He was bitter about the British subjection of his country. "India has been conquered more than once," he would say, "but when the conquest was over life would go on much as before. But this conquest is different; it is like a great steel hammer, crushing persistently the spirit of the people."

The wicker armchair which my sister gave us has seated many poets. One of the first after Tagore was that "big breezy cheerful troubadour, Nicholas Vachel Lindsay," who came swinging in from the wide spaces, his chin up, his curly sandy hair rampant over a beetling brow and deep-set blue eyes. He would boom out some of his early poems in a rich voice that shook the rafters and filled us with a sense of magnificent rhythms chanted for time and eternity in a manner inimitably original. A sharp contrast to this corn-fed poet was Arthur Ficke, tall and elegant, who came sauntering in from Davenport to see what the editors and their ideas were like and estimate their endurance, his report to be submitted to his friend Witter Bynner, who was slated to divide the February *Poetry* with him.

In those days there was an Italian restaurant around the corner, which served *vin ordinaire*, red or white, with its *table d'hôte* luncheon. Here we had parties when there were enough poets around to make an excuse for it, and our discussions would thrash out fine points of the art's province and technique. Lindsay used to say that he learned more in those talks than a whole college course or years of solitary study could have taught him—sparks flashed from the sharp encounter of sympathetic or opposing minds. And after lingering past luncheon most of us would adjourn to the *Poetry* office to carry on the arguments.

John Gould Fletcher, fresh from his English sojourn, was an early visitor, pausing for a few months in Chicago on his way to his native Arkansas, and telling us, in the falling cadences of his precisely rounded English, about his literary affiliations with Ezra's and Hueffer's groups in London, and his enthusiasm for Japan and Japanese prints.

Another new acquaintance was a stalwart slow-stepping Swede named Carl Sandburg, the son of illiterate sturdy immigrants who had reared their family on an Illinois farm. Alice had handed over to me a group of strange poems in very individual free verse, beginning with "Chicago" as the "hog-butcher of the world." This line was a shock at first, but I took a long breath and swallowed it, and was laughed at scornfully by critics and columnists when we gave it the lead in March, 1914. Carl was a typical Swedish peasant of proletarian sympathies in those days, with a massive frame and a face cut out of stone. He had earned his living at rough jobs ever since fourteen, had volunteered for the Spanish War, and during a lazy station in Puerto Rico had saved his pay to be used later for a few terms at Knox College; and at this time he was reporting for that early Chicago tabloid *The Day Book*. His delicate-featured very American wife told me that ours was the first acceptance of Carl's poems, although for two years she had been collecting rejection slips from a steady campaign against editors. Carl would come in often to sit solidly in our "poet's chair," and talk of life and poetry with whoever might be there, weighing his words before risking utterance in his rich, low-pitched, quiet voice.

There were women poets to join in the discussions. Agnes Lee, well-known through magazines and a volume or two, had come to Chicago from Boston after her marriage to Dr. Otto Freer, and we had become friendly neighbors months before *Poetry* accepted her verse play, *The Silent House*, for the last number of our first volume. The slight impediment in her speech seemed to point the thrust of her ideas, and her exacting criticisms were a help to us — for always we have let visiting poets read debatable manuscripts from the editor's drawer and write brief opinions on the envelope. Edith Wyatt, being a member of the advisory committee, came in often to discuss poets and policies; if we could not always agree, her Bryn Mawr-trained philosophic mind could usually get the better of mine in an argument. The three brilliant Dudley sisters — Helen and Dorothy poets, and Catherine a painter — were close friends of Alice's, and always stimulating visitors. Sara Teasdale, of St. Louis by birth and breeding, came in early on her way to or from New York, where she had been spending the winters ever since her early glamour-inspired volumes — *Sonnets to Duse* and *Helen of Troy* — had brought recognition of her talent from the critics and won sympathetic literary friends. She was as delicate as a lily, but under the white-petaled perfume one felt in her presence an impassioned intensity of feeling which her brief lyrics were then beginning to express; and a friendship began between her and the editor which only death, a score of years later, could seal with silence.

*Poetry* was for poets, and even the "business manager" had to be a poet to be worthy of her job. Eunice Tietjens was one of the first of these. After her return to a Chicago suburb from family life in Germany, a few of her poems had appeared in 1912, under the pseudonym "Eloise Britton," in Ferdinand Earle's *Lyric Year;* so, being a poet, she naturally drifted toward our office and joyfully gave up her kindergarten work for our small unlucrative post, later rising dizzily to associate editorship when ill health banished Alice Henderson to a softer climate in the spring of 1916. Eunice was as tall and dark as Alice was blond and little, and her olive skin and midnight eyes were emphasized by a heavy mass of dark brown hair. She was a clever talker in three or four languages, and she loved the new contacts, personal and by correspondence, with writers more or less provocative. She was less ruthless than Alice, more tender toward the hapless aspirants whose touching letters and worthless verses might move us to tears of sorrow or mirth, but never to acceptance.

Helen Hoyt also began as a mere recorder, a "subscription slavey." Her much-quoted poem "Ellis Park" arrived in 1913 from some South Side office where she was employed, and when she came over in response to our acceptance we found her a singularly free spirit who had escaped from a too narrow New England environment to lead her own life in the more spacious West. Soon she resigned her clerkship in favor of our ill-paid half-time job, managing to eke out her small salary with the aid of other work. The high spirits of these two young women, their undaunted sincerity which nothing could shake or frighten, were a tonic, not only to the editors but to unrecognized poets — good, bad, and indifferent — who would stray into the office for encouragement and consolation.

We women of the "staff" and our visitors used to have lively discussions during those first years, and each new letter from Ezra Pound sharpened the edge of them. Poetic technique was an open forum, in which everyone's theories differed from everyone's else, and the poems we accepted and published were a battleground for widely varying opinions. I have been much influenced by Lanier's *Science of English Verse*, and in November and December, 1913, I made an analysis (repeated in *Poets and Their Art*) of English poetic rhythms on the basis of quantity, illustrating metrical time values with musical notations, and showing that speech rhythm is a universal principle in the poetry of languages both classic and modern, and that accent marks poetic structure but does not make it. This view, which I still adhere to, aroused much discussion in our office and out of it. I remember one night, after a dinner I had given for Robert Frost, when he and I argued about poetic rhythms till three o'clock in the morning, against a background of cheers and jeers from three or four other poets who lingered as umpires, until at last Mrs. Moody called up my apartment and asked me to remind my guest of honor (her house guest) that she was waiting up for him. Three months after my rhythm editorials came Amy Lowell's carefully reasoned article on "Vers Libre and Metrical Prose," which analyzed with scholarly exactitude the practice of certain modern poets in French and English, and showed that there are numerous gradations, but no rigid dividing line, between prose and poetry. And so we all had an exciting time airing our different ideas of poetic technique, one of those inexhaustible subjects which will never be settled.

# Henry Blake Fuller

## (1857-1929)

*The scion of a wealthy Chicago family,* HENRY BLAKE FULLER *was born in the city in 1857, and his knowledge of and access to the world of wealthy businessmen and gentlemen authors inform much of his work.* The Cliff-Dwellers *(1893), his second novel, is probably the first novel ever set in a skyscraper, and certainly one of the first focusing on urban American life. Other notable works of fiction include the story collection* Under the Skylight *(1901),* On the Stairs *(1918), and* Bertram Cope's Year *(1919).*

*Fuller, who was too polite a writer to ever delve into the deepest recesses of the human psyche, nevertheless brought a small measure of renown to Chicago when its literature was at an early stage. He also provided friendship and encouragement to other Chicago literary figures, such as Hamlin Garland and Harriet Monroe. Fuller traveled in Europe in his later years, but he died in his hometown, in July 1929, a few months before the Great Depression forever transformed the city he found so fascinating.* With the Procession *(1895) traces the complex and troubled relationship between merchant David Marshall and his three children: Truesdale, the oldest; Jane, the dutiful daughter; and proud, pragmatic Roger. Though much of the novel is concerned with the nuances of social status, the book begins energetically enough with a description of Truesdale's return to Chicago. Like his character, Fuller came home after living abroad with an artistic sensibility and snobbish attitude, and* With the Procession *seems to gently satirize an earlier, less discerning version of the author himself.*

✦ ✦ ✦

## *from* WITH THE PROCESSION

The grimy lattice-work of the drawbridge swung to slowly, the steam-tug blackened the dull air and roiled the turbid water as it dragged its schooner on towards the lumber-yards of the South Branch, and a long line of waiting vehicles took up their interrupted course through the smoke and the stench as they filed across the stream into the thick of business beyond: first a yellow street-car; then a robust truck laden with rattling sheet-iron, or piled high with fresh wooden pails and willow baskets; then a junk-cart bearing a pair of dwarfed and bearded Poles, who bumped in unison with the jars of its clattering springs; then, perhaps, a bespattered buggy, with reins jerked by a pair of sinewy and impatient hands. Then more street-cars; then a butcher's cart loaded with the carcasses of calves — red, black, piebald — or an express wagon with a yellow cur yelping from its rear; then, it may be, an insolently venturesome landau, with crested panel and top-booted coachman. Then drays and omnibuses and more street-cars; then, presently, somewhere in the line, between the tail end of one truck and the menacing tongue of another, a family carry-all — a carry-all loaded with its family, driven by a man of all work, drawn by a slight and amiable old mare, and encumbered with luggage which shows the labels of half the hotels of Europe.

It is a very capable and comprehensive vehicle, as conveyances of that kind go. It is not new, it is not precisely in the mode; but it shows material and workmanship of the best grade, and it is washed, oiled, polished with scrupulous care. It advances with some deliberation, and one might fancy hearing in the rattle of its tires, or in the suppressed flapping of its rear curtain, a word of plaintive protest. "I am not of the great world," it seems to say; "I make no pretence to fashion. We are steady and solid, but we are not precisely in society, and we are far, very far indeed, from any attempt to cut a great figure. However, do not misunderstand our position; it is not that we are under, nor that we are exactly aside; perhaps we have been left just a little behind. Yes, that might express it — just a little behind."

How are they to catch up again — how rejoin the great caravan whose fast and furious pace never ceases, never slackens? Not, assuredly, by the help of the little sorrel mare, whose white mane swings to mildly, and whose pale eyelashes droop so diffidently when some official hand at a crowded crossing brings her to a temporary stand-still. Not by the help of the coachman, who wears a sackcoat and a derby hat, and whose frank, good-natured face turns about occasionally for a friendly participation in the talk that is going on behind. Can it be, then, that any hopes for an accelerated movement are packed away in the bulging portmanteau which rests squeezed in between the coachman's legs? Two stout straps keep it from bursting, and the crinkled brown leather of its sides is completely pasted over with the mementoes used by the hosts of the Old World to speed the parting guest. "London" and "Paris" shine in the lustre of the last fortnight; "Tangier" is distinctly visible; "Buda-Pest" may be readily inferred despite the overlapping labels of "Wien" and "Bâle"; while away off to one corner a crumpled and lingering shred points back, though uncertainly, to the Parthenon and the Acropolis. And in the midst of this flowery field is planted a large M after the best style of the White Star Line.

Who has come home bearing all these sheaves?

Is it, to begin with, the young girl who shares the front seat with the driver, and who faces with an innocent unconcern all the clamor and evil of a great city? There is a half-smile on her red lips, and her black eyes sparkle with a girlish gayety — for she does not know how bad the world is. At the same time her chin advances confidently, and her dark eyebrows contract with a certain soft imperiousness — for she does not know how hard the world is nor how unyielding. Sometimes she withdraws her glance from the jostling throng to study the untidy and overlapping labels on the big portmanteau; she betrays a certain curiosity, but she shows at the same time a full determination not to seem over-impressed. No, the returned traveller is not Rosy Marshall; all that *she* knows of life she has learned from the broadcast cheapness of English story-tellers and from a short year's schooling in New York.

Is it, then, the older girl who fills half of the rear seat and who, as the cruel phrase goes, will never see thirty again? She seems to be tall and lean, and one divines, somehow, that her back is narrow and of a slab-like flatness. Her forehead is high and full, and its bulging outlines are but slightly softened by a thin and dishevelled bang. Her eyes are of a light and faded blue, and have the peculiar stare which results from over-full eyeballs when completely bordered by white. Her long fingers show knotted joints and nails that seem hopelessly plebeian; sometimes she draws on open-work lace mitts, and then her hands appear to be embroiling each other in a mutual tragedy. No, poor Jane is thoroughly, incorruptibly indigenous; she is the best and dearest girl in half the world, as you shall see; but all her experiences have lain between Sandusky and Omaha.

Perhaps, then, the returned traveller is the elderly woman seated by her side. Perhaps — and perhaps not. For she seems a bit too dry and sapless and self-contained — as little susceptible, in fact, to the gentle dews of travel as an umbrella in a waterproof case. Moreover, it is doubtful if her bonnet would pass current beyond the national confines. One surmises that she became years ago the victim of arrested development; that she is a kind of antiquated villager — a geologic survival from an earlier age; that she is a house-keeper cumbered and encompassed by minute cares largely of her own making. It is an easy guess that, for Eliza Marshall, London is another world, that Tangier is but a remote and impracticable abstraction, and that all her strength and fortitude might be necessary merely to make the trip to Peoria.

There is but one other occupant of the carriage remaining — the only one, after all, who can or could be the owner of the baggage. He is a young man of twenty-three, and he sits with his back to the horse on a little seat which has been let down for the occasion between the usual two; his knees crowd one of the girls and his elbows the other. He seems uncommonly alert and genial; he focusses brilliantly the entire attention of the party. His little black mustache flaunts with a picturesque upward flourish, and it is supplemented by a small tuft at the edge of his underlip — an embellishment which overlays any slight trace of lingering juvenility with an effect which is most knowing, experienced, caprine, if you like, and which makes fair amends for the blanched cheeks, wrinkled brows and haggard eyes that the years have yet to accomplish for him. A navy-blue tie sprinkled with white interlacing circles spreads loosely and carelessly over the lapels of his coat; and while his clever eyes dart intelligently from one side to the other of the crowded thoroughfare, his admiring family make their own shy observations upon his altered physiognomy and his novel apparel — upon his shoes and his hat particularly; they become acquainted thus with the Florentine ideal of foot-wear, and the latest thing evolved by Paris in the way of head-gear.

This young man has passed back through London quite unscathed. Deduce from his costume the independence of his character and the precise slant of his propensities.

The carriage moves on, with a halt here, a spurt there, and many a jar and jolt between; and Truesdale Marshall throws over the shifting and resounding panorama an eye freshened by a four years' absence and informed by the contemplation of many strange and diverse spectacles. Presently a hundred yards of unimpeded travel ends in a blockade of trucks and street-cars and a smart fusillade of invective. During this enforced stoppage the young man becomes conscious of a vast unfinished structure that towers gauntly overhead through the darkening and thickening air, and for which a litter of iron beams in the roadway itself seems to promise an indefinite continuation skyward.

"Two, three, four — six, seven — nine," he says, craning his neck and casting up his eye. Then, turning with a jocular air to the elder lady opposite, "I don't suppose that Marshall & Belden, for instance, have got up to nine stories yet!"

"Marshall & Belden!" she repeated. Her enunciation was strikingly ejaculatory, and she laid an impatient and unforgiving emphasis upon the latter name. "I don't know what will happen if your father doesn't assert himself pretty soon."

"I should think as much!" observed the elder girl, explosively; "or they will never get up even to seven. The idea of Mr. Belden's proposing to enlarge by taking that ground adjoining! But of course poor pa didn't put up the building himself, nor anything; oh no! So *he* doesn't know whether the walls will stand a couple of extra stories or not. Upon my word," she went on with increased warmth, "I don't feel quite sure whether pa was the one to start the business in the first place and to keep it going along ever since, or whether he's just a new errand-boy, who began there a week ago! August, are we stuck here to stay forever?"

The little sorrel mare started up again and entered upon another stage of her journey. The first lights began to appear in the store-fronts; the newsboys were shrieking the last editions of the evening papers; the frenzied comedy of belated shopping commenced to manifest itself upon the pavements.

The throng of jostling women was especially thick and eager before a vast and vulgar front whose base was heaped with cheap truck cheaply ticketed, and whose long row of third-story windows was obscured by a great reach of cotton cloth tacked to a flimsy wooden frame. Unprecedented bargains were offered in gigantic letters by the new proprietors, "Eisendrath & Heide . . ." — the rest of the name flapped loosely in the wind.

"Alas, poor Wethersby, I knew him well," observed Marshall, absently. He cast a pensive eye upon the still-remaining name of the former proprietor, and took off his hat to weigh it in his hands with a pretence of deep speculation. "Well, the Philistines haven't got hold of *us* yet, have they?" he remarked, genially; he had not spent six months in Vienna for nothing. "I suppose we are still worth twenty sous in the franc, eh?"

"I suppose," replied his mother, with a grim brevity. She rather groped for his meaning, but she was perfectly certain of her own.

"I guess pa's all right," declared his sister, "as long as he is left alone and not interfered with."

The evening lights doubled and trebled — long rows of them appeared overhead at incalculable altitudes. The gongs of the cable cars clanged more and more imperiously as the crowds surged in great numbers round grip and trailer. The night life of the town began to bestir itself, and little Rosy, from her conspicuous place, beamed with a bright intentness upon its motley spectacle, careless of where her smiles might fall. For her the immodest theatrical poster drooped in the windows of saloons, or caught a transient hold upon the hoardings of uncompleted buildings; brazen blare and gaudy placards (disgusting rather than indecent) invited the passer-by into cheap museums and music-halls; all the unclassifiable riff-raff that is spawned by a great city leered from corners, or slouched along the edge of the gutters, or stood in dark doorways, or sold impossible rubbish in impossible dialects wherever the public indulgence permitted a foothold.

To Rosy's mother all this involved no impropriety. Eliza Marshall's Chicago was the Chicago of 1860, an Arcadia which, in some dim and inexplicable way, had remained for her an Arcadia still — bigger, noisier, richer, yet different only in degree, and not essentially in kind. She herself had traversed these same streets in the days when they were the streets of a mere town. Jane, accompanying her mother's courses as a child, had seen the town develop into a city. And now Rosy followed in her turn, though the *urbs in horto* of the earlier time existed only in the memory of "old settlers" and in the device of the municipal seal, while the great Black City stood out as a threatening and evil actuality. Mild old Mabel had drawn them all in turn or together, and had philosophized upon the facts as little as any of them; but Rosy's brother (who had been about, and who knew more than he was ever likely to tell) looked round at her now and then with a vague discomfort.

"There!" called their mother, suddenly; "did you see that?" A big lumpish figure on the crossing had loomed up at the mare's head, a rough hand had seized her bridle, and a raw voice with a rawer brogue had vented a piece of impassioned profanity on both beast and driver. "Well, I don't thank that policeman for hitting Mabel on the nose, I can tell him. August, did you get his number?"

"No'm," answered the coachman. He turned round familiarly. "I got his breath."

"I should think so," said Truesdale. "And such shoes as they have, and such hands, and such linen! Didn't that fellow see what we were? Couldn't he realize that we pay for the buttons on his coat? Mightn't he have tried to apprehend that we were people of position here long before he had scraped his wretched steerage-money together? And what was it he had working in his cheek?"

"I think I know," responded August mumblingly.

"Like enough," rejoined Truesdale, with his eye upon the coachman's own jaw.

His mother's sputter of indignation died rapidly away. It was, indeed, her notion that the guardians of the public peace should show some degree of sobriety, respect, neatness, and self-control, as well as a reasonable familiarity with the accents of the country; but her Arcadia was full of painful discrepancies, and she did not add to her own pain by too serious an attempt to reconcile them. Besides, what is a policeman compared with a detective?

Mabel, released from the arm of the law, jarred over another line of car tracks, whereon a long row of monsters glared at one another's slow advances with a single great red eye, and then she struck a freer gait on the succeeding stretch of Belgian blocks. Presently she passed a lofty building which rose in colonnades one above another, but whose walls were stained with smoke, whose windows were half full of shattered panes, and whose fraudulent metallic cornice curled over limply and jarred and jangled in the evening breeze — one more of the vicissitudes of mercantile life.

"Well, I'm glad the fire-fiend hasn't got Marshall & Co. yet," said the young man, restored to good-humor by the sight of another's misfortune. He used unconsciously the old firm name.

"But he'd get us fast enough if the insurance was taken off," declared Jane. "Do you know, Dicky," she went on, "how much that item cost us a year? Or have you any idea how much it has amounted to in the last twenty, without our ever getting one cent back? Well, there's ten thousand in the Hartford and eight in the Monongahela and eleven in — "

"Dear me, Jane!" exclaimed her brother, in some surprise; "where do you pick up all this?"

Rosy turned her head half round. "Mr. Brower tells her," she said, with a disdainful brevity.

Her face was indistinct in the twilight, but if its expression corresponded with the inflection of her voice, her nostrils were inflated and her lips were curled in disparagement. To Jane, in her dark corner of the carriage, this was patent enough. Indeed, it was sufficiently obvious to all that Jane's years availed little to save her from the searching criticism of her younger sister, and that Miss Rosamund Marshall bestowed but slight esteem — or, at least, but slight approval — upon Mr. Theodore Brower.

"Supposing he *does* tell me!" called Jane, absurdly allowing herself to be put on the defensive. "It's a mighty good thing, I take it. If there's anybody else in the family but me who knows or cares anything about poor pa's business, I should like to be told who it is!"

"That will do, Jane," sounded her mother's voice in cold correction. "There's no need for you to talk so. Your father has run his own business now for thirty-five years, with every year better than the year before, and I imagine he knows how to look out for himself. Thank goodness, we are on a respectable pavement once more."

Mabel, turning a sudden corner, had given them a quick transition from the rattle and jar of granite to the gentle palpitation that is possible on well-packed macadam. The carriage passed in review a series of towering and glittering hotels, told off a score or more of residences of the elder day, and presently drew up before the gate of an antiquated homestead in the neighborhood of the Panoramas.

"Just the same old place," murmured Truesdale, as he writhed out of his cramped quarters and stood on the carriage-block in the dusk to stretch his legs. "Wonderful how we contrive to stand stock-still in the midst of all this stir and change!"

"H'm!" said Jane, under her breath; "just wait and see!"

# Jane Addams

## (1860-1935)

*Although she wrote almost a dozen books,* JANE ADDAMS *will always be remembered more as a social activist than as an author. Born in tiny Cedarville, Illinois, in 1860, Addams founded Hull-House in 1889 (the building was named after the Chicago real estate developer who had built it and let it fall into disrepair). Modelled on London's Toynbee Hall, Hull-House provided a number of important services to residents of the impoverished West Side neighborhood in which it was located. Convinced that the poor were inherently as intelligent and capable as the rich, Addams focused on programs that emphasized education, fair and meaningful labor, civic cooperation, and exposure to the arts.*

*The public's perception of Addams was not unlike that of our own age toward Mother Teresa. While she had been condemned for her pacifism during World War I (much the same way that Mother Teresa was criticized for accepting money from despots), Addams was nevertheless generally regarded as a saintly figure. When she died in 1935, thousands of people came to Hull-House to pay their respects. Her legacy continues in Chicago at a number of activist neighborhood centers sponsored by the Hull-House Association.*

*Jane Addams's two best-known books are* Twenty Years at Hull-House *(1910) and* The Second Twenty Years at Hull-House *(1930). Our selection from the earlier book shows that Addams was not just a compassionate, clear-thinking woman, but also a writer of surprising grace. Measured yet forceful, her prose demonstrates how fully she understood the complex problems of poverty.*

✦ ✦ ✦

## *from* TWENTY YEARS AT HULL-HOUSE

That neglected and forlorn old age is daily brought to the attention of a Settlement which undertakes to bear its share of the neighborhood burden imposed by poverty, was pathetically clear to us during our first months of residence at Hull-House. One day a boy of ten led a tottering old lady into the House, saying that she had slept for six weeks in their kitchen on a bed made up next to the stove; that she had come when her son died, although none of them had ever seen her before; but because her son had "once worked in the same shop with Pa she thought of him when she had nowhere to go." The little fellow concluded by saying that our house was so much bigger than theirs that he thought we would have more room for beds. The old woman herself said absolutely nothing, but looking on with that gripping fear of the poorhouse in her eyes, she was a living embodiment of that dread which is so heart-breaking that the occupants of the County Infirmary themselves seem scarcely less wretched than those who are making their last stand against it.

This look was almost more than I could bear for only a few days before some frightened women had bidden me come quickly to the house of an old German woman, whom two men from the county agent's office were attempting to remove to the County Infirmary. The poor old creature had thrown herself bodily upon a small and battered chest of drawers and clung there, clutching it so firmly that it would have been impossible to remove her without also taking the piece of furniture. She did not weep nor moan nor indeed make any human sound, but between her broken gasps for breath she squealed shrilly like a frightened animal caught in a trap. The little group of women and children gathered at her door stood aghast at this realization of the black dread which always clouds the lives of the very poor when work is slack, but which constantly grows more imminent and threatening as old age approaches. The neighborhood women and I hastened to make all sorts of promises as to the support of the old woman and the county officials, only too glad to be rid of their unhappy duty, left her to our ministrations. This dread of the poorhouse, the result of centuries of deterrent Poor Law administration, seemed to me not without some justification one summer when I found myself perpetually distressed by the unnecessary idleness and forlornness of the old women in the Cook County Infirmary, many of whom I had known in the years when activity was still a necessity, and when they yet felt bustlingly important. To take away from an old woman whose life has been spent in household cares all the foolish little belongings to which her affections cling and to which her very fingers have become accustomed, is to take away her last incentive to activity, almost to life itself. To give an old woman only a chair and a bed, to leave her no cupboard in which her treasures may be stowed, not only that she may take them out when she desires occupation, but that her mind may dwell upon them in moments of revery, is to reduce living almost beyond the limit of human endurance.

The poor creature who clung so desperately to her chest of drawers was really clinging to the last remnant of normal living — a symbol of all she was asked to renounce. For several years after this summer I invited five or six old women to take a two weeks' vacation from the poorhouse which they eagerly and even gayly accepted. Almost all the old men in the County Infirmary wander away each summer taking their chances for finding food or shelter and return much refreshed by the little "tramp," but the old women cannot do this unless they have some help from the outside, and yet the expenditure of a very little money secures for them the coveted vacation. I found that a few pennies paid their car fare into town, a dollar a week procured a lodging with an old acquaintance; assured of two good meals a day in the Hull-House coffeehouse they could count upon numerous cups of tea among old friends to whom they would airily state that they had "come out for a little change" and hadn't yet made up their minds about "going in again for the winter." They thus enjoyed a two weeks' vacation to the top of their bent and returned with wondrous tales of their adventures, with which they regaled the other paupers during the long winter.

The reminiscences of these old women, their shrewd comments upon life, their sense of having reached a point where they may at last speak freely with nothing to lose because of their frankness, makes them often the most delightful of companions. I recall one of my guests, the mother of many scattered children, whose one bright spot through all the dreary years had been the wedding feast of her son Mike, — a feast which had become transformed through long meditation into the nectar and ambrosia of the very gods. As a farewell fling before she went "in" again, we dined together upon chicken pie, but it did not taste like "the chicken pie at Mike's wedding" and she was disappointed after all.

Even death itself sometimes fails to bring the dignity and serenity which one would fain associate with old age. I recall the dying house of one old Scotchwoman whose long struggle to "keep respectable" had so embittered her, that her last words were gibes and taunts for those who were trying to minister to her. "So you came in yourself this morning, did you? You only sent things yesterday. I guess you knew when the doctor was coming. Don't try to warm my feet with anything but that old jacket that I've got there; it belonged to my boy who was drowned at sea nigh thirty years ago, but it's warmer yet with human feelings than any of your damned charity hot-water bottles." Suddenly the harsh gasping voice was stilled in death and I awaited the doctor's coming shaken and horrified.

The lack of municipal regulation already referred to was, in the early days of Hull-House, paralleled by the inadequacy of the charitable efforts of the city and an unfounded optimism that there was no real poverty among us. Twenty years ago there was no Charity Organization Society in Chicago and the Visiting Nurse Association had not yet begun its beneficent work, while the relief societies, although conscientiously administered, were inadequate in extent and antiquated in method.

As social reformers gave themselves over to discussion of general principles, so the poor invariably accused poverty itself of their destruction. I recall a certain Mrs. Moran, who was returning one rainy day from the office of the county agent with her arms full of paper bags containing beans and flour which alone lay between her children and starvation. Although she had no money she boarded a street car in order to save her booty from complete destruction by the rain, and as the burst bags dropped "flour on the ladies' dresses" and "beans all over the place," she was sharply reprimanded by the conductor, who was further exasperated when he discovered she had no fare. He put her off, as she had hoped he would, almost in front of Hull-House. She related to us her state of mind as she stepped off the car and saw the last of her wares disappearing; she admitted she forgot the proprieties and "cursed a little," but, curiously enough, she pronounced her malediction, not against the rain nor the conductor, nor yet against the worthless husband who had been sent up to the city prison, but, true to the Chicago spirit of the moment, went to the root of the matter and roundly "cursed poverty."

This spirit of generalization and lack of organization among the charitable forces of the city was painfully revealed in that terrible winter after the World's Fair, when the general financial depression throughout the country was much intensified in Chicago by the numbers of unemployed stranded at the close of the exposition. When the first cold weather came the police stations and the very corridors of the city hall were crowded by men who could afford no other lodging. They made huge demonstrations on the lake front, reminding one of the London gatherings in Trafalgar Square.

It was the winter in which Mr. Stead wrote his indictment of Chicago. I can vividly recall his visits to Hull-House, some of them between eleven and twelve o'clock at night, when he would come in wet and hungry from an investigation of the levee district, and, while he was drinking hot chocolate before an open fire, would relate in one of his curious monologues, his experience as an out-of-door laborer standing in line without an overcoat for two hours in the sleet, that he might have a chance to sweep the streets; or his adventures with a crook, who mistook him for one of his own kind and offered him a place as an agent for a gambling house, which he promptly accepted. Mr. Stead was much impressed with the mixed goodness in Chicago, the lack of rectitude in many high places, the simple kindness of the most wretched to each other. Before he published "If Christ Came to Chicago" he made his attempt to rally the diverse moral forces of the city in a huge mass meeting, which resulted in a temporary organization, later developing into the Civic Federation. I was a member of the committee of five appointed to carry out the suggestions made in this remarkable meeting, and our first concern was to appoint a committee to deal with the unemployed. But when has a committee ever dealt satisfactorily with the unemployed? Relief stations were opened in various parts of the city, temporary lodging houses were established, Hull-House undertaking to lodge the homeless women who could be received nowhere else; employment stations were opened giving sewing to the women, and street sweeping for the men was organized. It was in connection with the latter that the perplexing question of the danger of permanently lowering wages at such a crisis, in the praiseworthy effort to bring speedy relief, was brought home to me. I insisted that it was better to have the men work half a day for seventy-five cents than a whole day for a dollar, better that they should earn three dollars in two days than in three days. I resigned from the street cleaning committee in despair of making the rest of the committee understand that, as our real object was not street cleaning but the help of the unemployed, we must treat the situation in such wise that the men would not be worse off when they returned to their normal occupations. The discussion opened up situations new to me and carried me far afield in perhaps the most serious economic reading I have ever done.

A beginning also was then made toward a Bureau of Organized Charities, the main office being put in charge of a young man recently come from Boston, who lived at Hull-House. But to employ scientific methods for the first time at such a moment involved difficulties, and the most painful episode of the winter for me came from an attempt on my part to conform to carefully received instructions. A shipping clerk whom I had known for a long time had lost his place, as so many people had that year, and came to the relief station established at Hull-House four or five times to secure help for his family. I told him one day of the opportunity for work on the drainage canal and intimated that if any employment were obtainable, he ought to exhaust that possibility before asking for help. The man replied that he had always worked indoors and that he could not endure outside work in winter. I am grateful to remember that I was too uncertain to be severe, although I held to my instructions. He did not come again for relief, but worked for two days digging on the canal, where he contracted pneumonia and died a week later. I have never lost trace of the two little children he left behind him, although I cannot see them without a bitter consciousness that it was at their expense I learned that life cannot be administered by definite rules and regulations; that wisdom to deal with a man's difficulties comes only through some knowledge of his life and habits as a whole; and that to treat an isolated episode is almost sure to invite blundering.

# Hamlin Garland

## (1860-1940)

*One of the central figures of the Chicago Literary Renaissance,* HAMLIN GARLAND *was born in Wisconsin in 1860 and lived in Iowa, Minnesota, North Dakota, and Boston before settling, at age thirty-three, in Chicago. Garland had begun writing about the difficult life of Midwestern farmers while teaching at the Boston School of Oratory, and he continued to do so for a good part of his career. In addition to his writing, Garland is also remembered as a founding member — with Henry Blake Fuller and others — of the Cliff Dwellers Club, Chicago's premier social club for literati. Garland's major works include the story collections* Main Travelled Roads *(1891) and* Book of the American Indian *(1923), and a book of essays entitled* Crumbling Idols *(1894). His autobiography,* Son of the Middle Border *(1917), was followed by the Pulitzer Prize–winning sequel* Daughter of the Middle Border *(1921). In 1930 Garland moved to Hollywood, where he lived for the next ten years before dying in his home of a cerebral hemorrhage.*

*The Rose of Dutcher's Coolly (1895), from which the passage below is taken, remains Garland's best known and best novel. Like so many classic works of Chicago fiction, the book traces the career of an ingenue who makes it big in the city. Creative, restless, Rose Dutcher, "an unaccountable child from the start," leaves her Wisconsin farm to pursue a career as a poet. Likeable and indomitable, Rose eventually marries, though she does so to a man, Warren Mason, who is willing to meet her on her own terms. The following passage from chapter 16, "Her First Conquest," describes Rose's initial meeting with Dr. Isabel Herrick, the woman who opens the doors of Chicago literary society for her.*

◆ ◆ ◆

## *from* THE ROSE OF DUTCHER'S COOLLY

The next day Rose went down town alone. The wind had veered to the south, the dust blew, and the whole terrifying panorama of life in the streets seemed some way blurred together, and forms of men and animals were like figures in tapestry. The grind and clang and clatter and hiss and howl of the traffic was all about her.

She came upon the river just as the bridge was being opened. Down toward the lake, which had to her all the wonder and expanse of the sea, boats lay thickly; steamers from deep water, long, narrow, and black, excursion boats, gleaming white, and trimmed with shining brass, lay beside the wharves, and low-lying tugs, sturdy, rowdyish little things, passed by, floating like ducks and pulling like bull-dogs, guiding great two-masted sailing boats and long, low grimy grain steamers, with high decks at the ends. The river ran below, gray-green, covered with floating refuse. Mountainous buildings stood on either side of the waterway.

The draw, as it began to move, made a noise precisely like an old-fashioned threshing machine — a rising howl, which went to Rose's heart like a familiar voice. Her eyes for a moment released hold upon the scene before her, and took a slant far over the town to the coolly farm, and the days when the threshing machine howled and rattled in the yard came back, and she was rushing to get dinner ready for the crew. When the bridge returned to its place she walked slowly across, studying each vista. To the west, other bridges, swarming with people, arched the stream — on each side was equal mystery. These wonderful great boats and their grim brave sailors she had read about, but had never seen. They came from far up the great tumultuous lake, and they were going to anchor somewhere in that wild tangle of masts and chimneys and towering big buildings to the west. They looked as if they might go to the ends of the earth. At the stern of an outgoing boat four sailors were pulling at a rope, the leader singing a wild, thrilling song in time to the action.

So it was that the wonderful and the terrifying appealed to her mind first. In all the city she saw the huge and the fierce. She perceived only contrasts. She saw the ragged newsboy and the towering policeman. She saw the rag-pickers, the street vermin, with a shudder of pity and horror, and she saw also the gorgeous show windows of the great stores. She saw the beautiful new gowns and hats, and she saw also the curious dresses of swart Italian girls scavenging with baskets on their arms. Their faces were old and grimy, their voices sounded like the chattered colloquies of the monkeys in the circus.

The street seemed a battle-field. There was no hint of repose or home in such a city. People were just staying here like herself, trying to get work, trying to make a living, trying to make a name. They had left their homes as she had, and though she conceived of them as having a foothold, she could not imagine them as having reached security. The home-life of the city had not revealed itself to her.

She made her way about the first few blocks below Water Street, looking for Dr. Herrick's address. It was ten o'clock, and the streets were in a frenzy of exchange. The sidewalks were brooks, the streets rivers of life, which curled into doors and swirled around mountainous buildings.

She was pathetically helpless in the midst of these alien sounds. It took away from her the calm, almost scornful, self-reliance which characterized her in familiar surroundings. Her senses were as acute as a hare's, and sluiced in upon her a bewildering flood of sights and sounds. She did not appear childish, but she seemed slow and stupid, which of course she was not. She thought and thought till she grew sick with thought. She struggled to digest all that came to her, but it was like trampling sand; she apparently gained nothing by her toil.

The streets led away into thunderous tunnels, beyond which some other strange hell of sound and stir imaginatively lay. The brutal voices of drivers of cabs and drays assaulted her. The clang of gongs drew her attention, now here, now there, and her anxiety to understand each sound and to appear calm added to her confusion.

She heard crashes and yells that were of murder and sudden death. It was the crash of a falling bundle of sheet iron, but she knew not that. She looked around thinking to see some savage, bloody battle-scene.

She saw women with painted faces and bleached hair whom she took to be those mysterious and appalling women who sell themselves to men. They were in fact simple-minded shop girls or vulgar little housewives with sad lack of taste.

Every street she crossed, she studied, looking both up and down it, in the effort to come at the end of its mystery — but they all vanished in lurid, desolate distance, save toward the lake. Out there, she knew, the water lay serene and blue.

This walk was to her like entrance into war. It thrilled and engaged her at every turn. She was in the centre of human life. To win here was to win all she cared to have.

It was a relief to pass into the rotunda of the splendid building in which Dr. Herrick's office was. Outside the war sounded, and around her men hastened as if to rescue. She entered the elevator as one in a dream. The man hustled her through the door without ceremony and clanged the door as if it were a prison gate. They soared to the ninth floor like a balloon suddenly liberated, and the attendant fairly pushed her out.

"Here's your floor — Herrick, to the left."

Rose was humiliated and indignant, but submitted. The hallway along which she moved was marble and specklessly clean. On each side doors of glass with letters in black set forth the occupations of the tenants.

She came at length to the half-open door of Dr. Herrick's office and timidly entered. A young girl came forward courteously.

"Would you like to see the Doctor?" she asked, in a soft voice.

"Yes, please. I have a letter to her from Dr. Thatcher of Madison."

"Oh! well, I will take it right in. Be seated, please."

This good treatment, and the soft voice of the girl, were very grateful after the hoarse war-cries of the street. Rose looked around the little room with growing composure and delight. It was such a dainty little waiting-room, and augured something attractive in Dr. Herrick.

"Come right in," the girl said on returning. "The Doctor is attending to her mail, but she will see you for a few moments."

Rose entered the second and larger room, and faced a small, graceful woman, of keen, alert glance. She appeared to be about thirty-five years of age. She shook hands briskly, but not warmly.

Her hand was small and firm and her tone quick and decisive. "How-d'-you-do? Sit down! I had a note from Dr. Thatcher the other day saying I might expect you."

Rose took a chair while the Doctor studied her, sitting meanwhile with small, graceful head leaning on one palm, her elbow on the corner of her desk. No woman's eyes ever searched Rose like those of this little woman, and she rebelled against it inwardly, as Dr. Herrick curtly asked:

"Well, now, what can I do for you? Dr. Thatcher thought I could do something for you."

Rose was too dazed to reply. This small, resolute, brusque woman was a world's wonder to her. She looked down and stammered.

"I don't know — I — thought maybe you could help me to find out what I *could* do."

The Doctor studied her for an instant longer. She saw a large, apparently inexperienced girl, a little sullen and a little embarrassed — probably stupid.

"Don't you know what you want to do?"

"No — that is, I want to write," confessed Rose.

"Write! My dear girl, every addle-pate wants to write. Have you friends in the city?"

"One; a classmate."

"Man?"

"No, a girl."

"Why did you leave home?"

Rose began to grow angry. "Because I couldn't live the life of a cow or a cabbage. I wanted to see the city."

The Doctor arose. "Come here a moment." Rose obeyed and stood beside her at the window, and they looked out across a stretch of roofs, heaped and humped into mountainous masses, blurred and blent and made appalling by smoke and plumes of steam. A scene as desolate as a burnt-out volcano — a jumble of hot bricks, jagged eave-spouts, gas-vomiting chimneys, spiked railings, glass skylights, and lofty spires, a hideous and horrible stretch of stone and mortar, cracked and seamed into streets. It had no limits and it palpitated under the hot September sun, boundless and savage. At the bottom of the crevasses men and women speckled the pavement like minute larvae.

"Is *that* what you came here to see?" asked the Doctor.

Rose drew a deep breath and faced her.

"Yes, and I'm not afraid of it. It's mighty! It is grander than I expected it to be — grand and terrible, but it's where things are done."

Isabel Herrick studied her a little closer.

"You'd leave your country home for this?"

Rose turned upon her and towered above her. Her eyes flashed and her abundant eyebrows drew down in a dark scowl.

"Would you be content to spend your life, day and night, summer and winter, in Dutcher's Coolly?"

"Pardon me," said Dr. Herrick, cuttingly, "the problem is not the same. I have not the same — I — the question — "

"Yes, *you* who are born in the city and who come up to see us on the farms for a couple of weeks in June — *you* take it on yourselves to advise us to stay there! *You* who succeed are always ready to discourage us when we come to try *our* fortunes. I can succeed just as well as you, and I'll make you bow your head to me before I am five years older."

She was magnificent, masterful, in the flaming heat of her wrath. This little woman had gone too far.

Dr. Herrick turned abruptly.

"I guess I've made a mistake; sit down again," she said, in softer tones.

Rose was not yet done. She kept her lofty pose.

"Yes, you certainly have. I am not afraid of this city; I can take care of myself. I wouldn't be under obligations to you now for the world. I want you to know I'm not a beggar asking for a dollar from you; I'm not a schoolgirl, either. I know what I can do and you don't. I wouldn't have troubled you, only for Dr. Thatcher." She moved toward the door, gloriously angry, too angry to say good-day.

The Doctor's cold little face lighted up. She smiled the most radiant smile, and it made her look all at once like a girl.

"My dear — I am crushed. I am an ant at your feet. Come here now, you great splendid creature, and let me hug you this minute."

Rose kept on to the door, where she turned: "I don't think I ought to trouble you further," she said coldly.

The Doctor advanced. "Come now, I beg your pardon. I'm knocked out. I took you for one of those romantic country girls, who come to the city — helpless as babes. Come back."

Rose came near going on. If she had, it would have lost her a good friend. She felt that, and so when the Doctor put an arm around her to lead her back to the desk she yielded, though she was still palpitating with the fervor of her wrath.

"My dear, you fairly scared me. I never was so taken by surprise in my life; tell me all about yourself; tell me how you came to come, where you are — and all about it."

Rose told her — not all, of course — she told her of her college work, of her father, of the coolly, and of her parting from her father.

"Oh, yes," the Doctor interrupted, "that's the way we go on — we new men and women. The ways of our fathers are not ours; it's tragedy either way you put it. Go on!"

At last she had the story, told with marvellous unconscious power, direct, personal, full of appeal. She looked at Rose with reflective eyes for a little space.

"Well, now we'll take time to consider. Bring me something of yours; I'll show it to a friend of mine, an editor here, and if it pleases him we'll know what to do. And come and see me. I'll introduce you to some nice people. Chicago is full of nice people if you only come at them. Come and see me to-morrow, can't you? Oh, you great, splendid creature! I wish I had your inches." She glowed with admiration.

"Come Sunday at six and dine with me," yielding to a sudden impulse. "Come early and let me talk to you."

Rose promised and they went out into the waiting-room.

"Etta, dear, this is Miss Dutcher; this is my sister. I want you to know each other." The little girl tiptoed up and took Rose's hand with a little inarticulate murmur.

There was a patient in waiting, but Dr. Herrick ignored her and conducted Rose to the door.

"Good-by, dear, I'm glad you came. You've given me a good shaking up. Remember, six, sharp!"

She looked after Rose with a wonderful glow in her heart.

"The girl is a genius — a jewel in the rough," she thought. "She must be guided. Heavens! How she towered."

When she stepped into the street Rose felt taller and stronger, and the street was less appalling. She raised her eyes to the faces of the men she met. Her eyes had begun their new search. The men streamed by in hundreds; impressive in mass, but comparatively uninteresting singly.

It was a sad comment upon her changing conceptions of life that she did not look at the poorly dressed men, the workmen. She put them aside as out of the question; not consciously, for the search at this stage was still unconscious, involuntary, like that of a bird seeking a mate, moved by a law which knows neither individuals nor time.

# Elia Peattie

# (1862-1935)

*She may be better known as the mother of naturalist Donald Culross Peattie, but in her day* ELIA WILKINSON PEATTIE *was a crusading reporter and editor for the* Chicago Tribune *and the author of more than thirty books. Born in 1862 to a proud, financially unsuccessful father, Elia Peattie was forced to quit school in seventh grade; her early poverty gave her a work ethic that never abated. She married a fellow writer, Robert, who was remarkably supportive of her career; in fact, she sometimes dictated stories to him in the evening as she sewed. Influential as a critic as well as social reformer, Peattie was an outspoken advocate of women's suffrage and women's rights. She died in 1935.*

*The Precipice (1914) is a novel of ideas. It chronicles Kate Barrington's escape from downstate Silvertree to Chicago, where she becomes involved in social welfare. Working for a time with Jane Addams (with whom Elia Peattie herself was friends), Kate, by the end of the novel, is offered the directorship of the Bureau of Children by the president of the United States. After deflecting a number of lesser proposals, she also manages to find a husband willing to honor her sense of independence.*

*Chapter 5 shows Kate balancing the demands of her own strong will and conscience with the constraints of early twentieth century society. She is carrying a neglected infant in her arms when she runs into two acquaintances, one of whom, Mrs. Barsaloux, is appalled that Kate would actually touch a poor child. After listening to Kate recount some of her troubles as a social worker to her friends David and Honora Fulham, we admire (or perhaps wince at) the way she is able to gracefully handle Dr. von Shierbrand, who "expected women to be amusing." One of Chicago literature's early feminist protagonists, Kate has the courage to wonder "what sort of world it would be if there were no men in it at all."*

◆ ◆ ◆

*from* THE PRECIPICE

A fortnight later she was established as an officer of the Children's Protective Association, an organization with a self-explanatory name, instituted by women, and chiefly supported by them. She was given an inexhaustible task, police powers, headquarters at Hull House, and a vocation demanding enough to satisfy even her desire for spiritual adventure.

It was her business to adjust the lives of children — which meant that she adjusted their parents' lives also. She arranged the disarranged; played the providential part, exercising the powers of intervention which in past times belonged to the priest, but which, in the days of commercial feudalism, devolve upon the social workers.

Her work carried her into the lowest strata of society, and her compassion, her efficiency, and her courage were daily called upon. Perhaps she might have found herself lacking in the required measure of these qualities, being so young and inexperienced, had it not been that she was in a position to concentrate completely upon her task. She knew how to listen and to learn; she knew how to read and apply. She went into her new work with a humble spirit, and this humility offset whatever was aggressive and militant in her. The death of her mother and the aloofness of her father had turned all her ardors back upon herself. They found vent now in her new work, and she was not long in perceiving that she needed those whom she was called upon to serve quite as much as they needed her.

Mrs. Barsaloux and Marna Cartan, who had been shopping, met Kate one day crossing the city with a baby in her arms and two miserable little children clinging to her skirts. Hunger and neglect had given these poor small derelicts that indescribable appearance of depletion and shame which, once seen, is never to be confused with anything else.

"My goodness!" cried Mrs. Barsaloux, glowering at Kate through her veil; "what sort of work is this you are doing, Miss Barrington? Aren't you afraid of becoming infected with some dreadful disease? Wherever do you find the fortitude to be seen in the company of such wretched little creatures? I would like to help them myself, but I'd never be willing to carry such filthy little bags of misery around with me."

Kate smiled cheerfully.

"We've just put their mother in the Bridewell," she said, "and their father is in the police station awaiting trial. The poor dears are going to be clean for once in their lives and have a good supper in the bargain. Maybe they'll be taken into good homes eventually. They're lovely children, really. You haven't looked at them closely enough, Mrs. Barsaloux."

"I'm just as close to them as I want to be, thank you," said the lady, drawing back involuntarily. But she reached for her purse and gave Kate a bill.

"Would this help toward getting them something?" she asked.

Marna laughed delightedly.

"I'm sure they're treasures," she said. "Mayn't I help Miss Barrington take them to wherever they're going, *tante?* I shan't catch a thing, and I love to know what becomes of homeless children."

Kate saw a look of acute distress on Mrs. Barsaloux's face.

"This isn't your game just now, Miss Cartan," Kate said in her downright manner. "It's mine. I'm moving my pawns here and there, trying to find the best places for them. It's quite exhilarating."

Her arms were aching and she moved the heavy baby from one shoulder to the other.

"A game, is it?" asked the Irish girl. "And who wins?"

"The children, I hope. I'm on the side of the children first and last."

"Oh, so am I. I think it's just magnificent of you to help them."

Kate disclaimed the magnificence.

"You mustn't forget that I'm doing it for money," she said. "It's my job. I hope I'll do it well enough to win the reputation of being honest, but you mustn't think there's anything saintly about me, because there isn't. Good-bye. Hold on tight, children!"

She nodded cheerfully and moved on, fresh, strong, determined, along the crowded thoroughfare, the people making way for her smilingly. She saw nothing of the attention paid her. She was wondering if her arms would hold out or if, in some unguarded moment, the baby would slip from them. Perhaps the baby was fearful, too, for it reached up its little clawlike hands and clasped her tight about the neck. Kate liked the feeling of those little hands, and was sorry when they relaxed and the weary little one fell asleep.

Each day brought new problems. If she could have decided these by mere rule of common sense, her new vocation might not have puzzled her as much as it did. But it was uncommon, superfine, intuitive sense that was required. She discovered, for example, that not only was sin a virtue in disguise, but that a virtue might be degraded into a sin.

She put this case to Honora and David one evening as the three of them sat in Honora's drawing-room.

"It's the case of Peggy Dunn," she explained. "Peggy likes life. She has brighter eyes than she knows what to do with and more smiles than she has a chance to distribute. She has finished her course at the parochial school and she's clerking in a downtown store. That is slow going for Peggy, so she evens things up by attending the Saturday night dances. When she's whirling around the hall on the tips of her toes, she really feels like herself. She gets home about two in the morning on these occasions and finds her mother waiting up for her and kneeling before a little statue of the Virgin that stands in the corner of the sitting-room. As soon as the mother sees Peggy, she pounces on her and weeps on her shoulder, and after Peggy's in bed and dead with the tire in her legs, her mother gets down beside the bed and prays some more. 'What would you do, please,' says Peggy to me, 'if you had a mother that kept crying and praying every time you had a bit of fun? Wouldn't you run away from home and get where they took things aisier?'"

David threw back his head and roared in sympathetic commendation of Peggy's point of view.

"Poor little mother," sighed Honora. "I suppose she'll send her girl straight on the road to perdition and never know what did it."

"Not if I can help it," said Kate. "I don't believe in letting her go to perdition at all. I went around to see the mother and I put the responsibility on her. 'Every time you make Peggy laugh,' I said, 'you can count it for glory. Every time you make her swear, — for she does swear, — you can know you've blundered. Why don't you give her some parties if you don't want her to be going out to them?'"

"How did she take that?" asked Honora.

"It bothered her a good deal at first, but when I went down to meet Peggy the other day as she came out of the store, she told me her mother had had the little bisque Virgin moved into her own bedroom and that she had put a talking-machine in the place where it had stood. I told Peggy the talking-machine was just a new kind of prayer, meant to make her happy, and that it wouldn't do for her to let her mother's prayers go unanswered. 'Any one with eyes like yours,' I said to her, 'is bound to have beaux in plenty, but you've only one mother and you'd better hang on to her.'"

"Then what did she say?" demanded the interested Honora.

"She's an impudent little piece. She said, 'You've some eyes yourself, Miss Barrington, but I suppose you know how to make them behave.'"

"Better marry that girl as soon as you can, Miss Barrington," counseled David; "that is, if any hymeneal authority is vested in you."

"That's what Peggy wanted to know," admitted Kate. "She said to me the other day: 'Ain't you Cupid, Miss Barrington? I heard about a match you made up, and it was all right — the real thing, sure enough.' 'Have you a job for me — supposing I was Cupid?' I asked. That set her off in a gale. So I suppose there's something up Peggy's very short sleeves."

The Fulhams liked to hear her stories, particularly as she kept the amusing or the merely pathetic ones for them, refraining from telling them of the unspeakable, obscene tragedies which daily came to her notice. It might have been supposed that scenes such as these would so have revolted her that she could not endure to deal with them; but this was far from being the case. The greater the need for her help, the more determined was she to meet the demand. She had plenty of superiors whom she could consult, and she suffered less from disgust or timidity than any one could have supposed possible.

The truth was, she was grateful for whatever absorbed her and kept her from dwelling upon that dehumanized house at Silvertree. Her busy days enabled her to fight her sorrow very well, but in the night, like a wailing child, her longing for her mother awoke, and she nursed it, treasuring it as those freshly bereaved often do. The memory of that little frustrated soul made her tender of all women, and too prone, perhaps, to lay to some man the blame of their shortcomings. She had no realization that she had set herself in this subtle and subconscious way against men. But whether she admitted it or not, the fact remained that she stood with her sisters, whatever their estate, leagued secretly against the other sex.

By way of emphasizing her devotion to her work, she ceased answering Ray McCrea's letters. She studiously avoided the attentions of the men she met at the Settlement House and at Mrs. Dennison's Caravansary. Sometimes, without her realizing it, her thoughts took on an almost morbid hue, so that, looking at Honora with her chaste, kind, uplifted face, she resented her close association with her husband. It seemed offensive that he, with his curious, half-restrained excesses of temperament, should have domination over her friend who stood so obviously for abnegation. David manifestly was averse to bounds and limits. All that was wild and desirous of adventure in Kate informed her of like qualities in this man. But she held — and meant always to hold — the restless falcons of her spirit in leash. Would David Fulham do as much? She could not be quite sure, and instinctively she avoided anything approaching intimacy with him.

He was her friend's husband. "Friend's husband" was a sort of limbo into which men were dropped by scrupulous ladies; so Kate decided, with a frown at herself for having even thought that David could wish to emerge from that nondescript place of spiritual residence. Anyway, she did not completely like him, though she thought him extraordinary and stimulating, and when Honora told her something of the great discovery which the two of them appeared to be upon the verge of making concerning the germination of life without parental interposition, she had little doubt that David was wizard enough to carry it through. He would have the daring, and Honora the industry, and — she reflected — if renown came, that would be David's beyond all peradventure.

No question about it, Kate's thoughts were satiric these days. She was still bleeding from the wound which her father had inflicted, and she did not suspect that it was wounded affection rather than hurt self-respect which was tormenting her. She only knew that she shrank from men, and that at times she liked to imagine what sort of a world it would be if there were no men in it at all.

Meantime she met men every day, and whether she was willing to admit it or not, the facts were that they helped her on her way with brotherly good will, and as they saw her going about her singular and heavy tasks, they gave her their silent good wishes, and hoped that the world of pain and shame would not too soon destroy what was gallant and trustful in her.

But here has been much anticipation. To go back to the beginning, at the end of her first week in the city she had a friend. It was Marna Cartan. They had fallen into the way of talking together a few minutes before or after dinner, and Kate would hasten her modest dinner toilet in order to have these few marginal moments with the palpitating young creature who moved to unheard rhythms, and whose laughter was the sweetest thing she had yet heard in a city of infinite dissonances.

"You don't know how to account for me very well, do you?" taunted Marna daringly, when they had indulged their inclination for each other's society for a few days. "You wonder about me because I'm so streaked. I suppose you see vestiges of the farm girl peeping through the operatic student. Wouldn't you like me to explain myself?"

She had an iridescent personality, made up of sudden shynesses, of bright flashes of bravado, of tenderness and hauteur, and she contrived to be fascinating in all of them. She held Kate as the Ancient Mariner held the wedding-guest.

"Of course I'd love to know all about you," answered Kate. "Inquisitiveness is the most marked of my characteristics. But I don't want you to tell me any more than I deserve to hear."

"You deserve everything," cried Marna, seizing Kate's firm hand in her own soft one, "because you understand friendship. Why, I always said it could be as swift and surprising as love, and just as mysterious. You take it that way, too, so you deserve a great deal. Well, to begin with, I'm Irish."

Kate's laugh could be heard as far as the kitchen, where Mrs. Dennison was wishing the people would come so that she could dish up the soup. Marna laughed, too.

"You guessed it?" she cried. She didn't seem to think it so obvious as Kate's laugh indicated.

"You don't leave a thing to the imagination in that direction," Kate cried. "Irish? As Irish as the shamrock! Go on."

"Dear me, I want to begin so far back! You see, I don't merely belong to modern Ireland. I'm — well, I'm traditional. At least, Great-Grandfather Cartan, who came over to Wisconsin with a company of immigrants, could tell you things about our ancestors that would make you feel as if we came up out of the Irish hills. And great-grandfather, he actually looked legendary himself. Why, do you know, he came over with these people to be their story-teller!"

"Their story-teller?"

"Yes, just that—their minstrel, you understand. And that's what my people were, 'way back, minstrels. All the way over on the ship, when the people were weeping for homesickness, or sitting dreaming about the new land, or falling sick, or getting wild and vicious, it was great-granddaddy's place to bring them to themselves with his stories. Then when they all went on to Wisconsin and took up their land, they selected a small beautiful piece for great-grandfather, and built him a log house, and helped him with his crops. He, for his part, went over the countryside and was welcomed everywhere, and carried all the friendly news and gossip he could gather, and sat about the fire nights, telling tales of the old times, and keeping the ancient stories and the ancient tongue alive for them."

"You mean he used the Gaelic?"

"What else would he be using, and himself the descendant of minstrels? But after a time he learned the English, too, and he used that in his latter years because the understanding of the Gaelic began to die out."

"How wonderful he must have been!"

"Wonderful? For eighty years he held sway over the hearts of them, and was known as the best story-teller of them all. This was the more interesting, you see, because every year they gathered at a certain place to have a story-telling contest; and great-grandfather was voted the master of them until—"

Marna hesitated, and a flush spread over her face.

"Until—" urged Kate.

"Until a young man came along. Finnegan, his name was. He was no more than a commercial traveler who heard of the gathering and came up there, and he capped stories with great-grandfather, and it went on till all the people were thick about them like bees around a flower-pot. Four days it lasted, and away into the night; and in the end they took the prize from great-grandfather and gave it to Gerlie Finnegan. And that broke great-granddad's heart."

"He died?"

"Yes, he died. A hundred and ten he was, and for eighty years had been the king of them. When he was gone, it left me without anybody at all, you see. So that was how I happened to go down to Baraboo to earn my living."

"What were you doing?"

Marna looked at the tip of her slipper for a moment, reflectively. Then she glanced up at Kate, throwing a supplicating glance from the blue eyes which looked as if they were snared behind their long dark lashes.

"I wouldn't be telling everybody that asked me," she said. "But I was singing at the moving-picture show, and Mrs. Barsaloux came in there and heard me. Then she asked me to live with her and go to Europe, and I did, and she paid for the best music lessons for me everywhere, and now—"

She hesitated, drawing in a long breath; then she arose and stood before Kate, breathing deep, and looking like a shining butterfly free of its chrysalis and ready to spread its emblazoned wings.

"Yes, bright one!" cried Kate, glowing with admiration. "What now?"

"Why, now, you know, I'm to go in opera. The manager of the Chicago Opera Company has been Mrs. Barsaloux's friend these many years, and she has had him try out my voice. And he likes it. He says he doesn't care if I haven't had the usual amount of training, because I'm really born to sing, you see. Perhaps that's my inheritance from the old minstrels — for they chanted their ballads and epics, didn't they? Anyway, I really can sing. And I'm to make my début this winter in 'Madame Butterfly.' Just think of that! Oh, I love Puccini! I can understand a musician like that — a man who makes music move like thoughts, flurrying this way and blowing that. It's to be very soon — my début. And then I can make up to Mrs. Barsaloux for all she's done for me. Oh, there come all the people! You mustn't let Mrs. Fulham know how I've chattered. I wouldn't dare talk about myself like that before her. This is just for you — I *knew* you wanted to know about me. I want to know all about you, too."

"Oh," said Kate, "you mustn't expect me to tell my story. I'm different from you. I'm not born for anything in particular — I've no talents to point out my destiny. I keep being surprised and frustrated. It looks to me as if I were bound to make mistakes. There's something wrong with me. Sometimes I think that I'm not womanly enough — that there's too much of the man in my disposition, and that the two parts of me are always going to struggle and clash."

Chairs were being drawn up to the table.

"Come!" called Dr. von Shierbrand. "Can't you young ladies take time enough off to eat?"

He looked ready for conversation, and Kate went smilingly to sit beside him. She knew he expected women to be amusing, and she found it agreeable to divert him. She understood the classroom fag from which he was suffering; and, moreover, after all those austere meals with her father, it really was an excitement and a pleasure to talk with an amiable and complimentary man.

# George Ade

## (1866-1944)

GEORGE ADE *was born in Kentland, Indiana, in 1866 and moved to Chicago in 1890. By 1893 he was writing a feature column for the* Chicago Morning News *(later the* Chicago Record*) entitled "Stories of the Streets and of the Town." In 1897 Ade began publishing a series of fables in slang, evetually bringing out ten such books. He also wrote for the theater, and his comic opera* The Sultan of Sulu *(1902) had a long run in New York. A humorist from beginning to end, Ade's life was, by all accounts, a remarkably pleasant one. He spent the last twenty-four years of his life in retirement at an estate near his Indiana hometown, where he died in 1944.*

*Among Ade's fictional creations are Doc Horne, Pink Marsh, and Artie Blanchard. Artie (1896) is highly episodic, which is not surprising considering the nature of its composition: the chapters originally appeared as newspaper columns (Ade churned out six pieces a week in his heyday) that were pasted together to form a novel. Nearly every scene is set in a Chicago office where the street-smart, wisecracking Artie works; the book takes the form of a dialogue between the protagonist and his conservative and timid (but loyal) friend Miller. In colorful, colloquial diction, Artie recounts his latest exploits to the fascinated Miller. Admittedly, the main characters in* Artie *are flat and the plot is minimal, tracing the rather predictable romance between Artie and his best girl, Mamie Carroll. The pleasure of the novel comes from Artie's use of language and the insights we are given into Chicago life in the late nineteenth century. In chapter 17, excerpted below, Artie recounts his and Mamie's passion for a new craze sweeping the nation—bicycle riding.*

✦ ✦ ✦

*from* ARTIE

"Well, I'm goin' to be one o' them boys," said Artie, after he had seated himself and turned half-way around so that he could see Miller.

"What boys?" asked Miller.

"Them bike people with the fried-egg caps and the wall-paper stockins'. I'm goin' to be the sassiest club boy in the whole push. You just wait. In about a week I'll come hot-footin' in here with my knee-pants and a dinky coat, and do the club yell."

"I knew you'd get it sooner or later."

"This thing got the half-Nelson on me before I know it. One night I goes to bed feelin' all right and the next mornin' when I woke up I was wrong. There was somethin' ailed me, but I wasn't wise to it. The first thing I know I was stoppin' along the street lookin' at the wheels in the windows and gettin' next to the new kinds o' saddles and rubber-neckin' to read the names on the tires, and all that business. Then I begin to see that I had it the same as everybody else."

"I noticed that you'd been talking bicycle lately, but I didn't know you were going to get one."

"I'll tell you. I had a spiel with Mame last night and we fixed it up that if we didn't ride wheels this summer we wouldn't be in it at all, so I'm goin' to do the sucker act and blow myself."

"Does Mamie ride?"

"Does she? She's a scorchalorum. You ought o' seen her pushin' around the block last night on the Connelly girl's wheel. I told her if she ever went through the park speedin' like that she'd have all the sparrow cops layin' for her."

"How did she learn if she hasn't a wheel?"

"Just picked it up. Ain't I told you she's a world-beater? She's got the dough saved up to buy a wheel, too. There's a funny thing. A girl has to work for nothin', but she can always keep herself dressed right and show a little bank roll to the good. A man gets two or three times as much coin — always on the hog, and goin' around lookin' like a tramp. If Mame had my salary she'd be collectin' rent on flat buildin's."

"What kind of a wheel are you going to get?"

"Now you've got me guessin'. I've talked to twenty wise guys that've been ridin', and every one of 'em sings a different song. Every guy cracks up his own wheel, and says all the others is made out o' sheet iron and bum castin's. I've had five or six chances to get inside prices. A friend o' mine fixed it so I can get a purty fair wheel for fifty and pay for it at five a week, and I think I'll take it."

"Can you ride?"

"I can stay on, but when it comes to stickin' to a straight line or turnin' around to come back I'm purty tart. The only practice I've had is on some o' the wheels that belong to the boys out at the boathouse. Anybody that gets on the same street with me is takin' horrible chances. I never know what I'm goin' to carom against. The other day I tried to climb a lamp-post and a lot of fresh kids stood around and give me the laugh."

"How does it happen that you never wanted a wheel before? I've been riding for two years."

"There was too many Charley-boys ridin'. You know the kind I mean — them dubs with the long hair and the badges all over the coats. W'y I've seen 'em with tobacco tags, campaign buttons and little ribbons hung all over the front of 'em. I couldn't stand for nothin' like that. They was out just to make a show o' themselves. This year it's different. Everybody's gone nutty on the proposition. You can go out on a bike now without every driver tryin' to upset you and all the people joshin' you about your knee-pants."

"It's wonderful, the number of people riding wheels this spring," said Miller.

"I'll tell you they've gone daffy and I'm one of 'em. I'm goin' to be the worst fan in the whole bunch. What do you think last Sunday out at Lincoln Park? Old geezers — ye-e-s, the white-haired boys that you'd think was too stiff to back a wheel out of a shed, they was out there in them dizzy togs cuttin' up and down the track like two-year-olds. And old girls, too — girls from away back, about the crop o' '45 — fat ones, too — poundin' the pedals and duckin' in and out past the rigs! W'y, when I see it I put both hands in the air and I says: 'Well, when the old people can cut in on this game it's about time for me to begin to associate.' I'll be with 'em, too, next Sunday."

"Are you going to wear a suit?" asked Miller.

"Well, I'm a little leary on that. I don't want to get too gay on the jump. Mame wants me to get one and be right in line with all them club boys, but when she first sprung it on me I said: 'Nix; if I ever come up here with one o' them funny suits on the old man might take a shot at me.' Here's a funny thing about that. Here's somethin' that'll knock you cold. Last night when I gets to the house to see the girl, Mrs. Carroll's on the front porch and I could see she was hot about something. I asked her if anything had gone wrong and she says, 'Mr. Blanchard, there's an old man around the corner makin' a fool of himself. If you've got any drag with him I wish you'd go and get him in the house before he breaks his neck.' I wasn't on to what she was talkin' about, but she pointed to the corner and I walked over there and say — this is a good thing — if there wasn't Mame's old man takin' a fall out of a wheel. He'd borrowed it from one o' the neighbors, and this guy was holdin' him on and jollyin' him along. 'Don't be afraid,' he says, 'you won't fall.' The old man's eyes was hangin' out, and he was workin' them handle-bars like a man twistin' a brake. Gee, he was a sight. I had to holler and then he looked up and saw me. Course that rattled him and over he went. He made a fair fall, too, both shoulders on the ground and Mr. Bike on top of him. You ought o' heard some o' the large blue language the old man got rid of soon as we took the wheel off of him. I didn't know it was in him. 'Try it again,' this neighbor says, and he was takin' long chances on gettin' his wheel smashed at that. But the old man wouldn't listen to it. He went limpin' back to the house, and Mrs. Carroll says:

'Well, I hope you're satisfied now.' The old man give her the cold eye, and then he says to me: 'She'd talk that way if I'd been killed.' I guess Mame's mother is the only people on the North Side that ain't monkeyin' with a wheel."

"When do you and Mamie make your first appearance?"

"As soon as we can get the wheels. If I don't get mine inside of a week I'll go bug-house. I'm dreamin' wheels, I tell you. Last night I dreamt I was goin' along at about forty miles an hour and run into a steam roller."

"Did it break the wheel?"

"I give it up. I woke up and found myself tryin' to get the strangle hold on the pillow."

"Is Mamie going to wear bloomers?"

"Is she? Is she goin' to wear 'em — bloomers? Not on your facial expression. The first time we talked wheel I got up and declared myself on the bloomer business. I done the tall talk. I told her any time she sprung them Turkish village clothes on her Artie boy, all bets was goin' to be declared off."

"Why, what's the matter? Bloomers are all right."

"They're all right on some other guy's girl, but they don't go in my set. When I see my girl come on a wheel I want to know whether it's her or some Board o' Trade clerk. I don't want to be kept guessin'.'"

"Why, what's wrong with bloomers?"

"I'll tell you. The first one I ever see in bloomers was a lemon-faced fairy that ought o' been picked along about centennial year. She come peltin' along Michigan avenue with one o' them ballet-girl smiles splittin' that face o' hers, and I aint kiddin' when I tell you that a horse jumped up on the sidewalk and tried to get in the Risholoo hotel so as to pass it up. For a month afterwards I'd see that face at night and I'd wake up and holler: 'Take it away!' From the minute I see this good thing on Michigan I'm dead sore on all bloomers. I never see a good-lookin' girl wear 'em yet. Some of 'em might have been good lookers before they got into 'em, but after that — nit. You needn't be afraid o' Mame, and what's more, I don't want to talk about her wearin' them things at all. I like her too well. Do you think I'm goin' out ridin' with her and have a lot o' cheap skates stoppin' to play horse with her everywhere we go? Not in a thousand years. Besides, she don't have to make up like a man to make people look at her. She ain't like some o' the others. W'y, she kills 'em dead in her street clothes. Bloomers! Well, if Mame goes with me she goes as a girl, and that ain't no lie, neither."

# Finley Peter Dunne
## (1867-1936)

FINLEY PETER DUNNE *was born on the West Side of Chicago in 1867 and began work as a reporter at the* Chicago Herald *seventeen years later, after graduating at the bottom of his high school class. From 1893 to 1905, Dunne wrote over seven hundred columns in the dialect of an immigrant Irish bartender named Martin Dooley (though Mr. Dooley began his fictional life as Colonel McNeery). While many of the columns seem dated today, and Mr. Dooley's brogue can at times be impenetrable, during the early part of the twentieth century Dunne was considered one of the most famous columnists in the country. The first Mr. Dooley anthology was* Mr. Dooley in Peace and War *(1898); the last was the posthumously published* Mr. Dooley at His Best *(1936). There were eight others in between. Dissertations by Mr. Dooley, from which "The American Family" is taken, appeared in 1906.*

*The column is a good-natured lampoon of intellectuals, such as Harvard president Charles Eliot, as well as the working-class denizens of Archey (i.e., Archer) Road, where Mr. Dooley's mythical bar was supposedly located. The cynical bartender contrasts the size of the average family on wealthy Michigan Avenue with those in his Irish neighborhood, where Father Kelly, the parish priest, estimates "twelve births to wan marredge." In pieces such as this one, Dunne's use of dialect admirably complements his subject matter.*

*Dunne's popularity waned after World War I. He had moved to New York in 1900 when he was becoming nationally renowned; he died there, nearly forgotten, in 1936.*

✦ ✦ ✦

## The American Family

*from* DISSERTATIONS BY MR. DOOLEY

"Is th' race dyin' out?" asked Mr. Dooley.

"Is it what?" replied Mr. Hennessy.

"Is it dyin' out?" said Mr. Dooley. "Th' ministhers an' me frind Dock Eliot iv Harvard say it is. Dock Eliot wud know diff'rent if he was a rale dock an' wint flying up Halsted Sthreet in a buggy, floggin' a white horse to be there on time. But he ain't, an' he's sure it's dyin' out. Childher ar-re disappearin' fr'm America. He took a squint at th' list iv Harvard gradjates th' other day, an' discovered that they had ivrything to make home happy but kids. Wanst th' wurruld was full iv little Harvards. Th' counthry swarmed with thim. Ye cud tell a Harvard man at wanst be a look at his feet. He had th' unmistakable cradle fut. It was no sthrange thing to see an ol' Harvard man comin' back to his almy mather pushin' a baby-carredge full iv twins an' ladin' a fam'ly that looked like an advertisemint in th' newspapers to show th' percintage iv purity iv bakin'-powdhers. Prisidint Eliot was often disturbed in a discoorse, pintin' out th' dangers iv th' counthry, be th' outcries iv th' progeny iv fair Harvard. Th' campus was full iv baby-carredges on commincemint day, an' specyal accomodations had to be took f'r nurses. In thim happy days some wan was always teethin' in a Harvard fam'ly. It looked as if ivinchooly th' wurruld wud be peopled with Harvard men, an' th' Chinese wud have to pass an Exclusion Act. But something has happened to Harvard. She is projoocin' no little rah-rahs to glad th' wurruld. Th' av'rage fam'ly iv th' Harvard gradjate an' th' jackass is parctically th' same. Th' Harvard man iv th' prinsint day is th' last iv his race. No artless prattle is heerd in his home.

"An' me frind Prisidint Eliot is sore about it, an' he has communicated th' sad fact to th' clargy. Nawthin' th' clargy likes so much as a sad fact. Lave wan iv me frinds iv th' clargy know that we're goin' to th' divvle in a new way an' he's happy. We used to take th' journey be covetin' our neighbor's ox or his ass or be disobeyin' our parents, but now we have no parents to disobey or they have no chidher to disobey thim. Th' American people is becomin' as unfruitful as an ash-heap. We're no betther thin th' Fr-rinch. They say th' pleasin' squawk iv an infant hasn't been heerd in France since th' Franco-Prooshun war. Th' governmint offers prizes f'r families, but no wan claims thim. A Frinch gintleman who wint to Germany wanst has made a good deal iv money lecturin' on 'Wild Babies I have Met,' but ivry wan says he's a faker. Ye can't convince anny wan in France that there ar're anny babies. We're goin' th' same way. Less thin three millyon babies was bor'rn in this counthry las' year. Think iv it, Hinnissy — less thin three millyon, hardly enough to consume wan-tenth iv th' output iv pins! It's a horrible thought. I don't blame ivry wan, fr'm Tiddy Rosenfelt down, f'r worryin' about it.

"What's th' cause, says ye? I don't know. I've been readin' th' newspapers, an' ivrybody's been tellin' why. Late marredges, arly marredges, no marredges, th' cost iv livin', th' luxuries iv th' day, th' tariff, th' thrusts, th' spots ion th' sun, th' difficulty iv obtainin' implyemint, th' growth iv culture, th' pitcher-hat, an' so on. Ivrybody's got a raison, but none iv thim seems to meet th' bill. I've been lookin, at th' argymints pro an' con, an' I come to th' conclusion that th' race is dyin' out on'y in spots. Th' av'rage size iv th' fam'ly in Mitchigan Avnoo is .000001, but th' av'rage size iv th' fam'ly in Ar-rchey R-road is somewhat larger. Afther I r-read what Dock Eliot had to say I ast me frind Dock Grogan what he thought about it. He's a rale dock. He has a horse an' buggy. He's out so much at night that th' polis ar-re always stoppin' him, thinkin' he is a burglar. Th' dock has prepared some statistics f'r me, an' here they ar're: Number iv twins bor-rn in Ar-rchey Road fr'm Halsted Sthreet to Westhern Avnoo, fr'm Janooary wan to Janooary wan, 355 pairs; number iv thrips iv thriplets in th' same fiscal year, nine; number iv individjool voters, eighty-three thousan' nine hundherd an' forty two; av'rage size iv fam'ly, fourteen; av'rage weight iv parents, wan hundherd an' eighty-five; av'rage size iv rooms, nine be eight; av'rage height iv ceilin', nine feet; av'rage wages, wan dollar sivinty-five; av'rage duration iv doctor's bills, two hundherd years.

"I took th' statistics to Father Kelly. He's an onprejudiced man, an' if th' race was dyin' out he wud have had a soundin'boord in his pulpit long ago, so that whin he mintioned th' wurrud 'Hell,' ivry wan in th' congregation wud have though he meant him or her. 'I think,' says Father Kelly, 'that Dock Grogan is a little wrong in his figures. He's boastin'. In this parrish I allow twelve births to wan marredge. It varies, iv coorse, bein' sometimes as low as nine, an' sometimes as high as fifteen. But twelve is about th' av'rage,' he says. 'If ye see Dock Eliot,' he says, 'ye can tell him th' race ain't dyin' out very bad in this here part iv the wurruld. On th' conthry. It ain't liable to, ayether,' he says, 'onless wages is raised,' he says. 'Th' poor ar-re becomin' richer in child-her, an' th' rich poorer,' he says. 'Tis always th' way,' he says. 'Th' bigger th' house th' smaller th' fam'ly. Mitchigan Avnoo is always thinnin' out fr'm itsilf, an' growin' frm', th' efforts iv Ar-rchey R-road. 'Tis a way Nature has iv get-tin' even with th' rich an' pw'rful. Wan part iv town has nawthin' but money, an' another nawthin' but childher. A man with tin dollars a week will have tin childher, a man with wan hundherd dollars will have five, an' a man with a millyon will buy an autymobill. Ye can ell Schwartzmeister, with his thirteen little Hanses an' Helenas, that he don't have to throw no bombs to make room f'r his childher. Th' people over in Mitchigan Avnoo will do that thim-silves. Nature,' he says, 'is a wild dimmycrat,' he says.

"I guess he's right. I'm goin' to ask Dock Eliot, Tiddy Rosenfelt, an' all th' rest iv thim to come up Ar-rchey R-road some summer's afthernoon an' show thim th' way th r-race is dyin' out. Th' front stoops is full iv childher; they block th' throlley-cars; they're shyin' bricks at th' polis, pullin' up coal-hole covers, playin' ring-around-th'-rosy, makin' paper dolls, goin' to Sundah-school, hurryin' with th' sprinklin'-pot to th' place at th' corner, an' indulgin' in other spoorts iv childhood. Pah-pah is settin' on th' steps, ma is lanin' out iv th' window gassin' with th' neighbors, an' a squad iv polis ar-re up at th' church, keepin' th' christenin' parties fr'm mobbin' Father Kelly while he inthrajooces wan thousan' little howlin' dimmycrats to Christyan s'ciety. No, sir, th' race, far fr'm dyin' out in Ar-rchey R-road, is runnin' aisy an' comin' sthrong."

"Ye ought to be ashamed to talk about such subjicks, ye, an ol' batch," said Mr. Hennessy. "It's a seeryous question."

"How many childher have ye?" asked Mr. Dooley.

"Lave me see," said Mr. Hennessy. "Wan, two, four, five, eight, siven, eight, tin, — no, that's not right. Lave me see. Ah, yes, I f'rgot Terence. We have fourteen."

"If th' race iv Hinnissys dies out," said Mr. Dooley, "'twill be fr'm overcrowdin'."

# Robert Herrick

## (1868-1938)

*Born in Cambridge, Massachusetts, in 1868, and educated at Harvard,* ROBERT
HERRICK *drew all his life on what he called "the puritan faith" of his New England
upbringing. Herrick came to Chicago in 1893 and taught at the University of
Chicago until 1923. Despite the fact that he was considered a member of the Chicago
school of writing, he was always critical of the city's avarice and lack of scruples.
Among Herrick's many novels that disparage business life in Chicago are* The Gospel of Freedom *(1898),* The Web of Life *(1900),* The Common Lot *(1904),
and* Together *(1908). In addition to fiction, Herrick also published political and historical works, and he remained outspoken all his life about the dangers of unchecked
materialism and the necessity of moral rehabilitation. In 1935 Herrick was appointed Government Secretary of the Virgin Islands by the Roosevelt administration.
After a brief but successful term as a public servant, he died in St. Thomas in 1938.*

 The Memoirs of an American Citizen, *Herrick's most readable and enduring novel, was published in 1905. Van Harrington, the narrator and protagonist,
leaves his hometown of Jasonville, Indiana, in disgrace after he is falsely accused of
setting a barn on fire. He spends his first night in Chicago among the hoboes on the
lakefront and the next day is arrested for stealing the purse of a woman he eventually
marries. After this tumultuous beginning, however, Harrington's name is cleared
and his destiny takes a turn for the better. He becomes a successful, if amoral, businessman and is eventually elected to the United States Senate. The following excerpt
is chapter 12 of* Memoirs, *entitled "An Honorable Merchant." In it, the naivete of
Harrington's boss, Henry Dround, comes into conflict with the unscrupulous pragmatism of John Carmichael, the "junior partner" of their meatpacking firm. Forced
to decide between the two, Harrington, like most Chicago businessmen of the time,
Herrick implies, unhesitatingly chooses profit over ethical concerns.*

◆ ◆ ◆

"Mr. Dround seems to be doing a good deal of talking for the benefit of his neighbors," Slocum observed one day when I was in his office.

"Oh, he likes the job of making the country over! It suits him to talk more than to sell pork."

"Did you see what he said last night?" Slocum continued.

"No, what was it? Free trade or college education?" For Mr. Henry I. Dround was long on both subjects. He had always fooled more or less with politics, having come out as a mugwump and free-trader under Cleveland. That kind of doctrine wasn't much in favor among the business men of Chicago, but Dround liked being in the minority. He was an easy, scholarly speaker, and was always ready to talk at dinners and public meetings. "It seems to me I saw something in the papers of his speaking at the Jefferson Club banquet," I went on; "but I didn't pay attention to it. The old man is rather long on wind."

"The papers missed most of the ginger. But I was there, and it was lively. Jimmy Birdsell, Hart's man, was there, too. It was this new Civil Service Bill that the silk stockings are trying to push through the legislature. Of course, Hart and the machine are fighting it like fire. Well, your boss made the chief speech, a good little talk about purity and business methods in government and the rest of it. Birdsell sat just across the table from me, and I could see from the way he knocked his glasses about that he was getting hot. Maybe he came there for a fight. At last he boiled over.

"'Say, Mr. Dround,' he sang out in a pause between two periods, 'how about your new switch-track over in Ada Street?'

"Dround looked toward him over his glasses for a moment, as though he hadn't heard what was said, and then he went ahead with his talk. But Birdsell was some drunk and too mad to care what he did. The men beside him couldn't keep him quiet. 'I say, Dround,' he broke out again pretty soon, 'we should like to hear what your firm does when it wants any little favors from the city? That might be to the point just now!'

"This time Dround couldn't pass it over. He took a drink of water and his hand shook. Then he said: 'I do not see that this is the proper time to introduce a personal matter, but since the gentleman seems concerned about my business honor, I am glad to set his mind at rest. To the best of my knowledge, Henry I. Dround & Co. have never asked and never accepted any favors from the city. Is that satisfactory?'

"'Come, now, Mr. Dround,' Birdsell sneered, 'that isn't generally believed, you know.'

"'I said,' your boss ripped back, '*to the best of my knowledge*, your insinuation is a lie!' He leaned forward and glared at Birdsell. Well, there was a kind of awkward pause, everybody waiting to see what would come next; and then Birdsell, who must have been pretty drunk, called back: 'Ask your man John Carmichael what he does when he wants anything from the city. Ask him about your rebates, too. Then the next time you come here telling us how to be good, you'll know more.' There was a cat-and-dog time after that, some yelling to put Birdsell out, and others laughing and clapping."

Slocum paused, and then added: —

"It put Mr. Dround in a tight place."

"What of it, anyhow?" said I. "Birdsell is nothing but a yellow dog. Hart keeps him to lick his platters. Every one knows that."

"Yes, that's so. But he said what most every one believes is true."

"That kissing goes by favor, and most other things in this world, too. Well, what of it?"

Slocum leaned back in his chair and laughed. Then he said to me seriously: —

"You aren't much troubled with scruples, Van!"

"Come, what's the use of talking good? You and I know well enough that there isn't any other way of doing business, not in any city in the country. You have got to pay for what you get, the same as elsewhere. Dround ought to know it, too, by this time, and not go 'round preaching loose — or else get out of business, which might be better!"

"I suppose so," Slocum replied solemnly. "But I always liked his sermons. Perhaps you and Carmichael could tone him down a bit just now."

"Oh, John don't mind his speeches, so long as he don't interfere with the business!"

We went out to lunch, and talked of other matters, and for several days I thought no more of the incident that Slocum had related. The switch-track business did not seem to me important. If the reformers wanted to get after us, or any other big firm, there were many more vulnerable points than that. Special privileges from the city we regarded as our rights. But there was the graft of railroad rates. Any fool could tell that, at the published tariff rates, there would be little business for the packers outside of Chicago. It was common knowledge that the trade was honeycombed with private agreements and rebate privileges, and that the fiercest part of the business was to get the right rate from the roads. Then there were the secret agreements between the packers, which were all illegal, but necessary to keep the trade from cutting prices all the time.

Carmichael attended to this end of the business for Dround, as he did of everything of real importance. He was a member of the firm now, and the wonder to me was that this smart Irishman could put up with Dround. It could hardly be a matter of sentiment with him. I had a warm feeling for the illiterate junior member, with a temper about an inch long, but a big, round heart open to any friend. He had bucked his way up in the world by main force, and I admired him. Besides, he had taught me how to eat, so to speak. In a word, I liked his way of doing things better than Mr. Dround's college talk.

Well, it happened that the cur Birdsell set some of the civil service reformers on the tracks of Brother Dround, and they got a smart newspaper reporter to work over the whole matter. There was a lively write-up in one of the papers, all about our switch-track over in Ada Street, with photographs and figures, and a lot more about the way the packers did business with the city. When I read the piece in the paper I took the trouble to pass by our new warehouse on my way to the office. The trackage was in, sure enough. Carmichael was just the man to have a thing done and settled by the time the public got around to talk about it!

Mr. Dround was in his office bright and early this morning, and sent for me.

"Harrington," he began, "what do you know about this talk in the papers?" Mr. Dround seemed very nervous, not sure of himself.

"Why," I smiled, "I don't know much more than what the papers said. Mr. Carmichael, you know — "

"Yes," Mr. Dround interrupted impatiently, "Mr. Carmichael is in New York, gets back this morning; but I thought you might — " He hesitated, not wishing to admit his own ignorance. "I will send for you later when Mr. Carmichael comes in," he concluded.

So when John arrived he had us both in his office.

"You want to see me?" Carmichael asked gruffly, as if he hadn't much time that morning to waste on the senior member.

"Yes, I wish to talk over certain matters that concern us all, even though they may have no immediate bearing upon the business." Mr. Dround always talked like that when he got the least nervous.

"Well, what is it?" Carmichael asked. He had just arrived, and I suppose his letters interested him more than Mr. Dround's talk.

"You may not have seen the articles in the morning papers — about — about certain privileges which it is alleged — "

"What are the boys yapping about now?" Carmichael demanded, taking up a newspaper from the desk and thrusting his shoulders forward in an ugly fashion.

"It concerns our permit to lay that new switch-track," Mr. Dround explained.

Carmichael laid the paper down and looked at the senior member in a curious way, as if he were trying to make out just what kind of a fool he had to deal with. But as he said nothing, Mr. Dround continued: —

"Recently I had occasion to deny categorically that, so far as I knew, our firm ever made any such kind of arrangement as is here described. My word was challenged. It was a very painful situation, I need not say. Since then I have been thinking — I have been wondering whether this charge — "

He floundered pitifully, disliking to mouth the dreadful words. John helped him out brutally: —

"You wonder whether we had to grease anybody's paw about that switch-track over in Ada Street?"

Dround nodded. "The papers say so!"

"They have to print something, don't they? What harm does that do us? I wouldn't trust the whole d — n bunch of papers with a ten-dollar bill. They're a lot of blackmailers — that's what they are!"

John bit off the end of a cigar and spat it out in front of Mr. Dround.

"We are not concerned with the newspapers or their motives, Mr. Carmichael," the senior member observed with considerable dignity. "What I want is your assurance that this firm — that, so far as we are concerned, this accusation is false."

We waited for the Irishman's reply. It would be an easy matter to tell a fib and set Mr. Dround's mind at rest. But Carmichael seemed to be in a specially bad temper this morning. When he went to New York he was accustomed to enjoy himself, and it was not the right time to badger a man just off the cars. Pretty soon John said fiercely: —

"It's my business to look after such matters?"

Mr. Dround nodded.

"Don't I do it satisfactorily?"

Mr. Dround waived this point.

"Well, I guess you'll have to be content with that."

"Mr. Carmichael," the senior member leaped to his feet, "you forget yourself! You will be good enough to answer me yes or no, to my direct question. Did you or did you not pay money for this privilege?"

Carmichael's voice shook as he replied: —

"See here, Dround! If you don't know your own business enough to know the answer, I don't see why I should tell you." His temper was going with every word he said. "But if you want to know, you shall! There hasn't been such a thing as a private switch-track put down in this city since you began doing business for less than seven thousand dollars. I paid the right people ninety-five hundred dollars for ours. There, you've got it! Now what are you going to do about it?"

The big Irishman plumped his two red fists on Mr. Dround's desk and glared at him. At that moment I pitied the old gentleman heartily; he was never born to do business, at least in our day. He seemed to shrivel up under Carmichael's words.

"How, may I ask," he said at last in a low tone, "was this done without my knowledge? How does it appear on the books?"

Carmichael laughed at the simple question.

"Charity! We are a very charitable concern!"

Mr. Dround's lips trembled, and he cried out rather than spoke: —

"No, never! Better to fail! Better to go bankrupt at once!"

He was talking to himself. Then he recollected us and said with dignity: —

"That is all, Mr. Carmichael. After this I shall attend to all such matters myself. Good morning, gentlemen."

He sat down at his desk, dismissing us. Carmichael was shaking with anger.

"No!" he cried, "it isn't all! Turn me out of your office like a boy, with my orders, when it's me that have stood between you and ruin any day these ten years! What would your business be worth if it weren't for John Carmichael? Ask Harrington here. Go out and ask your bank — "

"I don't believe we need to discuss this any further — " Mr. Dround began.

"Yes, we will! Get somebody else to do your dirty business for you. For, let me tell you right here, Henry I. Dround, that I don't go broke with you, not for all your college talk and prin-ci-ples."

Mr. Dround pointed to the door. He was trembling again. I took the big Irishman by the arm and led him from the office. Outside the door he shook me off, and hurled himself into his own office.

That was the first wind of the storm, and the rest wasn't long in coming. Somebody told me that Carmichael had been seen with one of Strauss's lieutenants going into a law office that did some of the big packer's work. It looked as though he were making a deal with the Strauss crowd. It seemed natural enough to me that Carmichael should do this, but I was sorry for what must come. Meantime, Mr. Dround was more assiduous at business than I had ever known him to be. He came early, and instead of driving over to his club for luncheon took a bite in his office, and put in the afternoons going into all departments of the business.

In the end, the trouble came to a head in this way: in company with every large shipper at that period we made our bargain with the roads; no large firm and no railroad pretended to live up to the law in the matter of rates. The roads sold their transportation, as we sold ribs and lard — for the highest figure they could get. Before any considerable contract was entered into the thrifty shipper saw to his rate in advance. And some time later there came along from the railroad that got the business a check in the way of "adjustment." The senior member, in his new energy, discovered one of these rebates. He sent it back to the traffic manager of the road with a letter such as the roads were not in the habit of getting from their favored shippers. The second vice-president and general traffic manager of that line attended the same church the Drounds went to, and the president of the road, also, was one of Dround's friends. I wonder what they thought when their attention was called to this little matter!

Carmichael told me what had happened with a wicked grin on his face.

"Righteous man, Henry I. Dround, all right! D—n good business man, too," he commented. "What do you think is going to happen to this concern? He's chucked away the profits of that contract!"

"You aren't planning to stay, John?" I remarked casually.

He looked at me and laughed.

"Do you want to come with me when I get out?"

I smiled, but said nothing. There was no open row between Mr. Dround and the junior member of the firm this time. But a few weeks later Mr. Dround told me what I already knew—that he and Carmichael were about to part. I advised him bluntly to make it up with the Irishman if he could, — not to part with him at any cost.

"For, Mr. Dround, you will find him fighting on the other side; Strauss will have him."

He knew as well as I what that meant to his business, but he said with new determination: —

"Mr. Carmichael and I can never do business together again."

Then he offered to take me into partnership on the same basis that Carmichael had. I suppose he expected me to jump at my chance, but the prospect was not altogether inviting.

"I ought to say, Mr. Dround," I replied hesitatingly, "that I think Carmichael was right in this rebate business, and in the other matter, too. If I had been in his place I should have done the same thing—any man would. It's against human nature to sit still and be eaten alive!"

Mr. Dround's eyes lowered, and he turned his face away from me. His spirit was somewhat daunted: perhaps he began to realize what it meant to stand out alone against the commercial system of the age. Nevertheless, he said some things, perfectly true, about the honor and integrity of his firm. As it had been handed over to him by his father, so he would keep it, please God.

"That's all right," I said a little impatiently. "That might do in times gone by. But Carmichael and I have got to live in the present. That means a fight. I would like to stay on and fight it with you. But I can't see the use on your basis. Look!"

I pointed out of his window to a new refrigerator building that Strauss was putting up under our noses.

"That is only one: you know the others. He is growing every day. You can't expect us to sit here twiddling our thumbs and thinking of our virtue while he gets the business! Better to sell out to Strauss right here and now, while there is something to sell."

"Never!" Mr. Dround cried with unaccustomed vehemence.

"Never to him!"

"Well, then, we've got our work cut out for us, and let us waste no more time talking rebates and the rest of it."

"Yet that horrid scandal about the switch-track," he resumed in his old weak way. "Nothing has done so much to hurt my position in the city as that!"

"But what are you going to do about it?" I asked in Carmichael's very words. "Those thieves over there in the council hold you up. What good does it do the public for you to refuse their price? It's like paying for the right to put up a house on your own lot — it's tough, but you had better pay and not worry."

"Mr. Harrington, I refuse to believe that in our country an honorable business cannot be conducted successfully by honorable methods."

"That depends on what you choose to call honorable methods. At any rate," I concluded in disgust, "you are likely to have a good chance to try that proposition to the bitter end, unless you take my advice and sell to your chief competitor."

He waived this aside impatiently.

"Well, then, look for the fight of your life just to survive, not to make money. I tell you, Mr. Dround, Strauss is out there waiting to eat us all up. And you have thrown him your general for a beginning."

"But I trust that I have another as good or better," he said with his usual flourish of courtesy.

We had some more talk, he urging me to stay with him, although I let him see plainly where I stood on the matter of rebates, private agreements, and all the rest of the underground machinery of business.

"If I take your offer," I said at last, "I shall use the old weapons — you must know that. There are no morals in business that I recognize except those that are written on the statute book. It is dog eat dog, Mr. Dround, and I don't propose to be the dog that's eaten."

Even then he did not stop urging me, salving his conscience by saying: "It saddens me to hear as young a man as you take that cynical view. It is a strange time we are coming to. I pray it may not be a worse time for the country!"

To my mind there was something childish in the use of those words "better" and "worse." Every age is a new one, and to live in any age you have got to have the fingers and toes necessary for that age. The forces which lie in us and make those triumph who do triumph in the struggle have been in men from the beginning of time. There's little use in trying to stop their sweep, or to sit and cry like Dround by the roadside, because you don't like the game. For my part, I went with the forces that are, willingly, gladly, believing in them no matter how ugly they might look. So history reads: the men who lead accept the conditions of their day. And the others follow along just the same; while the world works and changes and makes itself over according to its destiny.

# Edgar Lee Masters

## (1869-1950)

*Born in Garnett, Kansas, in 1869,* EDGAR LEE MASTERS *moved to Lewiston, Illinois, located near the Spoon River, when he was eleven. He attended Knox College, was admitted to the Illinois bar in 1891, and moved to Chicago. In 1903 he became law partners with Clarence Darrow. During this time, he was writing seriously, having published his first book of poems,* A Book of Verses, *in 1898 and, later, a collection of essays and several plays.*

*In 1914 his friend and editor William Marion Reedy began publishing Masters's* Spoon River *poems under the pseudonym Webster Ford. These poems, which were collected in* Spoon River Anthology *(1915), proved to be the work that immortalized him, much to Masters's chagrin. Spoken by former citizens now buried in the Spoon River graveyard, the poems present a cross section of occupations and attitudes. On the whole, though,* Spoon River Anthology *paints small town life as covetous, hypocritical, and mean. Because Masters dared explode one of America's most cherished myths — the sanctity of rural life — he was both reviled and celebrated.*

*Although he continued to publish into his seventies, Masters's work never again achieved such widespread popularity. Among his many books of poems are* Domesday Book *(1920),* The New Spoon River *(1924), and* The Fate of the Jury *(1929). He also wrote biographies of Vachel Lindsay, Abraham Lincoln, Walt Whitman, and Mark Twain. His novels include* Mitch Miller *(1920),* The Nuptial Flight *(1923), and* The Tide of Time *(1937). Of his autobiography,* Across Spoon River *(1936), John and Margaret Wrenn wrote that it is "a rationalization of his career, which he saw as a struggle between will and fate, with himself making his way through sheer determination." Masters moved to New York in 1923 and died in Philadelphia in 1950.*

✦ ✦ ✦

## THE HILL

Where are Elmer, Herman, Bert, Tom and Charley,
The weak of will, the strong of arm, the clown, the boozer, the fighter?
All, all, are sleeping on the hill.

One passed in a fever,
One was burned in a mine,
One was killed in a brawl,
One died in a jail,
One fell from a bridge toiling for children and wife —
All, all are sleeping, sleeping, sleeping on the hill.

Where are Ella, Kate, Mag, Lizzie and Edith,
The tender heart, the simple soul, the loud, the proud, the happy one? —
All, all, are sleeping on the hill.

One died in shameful child-birth,
One of a thwarted love,
One at the hands of a brute in a brothel,
One of a broken pride, in the search for heart's desire,
One after life in far-away London and Paris
Was brought to her little space by Ella and Kate and Mag —
All, all are sleeping, sleeping, sleeping on the hill.

Where are Uncle Isaac and Aunt Emily,
And old Towny Kincaid and Sevigne Houghton,
And Major Walker who had talked
With venerable men of the revolution? —
All, all, are sleeping on the hill.

They brought them dead sons from the war,
And daughters whom life had crushed,
And their children fatherless, crying —
All, all are sleeping, sleeping, sleeping on the hill.

Where is Old Fiddler Jones
Who played with life all his ninety years,
Braving the sleet with bared breast,
Drinking, rioting, thinking neither of wife nor kin,
Nor gold, nor love, nor heaven?
Lo! he babbles of the fish-frys of long ago,
Of the horse-races of long ago at Clary's Grove,
Of what Abe Lincoln said
One time at Springfield.

## Fiddler Jones

The earth keeps some vibration going
There in your heart, and that is you,
And if the people find you can fiddle,
Why, fiddle you must, for all your life.
What do you see, a harvest of clover?
Or a meadow to walk through to the river?
The wind's in the corn; you rub your hands
For beeves hereafter ready for market;
Or else you hear the rustle of skirts
Like the girls when dancing at Little Grove.
To Cooney Potter a pillar of dust
Or whirling leaves meant ruinous drouth;
They looked to me like Red-Head Sammy
Stepping it off, to "Toor-a-Loor."
How could I till my forty acres
Not to speak of getting more,
With a medley of horns, bassoons and piccolos
Stirred in my brain by crows and robins
And the creak of a wind-mill — only these?
And I never started to plow in my life
That some one did not stop in the road
And take me away to a dance or picnic.
I ended up with forty acres;
I ended up with a broken fiddle —
And a broken laugh, and a thousand memories,
And not a single regret.


## Petit, the Poet

Seeds in a dry pod, tick, tick, tick,
Tick, tick, tick, like mites in a quarrel —
Faint iambics that the full breeze wakens —
But the pine tree makes a symphony thereof.
Triolets, villanelles, rondels, rondeaus,
Ballades by the score with the same old thought:
The snows and the roses of yesterday are vanished;
And what is love but a rose that fades?
Life all around me here in the village:
Tragedy, comedy, valor and truth,

Courage, constancy, heroism, failure —
All in the loom, and oh what patterns!
Woodlands, meadows, streams and rivers —
Blind to all of it all my life long.
Triolets, villanelles, rondels, rondeaus,
Seeds in a dry pod, tick, tick, tick,
Tick, tick, tick, what little iambics,
While Homer and Whitman roared in the pines?


## Pauline Barrett

Almost the shell of a woman after the surgeon's knife!
And almost a year to creep back into strength,
Till the dawn of our wedding decennial
Found me my seeming self again.
We walked the forest together,
By a path of soundless moss and turf.
But I could not look in your eyes,
And you could not look in my eyes,
For such sorrow was ours — the beginning of gray in your hair,
And I but a shell of myself.
And what did we talk of? — sky and water,
Anything, 'most, to hide our thoughts.
And then your gift of wild roses,
Set on the table to grace our dinner.
Poor heart, how bravely you struggled
To imagine and live a remembered rapture!
Then my spirit drooped as the night came on,
And you left me alone in my room for a while,
As you did when I was a bride, poor heart.
And I looked in the mirror and something said:
"One should be all dead when one is half-dead —
Nor ever mock life, nor ever cheat love."
And I did it looking there in the mirror —
Dear, have you ever understood?


## Hannah Armstrong

I wrote him a letter asking him for old times' sake
To discharge my sick boy from the army;

But maybe he couldn't read it.
Then I went to town and had James Garber,
Who wrote beautifully, write him a letter;
But maybe that was lost in the mails.
So I traveled all the way to Washington.
I was more than an hour finding the White House.
And when I found it they turned me away,
Hiding their smiles. Then I thought:
"Oh, well, he ain't the same as when I boarded him
And he and my husband worked together
And all of us called him Abe, there in Menard."
As a last attempt I turned to a guard and said:
"Please say it's old Aunt Hannah Armstrong
From Illinois, come to see him about her sick boy
In the army."
Well, just in a moment they let me in!
And when he saw me he broke in a laugh,
And dropped his business as president,
And wrote in his own hand Doug's discharge,
Talking the while of the early days,
And telling stories.


## LUCINDA MATLOCK

I went to the dances at Chandlerville,
And played snap-out at Winchester.
One time we changed partners,
Driving home in the moonlight of middle June,
And then I found Davis.
We were married and lived together for seventy years,
Enjoying, working, raising the twelve children,
Eight of whom we lost
Ere I had reached the age of sixty.
I spun, I wove, I kept the house, I nursed the sick,
I made the garden, and for holiday
Rambled over the fields where sang the larks,
And by Spoon River gathering many a shell,
And many a flower and medicinal weed—
Shouting to the wooded hills, singing to the green valleys.
At ninety-six I had lived enough, that is all,

And passed to a sweet repose.
What is this I hear of sorrow and weariness,
Anger, discontent and drooping hopes?
Degenerate sons and daughters,
Life is too strong for you—
It takes life to love Life.

# Frank Lloyd Wright

## (1869-1959)

*The Imperial Hotel (Tokyo), the Guggenheim Museum (New York), Wingspread (Racine, Wisconsin), Taliesin (Spring Green, Wisconsin), the Robie House (Chicago) — the list of important buildings goes on and on for* FRANK LLOYD WRIGHT, *a giant of American architecture. Born in Richland Center, Wisconsin, his work in Chicago with Louis Sullivan (whom he referred to as "The Master") and his "prairie" style marked radical innovation in both the structural methods and the aesthetics of architecture.*

*In a 1918 article read to the Women's Aid Organization, his love/hate relationship with Chicago burns brightly. "Chicago is the national capital of the American spirit," he would say. Then, as in the passage quoted in the introduction to this book, he goes on to deride Chicago's surface, "stuck on" culture, calling it "dirt." In the following excerpt from his autobiography, he recounts the events and ideas behind the building of Oak Park's Unity Temple. Here his passion, genius, even arrogance, show clearly through as he applies his principle of organic form to the building of yet another great landmark in American architecture.*

✦ ✦ ✦

*from* AN AUTOBIOGRAPHY

Concerning the traditional church as a modern building! Religion and art are forms of inner-experience — growing richer and deeper as the race grows older. We will never lose either. But I believe religious experience is outgrowing the church — not outgrowing religion but outgrowing the church as an institution, just as architecture has outgrown the Renaissance and for reasons human, scientific and similar. I cannot see the ancient institutional form of any church building as anything but sentimental survival for burial. The Temple as a forum and good-time place — beautiful and inspiring as such — yes. As a religious edifice raised in the sense of the old ritual? No. I cannot see it at all as living. It is no longer free. . . .

Let us take Unity Temple to pieces in the thought of its architect and see how it came to be the Unity Temple you now see.

Had Doctor Johonnot, the Universalist pastor of Unity Church, been Fra Junipero the style of Unity Temple would have been predetermined — "Mission." Had he been Father Latour it would have been Midi-Romanesque. Yes, and perhaps being what he was, he was entitled to the only tradition he knew — that of the little white New England church, lean spire pointing to heaven — "back East." If sentimentality were sense this might be so.

But the pastor was out of luck. Circumstances brought him to yield himself up in the cause of architecture. And to that cause everyone who undertakes to read what follows is called upon to yield a little.

Our building committee were all good men and true. One of them, Charles E. Roberts, the mechanical engineer and inventor I have mentioned, was himself enlightened in creation. One, enlightened, is leaven enough in any Usonian committee lump. The struggle began. It is always a struggle in architecture for the architect where good men and true are concerned.

First came the philosophy of the building in my own mind.

I said, let us abolish, in the art and craft of architecture, literature in any symbolic form whatsoever. The sense of inner rhythm deep planted in human sensibility lives far above all other considerations in art. Then why the steeple of the little white church? Why *point* to heaven?

I told the committee a story. Did they know the tale of the holy man who, yearning to see God, climbed up and up the highest mountain — climbed to the highest relic of a tree there was on the mountain? There, ragged and worn, he lifted up his eager perspiring face to heaven and called upon God. He heard a voice bidding him get down . . . go back!

Would he really see God's face? Then he should go back, go down there in the valley below where his own people were — there only could *he* look upon God's countenance. . . .

Why not, then, build a temple, not to God in that way — more sentimental than sense — but build a temple to man, appropriate to his uses as a meeting place, in which to study man himself for his God's sake? A modern meeting-house and a good-time place.

The pastor was liberal. His liberality was thus challenged, his reason was piqued and the curiosity of all was aroused. What would such a building look like? They said they could imagine no such thing.

"That's what you came to me for," I ventured. "I can imagine it and I will help you create it." Promising the building committee something tangible to look at soon — I sent them away.

The first idea was to keep a noble room for worship in mind, and let that sense of the great room shape the whole edifice. Let the room inside be the architecture outside.

What shape? Well, the answer lay in the material. There was only one material to choose—as the church funds were $45,000—to "church" 400 people in 1906. Concrete was cheap.

Why not make the wooden boxes or forms so the concrete could be cast in them as separate blocks and masses, these grouped about an interior space in some such way as to preserve this sense of the interior space, the great room, in the appearance of the whole building? And the block-masses might be left as themselves with no facing at all? That would be cheap and permanent and not ugly either.

What roof? What had concrete to offer as a cover shelter? The concrete slab—of course. The reinforced slab. Nothing else if the building was to be thoroughbred, meaning built in character out of one material.

Too monumental, all this? Too forthright for my committee I feared. Would a statement so positive as that final slab over the whole seem irreligious to them? Profane in their eyes? Why? But the flat slab was cheap and direct. It would be nobly simple. The wooden forms or molds in which concrete buildings must at that time be cast were always the chief item of expense, so to repeat the use of a single form as often as possible was necessary. Therefore a building, all four sides alike, looked like the thing. This, reduced to simplest terms, meant a building square in plan. That would make their temple a cube—a noble form in masonry.

The slab, too, belonged to the cube by nature. *"Credo simplicitatem."* That form is most imaginative and happy that is most radiant with the aura or overtone of super-form. Integrity.

Then the Temple itself—still in my mind—began to take shape. The site was noisy, by the Lake Street car-tracks. Therefore it seemed best to keep the building closed on the three front sides and enter it from a court to the rear at the center of the lot. Unity Temple itself with the thoughts in mind I have just expressed, arrived easily enough, but there was a secular side to Universalist church activities—entertainment often, Sunday school, feasts, and so on.

To embody these with the temple would spoil the simplicity of the room—the noble Room in the service of man for the worship of God. So I finally put the secular space designated as "Unity House," a long free space to the rear of the lot, as a separate building to be subdivided by movable screens for Sunday school or on occasion. It thus became a separate building but harmonious with the Temple—the entrance to both to be the connecting link between them. That was that.

And why not put the pulpit at the entrance side at the rear of the square Temple, and bring the congregation into the room at the sides on a lower level so those entering would be imperceptible to the audience? This would preserve the quiet and the dignity of the room itself. Out of that thought came the depressed foyer or cloister corridor on either side, leading from the main lobby at the center to the stairs in the near and far corners of the room. Those entering the room in this way could see into the big room but not be seen by those already seated within it.

And, important to the pastor, when the congregation rose to disperse, here was opportunity to move forward toward their pastor and by swinging wide doors open beside the pulpit allow the entire flock to pass out by him and find themselves directly in the entrance loggia from which they had first come in. They had gone into the depressed entrances at the sides from this same entrance to the big room. But it seemed more respectful to let them go out thus toward the pulpit than turn their backs upon their minister as is usual in most churches.

So this was done.

The room itself — size determined by comfortable seats with leg-room for four hundred people — was built with four interior free standing posts to carry the overhead structure. These concrete posts were hollow and became free-standing ducts to insure economic and uniform distribution of heat. The large supporting posts were so set in plan as to form a double tier of alcoves on four sides of the room. I flooded these side-alcoves with light from above to get a sense of a happy cloudless day into the room. And with this feeling for light the center ceiling between the four great posts became skylight, daylight sifting through between the intersecting concrete beams, filtering through amber glass ceiling lights. Thus managed, the light would, rain or shine, have the warmth of sunlight. Artificial lighting took place there at night as well. This scheme of lighting was integral, gave diffusion and kept the room-space clear.

Now for proportion — for the concrete expression of concrete in this natural arrangement — the ideal of an organic whole well in mind. And we have arrived at the question of *style*. For observe, so far, what has actually taken place is only reasoned *arrangement*. The "plan" with an eye to an exterior in the realm of ideas but meantime "felt" in imagination as a whole.

First came the general philosophy of the thing as repeated in the little story to the trustees. All artistic creation has its own philosophy. It is the first condition of creation. However, some would smile and say, "the result of it."

Second there was the general purpose of the whole to consider in each part: a matter of reasoned arrangement. This arrangement must be made with a sense of the yet-unborn-whole in mind, to be blocked out as appropriate to concrete masses cast in wooden boxes. Holding all this diversity together in a preconceived direction is really no light matter but is the condition of creation. Imagination conceives here the PLAN suitable to the material and the purpose of the whole, seeing the probable possible form clearer all the time.

Imagination reigns supreme, until now the form the whole will naturally take must be seen.

But if all this preliminary planning has been well conceived that question in the main is settled. This matter of style is organic now.

We do not choose the style. No. Style is what is coming now and it will be what we *are* in all this. A thrilling moment in any architect's experience. He is about to see the countenance of something he is invoking with intense concentration. Out of this inner sense of order and love of the beauty of life something is to be born — maybe to live long as a message of hope and be a joy or a curse to his kind. *His* message he feels. None the less will it be "theirs," and rather more. And it is out of love and understanding that any building is born to bless or curse those it is built to serve. Bless them if they will see, understand and aid. Curse them as it will be cursed by them if either they or the architect fail to understand each other. This is the faith and the fear in the architect as he makes ready — to draw his design.

In all artists it is somewhat the same fear and the same faith.

# Theodore Dreiser

## (1871-1945)

*One of thirteen children born into an impoverished Terre Haute, Indiana, family in 1871,* THEODORE DREISER *taught himself and his mother to read and write before running away from home, at age fifteen, to Chicago. Acclaimed as the greatest American practitioner of "naturalistic" fiction, Dreiser lived for a time on Chicago's streets before finally getting a job as a reporter for the* Chicago Daily Globe. *Sister* Carrie, *Dreiser's first novel, received a cool reception when it originally was published in 1900, many readers objecting that its actress heroine, Carrie Meeber (who was purportedly based on Dreiser's own sister, Emma), lives a sexually permissive life yet is rewarded with financial success rather than punished with social condemnation. Despite the book's lack of sales, Dreiser flourished as an editor of women's magazines until 1910, when he was forced to resign because of an affair with a co-worker's daughter. Other major works include the Frank Cowperwood trilogy:* The Titan *(1912),* The Financier *(1914), and* The Stoic *(1947).* The Genius *(1915), a semiautobiographical novel, was condemned by the New York Society for the Suppression of Vice. His most celebrated book,* An American Tragedy *(1925), provided the scenario for the 1951 film* A Place in the Sun, *starring Montgomery Clift and Elizabeth Taylor.*

*Dreiser died in Hollywood in 1945. The famous opening passage of* Sister Carrie, *excerpted below, evokes a scene described by a number of other Chicago writers: the passage from country to city. Unlike immigrants to New York, who typically arrived on a ship and saw that city in its most spectacular light, newcomers to Chicago gradually become subsumed by suburban and then urban ugliness. Nevertheless, there was an excitement about arriving by train, especially if one's fellow passengers were interesting, and Dreiser's prose vividly captures the experience.*

✦ ✦ ✦

## *from* SISTER CARRIE

When Caroline Meeber had boarded the afternoon train for Chicago, her total outfit consisted of a small trunk, a cheap imitation alligator-skin satchel, a small lunch in a paper box, and a yellow leather snap purse, containing her ticket, a scrap of paper with her sister's address in Van Buren Street, and four dollars in money. It was August, 1889. She was eighteen years of age, bright, timid, and full of the illusions of ignorance and youth. Whatever touch of regret at parting characterized her thoughts, it was certainly not for advantages now being given up. A gush of tears at her mother's farewell kiss, a touch in her throat when the cars clacked by the flour mill where her father worked by day, a pathetic sigh as the familiar green environs of the village passed in review, and the threads which bound her so lightly to girlhood and home were irretrievably broken.

To be sure there was always the next station, where one might descend and return. There was the great city, bound more closely by these very trains which came up daily. Columbia City was not so very far away, even once she was in Chicago. What, pray, is a few hours — a few hundred miles? She looked at the little slip bearing her sister's address and wondered. She gazed at the green landscape, now passing in swift review, until her swifter thoughts replaced its impression with vague conjectures of what Chicago might be.

When a girl leaves her home at eighteen, she does one of two things. Either she falls into saving hands and becomes better, or she rapidly assumes the cosmopolitan standard of virtue and becomes worse. Of an intermediate balance, under the circumstances, there is no possibility. The city has its cunning wiles, no less than the infinitely smaller and more human tempter. There are large forces which allure with all the soulfulness of expression possible in the most cultured human. The gleam of a thousand lights is often as effective as the persuasive light in a wooing and fascinating eye. Half the undoing of the unsophisticated and natural mind is accomplished by forces wholly superhuman. A blare of sound, a roar of life, a vast array of human lives, appeal to the astonished senses in equivocal terms. Without a counsellor at hand to whisper cautious interpretations, what falsehoods may not these things breathe into the unguarded ear! Unrecognized for what they are, their beauty, like music, too often relaxes, then weakens, then perverts the simpler human perceptions.

Caroline, or Sister Carrie, as she had been half affectionately termed by the family, was possessed of a mind rudimentary in its power of observation and analysis. Self-interest with her was high, but not strong. It was, nevertheless, her guiding characteristic. Warm with the fancies of youth, pretty with the insipid prettiness of the formative period, possessed of a figure promising eventual shapeliness and an eye alight with certain native intelligence, she was a fair example of the middle American class — two generations removed from the emigrant. Books were beyond her interest — knowledge a sealed book. In the intuitive graces she was still crude. She could scarcely toss her head gracefully. Her hands were almost ineffectual. The feet, though small, were set flatly.

And yet she was interested in her charms, quick to understand the keener pleasures of life, ambitious to gain in material things. A half-equipped little knight she was, venturing to reconnoiter the mysterious city and dreaming wild dreams of some vague, far-off supremacy, which should make it prey and subject — the proper penitent, grovelling at a woman's slipper.

"That," said a voice in her ear, "is one of the prettiest little resorts in Wisconsin."

"Is it?" she answered nervously.

The train was just pulling out of Waukesha. For some time she had been conscious of a man behind. She felt him observing her mass of hair. He had been fidgeting, and with natural intuition she felt a certain interest growing in that quarter. Her maidenly reserve, and a certain sense of what was conventional under the circumstances, called her to forestall and deny this familiarity, but the daring and magnetism of the individual, born of past experiences and triumphs, prevailed. She answered.

He leaned forward to put his elbows upon the back of her seat and proceeded to make himself volubly agreeable.

"Yes, that is a great resort for Chicago people. The hotels are swell. You are not familiar with this part of the country, are you?"

"Oh, yes, I am," answered Carrie. "That is, I live at Columbia City. I have never been through here, though."

"And so this is your first visit to Chicago," he observed.

All the time she was conscious of certain features out of the side of her eye. Flush, colourful cheeks, a light moustache, a grey fedora hat. She now turned and looked upon him in full, the instincts of self-protection and coquetry mingling confusedly in her brain.

"I didn't say that," she said.

"Oh," he answered, in a very pleasing way and with an air of assumed mistake, "I thought you did."

Here was a type of the travelling canvasser for a manufacturing house — a class which at that time was first being dubbed by the slang of the day "drummers." He came within the meaning of a still newer term, which had sprung into general use among Americans in 1880, and which concisely expressed the thought of one whose dress or manners are calculated to elicit the admiration of susceptible young women — a "masher." His suit was of a striped and crossed pattern of brown wool, new at that time, but since become familiar as a business suit. The low crotch of the vest revealed a stiff shirt bosom of white and pink stripes. From his coat sleeves protruded a pair of linen cuffs of the same pattern, fastened with large, gold plate buttons, set with the common yellow agates known as "cat's-eyes." His fingers bore several rings — one, the ever-enduring heavy seal — and from his vest dangled a neat gold watch chain, from which was suspended the secret insignia of the Order of Elks. The whole suit was rather tight-fitting, and was finished off with heavy-soled tan shoes, highly polished, and the grey fedora hat. He was, for the order of intellect represented, attractive, and whatever he had to recommend him, you may be sure was not lost upon Carrie, in this, her first glance.

Lest this order of individual should permanently pass, let me put down some of the most striking characteristics of his most successful manner and method. Good clothes, of course, were the first essential, the things without which he was nothing. A strong physical nature, actuated by a keen desire for the feminine, was the next. A mind free of any consideration of the problems or forces of the world and actuated not by greed, but by an insatiable love of variable pleasure. His method was always simple. Its principal element was daring, backed, of course, by an intense desire and admiration for the sex. Let him meet with a young woman twice and he would straighten her necktie for her and perhaps address her by her first name. In the great department stores he was at his ease. If he caught the attention of some young woman while waiting for the cash boy to come back with his change, he would find out her name, her favourite flower, where a note would reach her, and perhaps pursue the delicate task of friendship until it proved unpromising, when it would be relinquished. He would do very well with more pretentious women, though the burden of expense was a slight deterrent. Upon entering a parlour car, for instance, he would select a chair next to the most promising bit of femininity and soon inquire if she cared to have the shade lowered. Before the train cleared the yards he would have the porter bring her a footstool. At the next lull in his conversational progress he would find her something to read, and from then on, by dint of compliment gently insinuated, personal narrative, exaggeration and service, he would win her tolerance, and, mayhap, regard.

A woman should some day write the complete philosophy of clothes. No matter how young, it is one of the things she wholly comprehends. There is an indescribably faint line in the matter of man's apparel which somehow divides for her those who are worth glancing at and those who are not. Once an individual has passed this faint line on the way downward he will get no glance from her. There is another line at which the dress of a man will cause her to study her own. This line the individual at her elbow now marked for Carrie. She became conscious of an inequality. Her own plain blue dress, with its black cotton tape trimmings, now seemed to her shabby. She felt the worn state of her shoes.

"Let's see," he went on, "I know quite a number of people in your town. Morgenroth the clothier and Gibson the dry goods man."

"Oh, do you?" she interrupted, aroused by memories of longings their show windows had cost her.

At last he had a clue to her interest, and followed it deftly. In a few minutes he had come about into her seat. He talked of sales of clothing, his travels, Chicago, and the amusements of that city.

"If you are going there, you will enjoy it immensely. Have you relatives?"

"I am going to visit my sister," she explained.

"You want to see Lincoln Park," he said, "and Michigan Boulevard. They are putting up great buildings there. It's a second New York — great. So much to see — theatres, crowds, fine houses — oh, you'll like that."

There was a little ache in her fancy of all he described. Her insignificance in the presence of so much magnificence faintly affected her. She realized that hers was not to be a round of pleasure, and yet there was something promising in all the material prospect he set forth. There was something satisfactory in the attention of this individual with his good clothes. She could not help smiling as he told her of some popular actress of whom she reminded him. She was not silly, and yet attention of this sort had its weight.

"You will be in Chicago some little time, won't you?" he observed at one turn of the now easy conversation.

"I don't know," said Carrie vaguely — a flash vision of the possibility of her not securing employment rising in her mind.

"Several weeks, anyhow," he said looking steadily into her eyes.

There was much more passing now than the mere words indicated. He recognized the indescribable thing that made up for fascination and beauty in her. She realized that she was of interest to him from the one standpoint which a woman both delights in and fears. Her manner was simple, though for the very reason that she had not yet learned the many little affectations with which women conceal their true feelings. Some thing she did appeared bold. A clever companion — had she ever had one — would have warned her never to look a man in the eyes so steadily.

"Why do you ask?" she said.

"Well, I'm going to be there several weeks. I'm going to study stock at our place and get new samples. I might show you 'round."

"I don't know whether you can or not. I mean I don't know whether I can. I shall be living with my sister, and — "

"Well, if she minds, we'll fix that." He took out his pencil and a little pocket note-book as if it were all settled. "What is your address there?"

She fumbled her purse which contained the address slip.

He reached down in his hip pocket and took out a fat purse. It was filled with slips of paper, some mileage books, a roll of greenbacks. It impressed her deeply. Such a purse had never been carried by any one attentive to her. Indeed, an experienced traveler, a brisk man of the world, had never come within such close range before. The purse, the shiny tan shoes, the smart new suit, and the *air* with which he did things, built up for her a dim world of fortune, of which he was the center. It disposed her pleasantly toward all he might do.

He took out a neat business card, on which was engraved Bartlett, Caryoe & Company, and down in the left-hand corner, Chas. H. Drouet.

"That's me," he said, putting the card in her hand and touching his name. "It's pronounced Drew-eh. Our family was French, on my father's side."

She looked at it while he put up his purse. Then he got out a letter from a bunch in his coat pocket. "This is the house I travel for," he went on, pointing to a picture on it, "corner of State and Lake." There was pride in his voice. He felt that it was something to be connected with such a place, and he made her feel that way.

"What is your address?" he began again, fixing his pencil to write.

She looked at his hand.

"Carrie Meeber," she said slowly. "Three hundred and fifty four West Van Buren Street, care S. C. Hanson."

He wrote it carefully down and got out the purse again. "You'll be home if I come around Monday night?" he said.

"I think so," she answered.

How true it is that words are but the vague shadows of the volumes we mean. Little audible links, they are, chaining together great inaudible feelings and purposes. Here were these two, bandying little phrases, drawing purses, looking at cards, and both unconscious of how inarticulate all their real feelings were. Neither was wise enough to be sure of the working of the mind of the other. He could not tell how his luring succeeded. She could not realize that she was drifting, until he secured her address. Now she felt that she had yielded something—he, that he had gained a victory. Already they felt that they were somehow associated. Already he took more control in directing the conversation. His words were easy. Her manner was relaxed.

They were nearing Chicago. Signs were everywhere numerous. Trains flashed by them. Across wide stretches of flat, open prairie they could see lines of telegraph poles stalking across the fields toward the great city. Far away were indications of suburban towns, some big smoke-stacks towering high in the air.

Frequently there were two-story frame houses standing out in the open fields, without fence or trees, lone outposts of the approaching army of homes.

To the child, the genius with imagination, or the wholly untravelled, the approach of a great city for the first time is a wonderful thing. Particularly if it be evening—that mystic period between the glare and gloom of the world when life is changing from one sphere or condition to another. Ah, the promise of the night. What does it not hold for the weary! What old illusion of hope is not here forever repeated! Says the soul of the toiler to itself, "I shall soon be free. I shall be in the ways and the hosts of the merry. The streets, the lamps, the lighted chamber set for dining, are for me. The theatre, the halls, the parties, the ways of rest and the paths of song — these are mine in the night." Though all humanity be still enclosed in the shops, the thrill runs abroad. It is in the air. The dullest feeling something which they may not always express or describe. It is the lifting of the burden of toil.

Sister Carrie gazed out of the window. Her companion, affected by her wonder, so contagious are all things, felt anew some interest in the city and pointed out its marvels.

"This is Northwest Chicago," said Drouet. "This is the Chicago River," and he pointed to a little muddy creek, crowded with the huge masted wanderers from far-off waters nosing the black-posted banks. With a puff, a clang, and a clatter of rails it was gone. "Chicago is getting to be a great town," he went on. "It's a wonder. You'll find lots to see here."

She did not hear this very well. Her heart was troubled by a kind of terror. The fact that she was alone, away from home, rushing into a great sea of life and endeavour, began to tell. She could not help but feel a little choked for breath — a little sick as her heart beat so fast. She half closed her eyes and tried to think it was nothing, that Columbia City was only a little way off.

"Chicago! Chicago!" called the brakeman, slamming open the door. They were rushing into a more crowded yard, alive with the clatter and clang of life. She began to gather up her poor little grip and closed her hand firmly upon her purse. Drouet arose, kicked his legs to straighten his trousers, and seized his clean yellow grip.

"I suppose your people will be here to meet you?" he said. "Let me carry your grip."

"Oh, no," she said. "I'd rather you wouldn't. I'd rather you wouldn't be with me when I meet my sister."

"All right," he said in all kindness. "I'll be near, though, in case she isn't here, and take you out there safely."

"You're so kind," said Carrie, feeling the goodness of such attention in her strange situation.

"Chicago!" called the brakeman, drawing the word out long. They were under a great shadowy train shed, where the lamps were already beginning to shine out, with passenger cars all about and the train moving at a snail's pace. The people in the car were all up and crowding about the door.

"Well, here we are," said Drouet, leading the way to the door. "Good-bye, till I see you Monday."

"Good-bye," she answered, taking his proffered hand.

"Remember, I'll be looking till you find your sister."

She smiled into his eyes.

They filed out, and he affected to take no notice of her. A lean-faced, rather commonplace woman recognized Carrie on the platform and hurried forward.

"Why, Sister Carrie!" she began, and there was a perfunctory embrace of welcome.

Carrie realized the change of affectional atmosphere at once. Amid all the maze, uproar, and novelty she felt cold reality taking her by the hand. No world of light and merriment. No round of amusement. Her sister carried with her most of the grimness of shift and toil.

"Why, how are all the folks at home?" she began, "how is father, and mother?"

Carrie answered, but was looking away. Down the aisle, toward the gate leading into the waiting-room and the street, stood Drouet. He was looking back. When he saw that she saw him and was safe with her sister he turned to go, sending back the shadow of a smile. Only Carrie saw it. She felt something lost to her when he moved away. When he disappeared she felt his absence thoroughly. With her sister she was much alone, a lone figure in a tossing, thoughtless sea.

# Willa Cather

## (1873-1947)

*Born in Virginia in 1873, the oldest of seven children,* WILLA CATHER *moved to Nebraska at age nine. The move had profound consequences for Cather as an artist; the challenge of life on the prairie proved to be an experience she returned to again and again in her fiction. Independent and intelligent, she graduated in 1895 from the University of Nebraska, where she had begun writing for the school newspaper. This, in turn, led to a job with a Pittsburgh paper and later with* McClure's Magazine *in New York, where she lived for the next forty years. Her major novels include* O Pioneers! *(1913),* My Antonia *(1918),* One of Ours *(1922),* Death Comes for the Archbishop *(1927), and* Sapphira and the Slave Girl *(1940). Cather died in 1947.*

*It must be admitted that Willa Cather cannot be considered a Chicago writer in the same sense as most of the other authors in this anthology; she gathered the material for the passage below during several weeks' visit to the city. Yet the editors feel compelled to include her work based on her vivid portrayal of Chicago in the middle section of* The Song of the Lark *(1915). The novel follows the career of Thea Kronborg from the tiny town of Moonstone, Colorado, to her early success in Chicago, to opera stardom in New York City. As was the case with Dreiser's Carrie Meeber, Chicago represents only an intermediate stop on Thea's road to fame. Nevertheless, it is in Chicago that she has her first real success as a singer, and it is at the Art Institute that she encounters the painting that gives the novel its title.*

◆ ◆ ◆

## *from* THE SONG OF THE LARK

By the first of February Thea had been in Chicago almost four months, and she did not know much more about the city than if she had never quitted Moonstone. She was, as Harsanyi said, incurious. Her work took most of her time, and she found that she had to sleep a good deal. It had never before been so hard to get up in the morning. She had the bother of caring for her room, and she had to build her fire and bring up her coal. Her routine was frequently interrupted by a message from Mr. Larsen summoning her to sing at a funeral. Every funeral took half a day, and the time had to be made up. When Mrs. Harsanyi asked her if it did not depress her to sing at funerals, she replied that she "had been brought up to go to funerals and didn't mind."

Thea never went into shops unless she had to, and she felt no interest in them. Indeed, she shunned them, as places where one was sure to be parted from one's money in some way. She was nervous about counting her change, and she could not accustom herself to having her purchases sent to her address. She felt much safer with her bundles under her arm.

During this winter Thea got no city consciousness. Chicago was simply a wilderness through which one had to find one's way. She felt no interest in the general briskness and zest of the crowds. The crash and scramble of that big, rich, appetent Western city she did not take in at all, except to notice that the noise of the drays and street-cars tired her. The brilliant window displays, the splendid furs and stuffs, the gorgeous flower-shops, the gay candy-shops, she scarcely noticed. At Christmas-time she did feel some curiosity about the toy-stores, and she wished she held Thor's little mittened fist in her hand as she stood before the windows. The jewelers' windows, too, had a strong attraction for her — she had always liked bright stones. When she went into the city she used to brave the biting lake winds and stand gazing in at the displays of diamonds and pearls and emeralds; the tiaras and necklaces and earrings, on white velvet. These seemed very well while to her, things worth coveting.

Mrs. Lorch and Mrs. Andersen often told each other it was strange that Miss Kronborg had so little initiative about "visiting points of interest." When Thea came to live with them she had expressed a wish to see two places: Montgomery Ward and Company's big mail-order store, and the packing-houses, to which all the hogs and cattle that went through Moonstone were bound. One of Mrs. Lorch's lodgers worked in a packing-house, and Mrs. Andersen brought Thea word that she had spoken to Mr. Eckman and he would gladly take her to Packingtown. Eckman was a toughish young Swede, and he thought it would be something of a lark to take a pretty girl through the slaughter-houses. But he was disappointed. Thea neither grew faint nor clung to the arm he kept offering her. She asked innumerable questions and was impatient because he knew so little of what was going on outside of his own department. When they got off the street-car and walked back to Mrs. Lorch's house in the dusk, Eckman put her hand in his overcoat pocket — she had no muff — and kept squeezing it ardently until she said, "Don't do that; my ring cuts me." That night he told his roommate that he "could have kissed her as easy as rolling off a log, but she wasn't worth the trouble." As for Thea, she had enjoyed the afternoon very much, and wrote her father a brief but clear account of what she had seen.

One night at supper Mrs. Andersen was talking about the exhibit of students' work she had seen at the Art Institute that afternoon. Several of her friends had sketches in the exhibit. Thea, who always felt that she was behindhand in courtesy to Mrs. Andersen, thought that here was an opportunity to show interest without committing herself to anything. "Where is that, the Institute?" she asked absently.

Mrs. Andersen clasped her napkin in both hands. "The Art Institute? Our beautiful Art Institute on Michigan Avenue? Do you mean to say you have never visited it?"

"Oh, is it the place with the big lions out in front? I remember; I saw it when I went to Montgomery Ward's. Yes, I thought the lions were beautiful."

"But the pictures! Didn't you visit the galleries?"

"No. The sign outside said it was a pay-day. I've always meant to go back, but I haven't happened to be down that way since."

Mrs. Lorch and Mrs. Andersen looked at each other. The old mother spoke, fixing her shining little eyes upon Thea across the table. "Ah, but Miss Kronborg, there are old masters! Oh, many of them, such as you would not see anywhere out of Europe."

"And Corots," breathed Mrs. Andersen, tilting her head feelingly. "Such examples of the Barbizon school!" This was meaningless to Thea, who did not read the art columns of the Sunday *Inter-Ocean* as Mrs. Andersen did.

"Oh, I'm going there some day," she reassured them. "I like to look at oil paintings."

One bleak day in February, when the wind was blowing clouds of dirt like a Moonstone sandstorm, dirt that filled your eyes and ears and mouth, Thea fought her way across the unprotected space in front of the Art Institute and into the doors of the building. She did not come out again until the closing hour. In the street-car, on the long cold ride home, while she sat staring at the waistcoat buttons of a fat strap-hanger, she had a serious reckoning with herself. She seldom thought about her way of life, about what she ought or ought not to do; usually there was but one obvious and important thing to be done. But that afternoon she remonstrated with herself severely. She told herself that she was missing a great deal; that she ought to be more willing to take advice and to go to see things. She was sorry that she had let months pass without going to the Art Institute. After this she would go once a week.

The Institute proved, indeed, a place of retreat, as the sand hills or the Kohlers' garden used to be; a place where she could forget Mrs. Andersen's tiresome overtures of friendship, the stout contralto in the choir whom she so unreasonably hated, and even, for a little while, the torment of her work. That building was a place in which she could relax and play, and she could hardly ever play now. On the whole, she spent more time with the casts than with the pictures. They were at once more simple and more perplexing; and some way they seemed more important, harder to overlook. It never occurred to her to buy a catalogue, so she called most of the casts by names she made up for them. Some of them she knew; the Dying Gladiator she had read about in "Childe Harold" almost as long ago as she could remember; he was strongly associated with Dr. Archie and childish illnesses. The Venus di Milo puzzled her; she could not see why people thought her so beautiful. She told herself over and over that she did not think the Apollo Belvedere "at all handsome." Better than anything else she liked a great equestrian statue of an evil, cruel-looking general with an unpronounceable name. She used to walk round and round this terrible man and his terrible horse, frowning at him, brooding upon him, as if she had to make some momentous decision about him.

The casts, when she lingered long among them, always made her gloomy. It was with a lightening of the heart, a feeling of throwing off the old miseries and old sorrows of the world, that she ran up the wide staircase to the pictures. There she liked best the ones that told stories. There was a painting by Gérôme called "The Pasha's Grief" which always made her wish for Gunner and Axel. The Pasha was seated on a rug, beside a green candle almost as big as a telegraph pole, and before him was stretched his dead tiger, a splendid beast, and there were pink roses scattered about him. She loved, too, a picture of some boys bringing a newborn calf on a litter, the cow walking beside it and licking it. The Corot which hung next to this painting she did not like or dislike; she never saw it.

But in that same room there was a picture — oh, that was the thing she ran upstairs so fast to see! That was her picture. She imagined that nobody cared for it but herself, and that it waited for her. That was a picture indeed. She liked even the name of it, "The Song of the Lark." The flat country, the early morning light, the wet fields, the look in the girl's heavy face — well, they were all hers, anyhow, whatever was there. She told herself that that picture was "right." Just what she meant by this, it would take a clever person to explain. But to her the word covered the almost boundless satisfaction she felt when she looked at the picture.

Before Thea had any idea how fast the weeks were flying, before Mr. Larsen's "permanent" soprano had returned to her duties, spring came; windy, dusty, strident, shrill; a season almost more violent in Chicago than the winter from which it releases one, or the heat to which it eventually delivers one. One sunny morning the apple trees in Mrs. Lorch's back yard burst into bloom, and for the first time in months Thea dressed without building a fire. The morning shone like a holiday, and for her it was to be a holiday. There was in the air that sudden, treacherous softness which makes the Poles who work in the packing-houses get drunk. At such times beauty is necessary, and in Packing-town there is no place to get it except at the saloons, where one can buy for a few hours the illusion of comfort, hope, love, — whatever one most longs for.

Harsanyi had given Thea a ticket for the symphony concert that afternoon, and when she looked out at the white apple trees her doubts as to whether she ought to go vanished at once. She would make her work light that morning, she told herself. She would go to the concert full of energy. When she set off, after dinner, Mrs. Lorch, who knew Chicago weather, prevailed upon her to take her cape. The old lady said that such sudden mildness, so early in April, presaged a sharp return of winter, and she was anxious about her apple trees.

The concert began at two-thirty, and Thea was in her seat in the Auditorium at ten minutes after two — a fine seat in the first row of the balcony, on the side, where she could see the house as well as the orchestra. She had been to so few concerts that the great house, the crowd of people, and the lights, all had a stimulating effect. She was surprised to see so many men in the audience, and wondered how they could leave their business in the afternoon. During the first number Thea was so much interested in the orchestra itself, in the men, the instruments, the volume of sound, that she paid little attention to what they were playing. Her excitement impaired her power of listening. She kept saying to herself, "Now I must stop this foolishness and listen; I may never hear this again"; but her mind was like a glass that is hard to focus. She was not ready to listen until the second number, Dvorak's Symphony in E minor, called on the programme, "From the New World." The first theme had scarcely been given out when her mind became clear; instant composure fell upon her, and with it came the power of concentration. This was music she could understand, music from the New World indeed! Strange how, as the first movement went on, it brought back to her that high tableland above Laramie; the grass-grown wagon trails, the far-away peaks of the snowy range, the wind and the eagles, that old man and the first telegraph message.

When the first movement ended, Thea's hands and feet were cold as ice. She was too much excited to know anything except that she wanted something desperately, and when the English horns gave out the theme of the Largo, she knew that what she wanted was exactly that. Here were the sand hills, the grasshoppers and locusts, all the things that wakened and chirped in the early morning; the reaching and reaching of high plains, the immeasurable yearning of all flat lands. There was home in it, too; first memories, first mornings long ago; the amazement of a new soul in a new world; a soul new and yet old, that had dreamed something despairing, something glorious, in the dark before it was born; a soul obsessed by what it did not know, under the cloud of a past it could not recall.

If Thea had had much experience in concert-going, and had known her own capacity, she would have left the hall when the symphony was over. But she sat still, scarcely knowing where she was, because her mind had been far away and had not yet come back to her. She was startled when the orchestra began to play again—the entry of the gods into Walhalla. She heard it as people hear things in their sleep. She knew scarcely anything about the Wagner operas. She had a vague idea that "Rhinegold" was about the strife between gods and men; she had read something about it in Mr. Haweis's book long ago. Too tired to follow the orchestra with much understanding, she crouched down in her seat and closed her eyes. The cold, stately measures of the Walhalla music rang out, far away; the rainbow bridge throbbed out into the air, under it the wailing of the Rhine daughters and the singing of the Rhine. But Thea was sunk in twilight; it was all going on in another world. So it happened that with a dull, almost listless ear she heard for the first time that troubled music, ever-darkening, ever-brightening, which was to flow through so many years of her life.

When Thea emerged from the concert hall, Mrs. Lorch's predictions had been fulfilled. A furious gale was beating over the city from Lake Michigan. The streets were full of cold, hurrying, angry people, running for street-cars and barking at each other. The sun was setting in a clear, windy sky, that flamed with red as if there were a great fire somewhere on the edge of the city. For almost the first time Thea was conscious of the city itself, of the congestion of life all about her, of the brutality and power of those streams that flowed in the streets, threatening to drive one under. People jostled her, ran into her, poked her aside with their elbows, uttering angry exclamations. She got on the wrong car and was roughly ejected by the conductor at a windy corner, in front of a saloon. She stood there dazed and shivering. The cars passed, screaming as they rounded curves, but either they were full to the doors, or were bound for places where she did not want to go. Her hands were so cold that she took off her tight kid gloves. The street lights began to gleam in the dusk. A young man came out of the saloon and stood eyeing her questioningly while he lit a cigarette. "Looking for a friend to-night?" he asked. Thea drew up the collar of her cape and walked on a few paces. The young man shrugged his shoulders and drifted away.

Thea came back to the corner and stood there irresolutely. An old man approached her. He, too, seemed to be waiting for a car. He wore an overcoat with a black fur collar, his gray mustache was waxed into little points, and his eyes were watery. He kept thrusting his face up near hers. Her hat blew off and he ran after it—a stiff, pitiful skip he had—and brought it back to her. Then, while she was pinning her hat on, her cape blew up, and he held it down for her, looking at her intently. His face worked as if he were going to cry or were frightened. He leaned over and whispered something to her. It struck her as curious that he was really quite timid, like an old beggar. "Oh, let me *alone!*" she cried miserably between her teeth. He vanished, disappeared like the Devil in a play. But in the mean time something had got away from her; she could not remember how the violins came in after the horns, just there. When her cape blew up, perhaps — Why did these men torment her? A cloud of dust blew in her face and blinded her. There was some power abroad in the world bent upon taking away from her that feeling with which she had come out of the concert hall. Everything seemed to sweep down on her to tear it out from under her cape. If one had that, the world became one's enemy; people, buildings, wagons, cars, rushed at one to crush it under, to make one let go of it. Thea glared round her at the crowds, the ugly, sprawling streets, the long lines of lights, and she was not crying now. Her eyes were brighter than even Harsanyi had ever seen them. All these things and people were no longer remote and negligible; they had to be met, they were lined up against her, they were there to take something from her. Very well; they should never have it. They might trample her to death, but they should never have it. As long as she lived that ecstasy was going to be hers. She would live for it, work for it, die for it; but she was going to have it, time after time, height after height. She could hear the crash of the orchestra again, and she rose on the brasses. She would have it, what the trumpets were singing! She would have it, have it, — it! Under the old cape she pressed her hands upon her heaving bosom, that was a little girl's no longer.

# Edith Wyatt

## (1873-1958)

EDITH WYATT *was born in Tomah, Wisconsin, in 1873, but she spent most of her life, from 1884 until her death in 1958, in Chicago. In a 1903 article entitled "Certain of the Chicago School of Fiction," William Dean Howells praised Wyatt's fiction for its realism and common sense, arguing that it represented the "apotheosis of the democratic spirit." Like Elia Peattie, Wyatt was a fierce advocate of social justice and women's issues. She taught English classes to immigrants in Hull-House and was involved in the reformation of various labor laws throughout her long life. Other than the story collection,* Every One His Own Way *(1901), her most popular works were the novel* A True Love: A Comedy of the Affections *(1903), and* Great Companions *(1917), a collection of essays. As some of their titles — "The Fox and the Stork," "Jack Sprat," "A Beauty and the Beast" — might indicate, the stories in* Every One His Own Way *often have the quality of fables and fairy tales. Good usually triumphs over bad, and in Wyatt's world that means honest and unpretentious people prevail over those who are condescending and conceited. Though Wyatt was later to see and write about Chicago at its very worst, her early fiction presents us with a city where delicate issues of etiquette are the order of the day. "The Parent's Assistant," which gently mocks the women's clubs she herself found valuable, presents Wyatt at her tongue-in-cheek best.*

◆ ◆ ◆

## The Parent's Assistant

*from* EVERY ONE HIS OWN WAY

Far out on North Clark Street used to stand a square red brick house with green blinds, white stone trimmings, and a mansard roof of blue slate.

It had a large green yard enclosed by an iron fence, and geranium-beds bordering the plank walk leading to its piazza.

There was a swing in the side-yard and a side-porch where the servants whipped eggs and peeled apples. Smoke blew from the chimneys, children played on the grass, women talked and sewed on the piazza or at the long bay-windows. The place was instinct and radiant with life, and in its amplitude and soft brilliant coloring there seemed to lie the lovely expression of a house of peace.

Here lived Major and Mrs. Porter with their sons, their daughter, Mrs. Burden, their grandchild, Pearl, old General Baggs, Mrs. Porter's father, and transient hordes of visiting relatives.

These the major loved to take to see the Masonic Temple and the Columbian Museum, to climb the pen-fences at the Stockyards, and to stand on the State Street Bridge while it turned.

Meanwhile, at home, Mrs. Porter would sit talking to Sister Susies and Cousin Belles and Aunt Annies, while she ran up seams or featherstitched or herringboned.

She was a pretty and industrious woman, rather small and slightly freckled, with habits regular as those of a bee.

She arranged her soft gray hair in a neatly curled cliff of bang tied around with an invisible net, and inside the house, she always wore in the daytime little white cambric sacks. At about four in the afternoon she would dress in a black Bengaline with ruching in the neck and sleeves.

She had dinner for her family in the middle of the day and supped at about six o'clock on a tea of the proudest character, with hot biscuit and creamed chicken and several kinds of cake. She had no idea of adopting, nor of making them adopt, any alien or more sophisticated customs, and she spent all her time in sewing and in taking care of her family, always large and cumbersome.

She had a friend, a Mrs. La Grange, who gave talks at clubs, who used to come to see her and say: "Fanny, why don't you go into these newer things a little more? I sometimes think you are stagnating here, dear, and that we ought to do something to take you out of yourself and your own little concerns. They really are *very* little, don't you think so yourself?" A hortatory manner had indeed grown so accustomed with Mrs. La Grange that she adopted it with almost every one; but she felt that Fanny especially needed improvement, or, in other words, that Fanny ought to be more like herself.

Mrs. Porter would sit and sew and wonder why she didn't have such good times as she used with Addie La Grange. She could just as well have retorted by asking Mrs. La Grange why she didn't go into hemstitching and feather-boning and plain sewing for her niece's children, and by telling her that she ought to try to get out of her rut and work for others instead of occupying herself so much with her own papers and little concerns. But as her large and various family had made her more tolerant than Mrs. La Grange, she did not expect her friend to be just like herself, but was content she should go her own way.

Mrs. La Grange, however, finally persuaded Mrs. Porter to attend two or three club meetings of a kind rather disappointing to her.

She had, as a girl, belonged to a very sprightly and diverting Cook County cooking club, with prizes at every meeting; she had hoped that the little club of Mrs. La Grange's invitation would be somewhat like these gatherings, and she was surprised when she was obliged to listen all the afternoon to a paper on Romanism. It seemed to be a very unsociable arrangement, far inferior to the old one. If Romanism were the rallying-point of the entertainment and you knew nothing about it, you were rather stranded; while, at the old club, if the rallying-point of the evening were Mrs. General U. S. Grant's recipe for pocketbooks, and you knew nothing about it, you could yet eat and pronounce on the pocketbooks.

However, Mrs. La Grange finally induced her friend to join the club. The major and the boys joked a great deal about it. They had a family habit of unambitiously repeating the same jests again and again, and roaring contentedly over them.

Mrs. Porter loved their jokes, and she liked to tie on her best bonnet and start off in the afternoon, to return and tell them all about it in the evening, and listen to the jokes, maintaining her accustomed attitude of scornful inattention.

In her furthering of the good work, Mrs. La Grange at length induced Mrs. Porter to write a paper. She might take any subject she chose. *The Bringing up of Children* and *Homekeeping and Housekeeping*, were suggested.

The boys were very hilarious over this.

"Look here, mother," her eldest son, Tom, said one morning after breakfast, "it's a darned shame the way they treat you at that little club. I can see plainly these are old measly subjects a cat wouldn't look at. What do the high lights write about? What are the big guns' subjects, anyhow? That's what I want to know."

"Oh, mercy, Tom! I wouldn't have any of their subjects for anything."

"Well, what are they, anyhow?"

"Oh, things like Reform and Drainage. They really are splendid, you know. The people that write about them know all about them. And those are the best days."

"Oh, well, all right. Of course, where they write about what they know, you'd better keep out of that. But aren't there any highfalutin subjects? Art? That's certainly the place where you can put on the most airs."

"Now, Tom, go away. I want to begin writing my paper this morning."

"Mother, do you think I'd leave you to suffer and struggle alone with that paper?"

"Go along, Tom. Stop your nonsense."

"Art's the thing for you. Now, what kind do you prefer — Painting?"

"Goodness, no. I'd feel like a perfect idiot writing about painting."

"Architecture, Modelling, or Decorative Design?"

"Tom, go off. I want to start my sewing."

"Music or the Drama?"

Mrs. Porter maintained an ostentatious silence.

"Well, what about Literature? That's your card, mother."

"Tom, I don't know anything about it."

"Well, that's just what's necessary in enlightened criticism. The main thing is to judge impartially; the less you know what you like the better. I tell you, mother, you'll come out strong there."

"Well, what author could I take?"

"Oh, almost any author — Herrick, for instance."

"I never read one word of Herrick's."

"That doesn't make any difference. You don't need to bring in his writing. You want to say that it is as a man you wish to know and love him. Father will have to stand it as well as he can."

"Where does Herrick live? In this country?"

"Oh, no. There's no danger of his being in the audience. He died a long while ago."

"Does he come in much in history?"

"No. Not at all. You can say you know that the happiest men, like the happiest countries, are those that have no histories. Everybody likes to see in papers and literary criticism something they've heard twenty or thirty times before. You put on your best bonnet, hold up your chin, and after they've rapped on the table, you say in the silence, as sweetly as you can and just as though it were fresh from the mint: 'The happiest men, like the happiest countries, are those that have no histories,' and every one will cotton to you."

"But, Tom, if he didn't come into history, where can I find anything about him?"

"You can't. That's the beauty of it. Just a few little encyclopaedia scribs and some biographies. All the rest is airs. You have just as good a right to make up a lot about Herrick as any one else has, you know."

"Tom, you'll be late at the office."

"You can call it 'Herrick, and Country-Life,' or 'Herrick, the Man.' You want to say things like 'I love to picture the poet in his green Devonshire, cared for by his faithful housewife, Prue, tending his rose-trees, listening to his cow-bells.'"

"Sha'n't I say a word about the poetry?"

"Well, just mention it casually as revealing his personality."

"But I don't know a word of it."

"Yes, you do. He wrote that thing Charles sings, '*Bid Me to Live.*'"

"Why, I love that, Tom. Don't I say a word about its being pretty or good or something?"

"Not on your life. Don't you let on for an instant he ever wrote a syllable for anything but to reveal his personality."

"Perhaps they'd like to have Charles come and sing '*Bid Me to Live.*' I'd like to have some one besides myself there when I read this thing."

"I'll stand by you, mother. I tell you I wouldn't miss seeing you stand up and get off, 'The happiest men, like the happiest countries, are those that have no histories.'"

"Tom, you help me too much."

"No, mother. I see you catch the spirit of the idea. Now what question are you going to raise?"

"What question?"

"Why, yes. You want to express your opinion about something or other Herrick did that some people think wasn't exactly straight."

"In his writing?"

"Mother! mother! Heavens, no. Something about allowing his brother-in-law to pay his debts or his being a royalist in the civil broils. Have a pause in your paper and then say, 'And now we come to the consideration of Herrick's moral calibre and the long-mooted question of his debt to his brother-in-law, Sir Wilmot Shanklin.' Then say you think it was really all right and Sir Wilmot could very well afford it, or else, that you think it was selfish and inconsiderate in Herrick and that you don't like it at all. But you want it all terribly refined and rambling and sort of patronizing; put in as often as you can what a special pet of yours Herrick is and say things like, 'How well I remember my first dip into Herrick's sweets, and the day of my introduction to the dear old man.'"

Mrs. Porter's paper, "*Herrick, and Country-Life,*" was finally written and read at Mrs. La Grange's club with great success.

The committee had been at first a little startled when Mrs. Porter changed her subject from the field of domestic experience to the field of letters, but with the event they all were charmed, and Mrs. La Grange said, when she next came to see her old friend: "My dear, that club has certainly developed you wonderfully. I knew when I persuaded you to go into it how stimulating it would be."

# Sherwood Anderson

## (1876-1941)

SHERWOOD ANDERSON *was born in Camden, Ohio, in 1876 and, like Carl Sandburg, he served in the Spanish-American War. Although Anderson was a copywriter in Chicago at the beginning of the century, his career as president of a paint company took him back to Ohio. In 1912 he returned to the city and soon became an integral part of a literary scene that included Carl Sandburg, Ben Hecht, and Edgar Lee Masters. The 1916 publication of* Windy McPherson's Son *marked him as one of America's most promising novelists.*

*However, like so many writers before and after him, Anderson's residence in Chicago was not permanent. He left in 1922 and never again lived in the city. Among his important books are* Winesburg, Ohio *(1919), his most renowned work;* Dark Laughter *(1925); and his final volume of stories,* Death in the Woods *(1933). Indeed, his fiction might be claimed by any number of regional anthologists, including those of Ohio, New Orleans, and Virginia, but it is in Chicago that he first came to prominence, and he will always be associated with its literary renaissance.*

*"For What?" published in 1941, shortly after his death of peritonitis while traveling in Panama, recounts his early years of struggle and comradeship. The story's clipped syntax mirrors the diminished lives of its characters, the fiction writing narrator and his three painter friends. Like struggling artists everywhere, the four men feel unappreciated by the larger world; yet there is something about the vast rich Midwest that inspires them to think of themselves as "rather special human beings, men with a right to that curious happiness that comes sometimes, fleetingly enough, with accomplishment."*

✦ ✦ ✦

## For What?

The big German man came along the river bank to where I was lying on the brown grass at the river's edge. The book I had been reading was on the grass beside me. I had been gazing across the sluggish little river at the distant horizon.

I had hoped to spend the day working. There was a story I wanted to write. This was in a low flat country southwest of the city of Chicago. I had come there that morning by train with the others, Joe and George, and Jerry, the big German.

They all wanted to be painters. They were striving. The Sundays were very precious to the others and to me. We were all working during the week and looking forward to the weekends. There were certain canvases the others wanted to paint. If one of them could get a painting hung in the Chicago Art Institute, it might be a beginning.

We used to speak of it at the lunch hours during the week.

There was a certain story that had been in my mind for weeks, even months. We were all living about in little rooming houses. We were clerks. Jerry, the big German, had been a truck driver. Now he had a job as a shipping clerk in a cold storage warehouse.

I had tried time and again to write the particular story that was in my mind. I told the others about it. I didn't tell them the story. That would bring bad luck. I spoke instead of how I wanted the words and sentences to march.

"Like soldiers marching across a field," I said.

"Like a plow turning up its ribbon of earth across a field."

Fine phrases about work not done. There had been too much of that. You can kill any job so. Just keep talking about the great thing you are to do, some time in the future. That will kill it.

"Yes, and it is so also that paint should go on a canvas."

This would be one of the others, one of the painters speaking.

There was this big talk, plenty of that, words, too many words. Sometimes, after the day's work, in the hot Chicago summers, we all got together to dine in some cheap place. There was a chop suey joint to which we went often, soft-footed, soft-voiced Chinamen trotting up and down. Chop suey and then a couple of bottles of beer each. We lingered over that. Then a walk together along the lake front on the near North Side. There was a little strip of park up there facing the lake, a bathing beach; working men with wives and children came there to escape the heat, newspapers spread on the grass, whole families huddled together in the heat, even the moon, looking down, seeming to give forth heat.

We would be full of literary phrases, culled out of books. Some one of us had been reading Kipling.

"City of dreadful night," he said.

Only Jerry, the big German, was a little different. He had a wife and children.

"What's it all about? Why do I want to paint? Why can't I be satisfied driving a truck and working in my warehouse?

"Going home at night to the wife and kids.

"What is it keeps stirring in a man, making him want to do something out of just himself?"

He grew profane. He would be describing a scene. He had come to the Chinese place from his warehouse across the Chicago River, this before the river was beautified, in the days of the old wooden bridges over the river.

He had stood for a time on one of the bridges, seeing a lake boat pass, lake sailors standing on the deck of the boat and looking up at him standing there above on the moving bridge, the curiously lovely chrysoprase color of the river, the gulls floating over the river.

He would begin speaking of all that, the beauty of the smoky sky over buildings off to the west. Sometimes he pounded with his fists on the table in the chop suey joint. A string of oaths flowed from his lips. Sometimes tears came into his eyes.

He was, to be sure, ridiculous. There was in him something I knew so well later in another friend, Tom Wolfe — a determination, half physical, all his big body in it, like a man striving to push his way through a stone wall.

Out into what?

He couldn't have said what any more than I could of my own hopes, my own passionate desires, of which I was always half ashamed.

To get it in some way down, something felt.

A man was too much in a cage — in some way trapped.

A man got himself trapped. All this business of making a living. There were Jerry and Joe, both married. They both had children.

Joe had been a farmer boy, on his father's farm, somewhere in Iowa. He had come to Chicago filled with hope.

He was like Jerry, the German. He wanted to paint.

"That's what I want.

"I want something."

And why the hell did a man get married? They spoke of that. They weren't complaining of the particular women they had married. You knew they were both fond of their children.

A man got stuck on some dame. A man was made that way. When it got him, when it gripped him, he thought, he convinced himself, that in her, in that particular one, was the thing he sought.

Then the kids coming.

They trap you that way.

Joe speaking up. He wasn't as intense as Jerry. He said we couldn't blame them, the women, his own or any other man's woman.

How'd we know they weren't trapped too? They were wanting to be beautiful in some man's eyes, that was it. They had, Joe declared, as much right to want their thing as we had to want ours.

But what was it we were all wanting, the little group of us, there in that vast Chicago, who had in some way found each other?

Comradeship in hungers we couldn't express.

Anyway it wasn't really success. We knew that. We had got that far.

George said we ought to be skunks. "A man should be a skunk," he said. George wasn't married but had an old mother and father he was supporting. He was laying down a law he couldn't obey.

"So I'm a clerk, eh?

"And whose fault is it?

"Mine, I tell you.

"I ought to walk out on them, on everyone, let 'em go to hell.

"What I want is to wander up and down for a long time. Look and look.

"People think of it as a virtue, a man like me, sticking to a clerk's job, supporting my old father and mother, when it's just cowardice, that's all.

"If I had the courage to walk out on them, be a skunk."

It was something he couldn't do. We all knew that.

By the river bank, on the Sunday afternoon, after a morning trying to write the story I had for weeks been trying to write, I had torn up what I had written. There were the pages of meaningless words, that refused to march, thrown into the sluggish river, floating slowly away.

White patches on a background of yellow sluggish river.

"Patience, patience."

White clouds floating in a hot sky, over a distant cornfield.

"Oh, to hell with patience."

How many men like me, over the world, everywhere, all over America, in big towns like Chicago and New York, small towns or farms.

Trying for it.

For what?

There was something beyond money to be made, fame got, a big name. I was already past thirty. There were others, Joe, Jerry, and George, none of them any longer young.

The World War had not yet come. It was to scatter us, shatter us.

The big German, Jerry, came down to where I lay on my back on the dry grass by the sluggish stream. He had with him the canvas on which he had been working all day. Now it was growing late. At noon, when we had together eaten our lunches, he had been hopeful.

"I think I'll get something. By the gods, I think I will."

Now he sat beside me on the grass at the stream's edge. He had thrown his wet canvas aside. Across the stream from us we could see stretched away the vast cornfields.

The corn was ripening now. The stalks grew high, the long ears hanging down. Soon it would be corn cutting time.

It was a fat rich land — the Middle West. At noon Jerry, the German, son of a German immigrant, who had been a city man all his life, had suddenly begun talking.

He had been trying to paint the cornfield. For the time he had forgotten to be profane. We others had all come from farms or from country towns of the Middle West. He had said that he wanted to paint a cornfield in such a way that everyone looking at his painting would begin at once to think of the fatness and richness of all Middle Western America.

It would be something to give men new confidence in life. He had grown serious. He was the son of a German immigrant who had fled to America to escape military service. Germany believed in the army, in the brute power of arms, but he, Jerry, wanted by his painting to make people believe in the land.

I remember that, in his earnestness, he had shaken a big finger under our noses. "You fellows, your fathers and grandfathers were born on the land. You can't see how rich it all is, how gloriously men might live here." He had spoken of his father, the immigrant, now an old man. We others couldn't understand how hard and meagre life had become for the peasants in all the European lands. We didn't know our own richness — what a foundation, the land, on which to build.

But he would show them, through the richness of the fields. The skyscrapers in the cities, money piled in banks, men owning great factories, they were not the significant things.

The real significance was in the tall corn growing. There was the real American poetry.

He'd show them.


He sat beside me on the grass, by the stream. We sat a long time in silence. There was a grim look on his face, and I knew that he had failed as, earlier in the day, I had. I did not want to embarrass him by speaking. I stayed silent, occasionally looking up at him.

He sat staring at the sluggish stream and looking across the stream to where the cornfields began, and I thought I saw tears in his eyes.

He didn't want me to see.

Suddenly he jumped up. Profane words flew from his lips. He began to dance up and down on the canvas lying on the grass. I remember that the sun was going down over the tops of the tall cornstalks, and he shook his fists at it. He cursed the sun, the corn, himself. What was the use? He had wanted to say something he'd never be able to say. "I'm a shipping clerk in a lousy warehouse, and I'll always be just that, nothing else." It was a child's rage in a grown man. He picked up the canvas on which he had been at work all day and threw it far out into the stream.

We were on our way to the suburban station where we would get our train into the city. All the others, Joe, George, and Jerry, had their painting traps, their easels, boxes of color, palettes. They had little canvas stools on which they sat while painting, and Joe and George carried the wet canvases they had done during the day.

We went along in silence. Joe and George ahead while I walked with Jerry. Did he want me to carry some of his traps?

"Oh, to hell with them, and you too."

He was in this grim mood. Fighting back something in himself. We went along a dusty road beside a wood and cut across a field in which tall weeds grew. We were getting near the station where we were to take the train.

Back to the city.

To our clerkships.

To his being a shipping clerk in his warehouse.

To little hot and cold Chicago flats where some of us had wives and children waiting.

To be fed, clothed, housed.

"A man can't just live in his children. He can't, I tell you."

Something rebellious in all of us.

What is it a man wants, to be of some account in the world, in himself, in his own manhood?

The attempts to write, to paint — these efforts only a part of something we wanted.

All of us half knowing all our efforts would end in futility.

I am very sure the same thoughts were in all our minds that evening, in the field of tall weeds, in the half darkness, as we drew near the little prairie railroad station, the lights of the train already seen far off, across the flat prairies.

And then the final explosion from Jerry. He had suddenly put his painting traps down. He began to throw his tubes of paint about, hurling them into the tall weeds in the field.

"You get out of here, damn you. Go on about your business."

He had thrown his easel, his stool, his paintbrushes. He stood there dancing among the tall weeds.

"Go on. Go away. I'll kill you if you don't."

I moved away from him and joined the others on the platform by the station. It was still light enough to see the man out there in the field, where the tall weeds grew waist-high. He was still dancing with rage, his hands raised, no doubt still cursing his fate.

He was expressing something for us all. He was going through something we had all been through and before we died would all go through again and again.

And then the train came and we got silently aboard, but already we could see happening what I think we all knew would happen. We saw Jerry, that brusque, profane German, already down on his knees among the weeds in the field.

We knew what he was doing, but, when our train arrived in the city and we separated at the station, Joe and George still clinging to the canvases they both knew were no good, when the others had gone I hung about the station.

I had been a farm boy, an American small-town boy like Joe and George. I was curious. Jerry, the big German, had spoken of the land. We had, all of us, been thinking of ourselves as rather special human beings, men with a right to that curious happiness that comes sometimes, fleetingly enough, with accomplishment.

Forgetting the millions like us on farms, holding minor jobs in cities.

What old Abe Lincoln meant when he spoke of "the people."

I was remembering bad years when I was a small-town boy, working about on farms, farmers working all through the year, from daylight until dark.

Big Jerry wanted to express something out of the American land.

Droughts coming, hailstorms destroying crops, disease among the cattle, often a long year's work come to nothing.

Something else remembered out of my own boyhood.

Springs coming, after such disastrous years, and the farmers near my own Middle Western town out again in their fields, again plowing the land.

A kind of deep patient heroism in millions of men on the land, in cities too.

The government pensioning men who went out to kill other men but no pensions for men who spent long lives raising food to feed men.

Killers become heroes, the millions of others never thinking of themselves as heroes.

There would be another train in an hour, and I wanted to see what I did see, keeping myself unseen, the arrival of Jerry, most of his painting traps again collected.

Knowing, as I did know, that on another weekend he would be trying again.

# Carl Sandburg

## (1878-1967)

CARL SANDBURG *was born in Galesburg, Illinois, in 1878, and served in the 6th Illinois Infantry during the Spanish-American War. Before moving to Chicago in 1913, he was an organizer for the Social Democratic Party and secretary to the mayor of Milwaukee. Like many other figures in the Chicago Literary Renaissance, Sandburg made his living as a journalist, first as editor of and later on the staff of the* Chicago Daily News.

Chicago Poems, *from which the following selections are drawn, was published in 1916. Also noted as a songwriter, a folklorist, and as the biographer of Abraham Lincoln, Sandburg won two Pulitzer Prizes, one for* Lincoln: The War Years *(1939), the other for his* Complete Poems *(1950). Like so many others involved in the Renaissance, Sandburg arrived from somewhere else and eventually left Chicago. He died in Flat Rock, North Carolina, in 1967.*

*However, during his years in Chicago, Sandburg was one of the literary scene's most memorable figures. As the following poems show, he had a Whitmanesque love of the working world. Sandburg's experience as a newspaper reporter brought him in contact with the less glamorous side of city life, and the people he met and places he saw became the subjects of his poems. Plainspoken and sympathetic, the voice that emerges in* Chicago Poems *is that of a common man among other common men and women. While it is not widely read today, Sandburg's poetry displays the sort of vigor and passion seen in the best contemporary American free verse, where his influence, if not often acknowledged, nevertheless persists.*

◆ ◆ ◆

## CHICAGO

Hog Butcher for the World,
Tool Maker, Stacker of Wheat,
Player with Railroads and the Nation's Freight Handler;
Stormy, husky, brawling,
City of the Big Shoulders:

They tell me you are wicked and I believe them, for I have seen your painted
women under the gas lamps luring the farm boys.
And they tell me you are crooked and I answer: Yes, it is true I have seen the
gunman kill and go free to kill again.
And they tell me you are brutal and my reply is: On the faces of women and
children I have seen the marks of wanton hunger.
And having answered so I turn once more to those who sneer at this my city,
and I give them back the sneer and say to them:
Come and show me another city with lifted head singing so proud to be
alive and coarse and strong and cunning.
Flinging magnetic curses amid the toil of piling job on job, here is a tall bold
slugger set vivid against the little soft cities;
Fierce as a dog with tongue lapping for action, cunning as a savage pitted
against the wilderness,
      Bareheaded,
      Shoveling,
      Wrecking,
      Planning,
      Building, breaking, rebuilding,
Under the smoke, dust all over his mouth, laughing with white teeth,
Under the terrible burden of destiny laughing as a young man laughs,
Laughing even as an ignorant fighter laughs who has never lost a battle,
Bragging and laughing that under his wrist is the pulse, and under his ribs
the heart of the people,
         Laughing!
Laughing the stormy, husky, brawling laughter of Youth, half-naked,
sweating, proud to be Hog Butcher, Tool Maker, Stacker of Wheat,
Player with Railroads and Freight Handler to the Nation.

## THEY WILL SAY

Of my city the worst that men will ever say is this:
You took little children away from the sun and the dew,
And the glimmers that played in the grass under the great sky,
And the reckless rain; you put them between walls
To work, broken and smothered, for bread and wages,
To eat dust in their throats and die empty-hearted
For a little handful of pay on a few Saturday nights.

## Halsted Street Car

Come you, cartoonists,
Hang on a strap with me here
At seven o'clock in the morning
On a Halsted street car.

Take your pencils
And draw these faces.

Try with your pencils for these crooked faces,
That pig-sticker in one corner — his mouth —
That overall factory girl — her loose cheeks.

Find for your pencils
A way to mark your memory
Of tired empty faces.

After their night's sleep,
In the moist dawn
And cool daybreak,
    Faces
Tired of wishes,
Empty of dreams.

## Graceland

Tomb of a millionaire,
A multi-millionaire, ladies and gentlemen,
Place of the dead where they spend every year
The usury of twenty-five thousand dollars
    For upkeep and flowers
To keep fresh the memory of the dead.
The merchant prince gone to dust
Commanded in his written will
Over the signed name of his last testament
Twenty-five thousand dollars be set aside
For roses, lilacs, hydrangeas, tulips,
For perfume and color, sweetness of remembrance
Around his last long home.

(A hundred cash girls want nickels to go to the movies to-night.
In the back stalls of a hundred saloons, women are at tables
Drinking with men or waiting for men jingling loose silver dollars
    in their pockets.
In a hundred furnished rooms is a girl who sells silk or dress goods
    or leather stuff for six dollars a week wages
And when she pulls on her stockings in the morning she is reckless about
    God and the newspapers and the police, the talk of her home town
    or the name people call her.)


## Skyscraper

By day the skyscraper looms in the smoke and sun and has a soul.
Prairie and valley, streets of the city, pour people into it and they mingle
    among its twenty floors and are poured out again back to the streets,
    prairies and valleys.
It is the men and women, boys and girls so poured in and out all day that
    give the building a soul of dreams and thoughts and memories.
(Dumped in the sea or fixed in a desert, who would care for the building or
    speak its name or ask a policeman the way to it?)

Elevators slide on their cables and tubes catch letters and parcels and iron
    pipes carry gas and water in and sewage out.
Wires climb with secrets, carry light and carry words, and tell terrors
    and profits and loves — curses of men grappling plans of business
    and questions of women in plots of love.

Hour by hour the caissons reach down to the rock of the earth and hold the
    building to a turning planet.
Hour by hour the girders play as ribs and reach out and hold together the
    stone walls and floors.
Hour by hour the hand of the mason and the stuff of the mortar clinch the
    pieces and parts to the shape an architect voted.
Hour by hour the sun and the rain, the air and the rust, and the press of time
    running into centuries, play on the building inside and out and use it.

Men who sunk the pilings and mixed the mortar are laid in graves where the
    wind whistles a wild song without words
And so are men who strung the wires and fixed the pipes and tubes and
    those who saw it rise floor by floor.

Souls of them all are here, even the hod carrier begging at back doors
　　　hundreds of miles away and the bricklayer who went to state's prison
　　　for shooting another man while drunk.
(One man fell from a girder and broke his neck at the end of a straight
　　　plunge — he is here — his soul has gone into the stones of the building.)

On the office doors from tier to tier — hundreds of names and each name
　　　standing for a face written across with a dead child, a passionate lover,
　　　a driving ambition for a million dollar business or a lobster's ease of life.

Behind the signs on the doors they work and the walls tell nothing from
　　　room to room.
Ten-dollar-a-week stenographers take letters from corporation officers,
　　　lawyers, efficiency engineers, and tons of letters go bundled from the
　　　building to all ends of the earth.
Smiles and tears of each office girl go into the soul of the building just the
　　　same as the master-men who rule the building.

Hands of clocks turn to noon hours and each floor empties its men and
　　　women who go away and eat and come back to work.
Toward the end of the afternoon all work slackens and all jobs go slower as
　　　the people feel day closing on them.
One by one the floors are emptied . . . The uniformed elevator men are
　　　gone. Pails clang . . . Scrubbers work, talking in foreign tongues. Broom
　　　and water and mop clean from the floors human dust and spit, and
　　　machine grime of the day.
Spelled in electric fire on the roof are words telling miles of houses and
　　　people where to buy a thing for money. The sign speaks till midnight.

Darkness on the hallways. Voices echo. Silence holds . . . Watchmen walk
　　　slow from floor to floor and try the doors. Revolvers bulge from their
　　　hip pockets . . . Steel safes stand in corners. Money is stacked in them.
A young watchman leans at a window and sees the lights of barges butting
　　　their way across a harbor, nets of red and white lanterns in a railroad
　　　yard, and a span of glooms splashed with lines of white and blurs of
　　　crosses and clusters over the sleeping city.
By night the skyscraper looms in the smoke and the stars and has a soul.

# Upton Sinclair

## (1878-1968)

*For most of his long life,* UPTON SINCLAIR *was a progressive idealist. Sinclair invested the money he made from his most famous book,* The Jungle *(1906), in the Utopian Helicon Hall Colony in New Jersey, which nevertheless did not succeed. In 1915 he moved from the East Coast to California, and in 1934 his EPIC (End Poverty in California) league helped him almost become elected governor of the state. His major novels include the topical* Oil! *(1927), a fictionalization of the Teapot Dome scandal, and* Boston *(1928), which focuses on the Sacco and Vanzetti trial.*

*While Upton Sinclair's residence in Chicago was temporary—just long enough to do the research for* The Jungle*—no anthology of Chicago literature would be complete without an excerpt from that classic "muckraking" novel. One of the most unremittingly grim books in modern American literature,* The Jungle, *published initially at Sinclair's own expense but later a huge best-seller, recounts the grueling lives of Lithuanian immigrant Jurgis Rudkus and his family.*

*Chapter 13 begins with the death of a child, apparently after eating tainted pork from the slaughterhouse where Jurgis had recently worked, and goes on to describe the protagonist's employment at the "place that waits for the lowest man—the fertilizer plant!" Although this section of the novel shows the family in relative prosperity— they are not, at any rate, actually starving—it also provides an unflinching look at the lives of the working poor in early-twentieth-century Chicago: Jurgis's sons are becoming juvenile delinquents, his relatives are quickly losing their health, and disaster lurks around every corner.*

♦ ♦ ♦

*from* THE JUNGLE

During this time that Jurgis was looking for work occurred the death of little Kristoforas, one of the children of Teta Elzbieta. Both Kristoforas and his brother, Juozapas, were cripples, the latter having lost one leg by having it run over, and Kristoforas having congenital dislocation of the hip, which made it impossible for him ever to walk. He was the last of Teta Elzbieta's children, and perhaps he had been intended by nature to let her know that she had had enough. At any rate he was wretchedly sick and undersized; he had the rickets, and though he was over three years old, he was no bigger than an ordinary child of one. All day long he would crawl around the floor in a filthy little dress, whining and fretting; because the floor was full of draughts he was always catching cold, and snuffling because his nose ran. This made him a nuisance, and a source of endless trouble in the family. For his mother, with unnatural perversity, loved him best of all her children, and made a perpetual fuss over him — would let him do anything undisturbed, and would burst into tears when his fretting drove Jurgis wild.

And now he died. Perhaps it was the smoked sausage he had eaten that morning — which may have been made out of some of the tubercular pork that was condemned as unfit for export. At any rate, an hour after eating it, the child had begun to cry with pain, and in another hour he was rolling about on the floor in convulsions. Little Kotrina, who was all alone with him, ran out screaming for help, and after a while a doctor came, but not until Kristoforas had howled his last howl. No one was really sorry about this except poor Elzbieta, who was inconsolable. Jurgis announced that so far as he was concerned the child would have to be buried by the city, since they had no money for a funeral; and at this the poor woman almost went out of her senses, wringing her hands and screaming with grief and despair. Her child to be buried in a pauper's grave! And her stepdaughter to stand by and hear it said without protesting! It was enough to make Ona's father rise up out of his grave to rebuke her! If it had come to this, they might as well give up at once, and be buried all of them together! . . . In the end Marija said that she would help with ten dollars; and Jurgis being still obdurate, Elzbieta went in tears and begged the money from the neighbors, and so little Kristoforas had a mass and a hearse with white plumes on it, and a tiny plot in a graveyard with a wooden cross to mark the place. The poor mother was not the same for months after that; the mere sight of the floor where little Kristoforas had crawled about would make her weep. He had never had a fair chance, poor little fellow, she would say. He had been handicapped from his birth. If only she had heard about it in time, so that she might have had that great doctor to cure him of his lameness! . . . Some time ago, Elzbieta was told, a Chicago billionaire had paid a fortune to bring a great European surgeon over to cure his little daughter of the same disease from which Kristoforas had suffered. And because this surgeon had to have bodies to demonstrate upon, he announced that he would treat the children of the poor, a piece of magnanimity over which the papers became quite eloquent. Elzbieta, alas, did not read the papers, and no one had told her; but perhaps it was as well, for just then they would not have had the carfare to spare to go every day to wait upon the surgeon, nor for that matter anybody with the time to take the child.

All this while that he was seeking for work, there was a dark shadow hanging over Jurgis; as if a savage beast were lurking somewhere in the pathway of his life, and he knew it, and yet could not help approaching the place. There are all stages of being out of work in Packingtown, and he faced in dread the prospect of reaching the lowest. There is a place that waits for the lowest man — the fertilizer plant!

The men would talk about it in awe-stricken whispers. Not more than one in ten had ever really tried it; the other nine had contented themselves with hearsay evidence and a peep through the door. There were some things worse than even starving to death. They would ask Jurgis if he had worked there yet, and if he meant to; and Jurgis would debate the matter with himself. As poor as they were, and making all the sacrifices that they were, would he dare to refuse any sort of work that was offered to him, be it as horrible as ever it could? Would he dare to go home and eat bread that had been earned by Ona, weak and complaining as she was, knowing that he had been given a chance, and had not had the nerve to take it? — And yet he might argue that way with himself all day, and one glimpse into the fertilizer works would send him away shuddering. He was a man, and he would do his duty; he went and made application — but surely he was not also required to hope for success!

The fertilizer works of Durham's lay away from the rest of the plant. Few visitors ever saw them, and the few who did would come out looking like Dante, of whom the peasants declared that he had been into hell. To this part of the yards came all the "tankage," and the waste products of all sorts; here they dried out the bones — and in suffocating cellars where the daylight never came you might see men and women and children bending over whirling machines and sawing bits of bone into all sorts of shapes, breathing their lungs full of the fine dust, and doomed to die, every one of them, within a certain definite time. Here they made the blood into albumen, and made other foul-smelling things into things still more foul-smelling. In the corridors and caverns where it was done you might lose yourself as in the great caves of Kentucky. In the dust and the steam the electric lights would shine like far-off twinkling stars — red and blue, green and purple stars, according to the color of the mist and the brew from which it came. For the odors in these ghastly charnel houses there may be words in Lithuanian, but there are none in English. The person entering would have to summon his courage as for a cold-water plunge. He would go on like a man swimming under water; he would put his handkerchief over his face, and begin to cough and choke; and then, if he were still obstinate, he would find his head beginning to ring, and the veins in his forehead to throb, until finally he would be assailed by an overpowering blast of ammonia fumes, and would turn and run for his life, and come out half-dazed.

On top of this were the rooms where they dried the "tankage," the mass of brown stringy stuff that was left after the waste portions of the carcasses had had the lard and tallow tried out of them. This dried material they would then grind to a fine powder, and after they had mixed it up well with a mysterious but inoffensive brown rock which they brought in and ground up by hundreds of carloads for that purpose, the substance was ready to be put into bags and sent out to the world as any one of a hundred different brands of standard bone phosphate. And then the farmer in Maine or California or Texas would buy this, at say twenty-five dollars a ton, and plant it with his corn; and for several days after the operation the fields would have a strong odor, and the farmer and his wagon and the very horses that had hauled it would all have it too. In Packingtown the fertilizer is pure, instead of being a flavoring, and instead of a ton or so spread out on several acres under the open sky, there are hundreds and thousands of tons of it in one building, heaped here and there in haystack piles, covering the floor several inches deep, and filling the air with a choking dust that becomes a blinding sand storm when the wind stirs.

It was to this building that Jurgis came daily, as if dragged by an unseen hand. The month of May was an exceptionally cool one, and his secret prayers were granted; but early in June there came a record-breaking hot spell, and after that there were men wanted in the fertilizer mill.

The boss of the grinding room had come to know Jurgis by this time, and had marked him for a likely man; and so when he came to the door about two o'clock this breathless hot day, he felt a sudden spasm of pain shoot through him — the boss beckoned to him! In ten minutes more Jurgis had pulled off his coat and overshirt, and set his teeth together and gone to work. Here was one more difficulty for him to meet and conquer!

His labor took him about one minute to learn. Before him was one of the vents of the mill in which the fertilizer was being ground — rushing forth in a great brown river, with a spray of the finest dust flung forth in clouds. Jurgis was given a shovel, and along with half a dozen others it was his task to shovel this fertilizer into carts. That others were at work he knew by the sound, and by the fact that he sometimes collided with them; otherwise they might as well not have been there, for in the blinding dust storm a man could not see six feet in front of his face. When he had filled one cart he had to grope around until another came, and if there was none on hand he continued to grope till one arrived. In five minutes he was, of course, a mass of fertilizer from head to feet; they gave him a sponge to tie over his mouth, so that he could breathe, but the sponge did not prevent his lips and eyelids from caking up with it and his ears from filling solid. He looked like a brown ghost at twilight — from hair to shoes he became the color of the building and of everything in it, and for that matter a hundred yards outside it. The building had to be left open, and when the wind blew Durham and Company lost a great deal of fertilizer.

Working in his shirtsleeves, and with the thermometer at over a hundred, the phosphates soaked in through every pore of Jurgis's skin, and in five minutes he had a headache, and in fifteen was almost dazed. The blood was pounding in his brain like an engine's throbbing; there was a frightful pain in the top of his skull, and he could hardly control his hands. Still, with the memory of his four months' siege behind him, he fought on, in a frenzy of determination; and half an hour later he began to vomit — he vomited until it seemed as if his inwards must be torn into shreds. A man could get used to the fertilizer mill, the boss had said, if he would only make up his mind to it; but Jurgis now began to see that it was a question of making up his stomach.

At the end of the day of horror, he could scarcely stand. He had to catch himself now and then, and lean against a building and get his bearings. Most of the men, when they came out, made straight for a saloon — they seemed to place fertilizer and rattlesnake poison in one class. But Jurgis was too ill to think of drinking — he could only make his way to the street and stagger on to a car. He had a sense of humor, and later on, when he became an old hand, he used to think it fun to board a street car and see what happened. Now, however, he was too ill to notice it — how the people in the car began to gasp and sputter, to put their handkerchiefs to their noses, and transfix him with furious glances. Jurgis only knew that a man in front of him immediately got up and gave him a seat; and that half a minute later the two people on each side of him got up; and that in a full minute the crowded car was nearly empty — those passengers who could not get room on the platform having gotten out to walk.

Of course Jurgis had made his home a miniature fertilizer mill a minute after entering. The stuff was half an inch deep in his skin — his whole system was full of it, and it would have taken a week not merely of scrubbing, but of vigorous exercise, to get it out of him. As it was, he could be compared with nothing known to men, save that newest discovery of the savants, a substance which emits energy for an unlimited time, without being itself in the least diminished in power. He smelt so that he made all the food at the table taste, and set the whole family to vomiting; for himself it was three days before he could keep anything upon his stomach — he might wash his hands, and use a knife and fork, but were not his mouth and throat filled with the poison?

And still Jurgis stuck it out! In spite of splitting headaches he would stagger down to the plant and take up his stand once more, and begin to shovel in the blinding clouds of dust. And so at the end of the week he was a fertilizer man for life — he was able to eat again, and though his head never stopped aching, it ceased to be so bad that he could not work.

So there passed another summer. It was a summer of prosperity, all over the country, and the country ate generously of packing-house products, and there was plenty of work for all the family, in spite of the packers' efforts to keep a superfluity of labor. They were again able to pay their debts and to begin to save a little sum; but there were one or two sacrifices they considered too heavy to be made for long — it was too bad that the boys should have to sell papers at their age. It was utterly useless to caution them and plead with them; quite without knowing it, they were taking on the tone of their new environment. They were learning to swear in voluble English; they were learning to pick up cigar stumps and smoke them, to pass hours of their time gambling with pennies and dice and cigarette cards; they were learning the location of all the houses of prostitution on the "Lêvée," and the names of the "madames" who kept them, and the days when they gave their state banquets, which the police captains and the big politicians all attended. If a visiting "country customer" were to ask for them, they could show him which was "Hinkydink's" famous saloon, and could even point out to him by name the different gamblers and thugs and "hold-up men" who made the place their headquarters. And worse yet, the boys were getting out of the habit of coming home at night. What was the use, they would ask, of wasting time and energy and a possible carfare riding out to the stockyards every night when the weather was pleasant and they could crawl under a truck or into an empty doorway and sleep exactly as well? So long as they brought home a half dollar for each day, what mattered it when they brought it? But Jurgis declared that from this to ceasing to come at all would not be a very long step, and so it was decided that Vilimas and Nikalojus should return to school in the fall, and that instead Elzbieta should go out and get some work, her place at home being taken by her youngest daughter.

Little Kotrina was like most children of the poor, prematurely made old; she had to take care of her little brother, who was a cripple, and also of the baby; she had to cook the meals and wash the dishes and clean house, and have supper ready when the workers came home in the evening. She was only thirteen, and small for her age, but she did all this without a murmur; and her mother went out, and after trudging a couple of days about the yards, settled down as a servant of a "sausage machine."

Elzbieta was used to working, but she found this change a hard one, for the reason that she had to stand motionless upon her feet from seven o'clock in the morning till half-past twelve, and again from one till half-past five. For the first few days it seemed to her that she could not stand it — she suffered almost as much as Jurgis had from the fertilizer, and would come out at sundown with her head fairly reeling. Besides this, she was working in one of the dark holes, by electric light, and the dampness, too, was deadly—there were always puddles of water on the floor, and a sickening odor of moist flesh in the room. The people who worked here followed the ancient custom of nature, whereby the ptarmigan is the color of dead leaves in the fall and snow in the winter, and the chameleon, who is black when he lies upon a stump and turns green when he moves to a leaf. The men and women who worked in this department were precisely the color of the "fresh country sausage" they made.

The sausage room was an interesting place to visit, for two or three minutes, and provided that you did not look at the people; the machines were perhaps the most wonderful things in the entire plant. Presumably sausages were once chopped and stuffed by hand, and if so it would be interesting to know how many workers had been displaced by these inventions. On one side of the room were the hoppers, into which men shovelled loads of meat and wheelbarrows full of spices; in these great bowls were whirling knives that made two thousand revolutions a minute, and when the meat was ground fine and adulterated with potato flour, and well mixed with water, it was forced to the stuffing machines on the other side of the room. The latter were tended by women; there was a sort of spout, like the nozzle of a hose, and one of the women would take a long string of "casing" and put the end over the nozzle and then work the whole thing on, as one works on the finger of a tight glove. This string would be twenty or thirty feet long, but the woman would have it all on in a jiffy; and when she had several on, she would press a lever, and a stream of sausage meat would be shot out, taking the casing with it as it came. Thus one might stand and see appear, miraculously born from the machine, a wriggling snake of sausage of incredible length. In front was a big pan which caught these creatures, and two more women who seized them as fast as they appeared and twisted them into links. This was for the uninitiated the most perplexing work of all, for all that the woman had to give was a single turn of the wrist; and in some way she contrived to give it so that instead of an endless chain of sausages, one after another, there grew under her hands a bunch of strings, all dangling from a single centre. It was quite like the feat of a prestidigitator—for the woman worked so fast that the eye could literally not follow her, and there was only a mist of motion, and tangle after tangle of sausages appearing. In the midst of the mist, however, the visitor would suddenly notice the tense set face, with the two wrinkles graven in the forehead, and the ghastly pallor of the cheeks; and then he would suddenly recollect that it was time he was going on. The woman did not go on; she stayed right there—hour after hour, day after day, year after year; twisting sausage links and racing with death. It was piece work, and she was apt to have a family to keep alive; and stern and ruthless economic laws had arranged it that she could only do this by working just as she did, with all her soul upon her work, and with never an instant for a glance at the well-dressed ladies and gentlemen who came to stare at her, as at some wild beast in a menagerie.

# Vachel Lindsay
## (1879-1931)

NICHOLAS VACHEL LINDSAY *was born in Springfield, Illinois, in 1879. Family tradition had it that the room in which Lindsay was born was one in which Abraham Lincoln had slept, and this early spiritual connection with the sixteenth president was one the poet cultivated throughout his life. Raised in Springfield by a mother who loved the arts, Lindsay initially studied pre-medicine in college, but a lack of interest in becoming a doctor led him to the Art Institute of Chicago in 1901. Unhappy with the school's unimaginative curriculum, he transferred to the New York School of Art in 1903, and it was in New York that he had his first success as a writer, selling copies of his poetry on the street.*

*In 1912 Harriet Monroe published "General William Booth Enters into Heaven" in* Poetry *magazine and Lindsay's career took off. By this time he had perfected the role of Wandering Bard, and his performances, much like those of contemporary slam poets, were lively and directed toward people who didn't normally read poetry. Dancing, chanting, and even playing "poem games" that required audience participation, Lindsay remained popular through the early 1920s. However, in the final years of his life his reputation began to wane and he was saddled with heavy debts. In 1931 he poisoned himself, declaring, "They tried to get me. I got them first."*

*Among Vachel Lindsay's major volumes of poetry are* General William Booth Enters into Heaven *(1913),* The Congo and Other Poems *(1928), and* Johnny Appleseed and Other Poems *(1928).* Collected Poems *(1925) includes a number of striking drawings by the poet. The two poems that follow give the reader an idea of Lindsay's patriotic and public bent. While his connection with Chicago was not a permanent one, much of the city's early-century spirit of burgeoning populism informs his best work.*

✦ ✦ ✦

# Abraham Lincoln Walks at Midnight

*(In Springfield, Illinois)*

It is portentous, and a thing of state
That here at midnight, in our little town
A mourning figure walks, and will not rest,
Near the old court-house pacing up and down,

Or by his homestead, or in shadowed yards
He lingers where his children used to play,
Or through the market, on the well-worn stones
He stalks until the dawn-stars burn away.

A bronzed, lank man! His suit of ancient black,
A famous high top-hat and plain worn shawl
Make him the quaint great figure that men love,
The prairie-lawyer, master of us all.

He cannot sleep upon his hillside now.
He is among us: — as in times before!
And we who toss and lie awake for long
Breathe deep, and start, to see him pass the door.

His head is bowed. He thinks on men and kings.
Yea, when the sick world cries, how can he sleep?
Too many peasants fight, they know not why,
Too many homesteads in black terror weep.

The sins of all the war-lords burn his heart.
He sees the dreadnaughts scouring every main.
He carries on his shawl-wrapped shoulders now
The bitterness, the folly and the pain.

He cannot rest until a spirit-dawn
Shall come; — the shining hope of Europe free:
The league of sober folk, the Workers' Earth,
Bringing long peace to Cornland, Alp and Sea.

It breaks his heart that kings must murder still,
That all his hours of travail here for men

Seem yet in vain. And who will bring white peace
That he may sleep upon his hill again?


## GENERAL WILLIAM BOOTH ENTERS INTO HEAVEN

*(To be sung to the tune of "The Blood of the Lamb" with indicated instrument)*

I

*(Bass drum beaten loudly.)*
Booth led boldly with his big bass drum —
(Are you washed in the blood of the Lamb?)
The Saints smiled gravely and they said: "He's come."
(Are you washed in the blood of the Lamb?)
Walking lepers followed, rank on rank,
Lurching bravos from the ditches dank,
Drabs from the alleyways and drug fiends pale —
Minds still passion-ridden, soul-powers frail: —
Vermin-eaten saints with moldy breath,
Unwashed legions with the ways of Death —
(Are you washed in the blood of the Lamb?)


*(Banjos.)*
Every slum had sent its half-a-score
The round world over. (Booth had groaned for more.)
Every banner that the wide world flies
Bloomed with glory and transcendent dyes.
Big-voiced lasses made their banjos bang,
Tranced, fanatical they shrieked and sang: —
"Are you washed in the blood of the Lamb?"
Hallelujah! It was queer to see
Bull-necked convicts with that land make free.
Loons with trumpets blowed a blare, blare, blare
On, on upward thro' the golden air!
(Are you washed in the blood of the Lamb?)

II

*(Bass drum slower and softer.)*
Booth died blind and still by faith he trod,
Eyes still dazzled by the ways of God.
Booth led boldly, and he looked the chief
Eagle countenance in sharp relief,

Beard a-flying, air of high command
Unabated in that holy land.

*(Sweet flute music.)*
Jesus came from out the court-house door,
Stretched his hands above the passing poor.
Booth saw not, but led his queer ones there
Round and round the mighty court-house square.
Then, in an instant all that blear review
Marched on spotless, clad in raiment new.
The lame were straightened, withered limbs uncurled
And blind eyes opened on a new, sweet world.

*(Bass drum louder.)*
Drabs and vixens in a flash made whole!
Gone was the weasel-head, the snout, the jowl!
Sages and sibyls now, and athletes clean,
Rulers of empires, and of forests green!

*(Grand chorus of all instruments.*
*Tambourines to the foreground.)*
The hosts were sandalled, and their wings were fire!
(Are you washed in the blood of the Lamb?)
But their noise played havoc with the angel-choir.
(Are you washed in the blood of the Lamb?)
Oh, shout Salvation! It was good to see
Kings and Princes by the Lamb set free.
The banjos rattled and the tambourines
Jing-jing-jingled in the hands of Queens.

*(Reverently sung, no instruments.)*
And when Booth halted by the curb for prayer
He saw his Master thro' the flag-filled air.
Christ came gently with a robe and crown
For Booth the soldier, while the throng knelt down.
He saw King Jesus. They were face to face,
And he knelt a-weeping in that holy place.
Are you washed in the blood of the Lamb?

# H. L. Mencken

## (1880-1956)

HENRY LOUIS MENCKEN *can in no way be considered a "Chicago writer," yet he is included in this anthology because one of his essays, "The Literary Capital of the United States," was instrumental in validating the work of Chicago writers to a national audience. (The essay appeared in April 1920 as part of an American supplement to the* London Nation *and was reprinted in book form in the United States later that year.)*

*Mencken was born in Baltimore in 1880, and he lived there for most of his long life. His early work as a newspaperman for the* Baltimore Herald *led to work for* The Smart Set *magazine, which he eventually co-edited with George Jean Nathan. In 1924 Mencken co-founded* The American Mercury, *which he edited until 1933. Impertinent, caustic, narrow-minded, brash, and brilliant, H. L. Mencken was probably the most hated and admired literary, social, and political critic of his day. His chief works include six series of* Prejudices *(collections of his articles) and* The American Language *and its two supplements (1919, 1945, 1948), a study of the development of American English. He died in 1956.*

*Mencken's praise of Chicago literature in the first twenty years of the twentieth century is obviously motivated as much by his disdain for the effete "Europeanized" work of Eastern writers as it is by genuine admiration. Indeed, Mencken later came to believe that the city had lost much of its vitality, and even in "The Literary Capital of the United States" he acknowledges that Chicago "is overgrown, it is oafish, it shows many of the characters of the upstart and the bounder." Nevertheless, in the work of Dreiser and Anderson, Sandburg and Masters, Mencken found "a genuine earnestness, a real interest in ideas, a sound curiosity about the prodigal and colorful life of the people of the republic." Coming from Mencken, there could have been no higher praise.*

◆ ◆ ◆

# The Literary Capital of the United States

However largely New York may bulk in the imagination of Europe or in the sight of those Americans who hang upon the front and rear edges of the materialistic conception of history, it ceased long ago to hold any leadership in that department of the national life of the republic which has to do with beautiful letters, or even to bear a part of any solid consequence therein. There is no longer a New York school of writers, as there was in Irving's day, and in Poe's, and even in Whitman's and Mark Twain's; there are, indeed, not more than two or three New York writers in practice to-day who are worthy of serious consideration at all. Scarcely a book of capital importance to the national literature has come out of the town for a generation. Nearly every work of genuine and arresting originality published in the United States during that time, nearly every work authentically representative of the life and thought of the American people, from George Ade's "Fables in Slang," to Edgar Lee Masters's "The Spoon River Anthology," and from Frank Norris's "McTeague" to Theodore Dreiser's "Sister Carrie," has been put together in the hinterland and by a writer innocent of metropolitan influence.

The phenomenon, so far as I know, is unique. It is impossible to imagine saying that of London, or of Paris, or of Berlin, or even of such somnolent and second-rate capitals as Christiania and Berne. But New York itself is unique. Alone among the great cities of the world it has no definite intellectual life, no body of special ideals and opinions, no aristocratic attitudes. Even the common marks of nationality are few and faint; one half wonders, observing its prodigious crowds and noting their lethargic reactions, if it is actually American at all. Huge, Philistine, self-centered, ignorant and vulgar, it is simply a sort of free port, a Hansa town, a place where raw materials of civilization are received, sorted, baled, and reshipped. In all the fine arts it is a mere wholesaler, and vastly less the connoisseur than the auctioneer. It has in Central Park the western world's largest storehouse of artistic fossils and mummies, real and fraudulent, good and bad — and yet it seldom, if ever, produces a picture worth looking at. Its peculiarly obnoxious social pushers, Christian and Jew, pour out millions for music every year — and yet even Philadelphia has a better orchestra. It prints four-fifths of the books of the nation, and nine-tenths of its magazines — and yet the salient men among its native authors are Robert W. Chambers, Owen Johnson, and James Montgomery Flagg.

Life buzzes and coruscates on Manhattan Island, but the play of ideals is not there. The New York spirit, for all the gaudy pretentiousness of the town, is a spirit of timidity, of regularity, of safe mediocrity. The typical New Yorker, whether artist or mere trader, feels the heavy hand of the capitalistic *bourgeoisie* upon him at all times. He is always looking over his shoulder furtively, in fear that he may have done something that is not approved, and so brought down upon himself some inexplicable penalty. Here are the great rewards, but here also are the inviolable taboos. The individual, facing that relentless regimentation, is afraid to be himself. Above all, he is afraid to be an American. The town is shoddily cosmopolitan, second-rate European, extraordinarily cringing, a sort of international Jenkins.

The artist arriving from the provinces is confronted at once by that alarmed orderliness, that fear of ideas. If he is still young and full of gas and able to take a chance, he commonly throws himself gallantly into Greenwich Village, the tawdry Latin Quarter of the town — only to find presently that Greenwich Village has been regimented too, that its revolts are artificial and empty, that commercial Jews behind the door pull its wires. But if, as is more likely, he comes in with a bit of sound work behind him, and is eager to get firm earth under him, then his descent follows more swiftly. A subtle something wars upon the elements that make him what he is. His ideas are delicately flattened out. He learns to do things as they should be done. New York swarms with such wrecks of talents — men who arrived with one or two promising books behind them, and are now highly respectable inmates of publishers' bordellos.

But the United States, for all that, occasionally produces a good book. Now and then it even penetrates to Europe — Dreiser's "Sister Carrie," the Masters' "Anthology," London's "The Call of the Wild." More often it is hauled up by the Atlantic — Willa Cather's "My Antonia," Sherwood Anderson's "Winesburg, Ohio," Carl Sandburg's "Chicago Poems," Cabell's "The Cream of the Jest." Where do they come from? Not from New York: it produces nothing, as we have seen. Not from Boston: it is as tragically dead as Alexandria or Padua. Not from Philadelphia: it is an intellectual slum. Not from San Francisco: its old life and color are gone, and the Methodists, Baptists and other such vermin of God now dominate it. Not from Washington, or St. Louis, or New Orleans, or Baltimore: they are simply flabby and degraded villages. Nay, from none of these, but from Chicago! — Chicago the unspeakable and incomparable, at once the most hospitably cosmopolitan and the most thoroughly American of American cities: —

> Hog Butcher for the World,
> Tool Maker, Stacker of Wheat,
> Player with Railroads, and the Nation's Freight Handler;
> . . . . . . . . . . . . . . . . . . . . . . . . .
>
> Laughing the stormy, husky, brawling laughter of Youth,
> half-naked, sweating, proud to be Hog Butcher, Tool
> Maker, Stacker of Wheat, Player with Railroads, and
> Freight Handler.

In Chicago there is the mysterious something that makes for individuality, personality, charm; in Chicago a spirit broods upon the face of the waters. Find a writer who is indubitably an American in every pulse-beat, an American who has something new and peculiarly American to say and who says it in an unmistakably American way, and nine times out of ten you will find that he has some sort of connection with the gargantuan abattoir by Lake Michigan — that he was bred there, or got his start there, or passed through there in the days when he was young and tender.

It is, indeed, amazing how steadily a Chicago influence shows itself when the literary ancestry and training of present-day American writers are investigated. The brand of the sugar-cured ham seems to be upon all of them. With two exceptions, there is not a single American novelist of the younger generation — that is, a serious novelist, a novelist deserving a civilized reader's notice — who has not sprung from the Middle Empire that has Chicago for its capital. I nominate the two exceptions at once: Abraham Cahan, Lithuanian Jew, always vastly more Russian than American, and James Branch Cabell, last survivor of the old aristocracy of the South. All the rest have come from the Chicago palatinate: Dreiser, Anderson, Miss Cather, Mrs. Watts, Tarkington, Wilson, Herrick, Patterson, even Churchill. It was Chicago that produced Henry B. Fuller, the pioneer of the modern American novel. It was Chicago that inspired and developed Frank Norris, its first practitioner of genius. And it was Chicago that produced Dreiser, undoubtedly the greatest artist of them all.

The astounding literary productivity of Indiana, the most salient phenomenon of latter-day American literature, is largely ascribable to the influence of the inland capital by the lake. The limits of the city run almost to the Indiana frontier: the youth of the state turns to it instinctively; it as plainly dominates the energy and aspiration of all that fertile region as Boston dominates the six states of New England. From Ade to Dreiser nearly all the bright young Indianians have gone to Chicago for a semester or two, and not only the Indianians, but also the youngsters of all the other Middle Western States. It has drawn them in from their remote wheat-towns and far-flung railway junctions, and it has given them an impulse that New York simply cannot match — an impulse toward independence, toward honesty, toward a peculiar vividness and *naïveté* — in brief, toward the unaffected self-expression that is at the bottom of sound art. New York, when it lures such a recruit eastward, makes a pliant conformist of him, and so ruins him out of hand. But Chicago, however short the time it has him, leaves him irrevocably his own man, with a pride sufficient to carry through a decisive trial of his talents.

What lies at the bottom of all this, I dare say, is the elemental curiosity of a simple and somewhat ignorant people — the *naïve* delight of hog butchers, freight handlers, the stackers of wheat, in the grand clash and clatter of ideas.

New York affects a superior sophistication, and in part it is genuine; Boston is already senile; Philadelphia is too stupid to be interested. But in Chicago there is an eagerness to hear and see, to experience and experiment. The town is colossally rich; it is ever-changing; it yearns for distinction. The new-comers who pour in from the wheatlands want more than mere money; they want free play for their prairie energy; they seek more imaginative equivalent for the stupendous activity that they were bred to. It is thus a superb market for merchants of the new. And in particular it is a superb market for the merchant whose wares, though new, have a familiar air — which is to say, on the aesthetic plane — for the sort of art that is recognizably national in its themes and its idioms, and combines a Yankee sharpness of observation with a homely simplicity — the sort of art that one finds in a novel by Dreiser or a poem by Sandburg — the only sort that stands free of imitation and is absolutely American.

For such originality Chicago has a perennial welcome, and where the welcome is, there the guests are to be found. Go back twenty or thirty years, and you will scarcely find an American literary movement that did not originate under the shadow of the stockyards. In the eighteen-nineties New York turned its eyes toward England, but Chicago had *Savoys* of its own, and at least one publishing house that grandly proclaimed the doom of the old order, and trotted out its Fullers and Mary MacLanes, and imported Ibsen and Maeterlinck, then as strange as Heliogabalus. The new poetry movement is thoroughly Chicagoan; the majority of its chief poets are from the Middle West; *Poetry*, the organ of the movement, is published in Chicago. So with the little theater movement. Long before it was heard of in New York, it was firmly on its legs in Chicago. And to support these various reforms and revolts, some of them already of great influence, others abortive and quickly forgotten, there is in Chicago a body of critical opinion that is unsurpassed for discretion and intelligence in America. The New York newspapers, in the main, employ third-rate journalistic hacks as dramatic critics, and their book reviews are ignorant and ridiculous. But in Chicago there is an abundance of sound work in both fields, and even the least of the newspapers makes a palpable effort to be honest and well-informed. . . .

So much for the Chicagoiad. Lying out there where the prairie runs down to the Great Lakes lies the real capital of the United States. It is overgrown, it is oafish, it shows many of the characters of the upstart and the bounder, but under its surface there is a genuine earnestness, a real interest in ideas, a sound curiosity about the prodigal and colorful life of the people of the republic. The literature of the country, at the moment, is in a state bordering upon paralysis. The war greatly augmented its chronic imitativeness; worse, it greatly strengthened the Puritan machinery for putting down intellectual experiment and enterprise; the statute books are heavy to-day with ferociously repressive laws, and many of them bear harshly on the man of letters. But men of high hope look for a reaction toward freedom in ideas, and, what is more, toward a sane and self-respecting nationalism. If it ever comes, it will not come from New York: New York is too timorous. It will come, I think, from Chicago.

# Ring Lardner

## (1885-1933)

*Born in Niles, Michigan,* RING LARDNER *began his long, on-again, off-again association with Chicago as a journalist in 1907. Though he wrote the general column* "In the Wake of the News" *for the* Chicago Tribune *from 1913 to 1919, his beat was mainly sports, especially baseball, and he traveled with both the Cubs and Sox. These experiences led to the publication of his first big book,* You Know Me Al: A Busher's Letters *(1916), a series of sketches and stories first published in the* Saturday Evening Post. *From that time on he became known primarily as a writer of short stories—preeminently "Haircut" (collected in the 1926* The Love Nest and Other Stories*)—and humorous essays and sketches. The preface to his 1924* How to Write Short Stories *is reprinted here. He also dabbled in writing absurdist plays, like* Clemo Uti—"The Water Lilies", *which defined a kind of American Dada far ahead of its time. The absurdity arose from a rather dark, fatalistic streak in Lardner that often showed itself in such works as "The New Immigrants," an absurdist tale about a family falling apart as it moves from the Midwest to the East to seek the good life.*

*Often accused of not fully developing his serious talents, Lardner nonetheless created many seemingly affable, goofy characters who reflected a deep bitterness against human foibles that was at odds with their naive, even cornpone surfaces. In* The Ring Lardner Reader, *editor Max Geismar focuses on the last line of the play* Clemo Uti — "They want the show over again, but it looks useless" — and comments: "And this was the surrealistic description of Lardner's own deepest feeling about maturity and society alike — about life. There was no point in playing the show over again; it was useless."*

✦ ✦ ✦

### *from* HOW TO WRITE SHORT STORIES

A glimpse at the advertising columns of our leading magazines shows that whatever else this country may be shy of, there is certainly no lack of correspondence schools that learns you the art of short-story writing. The most notorious of these schools makes the boast that one of their pupils cleaned up $5000.00 and no hundreds dollars writing short stories according to the system learnt in their course, though it don't say if that amount was cleaned up in one year or fifty.

However, for some reason another when you skin through the pages of high class periodicals, you don't very often find them cluttered up with stories that was written by boys or gals who had win their phy beta skeleton keys at this or that story-writing college. In fact, the most of the successful authors of the short fiction of to-day never went to no kind of a college, or if they did, they studied piano tuning or the barber trade. They could of got just as far in what I call the literary game if they had of stayed home those four years and helped mother carry out the empty bottles.

The answer is that you can't find no school in operation up to date, whether it be a general institution of learning or a school that specializes in story writing, which can make a great author out of a born druggist.

But a little group of our deeper drinkers has suggested that maybe boys and gals who wants to take up writing as their life work would be benefited if some person like I was to give them a few hints in regards to the technic of the short story, how to go about planning it and writing it, when and where to plant the love interest and climax, and finally how to market the finished product without leaving no bad taste in the mouth.

Well, then, it seems to me like the best method to use in giving out these hints is to try and describe my own personal procedure from the time I get inspired till the time the manuscript is loaded on the trucks.

The first thing I generally always do is try and get hold of a catchy title, like for instance, "Basil Hargrave's Vermifuge," or "Fun at the Incinerating Plant." Then I set down to a desk or flat table of any kind and lay out 3 or 4 sheets of paper with as many different colored pencils and look at them cockeyed a few moments before making a selection.

How to begin — or, as we professionals would say, "how to commence" — is the next question. It must be admitted that the method of approach ("L'approchement") differs even among first class fictionists. For example, Blasco Ibañez usually starts his stories with a Spanish word, Jack Dempsey with an "I" and Charley Peterson with a couple of simple declarative sentences about his leading character, such as "Hazel Gooftree had just gone mah jong. She felt faint."

Personally it has been my observation that the reading public prefers short dialogue to any other kind of writing and I always aim to open my tale with two or three lines of conversation between characters — or, as I call them, my puppets — who are to play important rôles. I have often found that something one of these characters says, words I have perhaps unconsciously put into his or her mouth, directs my plot into channels deeper than I had planned and changes, for the better, the entire sense of my story.

To illustrate this, let us pretend that I have laid out a plot as follows: Two girls, Dorothy Abbott and Edith Quaver, are spending the heated term at a famous resort. The Prince of Wales visits the resort, but leaves on the next train. A day or two later, a Mexican reaches the place and looks for accommodations, but is unable to find a room without a bath. The two girls meet him at the public filling station and ask him for a contribution to their autograph album. To their amazement, he utters a terrible oath, spits in their general direction and hurries out of town. It is not until years later that the two girls learn he is a notorious forger and realize how lucky they were after all.

Let us pretend that the above is the original plot. Then let us begin the writing with haphazard dialogue and see whither it leads:

"Where was you?" asked Edith Quaver.

"To the taxidermist's," replied Dorothy Abbott.

The two girls were spending the heated term at a famous watering trough. They had just been bathing and were now engaged in sorting dental floss.

"I am getting sick in tired of this place," went on Miss Quaver.

"It is mutual," said Miss Abbott, shying a cucumber at a passing paper-hanger.

There was a rap at their door and the maid's voice announced that company was awaiting them downstairs. The two girls went down and entered the music room. Garnett Whaledriver was at the piano and the girls tiptoed to the lounge.

The big Nordic, oblivious to their presence, allowed his fingers to form weird, fantastic minors before they strayed unconsciously into the first tones of Chopin's 121st Fugue for the Bass Drum.

From this beginning, a skilled writer could go most anywheres, but it would be my tendency to drop these three characters and take up the life of a mule in the Grand Canyon. The mule watches the trains come in from the east, he watches the trains come in from the west, and keeps wondering who is going to ride him. But she never finds out.

The love interest and climax would come when a man and a lady, both strangers, got to talking together on the train going back east.

"Well," said Mrs. Croot, for it was she, "what did you think of the Canyon?"

"Some cave," replied her escort.

"What a funny way to put it!" replied Mrs. Croot. "And now play me something."

Without a word, Warren took his place on the piano bench and at first allowed his fingers to form weird, fantastic chords on the black keys. Suddenly and with no seeming intention, he was in the midst of the second movement of Chopin's Twelfth Sonata for Flute and Cuspidor. Mrs. Croot felt faint.

That will give young writers an idea of how an apparently trivial thing such as a line of dialogue will upset an entire plot and lead an author far from the path he had pointed for himself. It will also serve as a model for beginners to follow in regards to style and technic. I will not insult my readers by going on with the story to its obvious conclusion. That simple task they can do for themselves, and it will be good practice.

So much for the planning and writing. Now for the marketing of the completed work. A good many young writers make the mistake of enclosing a stamped, self-addressed envelope, big enough for the manuscript to come back in. This is too much of a temptation to the editor.

Personally I have found it a good scheme to not even sign my name to the story, and when I have got it sealed up in its envelope and stamped and addressed, I take it to some town where I don't live and mail it from there. The editor has no idea who wrote the story, so how can he send it back? He is in a quandry.

In conclusion let me warn my pupils never to write their stories — or, as we professionals call them, "yarns" — on used paper. And never to write them on a post-card. And never to send them by telegraph (Morse code).

Stories ("yarns") of mine which have appeared in various publications — one of them having been accepted and published by the first editor that got it — are reprinted in the following pages and will illustrate in a half-hearted way what I am trying to get at.

RING LARDNER

"The Mange"
Great Neck, Long Island, 1924

# Vincent Starrett

## (1886-1974)

*One of the leading figures of the Chicago Literary Renaissance,* CHARLES VINCENT EMERSON STARRETT *was born in Toronto in 1886. After attending public schools in Toronto and Chicago, he began freelancing and working as a journalist for papers like the* Chicago Inter-Ocean, Chicago Daily News, *and the* Chicago Tribune. *Starrett wrote a number of volumes of poetry, including* Ebony Flame *(1922),* Flame and Dust *(1924), and* Autolycus in Limbo *(1943), and he was the author of more than a dozen nonfiction books such as* Ambrose Bierce *(1920),* The Private Life of Sherlock Holmes *(1933), and* Bookman's Holiday: The Private Satisfactions of an Incurable Collector *(1942).*

*Starrett was best known, however, as a writer of mysteries. His most famous sleuth was Jimmie Lavender, who appeared in a series of novels. One of the great twentieth-century experts on Arthur Conan Doyle's celebrated sleuth, Starrett created the sort of world in which Sherlock Holmes would have felt comfortable — a place where arcane knowledge of physical evidence and keen common sense combine to solve incredibly complex crimes. Starrett's mystery novels include* Murder on "B" Deck *(1929),* The Great Hotel Murder *(1935), and* The Laughing Buddha *(1937); his stories are collected in* Coffins for Two *(1924),* The Case Book of Jimmie Lavender *(1944),* The Quick and the Dead *(1965), and others. He received the first Edgar Award from the Mystery Writers of America and was presented with that organization's Grand Master Award in 1957.*

*The following selection from* Born in a Bookshop: Chapters from the Chicago Renascence *(1965) is, as its author claims, "an interesting essay . . . on why young men enter the newspaper business." Starrett takes us behind the scenes of the "fascinating maelstrom of vice and virture" as it appeared to a naive young reporter not long after the turn of the century. Both historians and lovers of good writing will appreciate this acute, sometimes graphic, portrait of Starrett's adopted hometown.*

*Vincent Starrett died in 1974 and was buried in Chicago's Graceland Cemetery.*

✦ ✦ ✦

An interesting essay might be written on why young men enter the newspaper business. I have known reporters who, before they became reporters, were post-office clerks, bank tellers, bond salesmen, pugilists, clergymen. For years I worked with one who had been an undertaker's assistant, and with another who had been a tramp. Nowadays many young fellows go directly from their journalism classes into their chosen profession; but I don't remember meeting many such graduates in my time. I think they were suspect. Chicago was a tough city in those days, as it is today, and tough newspapermen were required to cope with the city's reputation. In my own case, I became a journalist after I had failed at nearly everything else.

The story begins on a morning in 1906, a few months before my twentieth birthday. I had set out to find a job in the Chicago newspaper world. But the city editor of the *Daily News* could not use a young man without experience, and harrassed young men at the *Tribune* and the *Record-Herald* said much the same thing in much the same words. There was no job for me at the *Journal* or the *Evening Post*. Even the unimportant *Dispatch* could find no merit in me. At length there was only one newspaper left, the *Inter-Ocean*. Shortly I was seated with the city editor, a handsome young man with steel gray hair; his name was Harry Daniel. The business of the day had not begun for Mr. Daniel; he was kind enough to talk with me for some time. His remarks ran somewhat as follows:

"So you'd like to be a newspaper reporter, would you, Starrett? Let me tell you how you've gone about it. You went to the *Tribune* or the *Daily News* first, and they told you they couldn't use you because you had no experience. After that you went to every other newspaper in Chicago except the *Inter-Ocean*, and they all sang you the same song. You came here last because you thought this was the least important newspaper in Chicago. You'd rather work for one of the other papers, but you're willing to start here if you have to." He was grinning cheerfully throughout this recital; I was not offended. "And now," continued Mr. Daniel, "you're a bit discouraged. You wonder how the hell you're ever going to get experience unless somebody gives you a chance. Isn't that about it?"

I nodded uncomfortably.

"Well," he said in friendly fashion, "we've all been through it, Starrett. That's the way we all begin, and I'll tell you what I'll do. I like your looks and I think you may make a newspaperman. I'll give you a chance. I need a couple of young reporters just now and maybe you'll be one of them. I can't pay you very much. My budget doesn't allow it. How would you like to work for me for two weeks for your expenses, until you see how you like it, and I see how good you are? We'll pay you whatever it costs you out of your own pocket, carfare and telephone calls and that sort of thing. At the end of two weeks, if you've made good, I'll give you twelve dollars a week to start. Then if we decide to let you out, you can go back to the other papers and, when they ask you their trick question about previous experience, you can say you were on the *Inter-Ocean.* How about it?"

Even then I knew it was a decent offer from a decent fellow, and I lost no time in closing with it. I have never regretted the step I took that afternoon and I am still grateful to Harry Daniel, a good newspaperman and an even better human being.

I reported at one o'clock the following afternoon and was put to work at once. The trivial nature of my first assignments surprised me; I had hoped to be asked to understudy the drama critic, at least. Actually, I became a "picture chaser," although occasionally I was permitted to type a few paragraphs to accompany the photographs I had solicited. The other reporters, experienced men, had all started the same way, they said. They were friendly when they had time to be, and some of them were helpful — when they had time to be.

My first assignments, although unimportant, were educational and illuminating. When a citizen was murdered, when a young woman committed suicide, when somebody was injured in an unusual accident, when a high-school girl won a beauty contest, when an old couple celebrated fifty years of wedlock, the cry was for photographs to illustrate these notable events in human history, and I was one of several youngsters whose principal duty it was to visit the homes of such celebrities and ask for pictures. If these could not be obtained by solicitation, it was our duty to obtain them by cunning; that is to say, by whatever stealthy means occurred to us. At the end of a fortnight I became a member of the regular staff, at twelve dollars a week, and I remained with the paper for the next eleven months. By that time I had acquired enough experience to dazzle any editor in the world, for the *Inter-Ocean* was a wonderful proving ground.

Our night city editor was the fabulous Walter Howey who, as the newspaper world knows, went onward and upward in the profession until he became one of the greatest of Hearst's editors. It is common knowledge, too, that he figured largely and profanely, under another name, in Ben Hecht's and Charles MacArthur's newspaper drama, *The Front Page.* When I knew him first he was a slender young man of almost angelic appearance, with blond curls and an ironic blue eye — only one; the other was blind. But he had a chain-lightning mind, I realized quickly, and was not the night editor of a Chicago morning newspaper because of his good looks. It was, I know now, a privilege to begin a career under Walter Howey. It was, in fact, a whole newspaper education. It was he who taught me to write acceptably. At first my style was florid and my stories were over-written. I used to open the morning paper eagerly, hoping to find one of my pyrotechnic accounts of an unimportant fire featured prominently on the front page; but too often I found it hidden away on a back page, so mutilated by the copy desk that it hurt. And it was hard for me to understand the necessity for crowding all the vital facts of a story into the first paragraph. In my philosophy of writing, the facts were relatively unimportant; I liked to lead up to them in leisurely fashion, keeping the reader in suspense about what had happened. Howey was more patient with me than the copy desk. I suspect he had once written that way himself. His approach was kindly and cunning; it was at once benevolent and satirical. "Why, this is wonderful, Starrett!" he would say. "In a novel it would be simply grand. I particularly like your verbs. Your people always 'declare,' or 'vouchsafe,' or 'explode,' or something like that. However, I have a suggestion to make. The strongest verb in any dialogue is the little word *said*. Say 'he said' and 'she said.' That way the half-witted reader isn't so lost in admiration of your prose that he misses the point of your story." And then he would grin like a friendly crocodile and pat my shoulder and tell me I was coming on fine.

Among my colleagues in those memorable first months were Ring Lardner and his brother Rex; Newton Fuessle, later a successful novelist; Oliver Marble Gale, later an unsuccessful novelist; William L. Bliss, a remarkable crime reporter; Oswald Schuette, later a well-known Washington correspondent; and a dozen other sterling characters who attained at least local fame in their profession. Our drama critic was Burns Mantle, who went on to greater celebrity in New York. Our leading cartoonist was long, lean, quizzical, friendly H. T. Webster, whose humorous creations, including "Caspar Milquetoast," in time attained nation-wide popularity.

Lardner and his brother were cubs like myself; we drew the humbler assignments. I can remember only one story that Ring and I covered together, and it was unimportant; but he was a delightful companion. Except that he was younger then, he looked very much as he did years afterward when his photograph appeared frequently in the magazines; he was excessively tall, gangling, and owl-eyed, with a high bald forehead that made him look rather like a schoolmaster or a magician. I think he laughed more often in his *Inter-Ocean* days than later, when even his most humorous conversation was deadpan. But although I knew him well enough, we did not become intimates. A closer companion was Tristram Tupper, a romantic Virginian, a sort of Galahad of the news lanes, whose ambitions were as impossibly literary as my own. I lost touch with him when I left the *Inter-Ocean*, but years afterward I learned that he had published half a dozen romantic novels, all popular in their time. Then one day I saw a dispatch from Europe — it was during World War II — and found in it a line about the meritorious conduct of a Brigadier General Tristram Tupper, who could only be my old friend and companion, Tris Tupper, or so I supposed. I have had no further word of him. Possibly he is a major-general now, and I can think of nobody more admirably suited to the life of a major-general.

It was an interesting newspaper office in which I received my first training, and as I pass the old building today — it is now a motion picture theater, but the old name is still cut in stone over the arch — I like to stop and let the years roll back to the lively days when it housed as exhilarating a collection of characters as any novelist has dared to invent.

It was an interesting city, too, in which I received my first newspaper training. Judge Dunne, a Democrat, was mayor and was trying to be a good one. He had been a reform candidate, and clean-ups of every kind were impending or in progress. The newspapers called them "crusades," and took a lively part in them. Nevertheless, there was plenty of crime that went uncorrected and unpunished. One read of gambling syndicates, liquor syndicates, and vice lords, much as one reads of them today. Presumably, the lawbreakers were in league with the "higher-ups" — possibly with the city hall and the police. There were plenty of scandals. Undoubtedly, vice and gambling existed on a then almost unparalleled scale and were commercially profitable to all concerned. On the other side were a dozen picturesque reformers, including the women's clubs, important social workers like Jane Addams, and a number of well-known clergymen. Gangs as we came to know them had yet, I think, to arrive; but there were adumbrations of that development. It has been said that they began with the newspaper wars for place and circulation that followed the coming of Hearst in the first years of the century, and possibly there is some truth in the charge. Chicago was then called a "frontier town," an apt enough description; but as I think of its other aspects — cultural, educational and religious — it was a medieval city in which the good and the bad dwelt side by side, cheek by jowl, as in old Rome and Florence.

Into this fascinating maelstrom of vice and virtue, euphemistically called the "melting pot," I plunged with youthful rapture, happy to be on the side of the angels, but almost equally happy to have a front seat for the other side of the show. My greatest pride was my police and fire badge — then issued to all members of the working press — by displaying which I was able to barge my way through fire lines and police cordons and make a nuisance of myself. The feeling of importance it gave me was like nothing I had ever experienced before. Even when it was not actively in use, I wore it under my coat lapel, with one metal point showing. The home boys of our neighborhood were green with envy. It never impressed Mother, but for two cents Dad would have borrowed it every time he heard the fire engines pass the house. He said he had once owned a sheriff's star, himself, but had lost it in a fight with six thugs who sprang at him from the mouth of an alley.

My first police assignment was a murder case somewhere on the West Side, where a homicidal butcher had used his cleaver to hack off his wife's head. Happily, he was in custody. Another reporter was handling the story; my only task was to obtain photographs of the butcher, his wife, and members of the family circle. The shop occupied the ground floor of a three-story building and the butcher lived on the top level. I rang the downstairs front doorbell for some time, then climbed the long stairway, and thumped on the upstairs door. Apparently, there was nobody in the house, but I strolled around to the back anyway. Again I climbed three flights of stairs and thumped on the back door, and still there was no response. Then I noted that a rear window was open a few inches at the bottom. Obviously it gave on to a back bedroom; but the blind was down—I could not see within. My duty seemed plain enough, but one's first burglary is always a nervous occasion. Cautiously I eased up the window until it was possible to crawl through, pushed the blind aside without releasing it, blundered on all fours into a bed that lay beneath the window, and stepped gingerly to the floor. Then I turned and leaned across the bed to release the blind. Sunlight flooded the room and revealed the bed more clearly. I saw that it had an occupant. *She* was there—the murdered woman herself—clad only in her gore. The severed head and body had been reunited, but there was an appreciable gap between, and the whole spectacle was appalling. . . . Without further ado, I climbed back through my window and fled the neighborhood. I have seen many mutilated bodies since, but never with the same sense of shock.

Not long afterward I entered a cottage in Irving Park one night and experienced another kind of fright. An entire family had been poisoned, nobody knew how, and it was thought one of the dear people themselves might have been responsible. It was the classic situation, indeed: one of the sons was less dangerously ill than the others and was therefore suspect. Several members of the family were dead; the rest were in hospitals. I am not sure that a solution ever was found, but in any case it was not my business to seek a solution. My job, as usual, was to obtain photographs. I entered this time through a front window and found myself in the usual clutter of living room furniture, through which I picked my way with a flashlight. The mantelpiece was alive with photographs and, as I had no idea which was which, I seized them all. A dresser in the front bedroom held another gallery of photographs which I added to the collection. It was at this point, as I stood spraying my small light about the chamber, that I heard alarming sounds from the rear of the cottage. A door closed softly somewhere and light footsteps approached the front of the house. I shut off my light and tiptoed to the bedroom door, intending to make a quick getaway: but now the footsteps were in the dining room, only a few feet away. It was impossible to reach my front window without being caught. Then the footsteps stopped and someone stood in the doorway leading to the living room, breathing lightly. I realized that the intruder had become aware of *me*. Blackness lay all around us; I half expected a shot out of the dark. The silence was suddenly intolerable. Then, two minds functioned brilliantly at the same instant. Two flashlights split the darkness simultaneously; and there we were, almost face to face — the intruder and I. *"My God!"* he said.

He was Billy Black, the crack crime reporter from my own newspaper, seeking clues for a solution.

Not all my adventures were of this sort, however, and after a time I was permitted to write my own stories instead of telephoning them in for a rewrite man to mutilate. One of the most amusing of these assignments took me to the scene of an elopement. A boy and girl of tender years, well under the legal age for marriage, were the principals. The *Inter-Ocean* heard of the project from one of the bride's friends, who thought it would be nice to have a reporter at the wedding. Howey, too, thought it was a good idea. "Help them to elope, Starrett," he ordered, his single eye twinkling roguishly. "Go with them every step of the way until they go to bed. You needn't go to bed with them, but stay as long as possible. I want the best feature story we ever printed. Hop to it, kid!"

I managed to get them married before press time, and years afterward I used the innocent episode as the basis for a hilarious short story called "Advice to the Lovelorn." In my fiction the bride's father pursued us all over town; in cabs, on streetcars, on merry-go-rounds, in everything but airplanes — and was ultimately slugged by the bridegroom — but the actuality was unaccompanied by pursuit or violence.

One memorable assignment, after I had won my spurs, took me on a tour of the notorious "Red Light District," then centered in and around Twenty-second Street. A conference of state's attorneys from all parts of Illinois was being held in Chicago. After the inevitable banquet Captain McCann, who was in charge of the police district in which the levee was located, took the down-state lawyers through the vice area. It was intended to be a sort of educational tour, I think, and certainly it was educational to me. I had never been inside a house of prostitution before, and to find myself in a dozen of them in the course of a single evening was astonishing and a little terrifying. Reporters from all the newspapers accompanied the party. We visited all the more famous or infamous houses, including the Everleigh Club, which was the most famous and infamous of them all. As all had been warned of our coming, they were on their best behavior.

We reached the Everleigh Club fairly late. Although I had heard much about the splendors of this notorious house of entertainment, it eclipsed all descriptions. It was flagrantly luxurious. The actual business of the place went on upstairs. Most of the first floor seemed to be one vast living room and was, in fact, two living rooms, for the club occupied two adjoining houses that had been knocked into one. Expensive rugs and draperies were everywhere, creating the impression of an extravagant stage setting. There were some good oil paintings on the walls, not all of them nudes. As for the company, it would have been possible to imagine one's self as attending a distinguished social event. The girls looked much like other girls, except that they were prettier and more vivacious; and I suppose they were more sophisticated. They were scantily but attractively gowned and I saw little open vulgarity. We sat around the huge room in little nooks and alcoves, each with a Sadie Thompson for company, and drank the excellent liquor served by the house. On the whole, the entertainment was only a little more startling than might have been witnessed at a musical comedy.

We may have lost a state's attorney or two at the Everleigh Club — I wouldn't be surprised — but, for myself, I found the young woman who sat with me quiet, ladylike, and garrulous on many subjects, all of them in good taste. She was an actress, she told me, stopping at the club until she got another part, which may for all I know have been true. And of course I met the famous Everleigh sisters, Ada and Minna. They greeted us at the front door; but, except that they were tall and gracious, I have forgotten them. All in all, it was a fascinating experience for Mother's eldest son; but a little unnerving, too. Somehow I have never been able to sentimentalize or romanticize prostitutes. On a number of other occasions connected with my work, I visited houses of ill fame, as we called them in print. To tell the truth, though, I was always a little leery of the peccable ladies.

# Edna Ferber

## (1887-1968)

*Born in Kalamazoo, Michigan, in 1887,* EDNA FERBER *became a reporter in Wisconsin by the age of seventeen. She moved to Chicago in 1910 and remained in the city until the mid-1920s before settling in New York, where she made her home until she died in 1968.*

*Although she was never considered a major American writer, Ferber enjoyed a good deal of success during her lifetime. She won a Pulitzer Prize for* So Big *(1924), which is set in Chicago.* Show Boat *(1926) was made into a play that was still popular when it returned to Chicago for an extended run in the mid-1990s, and* Giant *(1952) was made into a movie starring Rock Hudson, James Dean, and Elizabeth Taylor.*

*Ferber began writing fiction after suffering a nervous breakdown, yet her work is marked by a tongue-in-cheek sense of humor and a generally optimistic tone.* Buttered Side Down *(1912), from which "The Frog and the Puddle" is taken, is typical of much of her early work. The two characters—romantic Gus and level-headed Gertie—engage in after-midnight repartee, and the piece comes to a neat, uncomplicated resolution. Nevertheless, Ferber's touch is deft and professional, and it is interesting to see a Chicago story in which the country girl heroine, rather than struggling on against enormous odds, admits the big city has defeated her and cheerfully heads for home.*

✦ ✦ ✦

## *The Frog and the Puddle*

*from* BUTTERED SIDE DOWN

Any one who has ever written for the magazines (nobody could devise a more sweeping opening; it includes the iceman who does a humorous article on the subject of his troubles, and the neglected wife next door, who journalizes) knows that a story the scene of which is not New York is merely junk. Take

Fifth Avenue as a framework, pad it out to five thousand words, and there you have the ideal short story.

Consequently I feel a certain timidity in confessing that I do not know Fifth Avenue from Hester Street when I see it, because I've never seen it. It has been said that from the latter to the former is a ten-year journey, from which I have gathered that they lie some miles apart. As for Forty-second Street, of which musical comedians carol, I know not if it be a fashionable shopping thoroughfare or a factory district.

A confession of this kind is not only good for the soul, but for the editor. It saves him the trouble of turning to page two.

This is a story of Chicago, which is a first cousin of New York, although the two are not on chummy terms. It is a story of that part of Chicago which lies east of Dearborn Avenue and south of Division Street, and which may be called the Nottingham curtain district.

In the Nottingham curtain district every front parlor window is embellished with a "Room With or Without Board" sign. The curtains themselves have mellowed from their original department-store-basement-white to a rich, deep tone of Chicago smoke, which has the notorious London variety beaten by several shades. Block after block the two-story-and-basement houses stretch, all grimy and gritty and looking sadly down upon the five square feet of mangy grass forming the pitiful front yard of each. Now and then the monotonous line of front stoops is broken by an outjutting basement delicatessen shop. But not often. The Nottingham curtain district does not run heavily to delicacies. It is stronger on creamed cabbage and bread pudding.

Up in the third floor back at Mis' Buck's (elegant rooms $2.50 and up a week. Gents preferred) Gertie was brushing her hair for the night. One hundred strokes with a bristle brush. Anyone who reads the beauty column in the newspapers knows that. There was something heroic in the sight of Gertie brushing her hair one hundred strokes before going to bed at night. Only a woman could understand her doing it.

Gertie clerked downtown on State Street, in a gents' glove department. A gents' glove department requires careful dressing on the part of its clerks, and the manager, in selecting them, is particular about choosing "lookers," with especial attention to figure, hair, and finger nails. Gertie was a looker. Providence had taken care of that. But you cannot leave your hair and finger nails to Providence. They demand coaxing with a bristle brush and an orange-wood stick.

Now clerking, as Gertie would tell you, is fierce on the feet. And when your feet are tired you are tired all over. Gertie's feet were tired every night. About eight-thirty she longed to peel off her clothes, drop them in a heap on the floor, and tumble, unbrushed, unwashed, unmanicured, into bed. She never did it.

Things had been particularly trying to-night. After washing out three handkerchiefs and pasting them with practised hand over the mirror, Gertie had taken off her shoes and discovered a hole the size of a silver quarter in the heel of her left stocking. Gertie had a country-bred horror of holey stockings. She darned the hole, yawning, her aching feet pressed against the smooth, cool leg of the iron bed. That done, she had had the colossal courage to wash her face, slap cold cream on it, and push back the cuticle around her nails.

Seated huddled on the side of her thin little iron bed, Gertie was brushing her hair bravely, counting the strokes somewhere in her sub-conscious mind and thinking busily all the while of something else. Her brush rose, fell, swept downward, rose, fell, rhythmically.

"Ninety-six, ninety-seven, ninety-eight, ninety — Oh, darn it! What's the use!" cried Gertie, and hurled the brush across the room with a crack.

She sat looking after it with wide, staring eyes until the brush blurred in with the faded red roses on the carpet. When she found it doing that she got up, wadded her hair viciously into a hard bun in the back instead of braiding it carefully as usual, crossed the room (it wasn't much of a trip), picked up the brush, and stood looking down at it, her under lip caught between her teeth. That is the humiliating part of losing your temper and throwing things. You have to come down to picking them up, anyway.

Her lip still held prisoner, Gertie tossed the brush on the bureau, fastened her nightgown at the throat with a safety pin, turned out the gas and crawled into bed.

Perhaps the hard bun at the back of her head kept her awake. She lay there with her eyes wide open and sleepless, staring into the darkness.

At midnight the Kid Next Door came in whistling, like one unused to boarding-house rules. Gertie liked him for that. At the head of the stairs he stopped whistling and came softly into his own third floor back just next to Gertie's. Gertie liked him for that, too.

The two rooms had been one in the fashionable days of the Nottingham curtain district, long before the advent of Mis' Buck. That thrifty lady, on coming into possession, had caused a flimsy partition to be run up, slicing the room in twain and doubling its rental.

Lying there Gertie could hear the Kid Next Door moving about getting ready for bed and humming "Every Little Movement Has a Meaning of Its Own" very lightly, under his breath. He polished his shoes briskly, and Gertie smiled there in the darkness of her room in sympathy. Poor kid, he had his beauty struggles, too.

Gertie had never seen the Kid Next Door, although he had come four months ago. But she knew he wasn't a grouch, because he alternately whistled and sang off-key tenor while dressing in the morning. She had also discovered that his bed must run along the same wall against which her bed was pushed. Gertie told herself that there was something almost immodest about being able to hear him breathing as he slept. He had tumbled into bed with a little grunt of weariness.

Gertie lay there another hour, staring into the darkness. Then she began to cry softly, lying on her face with her head between her arms. The cold cream and the salt tears mingled and formed a slippery paste. Gertie wept on because she couldn't help it. The longer she wept the more difficult her sobs became, until finally they bordered on hysterical. They filled her lungs until they ached and reached her throat with a force that jerked her head back.

"Rap-rap-rap!" sounded sharply from the head of her bed.

Gertie stopped sobbing, and her heart stopped beating. She lay tense and still, listening. Everyone knows that spooks rap three times at the head of one's bed. It's a regular high-sign with them.

"Rap-rap-rap!"

Gertie's skin became goose-flesh, and coldwater effects chased up and down her spine.

"What's your trouble in there?" demanded an unspooky voice so near that Gertie jumped. "Sick?"

It was the Kid Next Door.

"N-no, I'm not sick," faltered Gertie, her mouth close to the wall. Just then a belated sob that had stopped halfway when the raps began hustled on to join its sisters. It took Gertie by surprise, and brought prompt response from the other side of the wall.

"I'll bet I scared you green. I didn't mean to, but, on the square, if you're feeling sick, a little nip of brandy will set you up. Excuse my mentioning it, girlie, but I'd do the same for my sister. I hate like sin to hear a woman suffer like that, and, anyway, I don't know whether you're fourteen or forty, so it's perfectly respectable. I'll get the bottle and leave it outside your door."

"No you don't!" answered Gertie in a hollow voice, praying meanwhile that the woman in the room below might be sleeping. "I'm not sick, honestly I'm not. I'm just as much obliged, and I'm dead sorry I woke you up with my blubbering. I started out with the soft pedal on, but things got away from me. Can you hear me?"

"Like a phonograph. Sure you couldn't use a sip of brandy where it'd do the most good?"

"Sure."

"Well, then, cut the weeps and get your beauty sleep, kid. He ain't worth sobbing over, anyway, believe me."

"He!" snorted Gertie indignantly. "You're cold. There never was anything in peg-tops that could make me carry on like the heroine of the Elsie series."

"Lost your job?"

"No such luck."

"Well, then, what in Sam Hill could make a woman — "

"Lonesome!" snapped Gertie. "And the floorwalker got fresh to-day. And I found two gray hairs to-night. And I'd give my next week's pay envelope to hear the double click that our front gate gives back home."

"Back home!" echoed the Kid Next Door in a dangerously loud voice. "Say, I want to talk to you. If you'll promise you won't get sore and think I'm fresh, I'll ask you a favor. Slip on a kimono and we'll sneak down to the front stoop and talk it over. I'm as wide awake as a chorus girl and twice as hungry. I've got two apples and a box of crackers. Are you on?"

Gertie snickered. "It isn't done in our best sets, but I'm on. I've got a can of sardines and an orange. I'll be ready in six minutes."

She was, too. She wiped off the cold cream and salt tears with a dry towel, did her hair in a schoolgirl braid and tied it with a big bow, and dressed herself in a black skirt and a baby blue dressing sacque. The Kid Next Door was waiting outside in the hall. His gray sweater covered a multitude of sartorial deficiencies. Gertie stared at him, and he stared at Gertie in the sickly blue light of the boarding-house hall, and it took her one-half of one second to discover that she liked his mouth, and his eyes, and the way his hair was mussed.

"Why, you're only a kid!" whispered the Kid Next Door, in surprise.

Gertie smothered a laugh. "You're not the first man that's been deceived by a pig-tail braid and a baby blue waist. I could locate those two gray hairs for you with my eyes shut and my feet in a sack. Come on, boy. These Robert W. Chambers situations make me nervous."

Many earnest young writers with a flow of adjectives and a passion for detail have attempted to describe the quiet of a great city at night, when a few million people within it are sleeping, or ought to be. They work in the clang of a distant owl car, and the roar of an occasional "L" train, and the hollow echo of the footsteps of the late passer-by. They go elaborately into description, and are strong on the brooding hush, but the thing has never been done satisfactorily.

Gertie, sitting on the front stoop at two in the morning, with her orange in one hand and the sardine can in the other, put it this way:

"If I was to hear a cricket chirp now, I'd screech. This isn't really quiet. It's like waiting for a cannon cracker to go off just before the fuse is burned down. The bang isn't there yet, but you hear it a hundred times in your mind before it happens."

"My name's Augustus G. Eddy," announced the Kid Next Door, solemnly. "Back home they always called me Gus. You peel that orange while I unroll the top of this sardine can. I'm guilty of having interrupted you in the middle of what the girls call a good cry, and I know you'll have to get it out of your system some way. Take a bite of apple and then wade right in and tell me what you're doing in this burg if you don't like it."

"This thing ought to have slow music," began Gertie. "It's pathetic. I came to Chicago from Beloit, Wisconsin, because I thought that little town was a lonesome hole for a vivacious creature like me. Lonesome! Listen while I laugh a low mirthless laugh. I didn't know anything about the three-ply, double-barreled, extra heavy brand of lonesomeness that a big town like this can deal out. Talk about your desert wastes! They're sociable and snug compared to this. I know three-fourths of the people in Beloit, Wisconsin, by their first names. I've lived here six months and I'm not on informal terms with anybody except Teddy, the landlady's dog, and he's a trained rat-and-book-agent terrier, and not inclined to overfriendliness. When I clerked at the Enterprise Store in Beloit the women used to come in and ask for something we didn't carry just for an excuse to copy the way the lace yoke effects were planned in my shirtwaists. You ought to see the way those same shirtwaists stack up here. Why, boy, the lingerie waists that the other girls in my department wear make my best hand-tucked effort look like a simple English country blouse. They're so dripping with Irish crochet and real Val and Cluny insertions that it's a wonder the girls don't get stoop-shouldered carrying 'em around."

"Hold on a minute," commanded Gus. "This thing is uncanny. Our cases dovetail like the deductions in a detective story. Kneel here at my feet, little daughter, and I'll tell you the story of my sad young life. I'm no child of the city streets, either. Say, I came to this town because I thought there was a bigger field for me in Gents' Furnishings. Joke, what?"

But Gertie didn't smile. She gazed up at Gus, and Gus gazed down at her, and his fingers fiddled absently with the big bow at the end of her braid.

"And isn't there?" asked Gertie, sympathetically.

"Girlie, I haven't saved twelve dollars since I came. I'm no tightwad, and I don't believe in packing everything away into a white marble mausoleum, but still a gink kind of whispers to himself that some day he'll be furnishing up a kitchen pantry of his own."

"Oh!" said Gertie.

"And let me mention in passing," continued Gus, winding the ribbon bow around his finger, "that in the last hour or so that whisper has been swelling to a shout."

"Oh!" said Gertie again.

"You said it. But I couldn't buy a secondhand gas stove with what I've saved in the last half-year here. Back home they used to think I was a regular little village John Drew, I was so dressy. But here I look like a yokel on circus day compared to the other fellows in the store. All they need is a field glass strung over their shoulder to make them look like a clothing ad in the back of a popular magazine. Say, girlie, you've got the prettiest hair I've seen since I blew in here. Look at that braid! Thick as a rope! That's no relation to the piles of jute that the Flossies here stack on their heads. And shines! Like satin."

"It ought to," said Gertrude, wearily. "I brush it a hundred strokes every night. Sometimes I'm so beat that I fall asleep with my brush in the air. The manager won't stand for any romping curls or hooks-and-eyes that don't connect. It keeps me so busy being beautiful, and what the society writers call 'well groomed,' that I don't have time to sew the buttons on my underclothes."

"But don't you get some amusement in the evening?" marveled Gus. "What was the matter with you and the other girls in the store? Can't you hit it off?"

"Me? No. I guess I was too woodsy for them. I went out with them a couple of times. I guess they're nice girls all right; but they've got what you call a broader way of looking at things than I have. Living in a little town all your life makes you narrow. These girls! — Well, maybe I'll get educated up to their plane some day, but — "

"No, you don't!" hissed Gus. "Not if I can help it."

"But you can't," replied Gertie, sweetly. "My, ain't this a grand night! Evenings like this I used to love to putter around the yard after supper, sprinkling the grass and weeding the radishes. I'm the greatest kid to fool around with a hose. And flowers! Say, they just grow for me. You ought to have seen my pansies and nasturtiums last summer."

The fingers of the Kid Next Door wandered until they found Gertie's. They clasped them.

"This thing points one way, little one. It's just as plain as a path leading up to a cozy little three-room flat up here on the North Side somewhere. See it? With me and you married, and playing at housekeeping in a parlor and bedroom and kitchen? And both of us going down town to work in the morning just the same as we do now. Only not the same, either."

"Wake up, little boy," said Gertie, prying her fingers away from those other detaining ones. "I'd fit into a three-room flat like a whale in a kitchen sink. I'm going back to Beloit, Wisconsin. I've learned my lesson all right. There's a fellow there waiting for me. I used to think he was too slow. But say, he's got the nicest little painting and paper-hanging business you ever saw, and making money. He's secretary of the K. P.'s back home. They give some swell little dances during the winter, especially for the married members. In five years we'll own our home, with a vegetable garden in the back. I'm a little frog, and it's me for the puddle."

Gus stood up slowly. Gertie felt a little pang of compunction when she saw what a boy he was.

"I don't know when I've enjoyed a talk like this. I've heard about these dawn teas, but I never thought I'd go to one," she said.

"Good-night, girlie," interrupted Gus, abruptly. "It's the dreamless couch for mine. We've got a big sale on in tan and black seconds to-morrow."

# Ben Hecht
## (1894-1964)

*Born in New York City, but long associated with Chicago as a journalist and as founder of, among other things, the* Chicago Literary Times, BEN HECHT *is probably best remembered as a playwright, and, even more, a screenwriter of over sixty films, though he also published over thirty books of stories, sketches, and autobiography, as well as novels such as* The Florentine Dagger *(1923),* A Jew in Love *(1931), and* Miracle in the Rain *(1943). His film writing landed him many Academy Award nominations, including ones for* Wuthering Heights *(1939) and* Notorious *(1946). He won for 1927's* Underworld *and 1935's* The Scoundrel. *His most famous play,* The Front Page *(1928), co-written with Charles MacArthur, has been adapted to film at least three times. The play depicts the often cutthroat nature of the newspaper business, and critics sometimes complained that Hecht's work never escaped the rush and shallowness of that business.*

*"World Conquerors" is from his collection of stories and sketches titled* 1,001 Afternoons in Chicago *(1922), a work which, on the whole, shows that his journalistic style—often characterized as colorful, even "gaudy"—had its quiet, restrained side as well. Here we see a careful sense of dramatic situation that served him so well as a screenwriter. "World Conquerors" also reflects the significant presence of radical activity in the Chicago of the 1920s, as well as its problems.*

✦ ✦ ✦

## World Conquerors

### from 1,001 AFTERNOONS IN CHICAGO

The hall is upstairs. A non-committal sign has been tacked over the street entrance. It discloses that there is to be a discussion this night on the subject of the world revolution. The disclosure is made in English, Yiddish and Russian.

A thousand people have arrived. They are mostly west siders, with a sprinkling of north and south side residents. There seem to be two types. Shop workers and a type that classifies as the intelligentsia. The workers sit calmly and smoke. The intelligentsia are nervous. Dark-eyed women, bearded men, vivacious, exchanging greetings, cracking jokes.

The first speaker is a very bad orator. He is a workingman. An intensity of manner holds the audience in lieu of phrases. He says nothing. Yet every one listens. He says that workingmen have been slaves long enough. That there is injustice in the world. That the light of freedom has appeared on the horizon.

This, to the audience, is old stuff. Yet they watch the talker. He has something they one and all treasured in their own hearts. A faith in something. The workingmen in the audience have stopped smoking. They listen with a faint skepticism in their eyes. The intelligentsia, however, are warming up. For the moment old emotions are stirring in them. Sincerity in others — the martyr spirit in others — is something which thrills the insincerity of all intelligentsia.

Suddenly there is a change in the hall. Our stuttering orator with the forceful manner has made a few startling remarks. He has said, "And what we must do, comrades, is to use force. We can get nowhere without force. We must uproot, overthrow and seize the government."

Scandal! A murmur races around the hall. The residents from the north and south sides who have favored this discussion of world revolution with their uplifting presence are uneasy. Somebody should stop the man. It's one thing to be sincere, and another thing to be too sincere and tell them that they should use force.

Now, what's the matter? The orator has grown violent. It is somebody in the back of the hall. Heads turn. A policeman! The orator swings his arms, and in his foreign tongue, goes on. "They are stopping us. The bourgeoisie! They have sent the *polizei!* But we stand firm. The police are powerless against us. Even though they drive us from this hall."

The orator is all alone in his excitement. The audience has, despite his valorous pronouncements, grown nervous. And the policeman walking down the aisle seems embarrassed. He arrives at the platform finally. He hands a card to the orator. The orator glances at the card and then waves it in the air. Then he reads it slowly, his lips moving as he spells the words out. The audience is shifting around, acting as if it wanted to rise and bolt for the door.

"Ah," exclaims the orator, "the policeman says that an enemy of the revolution has smashed an automobile belonging to one of the audience that was standing in front of the hall. The number of the automobile is as follows." He recites the number slowly. And then: "If anybody has an automobile by that number standing downstairs he better go and look after it."

A substantial looking north sider arises and walks hurriedly through the hall. The orator decides to subside. There is a wait for the chief speaker, who has not yet arrived. During the wait an incident develops. There are two lights burning at the rear of the stage. A young woman calls one of the officials of the meeting.

"Look," she says, "those lights make it impossible for us to see the speaker who stands in front of them. They shine in our eyes."

The official wears a red sash across the front of his coat. He is one of the minor leaders among the west side soviet radicals. He blinks. "What do you want of me?" he inquires with indignation. "I should go and turn the lights out? You think I'm the janitor?"

"But can't you just turn the lights off?" persists the young woman.

"The janitor," announces our official with dignity, "turns the lights on and he will turn them off." Wherewith the Tarquin of the proletaire marches off. Two minutes later a man in his short sleeves appears, following him. This man is the janitor. The audience which has observed this little comedy begins to laugh as the janitor turns off the offending lights.

The chief speaker of the evening has arrived. He is a good orator. He is also cynical of his audience. A short wiry man with a pugnacious face and a cocksure mustache. He begins by asking what they are all afraid of. He accuses them of being more social than revolutionary. As long as revolution was the thing of the hour they were revolutionists. But now that it is no longer the thing of the hour, they have taken up other hobbies.

This appears to be rather the truth from the way the intelligentsia take it. They nod approval. Self-indictment is one thing which distinguishes the intelligentsia. They are able to recognize their faults, their shortcomings.

Now the speaker is on his real subject. Revolution. What we want, he cries, is for the same terrible misfortune to happen in this country that happened in Russia. Yes, the same marvelous misfortune. And he is ready. He is working toward that end. And he wishes in all sincerity that the audience would work with him. Start a reign of terror. Put the spirit of the masses into the day. The unconquerable will to overthrow the tyrant and govern themselves. He continues — an apostle of force. Of fighting. Of shooting, stabbing and barricades that fly the red flag. He is sardonic and sarcastic and everything else. And the audience is disturbed.

There are whispers of scandal. And half the faces of the intelligentsia frown in disapproval. They came to hear economic argument, not a call to arms. The other half is stirred.

It is almost eleven. The hall empties. The streets are alive. People hurry, saunter, stand laughing. Street cars, store fronts, mean houses, shadows and a friendly moon. These are part of the system. Three hours ago they seemed a powerful, impregnable symbol. Now they can be overthrown. The security that pervades the street is an illusion. Force can knock it out. A strange force that lies in the masses who live in this street.

The audience moves away. The intelligentsia will discuss the possibility of a sudden uprising of the proletaire and gradually they will grow cynical about it and say, "Well, he was a good talker."

The orator finally emerges from the building. He is surrounded by friends, questioners. For two blocks he has company. Then he is alone. He stands waiting for a street car. Some of the audience pass by without recognizing him.

The street car comes and the orator gets on. He finds a seat. His head drops against the window and his eyes close. And the car sweeps away, taking with it its load of sleepy men and women who have stayed up too late — including a messiah of the proletaire who dreams of leading the masses out of bondage.

# James T. Farrell

## (1904-79)

*In his* American Fiction, 1920 – 40, *Joseph Warren Beach characterized* JAMES T. FARRELL'*s work as "determined by his pity and loathing for all that was mean, ugly, and spiritually poverty-stricken in the mores and culture to which he was born." That culture was Chicago's South Side. His pity and loathing fueled a style unparalleled among the naturalists and radical 1930s novelists with whom he is most often associated for its headlong zest and its ability to render the grim atmospherics of city life.*

*His conviction that literature, as it led readers to a greater awareness of themselves and the conditions of their existence, could result in great social change drove him to produce an astonishingly large body of work: over sixty volumes of fiction, essays, and poetry, the most famous of which is, of course,* Studs Lonigan: A Trilogy *(1935). The germ of the story, as Farrell himself explains in a prefatory note, is the one printed here. Often controversial, and, especially for his later works, berated by critics for a certain ponderousness and fatalism, Farrell has nonetheless created an unusual number of American literary characters that continue to have an extraordinary life. This may be said of Farrell himself, as it were. Even while criticizing Farrell's 1966 prose poem* When Time Was Born, *the* Time *reviewer called Farrell "the most heroic figure in modern American letters."*

✦ ✦ ✦

## Studs

*from* THE SHORT STORIES OF JAMES T. FARRELL

AUTHOR'S NOTE: This, one of my first stories, is the nucleus out of which the Studs Lonigan trilogy was conceived, imagined, and written. It should suggest the experience and background of these books, and my own relationship to their background. But for the accident of this story, and of the impressions recorded in it, I should probably never have written the Studs Lonigan series.

After writing this story in the spring of 1929, before I had ever published any fiction, the impressions here recorded remained with me so vividly that I could not let them rest. It was then that both *Young Lonigan* and *The Young Manhood of Studs Lonigan* were begun. Originally they were planned as one volume, to end with a scene similar to the one presented in this story. As I worked over them, they were changed, split into two volumes, and finally they grew into the trilogy as it has been published. However, to repeat, this story is the nucleus of the entire work, and so I include it here.

—JTF

It is raining outside; rain pouring like bullets from countless machine guns; rain spat-spattering on the wet earth and paving in endless silver crystals. Studs' grave out at Mount Olivet will be soaked and soppy, and fresh with the wet, clean odors of watered earth and flowers. And the members of Studs' family will be looking out of the windows of their apartment on the South Side, thinking of the cold, damp grave and the gloomy, muddy cemetery, and of their Studs lying at rest in peaceful acceptance of that wormy conclusion which is the common fate.

At Studs' wake last Monday evening everybody was mournful, sad that such a fine young fellow at twenty-six should go off so suddenly with double pneumonia; blown out of this world like a ripped leaf in a hurricane. They sighed and the women and girls cried, and everybody said that it was too bad. But they were consoled because he'd had the priest and had received Extreme Unction before he died, instead of going off like Sport Murphy who was killed in a saloon brawl. Poor Sport! He was a good fellow, and tough as hell. Poor Studs!

The undertaker (it was probably old man O'Reedy who used to be usher in the old parish church) laid Studs out handsomely. He was outfitted in a sombre black suit and a white silk tie. His hands were folded over his stomach, clasping a pair of black rosary beads. At his head, pressed against the satin bedding, was a spiritual bouquet, set in line with Studs' large nose. He looked handsome, and there were no lines of suffering on his planed face. But the spiritual bouquet (further assurance that his soul would arrive safely in Heaven) was a dirty trick. So was the administration of the last sacraments. For Studs will be miserable in Heaven, more miserable than he was on those Sunday nights when he would hang around the old poolroom at Fifty-eighth and the elevated station, waiting for something to happen. He will find the land of perpetual happiness and goodness dull and boresome, and he'll be resentful. There will be nothing to do in Heaven but to wait in timeless eternity. There will be no can houses, speakeasies, whores (unless they are reformed) and gambling joints; and neither will there be a shortage of plasterers. He will loaf up and down gold-paved streets where there is not even the suggestion of a poolroom, thinking of Paulie Haggerty, Sport Murphy, Arnold Sheehan and Hink Weber, who are possibly in Hell together because there was no priest around to play a dirty trick on them.

I thought of these things when I stood by the coffin, waiting for Tommy Doyle, Red Kelly, Les, and Joe to finish offering a few perfunctory prayers in memory of Studs. When they had showered some Hail Marys and Our Fathers on his already prayer-drenched soul, we went out into the dining room.

Years ago when I was a kid in the fifth grade in the old parish school, Studs was in the graduating class. He was one of the school leaders, a light-faced, blond kid who was able to fight like sixty and who never took any sass from Tommy Doyle, Red Kelly, or any of those fellows from the Fifty-eighth Street gang. He was quarterback on the school's football team, and liked by the girls.

My first concrete memory of him is of a rainy fall afternoon. Dick Buckford and I were fooling around in front of Helen Shires' house bumping against each other with our arms folded. We never thought of fighting but kept pushing and shoving and bumping each other. Studs, Red O'Connell, Tubby Connell, the Donoghues, and Jim Clayburn came along. Studs urged us into fighting, and I gave Dick a bloody nose. Studs congratulated me, and said that I could come along with them and play tag in Red O'Connell's basement, where there were several trick passageways.

After that day, I used to go around with Studs and his bunch. They regarded me as a sort of mascot, and they kept training me to fight other kids. But any older fellows who tried to pick on me would have a fight on their hands. Every now and then he would start boxing with me.

"Gee, you never get hurt, do you?" he would say.

I would grin in answer, bearing the punishment because of the pride and the glory.

"You must be goofy. You can't be hurt."

"Well, I don't get hurt like other kids."

"You're too good for Morris and those kids. You could trim them with your eyes closed. You're good," he would say, and then he would go on training me.

I arranged for a party on one of my birthdays, and invited Studs and the fellows from his bunch. Red O'Connell, a tall, lanky, cowardly kid, went with my brother, and the two of them convinced my folks that Studs was not a fit person for me to invite. I told Studs what had happened, and he took such an insult decently. But none of the fellows he went with would accept my invitation, and most of the girls also refused. On the day of the party, with my family's permission, I again invited Studs but he never came.

I have no other concrete recollections of Studs while he was in grammar school. He went to Loyola for one year, loafed about for a similar period; and then he became a plasterer for his father. He commenced going round the poolroom. The usual commonplace story resulted. What there was of the boy disappeared in slobbish dissipation. His pleasures became compressed within a hexagonal of whores, movies, pool, alky, poker, and craps. By the time I commenced going into the poolroom (my third year in high school) this process had been completed.

Studs' attitude toward me had also changed to one of contempt. I was a goofy young punk. Often he made cracks about me. Once, when I retaliated by sarcasm, he threatened to bust me, and awed by his former reputation I shut up. We said little to each other, although Studs occasionally condescended to borrow fifty or seventy-five cents from me, or to discuss Curley, the corner imbecile.

Studs' companions were more or less small-time amateur hoodlums. He had drifted away from the Donoghues and George Gogarty, who remained bourgeois young men with such interests as formal dances and shows. Perhaps Slug Mason was his closest friend; a tall, heavy-handed, good-natured, child-minded slugger, who knew the address and telephone number of almost every prostitute on the South Side. Hink Weber, who should have been in the ring and who later committed suicide in an insane asylum, Red Kelly, who was a typical wisecracking corner habitué, Tommy Doyle, a fattening, bull-dozing, half-good-natured moron, Stan Simonsky and Joe Thomas were his other companions.

I feel sure that Studs' family, particularly his sisters, were appalled by his actions. The two sisters, one of whom I loved in an adolescently romantic and completely unsuccessful manner, were the type of middle-class girls who go in for sororities and sensibilities. One Saturday evening, when Studs got drunk earlier than usual, his older sister (who the boys always said was keen) saw him staggering around under the Fifty-eighth Street elevated station. She was with a young man in an automobile, and they stopped. Studs talked loudly to her, and finally they left. Studs reeled after the car, cursing and shaking his fists. Fellows like Johnny O'Brien (who went to the U. of C. to become a fraternity man) talked sadly of how Studs could have been more discriminating in his choice of buddies and liquor; and this, too, must have reached the ears of his two sisters.

Physical decay slowly developed. Studs, always a square-planed, broad person, began getting soft and slightly fat. He played one or two years with the corner football team. He was still an efficient quarterback, but slow. When the team finally disbanded, he gave up athletics. He fought and brawled about until one New Year's Eve he talked out of turn to Jim McGeoghan, who was a boxing champ down at Notre Dame. Jim flattened Studs' nose, and gave him a wicked black eye. Studs gave up fighting.

My associations with the corner gradually dwindled. I went to college, and became an atheist. This further convinced Studs that I wasn't right, and he occasionally remarked about my insanity. I grew up contemptuous of him and the others; and some of this feeling crept into my overt actions. I drifted into other groups and forgot the corner. Then I went to New York, and stories of legendary activities became fact on the corner. I had started a new religion, written poetry, and done countless similar monstrous things. When I returned, I did not see Studs for over a year. One evening, just before the Smith-Hoover election day, I met him as he came out of the I. C. station at Randolph Street with Pat Carrigan and Ike Dugan. I talked to Pat and Ike, but not to Studs.

"Aren't you gonna say hello to me?" he asked in friendly fashion, and he offered me his hand.

I was curious but friendly for several minutes. We talked of Al Smith's chances in an uninformed, unintelligent fashion and I injected one joke about free love. Studs laughed at it; and then they went on.

The next I heard of him, he was dead.

When I went out into the dining room, I found all the old gang there, jabbering in the smoke-thick, crowded room. But I did not have any desire or intention of giving the world for having seen them. They were almost all fat and respectable. Cloddishly, they talked of the tragedy of his death, and then went about remembering the good old days. I sat in the corner and listened.

The scene seemed tragi-comical to me. All these fellows had been the bad boys of my boyhood, and many of them I had admired as proper models. Now they were all of the same kidney. Jackie Cooney (who once stole fifteen bottles of grape juice in one haul from under the eyes of a Greek proprietor over at Sixty-fifth and Stony Island), Monk McCarthy (who lived in a basement on his pool winnings and peanuts for over a year), Al Mumford (the good-natured, dumbly well-intentioned corner scapegoat), Pat Carrigan, the roly-poly fat boy from Saint Stanislaus high school — all as alike as so many cans of tomato soup.

Jim Nolan, now bald-headed, a public accountant, engaged to be married, and student in philosophy at Saint Vincent's evening school, was in one corner with Monk.

"Gee, Monk, remember the time we went to Plantation and I got drunk and went down the alley over-turning garbage cans?" he recalled.

"Yeh, that was some party," Monk said.

"Those were the days," Jim said.

Tubby Connell, whom I recalled as a moody, introspective kid, singled out the social Johnny O'Brien and listened to the latter talk with George Gogarty about Illinois U.

Al Mumford walked about making cracks, finally observing to me, "Jim, get a fiddle and you'll look like Paderwooski."

Red Kelly sat enthroned with Les, Doyle, Simonsky, Bryan, Young Floss Campbell (waiting to be like these older fellows), talking oracularly.

"Yes, sir, it's too bad. A young fellow in the prime of life going like that. It's too bad," he said.

"Poor Studs!" Les said.

"I was out with him a week ago," Bryan said.

"He was all right then," Kelly said.

"Life is a funny thing," Doyle said.

"It's a good thing he had the priest," Kelly said.

"Yeh," Les said.

"Sa-ay, last Saturday I pushed the swellest little baby at Rosy's," Doyle said.

"Was she a blonde?" Kelly said.

"Yeh," Doyle said.

"She's cute. I jazzed her, too," Kelly said.

"Yeh, that night at Plantation was a wow," Jim Nolan said.

"We ought to pull off a drunk some night," Monk said.

"Let's," Nolan said.

"Say, Curley, are you in love?" Mumford asked Curley across the room.

"Now, Duffy," Curley said with imbecilic superiority.

"Remember the time Curley went to Burnham?" Carrigan asked.

Curley blushed.

"What happened, Curley?" Duffy asked.

"Nothing, Al," Curley said, confused.

"Go on, tell him, Curley! Tell him! Don't be bashful now! Don't be bashful! Tell him about the little broad!" Carrigan said.

"Now, Pat, you know me better than that," Curley said.

"Come on, Curley, tell me," Al said.

"Some little girl sat on Curley's knee, and he shoved her off and called her a lousy whore and left the place," Carrigan said.

"Why, Curley, I'm ashamed of you," Al said.

Curley blushed.

"I got to get up at six every morning. But I don't mind it. This not workin' is the bunk. You ain't got any clothes or anything when you ain't got the sheets. I know. No, sir, this loafin' is all crap. You wait around all day for something to happen," Jackie Cooney said to Tommy Rourke.

"Gee, it was tough on Studs," Johnny O'Brien said to George Gogarty.

Gogarty said it was tough, too. Then they talked of some student from Illinois U. Phil Rolfe came in. Phil was professional major-domo of the wake; he was going with Studs' kid sister. Phil used to be a smart Jewboy, misplaced when he did not get into the furrier business. Now he was sorry with everybody, and thanking them for being sorry. He and Kelly talked importantly of pall-bearers. Then he went out. Some fellow I didn't know started telling one of Red Kelly's brothers what time he got up to go to work. Mickey Flannagan, the corner drunk, came in and he, too, said he was working.

They kept on talking, and I thought more and more that they were a bunch of slobs. All the adventurous boy that was in them years ago had been killed. Slobs, getting fat and middle-aged, bragging of their stupid brawls, reciting the commonplaces of their days.

As I left, I saw Studs' kid sister. She was crying so pitifully that she was unable to recognize me. I didn't see how she could ever have been affectionate toward Studs. He was so outside of her understanding. I knew she never mentioned him to me the few times I took her out. But she cried pitifully.

As I left, I thought that Studs had looked handsome. He would have gotten a good break, too, if only they hadn't given him Extreme Unction. For life would have grown into fatter and fatter decay for him, just as it was starting to do with Kelly, Doyle, Cooney and McCarthy. He, too, was a slob; but he died without having to live countless slobbish years. If only they had not sent him to Heaven where there are no whores and poolrooms.

I walked home with Joe, who isn't like the others. We couldn't feel sorry over Studs. It didn't make any difference.

"Joe, he was a slob," I said.

Joe did not care to use the same language, but he did not disagree.

And now the rain keeps falling on Studs' new grave, and his family mournfully watches the leaden sky, and his old buddies are at work wishing that it was Saturday night, and that they were just getting into bed with a naked voluptuous blonde.

# Albert Halper
## (1904-84)

ALBERT HALPER *was born in Chicago in 1904. He grew up on the West Side and held a variety of poorly paid blue-collar jobs before turning to writing full time. With the exception of* Union Square *(1933), which was set in New York, most of Halper's major fiction takes place in Chicago. The* Foundry *(1934),* The Chute *(1937),* The Little People *(1942),* Sons of the Fathers *(1940), and* The Golden Watch *(1953) all make substantial use of local color to tell their stories.*

*Always a booster of the city's literary life, Halper's anthology* This Is Chicago *(1952) was, until the publication of* Smokestacks and Skyscrapers, *the most complete collection of Chicago writing available. He also edited an anthology of nonfiction narratives about the city's criminals entitled* The Chicago Crime Book *(1967). When Halper died in Poughkeepsie, New York, in 1984, Joseph Epstein, editor of* The American Scholar, *wrote: "If there is such a thing as a Chicago point of view, Albert Halper had it in the best sense."*

*Halper was certainly at his best when writing about the city he loved. "Young Writer Remembering Chicago," from* On the Shore *(1934), contrasts New York with Chicago and gives a vivid account of how the latter city's four seasons shaped him as a writer. Like so many other Chicago writers, Halper is both cynical and sentimental, trenchant and dreamy. As he says, "If I was born in a raw slangy town, if I happened to see raw slangy things, why shouldn't my stuff be raw slangy?"*

◆ ◆ ◆

## *Young Writer Remembering Chicago*

*from* ON THE SHORE

*I. Fall*

Stark days these. Stark nights too. In the parks the trees stand firm, the bare boughs creaking in the wind. The gravel paths, clean from many rains, are neat against the dead brown of faded grass. The wind blows, the leaves fall, and smoke rolls up from factories.

Through the South Side the trains come in at night, long gray metal monsters, racing from off the plains, thundering over viaducts, small squares of light flittering from their windowed steel bodies.

And mist hangs over the lake, drifting to the shore. Tugs creep up the river like water beetles, blunt-nosed, going under bridges, chugging. Fog hangs over the Loop all night. The empty iron streets are gray and dead.

Rearing themselves in the morning, big buildings go up, the steel framework clear against a dirty sky. The chatter of pneumatic hammers, the coarse casual language of men who earn two dollars an hour and like hot beans, drop from the height, but never reach the street.

The nights are blue and chill, with foggy air to breathe. The Elevated goes west, south, and north, spanning the miles, returning to the Loop, the crowded Loop, where big buildings stand lank, showing their thin sides, their flat buttocks. Cool shadows fall against the walls and the bricks are pressed down hard for strength.

Well, what about the town, what about the Windy City, the tough burg with the bad reputation? What about Chicago in the fall? Who knows Chicago? There's no wind. No answer.

A sprawl of shacks nibbling at the prairie, then came the smoke-stacks and the noise. A blare, a crash, and the hum of turbines all day long.

Fall comes, the hurly-burly season, the windy-shrieking season. The freights roll in from Texas, loaded to the doors with fat steers who stamp upon the flooring, rubbing sides, grunting in the swaying, roaring trains. Everything comes into Chicago. The long-legged cowboys in charge of the cattle, lads who are fond of plug tobacco, walk through the Loop on high-heeled boots, see the classy legs on Michigan Avenue, feel their bluish chins, and swallow. Oh, you Panhandle boys, how do you like the Windy City? What do you think of the big noisy town?

And after harvest the farm boys come in, big lanky fellers in overalls, with wide mouths and great brown hands, all eager to bite into Chicago, all hoping to get a job. They walk south along State Street, reach Harrison, stare at the photos in front of the cheap burlesque shows, see the penny arcades, the pimps standing in the doorways. They walk slowly under the lamps at night. Chicago has enough women to go around, women whose job it is to make big awkward farm boys happy, women with hard eyes and tight mouths, sloppy dames with loose breasts. The cops say nothing, look the other way, twirl their clubs, and think about getting on the day shift.

Oh, you farm boys, what do you think of the tough town by the lake? Corn sways when the wind blows over the prairie, but the wind in Chicago howls down the street; it howls over the rooftops of factories and office build-ings; and during lunch hour the young fellers stand on the corners with tooth-picks in their mouths and watch the girls waiting for the traffic signal, watch the wind act naughty-naughty. Why go to a burlesque show, folks, when you live in the Windy City? Why? You see, my friends, I am a booster for Chicago, I want my town to become the biggest in the land.

And now, folks, my own people, let me tell you my story. I was born on the West Side near the Northwestern tracks; there were factories and big liv-ery stables in the neighborhood. My old man ran a grocery and once a week I sprinkled sawdust on the floor, throwing out the grains like golden seeds. That was before the chain-stores were popular, that was a long time ago. In those days my old man carried a lot of book-trade, customers who paid every Satur-day; but if the wage-earner of the family came home drunk, why of course my old man had to wait until the next Saturday. He marked down the items in his big book, then marked them in duplicate in the customer's. Everybody was satisfied, it was fair enough, fair enough.

I remember the Polish janitress who lived on Lake Street near St. John's Place. She bought a half-dozen rolls every morning; she used to pinch my cheeks and feel my buttocks and say it was too bad I was only nine years old. I remember she had a rosy face and dark eyes and was always walking fast, al-ways out of breath. Her husband was a plumber's helper; he was tall and skinny and had the piles. One day she ran away with a husky shipping clerk.

We kids used to make fun of Lumpy Louie, the old cracked gent who had three bumps on his head that looked like three small eggs. He used to stand in front of the wooden Indian in front of Sutton's candy store, arguing and lifting his cane at it; sometimes he scolded the Indian for not keeping his appoint-ment the evening before. He would rap the fire-plugs sharply too and grow angry, and once in a while, when we hit him in the back with stones, he cried.

I used to go swimming in Union Park, in the old lagoon with the cement bottom, that bottom that got slippery because the water wasn't changed often enough. There was a stone bridge over the neck of the pond and people used to toss pennies down into the water on Saturday afternoons and we dived for them. There was quite a scramble. When we got a few we stuck them in our mouths, took a breath and dived for some more. One day a husky girl, a good diver, pushed us little fellers aside and got almost all the pennies. I remember she didn't wear a bathing suit, but an old dirty suit of clinging underwear; she was about twelve years old. We ducked her and kicked her, but she wouldn't go away, and the men on the bridge tossed pennies near her all the time.

George Hurrel, the kid who turned out to be an artist, the short, strong kid who was always drawing pictures on the sidewalks, was my buddy. Every night we went up the alley, crept near the rear window of Healy's, and looked into the back room. The window had a coat of black paint, but there were a few scratches that allowed us to see fairly well. We saw two women showing a few men a good time, and though the men changed from night to night, the women were always the same ones — the tall stout one and the one with black hair; they sat on the laps of the men, squeezed the boys hard, and made them dance to the tune of the old mechanical piano. We watched them drinking, saw old hunch-backed Paddy Curley bring in the bottles, and when the women started smoking our eyes popped. That was the first time I had ever seen ladies smoke, that was when I was a kid. Sometimes the dancing looked like wrestling; and when I told my mother about it, she slapped my face, telling me not to go back in that alley any more.

Yes, folks, I know many stories. And once I was acquainted with a very clever fellow. He told me that if you place a chair upon a table you create a new height. The world is full of clever folk, and I'm not so bad myself. Only I am too modest, I am not aggressive enough.

I go away to a town, a big strange town, and try to hammer out a good book. The days come, the days go, and big ships sail into the harbor. . . .

Speed is in the wind, all right, but the world rolls dead and heavy. Here in this Manhattan rooming-house, a thousand miles from home, it's hell to stare at brown bare walls, with your money almost gone. The place is chilly, and two limp towels hang from a rod. My arms are heavy, I've got the blues; there's a locomotive in my chest, and that's a fact.

Rain falls upon the asphalt and in Central Park the rocks are wet. Autos hurry over bridges, skimming along, while cops swear, mud is dashed onto the sidewalk, and a guy doesn't feel heroic when he gets some in the eye.

"For every shout upon the mountain top there's a million miles of wailing wind." This is from the book of Success, from the wide open door of Opportunity. Panes of glass rattle in their sockets, a roomer from the third floor goes tramping down the stairs, turns the knob, and slams the door, while outside the street lamps throw their cold white glare.


*II. Winter*

In the winter all things do not die. The waves leap up along a cold shore and the wind blows hard. The gulls band in flocks, swerving, wheeling to the right, and the bright sunlight glances from their bellies.

Oh, the iron streets are cold, cold. The raw wind whistles over buildings, rattles the laundry signs, swirls the snow into high drifts in the alleys, and long, blue sparks fly from the third rail as the Elevated goes over the frosty tracks.

Jake Bowers, coming from down-state, walks along Madison Street, stands on the corner of Clinton, takes his hands from his pockets and begins blowing on his fists. Jake is broke. His overalls are getting frayed, his hair is long, and he's getting thin. He shuffles in the cold, bucks the wind, thinks about the big wheat-cakes he has eaten all summer, thinks about the farmer's big stout wife, and when he reaches the Salvation Army headquarters his mind is warm all right, but his legs are like wood. He sees the long line of broken men, all anxious to get a bed, and, when he blows on his fists again, his chapped lips split open in several places and he begins sucking the blood coming from the cracks.

When the wind blows over the prairie, the cornstalks make a dry rustling sound, but in Chicago the wind whistles through your pants and you shiver plenty. Ask Jake Bowers, the tall, lanky boy from down-state. Hey, Jake, how do you like Chicago? Tell the folks about it. Jake doesn't answer; he wets his dry, cracked lips, stands in line with the others, and thinks about a bed for the night.

At dawn the day breaks, the cold, dark sky cracks slowly. Now the iron streets are noisy, the trucks pound hard, teamsters swing their heavy whips through the frosty air, and long columns of vapor come from the nostrils of the horses.

Hey, hey, my buckos. Go on, you bastards. Drag your loads, pull them through the streets, pull them along the shiny car tracks. At night I'll turn you toward the barn, I'll give you hay and water, I'll whack your steamy rumps. Hey, hey, my buckos. Go on, you big fat bastards.

And the long whips swing through the frosty air while the Elevated booms by overhead. The rear legs of the horse bulge with strength.

When I was a small kid, only a few autos were on the streets. I saw the big horses leaning forward, pulling; I heard the swearing teamsters swaying on their seats. Race-horses are nice to look at and pretty nice to write about, but what of the brutes who pull heavy loads, what of the animals that fall and break their legs on slippery streets, kicking weakly until a cop comes running with a gun in his hand? Hey, hey, my buckos. What about those poor bastards, pulling?

At noon the cracked sky is wide open. Small-faced flappers hurry in the cold, their long thin legs moving very fast. They head for the drug-stores, the long narrow stores lined with high stools. They crowd at the counters where prim sandwiches are sold, nicely decorated, good stuff to nibble at with small teeth. Some gals smoke now, swing their legs, and eye the soda-jerker, a tall slick lad with a turned-up shiny nose. The gals look from the windows, hoping for a rich feller, hoping the boss won't have too many letters to dictate.

I once worked in a factory. There were punch-presses near the wall. One noon I sat talking to a man who spoke broken English, but had good jaws. It was snowing outside and we watched the big flakes floating down. Next to me another fellow, a big Swede, yawned, closed his mouth slowly, sighted at the factory cat like at a target, then spat a good stream of rich brown tobacco juice.

The cat was white. But it was half brown as it sprang away. The Swede did not laugh; he yawned again, hoping the snow would stop at half-past five.

And I once had a job as order-picker for a mail-order house, my first job after graduating from high school, when I was eager to conquer the world, to advance with the times, as it were. I went along aisles of merchandise and picked the orders, reading the sheets sent in by customers from Arkansas and Minnesota. There were many items to pick, cheap work shirts, rubber collars, corduroy pants, fedora hats that the firm picked up at auction. I used to stand in the aisles when the supervisor wasn't looking and read the letters accompanying the orders. Some of the customers couldn't spell properly; they had scrawly handwriting and wrote in the personal vein; they told the firm that the last pair of pants was a bit too small for Tom — Tom liked more room around the seat. Yes, folks, those were the days. Another fellow worked with me, a huge Hollander, and his name was Big Bill Mesland; he had to leave Holland because of a girl there. Big Bill was fiery when the boss was not around, but as soon as Kerton walked by Bill became meek in manner. He used to coax the packing girls into the darker aisles, and none of them hollered very much. And at Christmas, when the orders grew heavy, when we had to work overtime until our eyes were so red we could hardly read the customers' writing, Big Bill cursed the firm, standing in the aisle. He shot off all the high-pressure oratory at his command. And one night, a clear starry night, as the poets say, after we had checked out, he and I walked toward the car-line and at the corner Bill wheeled around, raised his big fist in the air, and cursed the building behind us, cursed it in his broken English. I laughed at him. But one year later, while I was working at another job, I heard that the firm of Philipsborn had gone bankrupt. Well, maybe Bill was a medicine man after all. Who knows? He went away to California and wrote me a letter, but I didn't answer it and I don't know why.

And I once had another good friend, but he left town, left his job at the Post Office and is now working as a seaman; he once wrote me from Brussels. Before he left, he told me this: he said big hills are not small mountains. We had a long argument, but I don't recall who won. I told him he was a fathead, called him a mystic, but now I'm beginning to understand what he meant.

The point is, never go to New York, my friends. Stick in Chicago where you belong. They say New York is a great town, that it's the greatest thing in America, but that's all a lie, and a bloody lie at that.

Let the subways roar on, let them rumble underground, let the big boats sail into the harbor bringing freight and people. But the wide mouth of the continent can swallow it whole for all I care. Folks, if you'll please step closer, I'll tell you something; I want to tell you that New York is just a big small town, a burg full of suckers, swollen with yokels. Dear old Manhattan, sweet papa Knickerbocker. Eighty black years on you and yours.

But now it's winter, good old winter in Chicago. The wind howls and snow is whirled into drifts back in the alleys. A strong boat goes up the Chicago River, breaking the ice, keeping the way clear. And every Saturday afternoon races are held in the parks, the bands play on platforms, a few cops on skates keep the crowds back, and sometimes the favorite falls on the last lap and the people feel sorry for him. The wide oval pond glitters dully under the sun and the wind blows fine snow over the ice. People stamp to keep warm, some slap their sides. . . .

Here in New York the gusts blow in from the Battery; and sirens howl, and the bells of the Greek Catholic church over on Twelfth Street go bong-bong-bong all day long. When the air grows raw and damp here, the keys of my typewriter stick a little and I have to pound a bit harder; so hard in fact that some folks will say, "Too raw and awkward, too unfinished and slangy."

But I was born in a raw slangy city, in a raw slangy neighborhood. I lived near railroads, and on warm nights I could smell the strong odor from the stockyards rolling in heavy waves all the way from the South Side. Just try to write in the classic tradition with that stink in your nostrils, sit down and spin out smooth poetic sentences with the roar of railroads in your ears.

When I was a kid I saw sluggers pull down teamsters from the seats of wagons during the big strikes. I watched the bloody brawls at the polls at election time, and some of my old buddies are now successful gangsters. I was an errand-boy working after school when the race riots broke out on the South Side, and, coming from a home where I had just delivered a package, I saw five whites chasing a Negro up the street. The Negro was howling, waving his arms. He ran so hard his shirt worked loose from his pants and flapped in the summer wind. They chased him up an alley off Indiana Avenue, cornered him near a shed, and one white kicked the coon in the mouth as the dark boy got down on his knees to beg for mercy. The nigger begged hard. He said he had never done harm to any white man; he howled and then stopped, and for a while it looked as if he were trying to swallow his own lips. That was when one of the whites pulled out a gun, a shiny revolver that caught the sun. It took two shots to finish the business. The whites stood grim. The coon, his arms spread out as if nailed to a cross, lay quiet near a pile of horse manure. The whites chased me out of the alley, told me to beat it, to keep my mouth shut. Then the cops came, didn't ask me a question, and forced me to ride in the patrol wagon until we passed the danger zone. Soldiers of the National Guard stood on the corners. Many papers were sold.

I'm not a snooper, I don't go around looking for stories, but I know what I know, I know what I have seen. If I was born in a raw slangy town, if I happened to see raw slangy things, why shouldn't my stuff be raw slangy?

The wind shrieks and howls, and there's no answer, folks.

And meanwhile it's winter back in Chicago. Cold air blows over the frozen lagoons, whirls thin fine snow toward the pavilion, and out on the ice a small man wearing a fur cap tries to perform fancy turns on dull skates.

And the weeks slip by, with two limp towels hanging from a rod. The windows rattle. I've got a locomotive in my chest, and that's a fact. It's a gray day, my friends, and the traffic pounds down Eighth Avenue. Across the way, level with my window, a woman sticks a mop out and shakes it hard; but she's not much to look at, no shape at all, kind of middle-aged and her hair is hidden in an old house-cap.

Now a few peeps of steam come up, thin and faint, a drawn-out whistling sound. The landlady's heart has melted, she's a good sport after all. When I become famous, in forty years or so, when I learn to write that slick tricky stuff, I'll type her a nice letter, a letter that will make her proud. "Dear Madam," I will say, and I'll say plenty of nice things. She's a tall thin old lady, and once upon a time a young writer from Kentucky beat her out of two weeks' rent. A few more peeps come up, drearily, like lost pieces of fog drifting down a river on a sunny day.

*III. Spring*

The wind blows, but it is not so cold now; its howling mood is gone, gone down that twining river which disappears into the trees. On the left bank lies a rowboat, bottom up, like a fat man's belly. The paint is peeling, small worms crawl along the seams.

The wind is warm now, a little wet too, and small buds, hanging from the branches, tremble there like heavy drops of water.

When the damp air blows over the prairie, the tall new grass nods in the breeze, but in Chicago people sniff the air, begin walking through the parks again, and a few married young fellers hit the bosses for a raise.

And it's nice to walk up a street late at night when the warm wind blows. There goes the Windy City Kid, coming from work on the night shift down at the Post Office. It's four o'clock in the morning, folks, the street is quiet. He takes his time, walks with his hands in his pockets, and when he sees a police squad whiz around the corner he pretends he's in a hurry, luring them on, smiling a little to himself. Ah, Windy City Kid, you're no greenhorn, you know your onions. The police car bears down, swings over toward the curb, the cops leaning out. And then they call halt! The Windy City Kid halts; he recognizes the voice of authority. He stands firm but feels frisky, and has a mocking look around the eyes. The cops get out heavily, slap his body to feel for weapons, maybe he's a dangerous guy, they question him, tell him to talk up, threaten to run him in. But the Windy City Kid holds a trump card; he works nights, sleeps days, and he's got to have his little joke now and then. When the cops grow ugly, he pulls out his government Post Office badge, flashes it under their noses, tells them he works on the night shift, dares them to call up the supervisor if they doubt it. The cops swear. They get into their auto and drive away. And the Windy City Kid stands on the curb grinning. He calls himself a crazy nut, but he feels pretty good. Then he resumes walking up the dark silent street toward home. He has turned this trick a few times; he works nights, he's got to have his little joke once in a while.

And so spring comes to Chicago. The lake boats sail away like ocean liners, cruise a few hundred miles along Lake Michigan and bring back a load. Smoke trails them, hangs in the air, follows them over the water, and on clear days the horizon seems as boundless as the open sea.

And the warm wind blows, whirling dust along the street, into the public's eyes, into the eyes of those young fellers who stand on the corners during lunch hour, chewing on their toothpicks and looking for a free show.

Yes, folks, it's spring. The curbs along Madison are lined with men, husky fellers and broken geezers. It's spring and they also taste the warm wind. They stand east of Halsted Street, where the cheap employment agencies, with their signs posted outside, are doing a big business. Men are wanted, big raw fellers for the railroad gangs, men for road building, men to go north to the lumber mills. Forty dollars a month, board free. Well, bohunks, what do you say? Come on, what do you say? Take it or leave it. Hey, you, the big guy with the high shoulders, do you want a job? Your fists are big, you've got small angry eyes, maybe you've had a tough time this winter, eh? Want a job, want work? Here we are, forty bucks a month up north in the camps, or forty-five with the road gang. Hey, bohunks, what do you say? Hurry, hurry, hurry, men, the train pulls out when the sun stands in the sky like a fried egg on high.

But Jake Bowers from down-state says nothing. There he stands, his eyes half-sunken, pretty thin now, his country color gone, his big brown hands a dirty white. Hey, Jake, what do you think of Chicago? Tell the folks about it. Send your story singing against the wind. The breeze blows gently over the prairie, but in Chicago a man's got to think about a job. Hey, Jake, how about a job up north? Forty bucks a month and cheap booze every other Saturday. How about it? Jake says nothing. He stands lank, shoves his hands in his pockets, then shuffles away. Jake wants to go back home on the farm, Jake wants his wheat-cakes every morning and the sight of the farmer's tall stout wife. Jake wants to go home. He has had a tough winter, the raw lake wind has whistled through his pants for a long time. Now he wants to go back to the soil. He has been going to a quack doctor, trying to get cured of a dose, and he wants to go back awfully bad.

Spring comes. The brisk wind flaps the colored signs of the employment agencies, and the men walk by. Merchants wash their windows, advertise bargains, hire extra clerks, and stand behind the counters waiting for business.

Oh, blow, wind, go on blowing. Whistle through their Danish whiskers, blow the black smoke away from factories, sweep it out upon the lake.

The hard spring rains go drumming down the street, and wooden men and women go walking on their wooden feet. The water gurgles in the gutters, and on the corner the fat cop mutters.

And this is what I say, yes, this is what I say:

If you have seen pigeons wheeling in the sky, if you have looked at heavy sunlight warming the naked branches of trees, if all the sounds of a city merge, swelling into one great tone, if after you come back to your room, that room with the two towels hanging from a rod, if after all this has come about and you sit on your chair, your arms heavy, the keys of the typewriter staring at you — if you've gone as far as this, I want to tell you that in the winter all things do not die, but death takes many things in the spring. I want to tell you that if warm wind is sticky with new life, it also suffocates the old. It drives the young writers home, the brave boys, the heroic lads with epics in their chests, who came to New York. The young lads pack their grips, pay the landladies, take the subway to the station, and stand waiting for their trains. Youth does not always win, it rides home and tells the folks nothing, gets a job and lets the days go by.

Spring comes. The wharves along the coast lose their hard lines. Ferry boats plow away like dumpy washerwomen, and the heights of Jersey City are blue-gray in the distance. But the hard shiny railroad tracks go grinning west, mile after mile. The tank towns and the jerkwater towns, the junctions and the sidings blur, while the locomotive, like a bullet in a groove, whistles along the rails.

Folks, please listen. Once upon a time I thought that sincerity and simplicity were all that mattered, that if a young writer was honest and had a little talent, that was enough. In my high school days our composition teacher, a tall strong woman of Scotch descent, was always talking to us of honesty. That's how I got a bum steer, that's how I learned out-dated stuff. Like all young fools who lived away from the racket of Manhattan, I thought the wise men of the East were a noble group, and with my sweat I brought them every gift I had. When I crept up to the manger, there was no pure or holy thing in sight; the feed-trough was overturned and the wise boys were slapping down cards, a poker game was going strong. "It's a tough racket," one of them said. "War novels are going good this season, but I'll place a few chips on mystery books for the spring."

In the Sahara there's a sand storm, and in Chicago Hymie Katz gets taken for a ride for squealing on his pals. Women in back yards hang clothes out to dry and old man Sutton thinks about painting his wooden Indian.

I do not believe in heroes, I do not believe in valorous deeds. But why must death take so many things in the spring, why must the young grow weak fighting the old? The walls of New York are high and thick, and many lads have fired their loads of buckshot at them. Out of the west they come, up from the south, but they all go back, they all go back to where they belong.

And upon the upturned manger the wise men of the East slap their cards down. One guy moves a small pile of chips and another spits into the hay.

Roar, New York, keep on roaring. Some day I'll write a book that'll interrupt the poker game — a big raw slangy piece of work that'll set the chips to flying. So roar, New York, go on and roar. Your rumbling dies over the harbor, fades away in Brooklyn, disappears in Astoria.

And all the while the wind blows toward Chicago. People come home from work and eat big meals; roast beef and fried potatoes are washed down with strong coffee. Eat, Chicago, sock it in your belly. You'll need plenty of meat, lots of coffee in the spring.

For in the winter all things do not die, but death takes many things in the spring.

*IV. Summer*

Now the days are hot, the sunlight is intense. Heat quivers upward from the asphalt in crinkly lines. The tin roofs of garages glitter in the light. When the sun goes down, women take their clothes from the lines and the windows in the east are blood-red. The street cars during late rush hours are jammed to the doors, boxcars for human freight, swaying packing cases made of steel and glass.

The days are hot in Chicago, even though a breeze blows off the lake. The green grass in the parks is short and thick, and oars dip slowly as the rowboats go along.

And every evening pop-corn venders take their stands near the parks, draw their small white wagons toward the curb, and send their little whistling sounds into the hot dark night. Pop, kernels, keep on popping. The Greek puts another scoop of kernels over the gas-flame, gazes at it vaguely, shakes the pan a bit, then begins twisting his big mustaches very slowly.

Folks, did you ever go strolling with a gal through the park? Did you ever stop with her at the curb, hand the Greek a nickel, sit on the bench under those thickly set bushes where it was dark, and have your girl shake small handfuls of pop-corn and give them to you? When the bag was empty, you blew it up, then smashed it with your fist; there was a great noise. Your girl laughed. She gave you a shove and, when you kissed her, you tasted the butter from the pop-corn on her lips. The night was dark, brethren, and warm.

Oh, pop, kernels, keep on popping. Pop in the summer for dear old Chicago.

And there's outdoor public dancing in the West Side parks. Workmen have laid a cement floor and built a little platform, and a small, peppy orchestra spurts hot music. Hey, hey, sister, let's go.

And around the wire enclosure stand the middle-aged men, eying the young gals dancing, those fifteen- and sixteen-year-old gals. The middle-aged men have their cars parked a short distance away, those men who take the kids for long rides past the city limits, those men who know their onions. Yes, folks, such is life in the big city. Lift your glass and drain it down, the sour with the sweet, the good with the not-so-good.

And a few yards away from the dance floor boys and girls get together, hold hands as they sit on benches, make a little progress in the humanities. Then they walk along empty streets, thinking things over. Insects swarm about the arc lamps. And they reach her home.

"Farewell, farewell," he tells her mournfully.

"Good night, good night," she answers softly, then climbs the stairs, going around the back way, tells the little doggie not to bark, not even to make a squeal, then up to her room to undress, takes off her clothes, gazes at herself in the cracked mirror, feeling her breasts meanwhile, and so to bed, alone.

Yes, folks, that's the way things go in the summer, in the good old summertime.

When I was a kid band-concerts were held in Union Park. That was when Flo Jacobson had a reputation as a sweet singer, that was when music publishers hired her to plug their numbers at the concerts. She wore a big white floppy hat, stood on the platform, and sang the new songs. I copped a handful of navy beans from the store when my father wasn't looking, and at the concert George Hurrel and I tossed the beans at the band, aiming for the brass instruments. When the music was soft you could hear those hard navy beans hit the cornets and trombones, then go rattling to the wooden floor. One night a cop caught us, but that's another story, and a long sad one at that.

Oh, grow, navy beans, keep on growing. Grow hard and firm for dear old Chicago.

And one summer I worked nights in the Post Office, that great gray building wherein are many stories. I sweated with the others, tossed mail hour on hour, my body swaying, my arms moving, my mind going dead, my eyes reading the addresses. We were supposed to sort fifty letters a minute. Figure that out, folks. I must have tossed a few billion while I was there, and where those letters went I did not care, and if the letters had black borders, if they carried sad news, I didn't care either; I kept on tossing them into the small squares. It was some job, and it taught me plenty. It taught me how to stand on one spot until the bell rang. There were long lines of mail-cases and a thousand men on the floor, and the hard chatter of over a hundred canceling machines went on all night. Who knows big business? Who knows all the big mail-order firms, those houses that dump loads and loads of mail into the Post Office? The belts rumbled on, carrying the mail away, and merchandise rattled down the chutes. Some music, folks, a symphony in the blues: the Negroes humming as they tossed the mail, the sweat rolling down their faces, the dust whirling under the lights. Can a man dance standing still? He can. He can if he's a Negro, if he's throwing mail down at the Post Office. He stands at the case, hums and sways, and pretty soon it's dancing.

Oh, dance, dark boys, go on dancing. Dance on the night shift for dear old Chicago.

The windows were opened, but no wind came inside. At eleven o'clock we ate, went across the street for a big hamburger on rye, told the Greek to hurry up, folded the bread over a big slice of onion, then sank our fangs into onion, hamburger, and bread. The cashier, an old guy with three teeth in his mouth, grinned at us, showing his caved-in gums. "Is the meat juicy, is the onion strong enough?" he asked.

Ha-ha, folks, I have to laugh when I remember that old boy, that ancient guy who sat behind the register grinning at us, no hair on his head. That was a long time ago, that was a thousand years ago. We left the lunchroom, crossed the street again, sat on the wide stone stairs at the Jackson Boulevard entrance, and felt the hot wind blowing up the street. We wore short aprons to protect our clothes, and Christ knows why; they flapped in the hot wind. We waved at autos going by, whistled to a few whores coming from the cheap hotel on Clark Street, and smoked a cigarette or two. There we sat on the cool stone stairs, whites, Negroes, and Filipinos, all in the same boat, our hands moist, our shirts sticking to our backs, all waiting for the bell to ring. And it rang. It rang on time too. We dribbled through the small doorway, showed our badges to the watchman, checked in again at the desk, got another tray of mail, and our arms began tossing the letters again. We worked up a swaying movement. Our legs, restless at first, grew steady, and our arms seemed to flow on forever. And under the lights, those strong glaring bulbs, the dust from the dirty mail-sacks whirled in the air.

Yes, folks, I've held down some mighty fine jobs; you've got to hand it to me.

I once worked for an electrotype foundry, stood in the office, checking cuts, making out statements. When work was slack, I went into the shop, near the big twin dynamos where I could hear the whir of power, the deep hum of current. Back in the rear the hydraulic presses were making wax molds for printing plates, and up in front, along the windows, the air hammers were smoothening out the casts. The gang of workmen were a swell bunch. I worked in the office, wore a white collar, but they treated me as an equal. Sometimes we talked about baseball. But back in the rear was a man who didn't give a hang about the game. He stood over the pots of boiling lead, pouring the hot liquid upon the copper shells. He was Pete the caster, and he had hair on his chest. All the men liked him; they called him the bloody barstard. Pete was blind on one side, he had only one eye, but that optic was so sharp that few men would sit down with him at a game of cards during lunch hour. And you couldn't blame them. He was lucky in cards and love, a tall lean man with wide shoulders, and there was hair on his chest. Every Saturday he got shaved at the lady barber's around the corner, the shop near Polk Street.

And he always sat in Kitty's chair. She was the first barber, the big stout one, the one whose hair was dyed so red it knocked your eye out. She shaved Pete. She swung the chair back, and as the razor went over his face her big breasts nuzzled his shoulder. Every Monday morning Pete told me about it. He was a married man, had grown children, but he worked mighty hard and had to have a change once in a while. He stood half-naked over the pots, and the muscles stood out on his lean powerful arms.

And in the office were three bosses, men who fought among themselves. One was a woman-hound, he used to tell me dirty stories and watch me narrowly; another was impotent; and the third was absent-minded and had five grown daughters. This third one looked over my shoulder as I stood checking the cuts, to make sure I wasn't making mistakes.

And that's not all the jobs I've had.

I was a salesman representing a southern tobacco house, doing pioneer work, as it were. I sold a brand of chewing tobacco that the public didn't want to buy, a brand I pushed onto the dealers. When I came around to take re-orders, I was thrown out of the stores. The plug tobacco tasted like sour apples mixed with dried oatmeal. I tried it once just for fun; that was the time I went into a candy store run by a widow. She dared me to chew it, and I told her the Irish never say die. We had a good laugh together.

And I was once a salesman for a house selling beauty parlor supplies. Cripes, what a racket. Plenty life, plenty hot stuff in that game, folks. I sold supplies to the little manicure gals, to the hair-dressers, the big stout women who had tasted everything in life there was to be tasted, who had been married three or four times and were still game, who were good sports for all that. In those days I knew all about mud-packs, astringent lotions, permanent waves, and skin rejuvenator. In those days I met a hair-dresser, a handsome German girl whose father ran a farm in Iowa. She lived in a strict rooming-house and had to meet me on the corner. Sometimes I think she was the finest kid I ever knew. Her name was Thelma.

That was a long time ago. . . .

Folks, I'm going strong, mighty strong indeed. I'd like to tell you more, like to go on forever. But here we are in Chicago and it's summer. The heat is terrific. When a gal dances with you, her dress sticks to her back. And the small excursion boats ply between Navy Pier and Lincoln Park, twenty-five cents one way, a half a dollar up and back. Hurry, hurry, hurry, folks, the big steamer leaves in three minutes, takes you out upon the ample bosom of the lake. Kids free, madam, take 'em along. The sea air is good for their tummies, it's good for their constitutions, too.

If you stand on the Pier, you hear the dinky orchestra playing as the whistle blows, you hear the banjos strummin', the darkies hummin', and once I saw a nigger gal shake her Swedish movement to get the customers on board. Then another boat docks, more playin', and the whistle blows, the boat plows away, short and heavy toward the break-water, and a few more Chicago souls are made happy.

Oh, sail, boats, sail away. Sail out upon the lake and buck the wind. Let the dinky music hit the water sharply with a sweet smack, sail away for dear old Chicago. . . .

And what about Jake Bowers, you say, the farm boy from down-state? Well, Jake went home, got his old job back, now eats big wheat-cakes and gazes at the farmer's fat wife, but his stare is rather empty. Hey, Jake, how did you like Chicago? Tell the folks about it, tell them how you stood in line, waiting for a bed while the wind went whistling through your pants. Go on, Jake, tell the folks. Jake doesn't answer. He shoves his plate away, gets up, walks behind the barn, and gulps down a pink pill. He has to take two pills a day, that's what the quack doctor back in Chicago said, the doc who has his office in back of the dental parlors.

And the summer wind tosses the new corn playfully about, bends it slightly so that it curves golden in the sun, but in Chicago the wind is damn hot and folks walk up the streets wiping their faces.

Well, folks, I won't keep you any longer. I am sorry, very sorry that my time is up. I've got a lot more to say, many stories to tell, but there's no time, and so I'm sorry. Believe me, I am sorry.

I am sorry for many things in life. I am sorry for the small folk who live thin twisted lives, who have to hold onto their jobs and look alive when the big chief passes by. I am sorry for the broken men who stand against buildings when the wind howls down the street and the snow whirls past the arc lamps. I am sorry for clerks working in big stockrooms, for all my old buddies down at the Post Office—the whites, the Negroes, and the Filipinos, who stand hour on hour tossing mail, their armpits stinking, going to the whorehouses every pay-day, walking down the stairs after being with the girls, going slowly, thinking things over.

I tell you I am sorry for many things. I am sorry for all the dead jobs I have held, for lonely days in a big strange town, for long walks at night past the blazing signs of Broadway, for the dark side streets near the river. I am sorry too for the men who jam the burlesque houses in the afternoons, who lean forward as the girls kick their powdered legs, those girls who are always worrying about future bookings, who sing songs of happiness so loudly that big veins stand out in their necks. I tell you I am sorry. I have slept alone in a narrow bed in a small New York room many nights and have tried to think a few things out.

And now it is summer and I am sorry in the summer for many things, for those hot nights of open-air dancing that had to fade, for the fall that is coming. And for all the gray dead things in life, the things that drag themselves slowly along, I am sorry.

Folks, please listen. I would like to close this little piece with a grand flourish, with a blare of bugles, but I've got a locomotive in my chest, and that's a fact. . . .

When I was a kid, I went camping alone in the pine woods of upper Michigan. I was sixteen years old and carried a heavy pack upon my shoulder blades. Down past an old sawmill I hit a crooked trail that didn't seem to have any ending, and now all my years seem to be going down that trail. There were short bushes on either side, like the stunted lives of small folk, the branches warped and crooked, no buds showing, though it was already mid-summer.

When I reached the bottom of the hill, I struck an old railroad spur that curved away, then straightened out into a direct line. The shiny steel tracks, giving off a harsh glitter in the sun, grew small and taut, meeting at the horizon; and as I began walking over the wooden ties I heard the faint sound of a train. I didn't see the locomotive for a long time, but heard it coming closer and closer. Finally it showed at the end of the tracks, a small black beetle against the horizon. I stepped off to one side to let it pass, hearing the sound increase, seeing the far-off smoke.

It whirled past me, shot round the curve, and went out of sight, but I still heard it. I can hear it yet.

*Chug-chug-chug. Chug-chug-chug.*

Listen to it.

# Meyer Levin
## (1905-81)

*Born in Chicago near Maxwell Street, raised on Racine Avenue, and, by age eighteen a reporter, feature writer, and columnist for the* Chicago Daily News, MEYER LEVIN *went on to write over twenty books in one of America's stormiest literary careers. So often was he in court, suing or being sued, that he even referred to himself as "litigious Levin." Perhaps his most famous legal battle came over* The Diary of Anne Frank. *Working on behalf of Otto Frank, Anne's father and the only family member to survive the war, Levin arranged for the book's publication in America and wrote a stage adaptation of it. That adaptation was rejected and the project turned over to Frances Goodrich and Albert Hackett. It opened to tremendous popular and critical acclaim in 1955, winning a Pulitzer Prize, Tony, and the New York Drama Critics Circle Award. But it contained substantial portions of Levin's original version, so he sued, winning a partial victory when he was awarded $15,000 in damages. His main complaint, however, was that the Goodrich-Hackett version had eliminated or drastically downplayed the diary's "Jewishness."*

*Levin himself recalls that his most compelling childhood memory was "fear and shame at being a Jew," so his later, fierce dedication to Jewish themes came from hard-won personal struggles, though the results in turn often led to his work being labeled sentimental and "too Jewish."* Yehuda *(1931) was the first fictionalized account of life on a kibbutz;* The Old Bunch, *a classic of American-Jewish life;* The Settlers *(1972) and* The Harvest *(1978) about Zionist pioneers.*

*His most famous book, the 1956 novel* Compulsion, *is based on the infamous case of Richard Loeb and Nathan Leopold, sons of wealthy German Jews, who kidnapped and killed fourteen-year-old Bobby Franks "for kicks." The novel displays efficient, sometimes riveting, storytelling layered with philosophical musings over causation, truth, and beauty, the "idea of actuality," and the reality of evil. It too resulted in a famous lawsuit, when Nathan Leopold sued Levin in 1964 for invasion of privacy. Leopold lost.*

✦ ✦ ✦

## *from* COMPULSION

*Nothing ever ends. I had imagined that my part in the Paulie Kessler story was long ago ended, but now I am to go and talk to Judd Steiner, now that he has been thirty years in prison. I imagined that my involvement with Judd Steiner had ended when the trial was over and when he and Artie Straus were sentenced to life imprisonment plus additional terms longer than ordinary human life — ninety-nine years — as if in the wisdom of the law, too, there was this understanding that nothing ever ends, that it is a risk to suppose even that a prison sentence may end with the end of a life. And then as though to add more locks and barriers to exclude those two forever from human society, the judge recommended that they might permanently be barred from parole.*

*Walls and locks, sentences and decrees do not keep people out of your mind, and in my mind, as in the minds of many others, Judd Steiner and Artie Straus have not only stayed on but have lived with the same kind of interaction and extension that people engender in all human existence.*

*For years they seemed to sit quietly in my mind, as though waiting for me some day to turn my attention to them. Yes, I must someday try to understand what it was that made them do what they did. And once, in the war, I believed I understood. Perhaps that too was only what the psychiatrists call displacement; perhaps I was only putting upon them my own impulses and inner processes. But at that moment in the war — which I shall tell about in its place — those two, from their jail in my mind, and even though one of them had long been dead, rose up to influence an action of mine.*

*That was the last time, and I thought I was done with them, since Artie was gone and Judd too would eventually die in prison, doomed to his century beyond life. But now a governor has made Judd Steiner actually eligible for parole. He is to receive a hearing.*

*Somewhere in the chain of command of our news service an editor has remembered my particular role as a reporter on this story, and he has quite naturally conceived the idea that it would be interesting for me to interview Judd Steiner and to write my impression about his suitability to return to the world of men.*

We waited half through the night, with the news leaking out to us. The confessions were going well. The time was long because the state's attorney was going over each fact, nailing down the evidence so every point could be proven even if later some smart lawyers had the boys withdraw their statements.

Thus we hovered between the two confession rooms, catching bits of the story, certain it was turning out to be a sex murder, perversion, with the ransom plan tacked on to cover the act. Just as Tom and I had thought. We waited, the hours broken only by a call from Louisville informing the state's attorney that the miserable, almost forgotten drug clerk, Holmes, had died without talking.

Behind each door the story was pouring forth; each of the culprits seemed bent on getting ahead of the other. And as usual when it came right down to the end, Horn's assistants let us know, these smarties were like everyone else — they were frantically blaming each other.

Then gradually a new and curious idea came out to us. It was that there was something else to the crime, something other than a motive of lust. This different idea was being insisted upon especially by Judd, with a kind of triumphant disdain for the authorities who, even with the murderers in their hands, failed to see the real nature of the crime. Judd vowed that lust really had nothing to do with it. And as for money — would two millionaire boys risk their lives for ten thousand dollars? He had a strange explanation to offer. This was a crime for its own sake. It was a crime in a vacuum, a crime in a perfectly frozen nothingness, where the atmosphere of motive was totally absent.

And as we learned how Artie and Judd thought of their crime, the whole event again became a mystery. For was even their own notion of it the truth?

We could, in that night, only grasp their claim of an experiment, an intellectual experiment, as Judd put it, in creating a perfect crime. They would avow no other motive; their act sought to isolate the pure essence of murder.

Before, we had thought the boys could only have committed the murder under some sudden dreadful impulse. But now we learned how the deed had been marked by a long design developed in full detail. What was new to us was this entry into the dark, vast area of death as an abstraction. Much later, we were to seek the deeper cause that compelled these two individuals to commit this particular murder under the guise, even the illusion, that it was an experiment.

Just as there is no absolute vacuum, there is no absolute abstraction. But one approaches a vacuum by removing atmosphere, and so, in the pretentious excuse offered by Judd, it seemed that by removing the common atmospheres of lust, hatred, greed, one could approach the perfect essence of crime.

Thus one might come down to an isolated killing impulse in humanity. To kill, as we put it in the headlines, for a thrill! For an excitation that had no emotional base. I think the boys themselves believed this was what they had done.

At first their recital sounded much like an account of daydreams that all could recognize. They had been playing with the idea of the "perfect murder." Is not the whole of detective-story literature built on this common fantasy? True, in such stories we always supply a conventional motive. We accept that a man may kill for a legacy or for jealousy or for revenge, though inwardly we may make the reservation — that's foolish, the butler wouldn't go so far. We accept that a dictator may unleash a war out of "economic needs" or "lust for power" but inwardly we keep saying, "Why? Why? Why?"

In this case, the conventional motivation was omitted. Judd Steiner and Artie Straus were saying that they had killed the boy, a victim chosen at random, truly for the deed alone, for the fascinating experiment of committing a perfect crime. At first we hooted at their explanation because we felt it was offered with an account of superiority, even in a kind of triumph, as in a game where the puzzler says, "You didn't guess the right answer!" They had been caught, yes, but by a fluke, and not because we had discovered the right answer.

As the details emerged, we took apart their "perfect" action; how clumsy, how imperfect it was! We saw in each step of their scheme mistakes of construction, as any scientist, any engineer, sees clumsiness in any prototype machine and is led to wonder how a universal law could have been exposed with such a blundering device.

So each related how the plan had begun, Artie vaguely saying "a few months ago," but Judd, with his passion for precision, saying "the first time we thought of a thing like this was on the twenty-eighth of November" and telling us how on that night they had robbed the fraternity house in Ann Arbor, and how they had quarreled on their weird drive homeward. Quarreling lovers must break, or bind themselves into deeper intimacy, and so their pact was made to do some great and perfect crime together. That it should be a kidnapping came out in Artie's thought — perhaps it had been waiting in him. Now it emerged as a crime whose accomplishment would be the highest test of skill, of perfection.

Then, the step of pure logic: for security, the victim must never be able to identify the kidnapers; therefore he must be killed at the earliest moment. Thus the killing was nonemotionally arrived at; it was incidental to the perfection of an idea.

How needlessly emotional people had always been about death! In the pursuit of an impersonal plan, it was nothing, as Judd was to insist; it was no more meaningful than impaling a beetle, than mounting a bird.

The truly intriguing element of the problem would follow: how to secure the ransom, without risk of contact? Though money was not the actual motivating force, still it was part of the set exercise, and as the boys were to say, ten thousand dollars is ten thousand dollars. After the feat of a perfect murder came the feat of a perfect transfer of ransom. And so came the idea of a transfer in moving space — the train, the rented car, an abstract identity.

"And so you registered at the Morrison Hotel as James Singer?"

"Yes, Artie brought an old valise. It was of no value, less than the bill — we left it there."

Instantly, McNamara was hurried over to the Morrison. The registration was found: James Singer. In the storeroom, the tagged, abandoned valise. For weight, a few books. So clever, so careless the perfect plan — books from the university library, one of them containing a library card made out to Artie Straus.

By such tangible items the whole nightmarish, incredible tale began to become real even while the recital continued, behind each door. The rented car — and putting up the side curtains so no one could see into the rear.

"And even then you still could have stopped, desisted from the whole idea?"

"Yes." And then the lunch with Willie Weiss, and then hunting the victim, and the boy coming into the car.

"And at that moment it was not too late to stop?"

Was it? You could think it was too late from the moment Judd first met Artie, from the moment when he was born so bright, born a boy though a girl was wanted. Or you could believe that even with an arm upraised, holding the taped chisel, it was not yet too late. . . . The striking arm raised as in one of those movies where the action is frozen. How many murders are halted only as a thought in our minds? *I could kill that sonofabitch!* In how many tales do we have the moment of the pointed gun, the *Go ahead and shoot,* and instead, the dropping arm? And so from buying the chisel to the act of wrapping it in tape it had seemed that the arm would never really strike. When the first chosen victim, Dickie Weiss, had disappeared on 49th Street, it had seemed the end of their adventure. And yet the arm came to be raised.

"And in that moment you were still able to distinguish between right and wrong?"

"Right and wrong in the conventional sense, yes," Judd answered.

And so the blow was struck and perhaps even directly afterward it seemed not to have happened and that the deed could still be halted. But then they were driving the body through the streets. And then came that strange burial, the vain attempt at effacement.

"Then it was our plan to pour acid on the face in order to obliterate the identity, in case of the finding of the body."

But in the actual deed, suddenly it had seemed necessary, essential to go on pouring. "And when we were doing it, we continued pouring it also on another part of the body — "

"Where?"

"The private parts."

Then wasn't it after all a sex crime? Something sickening, to be hastily covered up, and turned away from? But the questioners had to be relentless. In that closed room, Judd was asked, "What made you do that?"

"We believed — yes, we were under the impression that a person could also be identified by — " He stopped. Perhaps he was seeing the moment more clearly than during the actual deed.

"Surely, university graduates like you couldn't really have believed that."

"We were under the impression at that moment."

But why? Why had this strange idea come over him, and why had the ether obliteration seemed so absolutely necessary? In that intensely charged confession room, with all the men staring at him — Horn, Czewicki, the stenographer, as though staring through his clothes, and with all the dirty meanings in their eyes — could there then have flashed through Judd's mind some image from his childhood, seemingly disconnected, undressing somewhere, naked, and fellows, maybe even his brother, making crude jokes? For myself, I recall an incident as a boy, in a shower room — one of the kids closing his legs so that only the hair showed and jumping around yelling, "I'm a girl! A girl!" And the ribald laughter. Could some such image have pressed itself forward? Could it perhaps have given Judd a shadowy hint as to the meaning of that attempted obliteration?

Thus, there was the deed, poured out, relived in that night of confession. The body dissolvingly anointed over mouth and genitalia, then pulled into the mire, pulled blood-flecked through the swamp water and pressed into the dark tube.

Then hurriedly away, dragging the bloodied robe, bits of garments trailing, up the night lane. Wait. To scoop the earth with the sharp tool, the chisel, and bury the belt buckle which never would burn. And farther on a piece, stop, wait, bury the shoes under a crust of earth. Then as far as the road, the city, returned from the swamp to the city streets and lights. And stopping at a drugstore, Judd to phone home — the dutiful son, "I'll be a little late," to drive his aunt and uncle to their house — and Artie in the meanwhile calling a girl — "I got held up, babe, detained, puss, make it tomorrow," kidding as if he were drunk and maybe out with some other babe. Then to Judd's house, and parking the Willys a few doors away while pulling out his Stutz to drive his aunt and uncle home, leaving Artie calmly playing a hand of casino with Judah Steiner, Sr. And then Judd back — "Good night, sir," as Pater retires upstairs — then both into the Willys, the robe, the clothes still inside it. (Couldn't Paulie's father, out scouring the streets that night, have looked into the car standing only a few blocks from his house?) Then to Artie's house, sneaking down to the basement, the clothes bundled into the furnace, but not the lap robe — "It'll make a stench. We'll stuff it behind a bush, get rid of it tomorrow. If anyone finds it, that's virgin blood — boys will be boys, ha ha." But wait — the blood in the car. Take the gardener's watering pail, wash off the worst of it — "Can't see, that's good enough," says Artie. "Park the damn Willys in front of some damn apartment house. Clear the stuff out of it." The ether can, never used. Rope. Chisel. Thrown into the Stutz. Then drive Artie home. "Wait — get rid of the frigging tool!" And driving along Ellis Avenue, Artie flinging the taped chisel out upon the stupid world . . .

# Richard Wright
## (1908-60)

*As a novelist, short story writer, poet, and essayist, Mississippi-born* RICHARD
WRIGHT *became one of the towering figures in American literature. His writings on
racism and its consequences hit America harder than anything ever written by a black
American before him, and few match his impact even today. He moved to Chicago in
the 1920s and many of his most powerful works, including* Native Son *(1940), are
set against the city's backdrop. His outrage over racism and his concern for its socio-
economic roots led him to join the Communist Party, and until 1938 most of his writing appeared only in left-wing publications. In that year, however, his collection of
four stories about a Chicago black communist won a* Story *magazine prize and was
published as* Uncle Tom's Children *(1938).*

*Much of Wright's work revealed not only the terrifying depth of racial hatred,
but, as with the excerpt printed here from* Native Son, *the prying, condescending,
and ultimately damaging nature of a white liberalism that is supposedly on the side of
the oppressed. From 1947 on he lived a kind of self-exile in France, where, among
writers like Sartre and de Beauvoir, he produced* The Outsider *(1953), considered
by some to be the first consciously existential novel written by an American.*

*Constantly controversial and often criticized for being too ideological, too sensa-
tionalistic, too sociological, Wright's place in American literature nevertheless seems
secure, not only among the Dreisers and Farrells with whom he is often compared
because of naturalism and the Chicago connection, but also because of the virtually
unparalleled impact his work has had on the way we view issues of race, class, and
humanity that haunt us still today.*

✦ ✦ ✦

## *from* NATIVE SON

Jan swung the car off the Outer Drive at Thirty-first Street and drove westward to Indiana Avenue. Bigger wanted Jan to drive faster, so that they could
reach Ernie's Kitchen Shack in the shortest possible time. That would allow
him a chance to sit in the car and stretch out his cramped and aching legs while

they ate. Jan turned onto Indiana Avenue and headed south. Bigger wondered what Jack and Gus and G.H. would say if they saw him sitting between two white people in a car like this. They would tease him about such a thing as long as they could remember it. He felt Mary turn in her seat. She placed her hand on his arm.

"You know, Bigger, I've long wanted to go into these houses," she said, pointing to the tall, dark apartment buildings looming to either side of them, "and just *see* how your people live. You know what I mean? I've been to England, France and Mexico, but I don't know how people live ten blocks from me. We know so *little* about each other. I just want to *see*. I want to *know* these people. Never in my life have I been inside of a Negro home. Yet they *must* live like we live. They're *human*. . . . There are twelve million of them. . . . They live in our country. . . . In the same city with us. . . ." her voice trailed off wistfully.

There was silence. The car sped through the Black Belt, past tall buildings holding black life. Bigger knew that they were thinking of his life and the life of his people. Suddenly he wanted to seize some heavy object in his hand and grip it with all the strength of his body and in some strange way rise up and stand in naked space above the speeding car and with one final blow blot it out — with himself and them in it. His heart was beating fast and he struggled to control his breath. This thing was getting the better of him; he felt that he should not give way to his feelings like this. But he could not help it. Why didn't they leave him alone? What had he done to them? What good could they get out of sitting here making him feel so miserable?

"Tell me where it is, Bigger," Jan said.

"Yessuh."

Bigger looked out and saw that they were at Forty-sixth Street.

"It's at the end of the next block, suh."

"Can I park along here somewhere?"

"Oh; yessuh."

"Bigger, *please!* Don't say sir to me. . . . I don't *like* it. You're a man just like I am; I'm no better than you. Maybe other white men like it. But I don't. Look, Bigger. . . . "

"Yes. . . . " Bigger paused, swallowed, and looked down at his black hands. "O.K.," he mumbled, hoping that they did not hear the choke in his voice.

"You see, Bigger. . . . " Jan began.

Mary reached her hand round back of Bigger and touched Jan's shoulder.

"Let's get out," she said hurriedly.

Jan pulled the car to the curb and opened the door and stepped out. Bigger slipped behind the steering wheel again, glad to have room at last for his arms and legs. Mary got out of the other door. Now, he could get some rest. So intensely taken up was he with his own immediate sensations, that he did not look up until he felt something strange in the long silence. When he did look he saw, in a split second of time, Mary turn her eyes away from his face. She was looking at Jan and Jan was looking at her. There was no mistaking the meaning of the look in their eyes. To Bigger it was plainly a bewildered and questioning look, a look that asked: What on earth is wrong with him? Bigger's teeth clamped tight and he stared straight before him.

"Aren't you coming with us, Bigger?" Mary asked in a sweet tone that made him want to leap at her.

The people in Ernie's Kitchen Shack knew him and he did not want them to see him with these white people. He knew that if he went in they would ask one another: *Who're them white folks Bigger's hanging around with?*

"I—I. . . . I don't want to go in. . . . " he whispered breathlessly.

"Aren't you hungry?" Jan asked.

"Naw; I ain't hungry."

Jan and Mary came close to the car.

"Come and sit with us anyhow," Jan said.

"I. . . . I. . . . " Bigger stammered.

"It'll be all right," Mary said.

"I can stay here. Somebody has to watch the car," he said.

"Oh, to hell with the car!" Mary said. "Come on in."

"I don't want to eat," Bigger said stubbornly.

"Well," Jan sighed. "If that's the way you feel about it, we won't go in."

Bigger felt trapped. Oh, Goddamn! He saw in a flash that he could have made all of this very easy if he had simply acted from the beginning as if they were doing nothing unusual. But he did not understand them; he distrusted them, really hated them. He was puzzled as to why they were treating him this way. But, after all, this was his job and it was just as painful to sit here and let them stare at him as it was to go in.

"O.K.," he mumbled angrily.

He got out and slammed the door. Mary came close to him and caught his arm. He stared at her in a long silence; it was the first time he had ever looked directly at her, and he was able to do so only because he was angry.

"Bigger," she said, "you don't have to come in unless you really want to. Please, don't think. . . . Oh, Bigger. . . . We're not trying to make you feel badly. . . . "

Her voice stopped. In the dim light of the street lamp Bigger saw her eyes cloud and her lips tremble. She swayed against the car. He stepped backward, as though she were contaminated with an invisible contagion. Jan slipped his arm about her waist, supporting her. Bigger heard her sob softly. Good God! He had a wild impulse to turn around and walk away. He felt ensnared in a tangle of deep shadows, shadows as black as the night that stretched above his head. The way he had acted had made her cry, and yet the way she had acted had made him feel that he had to act as he had toward her. In his relations with her he felt that he was riding a seesaw; never were they on a common level; either he or she was up in the air. Mary dried her eyes and Jan whispered something to her. Bigger wondered what he could say to his mother, or the relief, or Mr. Dalton, if he left them. They would be sure to ask why he had walked off his job, and he would not be able to tell.

"I'm all right, now, Jan," he heard Mary say. "I'm sorry. I'm just a fool, I suppose. . . . I acted a ninny." She lifted her eyes to Bigger. "Don't mind me, Bigger. I'm just silly, I guess. . . . "

He said nothing.

"Come on, Bigger," Jan said in a voice that sought to cover up everything. "Let's eat."

Jan caught his arm and tried to pull him forward, but Bigger hung back. Jan and Mary walked toward the entrance of the café and Bigger followed, confused and resentful. Jan went to a small table near a wall.

"Sit down, Bigger."

Bigger sat. Jan and Mary sat in front of him.

"You like fried chicken?" Jan asked.

"Yessuh," he whispered.

He scratched his head. How on earth could he learn not to say *yessuh* and *yessum* to white people in one night when he had been saying it all his life long? He looked before him in such a way that his eyes would not meet theirs. The waitress came and Jan ordered three beers and three portions of fried chicken.

"Hi, Bigger!"

He turned and saw Jack waving at him, but staring at Jan and Mary. He waved a stiff palm in return. Goddamn! Jack walked away hurriedly. Cautiously, Bigger looked round; the waitresses and several people at other tables were staring at him. They all knew him and he knew that they were wondering as he would have wondered if he had been in their places. Mary touched his arm.

"Have you ever been here before, Bigger?"

He groped for neutral words, words that would convey information but not indicate any shade of his own feelings.

"A few times."

"It's very nice," Mary said.

Somebody put a nickel in an automatic phonograph and they listened to the music. Then Bigger felt a hand grab his shoulder.

"Hi, Bigger! Where you been?"

He looked up and saw Bessie laughing in his face.

"Hi," he said gruffly.

"Oh, 'scuse me. I didn't know you had company," she said, walking away with her eyes upon Jan and Mary.

"Tell her to come over, Bigger," Mary said.

Bessie had gone to a far table and was sitting with another girl.

"She's over there now," Bigger said.

The waitress brought the beer and chicken.

"This is simply grand!" Mary exclaimed.

"You got something there," Jan said, looking at Bigger. "Did I say that right, Bigger?"

Bigger hesitated.

"That's the way they say it," he spoke flatly.

Jan and Mary were eating. Bigger picked up a piece of chicken and bit it. When he tried to chew he found his mouth dry. It seemed that the very organic functions of his body had altered; and when he realized why, when he understood the cause, he could not chew the food. After two or three bites, he stopped and sipped his beer.

"Eat your chicken," Mary said. "It's good!"

"I ain't hungry," he mumbled.

"Want some more beer?" Jan asked after a long silence.

Maybe if he got a little drunk it would help him.

"I don't mind," he said.

Jan ordered another round.

"Do they keep anything stronger than beer here?" Jan asked.

"They got anything you want," Bigger said.

Jan ordered a fifth of rum and poured a round. Bigger felt the liquor warming him. After a second drink Jan began to talk.

"Where were you born, Bigger?"

"In the South."

"Whereabouts?"

"Mississippi."

"How far did you go in school?"

"To the eighth grade."

"Why did you stop?"

"No money."

"Did you go to school in the North or South?"

"Mostly in the South. I went two years up here."

"How long have you been in Chicago?"

"Oh, about five years."

"You like it here?"

"It'll do."

"You live with your people?"

"My mother, brother, and sister."

"Where's your father?"

"Dead."

"How long ago was that?"

"He got killed in a riot when I was a kid — in the South."

There was silence. The rum was helping Bigger.

"And what was done about it?" Jan asked.

"Nothing, far as I know."

"How do you feel about it?"

"I don't know."

"Listen, Bigger, that's what we want to *stop*. That's what we Communists are fighting. We want to stop people from treating others that way. I'm a member of the Party. Mary sympathizes. Don't you think if we got together we could stop things like that?"

"I don't know," Bigger said; he was feeling the rum rising to his head. "There's a lot of white people in the world."

"You've read about the Scottsboro boys?"

"I heard about 'em."

"Don't you think we did a good job in helping to keep 'em from killing those boys?"

"It was all right."

"You know, Bigger," said Mary, "we'd like to be friends of yours."

He said nothing. He drained his glass and Jan poured another round. He was getting drunk enough to look straight at them now. Mary was smiling at him.

"You'll get used to us," she said.

Jan stoppered the bottle of rum.

"We'd better go," he said.

"Yes," Mary said. "Oh, Bigger, I'm going to Detroit at nine in the morning and I want you to take my small trunk down to the station. Tell father and he'll let you make up your time. You better come for the trunk at eight-thirty."

"I'll take it down."

Jan paid the bill and they went back to the car. Bigger got behind the steering wheel. He was feeling good. Jan and Mary got into the back seat. As Bigger drove he saw her resting in Jan's arms.

"Drive around in the park awhile, will you, Bigger?"

"O.K."

He turned into Washington Park and pulled the car slowly round and round the long gradual curves. Now and then he watched Jan kiss Mary in the reflection of the rear mirror above his head.

"You got a girl, Bigger?" Mary asked.

"I got a girl," he said.

"I'd like to meet her some time."

He did not answer. Mary's eyes stared dreamily before her, as if she were planning future things to do. Then she turned to Jan and laid her hand tenderly upon his arm.

"How was the demonstration?"

"Pretty good. But the cops arrested three comrades."

"Who were they?"

"A Y. C. L.-er and two Negro women. Oh, by the way, Mary. We need money for bail badly."

"How much?"

"Three thousand."

"I'll mail you a check."

"Swell."

"Did you work hard today?"

"Yeah. I was at a meeting until three this morning. Max and I've been trying to raise bail money all day today."

"Max is a darling, isn't he?"

"He's one of the best lawyers we've got."

Bigger listened; he knew that they were talking Communism and he tried to understand. But he couldn't.

"Jan."

"Yes, honey."

"I'm coming out of school this spring and I'm going to join the Party."

"*Gee*, you're a brick!"

"But I'll have to be careful."

"Say, how's about your working with me, in the office?"

"No, I want to work among Negroes. That's where people are needed. It seems as though they've been pushed out of everything."

"That's true."

"When I see what they've done to those people, it makes me *so* mad. . . . "

"Yes; it's awful."

"And I feel so helpless and useless. I want to *do* something."

"I knew all along you'd come through."

"Say, Jan, do you know many Negroes? I want to meet some."

"I don't know any very well. But you'll meet them when you're in the Party."

"They have so much *emo*tion! What a people! If we could ever get them going. . . . "

"We can't have a revolution without 'em," Jan said. "They've got to be organized. They've got spirit. They'll give the Party something it needs."

"And their songs — the spirituals! Aren't they marvelous?" Bigger saw her turn to him. "Say, Bigger, can you sing?"

"I can't sing," he said.

"Aw, Bigger," she said, pouting. She tilted her head, closed her eyes and opened her mouth.

> Swing low, sweet chariot,
> Coming fer to carry me home. . . .

Jan joined in and Bigger smiled derisively. Hell, that ain't the tune, he thought.

"Come on, Bigger, and help us sing it," Jan said.

"I can't sing," he said again.

They were silent. The car purred along. Then he heard Jan speaking in low tones.

"Where's the bottle?"

"Right here."

"I want a sip."

"I'll take one, too, honey."

"Going heavy tonight, ain't you?"

"About as heavy as you."

They laughed. Bigger drove in silence. He heard the faint, musical gurgle of liquor.

# Nelson Algren

## (1909-81)

*Although* NELSON ALGREN *was born in Detroit in 1909, his family moved to Chicago when he was three, and he lived in the city for most of his life. Algren graduated with a degree in journalism from the University of Illinois and worked at a variety of jobs to support himself as a writer: salesman, gas station attendant, and fieldworker for the WPA Illinois Writer's Project. Among Algren's books of fiction are* Never Come Morning *(1942),* The Neon Wilderness *(1947), and* The Last Carousel *(1973).* The Man with the Golden Arm *(1949) won the National Book Award and was made into a film directed by Otto Preminger and starring Frank Sinatra.*

*Despite the fact that critic Leslie Fielder once dismissed Algren as "the bard of the stumblebum," many Chicago writers have found inspiration in his gritty portrayal of street life. Algren occasionally poked fun at the august figure of the great "white-haired poet" Carl Sandburg, yet he shared Sandburg's compassion for the city's marginalized citizens — its working people and those out of work, the barely adequate and the easily defeated. Although Algren drew heavily on Chicago for his inspiration, his feelings toward the city were ambivalent at best, as "Nobody Knows Where O'Connor Went," the final chapter of his book-length prose poem,* Chicago: City on the Make *(1951), makes clear. Certainly, there is a great love for Chicago: "Never once, on any midnight whatsoever, will you take off from here without a pang"; however, Algren also believes that all the city finally has to offer is nothing but a "rusty iron heart."*

*Toward the end of his life, Nelson Algren left Chicago for the east coast, rightfully convinced that the city he had described so vividly never truly appreciated him. He died of a heart attack in Sag Harbor, New York, in 1981.*

✦ ✦ ✦

## *from* CHICAGO: CITY ON THE MAKE

An October sort of city even in spring. With somebody's washing always whipping, in smoky October colors off the third-floor rear by that same wind that drives the yellowing comic strips down all the gutters that lead away from home. A hoarse-voiced extry-hawking newsie of a city.

By its padlocked poolrooms and its nightshade neon, by its carbon Christs punching transfers all night long; by its nuns studying gin-fizz ads in the Englewood Local, you shall know Chicago.

By nights when the yellow salamanders of the El bend all one way and the cold rain runs with the red-lit rain. By the way the city's million wires are burdened only by lightest snow; and the old year yet lighter upon them. When chairs are stacked and glasses are turned and arc-lamps all are dimmed. By days when the wind bangs alley gates ajar and the sun goes by on the wind. By nights when the moon is an only child above the measured thunder of the cars, you may know Chicago's heart at last:

You'll know it's the place built out of Man's ceaseless failure to overcome himself. Out of Man's endless war against himself we build our successes as well as our failures. Making the city of all cities most like Man himself—loneliest creation of all this very old poor earth.

And Shoeless Joe, who lost his honor and his job, is remembered now more fondly here, when stands are packed and a striped sun burns across them, than old Comiskey, who salvaged his own.

On hot and magic afternoons when only the press box, high overhead, divides the hustler and the square.

For there's a left-hander's wind moving down Thirty-fifth, rolling the summer's last straw kelly across second into center, where fell the winning single of the first winning Comiskey team in thirty-two seasons.

Thirty-two American League seasons (and Lord knows how many swindles ago), Nephew is doing thirty days for the fifteenth or the thirty-ninth time (this time for defacing private property), nobody knows where O'Connor went and a thousand Happy-Days-Are-Here-Again tunes have come and gone. And the one that keeps coming back softest of all, when tavern lights come on and the night is impaled by the high-tension wires, goes:

> It's only a paper moon
> Hanging over a cardboard sea

For everybody takes care of himself under this paper moon, and the hustlers still handle the cardboard. Joe Felso doesn't trouble his pointy little head just because somebody tossed a rock through some other Joe Felso's window two doors down. It wasn't his window and it wasn't his rock and we all have our own troubles, Jack.

The big town is getting something of Uncle Johnson's fixed look, like that of a fighter working beyond his strength and knowing it. "Laughing even as an ignorant fighter laughs, who has never lost a battle," the white-haired poet wrote before his hair turned white.

But the quality of our laughter has altered since that appraisal, to be replaced by something sounding more like a juke-box running down in a deserted bar. Chicago's laughter has grown metallic, the city no longer laughs easily and well, out of spiritual good health. We seem to have no way of judging either the laughter of the living or the fixed smirk of the dead.

The slums take their revenge. How much did he *have*, is what we demand to know when we hear good old Joe Felso has gone to his reward. Never what *was* he, in human terms. Was his income listed publicly? Was there a Ford in his future at the very moment he was snatched? And whether he was of any use or any joy to himself, when he had his chance for use and joy, we never seem to wonder. It's hustle and bustle from day to day, chicken one day and feathers the next, and nobody knows where O'Connor went.[1]

Nobody will tell how Tommy got free.

Nor whether there are well-springs here for men beneath the rubble of last year's revelry.

The pig-wallows are paved, great Diesels stroke noiselessly past the clamorous tenements of home. The Constellations move, silently and all unseen, through blowing seas above the roofs. Only the measured clatter of the empty cars, where pass the northbound and the southbound Els, comes curving down the constant boundaries of night.

The cemetery that yet keeps the Confederate dead is bounded by the same tracks that run past Stephen A. Douglas' remains. The jail where Parsons hung is gone, and the building from which Bonfield marched is no more. Nobody remembers the Globe on Desplaines, and only a lonely shaft remembers the four who died, no one ever understood fully why.[2] And those who went down with the proud steamer *Chicora* are one with those who went down on the *Eastland*. And those who sang "My God, How the Money Rolls In" are one with those who sang, "Brother, Can You Spare a Dime?"

And never once, on any midnight whatsoever, will you take off from here without a pang. Without forever feeling something priceless is being left behind in the forest of furnished rooms, lost forever down below, beneath the miles and miles of lights and lights. With the slow smoke blowing compassionately across them like smoke across the spectrum of the heart. As smoky

---

1. Tommy O'Connor was scheduled to be hanged on December 19, 1921, for the murder of Maxwell Street detective Paddy O'Neil. He escaped before the execution. (Eds.)
2. Haymarket martyrs Albert Parsons, August Spies, Adolph Fischer, and George Engel were executed on November 11, 1887. (Eds.)

rainbows dreaming, and fading as they dream, across those big fancy South-side jukes forever inviting you to put another nickel in, put another nickel in whether the music is playing or not.

As the afternoon's earliest juke-box beats out rumors of the Bronzeville night.

A rumor of neon flowers, bleeding all night long, along those tracks where endless locals pass.

Leaving us empty-handed every hour on the hour.

Remembering nights, when the moon was a buffalo moon, that the narrow plains between the billboards were touched by an Indian wind. Littered with tin cans and dark with smoldering rubble, an Indian wind yet finds, between the shadowed canyons of The Loop, patches of prairie to touch and pass.

Between the curved street of the El and the nearest Clark Street hock-shop, between the penny arcade and the shooting gallery, between the basement ginmill and the biggest juke in Bronzeville, the prairie is caught for keeps at last. Yet on nights when the blood-red neon of the tavern legends tether the arc-lamps to all the puddles left from last night's rain, somewhere between the bright carnival of the boulevards and the dark girders of the El, ever so far and ever so faintly between the still grasses and the moving waters, clear as a cat's cry on a midnight wind, the Pottawattomies mourn in the river reeds once more.

The Pottawattomies were much too square. They left nothing behind but their dirty river.

While we shall leave, for remembrance, one rusty iron heart.

The city's rusty heart, that holds both the hustler and the square.

Takes them both and holds them there.

For keeps and a single day.

# Cyrus Colter
## (b. 1910)

CYRUS COLTER *was born in Noblesville, Indiana, in 1910. He received his LL.B. from the Chicago-Kent College of Law in 1940, and was a deputy collector of internal revenue in Chicago from 1940 to 1942. In 1946 he began practicing law, and from 1950 to 1973 he was the Commissioner of the Illinois Commerce Commission. Colter began teaching at Northwestern University in 1973, where he was the Chester D. Tripp Professor of Humanities until 1978.*

*Cyrus Colter was still very much involved in the world of business and government when his first collection of stories,* The Beach Umbrella *(1970), received a fiction prize from the University of Iowa's School of Letters. The subsequent success of his novels* The River of Eros *(1972) and* The Hippodrome *(1973) led to his position at Northwestern, where he had more time to write. Colter's other works of fiction include* Night Studies *(1979), winner of the 1980 Carl Sandburg prize for fiction;* A Chocolate Soldier *(1988);* The Amoralist and Other Tales *(1988), his collected stories; and* City of Light *(1993).*

*"The Beach Umbrella" is one of Colter's earliest published works, yet the story remains a powerful exploration of one of Chicago literature's most enduring themes: class-consciousness. Watching Elijah juggle the reality of his blue-collar existence and the fantasy world he has created at the Thirty-first Street beach, we can't help but sympathize with the plight of this South Side Everyman.*

✦ ✦ ✦

## The Beach Umbrella

*from* THE BEACH UMBRELLA

The Thirty-first Street beach lay dazzling under a sky so blue that Lake Michigan ran to the horizon like a sheet of sapphire silk, studded with little barbed white sequins for sails; and the heavy surface of the water lapped gently at the boulder "sea wall" which had been cut into, graded, and sanded to make the beach. Saturday afternoons were always frenzied: three black lifeguards, giants in sunglasses, preened in their towers and chaperoned the bathers—adults, teen-agers, and children—who were going through every physical gyration of which the human body is capable. Some dove, swam, some hollered, rode inner tubes, or merely stood waistdeep and pummeled the water; others—on the beach—sprinted, did handsprings and somersaults, sucked Eskimo pies, or just buried their children in the sand. Then there were the lollers—extended in their languor under a garish variety of beach umbrellas.

Elijah lolled too—on his stomach in the white sand, his chin cupped in his palm; but under no umbrella. He had none. By habit, though, he stared in awe at those who did, and sometimes meddled in their conversation: "It's gonna be gettin' *hot* pretty soon—if it ain't careful," he said to a Bantu-looking fellow and his girl sitting near by with an older woman. The temperature was then in the nineties. The fellow managed a negligent smile. "Yeah," he said, and persisted in listening to the women. Buoyant still, Elijah watched them. But soon his gaze wavered, and then moved on to other lollers of interest. Finally he got up, stretched, brushed sand from his swimming trunks, and scanned the beach for a new spot. He started walking.

He was not tall. And he appeared to walk on his toes—his walnut-colored legs were bowed and skinny and made him hobble like a jerky little spider. Next he plopped down near two men and two girls—they were hilarious about something—sitting beneath a big purple-and-white umbrella. The girls, chocolate brown and shapely, emitted squeals of laughter at the wisecracks of the men. Elijah was enchanted. All summer long the rambunctious gaiety of the beach had fastened on him a curious charm, a hex, that brought him gawking and twiddling to the lake each Saturday. The rest of the week, save Sunday, he worked. But Myrtle, his wife, detested the sport and stayed away. Randall, the boy, had been only twice and then without little Susan, who during the summer was her mother's own midget reflection. But Elijah came regularly, especially whenever Myrtle was being evil, which he felt now was almost always. She was getting worse, too—if that was possible. The woman was money-*crazy*.

"You gotta sharp-lookin' umbrella there!" he cut in on the two laughing couples. They studied him—the abruptly silent way. Then the big-shouldered fellow smiled and lifted his eyes to their spangled roof. "Yeah? . . . Thanks," he said. Elijah carried on: "I see a lot of 'em out here this summer—much more'n last year." The fellow meditated on this, but was non-committal. The others went on gabbing, mostly with their hands. Elijah, squinting in the hot sun, watched them. He didn't see how they could be married; they cut the fool too much, acted like they'd itched to get together for weeks and just now made it. He pondered going back in the water, but he'd already had an hour of that.

His eyes traveled the sweltering beach. Funny about his folks; they were every shape and color a God-made human could be. Here was a real sample of variety — pink white to jetty black. Could you any longer call that a *race* of people? It was a complicated complication — for some real educated guy to figure out. Then another thought slowly bore in on him: the beach umbrellas blooming across the sand attracted people — slews of friends, buddies; and gals, too. Wherever the loudest-racket tore the air, a big red, or green, or yellowish umbrella — bordered with white fringe maybe — flowered in the middle of it all and gave shade to the happy good-timers.

Take, for instance, that tropical-looking pea-green umbrella over there, with the Bikini-ed brown chicks under it, and the portable radio jumping. A real beach party! He got up, stole over, and eased down in the sand at the fringe of the jubilation — two big thermos jugs sat in the shade and everybody had a paper cup in hand as the explosions of buffoonery carried out to the water. Chief provoker of mirth was a bulging-eyed old gal in a white bathing suit who, encumbered by big flabby overripe thighs, cavorted and pranced in the sand. When, perspiring from the heat, she finally fagged out, she flopped down almost on top of him. So far, he had gone unnoticed. But now, as he craned in at closer range, she brought him up: "Whatta you want, Pops?" She grinned, but with a touch of hostility.

Pops! Where'd she get that stuff? He was only forty-one, not a day older than that boozy bag. But he smiled. "Nothin'," he said brightly, "but you sure got one goin' here." He turned and viewed the noise-makers.

"An' you wanta get in on it!" she wrangled.

"Oh, I was just lookin' — ."

" — You was just lookin'. Yeah, you was just lookin' at them young chicks there!" She roared a laugh and pointed at the sexy-looking girls under the umbrella.

Elijah grinned weakly.

"Beat it!" she catcalled, and turned back to the party.

He sat like a rock — the hell with her. But soon he relented, and wandered down to the water's edge — remote now from all inhospitality — to sit in the sand and hug his raised knees. Far out, the sailboats were pinned to the horizon and, despite all the close-in fuss, the wide miles of lake lay impassive under a blazing calm; far south and east down the long-curving lake shore, miles in the distance, the smoky haze of the Whiting plant of the Youngstown Sheet and Tube Company hung ominously in an otherwise bright sky. And so it was that he turned back and viewed the beach again — and suddenly caught his craving. Weren't they something — the umbrellas! The flashy colors of them! And the swank! No wonder folks ganged round them. Yes . . . yes, he too must have one. The thought came slow and final, and scared him. For there stood

Myrtle in his mind. She nagged him now night and day, and it was always money that got her started; there was never enough — for Susan's shoes, Randy's overcoat, for new kitchen linoleum, Venetian blinds, for a better car than the old Chevy. "I just don't understand you!" she had said only night before last. "Have you got any plans at all for your family? You got a family, you know. If you could only bear to pull yourself away from that deaf old tightwad out at that warehouse, and go get yourself a *real* job . . . But no! Not *you!*"

She was talking about old man Schroeder, who owned the warehouse where he worked. Yes, the pay could be better, but it still wasn't as bad as she made out. Myrtle could be such a fool sometimes. He had been with the old man nine years now; had started out as a freight handler, but worked up to doing inventories and a little paper work. True, the business had been going down recently, for the old man's sight and hearing were failing and his key people had left. Now he depended on *him*, Elijah — who of late wore a necktie on the job, and made his inventory rounds with a ball-point pen and clipboard. The old man was friendlier, too — almost "hat in hand" to him. He liked everything about the job now — except the pay. And that was only because of Myrtle. She just wanted so much; even talked of moving out of their rented apartment and buying out in the Chatham area. But one thing had to be said for her: she never griped about anything for herself; only for the family, the kids. Every payday he endorsed his check and handed it over to her, and got back in return only gasoline and cigarette money. And this could get pretty tiresome. About six weeks ago he'd gotten a thirty-dollar-a-month raise out of the old man, but that had only made her madder than ever. He'd thought about looking for another job all right; but where would he go to get another white-collar job? There weren't many of them for him. *She* wouldn't care if he went back to the steel mills, back to pouring that white-hot ore out at Youngstown Sheet and Tube. It would be okay with *her* — so long as his pay check was fat. But that kind of work was no good, undignified; coming home on the bus you were always so tired you went to sleep in your seat, with your lunch pail in your lap.

Just then two wet boys, chasing each other across the sand, raced by him into the water. The cold spray on his skin made him jump, jolting him out of his thoughts. He turned and slowly scanned the beach again. The umbrellas were brighter, gayer, bolder than ever — each a hiving center of playful people. He stood up finally, took a long last look, and then started back to the spot where he had parked the Chevy.

The following Monday evening was hot and humid as Elijah sat at home in their plain living room and pretended to read the newspaper; the windows were up, but not the slightest breeze came through the screens to stir Myrtle's fluffy curtains. At the moment she and nine-year-old Susan were in the kitchen finishing the dinner dishes. For twenty minutes now he had sat waiting for the furtive chance to speak to Randall. Randall, at twelve, was a serious, industrious boy, and did deliveries and odd jobs for the neighborhood grocer. Soon he came through — intent, absorbed — on his way back to the grocery for another hour's work.

"Gotta go back, eh, Randy?" Elijah said.

"Yes, sir." He was tall for his age, and wore glasses. He paused with his hand on the doorknob.

Elijah hesitated. Better wait, he thought — wait till he comes back. But Myrtle might be around then. Better ask him now. But Randall had opened the door. "See you later, Dad," he said — and left.

Elijah, shaken, again raised the newspaper and tried to read. He should have called him back, he knew, but he had lost his nerve — because he couldn't tell how Randy would take it. Fifteen dollars was nothing though, really — Randy probably had fifty or sixty stashed away somewhere in his room. Then he thought of Myrtle, and waves of fright went over him — to be even thinking about a beach umbrella was bad enough; and to buy one, especially now, would be to her some kind of crime; but to borrow even a part of the money for it from Randy . . . well, Myrtle would go out of her mind. He had never lied to his family before. This would be the first time. And he had thought about it all day long. During the morning, at the warehouse, he had gotten out the two big mail-order catalogues, to look at the beach umbrellas; but the ones shown were all so small and dinky-looking he was contemptuous. So at noon he drove the Chevy out to a sporting-goods store on West Sixty-third Street. There he found a gorgeous assortment of yard and beach umbrellas. And there he found his prize. A beauty, a big beauty, with wide red and white stripes, and a white fringe. But oh the price! Twenty-three dollars! And he with nine.

"What's the matter with you?" Myrtle had walked in the room. She was thin, and medium brown-skinned with a saddle of freckles across her nose, and looked harried in her sleeveless housedress with her hair unkempt.

Startled, he lowered the newspaper. "Nothing," he said.

"How can you read looking *over* the paper?"

"Was I?"

Not bothering to answer, she sank in a chair. "Susie," she called back into the kitchen, "bring my cigarettes in here, will you, baby?"

Soon Susan, chubby and solemn, with the mist of perspiration on her forehead, came in with the cigarettes. "Only three left, Mama," she said, peering into the pack.

"Okay," Myrtle sighed, taking the cigarettes. Susan started out. "Now, scour the sink good, honey—and then go take your bath. You'll feel cooler."

Before looking at him again, Myrtle lit a cigarette. "School starts in three weeks," she said, with a forlorn shake of her head. "Do you realize that?"

"Yeah? . . . Jesus, time flies." He could not look at her.

"Susie needs dresses, and a couple of pairs of *good* shoes—and she'll need a coat before it gets cold."

"Yeah, I know." He patted the arm of the chair.

"Randy—bless his heart—has already made enough to get most of *his* things. That boy's something; he's all business—I've never seen anything like it." She took a drag on her cigarette. "And old man Schroeder giving you a thirty-dollar raise! What was you thinkin' about? What'd you *say* to him?"

He did not answer at first. Finally he said, "Thirty dollars are thirty dollars, Myrtle. *You* know business is slow."

"*I'll* say it is! And there won't be any business before long—and then where'll you be? I tell you over and over again, you better start looking for something *now!* I been preaching' it to you for a year."

He said nothing.

"Ford and International Harvester are hiring every man they can lay their hands on! And the mills out in Gary and Whiting are going full blast—you see the red sky every night. The men make *good* money."

"They earn every nickel of it, too," he said in gloom.

"But they *get* it! Bring it home! It spends! Does that mean anything to you? Do you know what some of them make? Well, ask Hawthorne—or ask Sonny Milton. Sonny's wife says his checks some weeks run as high as a hundred sixty, hundred eighty, dollars. One week! Take-home pay!"

"Yeah? . . . And Sonny told me he wished he had a job like mine."

Myrtle threw back her head with a bitter gasp. "Oh-h-h, God! Did you tell him what you made? Did you tell him that?"

Suddenly Susan came back into the muggy living room. She went straight to her mother and stood as if expecting an award. Myrtle absently patted her on the side of the head. "Now, go and run your bath water, honey," she said.

Elijah smiled at Susan. "Susie," he said, "d'you know your tummy is stickin' way out—you didn't eat too much, did you!" He laughed.

Susan turned and observed him; then looked at her mother. "No," she finally said.

"Go on, now, baby," Myrtle said. Susan left the room.

Myrtle resumed. "Well, there's no use going through all this again. It's plain as the nose on your face. You got a family—a good family, *I* think. The only question is, do you wanta get off your hind end and do somethin' for it. It's just that simple."

Elijah looked at her. "You can talk real crazy sometimes, Myrtle."

"I think it's that old man!" she cried, her freckles contorted. "He's got you answering the phone, and taking inventory—wearing a necktie and all that. You wearing a necktie and your son mopping in a grocery store, so he can buy his own clothes." She snatched up her cigarettes, and walked out of the room.

His eyes did not follow her, but remained off in space. Finally he got up and went back into the kitchen. Over the stove the plaster was thinly cracked, and, in spots, the linoleum had worn through the pattern; but everything was immaculate. He opened the refrigerator, poured a glass of cold water, and sat down at the kitchen table. He felt strange and weak, and sat for a long time sipping the water.

Then after a while he heard Randall's key in the front door, sending tremors of dread through him. When Randall came into the kitchen, he seemed to him as tall as himself; his glasses were steamy from the humidity outside, and his hands were dirty.

"Hi, Dad," he said gravely without looking at him, and opened the refrigerator door.

Elijah chuckled. "Your mother'll get after you about going in there without washing your hands."

But Randall took out the water pitcher and closed the door.

Elijah watched him. Now was the time to ask him. His heart was hammering. Go on—now! But instead he heard his husky voice saying, "What'd they have you doing over at the grocery tonight?"

Randall was drinking the glass of water. When he finished he said, "Refilling shelves."

"Pretty hot job tonight, eh?"

"It wasn't so bad." Randall was matter-of-fact as he set the empty glass over the sink, and paused before leaving.

"Well . . . you're doing fine, son. Fine. Your mother sure is proud of you. . . ." Purpose had lodged in his throat.

The praise embarrassed Randall. "Okay, Dad," he said, and edged from the kitchen.

Elijah slumped back in his chair, near prostration. He tried to clear his mind of every particle of thought, but the images became only more jumbled, oppressive to the point of panic.

Then before long Myrtle came into the kitchen—ignoring him. But she seemed not so hostile now as coldly impassive, exhibiting a bravado he had not seen before. He got up and went back into the living room and turned on the television. As the TV-screen lawmen galloped before him, he sat oblivious, admitting the failure of his will. If only he could have gotten Randall to himself long enough — but everything had been so sudden, abrupt; he couldn't just ask him out of the clear blue. Besides, around him, Randall always seemed so busy, too busy to talk. He couldn't understand that; he had never mistreated the boy, never whipped him in his life; had shaken him a time or two, but that was long ago, when he was little.

He sat and watched the finish of the half-hour TV show. Myrtle was in the bedroom now. He slouched in his chair, lacking the resolve to get up and turn off the television.

Suddenly he was on his feet.

Leaving the television on, he went back to Randall's room in the rear. The door was open and Randall was asleep, lying on his back on the bed, perspiring, still dressed except for his shoes and glasses. He stood over the bed and looked at him. He was a good boy; his own son. But how strange — he thought for the first time — there was no resemblance between them. None whatsoever. Randy had a few of his mother's freckles on his thin brown face, but he could see none of himself in the boy. Then his musings were scattered by the return of his fear. He dreaded waking him. And he might be cross. If he didn't hurry, though, Myrtle or Susie might come strolling out any minute. His bones seemed rubbery from the strain. Finally he bent down and touched Randall's shoulder. The boy did not move a muscle, except to open his eyes. Elijah smiled at him. And he slowly sat up.

"Sorry, Randy — to wake you up like this."

"What's the matter?" Randall rubbed his eyes.

Elijah bent down again, but did not whisper. "Say, can you let me have fifteen bucks — till I get my check? . . . I need to get some things — and I'm a little short this time." He could hardly bring the words up.

Randall gave him a slow, queer look.

"I'll get my check a week from Friday," Elijah said, ". . . and I'll give it back to you then — sure."

Now instinctively Randall glanced toward the door, and Elijah knew Myrtle had crossed his thoughts. "You don't have to mention anything to your mother," he said with casual suddenness.

Randall got up slowly off the bed, and, in his socks, walked to the little table where he did his homework. He pulled the drawer out, fished far in the back a moment, and brought out a white business envelope secured by a rubber band. Holding the envelope close to his stomach, he took out first a ten-dollar bill, and then a five, and, sighing, handed them over.

"Thanks, old man," Elijah quivered, folding the money. "You'll get this back the day I get my check. . . . That's for sure."

"Okay," Randall finally said.

Elijah started out. Then he could see Myrtle on payday — her hand extended for his check. He hesitated, and looked at Randall, as if to speak. But he slipped the money in his trousers pocket and hurried from the room.

The following Saturday at the beach did not begin bright and sunny. By noon it was hot, but the sky was overcast and angry, the air heavy. There was no certainty whatever of a crowd, raucous or otherwise, and this was Elijah's chief concern as, shortly before twelve o'clock, he drove up in the Chevy and parked in the bumpy, graveled stretch of high ground that looked down eastward over the lake and was used for a parking lot. He climbed out of the car, glancing at the lake and clouds, and prayed in his heart it would not rain — the water was murky and restless, and only a handful of bathers had showed. But it was early yet. He stood beside the car and watched a bulbous, brown-skinned woman, in bathing suit and enormous straw hat, lugging a lunch basket down toward the beach, followed by her brood of children. And a fellow in swimming trunks, apparently the father, took a towel and sandals from his new Buick and called petulantly to his family to "just wait a minute, please." In another car, two women sat waiting, as yet fully clothed and undecided about going swimming. While down at the water's edge there was the usual cluster of dripping boys who, brash and boisterous, swarmed to the beach every day in fair weather or foul.

Elijah took off his shirt, peeled his trousers from over his swimming trunks, and started collecting the paraphernalia from the back seat of the car: a frayed pink rug filched from the house, a towel, sunglasses, cigarettes, a thermos jug filled with cold lemonade he had made himself, and a dozen paper cups. All this he stacked on the front fender. Then he went around to the rear and opened the trunk. Ah, there it lay — encased in a long, slim package trussed with heavy twine, and barely fitting athwart the spare tire. He felt prickles of excitement as he took the knife from the tool bag, cut the twine, and pulled the wrapping paper away. Red and white stripes sprang at him. It was even more gorgeous than when it had first seduced him in the store. The white fringe gave it style; the wide red fillets were cardinal and stark, and the white stripes glared. Now he opened it over his head, for the full thrill of its colors, and looked around to see if anyone else agreed. Finally after a while he gathered up all his equipment and headed down for the beach, his short, nubby legs seeming more bowed than ever under the weight of their cargo.

When he reached the sand, a choice of location became a pressing matter. That was why he had come early. From past observation it was clear that the center of gaiety shifted from day to day; last Saturday it might have been nearer the water, this Saturday, well back; or up, or down, the beach a ways.

He must pick the site with care, for he could not move about the way he did when he had no umbrella; it was too noticeable. He finally took a spot as near the center of the beach as he could estimate, and dropped his gear in the sand. He knelt down and spread the pink rug, then moved the thermos jug over onto it, and folded the towel and placed it with the paper cups, sunglasses, and cigarettes down beside the jug. Now he went to find a heavy stone or brick to drive down the spike for the hollow umbrella stem to fit over. So it was not until the umbrella was finally up that he again had time for anxiety about the weather. His whole morning's effort had been an act of faith, for, as yet, there was no sun, although now and then a few azure breaks appeared in the thinning cloud mass. But before very long this brighter texture of the sky began to grow and spread by slow degrees, and his hopes quickened. Finally he sat down under his umbrella, lit a cigarette, and waited.

It was not long before two small boys came by — on their way to the water. He grinned, and called to them, "Hey, fellas, been in yet?" — their bathing suits were dry.

They stopped, and observed him. Then one of them smiled, and shook his head.

Elijah laughed. "Well, whatta you waitin' for? Go on in there and get them suits wet!" Both boys gave him silent smiles. And they lingered. He thought this a good omen — it had been different the Saturday before.

Once or twice the sun burst through the weakening clouds. He forgot the boys now in watching the skies, and soon they moved on. His anxiety was not detectable from his lazy posture under the umbrella, with his dwarfish, gnarled legs extended and his bare heels on the little rug. But then soon the clouds began to fade in earnest, seeming not to move away laterally, but slowly to recede into a lucent haze, until at last the sun came through hot and bright. He squinted at the sky and felt delivered. They would come, the folks would come! — were coming now; the beach would soon be swarming. Two other umbrellas were up already, and the diving board thronged with wet, acrobatic boys. The lifeguards were in their towers now, and still another launched his yellow rowboat. And up on the Outer Drive, the cars, one by one, were turning into the parking lot. The sun was bringing them out all right; soon he'd be in the middle of a field day. He felt a low-key, welling excitement, for the water was blue, and far out the sails were starched and white.

Soon he saw the two little boys coming back. They were soaked. Their mother — a thin, brown girl in a yellow bathing suit — was with them now, and the boys were pointing to his umbrella. She seemed dignified for her youth, as she gave him a shy glance and then smiled at the boys.

"Ah, ha!" he cried to the boys. "You've been in *now* all right!" And then laughing to her, "I was kiddin' them awhile ago about their dry bathing suits."

She smiled at the boys again. "They like for me to be with them when they go in," she said.

"I got some lemonade here," he said abruptly, slapping the thermos jug. "Why don't you have some?" His voice was anxious.

She hesitated.

He jumped up. "Come on, sit down." He smiled at her and stepped aside.

Still she hesitated. But her eager boys pressed close behind her. Finally she smiled and sat down under the umbrella.

"You fellas can sit down under there too — in the shade," he said to the boys, and pointed under the umbrella. The boys flopped down quickly in the shady sand. He started at once serving them cold lemonade in paper cups.

"Whew! I thought it was goin' to rain there for a while," he said, making conversation after passing out the lemonade. He had squatted on the sand and lit another cigarette. "Then there wouldn't a been much goin' on. But it turned out fine after all — there'll be a mob here before long."

She sipped the lemonade, but said little. He felt she had sat down only because of the boys, for she merely smiled and gave short answers to his questions. He learned the boys' names, Melvin and James; their ages, seven and nine; and that they were still frightened by the water. But he wanted to ask *her* name, and inquire about her husband. But he could not capture the courage.

Now the sun was hot and the sand was hot. And an orange-and-white umbrella was going up right beside them — two fellows and a girl. When the fellow who had been kneeling to drive the umbrella spike in the sand stood up, he was string-bean tall, and black, with his glistening hair freshly processed. The girl was a lighter brown, and wore a lilac bathing suit, and, although her legs were thin, she was pleasant enough to look at. The second fellow was medium, really, in height, but short beside his tall, black friend. He was yellow-skinned, and fast getting bald, although still in his early thirties. Both men sported little shoestring mustaches.

Elijah watched them in silence as long as he could. "You picked the right spot all right!" he laughed at last, putting on his sunglasses.

"How come, man?" The tall, black fellow grinned, showing his mouthful of gold teeth.

"You see *every*body here!" happily rejoined Elijah. "They all come here!"

"Man, I been coming here for years," the fellow reproved, and sat down in his khaki swimming trunks to take off his shoes. Then he stood up. "But right now, in the water I goes." He looked down at the girl. "How 'bout you, Lois, baby?"

"No, Caesar," she smiled, "not yet; I'm gonna sit here awhile and relax."

"Okay, then — you just sit right there and relax. And Little Joe" — he turned and grinned to his shorter friend — "you sit there an' relax right along with her. You all can talk with this gentleman here" — he nodded at Elijah — "an' his nice wife." Then, pleased with himself, he trotted off toward the water.

The young mother looked at Elijah, as if he should have hastened to correct him. But somehow he had not wanted to. Yet too, Caesar's remark seemed to amuse her, for she soon smiled. Elijah felt the pain of relief — he did not want her to go; he glanced at her with a furtive laugh, and then they both laughed. The boys had finished their lemonade now, and were digging in the sand. Lois and Little Joe were busy talking.

Elijah was not quite sure what he should say to the mother. He did not understand her, was afraid of boring her, was desperate to keep her interested. As she sat looking out over the lake, he watched her. She was not pretty; and she was too thin. But he thought she had poise; he liked the way she treated her boys — tender, but casual; how different from Myrtle's frantic herding.

Soon she turned to the boys. "Want to go back in the water?" she laughed.

The boys looked at each other, and then at her. "Okay," James said finally, in resignation.

"Here, have some more lemonade," Elijah cut in.

The boys, rescued for the moment, quickly extended their cups. He poured them more lemonade, as she looked on smiling.

Now he turned to Lois and Little Joe sitting under their orange-and-white umbrella. "How 'bout some good ole cold lemonade?" he asked with a mushy smile. "I got plenty of cups." He felt he must get something going.

Lois smiled back, "No, thanks," she said, fluttering her long eyelashes, "not right now."

He looked anxiously at Little Joe.

"*I'll* take a cup!" said Little Joe, and turned and laughed to Lois: "Hand me that bag there, will you?" He pointed to her beach bag in the sand. She passed it to him, and he reached in and pulled out a pint of gin. "We'll have some *real* lemonade," he vowed, with a daredevilish grin.

Lois squealed with pretended embarrassment. "Oh, *Joe!*"

Elijah's eyes were big now; he was thinking of the police. But he handed Little Joe a cup and poured the lemonade, to which Joe added gin. Then Joe, grinning, thrust the bottle at Elijah. "How 'bout yourself, chief?" he said.

Elijah, shaking his head, leaned forward and whispered, "You ain't supposed to drink on the beach, y'know."

"*This* ain't a drink, man — it's a taste!" said Little Joe, laughing and waving the bottle around toward the young mother. "How 'bout a little taste for your wife here?" he said to Elijah.

The mother laughed and threw up both her hands. "No, not for me!"

Little Joe gave her a rakish grin. "What's a matter? You *'fraid* of that guy?" He jerked his thumb toward Elijah. "You 'fraid of getting' a whippin', eh?"

"No, not exactly," she laughed.

Elijah was so elated with her his relief burst up in hysterical laughter. His laugh became strident and hoarse and he could not stop. The boys gaped at him, and then at their mother. When finally he recovered, Little Joe asked him, "Whut's so funny 'bout *that?*" Then Little Joe grinned at the mother. "You beat *him* up sometimes, eh?"

This started Elijah's hysterics all over again. The mother looked concerned now, and embarrassed; her laugh was nervous and shadowed. Little Joe glanced at Lois, laughed, and shrugged his shoulders. When Elijah finally got control of himself again he looked spent and demoralized.

Lois now tried to divert attention by starting a conversation with the boys. But the mother showed signs of restlessness and seemed ready to go. At this moment Caesar returned. Glistening beads of water ran off his long, black body; and his hair was unprocessed now. He surveyed the group and then flashed a wide, gold-toothed grin. "One big, happy family, like I said." Then he spied the paper cup in Little Joe's hand. "Whut you got there, man?"

Little Joe looked down into his cup with a playful smirk. "Lemonade, lover boy, lemonade."

"Don't hand me that jive, Joey. You ain't never had any straight lemonade in your life."

This again brought uproarious laughter from Elijah. "I got the straight lemonade *here!*" He beat the thermos jug with his hand. "Come on — have some!" He reached for a paper cup.

"Why, sure," said poised Caesar. He held out the cup and received the lemonade. "Now, gimme that gin," he said to Little Joe. Joe handed over the gin, and Caesar poured three fingers into the lemonade and sat down in the sand with his legs crossed under him. Soon he turned to the two boys, as their mother watched him with amusement. "Say, ain't you boys goin' in any more? Why don't you tell your daddy there to take you in?" He nodded toward Elijah.

Little Melvin frowned at him. "My daddy's workin'," he said.

Caesar's eyebrows shot up. "Ooooh, la, la!" he crooned. "Hey, now!" And he turned and looked at the mother and then at Elijah, and gave a clownish little snigger.

Lois tittered before feigning exasperation at him. "There you go again," she said, "talkin' when you shoulda been listening."

Elijah laughed along with the rest. But he felt deflated. Then he glanced at the mother, who was laughing too. He could detect in her no sign of dismay. Why then had she gone along with the gag in the first place, he thought — if now she didn't hate to see it punctured?

"*Hold the phone!*" softly exclaimed Little Joe. "Whut is *this?*" He was staring over his shoulder. Three women, young, brown, and worldly-looking, wandered toward them, carrying an assortment of beach paraphernalia and looking for a likely spot. They wore very scant bathing suits, and were followed, but slowly, by an older woman with big, unsightly thighs. Elijah recognized her at once. She was the old gal who, the Saturday before, had chased him away from her beach party. She wore the same white bathing suit, and one of her girls carried the pea-green umbrella.

Caesar forgot his whereabouts ogling the girls. The older woman, observing this, paused to survey the situation. "How 'bout along in here?" she finally said to one of the girls. The girl carrying the thermos jug set it in the sand so close to Caesar it nearly touched him. He was rapturous. The girl with the umbrella had no chance to put it up, for Caesar and Little Joe instantly encumbered her with help. Another girl turned on their radio, and grinning, feverish Little Joe started snapping his fingers to the music's beat.

Within a half hour, a boisterous party was in progress. The little radio, perched on a hump of sand, blared out hot jazz, as the older woman — whose name turned out to be Hattie — passed around some cold, rum-spiked punch; and before long she went into her dancing-prancing act — to the riotous delight of all, especially Elijah. Hattie did not remember him from the Saturday past, and he was glad, for everything was so different today! As different as milk and ink. He knew no one realized it, but this was *his* party really — the wildest, craziest, funniest, and best he had ever seen or heard of. Nobody had been near the water — except Caesar, and the mother and boys much earlier. It appeared Lois was Caesar's girl friend, and she was hence more capable of reserve in face of the come-on antics of Opal, Billie, and Quanita — Hattie's girls. But Little Joe, to Caesar's tortured envy, was both free and aggressive. Even the young mother, who now volunteered her name to be Mrs. Green, got frolicsome, and twice jabbed Little Joe in the ribs.

Finally Caesar proposed they all go in the water. This met with instant, tipsy acclaim; and Little Joe, his yellow face contorted from laughing, jumped up, grabbed Billie's hand, and made off with her across the sand. But Hattie would not budge. Full of rum, and stubborn, she sat sprawled with her flaccid thighs spread in an obscene V, and her eyes half shut. Now she yelled at her departing girls: "You all watch out, now! Dont'cha go in too far. . . . Just wade! None o' you can swim a lick!"

Elijah now was beyond happiness. He felt a floating, manic glee. He sprang up and jerked Mrs. Green splashing into the water, followed by her somewhat less ecstatic boys. Caesar had to paddle about with Lois and leave Little Joe unassisted to caper with Billie, Opal, and Quanita. Billie was the prettiest of the three, and, despite Hattie's contrary statement, she could swim; and Little Joe, after taking her out in deeper water, waved back to Caesar in triumph. The sun was brazen now, and the beach and lake thronged with a variegated humanity. Elijah, a strong, but awkward, country-style swimmer, gave Mrs. Green a lesson in floating on her back, and, though she too could swim, he often felt obligated to place both his arms under her young body and buoy her up.

And sometimes he would purposely let her sink to her chin, whereupon she would feign a happy fright and utter faint simian screeches. Opal and Quanita sat in the shallows and kicked up their heels at Caesar, who, fully occupied with Lois, was a grinning water-threshing study in frustration.

Thus the party went — on and on — till nearly four o'clock. Elijah had not known the world afforded such joy; his homely face was a wet festoon of beams and smiles. He went from girl to girl, insisting she learn to float on his outstretched arms. Once begrudgingly Caesar admonished him, "Man, you gonna *drown* one o' them pretty chicks in a minute." And Little Joe bestowed his highest accolade by calling him "lover boy," as Elijah nearly strangled from laughter.

At last, they looked up to see old Hattie as she reeled down to the water's edge, coming to fetch her girls. Both Caesar and Little Joe ran out of the water to meet her, seized her by the wrists, and, despite her struggles and curses, dragged her in. "Turn me loose! You big galoots!" she yelled and gasped as the water hit her. She was in knee-deep before she wriggled and fought herself free and lurched out of the water. Her breath reeked of rum. Little Joe ran and caught her again, but she lunged backwards, and free, with such force she sat down in the wet sand with a thud. She roared a laugh now, and spread her arms for help, as her girls came sprinting and splashing out of the water and tugged her to her feet. Her eyes narrowed to vengeful, grinning slits as she turned on Caesar and Little Joe: "*I* know whut you two're up to!" She flashed a glance around toward her girls. "I been watchin' both o' you studs! Yeah, yeah, but your eyes may shine, an' your teeth may grit. . . ." She went limp in a sneering, raucous laugh. Everybody laughed now — except Lois and Mrs. Green.

They had all come out of the water now, and soon the whole group returned to their three beach umbrellas. Hattie's girls immediately prepared to break camp. They took down their pea-green umbrella, folded some wet towels, and donned their beach sandals, as Hattie still bantered Caesar and Little Joe.

"Well, you sure had *yourself* a ball today," she said to Little Joe, who was sitting in the sand.

"Comin' back next Saturday?" asked grinning Little Joe.

"I jus' might at that," surmised Hattie. "We wuz here last Saturday."

"Good! Good!" Elijah broke in. "Let's *all* come back — next Saturday!" He searched every face.

"*I'll* be here," chimed Little Joe, grinning to Caesar. Captive Caesar glanced at Lois, and said nothing.

Lois and Mrs. Green were silent. Hattie, insulted, looked at them and started swelling up. "Never mind," she said pointedly to Elijah, "you jus' come on anyhow. You'll run into a slew o' folks lookin' for a good time. You don't need no *certain* people." But a little later, she and her girls all said friendly goodbyes and walked off across the sand.

The party now took a sudden downturn. All Elijah's efforts at resuscitation seemed unavailing. The westering sun was dipping toward the distant buildings of the city, and many of the bathers were leaving. Caesar and Little Joe had become bored; and Mrs. Green's boys, whining to go, kept a reproachful eye on their mother.

"Here, you boys, take some more lemonade," Elijah said quickly, reaching for the thermos jug. "Only got a little left — better get while gettin's good!" He laughed. The boys shook their heads.

On Lois he tried cajolery. Smiling, and pointing to her wet, but trim bathing suit, he asked, "What color would you say that is?"

"Lilac," said Lois, now standing.

"It sure is pretty! Prettiest on the beach!" he whispered.

Lois gave him a weak smile. Then she reached down for her beach bag, and looked at Caesar.

Caesar stood up, "Let's cut," he turned and said to Little Joe, and began taking down their orange-and-white umbrella.

Elijah was desolate. "Whatta you goin' for? It's gettin' cooler! Now's the time to *enjoy* the beach!"

"I've got to go home," Lois said.

Mrs. Green got up now; her boys had started off already. "Just a minute, Melvin," she called, frowning. Then, smiling, she turned and thanked Elijah.

He whirled around to them all. "Are we comin' back next Saturday? Come on — let's all come back! Wasn't it *great!* It was great! Don't you think? Whatta you say?" He looked now at Lois and Mrs. Green.

"We'll see," Lois said smiling. "Maybe."

"Can *you* come?" He turned to Mrs. Green.

"I'm not sure," she said. "I'll try."

"Fine! Oh, that's fine!" He turned on Caesar and Little Joe. "I'll be lookin' for you guys, hear?"

"Okay, chief," grinned Little Joe. "An' put somethin' in that lemonade, will ya?"

Everybody laughed . . . and soon they were gone.

Elijah slowly crawled back under his umbrella, although the sun's heat was almost spent. He looked about him. There was only one umbrella on the spot now, his own; where before there had been three. Cigarette butts and paper cups lay strewn where Hattie's girls had sat, and the sandy imprint of

Caesar's enormous street shoes marked his site. Mrs. Green had dropped a bobby pin. He too was caught up now by a sudden urge to go. It was hard to bear much longer—the lonesomeness. And most of the people were leaving anyway. He stirred and fidgeted in the sand, and finally started an inventory of his belongings. . . . Then his thoughts flew home, and he reconsidered. Funny—he hadn't thought of home all afternoon. Where had the time gone anyhow? . . . It seemed he'd just pulled up in the Chevy and unloaded his gear; now it was time to go home again. Then the image of solemn Randy suddenly formed in his mind, sending waves of guilt through him. He forgot where he was as the duties of his existence leapt on his back—where would he ever get Randy's fifteen dollars? He felt squarely confronted by a great blank void. It was an awful thing he had done—all for a day at the beach . . . with some sporting girls. He thought of his family and felt tiny—and him itching to come back next Saturday! Maybe Myrtle was right about him after all. Lord, if she knew what he had done. . . .

He sat there for a long time. Most of the people were gone now. The lake was quiet save for a few boys still in the water. And the sun, red like blood, had settled on the dark silhouettes of the housetops across the city. He sat beneath the umbrella just as he had at one o'clock . . . and the thought smote him. He was jolted. Then dubious. But there it was—quivering, vital, swelling inside his skull like an unwanted fetus. So this was it! He mutinied inside. So he must sell it . . . his *umbrella*. Sell it for anything—only as long as it was enough to pay back Randy. For fifteen dollars even, if necessary. He was dogged; he couldn't do it; that wasn't the answer anyway. But the thought clawed and clung to him, rebuking and coaxing him by turns, until it finally became conviction. He must do it; it was the right thing to do; the only thing to do. Maybe then the awful weight would lift, the dull commotion in his stomach cease. He got up and started collecting his belongings; placed the thermos jug, sunglasses, towel, cigarettes, and little rug together in a neat pile, to be carried to the Chevy later. Then he turned to face his umbrella. Its red and white stripes stood defiant against the wide, churned-up sand. He stood for a moment mooning at it. Then he carefully let it down and, carrying it in his right hand, went off across the sand.

The sun now had gone down behind the vast city in a shower of crimson-golden glints, and on the beach only a few stragglers remained. For his first prospects, he approached two teen-age boys, but suddenly realizing they had no money, he turned away and went over to an old woman, squat and black, in street clothes—a spectator—who stood gazing eastward out across the lake. She held in her hand a little black book, with red-edged pages, which looked like the *New Testament*. He smiled at her. "Wanna buy a nice new beach umbrella?" He held out the collapsed umbrella toward her.

She gave him a beatific smile, but shook her head. "No, son," she said, "that ain't what *I* want." And she turned to gaze out on the lake again.

For a moment he still held the umbrella out, with a question mark on his face. "Okay, then," he finally said, and went on.

Next he hurried to the water's edge, where he saw a man and two women preparing to leave. "Wanna buy a nice new beach umbrella?" His voice sounded high-pitched, as he opened the umbrella over his head. "It's brand-new. I'll sell it for fifteen dollars — it cost a lot more'n that."

The man was hostile, and glared. Finally he said, "Whatta you take me for — a fool?"

Elijah looked bewildered, and made no answer. He observed the man for a moment. Finally he let the umbrella down. As he moved away, he heard the man say to the women, "It's hot — he stole it somewhere."

Close by, another man sat alone in the sand. Elijah started toward him. The man wore trousers, but was stripped to the waist, and bent over intent on some task in his lap. When Elijah reached him, he looked up from half a hatful of cigarette butts he was breaking open for the tobacco he collected in a little paper bag. He grinned at Elijah, who meant now to pass on.

"No, I ain't interested either, buddy," the man insisted as Elijah passed him. "Not me. I jus' got *outa* jail las' week — an' ain't goin' back for no umbrella." He laughed, as Elijah kept on.

Now he saw three women, still in their bathing suits, sitting together near the diving board. They were the only people he had not yet tried — except the one lifeguard left. As he approached them, he saw that all three wore glasses and were sedate. Some schoolteachers maybe, he thought, or office workers. They were talking — until they saw him coming; then they stopped. One of them was plump, but a smooth dark brown, and sat with a towel around her shoulders. Elijah addressed them through her: "Wanna buy a nice beach umbrella?" And again he opened the umbrella over his head.

"Gee! It's beautiful," the plump woman said to the others. "But where'd you get?" she suddenly asked Elijah, polite mistrust entering her voice.

"I bought it — just this week."

The three women looked at each other. "Why do you want to sell it so soon, then?" a second woman said.

Elijah grinned. "I need the money."

"Well!" The plump woman was exasperated. "*No*, we don't want it." And they turned from him. He stood for a while, watching them; finally he let the umbrella down and moved on.

Only the lifeguard was left. He was a huge youngster, not over twenty, and brawny and black, as he bent over cleaning out his beached rowboat. Elijah approached him so suddenly he looked up startled.

"Would you be interested in this umbrella?" Elijah said, and proffered the umbrella. "It's brand-new — I just bought it Tuesday. I'll sell it cheap." There was urgency in his voice.

The lifeguard gave him a queer stare; and then peered off toward the Outer Drive, as if looking for help. "You're lucky as hell," he finally said. "The cops just now cruised by — up on the Drive. I'd have turned you in so quick it'd made your head swim. Now you get the hell outa here." He was menacing.

Elijah was angry. "Whatta you mean? I *bought* this umbrella — it's mine."

The lifeguard took a step toward him. "I said you better get the hell outa here! An' I mean it! *You thievin' bastard, you!*"

Elijah, frightened now, gave ground. He turned and walked away a few steps; and then slowed up, as if an adequate answer had hit him. He stood for a moment. But finally he walked on, the umbrella drooping in his hand.

He walked up the gravelly slope now toward the Chevy, forgetting his little pile of belongings left in the sand. When he reached the car, and opened the trunk, he remembered; and went back down and gathered them up. He returned, threw them in the trunk and, without dressing, went around and climbed under the steering wheel. He was scared, shaken; and before starting the motor sat looking out on the lake. It was seven o'clock; the sky was waning pale, the beach forsaken, leaving a sense of perfect stillness and approaching night; the only sound was a gentle lapping of the water against the sand — one moderate *hallo-o-o-o* would have carried across to Michigan. He looked down at the beach. Where were they all now — the funny, proud, laughing people? Eating their dinners, he supposed, in a variety of homes. And all the beautiful umbrellas — where were they? Without their colors the beach was so deserted. Ah, the beach . . . after pouring hot ore all week out at the Youngstown Sheet and Tube, he would probably be too fagged out for the beach. But maybe he wouldn't — who knew? It was great while it lasted . . . great. And his umbrella . . . he didn't know what he'd do with that . . . he might never need it again. He'd keep it, though — and see. Ha! . . . hadn't he sweat to get it! . . . and they thought he had stolen it . . . stolen it . . . ah . . . and maybe they were right. He sat for a few moments longer. Finally he started the motor, and took the old Chevy out onto the Drive in the pink-hued twilight. But down on the beach the sun was still shining.

# Willard Motley

## (1912-65)

WILLARD MOTLEY *was born in Chicago in 1912 and grew up in an all-white neighborhood on the South Side. Between 1929 and 1940, he traveled to both coasts and held a variety of menial jobs before he began working for the WPA Writer's Project. His experience in the West Side slums provided him with valuable material that he was eventually to incorporate into his first and most successful novel,* Knock on Any Door *(1947). Motley's other works of fiction include* We Fished All Night *(1951),* Let No Man Write My Epitaph *(1958), and the posthumously published* Let Noon Be Fair *(1966). He moved to Mexico in 1951 and died in Mexico City of gangrene in 1965 at the age of fifty-two.*

*While Motley, an African American, benefitted from the publication of Richard Wright's* Native Son *(1940) — a national best-seller and the first novel by an African American to be selected by the Book of the Month Club — his work more closely resembles that of Nelson Algren than of Wright. Indeed, Algren, an early editor and mentor, once noted that Motley "wrote about white people for white people." This is undeniably an exaggeration, yet it is true that compared to Wright, or to other African-American writers from Chicago like Cyrus Colter, Lorraine Hansberry, and Leon Forrest, Motley seems relatively uninterested in questions of race.*

Knock on Any Door *began as a huge sprawling work of 600,000 words; once edited into its present form at less than half that length, the book became a best-seller and eventually spawned a movie starring John Derek and Humphrey Bogart. The novel follows the descent into crime of Nick Romano, an Italian-American and former altar boy. Convicted for killing a cop, "Pretty Boy" Romano, whose motto is "Live fast, die young, and make a good-looking corpse," becomes something of a media star before he is finally electrocuted. In an unpublished introduction to* Knock on Any Door, *Motley outlined his aesthetic: "the writer approaches his subject matter — his fellow man — in humility and understanding, in sympathy and identification. And he tries — only the serious writer knows how hard — to tell the truth, frankly and unshrinkingly." That attempt to faithfully depict poverty in the city's rough West Side is clearly successful. Chapter 17, in which Nick wanders through the area around the old Maxwell Street market, shows Motley at his best.*

◆ ◆ ◆

*from* KNOCK ON ANY DOOR

On Halsted Street Nick heard a loud and continuous honking of automobile horns. He turned and saw a wedding procession. Streamers of colored tissue paper were wrapped around the cars. On the backs of the cars were big, unevenly lettered signs: WATCH CHICAGO GROW! WE CAN'T WAIT FOR TONIGHT. GRAND OPENING TONIGHT.

The cars stopped before a photographer's shop. The wedding party went across the sidewalk in front of Nick. The bride wasn't young; she was fat and wore a lacy white veil that trailed to widened-out hips. The bridesmaids wore pink and blue and green dresses made out of stuff that looked like curtains. The men were in tuxedos with flowers in the buttonholes and the women held their arms. Nick walked past them. He looked back at the dresses that swept against the dirty sidewalks, the hands holding them up a little and the men dressed like a dead man he had seen once.

Nick walked on, looking at everything. There were Italian stores crowded together, with spaghetti, olives, tomato purée for sale. He saw baskets with live snails in them: 10¢ A POUND. Nick, thinking of people eating them, spat on the sidewalk. At the corner of 12th Street taxi drivers stood in groups, smoking and talking. The streets were crowded with people. All kinds of people. Negroes in flashy clothes — high-waisted pants, wide-brimmed hats, loud shirts. Women dragging kids by the hand. Young Mexican fellows with black hair and blue sport shirts worn outside their pants and open at the neck. Kids, lots of kids. Two gypsy women passed Nick. They wore several different-colored skirts, red and blue, yellow, green. They had big yellow earrings, dangling, and long braids; and their dresses were so low in front that if they stooped over you could have seen their belly buttons. There were beggars with sad eyes, with mouth organs, with hands held out. A blind man's cane tapped the sidewalk. Dress shops, hat shops, men's clothing stores were crowded together along Halsted, hiding the slum streets behind them. Hiding the synagogues, the Greek church, the Negro storefront churches, the taverns, the maternity center, the public bath.

Nick turned onto Maxwell Street. Before him stretched the Maxwell Street Market extending between low, weather-grimed buildings that knelt to the sidewalk on their sagging foundations. On the sidewalk were long rows of stands set one next to the other as far as he could see. On the stands were dumped anything you wanted to buy: overalls, dresses, trinkets, old clocks, ties, gloves — anything. On what space was left near the curb were pushcarts that could be wheeled away at night. There were still other rough stands — just planks set up across loose-jointed wooden horses: hats for a quarter apiece, vegetables, curtains, pyramid-piled stacks of shoes tied together by their laces —

everything. From wooden beams over store fronts, over the ragged awnings, hung overcoats, dresses, suits and aprons waving in the air like pennants. The noises were radios turned as high as they could go, recordshop victrolas playing a few circles of a song before being switched to another, men and women shouting their wares in hoarse, rasping voices, Jewish words, Italian words, Polish and Russian words, Spanish, mixed-up English. And once in a while you heard a chicken cackling or a baby crying. The smells were hot dog, garlic, fish, steam table, cheese, pickle, garbage can, mould and urine smells.

Behind Hewitt's Restaurant Nick saw the stinking garbage cans pressed full and running over. Bums were picking through the garbage, carefully and without shame. They took out scraps of meat, bones, crusts of bread. They had wrinkled brown bags. Into the bags they dumped stale buns, blue-stencilled ham fat, chewed chops, soft tomatoes. The well-dressed people coming off the curb stared at them.

Down Maxwell the people were crowded in thick, shoulder to shoulder, tripping over each other, pushing down both sides of the street in a nosey, bargain-hunting crowd. The pavement had no rest from the shuffle of their feet. They even took up every bit of room in the middle of the street as they wove around the pushcarts. The venders gestured and lifted their wares for the people to see. They shouted back and forth to each other in Yiddish over their shoes, their aprons, their vegetables.

Three boys in old clothes walked along Maxwell. One of them had a sailor's white oval of cap on the back of his head. He was blond, bowlegged. He talked huskily. When Nick saw him later he was alone and ran out of a shop with two gesticulating and cursing Jews after him and a sweater in his hands. All the Jews along the lines of stalls shouted angrily, cursed, moaned. A couple of women, powdered-up and well-dressed, said, "A shame! A shame!" But when the kid ran down a side street with the Jews still after him the people squatting on the steps of the miserable little slum houses only laughed.

Nick turned off the market street. But he didn't get away from it. Down this street, on both sides, stood men in straw hats and vests and baggy pants with cages of pigeons at their feet. Foreign-appearing men, but lighter than Italians, stood around looking at the pigeons, taking them in their hands, spreading out their wings gently and examining their feet. The birds rested in the men's palms with caged tenseness. The venders talked, bargained, argued. And one vender released a homing pigeon. The pigeon flew slowly above his head, seemed to shake out his long-pinioned wings, hung there uncertainly a minute just over the heads of all the people on the street. Then, even with the factory building across the street, over the shacks and hovels, over the high-spired cross of St. Francis' Church the gray pigeon wheeled in large, widening circles. And out of sight.

Nick wandered around, up and down side streets. A short-haired, dirty-white puppy, tail working, looked back over his shoulder at his master and hopped down off a curbstone. The automobile was coming fast. It didn't stop, didn't slow. The dog yelped once, sharply, and lay in the street. "Oh!" Nick gasped, scared and with pity.

The puppy lay in the gutter belching blood. His skinny legs pawed the air. A crowd, staring, pushed in on tiptoe. The puppy's head lay in an oil puddle. His blood, spewing out of his mouth, mixed with the oil. The dog's master, unconcerned, walked on down the street. "See, that's what will happen to you if you don't stay out of the street," a woman told her small boy as she pulled him along by the hand. The boy looked back at the dog fearfully, his nose running and his eyes filling up.

Nick wandered on, not noticing things at first, thinking about the puppy. And underneath, farther from the surface, ran disconnected memories of Tommy, Jesse, Rocky.

It got later and it got more exciting. Down one street there was a fight. They were two niggers. Young guys. One was short and husky and black. The other was bigger and he was the one who pulled the knife that went zigzag in the air where the black one's face had been before he jerked it away. The black one ran. The guy with the knife was right on his tail with the knife held over his head, slashing. There were paving rocks in the alley. It didn't take the black guy long to get to them; and he starting throwing them at the fellow with the knife. Nick was on the small guy's side. Because he was little and because he didn't have a knife.

A crowd of Negroes watched from the sidewalk. As a rock sailed past the tall yellow nigger's head some fellow in the crowd yelled, "Ball! — little too wide." Everybody laughed. Another rock missed his head and the fellow shouted, "Ball two!" On the porch of one of the houses an old white couple sat on the seat cushions from an automobile. They weren't scared and didn't go into the house but just sat watching indifferently. A Negro sat on a sagging balcony with his feet propped up in front of him. He chewed an apple and watched the fight. The woolly heads of three Negro women came out of the first floor windows of a shack next door. Three black hands clutching beer mugs rested on the window sills. The bums and transients at the Shelter across the street lined the fence in front of the old school building that was their home. One transient lay sleeping in the doorway. His shoes were off. His dirty toes came up out of the holes of his socks. His head, in the crushed felt hat, was on the concrete. Over him, painted on the old boards of the door, was an unevenly lettered sign some bum had painted: HOOVER HOTEL. The words were faded from rain and some later hobo had drawn a chalk mark through the HOOVER and scrawled over it: ROOSEVELT.

On the stone step of a tenement sat a Mexican boy watching a crap game in the middle of the street. After an indecisive pause Nick sat next to him. After a while the Mexican kid pulled out a package of cigarettes, lit one, saw Nick there on the step and shoved the pack at him without saying anything. In the street the crap-shooters saw nothing but the black and white cubes tangoing across the dirty pavement.

"Two bits he don't come."

"You're covered!"

Two big-shouldered men in dark suits walked along the sidewalk, in the shadows, watching. Nick look at them uneasily and said to the Mexican boy, "They're going to be raided." The Mexican smiled and shook his head no. "You're not from around here, are you?"

"No," Nick said.

One of the dicks caught the eye of the teen-aged fellow who was running the game. The dick lifted a long, beckoning finger. The youth walked over to him with his hand in his pocket. They stood close together. Their hands touched. They walked their opposite ways.

"Come on seven, come on seven, baby needs shoes."

"See how we do things down here," the Mexican said to Nick a little proudly.

Nick, losing his way a dozen times, went home. Yes, they were smart down there.

Something pulled him back to Maxwell Street. Right after supper he got up and started for the door. "Where you going, Nick?" Ma wanted to know.

"Aw, for a walk," and outside the door, "for Christ sake!"

"You come back here! You might get lost," Ma called.

Nick had already hit the bottom step.

This was a *big* night. The crowd, gathering from all the slum houses, talked about the mayor coming to make a speech. The whole neighborhood was turning out.

They came across the cracked sidewalks and dirty street stones.

There was music at the carnival. And laughter.

The street lamps leaned drunkenly and were an easy target for the kids' rocks. Under the now deserted Maxwell stands the cats fought their fights. In an alley a bottle of fifteen-cents-a-pint wine went the rounds. On a stand, blotted out by the darkness, a boy had his arm around a girl. They looked up, through the threading trails of smoke, at the moon. In the alley an empty bottle crashed against a brick wall and tinkled in shattered glass to the ground.

Nick walked down the carnival street, edging his way through the crowd. One end of the street had been sectioned off. Wooden horses made an uneven circle around the part that was for dancing. A crayoned sign tacked to one of the horses read: 5¢ A DANCE. A string of sickly red bulbs crossed above the dance space. There was a jukebox playing constantly. Its long electric cord went across the sidewalk to a second story window. A group of young Italian boys, fourteen to eighteen years old, loafed near the wooden horses, straddling them, laughing, joking, poking fun. The jukebox beat its drums, moaned with its saxophones, swung the music out loudly —

> Come on and hear, come on and hear
> Alexander's rag-time band —
> Come on and hear, come on and hear, —
> It's the best band in the land. . . .

The boys each grabbed another boy and, outside the circle of wooden horses, went into their wild, imitative dance.

The music said —

> Come on along, come on along —
> Let me take you by the hand
> Up to the man, up to the man
> Who's the leader of the band. . . .

The boys protruded their rear ends. They kicked their toes against the street. Some postured like girls, smirking, touching their hair, putting their cheeks up against their partners'.

A youth escorted a girl to the dance floor entrance and, embarrassed, led her out to dance on the empty pavement. The ridiculing boys, recognizing him, hurdled the horses, clapped their hands in time to the music, patted their feet to its rhythm, began chanting the words.

The boys joined hands and circled him, shouting, laughing, ribbing him.

The shuffle of feet in broken shoes, in turned-over heels, came across the night pavement and under the electric wreath of lights over the middle of the street. Nick leaned against a stand and watched them. There were women ready to drop kids into the world. There were the tough faces of boys who had known no boyhood and the broadened bodies of girls who had known everything before they were fourteen. There were little kids, looking like they belonged to no one — with just a dress pulled over their heads, with their stockings hanging down over their shoes and their shoe laces dragging. Lots of kids. And young fellows. And girls. Boys, half-grown, with arms encircled, walked down the carnival pavement. Girls in slacks, in tight-fitting sweaters, whispered together or giggled. There were a couple of drunks staggering up to beer stalls. Negro youths, black, brown, yellow, walked down the middle of the street in baseball shirts and caps. They walked loose-jointed with all the ancient African grace retained. And when the sob of the music caught their ears it affected their feet.

Wheels of chance spun. Bingo games were in full swing with a loud voice coming out over the microphone to announce the numbers. At one stand Italian sausages on long, swordlike spears baked over charcoal pan-fires. The smoke curled up and was lost overhead. In the houses lining each side of the street people were leaning out the windows with their elbows on the sills.

The mayor came in a shiny new car, and a policeman opened up the wooden horses that blocked off the street to let his car pass.

The mayor said he had been raised in the neighborhood and pointed toward the street where his school was. The mayor said, "I came from the bottom and I'm still with the bottom!" And everybody cheered. The mayor said, "We can thank God for living in a great country and a great city." And everybody cheered. The mayor said, "Each boy in this neighborhood has the same chance I had to make his place in the world."

The mayor left. The crowd was good-natured and happy all over the carnival street. There was a colored orchestra by the dance floor now. It played hot music from the back of a truck. The crowd ringed a drunken Irishman who danced in the street, his hat sliding over his eyes. Then a colored boy and girl did a jitterbug dance while the crowd clapped hands, keeping time with the music. They could dance! Then a Jewish girl in a high school sweater with bumps and her skinny partner in loud-colored trousers and glasses took over. They were almost as good. Then, for a nickel you could dance inside the ring of wooden horses.

Only a few people danced. Fellows and girls stood around uncertain and half-embarrassed. A lean young Negro, black as the hat he wore, came out of the crowd and asked a pretty Italian girl in her teens for a dance. She smiled and nodded. Together they went under the strings of electric bulbs. Through the wild steps of the jitterbug dance he took her. They whirled across the dirty asphalt and back. They swayed to the music. They answered its harsh notes. The crowd, three-fourths white, watched, applauded when they were finished. The black boy escorted the Italian girl back to the fringe of the crowd, thanked her for the dance and went on his way.

Nick stayed late. When the carnival was no longer interesting he walked around the side streets. By the hot-dog stand on Newberry and Maxwell, propped against an empty stand were two women. One of them looked only about seventeen. She still had a childishness about her lips and an undefinable freshness. In the half-dark of the street they were smoking cigarettes.

One of the Maxwell Street merchants, a little round Jew in a straw hat, came along the sidewalk. When he saw the two women sitting there he tipped his hat to them. He said, "Hello, girls." Then he walked over closer, let his voice drop down and said confidentially, "Better be careful. The heat is on."

"How often do we have to pay them goddamn cops!" the older woman complained, half-whining.

Nick sat near where the women were, listening and smoking a cigarette he had sneaked out of Aunt Rosa's pack. The two women kicked their heels against the stand. They lit cigarettes and complained about "business." "I can't make fifty cents. If I was getting drunk I know I'd make it," said the older one. "I'd run up and grab somebody."

"You gotta eat," said the young one, laughing, but her eyes didn't match her laugh.

A man came through the shadows. The young whore whispered loud enough for his ear, "Want to go home with me, honey?"

The man walked slow. He hung on the corner, uncertain. The young whore's heels struck against the sidewalk. She dug her elbow into the other woman's side and said, matter-of-fact, "Here I go again."

The man waited on the corner. She caught up with him, said something under her breath, walked half a step in front. He followed her with one hand in his pocket.

Nick smoked the second half of his cigarette and went home. On the way he went to see if the dog was still there.

He was.

He lay in the gutter. The grime of the street had sooted his white coat. Red spots were crusted on it. Flies had already commenced to carry bits of him away.

And newspapers swirled around him like the withered petals of flowers.

In the street in the dark ahead of Nick were the reform school grounds. Again he was staring through the little diamonds of its tall wire fence.

# Studs Terkel
## (b. 1912)

*Though* LOUIS "STUDS" TERKEL *often speaks of his "wildly ambivalent" feelings for Chicago, he has lived here since he was ten, adopted his nickname from James T. Farrell's colorful Chicago character Studs Lonigan, and been a fixture on its cultural scene since the mid-1940s, especially as host of his ever-popular radio program at WFMT, a position which he held until 1998. For* Division Street, *from which the following excerpts come, Terkel said he was "on the prowl," tape recorder in hand, "for a cross-section of urban thought . . . aware it would take me to suburbs, upper, lower, and middle income, as well as to the inner city itself." Such inclusiveness, as well as his concentration on and celebration of, as he calls them, "real people" and "average Americans," has led to his often being called a national treasure and living legend himself.*

*While he has referred to "average men" as people of "inchoate thought," he has been remarkable in being able to extract not only extraordinary eloquence from them during his interviews, but also an intelligence, a wit, and a recounting and reflection on feelings, memories, hopes, and disappointments that have illuminated America's history, revealing astonishing inner landscapes of attitudes about work, war, race, and the American Dream itself.*

*Among his classic books are* Division Street: America *(1967),* Hard Times: An Oral History of the Great Depression *(1970),* Working: People Talk about What They Do All Day and How They Feel about What They Do *(1974),* The Great Divide: Second Thoughts on the American Dream *(1988), and* RACE: How Black and Whites Think and Feel about the American Obsession *(1992). His 1984* "The Good War": An Oral History of World War II, *won the 1985 Pulitzer Prize.*

✦ ✦ ✦

*Benny Bearskin, 45*

*The American Indian Center. It is on the North Side, an area of many transients —
elderly pensioners, Appalachians, and many of the nine thousand American Indians
who live in Chicago.*

*Here, on a winter's Saturday night, such as this one, are ceremonial dances,
songs, and stories. We're seated in the office; families are assembling in the hall.*

*It is the Center's purpose, in the words of Benny Bearskin, "to preserve and fos-
ter the cultural values of the American Indian, at the same time helping him to make
an adjustment to an urban society."*

Getting urbanized. I like this term. It means you have to learn the ropes, just
like a person moving out from prairie country into the woods. You know,
there are certain dangers in such a transition, and it's the same way in a city.
You have to learn the ropes. And once you become urbanized, this means to
me that you're gonna settle down, and you have to have a goal to look forward to. Otherwise, I think it would drive you crazy.

I'll tell you the extent to which I'm urbanized, after being here for seventeen years. Some years ago, we went back to Nebraska, to my wife's parents'
place. And for three or four nights in a row, I'd wake up in the middle of the
night, feeling there was something drastically wrong. And it puzzled me until
I began to realize: it was quiet, that's what was wrong. There's no fire engines
or police sirens passing by, no street noises. It's funny.

I was raised all the way from the Winnebago Indian reservation in north-
east Nebraska, to Iowa, Minnesota, and Wisconsin. My father was a laborer.
He moved his family whenever there was employment. So I got an early introduction to the melting pot.

In those days, I didn't give discrimination much thought. Since we moved
around quite a lot. The one thing that stands out in my mind is that every
new school we attended, we had to go through an ordeal. The toughest fellas
wanted to see how tough we were. So we got kind of oriented that way. And if
we could whip the toughest kid, why then, we had it made from then on. We
had a lot of friends. Of course, that didn't always happen that way, either.

I came to Chicago in 1947, after I had been married, and later on I sent
for my wife and my one child and since that time we've lived here in the city.
The most important reason was that I could at least feel confident that perhaps fifty paychecks a year here . . . and you can't always get that way. Even
though it might be more pleasant to be back home, for instance, Nebraska.

*What do you call home? Do you call Nebraska home?*

Yes, I think this is one feature most Indians have in common. They have a deep attachment for the land. This has been so for a long, long time. Many different tribes of Indians are now residing in Chicago, but most of them maintain ties with the people back home. Even in cases where the older members of their families have passed away, they still make a point to go home. Many of them make the trip twice a year to go back to the place where they were born and raised.

*Some Appalachian whites in this neighborhood feel the same way. Home is not the city, but where they came from.*

I guess there is that one similarity. When we were in Minnesota, we listened to the Grand Old Opry on these long winter nights. My brother and I used to play fiddle and guitar for square dances. I guess that was the only phase of my life when I was interested in music other than Indian music. As a matter of fact, I still own my violin. I kept it probably for sentimental reasons. I think the country fiddler was expressing some mood to his instrument. And Indian music is similar in that way, too. There are songs that we have which might have a sad mood to it. There are others that are very joyous and sort of light-hearted. And I found that this country and hill music had this sort of appeal for me.

. . . You know, the federal government has made mistakes . . . and one time, dating back to 1887, under the Allotment Act that Congress passed, they thought that evidently all the Indian needed was a plow and a pair of horses and harnesses and some seed and he'd become a farmer overnight. This didn't happen by any means. So judging by this, I would find it very difficult if I were used to the Southern hill country and then make an abrupt changeover and finding myself in a large city.

I was fortunate in that, as I grew up, at least part of my youth was spent in a city. I did a lot of common labor the first few years, and then the war came along, the Second World War. And I picked up the welding trade, worked in a shipyard, worked in a powder plant. And after following the welding trade for some seven years, I moved to Chicago, and I became a union boilermaker, which I am yet today.

I believe, in the long run, automation will affect my trade. Because in the length of time that I've been at it, design has changed so radically in the last few years. They can erect a powerhouse perhaps twice the size of a powerhouse that was built ten years ago, and they can do it with several thousand man-hours less. And, you know, in the long run, this process of change continues, it's gonna have a great effect on the tradesman.

On the basis of my experience, I'd say about nine out of ten companies judge you solely on your performance and only about one out of ten would have any reservation because of race. This doesn't say much, because I don't know what happens to anyone else.

The one out of ten? Well, they come up with some kind of excuse that we think you can do the work, and we'll call you whenever we have an opening, and that's the end of that.

*You put down on the application:* INDIAN?

Yes, always. I think that's a source of pride. I think a lot of fellas think this is a source of pride, because we enjoy the distinction that no other person has. We are at home, while everyone else came here from somewhere else.

And I believe that, as time goes on, that society becomes more and more complex, there is that need for a basic pride in order to have something on which to build character. If you don't have that pride, well, then you have no identity. We understand that all the states have these mental institutions that are bulging at the seams. This is evidence of social and psychological maladjustment. So we have to have some values, I believe.

There is possibly a class of Indian youth that doesn't have these values. I've seen signs of this in my travels. Back in 1961, I covered about ninety-five percent of the reservations to the north and a little to the west. During these times I saw the cultural deterioration that some of these children are growing up with.

There are some areas where the transition from Indian culture to white culture is going on, and some of the children are born into a situation where the old values are already lost. There being no basic economies in these areas, there's much poverty. And nothing of the white culture is available to them. So they're lost in between.

And it is this type of young Indian who is ashamed he is an Indian. Because he doesn't realize, there's nobody ever told him: his ancestors were a noble race of men, who developed over many centuries a way of life, primitive though it was; it existed without prisons, hospitals, jails, courts or anything, or insane asylums or currency or anything. Yet an Indian back in those days was able to live from babyhood till all the hair on his head became white, and he lived a life of complete fulfillment. With no regrets at the end. You rarely see that in this day and age.

Four of our children were born here in this city, and yet, I think, they're oriented as American Indians. I make it a point to take them on my vacation trips in the summer, always to a different reservation to get acquainted with the people of the tribe. We take photographs, we record the songs that are sung, we participate in dancing and compete for prizes. . . .

I have five now. My wife is a full-blooded Winnebago. I met her on the Nebraska reservation.

(Laughs.) Oh, one time we had a little trouble with housing. In 1960 the work was kind of slack, there wasn't anything going on about that time. So I got together with three other boilermakers, and we went up to Pierre, South Dakota, where the U.S. Army Corps of Engineers had this dam-construction project going on. While I was up there, the rents were raised where I had been living on the West Side. Well, my wife, with the help of the parish priest, found another apartment.

But I was kind of worried about being eight hundred miles from home, so I jumped on a train and came back to help her make the move. We made the move, and it happened that weekend the American Indian Center was holding a show. So after we got everything moved, we all went down to the theater. And after the show, we all went to the Center and had coffee and a good visit with everyone.

When we went back to the apartment on the West Side, the first thing we discovered that most of the windows were smashed. Well, I called the Chicago police. The police came out there, and we had a police car in front of the door for about two weeks, I guess. But . . .

I still don't know who did it, because it was done at night. They evidently thought we were Mexicans. Well, when the police asked me about this, I said I was sorry to disappoint anybody. As much as I admire Mexicans, I'm not a Mexican. I'm an American Indian.

And, well, during the following days, there were representatives of many different organizations who came out and talked to us. There was a man from the Chicago Commission on Human Relations, the Illinois Commission, from the National Conference of Christians and Jews, American Friends Service Committee, Bureau of Indian Affairs, Catholic Interracial Council. You know, there was very little that they could do.

If I didn't have any children to worry about — they would have to walk to school about four, five blocks — I think I would have stayed. It was one of those arrangements where the thing was operated by a trust. Even the newspapers couldn't find out who was the actual owner. But I found out later that this was right inside the battle lines that had already been established. It was an old Italian neighborhood, and just across the line east of us were Puerto Ricans, Southern whites, and to the South were Negroes. And since we were different, we posed a threat. They thought we were breaking the dike or something. It was kind of enlightening, really, after it was over.

The most amusing part of it was the Chicago *Defender*[1] ran a cartoon. Yeah, there was a picture of an Indian family leaving a neighborhood in an old jalopy, and the people were all shouting. And then the label said, the caption said:

_____

1. Chicago's leading Negro newspaper.

These fellas just got off the boat. (Laughs.) The fellas just got off the boat were running the first Americans out of the neighborhood.

If we go back three generations in any given family, you see that perhaps our grandfathers had no education at all. But your fathers had a little, and we've had a little more than our fathers have had, and our children are getting a college education. We also see the pattern in the last two states that granted the Indian the right to vote: New Mexico and Arizona. Strange, but these are the two areas where the Indians really get out and vote when an election comes up. They realize they can swing an election in some areas of the country.

The Indian has little in common with the Negro, other than they are both minority groups. The American Negro, according to Indian observation, is that the Negro's culture, his entire culture, is obtained from the white man. *Whereas*, the American Indian still retains his own culture. For instance, you go back to the first sit-ins at lunch counters. During these periods, Indians felt that this was kind of ridiculous, because I mean after all, what was a lunch counter from an Indian's point of view? Or the front seat of a bus? Or the freedom to sit in any railroad car you want to? The Indian, in his mind, possesses values that the white man never dreamed of, which are much more important to him.

Some Indians take a stand for or against the Negro Revolution. But there are many who do not take a stand, they want to wait and see, and watch with interest. I believe that they understand, because they have an innate sense of justice, because of their heritage.

I think those Indians who retain the greatest amount of their cultural heritage are really very fortunate, because they feel that it's more important to retain one's dignity and integrity and go through life in this manner, than spending all their energy on an accumulation of material wealth. They find this a frustrating situation. I think the Indian is the only nationality under the system who has resisted this melting-pot concept. Everybody else want to jump in, they view this idea, jumping in and becoming American or losing identity.

I don't think the flame has ever went out. Of course, we do have exceptions. We have many Indians who have been orphaned at an early age, who have become completely acculturated and know nothing of their heritage.

No, I don't think there's much bitterness retained toward the white man. I think that certainly some of the older people can recall some of the — *many* of the atrocities that were perpetrated against the various tribes. But they more or less view it as being part of an era.

I believe the Indian sees irony in specific situations. What appears to be ironic to him is the recent Supreme Court ruling on prayer in public schools. I think the Indians felt that we almost witnessed the white man meeting himself coming back, so to speak. Because in the beginning, the foundation of this nation is supposed to be a belief in God. I think that you read some of the historical accounts of how the Puritans wiped out whole Indian tribes, burned them out, and burnt everything to the ground, and then proclaimed to the world that this is a nation so founded under God.

We then arrived at the point where the Supreme Court said you can't do it in public schools. But whether you're an atheist or not, they put the Bible in your hotel room. Indians certainly have a view in regards to things like this. During the early periods, the main motivation in the building of these big schools was one of competition for the soul of the Indian. I was baptized a Christian. Episcopalian.

I think we all share the knowledge that the Bomb has grown all out of proportion to its creator. And certainly it's nothing like warfare in the early days when warfare was pretty much of a sporting proposition. Now it's just a matter of pressing a button. And some of the older Indians point out: in the earliest times, humility was preached and practiced, which was supposed to attain nearness to one's Creator. How in the world is a man who can kill thousands of people just by pressing a button going to be humble enough to think of his Creator? It can't be done.

It's so impersonal. I think this makes itself felt in many situations. For instance, when you become urbanized, you learn how to think in abstract terms. Now when you get here on Broadway, to catch a CTA bus going south, you subconsciously know there's a driver, but you take no interest in him at all as a person, he's more like an object. And it's the same way in schools. The teacher is there to do a certain function. And I think the teacher also feels that these pupils are like a bunch of bumps on a log. You know, this can be a difficult thing, especially for an Indian child, who, in his family life, he learns to establish relationships on a person-to-person basis. And he finds that this is absent in the classroom. And frequently parents go to talk to the principal, to talk to the teacher; it's just like going over there talking to a brick wall. They feel you just aren't hip. Something wrong with you, and if you don't conform, it's just too bad.

It would have to be a very unusual teacher, I think, who would see the capabilities of an unusual child. Unless the child came from an acculturated family, where you go by the rules, just rules only, instead of person-to-person. Then the Indian child would sail right through without any trouble because he'd be behaving just like the rest of the kids in school.

Of course, the adults accommodate to it, they can adjust to it. But there are exceptions to that, too, and this leads to personal problems: alcoholism and other such symptoms.

Poverty is not merely the lack of wealth, a lack of money. It goes much deeper than that. There's poverty in reservations and where there are no reservations, and where there are no Indians. What we try to do here, at the Center, is to some way, somehow, get people *involved*. Most of these people are coping with their problem on a day-to-day basis. The future is something rarely enters their minds.

I think that perhaps my early training in the home impressed me with the philosophy of our forebears. It was taught to us that if one could be of service to his people, this is one of the greatest honors there is. I think this has been a strong influence on my life. I'll never know all the answers. I'm still learning the answers.

I think there will be some radical changes taking place. We have a younger generation, in the age bracket of my oldest daughter. I think in the future Indians will make a bigger contribution. It's been pointed out that Indians should feel that if it was not for the land which *they* owned, this would not be the greatest nation on earth. . . .


*Jessie Binford, 90*

*Tall Corn Motor Motel, Marshalltown, Iowa: population, 23,000. She returned to her home town in 1963, "when Hull House went down." She had come to Chicago at the invitation of Jane Addams in 1906 and was a Hull House resident until the day of its demolition.*

*"The day isn't long enough for all I want to do. I can't begin to tell you my new interests: the people who work in this hotel, the college students from little towns around here, who come to see me and talk. And I have a tremendous correspondence with old friends from Chicago and from people I've come to know, when I was with the Juvenile Protective Association, perhaps twenty years ago. People don't forget.*

*"I'm usually alone and read a good deal in the evening. I rarely go to bed before midnight. Twilight are the hours I like best. I've been doing lots of thinking. . . ."*

*From her two-room suite, we see the brick building in which she was born.*

Here it stands, as fundamentally strong as the day it was built in 1874. And beautiful. The story we loved to hear my father tell was when his father came out from Ohio to see the new house. They sat out on the steps talking. And finally my father said to his father, "It's getting late, I think we'd better get to bed." And his father stood up and said, "I have yet slept in a house with a mortgage over my head and I don't intend to do it tonight." And he wouldn't do it. He was a Quaker. And my father often told us it was the proudest moment of his life when he said, "You don't have to go tonight, the house is paid for." That kind of morality, I hardly know how to express it. . . .

You think of the joy it must have been in those days, to build a house for his family, to help build a town. And what a wonderful beginning for a child's life. You can't get much joy out of the city any more. They've scattered the people, they're wrecking things. You'd have thought there'd be enough people in Chicago who wouldn't let them cut down those trees, just to change the route, to make it a little faster by car, to save a few minutes.[2] Our whole sense of values has changed. It's reflected here, too, in a small Iowa town.

Nobody walks here any more. He jumps into his car, of course. I walk more than anyone else in this town. I'd much rather get out in the evening at sunset and walk here then get into a car, with probably all the windows closed, because nobody wants her hair to be blown, and just drive around the city's streets. My sister gets into the car and drives to the grocery store instead of walking.

It applies to everything. Nobody seems to care about the things we feel are wrong. Take a town like this. Most people are pretty comfortable here now. They're putting lots of money into schools, especially gymnasiums. A huge, awfully expensive high school here, and the teachers complain about the lack of educational facilities. But people don't want to take any responsibility, you know. Don't bother us, we're comfortable.

Yet, the commonest thing I hear in a town like this is a fear of the unknown. They've got just that one word, Communism. Fear, fear. They don't even know what it means. They know something's wrong, why do we fight over there in Vietnam? They're just scared to death. I think they'd even accept the Bomb. I just stopped talking to lots of people, because I just didn't get anywhere. They say why worry about it? There's nothing we can do about it. That's the problem. I ask too many questions.

We began pretty well here in America, didn't we? When you think of all the promise in this country . . . I don't see how you could have found much greater promise. Or a greater beginning. So nothing stays the same. I don't know, do you? We should have the intelligence and courage to see the many changes that come into the world and will always come. But what are the intrinsic values we should not give up? That's the great challenge that faces us all.

Elmer is one of the so-called houseboys in the hotel. He's very quiet, no one pays much attention to him. But I've always liked him and we talked now and then. The other day, he said, "You have lots of books, haven't you?" And I said, "I have only a few. I wish I had all my books here." He went over and stood there, looking at the titles, and he took one book out and he said, "What's this book about?" It happened to be *What Can a Man Do?*[3] I tried very simply to explain and he put the book back. He didn't ask to take it. He could have if he wanted to. But I wasn't sure, because he's somewhat retarded. But of all the

2. The city authorities cut down 800 trees in Jackson Park to facilitate auto travel in the area.
3. Milton Mayer, *What Can a Man Do?* (Chicago: University of Chicago Press, 1964).

titles, that was the one that attracted him. It seemed to mean something to him: What can a man do?

Everything is so organized today. The corruption itself has become organized. Everything, it's part of our whole fabric. Drugs . . . the first day I came to Hull House in 1906, a mother came in and asked for Dr. Alice Hamilton, who was living there at the time. She was worried about her boy staying out of school, sleeping. Dr. Hamilton found he was taking cocaine. So we campaigned against the sale of drugs, which was carried on in the school yard. But those were individuals. It wasn't organized then.

I arrived in Chicago on an awfully hot July day. Every other place was a saloon, the streets were dirty. The air was heavy. I had left the beautiful Iowa countryside, and I wondered if I hadn't made a mistake. And no one paid much attention to me. The next morning I said to Miss Addams, "I want you to tell me what I am to do." And then she said what seemed to me the most wonderful introduction for a young person: "I wouldn't do anything if I were you for a while. Just look around and get acquainted and perhaps you'll think of something to do that none of the rest of us have thought of before." I don't know, it gave me a kind of freedom. Of not having to conform to an organization right away.

Miss Addams didn't start with any blueprints. She didn't start out with getting money for a foundation. Everything grew from the bottom up. We lived where we worked. And the place belonged to everybody. You learned life from life itself.

It was her understanding of why each person had become what he was. She didn't condemn because she understood what life does to people, to those of us who have everything and to those of us who have nothing. And now we're getting further and further away from this eternal foundation on which individual life must rest. And community life.

Miss Addams realized a whole world outside her gatepost. As a child of four, she heard her father talk of Lincoln, on the day he died. He wept when Mazzini died. And she realized then that we didn't have to live close together or know each other to be really brothers in things that matter most. Her dream of world peace became her life's goal. She paid a great price for this. Even her name was taken off the roll of the little church she belonged to, right next door to Hull House. They just struck it off. . . .

I feel most sorry today for our young people that are growing up just at this time, and the current despair they feel about lots of things. They're rebellious against they know not what. But I've come to feel, especially out here, that our great hope is in them, the youth who I think are concerned and even the ones who are confused. But they're getting a feeling of something that may affect the whole world. I don't know, I just feel it.

They know that in the huge colleges today, they're not getting what they want, what they long for. They have a feeling of sort of unreality about it.

I know a young boy who's just wandering around, a boy with Beatle haircut, a brilliant student. He's been through college. He'd rather hitchhike than take a plane, which he could easily do. He feels more comfortable. He hasn't any plans. He's like many young people today, he's restless. He's resentful about so many things which he feels are wrong — and they *are* wrong. I think there are thousands like him. But not all of them. Some just give it up, for something they don't really want. He's resentful, he can't tell you just what — but it's something pretty big.

When you look to the older people for what the young should find in them, it isn't there. Nothing's there. Do we have to wait for these young people to grow up and awaken those who are older? Or those who are in control and make all the decisions? To help us clarify the eternal truths which America seems to have forgotten? They'll meet opposition, no matter what they do.

Oh, the terrific waste! We've forgotten the spirit of youth, in things we permit to happen to them. I mean, if we're ever going to fulfill the possibility of life for all men, not only in Chicago, but in America and in the world, the spirit of youth must not be neglected. It must not be injured. It must not be killed.

*Postscript*

*Jessie Binford died July 9, 1966. She was buried in Marshalltown, Iowa.*

# John Frederick Nims
## (1913-99)

JOHN FREDERICK NIMS *was born in Muskegon, Michigan, in 1913. After attending DePaul University for two years, Nims graduated from the University of Notre Dame in 1937. He received his Master's degree and Ph.D. from the University of Chicago. Nims taught at the University of Notre Dame from 1946 to 1962. After a short time at the University of Illinois at Urbana, he moved to the University of Illinois at Chicago, where he taught for the next twenty years, with the exception of a two-year stint at the University of Florida.*

*In addition to a distinguished career as a teacher, Nims also served as the editor of* Poetry *magazine from 1978 to 1984. Moreover, his work as a translator has been highly praised. His versions of four tragedies by Euripides (1958),* Poems of St. John of the Cross *(1959),* Sappho to Valery: Poems in Translation *(1971), and the poems of Michelangelo (1998) show his intelligence and craftsmanship at work. Nims's own volumes of poetry include* The Iron Pastoral *(1947),* Knowledge of the Evening *(1960),* Of Flesh and Bone *(1967),* The Kiss: A Jambalaya *(1982),* The Six-Corned Snowflake *(1990), and* Zany in Denim *(1990).*

*While one branch of American poetry has veered off in a decidedly experimental direction, John Frederick Nims continued writing shrewd, witty, and engaging poems in traditional forms throughout his career. The small sample of his work we have included here gives an indication of his range: from the heartbreaking "The Evergreen" to the gently sardonic "Poetry Workshop (First Semester)."*

◆ ◆ ◆

## THE EVERGREEN

a.

*Under this stone, what lies?*
    A little boy's thistledown body.
*How, on so light a child*
    *Gravel hefted and hurled?*

Light? As a flower entwined
    In our shining arms. Heavy
Laid in this scale — it set
    Wailing the chains of the world.


           b.

*What did you say?* We said:
    Bedtime, dear, forever.
Time to put out the light.
    Time for the eyes to close.
*What did he do?* He lay
    In a crazyquilt of fever.
His hands were already like grasses.
    His cheek already a rose.


           c.

*How was that year?* His voice.
    Over sun on the rug, slow-turning,
Hung like a seabird lost the
    Lorn and bodiless cry.
Haunting the house. *And then?*
    I remember then. One morning
Silence like knives in the ear.
    A bird gone over the sea.


           d.

*What of his eyes?* Dark glow
    Furling the world's great surface.
Bubbles among tree lights;
    Bubbles of ferny dew.
*And his kiss?* On our cheek at evening
    Vintage: a fine bursting.
*This, and never dreamed his*
    *Span was a bubble too?*


           e.

Little head, little head,
    Frail in the air, gold aster —
Why did the great king stoop
    And smoothe those ringlets down?

*For a tinsel party-hat?*
  *It was Christmas then, remember?*
I remember grown men wept
  And couldn't lift that crown.


    f.

*Mother, these tears and tears?*
  The better to see you, darling.
*Mother, your golden glasses —*
  Have a sorry fault,
Being made for things, dear,
  Mostly: carts and marbles.
Mothers wear, for children,
  Better the stinging salt.


    g.

*What you remember most — ?*
  Is a way of death with fingers.
How they are cast in tallow
  — Lover! — webbed as one.
*Where was he going, with webs?*
  *A flying child? or a swimming?*
He knew, where he went,
  One way back to the sun.


    h.

"Tesoro!" implored the maid.
  "Treasure!" the tall signora.
*Under a distant heaven*
  *What struck the famous tower?*
Faults in the earth despairing.
  Worlds away, an orchard
Offered violets early.
  And we returned a flower.


    i.

*Where does he lie?* Hill-high
  In a vision of rolling river.
Where the dogwood curls in April
  And June is a dream of Greece.

Like a Christmas scene on china,
Snow and the stubborn myrtle.
*Those flakes from feathery heaven — ?*
Deepen all in peace.


j.

*Where does he rest, again?*
In a vision of rolling river.
*What does he know of river?*
What do we know of sea?
*Comfort? — when tomorrow's*
*Cheek by jowl with never?*
Never . . . in whose garden
Bloomed the used-to-be.


k.

*Under the snow, what lies?*
Treasure the hemlock covers —
Skysail of frost, and riding in
Starlight keen and steep.
*But the boy below?* What's here is
Gear in a sea-chest only.
Stowed for a season, then
Pleasure-bound on the deep.


## POETRY WORKSHOP (FIRST SEMESTER)

It's time. I find them waiting in the hall.
Sun-burnished Claire, with Jane not plain at all
— She's majoring in glamor. Gloria's here
With Megan, Liz, and Leila. Guenevere,
Already ripe for legend. That's our class.

In skirt or jeans they settle, start to pass
Poems around, assort them. Check their hair.
Then read their verse in turn.

                It's my despair,
That verse. For some relief, my reason flees
To plan harangues, in fantasy, like these:

"Dear, you start writing, you're an instant hag!
Wizened and blear, spine crooked, feet that drag.
From the crisp lip, what bulbous generality:
You write 'enamored of your personality'
When you mean *love;* for *naked* you write 'clad
In Nature's finery'; call yourself, when *sad,*
'Lost noodle in gloom's soup'; then soar to sing
Paeans to 'stellar orb' or 'vernal spring.'

Must your own words lampoon you — you of all! —
Gawky graffiti on a chapel wall?
Your figure, now, 's in high relief — not flat —
Incised here, and there salient. Learn from that:
Don't write on one dead level: emphasize.
Let your wit sparkle sometimes, like your eyes.
Fine turn of ankle — and why not of phrase?
Lips in live color — and yet talk in greys?

Words should be lithe and lean, compact as muscles
Our marathoners build — not stuffed in bustles.
Thought should be there like bone, that's best unseen;
Emotion run like blood through all. I mean,
Look at yourself: you're classic *Ars Poetica,*
For realms of gold (see Keats) the one right *Baedeker.*
There! — in your looking-glass The Vision's found
(Though here you're fragrant, warm, and in the round).
Study, as Yeats said, what your mirror shows:
Lines elegant with entelechy. Trust in those.
'To thine own self' — see what it means? — 'be true.'
Why? To show soul, as all fine bodies do."

But no! — no talking that way. Realler far
Than selves you play-act are the selves you are.
No: you'd be hurt, flick skirts and flounce your hair
— So ponies paw the earth. I see you there:
Head high, you stalk away. Such rhythms flow
As thrill the heart — then break it.

                              So don't go.
Just sit here with me, wordless, and effulge.
I've no more pet opinions to indulge.

Or, talk of what you will. Vacations spent,
Summers to come. Relax and loll, content
To be, if not our laureate, our delight:
The perfect poem none of us can write.

# Karl Shapiro
## (b. 1913)

*As professor of English at the University of Illinois at Chicago, and especially as editor of Chicago's influential* Poetry *magazine from 1950 to 1956,* KARL SHAPIRO *made some of his most important contributions to American poetry in Chicago. An early follower of the more formal and traditional verse of poets like W. H. Auden, and later a passionate champion of Walt Whitman and William Carlos Williams, Shapiro fashioned from these two poles a distinctive poetry — fluid and idiomatic, while still retaining much formal rigor.*

*Author of nearly twenty volumes of poetry, several volumes of literary criticism, and an autobiography; consultant in poetry for the Library of Congress from 1947 to 1948; winner of both the Bollingen and Pulitzer Prizes; a central figure in poetry education in America — despite all these achievements, Karl Shapiro considers himself the perpetual outsider. This feeling comes partly from his Jewish background, partly from his sense of the marginality of poetry in American society, and partly from his distaste of oppressive social strictures, such as the censoring of G.I. letters during World War II, which became a metaphor for oppression that animated his Pulitzer Prize – winning collection,* V-Letter and Other Poems *(1944).*

*He could be a strident social critic, but this stridency, showing through, for instance, in "The Fly" below, often combined with an unusual compassion to define another characteristic of his style — the blending of a detached, nearly cynical vision of human pride and folly with an empathy for the difficulties and disasters of life.*

◆ ◆ ◆

## The Fly

O hideous little bat, the size of snot,
With polyhedral eye and shabby clothes,
To populate the stinking cat you walk
The promontory of the dead man's nose,
Climb with the fine leg of a Duncan-Phyfe

The smoking mountains of my food
　　　And in a comic mood
In mid-air take to bed a wife.

Riding and riding with your filth of hair
On gluey feet or wing, forever coy,
Hot from the compost and green sweet decay,
Sounding your buzzer like an urchin toy —
You dot all whiteness with diminutive stool,
　　　In the tight belly of the dead
　　　　　Burrow with hungry head
And inlay maggots like a jewel.

At your approach the great horse stomps and paws
Bringing the hurricane of his heavy tail;
Shod in disease you dare to kiss my hand
Which sweeps against you like an angry flail;
Still you return, return, trusting your wing
　　　To draw you from the hunter's reach
　　　　　That learns to kill to teach
Disorder to the tinier thing.

My peace is your disaster. For your death
Children like spiders cup their pretty hands
And wives resort to chemistry of war.
In fens of sticky paper and quicksands
You glue yourself to death. Where you are stuck
　　　You struggle hideously and beg,
　　　　　You amputate your leg
Imbedded in the amber muck.

But I, a man, must swat you with my hate,
Slap you across the air and crush your flight,
Must mangle with my shoe and smear your blood,
Expose your little guts pasty and white,
Knock your head sidewise like a drunkard's hat,
　　　Pin your wings under like a crow's,
　　　　　Tear off your flimsy clothes
And beat you as one beats a rat.

Then like Gargantua I stride among
The corpses strewn like raisins in the dust,
The broken bodies of the narrow dead
That catch the throat with fingers of disgust.
I sweep. One gyrates like a top and falls
    And stunned, stone blind, and deaf
        Buzzes its frightful F
    And dies between three cannibals.

## THE CONSCIENTIOUS OBJECTOR

The gates clanged and they walked you into jail
More tense than felons but relieved to find
The hostile world shut out, the flags that dripped
From every mother's windowpane, obscene
The bloodlust sweating from the public heart,
The dog authority slavering at your throat.
A sense of quiet, of pulling down the blind
Possessed you. Punishment you felt was clean.

The decks, the catwalks, and the narrow light
Composed a ship. This was a mutinous crew
Troubling the captains for plain decencies,
A Mayflower brim with pilgrims headed out
To establish new theocracies to west,
A Noah's ark coasting the topmost seas
Ten miles above the sodomites and fish.
These inmates loved the only living doves.

Like all men hunted from the world you made
A good community, voyaging the storm
To no safe Plymouth or green Ararat;
Trouble or calm, the men with Bibles prayed,
The gaunt politicals construed our hate.
The opposite of all armies, you were best
Opposing uniformity and yourselves;
Prison and personality were your fate.

You suffered not so physically but knew
Maltreatment, hunger, ennui of the mind.

Well might the soldier kissing the hot beach
Erupting in his face damn all your kind.
Yet you who saved neither yourselves nor us
Are equally with those who shed the blood
The heroes of our cause. Your conscience is
What we come back to in the armistice.

## The First Time

Behind shut doors, in shadowy quarantine,
There shines the lamp of iodine and rose
That stains all love with its medicinal bloom.
This boy, who is no more than seventeen,
Not knowing what to do, takes off his clothes
As one might in a doctor's anteroom.

Then in a cross-draft of fear and shame
Feels love hysterically burn away,
A candle swimming down to nothingness
Put out by its own wetted gusts of flame,
And he stands smooth as uncarved ivory
Heavily cured for some expert caress.

And finally sees the always open door
That is invisible till the time has come,
And half falls through as through a rotten wall
To where chairs twist with dragons from the floor
And the great bed drugged with its own perfume
Spreads its carnivorous flower-mouth for all.

The girl is sitting with her back to him;
She wears a black thing and she rakes her hair,
Hauling her round face upward like moonrise;
She is younger than he, her angled arms are slim
And like a country girl her feet are bare.
She watches him behind her with old eyes,

Transfixing him in space like some grotesque,
Far, far from her where he is still alone
And being here is more and more untrue.

Then she turns round, as one turns at a desk,
And looks at him, too naked and too soon,
And almost gently asks: *Are you a Jew?*

## HOMEWRECK

By and large there is no blood,
Police reports to the contrary notwithstanding,
But lots of ichor, a few missing books,
A hasty and disproportionate money transaction
And a sudden enlargement of space.

Three parties form the usual cast,
One happy, one in a rage, and one in the wings,
A telephone rings and rings and rings,
Incinerators open and close and open
And the dramatis personae have all lost face

Though they themselves don't think so
Or try not to think so because the immediate public
Is immediately involved,
Greedy to know what kind of problem is solved
By a seriously departing suitcase.

The public waits for the party in the wings
Who is no longer incognito, who
Has achieved stardom in a matinee
And appears shyly to complete the play
And just as shyly is proferred — an ashtray.

# Saul Bellow

## (b. 1915)

The only Chicago writer to receive the Nobel Prize for Literature (1976), SAUL BELLOW is widely considered one of the greatest American novelists of the twentieth century. Bellow was born near Montreal, Canada, in 1915 and moved to Chicago when he was nine. Raised in an Orthodox Jewish household where he was fluent in Yiddish, Bellow was early on acutely conscious of the Jewish American experience. As an undergraduate, he attended the University of Chicago, where he was later a faculty member on the Committee for Social Thought. He received his B.S. from Northwestern University.

Bellow's novels include The Adventures of Augie March (1953), a picaresque work set largely in Chicago; Henderson the Rain King (1959); Herzog (1964), winner of the National Book Award; Mr. Sammler's Planet (1970), another National Book Award winner; and The Dean's December (1982). In all of them, Bellow's exuberance as an artist often seems in conflict with his cynical view of human nature. "Bellow is a moralist," critic Mark Schechner argues, "and his heroes' ability to face up to what is given, historically or psychologically, is usually the moral point of each book."

Although he is certainly an accomplished writer of short fiction, as Mosby's Memoirs (1968) and Him with His Foot in His Mouth and Other Stories (1984) make plain, it is Bellow's novels that highlight his expansive imagination and linguistic daring to best advantage. The excerpt below is from early on in the Pulitzer Prize–winning novel Humboldt's Gift (1975). The narrator, Charlie Citrine, a beleaguered writer whose best days appear to be behind him, is driven around Chicago by Rinaldo Cantabile, a small-time gangster to whom Citrine has stopped payment on a check after a crooked poker game. In a brilliant set piece that surveys life far above the city's streets, Citrine and Cantabile move from the Playboy Building (now 919 North Michigan Avenue) to the John Hancock Building to a skyscraper still under construction. Along the way, they encounter an illuminating cross section of Chicago life.

✦ ✦ ✦

I was now taken to the Playboy Club. Rinaldo was a member. He walked away from his supercar, the Bechstein of automobiles, leaving it to the car jockey. The checkroom Bunny knew him. From his behavior here I began to understand that my task was to make amends publicly. The Cantabiles had been defied. Maybe Rinaldo had been ordered at a family council to go out and repair the damage to their good bad name. And this matter of his reputation would consume a day — an entire day. And there were so many pressing needs, I had so many headaches already that I might justifiably have begged fate to give me a pass. I had a pretty good case.

"Are the people here?"

He threw over his coat. I also dropped mine. We stepped into the opulence, the semidarkness, the thick carpets of the bar where bottles shone, and sensual female forms went back and forth in an amber light. He took me by the arm into an elevator and we rose immediately to the top. Cantabile said, "We're going to see some people. When I give you the high sign, then you pay me the money and apologize."

We were standing before a table.

"Bill, I'd like to introduce Charlie Citrine," said Ronald to Bill.

"Hey, Mike, this is Ronald Cantabile," Bill said, on cue.

The rest was, Hey how are you, sit down, what'll you drink.

Bill was unknown to me, but Mike was Mike Schneiderman the gossip columnist. He was large heavy strong tanned sullen fatigued, his hair was razor styled, his cuff links were as big as his eyes, his necktie was a clumsy flap of silk brocade. He looked haughty, creased and sleepy, like certain oil-rich American Indians from Oklahoma. He drank an old-fashioned and held a cigar. His business was to sit with people in bars and restaurants. I was much too volatile for sedentary work like this, and I couldn't understand how it was done. But then I couldn't understand office jobs, either, or clerking or any of the confining occupations or routines. Many Americans described themselves as artists or intellectuals who should only have said that they were incapable of doing such work. I had many times discussed this with Von Humboldt Fleisher, and now and then with Gumbein the art critic. The work of sitting with people to discover *what was interesting* didn't seem to agree with Schneiderman either. At certain moments he looked blank and almost ill. He knew me, of course, I had once appeared on his television program, and he said, "Hello, Charlie." Then he said to Bill, "Don't you know Charlie? He's a famous person who lives in Chicago incognito."

I began to appreciate what Rinaldo had done. He had gone to great trouble to set up this encounter, pulling many strings. This Bill, a connection of his, perhaps owed the Cantabiles a favor and had agreed to produce Mike Schneiderman the columnist. Obligations were being called in all over the place. The accountancy must be very intricate, and I could see that Bill was not pleased. Bill had a Cosa Nostra look. There was something corrupt about his nose. Curving deeply at the nostrils it was powerful yet vulnerable. He had a foul nose. In a different context I would have guessed him to be a violinist who had become disgusted with music and gone into the liquor business. He had just returned from Acapulco and his skin was dark, but he was not exactly shining with health and well-being. He didn't care for Rinaldo; he appeared contemptuous of him. My sympathy at this moment was with Cantabile. He had attempted to organize what should have been a beautiful spirited encounter, worthy of the Renaissance, and only I appreciated it. Cantabile was trying to crash Mike's column. Mike of course was used to this. The would-be happy few were always after him and I suspected that there was a good deal of trading behind the scenes, *quid pro quo.* You gave Mike an item of gossip and he printed your name in bold type. The Bunny took our drink order. Up to the chin she was ravishing. Above, all was commercial anxiety. My attention was divided between the soft crease of her breasts and the look of business difficulty on her face.

We were on one of the most glamorous corners of Chicago. I dwelt on the setting. The lakeshore view was stupendous. I couldn't see it but I knew it well and felt its effect — the shining road beside the shining gold vacancy of Lake Michigan. Man had overcome the emptiness of this land. But the emptiness had given him a few good licks in return. And here we sat amid the flatteries of wealth and power with pretty maidens and booze and tailored suits, and the men wearing jewels and using scent. Schneiderman was waiting, most skeptically, for an item he could use in his column. In the right context, I was good copy. People in Chicago are impressed with the fact that I am taken seriously elsewhere. I have now and then been asked to cocktail parties by culturally ambitious climbing people and have experienced the fate of a symbol. Certain women have said to me, "You *can't* be Charles Citrine!" Many hosts are pleased by the contrast I offer. Why, I look like a man intensely but incompletely thinking. My face is no match for their shrewd urban faces. And it's especially the ladies who can't mask their disappointment when they see what the well-known Mr. Citrine actually looks like.

Whisky was set before us. I drank down my double Scotch eagerly and, being a quick expander, started to laugh. No one joined me. Ugly Bill said, "What's funny?"

I said, "Well, I just remembered that I learned to swim just down the way at Oak Street before all these skyscrapers went up, the architectural pride of P.R. Chicago. It was the Gold Coast then, and we used to come from the slums on the streetcar. The Division car only went as far as Wells. I'd come with a greasy bag of sandwiches. My mother bought me a girl's bathing suit at a sale. It had a little skirt with a rainbow border. I was mortified and tried to dye it with India ink. The cops used to jab us in the ribs to hurry us across the Drive. Now I'm up here, drinking whisky. . . . "

Cantabile gave me a shove under the table with his whole foot, leaving a dusty print on my trousers. His frown spread upward into his scalp, rippling under the close-cut curls, while his nose became as white as candle wax.

I said, "By the way, Ronald . . . " and I took out the bills. "I owe you money."

"What money?"

"The money I lost to you at that Poker game — it was some time back. I guess you forgot about it. Four hundred and fifty bucks."

"I don't know what you're talking about," said Rinaldo Cantabile. "What game?"

"You can't remember? We were playing at George Swiebel's apartment."

"Since when do you book guys play poker?" said Mike Schneiderman.

"Why? We have our human side. Poker has always been played at the White House. Perfectly respectable. President Harding played. Also during the New Deal. Morgenthau, Roosevelt, and so on."

"You sound like a West Side Chicago boy," said Bill.

"Chopin School, Rice and Western," I said.

"Well, put away your dough, Citrine," said Cantabile. "This is drink time. No business. Pay me later."

"Why not now, while I think of it and have the bills out? You know the whole thing slipped my mind, and last night I woke up with a start thinking, 'I forgot to pay Rinaldo his dough.' Christ, I could have blown my brains out."

Cantabile said violently, "Okay, okay, Charlie!" He snatched the money from me and crammed it without counting into his breast pocket. He gave me a look of high irritation, a flaming look. What for? I could not imagine why. What I did know was that Mike Schneiderman had power to put you in the paper and if you were in the paper you hadn't lived in vain. You were not just a two-legged creature, seen for a brief hour on Clark Street, sullying eternity with nasty doings and thoughts. You were —

"What'cha doing these days, Charlie," said Mike Schneiderman. "Another play maybe? A movie? You know," he said to Bill, "Charlie's a real famous guy. They made a terrific flick out of his Broadway hit. He's written a whole lot of stuff."

"I had my moment of glory on Broadway," I said, "I could never repeat it, so why try?"

"Now I remember. Somebody said you were going to publish some kind of highbrow magazine. When is it coming out? I'll give you a plug."

But Cantabile glared and said, "We've got to go."

"I'll be glad to phone when I have an item for you. It would be helpful," I said with a meaning glance toward Cantabile.

But he had already gone. I followed him and in the elevator he said, "What the fuck is the matter with you?"

"I can't think what I did wrong."

"You said you wanted to blow your brains out, and you know damn well, you creep, that Mike Schneiderman's brother-in-law blew *his* brains out two months ago."

"No!"

"You must have read it in the paper—that whole noise about phony bonds, the counterfeit bonds he gave for collateral."

"Oh, *that* one, you mean Goldhammer, the fellow who printed up his own certificates, the forger!"

"You knew it, don't pretend," said Cantabile. "You did it on purpose, to louse me up, to wreck my plan."

"I didn't, I swear I didn't. Blowing my brains out? That's a commonplace expression."

"Not in a case like this. You knew," he said violently, "you knew. You knew his brother-in-law killed himself."

"I didn't make the connection. It must have been a Freudian slip. Absolutely unintentional."

"You always pretend you never know what you're doing. I suppose you didn't know who that big-nosed fellow was."

"Bill?"

"Yes! Bill! Bill is Bill Lakin, the banker who was indicted with Goldhammer. He took the forged bonds as security."

"Why should he be indicted for that? Goldhammer put them over on him."

"Because, you bird-brain, don't you understand what you read in the news? He bought Lekatride from Goldhammer for a buck a share when it was worth six dollars. Haven't you heard of Kerner either? All these grand juries, all these trials? But you don't care about the things that other people knock themselves out over. You have contempt. You're arrogant, Citrine. You despise us."

"Who's us?"

"Us! People of the world . . ." said Cantabile. He spoke wildly. It was no time for argument. I was to respect and to fear him. It would be provoking if he didn't think I feared him. I didn't think that he would shoot me but a beating was surely possible, perhaps even a broken leg. As we left the Playboy Club he thrust the money again into my hand.

"Do we have to do this over?" I said. He explained nothing. He stood with his head angrily hooked forward until the Thunderbird came around. Once more I had to get in.

Our next stop was in the Hancock Building, somewhere on the sixtieth or seventieth story. It looked like a private apartment, and yet it seemed also to be a place of business. It was furnished in decorator style with plastic, trick art objects hanging on the walls, geometrical forms of the *trompe l'oeil* type that intrigue business people. They are peculiarly vulnerable to art racketeers. The gentleman who lived here was elderly, in a brown hopsack sports jacket with gold threads and a striped shirt on his undisciplined belly. White hair was slicked back upon his narrow head. The liver stains on his hands were large. Under the eyes and about the nose he did not look altogether well. As he sat on the low sofa which, judging by the way it gave under him, was stuffed with down, his alligator loafers extended far into the ivory shag carpet. The pressure of his belly brought out the shape of his phallus on his thigh. Long nose, gaping lip, and wattles went with all this velvet, the gold-threaded hopsack, brocade, satin, the alligator skin, and the *trompe l'oeil* objects. From the conversation I gathered that his line was jewelry and that he dealt with the underworld. Perhaps he was also a fence — how would I know? Rinaldo Cantabile and his wife had an anniversary coming and he was shopping for a bracelet. A Japanese houseboy served drinks. I am not a great drinker but today I understandably wanted whisky and I took another double shot of Black Label. From the skyscraper I could contemplate the air of Chicago on this short December afternoon. A ragged western sun spread orange light over the dark shapes of the town, over the branches of the river and the black trusses of bridges. The lake, gilt silver and amethyst, was ready for its winter cover of ice. I happened to be thinking that if Socrates was right, that you could learn nothing from trees, that only the men you met in the street could teach you something about yourself, I must be in a bad way, running off into the scenery instead of listening to my human companions. Evidently I did not have a good stomach for human companions. To get relief from uneasiness or heaviness of heart I was musing about the water. Socrates would have given me a low mark. I seemed to be on the Wordsworth end of things — trees, flowers, water. But architecture, engineering, electricity, technology had brought me to this sixty-fourth story. Scandinavia had put this glass in my hand, Scotland had filled it with whisky, and I sat there recalling certain marvelous facts about the sun, namely, that the light of other stars when it entered the sun's gravitational field, had to bend. The sun wore a shawl made of this universal light. So Einstein, sitting thinking of things, had foretold. And observations made by Arthur Eddington during an eclipse proved it. Finding before seeking.

Meantime, the phone rang continually and not a single call seemed local. It was all Las Vegas, L.A., Miami, and New York. "Send your boy over to Tiffany and find out what they get for an item like that," our host was saying. I then heard him speak of estate-jewels, and of an Indian prince who was trying to sell a whole lot of stuff in the USA and inviting bids.

At one interval, while Cantabile was fussing over a tray of diamonds (nasty, that white stuff seemed to me), the old gentleman spoke to me. He said, "I know you from somewhere, don't I?"

"Yes," I said. "From the whirlpool at the Downtown Health Club, I think."

"Oh yeah sure, I met you with that lawyer fellow. He's a big talker."

"Szathmar?"

"Alec Szathmar."

Cantabile said, fingering diamonds and not lifting his face from the dazzle of the velvet tray, "I know that son of a bitch Szathmar. He claims to be an old buddy of yours, Charlie."

"True," I said, "we were all boys at school. Including George Swiebel."

"In the old stone age that must have been," said Cantabile.

Yes, I had met this old gentleman in the hot chemical bath at the club, the circular bubbling whirlpool where people sat sweating, gossiping about sports, taxes, television programs, best sellers, or chatting about Acapulco and numbered bank accounts in the Cayman Islands. I didn't know but what this old fence had one of those infamous *cabañas* near the swimming pool to which young chicks were invited for the siesta. There had been some scandal and protest over this. What was done behind drawn drapes in the *cabañas* was no one's business, of course, but some of the old guys, demonstrative and exhibitionistic, had been seen fondling their little dolls on the sun-terrace. One had removed his false teeth in public to give a girl soul kisses. I had read an interesting letter in the *Tribune* about this. A retired History teacher living high up in the club building had written a letter saying that Tiberius — the old girl was showing off — Tiberius in the grottoes of Capri had had nothing on these grotesque lechers. But what did these old characters, in the rackets or in First Ward politics, care about indignant school-mams and classical allusions. If they had gone to see Fellini's *Satyricon* at the Woods Theater it was only to get more sex ideas not because they were studying Imperial Rome. I myself had seen some of these spider-bellied old codgers on the sundeck taking the breasts of teen-age hookers into their hands. It occurred to me that the Japanese houseboy was also a judo or karate expert as in *007* movies, there were so many valuables in the apartment. When Rinaldo said he'd like to see more Accutron watches, the fellow brought out a few dozen, flat as wafers. These may or may not have been stolen. My heated imagination couldn't be relied upon for guidance here. I was excited, I admit, by these currents of criminality. I could feel the need to laugh rising, mounting, always a sign that my weakness for the sensational, my American, Chicagoan (as well as personal) craving for high stimuli, for incongruities and extremes, was aroused. I knew that fancy thieving was a big thing in Chicago. It was said that if you knew one of these high-rise superrich Fagin-types you could obtain luxury goods at half the retail price. The actual shoplifting was done by addicts. They were compensated in heroin. As for the police, they were said to be paid off. They kept the merchants from making too much noise. Anyway there was insurance. There was also the well-known "shrinkage" or annual loss reported to the Internal Revenue Service. Such information about corruption, if you had grown up in Chicago, was easy to accept. It even satisfied a certain need. It harmonized with one's Chicago view of society. Naïveté was something you couldn't afford.

Item by item, I tried to asses what Cantabile wore as I sat there in soft up-holstery with my scotch on the rocks, his hat coat suit boots (the boots may have been unborn calf) his equestrian gloves, and I made an effort to imagine how he had obtained these articles through criminal channels, from Field's, from Saks Fifth Avenue, from Abercrombie & Fitch. He was not, so far as I could judge, taken absolutely seriously by the old fence.

Rinaldo was intrigued with one of the watches and slipped it on. His old watch he tossed to the Japanese who caught it. I thought the moment had come to recite my piece and I said, "Oh, by the way, Ronald, I owe you some dough from the other night."

"Where from?" said Cantabile.

"From the poker game at George Swiebel's. I guess it slipped your mind."

"Oh I know that guy Swiebel with all the muscles," said the old gentle-man. "He's terrific company. And you know he cooks a great bouillabaisse, I'll give him that."

"I inveigled Ronald and his cousin Emil into this game," I said. "It really was my fault. Anyhow, Ronald cleaned up on us. Ronald is one of the poker greats. I ended up about six hundred dollars in the hole and he had to take my IOU — I've got the dough on me, Ronald, and I better give it to you while we both remember."

"Okay." Again Cantabile, without looking, crumpled the notes into his jacket pocket. His performance was better than mine, though I was doing my very best. But then he had the honor side of the deal, the affront. To be angry was his right and that was no small advantage.

When we were out of the building again I said, "Wasn't that okay?"

"Okay — yes! Okay!" he said loud and bitter. Clearly he wasn't ready to let me off. Not yet.

"I figure that old pelican will pass the word around that I paid you. Wasn't that the object?"

I added, almost to myself, "I wonder who makes pants like the pants the old boy was wearing. The fly alone must have been three feet long."

But Cantabile was still stoking his anger. "Christ!" he said. I didn't like the way he was staring at me under those straight bodkin brows.

"Well, then, that does it," I said. "I can get a cab."

Cantabile caught me by the sleeve. "You wait," he said. I didn't really know what to do. After all, he carried a gun. I had for a long time thought about having a gun too, Chicago being what it is. But they'd never give me a license. Cantabile, without a license, packed a pistol. There was one index of the difference between us. Only God knew what consequences such differences might bring. "Aren't you enjoying our afternoon?" said Cantabile, and grinned.

Attempting to laugh this off I failed. The globus hystericus interfered. My throat felt sticky.

"Get in, Charlie."

Again I sat in the crimson bucket seat (the supple fragrant leather kept reminding me of blood, pulmonary blood) and fumbled for the seat belt—you never can find those cursed buckles.

"Don't fuck with the belt, we're not going that far."

Out of this information I drew what relief I could. We were on Michigan Boulevard, heading south. We drew up beside a skyscraper under construction, a headless trunk swooping up, swarming with lights. Below the early darkness now closing with December speed over the glistening west, the sun like a bristling fox jumped beneath the horizon. Nothing but a scarlet afterglow remained. I saw it between the El pillars. As the tremendous trusses of the unfinished skyscraper turned black, the hollow interior filled with thousands of electric points resembling champagne bubbles. The completed building would never be so beautiful as this. We got out, slamming the car doors, and I followed Cantabile over some plank-bedding laid down for the trucks. He seemed to know his way around. Maybe he had clients among the hardhats. If he was in the juice racket. Then again if he was a usurer he wouldn't come here after dark and risk getting pushed from a beam by one of these tough guys. They must be reckless. They drink and spend recklessly enough. I like the way these steeplejacks paint the names of their girlfriends on inaccessible girders. From below you often see DONNA or SUE. I suppose they bring the ladies on Sunday to point to their love-offerings eight hundred feet up. They fall to death now and then. Anyway Cantabile had brought his own hard hats. We put them on. Everything was prearranged. He said he was related by blood to some of the supervisory personnel. He also mentioned that he did lots of business hereabouts. He said he had connections with the contractor and the architect. He told me things much faster than I could discount them. However, we rose in one of the big open elevators, up, up.

How should I describe my feelings? Fear, thrill, appreciation, glee — yes I appreciated his ingenuity. It seemed to me, however, that we were rising too high, too far. Where were we? Which button had he pressed? By daylight I had often admired the mantis-like groups of cranes, tipped with orange paint. The tiny bulbs, which seemed so dense from below, were sparsely strung through. I don't know how far we actually went, but it was far enough. We had as much light about us as the time of day had left to give, steely and freezing, keen, with the wind ringing in the empty squares of wound-colored rust and beating against the hanging canvases. On the east, violently rigid was the water, icy, scratched, like a plateau of solid stone, and the other way was a tremendous effusion of low-lying color, the last glow, the contribution of industrial poisons to the beauty of the Chicago evening. We got out. About ten hard-hats who had been waiting pushed into the elevator at once. I wanted to call to them "Wait!" They went down in a group, leaving us nowhere. Cantabile seemed to know where he was going, but I had no faith in him. He was capable of faking anything. "Come on," he said. I followed, but I was going slowly. He waited for me. There were a few windbreaks up here on the fiftieth or sixtieth floor, and those, the wind was storming. My eyes ran. I held on to a pillar and he said, "Come on Granny, come on check-stopper."

I said, "I have leather heels. They skid."

"You'd better not chicken out."

"No, this is it," I said. I put my arms around the pillar. I wouldn't move.

Actually we had come far enough to suit him "Now," he said, "I want to show you just how much your dough means to me. You see this?" He held up a fifty-dollar bill. He rested his back on a steel upright and stripping off his fancy equestrian gloves began to fold the money. It was incomprehensible at first. Then I understood. He was making a child's paper glider of it. Hitching back his raglan sleeve, he sent the glider off with two fingers. I watched it speeding through the strung lights with the wind behind it out into the steely atmosphere, darker and darker below. On Michigan Boulevard they had already put up the Christmas ornaments, winding tiny bubbles of glass from tree to tree. They streamed down there like cells under a microscope.

My chief worry now was how to get down. Though the papers underplay it people are always falling off. But however scared and harassed, my sensation-loving soul also was gratified. I knew that it took too much to gratify me. The gratification-threshold of my soul had risen too high. I must bring it down again. It was excessive. I must, I knew, change everything.

He sailed off more of the fifties. Tiny paper planes. Origami (my knowledgeable mind, keeping up its indefatigable pedantry — my lexical busybody mind!), the Japanese paper-folder's art. An international congress of paper-aircraft freaks had been held, I think, last year. It seemed last year. The hobbyists were mathematicians and engineers.

Cantabile's green bills went off like finches, like swallows and butterflies, all bearing the image of Ulysses S. Grant. They brought crepuscular fortune to people down in the streets.

"The last two I'm going to keep," said Cantabile. "To blow them on drinks and dinner for us."

"If I ever get down alive."

"You did fine. Go on, lead the way, start back."

"These leather heels are awfully tricky. I hit an ordinary piece of wax paper in the street the other day and went down. Maybe I should take my shoes off."

"Don't be crazy. Go on your toes."

If you didn't think of falling, the walkways were more than adequate. I crept along, fighting paralysis of the calves and the thighs. My face was sweating faster than the wind could dry it as I took hold of the final pillar. I thought that Cantabile had been treading much too close behind. More hard-hats waiting for the elevator probably took us for union guys or architect's men. It was night now and the hemisphere was frozen all the way to the Gulf. Gladly I fell into the seat of the Thunderbird when we got down. He removed his hard hat and mine. He cocked the wheel and started the motor. He should really let me go now. I had given him enough satisfaction.

But he was off again, driving fast. He sped away toward the next light. My head hung back over the top of the seat in the position you take to stop a nosebleed. I didn't know exactly where we were. "Look, Rinaldo," I said. "You've made your point. You bashed my car, you've run me all day long, and you've just given me the scare of my life. Okay, I see it wasn't the money that upset you. Let's stuff the rest of it down a sewer so I can go home."

"You had it with me?"

"It's been a whole day of atonement."

"You've seen enough of the whatchamacallems? — I learned some new words at the poker game from you."

"Which words?"

"Proles," he said "*Lumps. Lumpenproletariat.* You gave us a little talk about Karl Marx."

"My lord, I did carry on, didn't I? Completely unbuttoned. What got into me!"

"You wanted to mix with riffraff and the criminal element. You went slumming, Charlie, and you had a great time playing cards with us dumbheads and social rejects."

"I see. I was insulting."

"Kind of. But you were interesting, here and there, about the social order and how obsessed the middle class was with the *Lumpenproletariat*. The other fellows didn't know what in hell you were talking about." For the first time, Cantabile spoke more mildly to me. I sat up and saw the river flashing night-lights on the right, and the Merchandise Mart decorated for Christmas. We were going to Gene and Georgetti's old steak house, just off the spur of the Elevated train. Parking among other sinister luxury cars we went into the drab old building where—hurrah for opulent intimacy!—a crash of jukebox music fell on us like Pacific surf. The high-executive bar was crowded with executive drinkers and lovely companions. The gorgeous mirror was peopled with bottles and resembled a group photograph of celestial graduates.

"Giulio," Rinaldo told the waiter. "A quiet table, and we don't want to sit by the rest rooms."

"Upstairs, Mr. Cantabile?"

"Why not?" I said. I was shaky and didn't want to wait at the bar for seating. It would lengthen the evening, besides.

Cantabile stared as if to say, Who asked you! But he then consented. "Okay, upstairs. And two bottles of Piper Heidsieck."

"Right away, Mr. Cantabile."

In the Capone days hoodlums fought mock battles with champagne at banquets. They jigged the bottles up and down and shot each other with corks and foaming wine, all in black tie, and like a fun-massacre.

"Now I want to tell you something," said Rinaldo Cantabile, "and it's a different subject altogether. I'm married, you know."

"Yes, I remember."

"To a marvelous beautiful intelligent woman."

"You mentioned your wife in South Chicago. That night . . . Do you have children? What does she do?"

"She's no housewife, buddy, and you'd better know it. You think I'd marry some fat-ass broad who sits around the house in curlers and watches TV? This is a real woman, with a mind, with knowledge. She teaches at Mundelein College and she's working on a doctoral thesis. You know where?"

"No."

"At Radcliffe, Harvard."

"That's very good," I said. I emptied the champagne glass and refilled it.

"Don't brush it off. Ask me what her subject is. Of the thesis."

"All right, what is it?"

"She's writing a study of that poet who was your friend."

"You're kidding. Von Humboldt Fleisher? How do you know he was my friend? . . . I see. I was talking about him at George's. Someone should have locked me in a closet that night."

"You didn't have to be cheated, Charlie. You didn't know what you were doing. You were talking away like a nine-year-old kid about lawsuits, lawyers, accountants, bad investments, and the magazine you were going to publish — a real loser, it sounded like. You said you were going to spend your own money on your own ideas."

"I never discuss these things with strangers. Chicago must be giving me arctic madness."

"Now, listen, I'm very proud of my wife. Her people are rich, upper class. . . ." Boasting gives people a wonderful color, I've noticed, and Cantabile's cheeks glowed. He said, "You're asking yourself what is she doing with a husband like me."

I muttered, "No, no," though it certainly was a natural question. However, it was not exactly news that highly educated women were excited by scoundrels criminals and lunatics, and that these scoundrels etcetera were drawn to culture, to thought. Diderot and Dostoevski had made us familiar with this.

"I want her to get her PhD," said Cantabile. "You understand? I want it bad. And you were a pal of this Fleisher guy. You're going to give Lucy the information."

"Now wait a minute —"

"Look this over." He handed me an envelope and I put on my glasses and glanced over the document enclosed. It was signed Lucy Wilkins Cantabile and it was the letter of a model graduate student, polite, detailed, highly organized, with the usual academic circumlocutions — three single-spaced pages, dense with questions, painful questions. Her husband kept me under close observation as I read. "Well, what do you think of her?"

"Terrific," I said. The thing filled me with despair. "What do you two want of me?"

"Answers. Information. We want you to write out the answers. What's your opinion of her project?"

"I think the dead owe us a living."

"Don't horse around with me, Charlie. I didn't like that crack."

"I couldn't care less," I said. "This poor Humboldt, my friend, was a big spirit who was destroyed . . . never mind that. The PhD racket is a very fine racket but I want no part of it. Besides, I never answer questionnaires. Idiots impose on you with their documents. I can't bear that kind of thing."

"Are you calling my wife an idiot?"

"I haven't had the pleasure of meeting her."

"I'll make allowances for you. You got hit in the guts by the Mercedes and then I ran you ragged. But don't be unpleasant about my wife."

"There are things I don't do. This is one of them. I'm not going to write answers. It would take weeks."

"Listen!"

"I draw the line."

"Just a minute!"

"Bump me off. Go to hell."

"All right, easy does it. Some things are sacred. I understand. But we can work everything out. I listened at the poker game and I know that you're in plenty of trouble. You need somebody tough and practical to handle things for you. I've given this a lot of thought, and I have all kinds of ideas for you. We'll trade off."

"No, I don't want to trade anything. I've had it. My heart is breaking and I want to go home."

"Let's have a steak and finish the wine. You need red meat. You're just tired. You'll do it."

"I won't."

"Take the order, Giulio," he said.

# Gwendolyn Brooks
## (b. 1917)

*There have been anthologies comprised, in whole or in large part, of tributes to* GWENDOLYN BROOKS *(see Haki Madhubuti's tribute in this anthology). Born in Topeka, Kansas, she has long made her home in Chicago, and is simply one of the most celebrated writers in American history. Author of a novel,* Maud Martha *(1953), and many short stories, children's books, memoirs, and other nonfiction, she is still best known for her poetry. From her stunning debut* A Street in Bronzeville *in 1945 through nearly twenty other volumes of poetry, including her latest,* Children Coming Home *(1991), Brooks's poems have maintained an astonishing level of power, a genius for celebration and criticism, and a knack for capturing the right nuance of language and finding the perfect subject for probing, reflecting on, and embodying concerns that go to the heart not only of black life in America, but of American life as a whole. These accomplishments and more have brought her, among many literary prizes, the 1950 Pulitzer Prize for* Annie Allen. *She thus became the first black American to win that coveted award.*

*Currently a professor at Chicago State University, Brooks has taught at many universities and received more than fifty honorary doctorates. She has been inducted into the National Women's Hall of Fame and received the Lifetime Achievement Award of the National Endowment for the Arts. She is Illinois's poet laureate and has been, as poetry consultant to the Library of Congress, America's poet laureate as well. She is known for her dedication to uplifting the young and for confronting social and political issues such as race and poverty. In 1972 she published her autobiography* Report from Part One.

*The magnificent long poem "A Bronzeville Mother Loiters in Mississippi. Meanwhile, a Mississippi Mother Burns Bacon" recounts the horrible tale of Emmett Till, a fourteen-year-old Chicago boy murdered for "talking fresh" to a white woman. "The* Chicago *Defender Sends a Man to Little Rock" is an often-anthologized classic of American poetry and the Civil Rights movement. The other poems included here attempt to suggest the extraordinary range of her interests and her poetic voice, from the cautiously celebratory tone of "The Chicago Picasso" to the knowing innocence and outrage of a child suffering abuse to the impishness of a black girl considering white girls' hair.*

✦ ✦ ✦

## A Bronzeville Mother Loiters in Mississippi. Meanwhile, a Mississippi Mother Burns Bacon

From the first it had been like a
Ballad. It had the beat inevitable. It had the blood.
A wildness cut up, and tied in little bunches,
Like the four-line stanzas of the ballads she had never quite
Understood — the ballads they had set her to, in school.

Herself: the milk-white maid, the "maid mild"
Of the ballad. Pursued
By the Dark Villain. Rescued by the Fine Prince.
The Happiness-Ever-After.
That was worth anything.
It was good to be a "maid mild."
That made the breath go fast.

Her bacon burned. She
Hastened to hide it in the step-on can, and
Drew more strips from the meat case. The eggs and sour-milk biscuits
Did well. She set out a jar
Of her new quince preserve.

. . . But there was a something about the matter of the Dark Villain.
He should have been older, perhaps.
The hacking down of a villain was more fun to think about
When his menace possessed undisputed breadth, undisputed height,
And a harsh kind of vice.
And best of all, when his history was cluttered
With the bones of many eaten knights and princesses.

The fun was disturbed, then all but nullified
When the Dark Villain was a blackish child
Of fourteen, with eyes still too young to be dirty,
And a mouth too young to have lost every reminder
Of its infant softness.

That boy must have been surprised! For
These were grown-ups. Grown-ups were supposed to be wise.

And the Fine Prince — and that other — so tall, so broad, so
Grown! Perhaps the boy had never guessed
That the trouble with grown-ups was that under the magnificent shell
    of adulthood, just under,
Waited the baby full of tantrums.
It occurred to her that there may have been something
Ridiculous in the picture of the Fine Prince
Rushing (rich with the breadth and height and
Mature solidness whose lack, in the Dark Villain, was impressing her,
Confronting her more and more as this first day after the trial
And acquittal wore on) rushing
With his heavy companion to hack down (unhorsed)
That little foe.
So much had happened, she could not remember now what that foe had done
Against her, or if anything had been done.
The one thing in the world that she did know and knew
With terrifying clarity was that her composition
Had disintegrated. That, although the pattern prevailed,
The breaks were everywhere. That she could think
Of no thread capable of the necessary
Sew-work.

She made the babies sit in their places at the table.
Then, before calling Him, she hurried
To the mirror with her comb and lipstick. It was necessary
To be more beautiful than ever.
The beautiful wife.
For sometimes she fancied he looked at her as though
Measuring her. As if he considered, Had she been worth It?
Had *she* been worth the blood, the cramped cries, the little stuttering bravado,
The gradual dulling of those Negro eyes,
The sudden, overwhelming *little-boyness* in that barn?
Whatever she might feel or half-feel, the lipstick necessity was something
    apart. He must never conclude
That she had not been worth It.

He sat down, the Fine Prince, and
Began buttering a biscuit. He looked at his hands.
He twisted in his chair, he scratched his nose.
He glanced again, almost secretly, at his hands.
More papers were in from the North, he mumbled. More meddling headlines.

With their pepper-words, "bestiality," and "barbarism," and
"Shocking."
The half-sneers he had mastered for the trial worked across
His sweet and pretty face.

What he'd like to do, he explained, was kill them all.
The time lost. The unwanted fame.
Still, it had been fun to show those intruders
A thing or two. To show that snappy-eyed mother,
That sassy, Northern, brown-black —

Nothing could stop Mississippi.
He knew that. Big Fella
Knew that.
And, what was so good, Mississippi knew that.
Nothing and nothing could stop Mississippi.
They could send in their petitions, and scar
Their newspapers with bleeding headlines. Their governors
Could appeal to Washington. . . .

"What I want," the older baby said, "is 'lasses on my jam."
Whereupon the younger baby
Picked up the molasses pitcher and threw
The molasses in his brother's face. Instantly
The Fine Prince leaned across the table and slapped
The small and smiling criminal.

She did not speak. When the Hand
Came down and away, and she could look at her child,
At her baby-child,
She could think only of blood.
Surely her baby's cheek
Had disappeared, and in its place, surely,
Hung a heaviness, a lengthening red, a red that had no end.
She shook her head. It was not true, of course.
It was not true at all. The
Child's face was as always, the
Color of the paste in her paste-jar.

She left the table, to the tune of the children's lamentations,
    which were shriller
Than ever. She
Looked out of a window. She said not a word. *That*
Was one of the new Somethings —
The fear,
Tying her as with iron.

Suddenly she felt his hands upon her. He had followed her
To the window. The children were whimpering now.
Such bits of tots. And she, their mother,
Could not protect them. She looked at her shoulders, still
Gripped in the claim of his hands. She tried, but could not resist the idea
That a red ooze was seeping, spreading darkly, thickly, slowly,
Over her white shoulders, her own shoulders,
And over all of Earth and Mars.

He whispered something to her, did the Fine Prince, something
About love, something about love and night and intention.

She heard no hoof-beat of the horse and saw no flash of the shining steel.

He pulled her face around to meet
His, and there it was, close close,
For the first time in all those days and nights.
His mouth, wet and red,
So very, very, very red,
Closed over hers.

Then a sickness heaved within her. The courtroom Coca-Cola,
The courtroom beer and hate and sweat and drone,
Pushed like a wall against her. She wanted to bear it.
But his mouth would not go away and neither would the
Decapitated exclamation points in that Other Woman's eyes.

She did not scream.
She stood there.
But a hatred for him burst into glorious flower,
And its perfume enclasped them — big,
Bigger than all magnolias.

The last bleak news of the ballad.
The rest of the rugged music.
The last quatrain.

## The Last Quatrain of the Ballad of Emmett Till

*after the murder,*
*after the burial*

Emmett's mother is a pretty-faced thing;
    the tint of pulled taffy.
She sits in a red room,
    drinking black coffee.
She kisses her killed boy.
    And she is sorry.
Chaos in windy grays
    through a red prairie.

## The Chicago *Defender* Sends a Man to Little Rock

*Fall, 1957*

In Little Rock the people bear
Babes, and comb and part their hair
And watch the want ads, put repair
To roof and latch. While wheat toast burns
A woman waters multiferns.

Time upholds or overturns
The many, tight, and small concerns.

In Little Rock the people sing
Sunday hymns like anything,
Through Sunday pomp and polishing.

And after testament and tunes,
Some soften Sunday afternoons
With lemon tea and Lorna Doones.

I forecast
And I believe
Come Christmas Little Rock will cleave

To Christmas tree and trifle, weave,
From laugh and tinsel, texture fast.

In Little Rock is baseball; Barcarolle.
That hotness in July . . . the uniformed figures raw and implacable
And not intellectual,
Batting the hotness or clawing the suffering dust.
The Open Air Concert, on the special twilight green . . .
When Beethoven is brutal or whispers to lady-like air.
Blanket-sitters are solemn, as Johann troubles to lean
To tell them what to mean. . . .

There is love, too, in Little Rock. Soft women softly
Opening themselves in kindness,
Or, pitying one's blindness,
Awaiting one's pleasure
In azure
Glory with anguished rose at the root. . . .
To wash away old semi-discomfitures.
They re-teach purple and unsullen blue.
The wispy soils go. And uncertain
Half-havings have they clarified to sures.

In Little Rock they know
Not answering the telephone is a way of rejecting life,
That it is our business to be bothered, is our business
To cherish bores or boredom, be polite
To lies and love and many-faceted fuzziness.

I scratch my head, massage the hate-I-had.
I blink across my prim and pencilled pad.
The saga I was sent for is not down.
Because there is a puzzle in this town.
The biggest News I do not dare
Telegraph to the Editor's chair:
"They are like people everywhere."

The angry Editor would reply
In hundred harryings of Why.

And true, they are hurtling spittle, rock,
Garbage and fruit in Little Rock.
And I saw coiling storm a-writhe
On bright madonnas. And a scythe
Of men harassing brownish girls.
(The bows and barrettes in the curls
And braids declined away from joy.)

I saw a bleeding brownish boy. . . .

The lariat lynch-wish I deplored.

The loveliest lynchee was our Lord.

## THE CHICAGO PICASSO

*August 15, 1967*

> "Mayor Daley tugged a white ribbon, loosing the
> blue percale wrap. A hearty cheer went up as the
> covering slipped off the big steel sculpture that
> looks at once like a bird and a woman."
> — Chicago *Sun-Times*

*(Seiji Ozawa leads the Symphony.*
*The Mayor smiles.*
*And 50,000 See.)*

Does man love Art? Man visits Art, but squirms.
Art hurts. Art urges voyages —
and it is easier to stay at home,
the nice beer ready.
　　In commonrooms
we belch, or sniff, or scratch.
Are raw.

But we must cook ourselves and style ourselves for Art, who
is a requiring courtesan.
We squirm.
We do not hug the Mona Lisa.

We
may touch or tolerate
an astounding fountain, or a horse-and-rider.
At most, another Lion.

Observe the tall cold of a Flower
which is as innocent and as guilty,
as meaningful and as meaningless as any
other flower in the western field.


## Uncle Seagram

My uncle likes me too much.

I am five and a half years old, and in kindergarten.
In kindergarten everything is clean.

My uncle is six feet tall with seven bumps on his chin.
My uncle is six feet tall, and he stumbles.
He stumbles because of his Wonderful Medicine
packed in his pocket all times.

Family is ma and pa and my uncle,
three brothers, three sisters, and me.

Every night at my house we play checkers and dominoes.
My uncle sits *close.*
There aren't any shoes or socks on his feet.
Under the table a big toe tickles my ankle.
Under the oilcloth his thin knee then beats into mine.
And mashes. And mashes.

When we look at TV
my uncle picks *me* to sit on his lap.
As I sit, he gets hard in the middle.
I squirm, but he keeps me, and kisses my ear.

I am not even a girl.

Once, when I went to the bathroom,
my uncle noticed, came in, shut the door,
put his long white tongue in my ear,

and whispered "We're Best Friends, and Family,
and we know how to keep Secrets."

My uncle likes me too much. I am worried.

I do not like my uncle anymore.

## WHITE GIRLS ARE PECULIAR PEOPLE

White girls are peculiar people.
They cannot keep their hands out of their hair.
Also
they are always shaking it away from their eyes
when it is not in their eyes.
Sometimes when it is braided they forget—
and shake and shake
and smooth what is nothing
away from their shameless eyes.

I laugh.

My hair is short.
It is close to my head.
It is almost a crown of dots.
My head is clean and free.
I do not shake my head to make
my brains like a crazy dust.

# Harry Mark Petrakis
## (b. 1923)

*Born in St. Louis, Missouri,* HARRY MARK PETRAKIS *has long been known as the interpreter of the Chicago Greek immigrant community, and it is this tie with Greece that gives his writing the air of a Hellenic epic even when he focuses on the most mundane of experiences. But the sense of epic quest has throughout most of his work been balanced against another Greek form — tragedy, so that his characters, even in the essentially comic story "The Journal of a Wife Beater" reprinted here, are pulled back and forth between expansive quest and confining loss.*

*Petrakis is the author of several novels, including* A Dream of Kings *(1966),* Nick the Greek *(1979),* Days of Vengeance *(1983), and* Ghost of the Sun *(1990); short story collections, including* Pericles on 31st Street *(1965) and* The Waves of Night *(1969); and a memoir,* Stelmark: A Family Recollection *(1970).*

✦ ✦ ✦

## *The Journal of a Wife Beater*

*from* COLLECTED STORIES

*October 2:* Today I beat my wife, Nitsa, for the first time! I preserve this momentous event for future generations by beginning this Journal and recording this first entry with some pride.

I did not beat her hard, really not hard at all. I gave her several clouts across her head with my open palm, enough to make her stagger and daze her a little. Then I led her courteously to a chair to show her I was not punishing her in anger.

"Why?" she asked, and there were small tears glistening in the corners of her eyes.

"Nothing of great significance," I said amiably. "The coffee you served me was not hot enough this morning and after the last few washings my shirts have not had enough starch. Yesterday and the day before you were late in arriving at the restaurant. All of these are small imprudences that display a growing laxity on your part. I felt it was time to suggest improvement."

She watched me with her lips trembling. How artfully women suffer!

"You have never struck me before," she said thoughtfully. "In the year since we married, Vasili, you have never stuck me before."

"One does not wish to begin correction too soon," I said. "It would be unjust to expect a new bride to attain perfection overnight. A period of flexibility is required."

Her big black eyes brooded, but she said nothing.

"You understand," I said consolingly. "This does not mean I do not love you." I shook my head firmly to emphasize my words. "It is exactly because I do care for you that I desire to improve you. On a number of occasions in my father's house I can remember him beating my mother. Not hard you understand. A clout across the head, and a box upon the ear. Once when she left the barn door open and the cows strayed out, he kicked her, but that was an exception. My mother was a happy and contented woman all her life."

The conversation ended there, but Nitsa was silent and meditative as we prepared for bed. She did not speak again until we were under the covers in the darkness.

"Vasili," she asked quietly, "will you strike me again?"

"Only when I feel you need it," I said. "It should not be required too often. You are a sensible girl and I am sure are most anxious to please me by being a good wife and a competent homemaker."

She turned away on her pillow and did not say another word.

*October 3:* I slept splendidly last night!

*October 5:* Since I have a few moments of leisure this evening, I will fill in certain background information about Nitsa and myself so that future generations may better understand this record of an ideal marriage relationship.

First I must record my immense satisfaction in the results of the beating. Nitsa has improved tremendously the past two days. She has taken the whole affair as sensibly as any man could have wished.

Her good sense was what first impressed me about Nitsa. I met her about a year ago at a dance in the church hall, sponsored by the Daughters of Athens. I drank a little beer and danced once with each of a number of young ladies whose zealous mothers beamed at me from chairs along the wall. I might add here that before my marriage a year ago I was a very desirable catch for some fortunate girl. I was just a year past forty, an inch above average height, with all of my own hair and most of my own teeth, a number of which have been capped with gold. I had, and of course still have, a prosperous restaurant on Dart Street and a substantial sum in United States Savings Bonds. Finally, I myself was interested in marriage to a well-bred young lady. My first inclination was to return to Greece and select some daughter born to respect the traditions of the family; but as our parish priest, Father Antoniou, pointed out with his usual keen discernment, this would have been grossly unfair to the countless girls in our community who hoped for me as a bridegroom. Although marriage to any one of them would dismay the others, it would be better than if I scorned them all for a wife from overseas.

Nitsa impressed me because she was not as young as most of the other girls, perhaps in her late twenties, a tall athletic-looking girl who appeared capable of bearing my sturdy sons. She was not as beautiful a girl as I felt I deserved, but she made a neat and pleasant appearance. Most attractive young girls are too flighty and arrogant. They are not sensible enough to be grateful when a successful man pays them attention. Bringing one of them into a man's home is much the same as bringing in a puppy that has not yet been housebroken. Too much time is spent on fundamentals!

Imagine my delight when, in inquiry regarding Nitsa's family that night, I learned that she was the niece of our revered priest, Father Antoniou, visiting him from Cleveland.

I danced several American dances with her to demonstrate that I was not old-fashioned and spoke to her at some length of my assets and my prospects. She listened with unconcealed interest. We sat and drank coffee afterward until a group of my friends called to me to lead one of the old country dances. Conscious of her watching me, I danced with even more than my usual grace and flourish, and leaped higher off the floor than I had in some time.

A day or two later I spoke seriously to Father Antoniou. He was frankly delighted. He phoned his sister, Nitsa's mother in Cleveland, and in no time at all the arrangements were made. As I had accurately surmised, the whole family, including Nitsa, were more than willing.

Several weeks later we were married. It was a festive affair and the reception cost a little over a thousand dollars which I insisted her father pay. He was a housepainter who worked irregularly, but in view of the fact that Nitsa brought me no dowry I felt he should demonstrate the good faith of the family by paying for the reception.

Nitsa and I spent a honeymoon weekend at the Mortimer Hotel so I could return to count the cash when the restaurant closed each evening. As it was, God only knows what the waitresses stole from me those two days. During our absence I had the bedroom of my apartment painted, and after considerable deliberation bought a new stove. I write this as proof of my thoughtfulness. The stove I had was only twelve years old, but I am worldly enough to understand how all women love new stoves. If permitted by weak and easily swayed husbands they would trade them in on newer models every year.

In recalling our first year together, while it was not quite what I expected, I was not completely disillusioned. There was a certain boldness and immodesty about Nitsa which I found displeasing, but one must bear with this in a healthy young woman.

As time went on she spent a good part of the day with me in the restaurant taking cash. She became familiar enough with my business so that when the wholesale produce and meat salesman called she could be trusted to order some of the staple items. But I noticed a certain laxity developing, a carelessness in her approach to her responsibilities, and remembering my father's success with my mother, it was then I beat her for the first time.

I am so pleased that it seems to have prompted unreserved improvement. Bravo, Vasili!

*October 7:* It is after midnight and I am alone in the restaurant which is closed until morning. I am sitting at the small table in the kitchen and can hardly bear to write the shameful and disgraceful episode which follows.

Last night after returning from the restaurant I went to bed because I was tired. Nitsa came into the room as I was slipping under the covers. I had noticed a rather somber quietness about her all that day, but I attributed it to that time of the female month. When she had donned her night clothes and gotten into bed beside me, I raised my cheek for her to kiss me goodnight. She turned her back on me and for a moment I was peeved, but remembering her indisposition, I turned off the lamp and said nothing.

I fell asleep shortly and had a stirring dream. I fought beside Achilles on the plains before Troy. I carried a mighty shield and a long sword. Suddenly a massive Trojan appeared before me and we engaged each other in combat. After I brilliantly parried a number of his blows he seemed to recognize he was doomed. He retreated and I pressed him hard. While we slashed back and forth, another Trojan rose beside me as if he had sprung from the earth, and swung his weapon at my head. I raised my shield swiftly but not quite in time and the flat of his sword landed across my head. The pain was so terrible I shrieked out loud, and suddenly the plains of Troy and the helmeted warriors were all swept away and my eyes exploded open to the sight of Nitsa bent over me, calmly preparing to strike again!

I bellowed and clawed to sit up, and tried desperately to flee from the bed. The stick she swung bounced again across my head and the pain was ferocious.

I fell off the bed in a tangle of sheets at her feet; then I jumped up frantically and ran to the other side of the bed, looking back in desperation to see if she followed. She stood dreadfully calm with the stick still in her hand.

"Are you mad!" I shouted. My nose seemed to be swelling and my head stung and I tasted blood from my cut lip. "You must be mad or in the employ of the devil! You have split me open!"

"I owed you one," she said quietly.

I looked at her in astonishment and rubbed my aching head. I could not comprehend the desecration of a wife striking her husband. "Your senses have come apart," I bellowed. "You might have broken my head!"

"I don't think so," she said. "You have an unusually dense head."

I was horrified. On top of my injuries her insolence could not be tolerated. I ran around the bed and pulled the stick from her hands. I swung it up and down. When it landed across her shoulders she winced and gave a shrill squeal. Then I went to bathe my swollen head. A harrowing and terrible experience indeed!

*October 11:* Plague and damnation! Blood and unspeakable horror! She has done it again.

That wench of evil design waited just long enough for the swelling of my nose to recede and my lip to heal. All week she had been quiet and reserved. She came to work promptly and performed her duties efficiently. While I could never forget that night in bed when she struck me, I was willing to forgive. Women are by nature as emotionally unstable as dogs under the mad light of a full moon. But I am a generous man and in this foul manner was my generosity rewarded.

It happened shortly after the rush at lunch was over. The restaurant was deserted except for Nitsa at the register and the waitresses chattering beside the urns of coffee. I was sitting at the small table in the kitchen, smoking a cigar, and pondering whether to order short ribs or pork loins for lunch on Thursday. Suddenly I was conscious of an uneasy chill in the center of my back. A strange quick dread possessed me and I turned swiftly around and Nitsa was there. Almost at the same instant the pot she was swinging landed with a horrible clatter on my head. I let out a roar of outrage and pain, and jumped up holding my thundering head. I found it impossible to focus my eyes, and for a frenzied moment I imagined I was surrounded by a dozen Nitsas. I roared again in fear and anger, and ran to seek sanctuary behind the big stove. She made no move to follow me but stood quietly by the table with the pot in her hand.

"You must be mad!" I shrieked. "I will call the doctor and have him exchange your bloody head!"

The dishwasher, who had come from the back room where he had been eating, watched us with his great idiot eyes, and the waitresses, cousins of imbeciles, peered through the porthole of the swinging door.

"I owed you one," Nitsa said quietly. She put down the pot and walked from the kitchen past the awed and silent waitresses.

As I write this now, words are inadequate to describe my distress. Fiercer by far than the abominable lump on my head is the vision of chaos and disorder. In the name of all that is sacred, where is the moral and ordered world of my father?

*October 15:* Disturbed and agitated as I have been for the past few days, tonight I decided something had to be done. I went to speak to Father Antoniou.

Nitsa, that shrew, has been at the restaurant for several days now acting as if nothing had happened. She joked with the customers and took cash calmly. Heartless wench without the decency to show some shred of remorse!

Last night I slept locked in the bathroom. Even then I was apprehensive and kept one eye open on the door. While it was true that by her immoral standards we were even, she could not be trusted. I feared she would take it into her stony soul to surge into a shameful lead. Finally tonight, because I knew the situation had become intolerable, I visited the priest.

He greeted me courteously and took me into his study. He brought out a bottle of good sherry. We sat silent for a moment, sipping the fine vintage.

"You may speak now, my dear friend," he said gently. "You are troubled."

"How can you tell, Father?" I asked.

He smiled sagely. He was indeed a fountain of wisdom.

"Well, Father," I struggled for the mortifying words. "It is Nitsa. To put it plainly, she has struck me not once, but twice, with a stout stick and a heavy pot."

He sat upright in his chair.

"May God watch over us!" he said. "Surely, Vasili, you are jesting!"

I made my cross and bent my head to show him the hard lump that still dwelt there. He rose from his chair and came to examine it. When he touched the lump, I jumped.

He paced the floor in agitation, his black cassock swirling about his ankles.

"She must be demented," he said slowly. "The poor girl must be losing her mind."

"That is what I thought at first," I said seriously. "But she seems so calm. Each time she strikes me she merely says, 'I owed you one.'"

"Aaaaah!" the priest said eagerly. "Now we approach the core of truth." His voice lowered. "What did you do to her for which she seeks revenge?" He winked slyly. "I know you hot-blooded Spartans. Perhaps a little too passionate for a shy young girl?"

"Nothing, Father!" I said in indignation, although I could not help being pleased at his suggestion. "Absolutely nothing."

"Nothing?" he repeated.

"I have clouted her several times across her head," I said. "My prerogative as husband to discipline my wife. Certainly nothing to warrant the violence of her blows."

"Incredible," the priest said. He sat silent and thoughtful, then shook his head. "A woman raising her hand to her husband in my parish, and that woman my niece. Incredible!" He wrung his hands fretfully. "A stain upon the sacred vows of marriage." He paused as if struck by a sudden thought. "Tell me, Vasili, has she been watching much television? Sometimes it tends to confuse a woman."

"Our picture tube is burned out now several months, Father," I said.

"Incredible," the priest said.

"Perhaps if you talk to her, Father," I said. "Explain what it is to be a dutiful wife. Define the rights of a husband."

The priest shook his head sadly. "When I first entered the priesthood," he said somberly, "I learned never to attempt to reason with a woman. The two words should never be used in the same sentence. The emancipation of these crafty scheming descendants of Eve has hurled man into a second Dark Ages."

I was impressed by the gravity of his words and had to agree I had spoken hastily.

"My son," the priest said finally, a thin edge of desperation in his voice. "I confess I am helpless to know what to advise. If you came to seek counsel because she drank to excess or because she had succumbed to the wiles of another man . . . but for this! I will have to contact the Bishop."

I sipped my sherry and felt anger coming to a head on my flesh as if it were a festered boil pressing to break. I, Vasili Makris, subjected to these indignities! Humiliated before my own dishwasher! Driving my parish priest to consult with the Bishop!

"There is only one answer, Father," I said, and my voice rang out boldly, a Homeric call to battle. "I have clouted her too lightly. There is nothing further to be done but for me to give her a beating she will not forget!" I waved my hand. "Rest assured I will remember my own strength. I will not break any bones, but I will teach her respect." I became more pleased with that solution by the moment. "That is the answer, Father," I said. "A beating that will once and for all end this insufferable mutiny!"

We watched each other for a long wordless moment. I could sense that good man struggling between a moral objection to violence and an awareness there was no other way.

"They who live by the sword," he said dolefully, and he paused to permit me to finish the quotation in my mind. "This cancer must be cut out," he said, "before it spreads infection through the parish."

He raised his glass of wine and toasted me gravely.

"Consider yourself embarked on a holy crusade," he said in a voice trembling with emotion. "Recapture the sanctity of your manhood. Go, Vasili Makris, with God."

I kissed his revered hand and left.

*October 17:* The promised retribution has been delayed because a waitress has been sick and I cannot afford to incapacitate Nitsa at the same time. But I vow her reprieve will be brief!

*October 19:* Tonight is the night! The restaurant is closed and we are alone. I am sitting in the kitchen making this entry while she finishes cleaning out the urns of coffee. When the work is all done I will call her into the kitchen for judgment.

Nitsa! Misguided and arrogant woman, your hour of punishment is here!

*October 23:* In the life of every noble man there are moments of decisive discovery and events of inspired revelation. I hasten with fire and zeal to record such an experience in this Journal!

That epic night when Nitsa came to the kitchen of the restaurant after finishing her work, without a word of warning I struck her. Quick as a flash she struck me back. I was prepared for that and hit her harder. She replied with a thump on my head that staggered me. I threw all hesitation to the winds and landed a fierce blow upon her. Instead of submitting, she became a flame of baleful fury. She twisted violently in search of some weapon to implement her rage, and scooped up a meat cleaver off the block! I let out a hoarse shout of panic and turned desperately and fled! I heard her pounding like a maddened mare after me, and I made the door leading to the alley and bounded out with a wild cry! I forgot completely the accursed stairs and spun like a top in the air and landed on my head. I woke in the hospital where I am at present and X-rays have indicated no damage beyond a possible concussion that still causes me some dizziness.

At the first opportunity I examined myself secretly for additional reassurance that some vital part of me had not been dismembered by that frightful cleaver. Then I sat and recollected each detail of that experience with somber horror. A blow now and then, delivered in good faith, is one of the prerogatives of marriage. Malevolent assault and savage butchery are quite another matter!

However, as my first sense of appalled outrage and angry resentment passed, I found the entire situation developing conclusive compensations. I had fancied myself married to a mortal woman and instead I was united to a

Goddess, a fierce Diana, a cyclonic Juno! I realized with a shock of recognition that one eagle had found another, perched on Olympian peaks, high above the obscure valley of pigeons and sheep.

O fortunate woman! You have gained my mercy and forbearance and have proven to my satisfaction that you deserve my virile love and are worthy of my intrepid manhood!

Nitsa, rejoice! You need no longer tremble or fear that I will ever strike you again!

# Richard Stern
## (b. 1928)

RICHARD STERN *is often referred to as a "writer's writer" for his gleaming intelli-gence, the lucidity of his prose, and his formidable command of technique. He has also been called "American letters' unsung comic writer about serious matters," and though he has somehow managed to evade the wider popularity of his former University of Chicago colleague Saul Bellow, with whom he shares many literary similarities, Stern sports a long and growing list of honors for his poetry, essays, and fiction that testifies to a widespread admiration of his work. These honors include an American Library Association Books of the Year selection for* Stitch *(1965), a Sandburg Award for* Natural Shocks *(1979), an Award of Merit for the Novel from the American Academy and Institute of Arts and Letters (1986), the* Chicago Sun-Times *book of the year award (1989) for his collection of stories* Noble Rot, *and the Heartland Award (1995) for best nonfiction work for* Sistermony, *a probing memoir of his re-lationship to his sister prompted by her battle with uterine cancer.*

*Though sometimes chided for valuing ideas over characters, he has just as often been praised for the way he directs those ideas, with affection and wit, toward a com-pact, precise rendering of a character's psychological particularity. Such is the case in "Packages," the last story in* Noble Rot, *about a man dealing with the death of his mother. Of this story, Philip Roth has said that Stern tosses it off "with the kind of simplicity and freedom that every writer who isn't Chekhov struggles to achieve."*

❖ ❖ ❖

## Packages

*from* NOBLE ROT

As I was staying in Aliber's place across from Campbell's, my sister asked me to pick up the package. "I guess it's the acknowledgment cards." Our mother had died five days before.

Campbell's is a wonderful funeral factory. It does it all for you, gets the notice into the *Times*, sends for the death certificates (needed by banks, lawyers, accountants), orders the printed acknowledgments of condolence, and, of course, works out the funeral; or, as in Mother's case, the cremation and memorial service.

We'd held the service there in the large upstairs salon. Lots of flowers and few mourners: Mother's friends — who were in New York and ambulatory (eight octogenarian widows) — cousins, many of whom we hadn't seen in decades, two of my children, Doris's, and my father with Tina and Leona, the two Trinidad ladies who kept him up to snuff. A black-gowned organist — the closest thing to a religious figure in attendance — played some of Dad's favorites, "Who," "Some Enchanted Evening," and "Smoke Gets in Your Eyes" (this one a bit much in view of Mother's chosen mode of disintegration).

The package was wrapped in rough brown paper tied with a strand of hemp which broke when I hoisted it. "Don't worry," I said to the shocked Mr. Hoffman. "I'm just across the street." I held it with one hand and shook his with the other. Outside, limousines and chauffeurs idled — it was a slow death day in New York.

Thursday. Garbage collection on East Eighty-First. A massif of sacks and cartons ranged the stony fronts of town and apartment houses. No one but me on the street. Across Fifth Avenue, the Museum fountains poured boredom into the July heat. I left the package in a half-empty carton, walked to Aliber's door, then returned and covered it with yesterday's *Times*. Back to the house, key in the door, then back again to the package, which I unwrapped. It was a silvery can, the size of a half-gallon of paint; labeled. Curious about the contents, I tried to open it. No lid. Nor was it worth the trouble of fetching a hammer and wedge from Aliber's. I stripped off the label, rewrapped the can, and covered it with the newspaper. On top of that, I put a plastic sack of rinds and fishbones.

Aliber's apartment is dark, leathery, high ceilinged, somberly turbulent. Its walls are books. Books litter tables, chairs, sills, floors. An investment counselor, Aliber is really a reader. His claim is that all intelligence has a monetary translation. A cover for sheer desire to know everything. (He does better than most. Of the hundreds of Aliber's books I've looked at, ninety percent bear his green-inked comments.)

There are hours to kill before Doris picks me up. I activate air conditioners and sound system and pick out some correct music. A cello suite of Poppa Bach. Naked on the leather couch, I listen until it overflows my capacity. You need weeks for such a piece. It should take as long to listen to as it did to compose. Or is the idea to reduce vastness into something portable?

A package.

I think I thought that then, though the notion may have come after I'd found *The Mind of Matter* in the wall behind my head. I read a chapter devoted to Planck's "famous lecture to the Berlin Academy in May of 1899," in which he described "that extraordinary quantity" which "for all times and cultures" made possible "the derivation of units for mass, length, time and temperature." Planck's constant. Not then called $h$. Only $6.625 \times 10^{-27}$ erg seconds, or, by our author, "that stubby transmitter of universal radiance . . . Nature's own package." Little as I understood of this package, I felt some connection between it and Bach's and the one which held what was left of what had once held me.

Six weeks earlier, back in Chicago, I'd written a letter in my head. *Dearest Mother. Last Saturday, I unbuttoned your dress and slipped it off your shoulders. Doris undid your bra, and for the first time in decades, I saw your sad breasts. We put the gauzy, small-flowered nightgown over your head and pulled it down the bony tunnel of your back, your seamed belly.*

*Before we taxied to Mount Sinai, Leona fixed your hair; tucked, curled, waved, and crimped it. (If her eight months of beauty school produce nothing else, they've been worth it.) It was your last home vanity. When we left you, sunk in the narrow bed, the piled hair survived. Your stake in the great world.*

I finished lunch with my spring wheat man in the Wrigley Restaurant and walked alone by the Chicago River. Immense brightness, the Sun-Times Building a cube of flame. All around, the steel-and-glass dumbness of this beautiful, cruel town. *I noticed, then noticed I noticed, the bodies of women, white and black. Thank you, Mother, for my pleasure in such sights.*

A girl in leotards the color of papaya meat jumped around a stage in front of the big nothing of Picasso's metal gift—bloodless heart, brainless head. Huffing, she explained arabesque and second position to the soft crowd of municipal workers, shoppers, tourists. It's splendid being part of a crowd like this, letting bored respect for art muzzle the interest in the dancer's body. Bless such civic gifts.

*There have been times I've wanted your death, Mother.* At least, did not much care.

It was money. That noise. Curse me for it.

I've walked through slums, *bustees, barriadas, callampas, favelas, suburbios* (the very names a misery). *In a Calcutta dump, I saw a darker you,* forty years younger, everything in her life within her reach: pot, shawl, kid. *What should a man do with money?* Getty, the billionaire, claimed he wasn't rich, didn't have a spare—an uninvested—nickel. I'm rich. So what am I doing in these glassy dollared Alps—reflections annihilating reflections—the money canyons of your town and mine?

Unearned dough. *It came to you without effort; it filled your head. (Should noise fill heads like yours? Or mine?)*

*Last week you said you wanted "to go," and you kissed me with the strength of goodbye.* (Goodbye is what's left.) *Soon you'll be nothing but your purses, your spoons, your china, your sheets, your doilies. Your money. You'll be an absence in Doris; in me; a shard in Dad's head.*

After Mother's death — which he does not acknowledge: she is *out for lunch* — his head is in more of a whirl than ever. He shuts himself in closets, undresses at three P.M., goes, pajamaed, into the street (brought back by the doormen). One night, he appears naked at Tina's bedside. He says he wishes to do things with her. Disused parts hang from his groin like rotten fruit. Tina gets a blanket around him, persuades him back to his own bed. "I was *so* scared, Miss Doris. Doctor is a strong mon. Yesterday, he moved the fuhniture round and round the living room."

Deprived of cigarettes — he sets clothes and furniture afire — and of the *Times* — there's a pressman's strike — his hours are spent walking from room to room, staring at Third Avenue, winding his wristwatch.

As the small shocks of his small world dislodge more and more of his brain, his speech shrivels to the poetry of the very young and old.

"How are you today, Daddy?"

"Rainy."

"What time do you make it?"

"Too late."

He lives by a few lines of verse which embody a creed and an old passion for eloquence. "For a' that and a' that, A man's a man for a' that." (We recite the Burns poem at his grave.) "Oh, lady bright, can it be right/This window open to the night?"

Decades of control slough off the frail body. He sits tensely in the living room. "What you doin', Doctor?"

"Waiting."

"May I ask what you waitin' *for?*"

"A girl is coming."

"What gull you talkin' of?"

"None of yours. Give her fifty dollars. A hundred dollars."

Tina has a grand laugh. (And laughs are scarce here.)

He is furious. "Out."

He waits an hour, then locks himself in the bathroom.

"You okay, Doctor?"

"Am I supposed to be?"

Doris calls Dr. Rice, who is not surprised. "It's the ones who've done the least who do the most now. I've known them to masturbate in front of people."

"Maybe we should get him a girl."

"I don't think that would do any good. And *he* certainly couldn't."

"What can be done?"

"An extra tranquilizer before bed."

Not a few times we would have liked to tranquilize him permanently. But senility too is part of life, one of the few remaining middle-class encounters with the Insoluble.

One afternoon, before I went back to Chicago, he came in while I was going over estate papers. He was in white pajamas. (The day's familiar diversions were no longer his.) "I have to talk with you, Son."

"What is it, Dad?"

He took a scrap of paper from his old billfold and gave it to me. "I want to go here."

"You are here. This is your address."

"No, dear. I want to go *home*."

"This is your home. No one else's."

"I don't think so."

And he was right. Home is where his wife lived. Or his mother — who died during the Spanish-American War.

The next day, his need to go home was so strong, we took a taxi four blocks to Doris's house. How happy he was. Doris was a segment of that female benevolence which had watched over him from birth, mother-stepmother-sisters-wife-daughter. They were a continuity of watchfulness. How he kissed Doris, and talked, until, noticing unfamiliar furniture, a different view, he grew weary. We taxied home, and now it was home, the place where his wife would be coming after lunch.

In Chicago, I got the day's bulletins by phone. "He peed in the dresser."

"Jesus."

"I think he confused drawer and door. They both open. I mean it wasn't totally irrational."

"Bless you, Doris."

He became incontinent. "I never thought I'd live to clean up my own father. I couldn't let the girls do it."

"How long can it go on?"

"Dr. Rice says he's strong as an ox. There's nothing organically wrong."

"Poor fellow."

"He misses you."

"How do you know?"

"He lights up when I say you're coming. Can't you come?"

"I'll try."

But didn't. At Christmas, I sent him a check for a billion dollars. "To the World's Best Father."

"Did he like it?"

"I don't think so. He tore it up."

"How dumb of me."

"He's still a human being, you know."

"I hadn't forgotten." *Despite those reports of yours*, I didn't say. *Which convert him into a pile of disasters.* "I should have come. He knew I should be there. And knew I knew it." Unable to say it directly, he tore up the check.

His last paternal correction.

At the end of the beautiful novella which Proust plants like an ice-age fragment in his novel, Swann thinks how terrible it is that the greatest love of his life has been for a woman who was not his type. (This thought—like the piano music of Ravel—detonates the world's pathos for me; though consciousness makes it as beautiful as the music.) My mother was not my type.

A month after Dad's death, I dreamed that she and I were having another of the small disputes which disfigured thousands of our hours. "I can't bear your nagging," I said. As always, my anger silenced hers. She said she'd tell my father to speak to me. But when he came in, he was the old man who died, and, instead of his slipper, I saw only the sad face of his last days.

Then my dream mother said, "I hope you'll be coming back to New York next summer."

"This one hasn't been very pleasant."

"I haven't had a good one either."

I knew this meant the ulcerous mouth, the colds, the drowsiness which disguised and expressed her cancer.

I was about to tell her that I would be back, when this part of the dream became a poem. (My dreams often conclude in poems and interpretations.) On a screen of air, I saw lines from George Herbert's "The Collar." "Forsake thy cage," they read,

> Thy rope of sands,
> Which petty thoughts have made, and made to thee
> Good cable, to enforce and draw,
> And be thy law . . .

My dream interpreter here let me know that my cable had turned to sand because my parents were dead. I was free.

I've been a father so long, I didn't know how much I was still a son; how onerous it was to be a son. Now my "lines and life were free." "But," the poem continued on the screen of inner air,

> as I raved and grew more fierce and wild
> At every word,
> Methought I heard one calling, *Child!*
> And I replied, *My Lord.*

My response was not *"My Lord"* but *My Duty.* The Duty which had raised and formed me.

Only at the beginning of my life and the end of hers did I love my mother wholly. When her life was over — like a simpleminded book — I pitied its waste.

There was much intelligence and much energy in her. Yet what was her life but an advertisement for idleness. And how could such a woman have failed to be a nagger, a boss, the idle driver of others, an anal neurotic for whom cleanliness was not a simple, commonsensical virtue but a compulsion nourished by her deepest need? *Wash your hands. Pick up your clothes. The room is filthy. Eat up. Mary wants to go out.* (The sympathy for Mary veiled the need to have the dining room inert, restored to preorganic purity. What counted was setting, stage, the scene before and after action. What drastic insecurity underlay this drive toward inertness?)

Too simple.

Mother loved learning, going, seeing. She loved shows, travel, games. She loved *doing good.*

Nor is this enough. She was the reliable, amiable center of a large group of women like herself, the one who remembered occasions and relationships, the one who knew *the right thing to do.*

Her telephone rang from eight A.M. on. Lunches, games, lectures, plays, visits. Lunch was a crucial, a beautiful event. One went *out.* (But where? Longchamps — before its fall — Schrafft's, but which one? *Or shall we try a new place?* What excitement.) Whose game was it? Beasie's? Marion B's? Justine's? Bridge, canasta, gin, mah-jongg (the small clicks of the tiles, "One dot"; "Two crack").

A smallish woman, five-four, brown haired. (Gray for the last twenty years, but I always *saw* her brown haired.) Not abundant, but crowded with soft, expressive waves. (Expressive of expense, of free time.) Clear brown eyes, scimitar nose, narrow lips; a sharp face, once soft, fine cheeked, pretty.

She died well. "What choice do I have?"

Not bad; for anyone, let alone a monument to redundance. (Bear two children, *cared for by others*, oversee an apartment, *cleaned by others*, shop for food, *cooked by others*.) She died bravely, modestly, with decorum. The decorum of practicality. (Her other tutelary deity.) She made up her mind to be as little trouble to those she loved as possible. (Cleanliness reborn as virtue.) She set her face to the wall, stopped taking medicine (without offending the nurses she loved so in the last weeks), and sank quietly into nonexistence. The last hours, teeth out, face caved in, the wrestler Death twisting the jaw off her face, she managed a smile (a human movement) when I said we were there, we loved her. She lay, tiny, at the bottom of tremendous loneliness.

Doris and I wait for a taxi at the corner of Eighty-First and Madison. Seven o'clock, the tail end of the day. Traffic flows north. Buses crap plumes of filth into the lovely street (where — I think for some reason — Washington's troops were chased by British redcoats two hundred years ago). A growl of horns to our left. A Rolls-Royce honks at a Department of Sanitation truck in front of Aliber's house. The garbage men are throwing sacks and cartons into great blades whirling in the truck's backside. A powerful little fellow throws in the carton with my package.

"What's the matter?"

"Nothing."

"You look funny."

"Tell you later."

*Goodbye, darling.*

And: Why not?

*You were a child of the city, born here, your mother born here. If I could have pried it open, I would have spread you in Central Park.* But this way is better than a slot in that Westchester mausoleum. Foolish, garish anteroom to no house. Egyptian stupidity.

And it was the *practical* thing to do.

*Wasn't it, Mother?*

# A. K. Ramanujan

## (1929-94)

ATTIPPAT KRISHNASWAMI RAMANUJAN *was born in Mysore, India, in 1929. The son of a mathematics professor, Ramanujan was educated at Maharaja's University in Mysore and at the University of Indiana, where he received his Ph.D. in linguistics. He taught in the Department of South Asian Languages and Civilizations and the Department of Linguistics at the University of Chicago from 1962 until his death in 1994. His books of original poetry in English are* The Striders *(1966),* Selected Poems *(1976),* Second Sight *(1986), and* The Black Hen: Complete Poems *(1995). In addition, he translated numerous classic works from Tamil and Kannada into English.*

*One of the leading post–World War II Indian poets writing in English, Ramanujan turned as often to memories of South India as to Chicago for inspiration. Nevertheless, as the five poems included below demonstrate, Ramanujan also found fascinating ways to incorporate elements of both East and West into his work. A careful craftsman, Ramanujan was also a sardonic observer of his own foibles as well as those of his homeland and his adopted country.*

*While some of Ramanujan's sentiments may be shared by Chicago's burgeoning South Asian population (as, for instance, in "Take Care"), it would be difficult for any group to claim him as a spokesman. Elliptical and intellectual, his poetry resists easy interpretation. Like the striders (the New England name for the water insect in the following poem) he admires, Ramanujan's poems often seem to walk on water while drowning in their "tiny strip/of sky."*

◆ ◆ ◆

## THE STRIDERS

And search
for certain thin-
stemmed, bubble-eyed water bugs.
See them perch
on dry capillary legs

weightless
on the ripple skin
of a stream.

No, not only prophets
walk on water. This bug sits
on a landslide of lights
and drowns eye-
deep
into its tiny strip
of sky.

## Epitaph on a Street Dog

On the hedges grew the low melon moons.
Before the crescent dark could sink her teeth
    our bitch had all her mangy suitors
        sparring for a wreath
        of the midnight noons
    in her womb. And they were no neuters.
She spawned in a hurry a score of pups,
all bald, blind, and growing old at her paps;
        some of them alive
enough to die in the cold of her love.

Peacocks may have eyes in their tails, and crests.
But She had in a row four pairs of breasts,
where blind mouths plucked and swilled their fill
till mouths had eyes, and She was full of flies.

## Take Care

In Chicago it blows
hot and cold. Trees
play fast and loose.
        Kittens and children
        have tics: the old
        have things in their
        eyes. So, do not breathe
deeply. Practise
analysis.

Invisible crabs
  scuttle the air.
  Small flies sit
  on aspirin and booze.
  Enemies have guns.
Friends have doubts.
Wives have lawyers.

Smudge your windows.
Draw the blinds.
All tall buildings
  use telescopes.
  Give daughters pills,
  learn karate.
  Prepare to get raped
bending for a book.
Go to the opera
in brown overalls,
  wear pure plastic
  on the daily bus.
  Think of the stink-
  bomb in the barber's
chair. Expect the knife
on the museum stair.

When you are there
take special care
not to stare
  at peppergrinders,
  salt shakers, or the box
  of matches on the black
  and white squares
of your kitchen cloth.
They take on the look
of meat grinders,
  cement shakers,
  boxes against boxes
  in the grilled
  city: intersections
of wet black splinter,
of houses burned

in the white oblongs
of winter, three T-
squares standing
 for the backstairs,
 the blacks black
 as the blacks
 in the Christmas snow
or the statistics
of City Hall
and Skid Row.
 In Chicago,
 do not walk slow.
 Find no time
 to stand and stare.
Down there, blacks look black.
And whites, they look blacker.

## CHICAGO ZEN

i

Now tidy your house,
dust especially your living room

and do not forget to name
all your children.

ii

Watch your step. Sight may strike you
blind in unexpected places.

The traffic light turns orange
on 57th and Dorchester, and you stumble,

you fall into a vision of forest fires,
enter a frothing Himalayan river,

rapid, silent.

 On the 14th floor,
Lake Michigan crawls and crawls

in the window. Your thumbnail
cracks a lobster louse on the windowpane

from your daughter's hair
and you drown, eyes open,

towards the Indies, the antipodes.
And you, always so perfectly sane.

iii

Now you know what you always knew:
the country cannot be reached

by jet. Nor by boat on jungle river,
hashish behind the Monkey-temple,

nor moonshot to the cratered Sea
of Tranquillity, slim circus girls

on a tightrope between tree and tree
with white parasols, or the one

and only blue guitar.

      Nor by any
other means of transport,

migrating with a clean valid passport,
no, not even by transmigrating

without any passport at all,
but only by answering ordinary

black telephones, questions
walls and small children ask,

and answering all calls of nature.

Watch your step, watch it, I say,
especially at the first high
threshold,

and the sudden low
one near the end
of the flight
of stairs,

and watch
for the last
step that's never there.

## THE BLACK HEN

It must come as leaves
to a tree
or not at all

yet it comes sometimes
as the black hen
with the red round eye

on the embroidery
stitch by stitch
dropped and found again

and when it's all there
the black hen stares
with its round red eye

and you're afraid

# Lorraine Hansberry

## (1930-65)

LORRAINE VIVIAN HANSBERRY *was born on the South Side of Chicago in 1930. After two years at the University of Wisconsin, she moved to New York in 1950, where she worked as a journalist on Paul Robeson's magazine,* Freedom. *Hansberry's first play,* A Raisin in the Sun *(1959), was the first play by an African American woman to be produced on Broadway. It won the New York Drama Critics Circle Award, and the 1961 film version, starring Sidney Poitier, received a special award at the Cannes Film Festival. However,* The Sign in Sidney Brustein's Window *(1964), set in Greenwich Village, was less successful, and Hansberry died of cancer in New York City the following year. Another play,* Les Blancs, *was unfinished at the time of her death but was later completed by her husband, Robert Nemiroff, and Charlotte Zaltzberg.* To Be Young, Gifted and Black, *a collection of her work — which includes journal entries, letters, and portions of her plays — was published in 1969.*

A Raisin in the Sun *explores what happens to people whose dreams have been deferred by racial prejudice and poverty. The play is set in a crowded Chicago apartment and tells the story of the Younger family's struggle to leave the city for a new home in the all-white (imaginary) suburb of Clybourne Park. The climax of the play comes after Walter, Mama's son and the nominal head of the family, is swindled out of the family's savings by a man who claimed to be his friend. Walter briefly considers selling the Younger honor to the head of a racist homeowner's association, but, ultimately, pride and heritage are triumphant.*

*In Scene 2, reprinted here, Walter's wife, Ruth, wrestles with the news that she is pregnant while Walter's sister, Beneatha, struggles with her identity as an American of African descent. Toward the end of the scene, the ten thousand dollar life insurance check the family has been waiting for arrives, followed shortly afterwards by Walter, who wants to invest the money in a liquor store. When Mama refuses, a conflict ensues, in the course of which Ruth, despairing over the imminent collapse of her marriage, is already planning to abort her unborn child.*

✦ ✦ ✦

*It is the following morning; a Saturday morning, and house cleaning is in progress at the* YOUNGERS. *Furniture has been shoved hither and yon and* MAMA *is giving the kitchen-area walls a washing down.* BENEATHA, *in dungarees, with a handkerchief tied around her face, is spraying insecticide into the cracks in the walls. As they work, the radio is on and a Southside disk-jockey program is inappropriately filling the house with a rather exotic saxophone blues.* TRAVIS, *the sole idle one, is leaning on his arms, looking out of the window.*

TRAVIS: Grandmama, that stuff Bennie is using smells awful. Can I go downstairs, please?

MAMA: Did you get all them chores done already? I ain't seen you doing much.

TRAVIS: Yes'm — finished early. Where did Mama go this morning?

MAMA: (*Looking at* BENEATHA) She had to go on a little errand.

TRAVIS: Where?

MAMA: To tend to her business.

TRAVIS: Can I go outside then?

MAMA: Oh, I guess so. You better stay right in front of the house though . . . and keep a good lookout for the postman.

TRAVIS: Yes'm. (*He starts out and decides to give his* AUNT BENEATHA *a good swat on the legs as he passes her*) Leave them poor little old cockroaches alone, they ain't bothering you none.

(*He runs as she swings the spray gun at him both viciously and playfully.* WALTER *enters from the bedroom and goes to the phone*)

MAMA: Look out there, girl, before you be spilling some of that stuff on that child!

TRAVIS: (*Teasing*) That's right — look out now!

(*He exits*)

BENEATHA: (*Drily*) I can't imagine that it would hurt him — it has never hurt the roaches.

WALTER: (*Into phone*) Hello — Let me talk to Willy Harris.

MAMA: You better get over there behind the bureau. I seen one marching out of there like Napoleon yesterday.

WALTER: Hello, Willy? It ain't come yet. It'll be here in a few minutes. Did the lawyer give you the papers?

BENEATHA: There's really only one way to get rid of them, Mama —

MAMA: How?

BENEATHA: Set fire to this building.

WALTER: Good. Good. I'll be right over.

BENEATHA: Where did Ruth go, Walter?

WALTER: I don't know.

(*He exits abruptly*)

BENEATHA: Mama, where did Ruth go?

MAMA: (*Looking at her with meaning*) To the doctor, I think.

BENEATHA: The doctor? What's the matter? (*They exchange glances*) You don't think—

MAMA: (*With her sense of drama*) Now I ain't saying what I think. But I ain't never been wrong 'bout a woman neither.

(*The phone rings*)

BENEATHA: (*At the phone*) Hay-lo . . . (*Pause, and a moment of recognition*) Well—when did you get back! . . . And how was it? . . . Of course I've missed you—in my way . . . This morning? No . . . house cleaning and all that and Mama hates it if I let people come over when the house is like this . . . You have? Well, that's different . . . What is it—Oh, what the hell, come on over . . . Right, see you then.

(*She hangs up*)

MAMA: (*Who has listened vigorously, as is her habit*) Who is that you inviting over here with this house looking like this? You ain't got the pride you was born with!

BENEATHA: Asagai doesn't care how houses look, Mama—he's an intellectual.

MAMA: Who?

BENEATHA: Asagai—Joseph Asagai. He's an African boy I met on campus. He's been studying in Canada all summer.

MAMA: What's his name?

BENEATHA: Asagai, Joseph. Ah-sah-guy . . . He's from Nigeria.

MAMA: Oh, that's the little country that was founded by slaves way back . . .

BENEATHA: No, Mama—that's Liberia.

MAMA: I don't think I never met no African before.

BENEATHA: Well, do me a favor and don't ask him a whole lot of ignorant questions about Africans. I mean, do they wear clothes and all that—

MAMA: Well, now, I guess if you think we so ignorant 'round here maybe you shouldn't bring your friends here—

BENEATHA: It's just that people ask such crazy things. All anyone seems to know about when it comes to Africa is Tarzan—

MAMA: (*Indignantly*) Why should I know anything about Africa?

BENEATHA: Why do you give money at church for the missionary work?

MAMA: Well, that's to help save people.

BENEATHA: You mean save them from Heathenism—

MAMA: (*Innocently*) Yes.

BENEATHA: I'm afraid they need more salvation from the British and the French.

(RUTH *comes in forlornly and pulls off her coat with dejection. They both turn to look at her*)

RUTH: (*Dispiritedly*) Well, I guess from all the happy faces—everybody knows.

BENEATHA: You pregnant?

MAMA: Lord have mercy, I sure hope it's a little old girl. Travis ought to have a sister. (BENEATHA *and* RUTH *give her a hopeless look for this grandmotherly enthusiasm*)

BENEATHA: How far along are you?

RUTH: Two months.

BENEATHA: Did you mean to? I mean did you plan it or was it an accident?

MAMA: What do you know about planning or not planning?

BENEATHA: Oh, Mama.

RUTH: (*Wearily*) She's twenty years old, Lena.

BENEATHA: Did you plan it, Ruth?

RUTH: Mind your own business.

BENEATHA: It is my business—where is he going to live, on the *roof?* (*There is silence following the remark as the three women react to the sense of it*) Gee—I didn't mean that, Ruth, honest. Gee, I don't feel like that at all. I—I think it is wonderful.

RUTH: (*Dully*) Wonderful.

BENEATHA: Yes, really.

MAMA: (*Looking at* RUTH, *worried*) Doctor say everything going to be all right?

RUTH: (*Far away*) Yes—she says everything is going to be fine . . .

MAMA: (*Immediately suspicious*) "She"—What doctor you went to?

(RUTH *folds over, near hysteria*)

MAMA: (*Worriedly hovering over* RUTH) Ruth honey—what's the matter with you—you sick?

(RUTH *has her fists clenched on her thighs and is fighting hard to suppress a scream that seems to be rising in her*)

BENEATHA: What's the matter with her, Mama?

MAMA: (*Working her fingers in* RUTH's *shoulder to relax her*) She be all right. Women gets right depressed sometimes when they get her way. (*Speaking softly, expertly, rapidly*) Now you just relax. That's right . . . just lean back, don't think 'bout nothing at all . . . nothing at all—

RUTH: I'm all right . . .

(*The glassy-eyed look melts and then she collapses into a fit of heavy sobbing. The bell rings*)

BENEATHA: Oh, my God—that must be Asagai.

MAMA: (*To* RUTH) Come on now, honey. You need to lie down and rest awhile . . . then have some nice hot food.

(*They exit,* RUTH's *weight on her mother-in-law.* BENEATHA, *herself profoundly disturbed, opens the door to admit a rather dramatic-looking young man
with a large package*)

ASAGAI: Hello, Alaiyo —

BENEATHA: (*Holding the door open and regarding him with pleasure*) Hello . . .
(*Long pause*) Well — come in. And please excuse everything. My mother
was very upset about my letting anyone come here with the place like this.

ASAGAI: (*Coming into the room*) You look disturbed too . . . Is something wrong?

BENEATHA: (*Still at the door, absently*) Yes . . . we've all got acute ghetto-itus.
(*She smiles and comes toward him, finding a cigarette and sitting*) So — sit
down? How was Canada?

ASAGAI: (*A sophisticate*) Canadian.

BENEATHA: (*Looking at him*) I'm very glad you are back.

ASAGAI: (*Looking back at her in turn*) Are you really?

BENEATHA: Yes — very.

ASAGAI: Why — you were quite glad when I went away. What happened?

BENEATHA: You went away.

ASAGAI: Ahhhhhhhh.

BENEATHA: Before — you wanted to be so serious before there was time.

ASAGAI: How much time must there be before one knows what one feels?

BENEATHA: (*Stalling this particular conversation. Her hands pressed together, in a
deliberately childish gesture*) What did you bring me?

ASAGAI: (*Handing her the package*) Open it and see.

BENEATHA: (*Eagerly opening the package and drawing out some records and the
colorful robes of a Nigerian woman*) Oh, Asagai! . . . You got them for me! . . .
How beautiful . . . and the records too! (*She lifts out the robes and runs to
the mirror with them and holds the drapery up in front of herself*)

ASAGAI: (*Coming to her at the mirror*) I shall have to teach you how to drape it
properly. (*He flings the material about her for the moment and stands back to
look at her*) Ah — Oh-pay-gay-day, oh-ghah-mu-shay. (*A Yoruba exclamation
for admiration*) You wear it well . . . very well . . . mutilated hair and all.

BENEATHA: (*Turning suddenly*) My hair — what's wrong with my hair?

ASAGAI: (*Shrugging*) Were you born with it like that?

BENEATHA: (*Reaching up to touch it*) No . . . of course not. (*She looks back to the
mirror, disturbed*)

ASAGAI: (*Smiling*) How then?

BENEATHA: You know perfectly well how . . . as crinkly as yours . . . that's how.

ASAGAI: And it is ugly to you that way?

BENEATHA: (*Quickly*) Oh, no — not ugly . . . (*More slowly, apologetically*) But
it's so hard to manage when it's, well — raw.

ASAGAI: And so to accommodate that—you mutilate it every week?

BENEATHA: It's not mutilation!

ASAGAI: (*Laughing aloud at her seriousness*) Oh . . . please! I am only teasing you because you are so very serious about these things. (*He stands back from her and folds his arms across his chest as he watches her pulling at her hair and frowning in the mirror*) Do you remember the first time you met me at school? . . . (*He laughs*) You came up to me and you said—and I thought you were the most serious little thing I had ever seen—you said: (*He imitates her*) "Mr. Asagai—I want very much to talk with you. About Africa. You see, Mr. Asagai, I am looking for my identity!"
(*He laughs*)

BENEATHA: (*Turning to him, not laughing*) Yes—(*Her face is quizzical, profoundly disturbed*)

ASAGAI: (*Still teasing and reaching out and taking her face in his hands and turning her profile to him*) Well . . . it is true that this is not so much a profile of a Hollywood queen as perhaps a queen of the Nile—(*A mock dismissal of the importance of the question*) But what does it matter? Assimilationism is so popular in your country.

BENEATHA: (*Wheeling, passionately, sharply*) I am not an assimilationist!

ASAGAI: (*The protest hangs in the room for a moment and* ASAGAI *studies her, his laughter fading*) Such a serious one. (*There is a pause*) So—you like the robes? You must take excellent care of them—they are from my sister's personal wardrobe.

BENEATHA: (*With incredulity*) You—you sent all the way home—for me?

ASAGAI: (*With charm*) For you—I would do much more . . . Well, that is what I came for. I must go.

BENEATHA: Will you call me Monday?

ASAGAI: Yes . . . We have a great deal to talk about. I mean about identity and time and all that.

BENEATHA: Time?

ASAGAI: Yes. About how much time one needs to know what one feels.

BENEATHA: You never understood that there is more than one kind of feeling which can exist between a man and a woman—or, at least, there should be.

ASAGAI: (*Shaking his head negatively but gently*) No. Between a man and a woman there need only be one kind of feeling. I have that for you . . . Now even . . . right this moment . . .

BENEATHA: I know—and by itself—it won't do. I can find that anywhere.

ASAGAI: For a woman it should be enough.

BENEATHA: I know—because that's what it says in all the novels that men write. But it isn't. Go ahead and laugh—but I'm not interested in being someone's little episode in America or — (*With feminine vengeance*) — one of them! (ASAGAI *has burst into laughter again*) That's funny as hell, huh!

ASAGAI: It's just that every American girl I have known has said that to me. White — black — in this you are all the same. And the same speech, too!

BENEATHA: (*Angrily*) Yuk, yuk, yuk!

ASAGAI: It's how you can be sure that the world's most liberated women are not liberated at all. You all talk about it too much!

(MAMA *enters and is immediately all social charm because of the presence of a guest*)

BENEATHA: Oh — Mama — this is Mr. Asagai.

MAMA: How do you do?

ASAGAI: (*Total politeness to an elder*) How do you do, Mrs. Younger. Please forgive me for coming at such an outrageous hour on a Saturday.

MAMA: Well, you are quite welcome. I just hope you understand that our house don't always look like this. (*Chatterish*) You must come again. I would love to hear all about — (*Not sure of the name*) — your country. I think it's so sad the way our American Negroes don't know nothing about Africa 'cept Tarzan and all that. And all that money they pour into these churches when they ought to be helping you people over there drive out them French and Englishmen done taken away your land.

(*The mother flashes a slightly superior look at her daughter upon completion of the recitation*)

ASAGAI: (*Taken aback by this sudden and acutely unrelated expression of sympathy*) Yes . . . yes . . .

MAMA: (*Smiling at him suddenly and relaxing and looking him over*) How many miles is it from here to where you come from?

ASAGAI: Many thousands.

MAMA: (*Looking at him as she would* WALTER) I bet you don't half look after yourself, being away from your mama either. I spec you better come 'round here from time to time and get yourself some decent home-cooked meals . . .

ASAGAI: (*Moved*) Thank you. Thank you very much. (*They are all quiet, then* —) Well . . . I must go. I will call you Monday, Alaiyo.

MAMA: What's that he call you?

ASAGAI: Oh — "Alaiyo." I hope you don't mind. It is what you would call a nickname, I think. It is a Yoruba word. I am a Yoruba.

MAMA: (*Looking at* BENEATHA) I — I thought he was from —

ASAGAI: (*Understanding*) Nigeria is my country. Yoruba is my tribal orgin —

BENEATHA: You didn't tell us what Alaiyo means . . . for all I know, you might be calling me Little Idiot or something . . .

ASAGAI: Well . . . let me see . . . I do not know how just to explain it . . . The sense of a thing can be so different when it changes languages.

BENEATHA: You're evading.

ASAGAI: No—really it is difficult . . . (*Thinking*) It means . . . it means One for Whom Bread Food—Is Not Enough. (*He looks at her*) Is that all right?

BENEATHA: (*Understanding, softly*) Thank you.

MAMA: (*Looking from one to the other and not understanding any of it*) Well . . . that's nice . . . You must come see us again—Mr.—

ASAGAI: Ah-sah-guy . . .

MAMA: Yes . . . Do come again.

ASAGAI: Good-bye.

(*He exits*)

MAMA: (*After him*) Lord, that's a pretty thing just went out here! (*Insinuatingly, to her daughter*) Yes, I guess I see why we done commence to get so interested in Africa 'round here. Missionaries my aunt Jenny!

(*She exits*)

BENEATHA: Oh, Mama! . . .

(*She picks up the Nigerian dress and holds it up to her in front of the mirror again. She sets the headdress on haphazardly and then notices her hair again and clutches at it and then replaces the headdress and frowns at herself. Then she starts to wriggle in front of the mirror as she thinks a Nigerian woman might. TRAVIS enters and regards her*)

TRAVIS: You cracking up?

BENEATHA: Shut up.

(*She pulls the headdress off and looks at herself in the mirror and clutches at her hair again and squinches her eyes as if trying to imagine something. Then, suddenly she gets her raincoat and kerchief and hurriedly prepares for going out*)

MAMA: (*Coming back into the room*) She's resting now. Travis, baby, run next door and ask Miss Johnson to please let me have a little kitchen cleanser. This here can is empty as Jacob's kettle.

TRAVIS: I just came in.

MAMA: Do as you told. (*He exits and she looks at her daughter*) Where you going?

BENEATHA: (*Halting at the door*) To become a queen of the Nile!

(*She exits in a breathless blaze of glory. RUTH appears in the bedroom doorway*)

MAMA: Who told you to get up?

RUTH: Ain't nothing wrong with me to be lying in no bed for. Where did Bennie go?

MAMA: (*Drumming her fingers*) Far as I could make out—to Egypt. (*RUTH just looks at her*) What time is it getting to?

RUTH: Ten twenty. And the mailman going to ring that bell this morning just like he done every morning for the last umpteen years.

(TRAVIS *comes in with the cleanser can*)

TRAVIS: She say to tell you that she don't have much.

MAMA: (*Angrily*) Lord, some people I could name sure is tight-fisted! (*Directing her grandson*) Mark two cans of cleanser down on the list there. If she that hard up for kitchen cleanser, I sure don't want to forget to get her none!

RUTH: Lena — maybe the woman is just short on cleanser —

MAMA: (*Not listening*) — Much baking powder as she done borrowed from me all these years, she could of done gone into the baking business!

(*The bell sounds suddenly and sharply and all three are stunned — serious and silent — mid-speech. In spite of all the other conversations and distractions of the morning, this is what they have been waiting for, even* TRAVIS, *who looks helplessly from his mother to his grandmother.* RUTH *is the first to come to life again*)

RUTH: (*To* TRAVIS) Get down them steps, boy!

(TRAVIS *snaps to life and flies out to get the mail*)

MAMA: (*Her eyes wide, her hand to her breast*) You mean it done really come?

RUTH: (*Excited*) Oh, Miss Lena!

MAMA: (*Collecting herself*) Well . . . I don't know what we all so excited about 'round here for. We known it was coming for months.

RUTH: That's a whole lot different from having it come and being able to hold it in your hands . . . a piece of paper worth ten thousand dollars . . .

(TRAVIS *bursts back into the room. He holds the envelope high above his head, like a little dancer, his face is radiant and he is breathless. He moves to his grandmother with sudden slow ceremony and puts the envelope into her hands. She accepts it, and then merely holds it and looks at it*) Come on! Open it . . . Lord have mercy, I wish Walter Lee was here!

TRAVIS: Open it, Grandmama!

MAMA: (*Still staring at it*) Now don't act silly . . . We ain't never been no people to act silly 'bout no money —

RUTH: (*Swiftly*) We ain't never had none before — open it!

(MAMA *finally makes a good strong tear and pulls out the thin blue slice of paper and inspects it closely. The boy and his mother study it raptly over* MAMA's *shoulders*)

MAMA: Travis! (*She is counting off with doubt*) Is that the right number of zeros.

TRAVIS: Yes'm . . . ten thousand dollars. Gaalee, Grandmama, you rich.

MAMA: (*She holds the check away from her, still looking at it. Slowly her face sobers into a mask of unhappiness*) Ten thousand dollars. (*She hands it to* RUTH) Put it away somewhere, Ruth. (*She does not look at* RUTH; *her eyes seem to be seeing something somewhere very far off*) Ten thousand dollars they give you. Ten thousand dollars.

TRAVIS: (*To his mother, sincerely*) What's the matter with Grandmama — don't she want to be rich?

RUTH: (*Distractedly*) You go on out and play now, baby. (TRAVIS *exits.* MAMA *starts wiping dishes absently, humming intently to herself.* RUTH *turns to her, with kind exasperation*) You've gone and got yourself upset.

MAMA: (*Not looking at her*) I spec if it wasn't for you all . . . I would just put that money away or give it to the church or something.

RUTH: Now what kind of talk is that. Mr. Younger would just be plain mad if he could hear you talking foolish like that.

MAMA: (*Stopping and staring off*) Yes . . . he sure would. (*Sighing*) We got enough to do with that money, all right. (*She halts then, and turns and looks at her daughter-in-law hard;* RUTH *avoids her eyes and* MAMA *wipes her hands with finality and starts to speak firmly to* RUTH) Where did you go today, girl?

RUTH: To the doctor.

MAMA: (*Impatiently*) Now, Ruth . . . you know better than that. Old Doctor Jones is strange enough in his way but there ain't nothing 'bout him make somebody slip and call him "she"—like you done this morning.

RUTH: Well, that's what happened—my tongue slipped.

MAMA: You went to see that woman, didn't you?

RUTH: (*Defensively, giving herself away*) What woman you talking about?

MAMA: (*Angrily*) That woman who—

(WALTER *enters in great excitement*)

WALTER: Did it come?

MAMA: (*Quietly*) Can't you give people a Christian greeting before you start asking about money?

WALTER: (*To* RUTH) Did it come? (RUTH *unfolds the check and lays it quietly before him, watching him intently with thoughts of her own.* WALTER *sits down and grasps it close and counts off the zeros*) Ten thousand dollars—(*He turns suddenly, frantically to his mother and draws some papers out of his breast pocket*) Mama—look. Old Willy Harris put everything on paper—

MAMA: Son—I think you ought to talk to your wife . . . I'll go on out and leave you alone if you want—

WALTER: I can talk to her later—Mama, look—

MAMA: Son—

WALTER: WILL SOMEBODY PLEASE LISTEN TO ME TODAY!

MAMA: (*Quietly*) I don't 'low no yellin' in this house, Walter Lee, and you know it—(WALTER *stares at them in frustration and starts to speak several times*) And there ain't going to be no investing in no liquor store. I don't aim to have to speak on that again.

(*A long pause*)

WALTER: Oh—so you don't aim to have to speak on that again? So you have decided . . . (*Crumpling his papers*) Well, you tell that to my boy tonight when you put him to sleep on the living room couch . . . (*Turning to* MAMA *and speaking directly to her*) Yeah — and tell it to my wife, Mama, tomorrow when she has to go out of here to look after somebody else's kids. And tell it to me, Mama, every time we need a new pair of curtains and I have to watch you go out and work in somebody's kitchen. Yeah, you tell me then!

(WALTER *starts out*)

RUTH: Where you going?

WALTER: I'm going out!

RUTH: Where?

WALTER: Just out of this house somewhere —

RUTH: (*Getting her coat*) I'll come too.

WALTER: I don't want you to come!

RUTH: I got something to talk to you about, Walter.

WALTER: That's too bad.

MAMA: (*Still quietly*) Walter Lee — (*She waits and he finally turns and looks at her*) Sit down.

WALTER: I'm a grown man, Mama.

MAMA: Ain't nobody said you wasn't grown. But you still in my house and my presence. And as long as you are — you'll talk to your wife civil. Now sit down.

RUTH: (*Suddenly*) Oh, let him go on out and drink himself to death! He makes me sick to my stomach! (*She flings her coat against him*)

WALTER: (*Violently*) And you turn mine too, baby! (RUTH *goes into their bedroom and slams the door behind her*) That was my greatest mistake —

MAMA: (*Still quietly*) Walter, what is the matter with you?

WALTER: Matter with me? Ain't nothing the matter with me!

MAMA: Yes there is. Something eating you up like a crazy man. Something more than me not giving you this money. The past few years I been watching it happen to you. You get all nervous acting and kind of wild in the eyes — (WALTER *jumps up impatiently at her words*) I said sit there now, I'm talking to you!

WALTER: Mama — I don't need no nagging at me today.

MAMA: Seem like you getting a place where you always tied up in some kind of knot about something. But if anybody ask you 'bout it you just yell at 'em and bust out the house and go out and drink somewheres. Walter Lee, people can't live with that. Ruth's a good, patient girl in her way — but you getting to be too much. Boy, don't make the mistake of driving that girl away from you.

WALTER: Why — what she do for me?

MAMA: She loves you.

WALTER: Mama — I'm going out. I want to go off somewhere and be by myself for a while.

MAMA: I'm sorry 'bout your liquor store, son. It just wasn't the thing for us to do. That's what I want to tell you about —

WALTER: I got to go out, Mama —

(*He rises*)

MAMA: It's dangerous, son.

WALTER: What's dangerous?

MAMA: When a man goes outside his home to look for peace.

WALTER: (*Beseechingly*) Then why can't there never be no peace in this house then?

MAMA: You done found it in some other house?

WALTER: No — there ain't no woman! Why do women always think there's a woman somewhere when a man gets restless. (*Coming to her*) Mama — Mama — I want so many things . . .

MAMA: Yes, son —

WALTER: I want so many things that they are driving me kind of crazy . . . Mama, look at me.

MAMA: I'm looking at you. You a good-looking boy. You got a job, a nice wife, a fine boy and —

WALTER: A job. (*Looks at her*) Mama, a job? I open and close car doors all day long. I drive a man around in his limousine and I say, "Yes, sir; no, sir; very good, sir; shall I take the Drive, sir?" Mama, that ain't no kind of job . . . that ain't nothing at all. (*Very quietly*) Mama, I don't know if I can make you understand.

MAMA: Understand what, baby?

WALTER: (*Quietly*) Sometimes it's like I can see the future stretched out in front of me — just plain as day. The future, Mama. Hanging over there at the edge of my days. Just waiting for me — a big, looming blank space — full of nothing. Just waiting for me. (*Pause*) Mama — sometimes when I'm downtown and I pass them cool, quiet-looking restaurants where them white boys are sitting back and talking 'bout things . . . sitting there turning deals worth millions of dollars . . . sometimes I see guys don't look much older than me —

MAMA: Son — how come you talk so much 'bout money?

WALTER: (*With immense passion*) Because it is life, Mama!

MAMA: (*Quietly*) Oh — (*Very quietly*) So now it's life. Money is life. Once upon a time freedom used to be life — now it's money. I guess the world really do change . . .

WALTER: No — it was always money, Mama. We just didn't know about it.

MAMA: No . . . something has changed. (*She looks at him*) You something new, boy. In my time we was worried about not being lynched and getting to the North if we could and how to stay alive and still have a pinch of dignity too . . . Now here come you and Beneatha — talking 'bout things we ain't never even thought about hardly, me and your daddy. You ain't satisfied or proud of nothing we done. I mean that you had a home; that we kept you out of trouble till you was grown; that you don't have to ride to work on the back of nobody's streetcar — You my children — but how different we done become.

WALTER: You just don't understand, Mama, you just don't understand.

MAMA: Son — do you know your wife is expecting another baby? (WALTER *stands, stunned, and absorbs what his mother has said*) That's what she wanted to talk to you about. (WALTER *sinks down into a chair*) This ain't for me to be telling — but you ought to know. (*She waits*) I think Ruth is thinking 'bout getting rid of that child.

WALTER: (*Slowly understanding*) No — no — Ruth wouldn't do that.

MAMA: When the world gets ugly enough — a woman will do anything for her family. The part that's already living.

WALTER: You don't know Ruth, Mama, if you think she would do that.

(RUTH *opens the bedroom door and stands there a little limp*)

RUTH: (*Beaten*) Yes I would too, Walter. (*Pause*) I gave her a five-dollar down payment.

(*There is total silence as the man stares at his wife and the mother stares at her son*)

MAMA: (*Presently*) Well — (*Tightly*) Well — son, I'm waiting to hear you say something . . . I'm waiting to hear how you be your father's son. Be the man he was . . . (*Pause*) Your wife say she going to destroy your child. And I'm waiting to hear you talk like him and say we a people who give children life, not who destroys them — (*She rises*) I'm waiting to see you stand up and look like your daddy and say we done give up one baby to poverty and that we ain't going to give up nary another one . . . I'm waiting.

WALTER: Ruth —

MAMA: If you a son of mine, tell her! (WALTER *turns, looks at her and can say nothing. She continues, bitterly*) You . . . you are a disgrace to your father's memory. Somebody get me my hat.

# Mike Royko

## (1932-97)

*When* MIKE ROYKO *died in 1997, the city mourned. Granted, a few of the many people he confronted in his no-nonsense manner may have secretly celebrated, but his death was seen by many as the end of an era, when newspaper columnists spoke their minds and weren't afraid to offend the sensibilities of their readers.*

*Royko was born in a Polish neighborhood on the Northwest Side of Chicago in 1932, the son of saloonkeepers. He grew up among drinkers and fighters and, not surprisingly, some of his best writing is set in the city's bars. After a stint in the Air Force, Royko became a columnist for the* Chicago Daily News *from 1959 until the paper closed in 1978. He wrote for the* Chicago Sun-Times *from 1978 – 84 and finally, in a move that coincided with national syndication, for the* Chicago Tribune *from 1984 until his death. Royko, whose higher education consisted of two years at Wright Junior College, was always skeptical of intellectuals; he saw himself as a champion of the common man, a debunker of frauds, and was perhaps most famous for his tough-talking, cynical alter ego Slats Grobnik.*

*Nearly all of Royko's books were collections of his newspaper columns, yet* Boss: Richard J. Daley of Chicago *(1971), winner of the Pulitzer Prize for commentary, shows that Royko's sometimes careless prose could truly shine when he was freed from the constraints of his daily essay assignment. As Roy Fisher wrote in a* New Republic *review, "Daley emerges as a complex mixture of integrity and debasement, of wisdom and stupidity, of vision and blindness, of compassion and brutality." Chapter 1, excerpted below, provides a vivid, detailed portrait of a day in the life of the late mayor.*

✦ ✦ ✦

## *from* Boss

WILLIAM KUNSTLER: What is your name?
WITNESS: Richard Joseph Daley.
WILLIAM KUNSTLER: What is your occupation?
WITNESS: I am the mayor of the city of Chicago.

The workday begins early. Sometime after seven o'clock a black limousine glides out of the garage of the police station on the corner, moves less than a block, and stops in front of a weathered pink bungalow at 3536 South Lowe Avenue. Policeman Alphonsus Gilhooly, walking in front of the house, nods to the detective at the wheel of the limousine.

It's an unlikely house for such a car. A passing stranger might think that a rich man had come back to visit his people in the old neighborhood. It's the kind of sturdy brick house, common to Chicago, that a fireman or printer would buy. Thousands like it were put up by contractors in the 1920s and 1930s from standard blueprints in an architectural style fondly dubbed "carpenter's delight."

The outside of that pink house is deceiving. The inside is furnished in expensive, Colonial-style furniture, the basement paneled in fine wood, and two days a week a woman comes in to help with the cleaning. The shelves hold religious figurines and bric-a-brac. There are only a few volumes — the Baltimore Catechism, the Bible, a leather-bound *Profiles in Courage*, and several self-improvement books. All of the art is religious, most of it bloody with crucifixion and crosses of thorns.

Outside, another car has arrived. It moves slowly, the two detectives peering down the walkways between the houses, glancing at the drivers of the cars that travel the street, then parks somewhere behind the limousine.

At the other end of the block, a blue squad car has stopped near the corner tavern, and the policemen are watching Thirty-sixth Street, which crosses Lowe.

In the alley behind the house, a policeman sits in a car. Like Gilhooly, he has been there all night, protecting the back entrance, behind the high wooden fence that encloses the small yard.

Down the street, in another brick bungalow, Matt Danaher is getting ready for work. He runs the two thousand clerical employees in the Cook County court system, and he knows the morning routine of his neighbor. As a young protégé he once drove the car, opened the door, held the coat, got the papers. Now he is part of the ruling circle, and one of the few people in the world who can walk past the policeman and into the house, one of the people who are invited to spend an evening, sit in the basement, eat, sing, dance the Irish jig. The blue-blooded bankers from downtown aren't invited, although they would like to be, and neither are men who have been governors, senators, and ambassadors. The people who come in the evening or on Sunday are old friends from the neighborhood, the relatives, people who take their coats off when they walk in the door, and loosen their ties.

Danaher is one of them, and his relationship to the owner of the house is so close that he has served as an emotional whipping boy, so close that he can yell back and slam the door when he leaves.

They're getting up for work in the little houses and flats all across the old neighborhood known as Bridgeport, and thanks to the man for whom the limousine waits, about two thousand of the forty thousand Bridgeport people are going to jobs in City Hall, the County Building, the courts, ward offices, police and fire stations. It's a political neighborhood, with political jobs, and the people can use them. It ranks very low among the city and suburban communities in education. Those who don't have government jobs work hard for their money, and it isn't much. Bridgeport ranks low in income, too.

It's a suspicious neighborhood, a blend of Irish, Lithuanian, Italian, Polish, German, and all white. In the bars, heads turn when a stranger comes in. Blacks pass through in cars, but are unwise to travel by on foot. When a black college student moved into a flat on Lowe Avenue in 1964, only a block north of the pink bungalow, there was a riot and he had to leave.

Well before eight o'clock, the door of the bungalow opens and a short, stout man steps out. His walk is brisk and bouncy. A nod and smile to Patrolman Gilhooly and he's in the limousine. It pulls out from the curb and the "tail car" with the two detectives trails it, hanging back to prevent the limousine from being followed.

It's a short drive to work. The house is about four miles southwest of the Loop, the downtown business district, within the problem area known as the "inner city." If the limousine went east, to Lake Shore Drive, it would go through part of the black ghetto. If it went straight north, it would enter a decaying neighborhood in transition from white to Latin and black. It turns toward an expressway entrance only a few blocks away.

The two cars take the Dan Ryan Expressway, twelve lanes at its widest point, with a rapid-transit train track down the center. It stretches from the Loop, past the old South Side ghetto, past the giant beehive public housing with its swarming children, furious street gangs, and weary welfare mothers.

He built that expressway, and he named it after Dan Ryan, another big South Side politician, who was named after his father, a big South Side politician.

The limousine crosses another expressway, this one cutting through the big, smokey, industrial belt, southwest toward white backlash country, where five years ago Dr. Martin Luther King was hit in the head with a brick when he led marchers into the neighborhood for the cause of open housing—which exists only on a few pages of the city's ordinance.

He built that expressway, too, and named it after Adlai Stevenson, whom he helped build into a presidential candidate, and whom he dropped when it was time.

The limousine passes an exit that leads to the Circle Campus, the city's branch of the University of Illinois, acres of modern concrete buildings that comprise one of the biggest city campuses in the country. It wasn't easy to build because thousands of families in the city's oldest Italian neighborhood had to be uprooted and their homes and churches torn down. They cried that they were betrayed because they had been promised they would stay. But he built it.

Another mile or so and the limousine crosses another expressway that goes straight west, through the worst of the ghetto slums, where the biggest riots and fires were ignited, for which the outraged and outrageous "shoot to kill" order was issued. Straight west, past the house where the Black Panthers were killed, some in their beds, by the predawn police raiders.

He opened that expressway and named it after Dwight D. Eisenhower, making it the city's only Republican expressway.

As the limousine nears the Loop, the Dan Ryan blends into still another expressway. This one goes through the Puerto Rican ghetto and the remnants of the old Polish neighborhood, where the old people remain while their children move away, then into the middle class far Northwest Side, where Dr. King's marchers walked through a shower of bottles, bricks and spit. It ends at O'Hare Airport, the nation's busiest jet handler.

He built that expressway, too, and he named it after John F. Kennedy, whom he helped elect president, and he built most of the airport and opened it, although he still calls it "O'Hara."

During the ride he reads the two morning papers, the *Chicago Sun-Times* and the *Chicago Tribune*, always waiting on the back seat. He's a fast but thorough reader and he concentrates on news about the city. He is in the papers somewhere every day, if not by name — and the omission is rare — at least by deed. The papers like him. If something has gone well, he'll be praised in an editorial. If something has gone badly, one of his subordinates will be criticized in an editorial. During the 1968 Democratic Convention, when their reporters were being bloodied, one of the more scathing newspaper editorials was directed at a lowly Police Department public relations man.

He, too, was criticized, but a week after the convention ended, his official version of what had happened on Chicago's streets was printed, its distortions and flat lies unchallenged. He dislikes reporters and writers, but gets on well with editors and publishers, a trait usually found in Republicans rather than Democrats. If he feels that he has been criticized unfairly, and he considers most criticism unfair, he doesn't hesitate to pick up a phone and complain to an editor. All four papers endorsed him for his fourth term — even the *Tribune*, the voice of Middle West Republicanism — but in general, he views the papers as his enemy. The reporters, specifically. They want to know things that are none of their business, because they are little men. Editors, at least, have power, but he doesn't understand why they let reporters exercise it.

The limousine leaves the expressway and enters the Loop, stopping in front of St. Peter's, a downtown church. When the bodyguards have parked and walked to his car, he gets out and enters the church. This is an important part of his day. Since childhood he has attended daily mass, as his mother did before him. On Sundays and some work days, he'll go to his own church, the Church of the Nativity, just around the corner from his home. That's where he was baptized, married, and the place from which his parents were buried. Before Easter, his wife will join the other neighborhood ladies for the traditional scrubbing of the church floors. Regardless of what he may do in the afternoon, and to whom, he will always pray in the morning.

After mass, it's a few steps to the side door of Maxim's, a glass and plastic coffee shop, where, in the event he comes in, a table is set up in the privacy of the rear. It is not to be confused with Chicago's other Maxim's which serves haute cuisine, has a discotheque, and enjoys a social-register clientele. He won't go to those kinds of places. He doesn't like them and people might think he was putting on airs. He eats at home most of the time, and for dinner out there are sedate private clubs with a table in a quiet corner.

He leaves a dollar for his coffee and roll and marches with his bodyguards toward City Hall — "the Hall," as it is called locally, as in "I got a job in the Hall," or "See my brother in the Hall and he'll fix it for you," or "Do you know anybody in the Hall who can take care of this?"

He glances at the new Civic Center, a tower of russet steel and glass, fronted by a gracious plaza with a fountain and a genuine Picasso-designed metalwork sculpture almost fifty feet high.

He put it all there, the Civic Center, the plaza, the Picasso. And the judges and county officials who work in the Civic Center, he put most of them there, too.

Wherever he looks as he marches, there are new skyscrapers up or going up. The city has become an architect's delight, except when the architects see the great Louis Sullivan's landmark buildings being ripped down for parking garages or allowed to degenerate into slums.

None of the new buildings were there before. His leadership put them there, his confidence, his energy. Everybody says so. If he kept walking north a couple more blocks, he'd see the twin towers of Marina City, the striking tubular downtown apartment buildings, a self-contained city with bars and restaurants, ice rinks, shops and clubs, and balconies on every apartment for sitting out in the smog.

His good friend Charlie Swibel built it, with financing from the Janitors' Union, run by his good friend William McFetridge. For Charlie Swibel, building the apartment towers was coming a long way from being a flophouse and slum operator. Now some of his friend Charlie's flophouses are going to be torn down, and the area west of the Loop redeveloped for office buildings and such. And his friend Charlie will do that, too. Let people wonder why out-of-town investors let Charlie in for a big piece of the new project, without Charlie having to put up any money or take any risk. Let people ask why the city, after acquiring the land under urban renewal powers, rushed through approval of Charlie's bid. Let them ask if there's a conflict of interest because Charlie is also the head of the city's public housing agency, which makes him a city official. Let them ask. What trees do they plant? What buildings do they put up?

Head high, shoulders back, he strides with his bodyguards at the pace of an infantry forced march. The morning walk used to be much longer than two blocks. In the quiet of the 1950s, the limousine dropped him near the Art Institute on Michigan Avenue, and he'd walk a mile and a half on Michigan Avenue, the city's jeweled thoroughfare, grinning at the morning crowds that bustled past the shops and hotels, along the edge of Grant Park. That ritual ended in the sixties, when people began walking and marching for something more than pleasure, and a man couldn't be sure who he'd meet on the street.

He rounds the corner and a bodyguard moves ahead to hold open the door. An elderly man is walking slowly and painfully close to the wall, using it as support. His name is Al, and he is a lawyer. Years ago he was just a ward boss's nod away from becoming a judge. He had worked hard for the party and had earned the black robe, and he was even a pretty good lawyer. But the ward boss died on him, and judgeships can't be left in wills. Now his health was bad and Al had an undemanding job in county government.

He spots Al, calls out his name, and rushes over and gives him a two-handed handshake, the maximum in City Hall affection. He has seen Al twice in ten years, but he quickly recalls all of his problems, his work, and a memory they shared. He likes old people and keeps them in key jobs and reslates them for office when they can barely walk, or even when they can't. Like the marriage vows, the pact between jobholder and party ends only in either's death, so long as the jobholder loves, honors, and obeys the party. Later that day, Al will write an eloquent letter in praise of his old friend to a paper, which will print it.

The bodyguard is still holding the door and he goes in at full stride. He never enters a room tentatively — always explosively and with a sense of purpose and direction, especially when the building is City Hall.

Actually, there are two identical buildings — City Hall and Cook County Building. At the turn of the century, the County Building was erected on half a city block, and shortly thereafter City Hall was put up. Although identical, City Hall cost substantially more. Chicago history is full of such oddities. Flip open any page and somebody is making a buck.

Although the main lobby and upstairs corridors extend through both buildings, he never goes through the County Building. That's a political courtesy, because the County Building is the domain of another politician, the president of the Cook County Board, known as "the mayor of Cook County," and, in theory, second only to him in power. But later in the day, the president of Cook County will call and ask how his domain should be run.

The elevator operators know his habits and are holding back the door of a car. The elevators are automated, but many operators remain on the job, standing in the lobby pointing at open cars and saying, "Next." Automation is fine, but how many votes can an automatic elevator deliver?

He gets off at the fifth floor, where his offices are. That's why he's known as "the Man on Five." He is also known as "duh mare" and "hizzoner" and "duh leader."

He marches past the main entrance to his outer offices, where people are already waiting, hoping to see him. They must be cleared first by policemen, then by three secretaries. He doesn't use the main entrance because the people would jump up, clutch at his hands, and overexcite themselves. He was striding through the building one day when a little man sprung past the bodyguards and kissed his hand.

Down the corridor, a bodyguard has opened a private door, leading directly to his three-room office complex. He almost always uses the side door.

The bodyguards quickly check his office then file into a smaller adjoining room, filled with keepsakes from presidents and his trip to Ireland. They use the room as a lounge, while studying his schedule, planning the routes and waiting. Another room is where he takes important phone calls when he has someone with him. Calls from President Kennedy and President Johnson were put through to that room.

Somewhere in the building, phone experts have checked his lines for taps. The limousine has been parked on LaSalle Street, outside the Hall's main entrance, and the tail car has moved into place. His key people are already in their offices, always on time or early, because he may call as soon as he arrives. And at 9 A.M. he, Richard Joseph Daley, is in his office and behind the big gleaming mahogany desk, in a high-backed dark green leather chair, ready to start another day of doing what the experts say is no longer possible — running a big American city. But as he, Daley, has often said to confidantes, "What in hell do the experts know?" He's been running a big American city for fifteen of the toughest years American cities have ever seen. He, Daley, has been running it as long or longer than any of the other famous mayors — Curley of Boston, LaGuardia of New York, Kelly of Chicago — ran theirs, and unless his health goes, or his wife says no, he, Daley, will be running it for another four years. Twenty is a nice, round figure. They give soldiers pensions after twenty years, and some companies give wristwatches. He'll settle for something simple, like maybe another jet airport built on a man-made island in the lake, and named after him, and maybe a statue outside the Civic Center, with a simple inscription, "The greatest mayor in the history of the world." And they might seal off his office as a shrine.

It's a business office. Like the man, the surroundings have no distracting frills. He wears excellently tailored business suits, buying six a year from the best shop on Michigan Avenue. The shirt is always radiant white, the tie conservative. Because his shoulders are narrow, he never works in his shirt sleeves, and is seldom seen publicly in casual clothes. The businesslike appearance carries through the office. The carpets, furniture, and walls are in muted shades of tan and green. The only color is provided by the flags of the United States and the city of Chicago, and a color photograph of his family. When a prominent cultural leader offered to donate some paintings for the office, an aide said, "Please, no, he can't accept them. People would think he's going high-hat."

The desk, with a green leather inset, is always clear of papers. He is an orderly man. Besides, he doesn't like to put things on paper, preferring the telephone. Historians will look in vain for a revealing memo, an angry note. He stores his information in his brain and has an amazing recall of detail.

The office is a place to work. And the work begins immediately. The first call will be to his secretary, checking the waiting visitors and asking that his press secretary be summoned, so he can let him know if he wants to talk to the press that morning. He holds more press conferences than any major public official in the country — at least two, and usually three, a week. In the beginning, they were often relaxed, casual, friendly and easy, with the reporters coming into his office, getting the q's and a's out of the way, and swapping fish stories and a few jokes, but always clean jokes because he walks away from the dirty ones. But with television, the press conferences became formal. They moved to a conference room, and became less friendly as the times became less friendly. He works at self-control, but it is impossible not to blow up and begin ranting. Reporters are like experts. What do they know?

If he is going to see them, Earl Bush, the press aide, will brief him on likely questions. The veteran City Hall reporters are not hostile, since they have to live with him, but the TV personalities sometimes ask questions that are calculated to cause a purple face and a fit of shouting rather than evoke information. He knows it, but sometimes it is hard not to get purple and shout.

If he doesn't feel like bothering, he'll just tell Bush, "To hell with them," and go on to other work. Bush never argues. He's been there since the beginning, a hungry journalist, operating a struggling neighborhood newspaper news service, who had a hunch that the quiet man running the county clerk's office was going to go somewhere. On the day after the first mayoralty election,

Daley threw three hundred-dollar bills in his rumpled lap and said, "Get yourself some decent-looking clothes." Bush has since slept a night in the White House.

After Bush will come someone like Deputy Mayor David Stahl, one of the young administrators the old politicians call "the whiz kids." Like the other "whiz kids," Stahl is serious, well educated, obedient, ambitious, and keeps his sense of humor out of sight. He was hired for these qualities and also because his father-in-law is a real estate expert and a close friend.

On a day when the City Council is meeting, Ald. Thomas Keane will slip in the side door to brief him on the agenda. Keane is considered to be second in party power, but it is a distant second. Keane wanted to be in front, but he was distracted by a craving for personal wealth. You can't do both if the man you're chasing is concentrating only on power. Now Keane is rich, but too old to ever be the successor.

If there is a council meeting, everybody marches downstairs at a few minutes before ten. Bush and the department heads and personal aides form a proud parade. The meeting begins when the seat of the mayor's pants touches the council president's chair, placed beneath the great seal of the city of Chicago and above the heads of the aldermen, who sit in a semi-bowl auditorium.

It is his council, and in all the years it has never once defied him as a body. Keane manages it for him, and most of its members do what they are told. In other eras, the aldermen ran the city and plundered it. In his boyhood they were so constantly on the prowl that they were known as "the Gray Wolves." His council is known as "the Rubber Stamp."

He looks down at them, bestowing a nod or a benign smile on a few favorites, and they smile back gratefully. He seldom nods or smiles at the small minority of white and black independents. The independents anger him more than the Republicans do, because they accuse him of racism, fascism, and of being a dictator. The Republicans bluster about loafing payrollers, crumbling gutters, inflated budgets — traditional, comfortable accusations that don't stir the blood.

That is what Keane is for. When the minority goes on the attack, Keane himself, or one of the administration aldermen he has groomed for the purpose, will rise and answer the criticism by shouting that the critic is a fool, a hypocrite, ignorant, and misguided. Until his death, one alderman could be expected to leap to his feet at every meeting and cry, "God bless our mayor, the greatest mayor in the world."

But sometimes Keane and his trained orators can't shout down the minority, so Daley has to do it himself. If provoked, he'll break into a rambling, ranting speech, waving his arms, shaking his fists, defending his judgment, defending his administration, always with the familiar "It is easy to criticize . . . to find fault . . . but where are your programs . . . where are your ideas . . ."

If that doesn't shut off the critics, he will declare them to be out of order, threaten to have the sergeant at arms force them into their seats, and invoke *Robert's Rules of Orders*, which, in the heat of debate, he once described as "the greatest book ever written."

All else failing, he will look toward a glass booth above the spectator's balcony and make a gesture known only to the man in the booth who operates the sound system that controls the microphones on each alderman's desk. The man in the booth will touch a switch and the offending critic's microphone will go dead and stay dead until he sinks into his chair and closes his mouth.

The meetings are seldom peaceful and orderly. The slightest criticism touches off shrill rebuttal, leading to louder criticism and finally an embarrassingly wild and vicious free-for-all. It can't be true, because Daley is a man who speaks highly of law and order, but sometimes it appears that he enjoys the chaos, and he seldom moves to end it until it has raged out of control.

Every word of criticism must be answered, every complaint must be disproved, every insult must be returned in kind. He doesn't take anything from anybody. While Daley was mediating negotiations between white trade unions and black groups who wanted the unions to accept blacks, a young militant angrily rejected one of his suggestions and concluded, "Up your ass!" Daley leaped to his feet and answered, "And up yours too." Would John Lindsay have become so involved?

Independent aldermen have been known to come up with a good idea, such as providing food for the city's hungry, or starting day-care centers for children of ghetto women who want to work; Daley will acknowledge it, but in his own way. He'll let Keane appropriate the idea and rewrite and resubmit it as an administration measure. That way, the independent has the satisfaction of seeing his idea reach fruition and the administration has more glory. But most of the independents' proposals are sent to a special subcommittee that exists solely to allow their unwelcome ideas to die.

The council meetings seldom last beyond the lunch hour. Aldermen have much to do. Many are lawyers and have thriving practices, because Chicagoans know that a dumb lawyer who is an alderman can often perform greater legal miracles than a smart lawyer who isn't.

Keane will go to a hotel dining room near City Hall, where at a large round table in a corner, he lunches each day with a clique of high-rise real estate developers, financiers, and political cronies. The things they plan and share will shape the future of the city, as well as the future of their heirs.

Daley has no such luncheon circle, and he eats only with old and close friends or one of his sons. Most afternoons, he darts across the street to the Sherman House hotel and his office in the Democratic headquarters, where as party chairman he will work on purely political business: somebody pleading to be slated for an office or advanced to a judgeship, a dispute between ward bosses over patronage jobs. He tries to separate political work from his duties as mayor, but nobody has ever been able to see where one ends and the other begins.

Lunch will be sent up and he might be joined by someone like Raymond Simon, the Bridgeport-born son of an old friend. Daley put him in the city legal department when he was fresh out of law school, and in a few years he was placed in charge, one of the highest legal jobs in the country. Now Simon has taken on an even bigger job: he resigned and went into private practice with Daley's oldest son, Richard Michael, not long out of law school. The name Daley and Simon on the office door possesses magic that has the big clients almost waiting in line. Daley's next oldest son, Michael, has gone into practice with a former law partner of the mayor, and has a surprisingly prosperous practice for so young and inexperienced an attorney. Daley filled Simon's place in his cabinet with another bright young lawyer, the mayor's first cousin.

When there is time, Daley is driven to the private Lake Shore Club for lunch, a swim, or a steam bath. Like most of the better private clubs in the fine buildings along the lake front, the Lake Shore Club accepts Jews and blacks. But you have to sit there all day to be sure of seeing one.

It's a pleasant drive to the club. Going north on Michigan Avenue, he passes the John Hancock Building, second in size only to the Empire State, and twice as high as anything near it. It was built during Daley's fourth term, despite cries of those who said it would bring intolerable traffic congestion to the gracious streets that can't handle it and lead to other oversized buildings that would destroy the unique flavor of the North Michigan Avenue district. It's happening, too, but the Hancock is another tall monument to his leadership.

From Michigan Avenue, he goes onto Lake Shore Drive, with the lake and beaches on the right, which were there when he started, and ahead the great wall of high-rise buildings beginning on the left, which wasn't. Dozens of them, hundreds, stretching mile after mile, all the way to the city limits, and almost all constructed during his administration, providing city living for the upper middle class, and billions in profits for the real estate developers. They are his administration's solution to keeping people in the city.

Behind the high-rises are the crumbling, crowded buildings where the lower-income people live. No answer has been found to their housing problems because the real estate people say there's not enough profit in building homes for them. And beyond them are the middle-income people, who can't make it to the high-rises and can't stay where they are because the schools are inadequate, the poor are pushing toward them, and nothing is being done about their problems, so they move to the suburbs. When their children grow up and they retire, maybe then they can move to a lake front high-rise.

By two o'clock he's back behind his desk and working. One of his visitors will be a city official unique to Chicago city government: the director of patronage. He brings a list of all new city employees for the day. The list isn't limited to the key employees, the professional people. All new employees are there — down to the window washer, the ditch digger, the garbage collector. After each person's name will be an extract of his background, the job, and most important, his political sponsor. Nobody goes to work for the city, and that includes governmental bodies that are not directly under the mayor, without Daley's knowing about it. He must see every name because the person becomes more than an employee: he joins the political Machine, part of the army numbering in the thousands who will help win elections. They damn well better, or they won't keep their jobs.

He scans the list for anything unusual. A new employee might be related to somebody special, an important businessman, an old political family. That will be noted. He might have been fired by another city office in a scandal. That won't keep him from being put to work somewhere else. Some bad ones have worked for half the governmental offices in the city. There might be a police record, which prompts a call to the political sponsor for an explanation. "He's clean now." "Are you sure?" "Of course, it was just a youthful mistake." "Three times?" "Give him a break, his uncle is my best precinct captain." "Okay, a break, but keep your eye on him." As he has said so often, when the subject of ex-cons on the city payroll comes up, "Are we to deny these men honest employment in a free society . . . are we to deprive them of the right to work . . . to become rehabilitated . . ." He will forgive anything short of Republicanism.

The afternoon work moves with never a minute wasted. The engineers and planners come with their reports on public works projects. Something is always being built, concrete being poured, steel being riveted, contractors being enriched.

"When will it be completed?" he asks.

"Early February."

"It would be a good thing for the people if it could be completed by the end of October."

The engineers say it can be done, but it will mean putting on extra shifts, night work, overtime pay, a much higher cost than was planned.

"It would be a good thing for the people if it could be completed by the end of October."

Of course it would be a good thing for the people. It would also be a good thing for the Democratic candidates who are seeking election in early November to go out and cut a ribbon for a new expressway or a water filtration plant or, if nothing else is handy, another wing at the O'Hare terminal. What ribbons do their opponents cut?

The engineers and planners understand, and they set about getting it finished by October.

On a good afternoon, there will be no neighborhood organizations to see him, because if they get to Daley, it means they have been up the ladder of government and nobody has been able to solve their problem. And that usually means a conflict between the people and somebody else, such as a politician or a business, whom his aides don't want to ruffle. There are many things his department heads can't do. They can't cross swords with ward bosses or politically heavy businessmen. They can't make important decisions. Some can't even make petty decisions. He runs City Hall like a small family business and keeps everybody on a short rein. They do only that which they know is safe and that which he tells them to do. So many things that should logically be solved several rungs below finally come to him.

Because of this, he has many requests from neighborhood people. And when a group is admitted to his office, most of them nervous and wide-eyed, he knows who they are, their leaders, their strength in the community. They have already been checked out by somebody. He must know everything. He doesn't like to be surprised. Just as he knows the name of every new worker, he must know what is going on in the various city offices. If the head of the office doesn't tell him, he has somebody there who will. In the office of other elected officials, he has trusted persons who will keep him informed. Out in the neighborhoods his precinct captains are reporting to the ward committeemen, and they in turn are reporting to him.

His police department's intelligence-gathering division gets bigger and bigger, its network of infiltrators, informers, and spies creating massive files on dissenters, street gangs, political enemies, newsmen, radicals, liberals, and anybody else who might be working against him. If one of his aides or handpicked officeholders is shacking up with a woman, he will know it. And if that man is married and a Catholic, his political career will wither and die. That is the greatest sin of all. You can make money under the table and move ahead, but you are forbidden to make secretaries under the sheets. He has dumped several party members for violating his personal moral standards. If something is leaked to the press, the bigmouth will be tracked down and punished. Scandals aren't public scandals if you get there before your enemies do.

So when the people come in, he knows what they want and whether it is possible. Not that it means they will get it. That often depends on how they act.

He will come from behind his desk all smiles and handshakes and charm. Then he returns to his chair and sits very straight, hands folded on his immaculate desk, serious and attentive. To one side will be somebody from the appropriate city department.

Now it's up to the group. If they are respectful, he will express sympathy, ask encouraging questions, and finally tell them that everything possible will be done. And after they leave, he may say, "Take care of it." With that command, the royal seal, anything is possible, anybody's toes can be stepped on.

But if they are pushy, antagonistic, demanding instead of imploring, or bold enough to be critical of him, to tell him how he should do his job, to blame him for their problem, he will rub his hands together, harder and harder. In a long, difficult meeting, his hands will get raw. His voice gets lower, softer, and the corners of his mouth will turn down. At this point, those who know him will back off. They know what's next. But the unfamiliar, the militant, will mistake his lowered voice and nervousness for weakness. Then he'll blow, and it comes in a frantic roar:

"I want *you* to tell *me* what to do. *You* come up with the answers. *You* come up with the program. Are we perfect? Are *you* perfect? We all make mistakes. We all have faults. It's easy to criticize. It's easy to find fault. But *you* tell me what to do. This problem is all over the city. We didn't create these problems. We don't want them. But we are doing what we can. *You* tell me how to solve them. *You* give me a program." All of which leaves the petitioners dumb, since most people don't walk around with urban programs in their pockets. It can also leave them right back where they started.

They leave and the favor seekers come in. Half of the people he sees want a favor. They plead for promotions, something for their sons, a chance to do some business with the city, to get somebody in City Hall off their backs, a chance to return from political exile, a boon. They won't get an answer right there and then. It will be considered and he'll let them know. Later, sometimes much later, when he has considered the alternatives and the benefits, word will get back to them. Yes or no. Success or failure. Life or death.

Some jobseekers come directly to him. Complete outsiders, meaning those with no family or political connections, will be sent to see their ward committeemen. That is protocol, and that is what he did to the tall young black man who came to see him a few years ago, bearing a letter from the governor of North Carolina, who wrote that the young black man was a rising political prospect in his state. Daley told him to see his ward committeeman, and if he did some precinct work, rang doorbells, hustled up some votes, there might be a government job for him. Maybe something like taking coins in a tollway booth. The Rev. Jesse Jackson, now the city's leading black civil rights leader, still hasn't stopped smarting over that.

Others come asking him to resolve a problem. He is the city's leading labor mediator and has prevented the kind of strikes that have crippled New York. His father was a union man, and he comes from a union neighborhood, and many of the union leaders were his boyhood friends. He knows what they want. And if it is in the city's treasury, they will get it. If it isn't there, he'll promise to find it. He has ended a teachers' strike by promising that the state legislature would find funds for them, which surprised the Republicans in Springfield, as well as put them on the spot. He is an effective mediator with the management side of labor disputes, because they respect his judgment, and because there are few industries that do not need some favors from City Hall.

There are disputes he won't bother with, such as that between two ranking party members, both lawyers, each retained by a rival business interest in a zoning dispute. That was the kind of situation that can drive judges, city agencies, and functionaries berserk. He angrily wiped his hands of the matter, bawled the lawyers out for creating the mess, and let them take their chances on a fair decision. There are so many clients, peace should exist among friends.

The afternoon is almost gone, but they still keep coming in the front door and those he summons through the side. The phone keeps ringing, bringing reports from his legislators in Springfield, his congressmen in Washington, and prominent businessmen, some of whom may waste a minute of his time for the status of telling dinner guests, "I mentioned that to Dick and he likes the idea . . ."

Finally the scheduled appointments have been cleared, the unscheduled hopefuls told to come back again, and a few late calls made to his closest aides. It's six o'clock, but he is still going, as if reluctant to stop. The workdays have grown longer over the years, the vacations shorter. There is less visible joy in it all, but he works harder now than ever before. Some of his friends say he isn't comfortable anywhere but in the office on five.

The bodyguards check the corridor and he heads downstairs to the limousine. Most of the people in the Hall have left, and the mop crews are going to work, but always on the sidewalk outside will be the old hangers-on, waiting to shout a greeting, to get a nod or a smile in return.

On the way out, Bush hands him a speech. That's for the next stop, a banquet of civic leaders, or a professional group, or an important convention. The hotel grand ballroom is a couple of minutes away and he'll speed-read the speech just once on the way, a habit that contributes to his strange style of public speaking, with the emphasis often on the wrong words, the sentences overlapping, and the words tumbling over each other. Regardless of where he goes, the speech will be heavy in boosterism, full of optimism for the future, pride in the city, a reminder of what he has done. Even in the most important of gatherings, people will seek out his handshake, his recognition. A long time ago, when they opposed him, he put out the hand and moved the few steps to them. Now they come to him. He arrives after dinner, in time to be introduced, speak, and get back to the car.

The afternoon papers are on the back seat and he reads them until the limousine stops in front of a funeral home. Wakes are still part of political courtesy and his culture. Since he started in politics, he's been to a thousand of them. On the way up, the slightest connection with the deceased or his family was enough reason to attend a wake. Now he goes to fewer, and only to those involving friends, neighbors. His sons fill in for him at others. Most likely, he'll go to a wake on the South Side, because that's where most of his old friends are from. The funeral home might be McInerney's, which has matchbooks that bear a poem beginning, "Bring out the lace curtains and call McInerney, I'm nearing the end of life's pleasant journey." Or John Egan's, one of the biggest, owned by his high school pal and one of the last of the successful undertaker-politicians. The undertaker-politicians and the saloon keeper – politicians have given way to lawyer-politicians, who are no better, and they don't even buy you a drink or offer a prayer.

He knows how to act at a wake, greeting the immediate family, saying the proper things, offering his regrets, somberly and with dignity. His arrival is as big an event as the other fellow's departure. Before leaving, he will kneel at the casket, an honor afforded few of the living, and sign the visitor's book. A flurry of handshakes and he is back in the car.

It's late when the limousine turns toward Bridgeport. His neighbors are already home watching TV or at the Pump Tavern having a beer, talking baseball, race or politics. His wife Eleanor, "Sis" as he calls her, knows his schedule and will be making supper. Something boiled, meat and potatoes, home-baked bread. She makes six loaves a week. His mother always made bread. And maybe ice cream for dessert. He likes ice cream. There's an old ice cream parlor in the neighborhood, and sometimes he goes there for a sundae, as he did when he was a boy.

The limousine passes Comiskey Park, where his beloved Sox play ball. He goes to Wrigley Field, too, but only to be seen. The Sox are his team. He can walk to the ball park from the house. At least he used to be able to walk there. Today it's not the same. A person can't walk anywhere. Maybe someday he'll build a big superstadium for all the teams, better than any other city's. Maybe on the Lake Front. Let the conservationists moan. It will be good for business, drawing conventioneers from hotels, and near an expressway so people in the suburbs can drive in. With lots of parking space for them, and bright lights so they can walk. Some day, if there's time, he might just build it.

Across Halsted Street, then a turn down Lowe Avenue, into the glow of the brightest street lights of any city in the country. The streets were so dark before, a person couldn't see who was there. Now all the streets have lights so bright that some people have to lower their shades at night. He turned on all those lights, he built them. Now he can see a block ahead from his car, to where the policeman is guarding the front of his home.

He tells the driver that tomorrow will require an even earlier start. He must catch a flight to Washington to tell a committee that the cities need more money. There are so many things that must be built, so many more people to be hired. But he'll be back the same day, in the afternoon, with enough time to maybe stop at the Hall. There's always something to do there. Things have to be done. If he doesn't do them, who will?

# Leon Forrest
## (1937-97)

*Born in Chicago,* LEON FORREST *was long associated with Northwestern University's African American Studies program, and gained an almost reverential following for his dedication to, research in, and contributions to black culture in the Chicago area and throughout the nation. Among those contributions were four novels:* There Is a Tree More Ancient than Eden *(1973),* The Bloodworth Orphans *(1977),* Two Wings to Veil My Face *(1984), and the monumental* Divine Days *(1992), which Harvard University professor Henry Louis Gates, Jr., referred to as the* War and Peace *of African American literature. Forrest's fusion of American myth, autobiography, black history, and religious doctrine and obsession creates an almost too-rich palette of shifting scenes, overlapping selves, and multivoiced meditations not dissimilar to two other writers to whom he has sometimes been compared: James Joyce and William Faulkner.*

*Faced with the difficulty of excerpting a fiction so densely textured, we have chosen instead an essay from Forrest's collection* Relocations of the Spirit *(1994). His account of some of Chicago's black churches rides, as much of his work does, on the "music of the spirit." Though it faces squarely the reality of evil, and even the commerce of religion, the essay radiates an ultimately calming transcendence that often characterized his work.*

✦ ✦ ✦

## Souls in Motion

*from* RELOCATIONS OF THE SPIRIT

Baptisms at the West Point Baptist Church, at 36th and Cottage Grove in Chicago, are conducted in a pool plainly in view of the congregation, in a small, glass-enclosed room high above the heads of the choir. The candidates—wearing a white cap and white linen blouse or shirt and white slacks, recalling a swimmer's outfit of the late nineteenth century—are ushered up a short flight of steps to the left of the altar, one by one. As the choir and the congregation sing out in a call and response, the Reverend Carroll J. Thompson conducts that ritual of baptism, calling forth—so that the microphone pitched just above the pool picks up his words of affirmation—"I do baptize you, my brother [or sister], upon the profession of your faith . . . "

The call and response continues as the candidate's body is deftly lowered into the tank of water:

> Choir call: "Have you got good religion?"
> Congregation: "Certainly, Lord. Certainly, Lord."
> Choir call: "Have you got *good* religion?"
> Congregation: "Certainly, Lord. *Certainly*, Lord."

This is a dramatic moment of witness bearing and conversion, and the congregation's role in the ritual is participatory, like that of the chorus in Greek drama. Each time the body of a baptismal candidate is carefully lowered and swiftly raised by Reverend Thompson, a throb of rapture and confirmation is heard charging through the more than 300 members present at this service. It is an ecstatic moment for many as they recall their own spiritual awakening— "I was blind, but now I see." Embossing the panel behind the tank of water is a landscape of the Holy Land, a view to paradise on this Sunday morning as the October light streams through the stained-glass windows of the church.

When the last of the four candidates is brought forth, a woman in the pew in front of me cries out, "My boy, that's my son!" He is a heavyset fellow, a rich, dark mahogany brown; he wears a jeri-curl. As Reverend Thompson holds the young man's slowly descending body in his arms, the candidate co-operatively tilts his full-back's frame; their movements are ever harmonious, recalling for me the Alvin Ailey dancers' performance of *Wade in the Water*.

Out of the corner of my eye, I observe the mother's face all aglow as her son goes under, ever so nimbly. Her hands reach out and tremble as he begins to emerge, and there is a sudden shout from the congregation as he is brought forth, drenched from head to toe. I hear the old Negro spiritual echoing through my soul: "Jordan river chilly and col', chills the body, not the soul."

The question at every turn in the service is how to keep the fire and the zeal up-tempo, how to let neither the body nor the soul cool off. The service is always bound up in a keening relationship between great solemnity and the furious rhythms of body and soul. There is a place here for the commingling of the sexual and the spiritual.

As the choir sings "Your Labor Is Not in Vain," all of the newly baptized souls have returned to their seats, except for the son of the woman in front of me. The choir and the congregation trumpet forth again and again:

Choir: "Your labor . . ."
Lead singer: "Hang on in there . . ."
Choir: "Your labor . . . "
Lead singer: "Hang on in there . . ."
Choir: "Your labor . . ."
All: "Your labor is not in vain."

Each round pitches us higher, so that when we reach the fiery climax of the last winging round, Reverend Thompson can exclaim, just before delivering his sermon: "Our choir sounds like it came to church, for church today."

The newly baptized son of the woman in front of me returns dressed in fashionable street clothes and touches his mother's hand. I see fresh pride in her burnished, autumn-brown face, the baptismal light still incandescent in her eyes.

At Mount Pisgah, at 46th Street and King Drive, the choir enters, singing along with the congregation "We Came This Far by Faith." Each member of the congregation clasps hands with the person on his left, and the service begins with the singing of The Lord's Prayer.

The choir looks like a delegation from the United Nations, culled from the bloodlines of Africa, Europe, and Native America. As the choir sings of a "new way of walking and a new way of talking," they rejoice that if you have the Lord, "it's wonderful, really wonderful." And you realize that this group, this remnant of the race, in this place on Sunday morning feel that they are a new kind of people "who came this far by faith." In this former Jewish synagogue, choir and congregation feel that *they* are the newly chosen people.

Lead singer: "I've got a new walk . . . "
Choir: "Over in glory."
Lead singer: "I've got a new talk . . . "
Choir: "Over in glory."

At Mount Pisgah the choir is directed by a young woman whose lightning-rod motions seem to be those of a winging eagle caught up in a sudden storm: calm, trembling, then vaulting into space. "I'm going to wear this world—I don't believe you know what I'm talking about—I'm going to wear this world like a loose garment," she sings, raising her arms and the balloon-like sleeves of her robe in a sweeping arc. Her very body seems disconnected from her backbone, superruled by her skullbone . . . "oh, hear the world of the Lord." In her declaiming, redeeming, recalling command over the choir, she appears to have more moves in her repertoire than Dr. "J." on one of his better nights in the NBA. The song is "Move Mountain."

Now the first lead singer and a second lead are having a battle of "antagonistic cooperation" as they wing it out over a mountain. They call and respond and then each outdoes the other in escalating rhythms with the church organs racing them on and the younger members of the church following in an avalanche of sound. . . .

Not all of the members are caught up in the frenzy, but many of the young people appear to be going through a religious moment, a seizure that is fitfully sexual and spiritually elevating, that lifts them to some imagined mountain. At this point we can see the importance of the church's nursing cadre.

These soul-soothing sisters move in to aid the spiritually seized members, whose bodies leap forth in convulsive spasms. Dressed in hospital white, the nurses attempt to revive, but not cool off, these swirling, mountain-moving souls. One young man proclaims, "In the Lord's good time" — and I recall that the precursors of the prophets were often wild, spinning dervishes caught up in the perceived moment of a miracle, in the revelation of radical faith.

This sets the stage for the Reverend Joseph Wells, who has just announced his text. He has a rich voice full of Negro grain and timbre — a rugged grain, fermented, it would appear, in the South. His voice is husky, vibrant, and gruff one moment and mellow the next, like the combined voices of Jimmy Rushing, Louis Armstrong, Ray Charles, and James Brown — all blues-brooding, full-bodied voice.

But Reverend Wells can't get started yet, because the nurses are still fanning several of the felled faithful, who have apparently moved that mountain out of their way but are drained by the action . . . *but coming through* . . . and trying to rise. After the first lead singer comes back for yet another chorus of the song, Reverend Wells is at the microphone and ready to preach. He says, "If it weren't for the grace of God, I don't know where I'd be." This works in beautifully, because it identifies him with what the fury-charged souls of the congregation are feeling — heelbone to backbone to skullbone.

Throughout his sermon Reverend Wells relates everything that has happened on this Sunday to the larger interests of his text, which is based on God's protection of the Israelites in Egypt in the Old Testament: "Going down the Dan Ryan — thinking about a mountain in my life and suddenly God moved it. I got happy in the car . . . Did the Lord bring you from somewhere, church? God brought me from the cottonfields of Mississippi, from behind the plow. What the Lord did for Israel — moved that mountain and protected them. The Lord brought us through . . . Some of you worrying about Reagan. Lord brought us through Hoover.

". . . But Israel had forgotten that God had worked in their interests. Israel had forgotten that God had divided the Red Sea."

The structure of a black Baptist sermon is orchestrated, with highly associative links to group memory, the Bible, Afro-American folklore, Negro spirituals, secular blues phrases, politics, and personal testimonial. A sermon is open-ended, allowing a preacher to expand new ideas or to cut out sections if they aren't working. The role of the congregation during a sermon is similar to that of a good audience at a jazz set—driving, responding, adding to the ever-rising level of emotion and intelligence. Ultimately, the preacher and the congregation reach one purifying moment, and a furious catharsis is fulfilled.

Several years ago at a Christmas party, I met the Reverend Morris Harrison Tynes. We had a brief but memorable exchange, and I was delighted and instructed by his many-sided intelligence. Reverend Tynes is a man who believes that all things happen for a deeper purpose, so I am certain that he felt our first conversation was fortuitous when I turned up late last fall at the Greater Mount Moriah Baptist Church, at 214 East 50th Street, where he is the pastor, and again the following week at his home for an interview.

Reverend Tynes is gifted with an exceptional flair for language, storytelling, and ideas, and he has an excellent singing voice; he is a powerful orator in the pulpit. He holds several degrees, including a Ph.D. in philosophy and ethics, and he is one of the most articulate men of the cloth in Chicago. As he speaks, one hears a preacher's voice ascending in layers of rhetorical eloquence.

FORREST: How is the divine moment of spiritual and emotional ecstasy that a preacher feels as he builds toward the climax of a sermon different from what an artist or composer feels during profound moments of creativity?

TYNES: I think that each man's historical perspective determines his response to this divine encounter. There is something in his life that exalts him to great inspiration. Take Handel writing the *Messiah* in less than 30 days. He must have ascended to heaven! There is no way possible that a human being could have written that alone.

FORREST: Is it the moment of a miracle?

TYNES: I think the same thing happens in preaching at its zenith; and, yes, I do think it is the moment of a miracle. I think that any time man can discover God, or God discloses to man, that's a miracle.

FORREST: What about the man in the street who doesn't go to church but who has developed a certain grit and fiber to deal with life, or so he thinks? Doesn't he feel he needs the support of the church?

TYNES: These street people have often told me that they'll be in church next Sunday, and I'll say, "You've been telling me that for two years." Then I'll pose this question: "Are you happy with your life the way it is? Because every time I see you, your eyes are full of whiskey and dissipation. Do you think that this is the highest fulfillment of your life?" Time and again the man or woman will say, "No, Doc, I'll tell you the way it is — I'm not happy with my life. To be frank with you, Doc, I'm not satisfied with myself."

FORREST: Those street people probably speak for a lot of lost souls at some very effete levels.

TYNES: You know St. Augustine said, "My soul shall not find fulfillment until it rests in Thee." He was alluding to this spiritual hunger.

FORREST: How do you deal with the mystery of iniquity and the absurdity of human misfortune? I'm thinking here of the high-school basketball player Ben Wilson, who was murdered by three young black men.

TYNES: Man's freedom is his glory and his shame, because God gave man the freedom to become like the God in whose image he was created or to sink to the level of the worst beast, the worst criminal on earth. In other words, man can be either a marvelous musician or a monster. Where does suffering come in? Where does pain come in? Job raises this question, Why do the righteous suffer, instead of the wicked? My simple answer is that since we are made in God's image, He wants us all to be like Him. If I share in the benefits of an illumination that I had nothing to do with creating, then I must also share in the consequences of an evil that I had no part in creating. When an airplane goes down, the nun and the gangster die together. That is the collectivity of man's basic freedom. That is the price we pay for freedom.

FORREST: But what would you say to Ben Wilson's mother if she were sitting across from you at this moment?

TYNES: I would say that your son — very precious in your sight and in God's sight — was caught up in the ambiguity of personal option. He did not have to be walking on that street, at that time of the day. He could have been in another place. But he chose to walk down that street. So I would say to her what the prophet Gibran; I think it was, said, "Your children are not your children. They come through you but not from you." That son of yours, though he was to be a great basketball star, perhaps shines more brightly now through the tragedy and the ambiguity of his untimely demise than he would have if he had been a basketball star *only*. Because his murder has highlighted another aspect of the human condition — black-on-black crime, which could not have been highlighted as effectively, nor more dramatically, than by seeing his beautiful, handsome face and body sacrificed on this altar of senseless, brutal killings in the black community. And since he was so great and so good, God said, I'm going to let you do this. But in the other life, in heaven, you will shine more brightly than you ever would have on the basketball court. There, you would have shined for only eight or ten years, but in eternity, in heaven, you'll shine with ever-increasing illumination.

FORREST: What would you say to the kids at Simeon High School if you were lecturing them about the punks who killed their star?

TYNES: There are two ways to look at those punks. Look at them as misguided children of God, who need sympathy, love, and forgiveness — just as Martin Luther King forgave that black woman who stabbed him. He said, Don't treat her harshly; Christ will forgive her. That is the ultimate Christian response. The other response is the human reflex: "Let's string them up. Let's have a public execution." But I believe the finality of death would be to them a blessing. They would be released from the agonizing shame and frustration that they will have to go through for the rest of their lives. As they get older they will see the dimension of what they've done, more than they do now in their little 19- and 20-year-old minds. And if they are in prison they are going to have a long time to think about their deeds. And the awesome dimension of that may turn them into saints.

So it could have been a two-edged sword of goodness. God using this boy, Ben Wilson, to highlight the many sons who have been lost and murdered, and then God using those other boys — ignominious as their crime was — to say what can become of two hideous individuals 20 years hence. Because Christ always looked at an individual as if he were what he ought to be so that he might become what he should be.

FORREST: But, Reverend Tynes, what can the church do about these gangs?

TYNES: Most of these gang people are peripheral to the church, at best. They know that the lives they are living are sordid and criminal, and they don't want any part of the church. I believe that the gang phenomenon is the manipulation of these teen-agers by older men, 27 to 35 years in age, who send these teen-agers out to sell dope. Then they bring the bounty back and give it to these bosses. So I believe that these boys, like the ones who killed young Wilson, are manipulated. You look in these kids' eyes and they look frightened. That's the way the bosses enforce; that's the way they control. They control them through fear. They have enforcers who beat the teen gang members with baseball bats.

The question of spiritual alienation from the Christian community surges through at central moments in *Native Son*, Richard Wright's Chicago-based novel. Published in 1940, it seems so prophetic now. Wright's Bigger Thomas is a gang member, a manchild deteriorating in the wasteland of the city slums. For Bigger Thomas, violence became the one symbolic action in which he could feel a sense of creative elevation, could attain a profane spiritual high.

Bigger's brief life of murder suggests the sort of wayward behavior that is open to a closed-off contemporary youth who is black, fatherless, undereducated most of his life, and churchless.

After Bigger's arrest for the murder of a white girl, he is visited in prison by a black minister. This scene isolates the growing cleavage — even then — between the unemployed slum dweller and the Negro church. The minister's words about moral redemption and the kingdom of God are hollow sounds that have lost all of their resonance for Wright's emptied-out Underman.

The Chicago-born playwright Lorraine Hansberry believed herself to be almost as far to the left ideologically as Richard Wright. She grew up in a complex black middle-class family but chose a Chicago working-class family emboldened by visions of the American Dream as the subject for *A Raisin in the Sun*. Hansberry's play introduced at least four black characters previously invisible upon the mainstream American stage: an intellectual African, meaning an African without a bone in his nose; a young female college student engaged in spinning out her identity; a chauffeur, who suggested the frustrated ambitions of an energetic black man — a long way from Wright's Bigger — who wants out of the slum mentality but whose options are limited to buying a liquor store in those slums. But none of the characters is more memorable than Lena Younger, the matriarch, whose spiritual core dominates the stage like Mahalia Jackson singing "How I Got Over."

At one point in the play, Lena Younger slaps her daughter, Beneatha, for saying, "There simply is no blasted God — there is only man who makes miracles!" Then she demands: "Now — you say after me, in my mother's house there is still God. . . . In my mother's house there is still God." Indeed, it is Lena Younger — created by an agnostic — who asks the central question of the play and perhaps the primary question that could be asked about the materialistic ambitions of some of today's young blacks, as well. In an exchange with her chauffeur son, Walter, Lena Younger finds an answer to that question:

MAMA: Son — how come you talk so much 'bout money?

WALTER: (*With immense passion*) Because it is life, Mama!

MAMA: (*Quietly*) Oh — (*very quietly*) So now it's life. Money is life. Once upon a time freedom used to be life — now it's money. I guess the world really do change. . . .

WALTER: No — it was always money, Mama. We just didn't know about it.

MAMA: No . . . Something has changed. (*She looks at him*) You something new, boy. In my time we was worried about not being lynched and getting to the North if we could and how to stay alive and still have a pinch of dignity too . . . Now here comes you and Beneatha — talking 'bout things we ain't never even thought about hardly, me and your daddy. You ain't satisfied or proud of nothing we done. I mean that you had a home; that we kept you out of trouble till you was grown; that you don't have to ride to work on the back of nobody's streetcar — You my children — but how different we done become.

There are several major black Baptist churches between 35th Street and 51st and King Drive, and each Sunday inner and outer traffic lanes in the area provide extra parking for a multitude of worshipers. And, oh, those ladies' hats. They are something of a fashion show on parade. Some are too outrageous to be audacious; others are too bodacious to be missed on Sunset and Vine. Take the gushing rainbow of a bonnet before me, climbing to God's kingdom in a babbling tower of colors. Many designer hats — and some redesigned by virtue of Afro-American reinvention — send the observer's head spinning, as when one tries to let the eye follow the layers of a wraparound turban. Rarely simple, these hats can often be as dazzling as the crack of daybreak on Lake Shore Drive.

If you want a prediction for the coming fashion season, you might drop in at the Liberty Baptist Church, at 49th Street and King Drive. The hats the ladies wear there are something to behold. The church is also deeply involved in a range of self-help and service programs, and on the Sunday of my visit, Liberty is getting an award for its donation to the relief effort in Ethiopia. Spencer Leak, one of the leading morticians on the South Side and a church activist, leads a group of members to the altar for this homage.

The black middle class, recalling the heightened consciousness of upwardly mobile Poles, Jews, and Irish, is reaching a growing awareness of those brethren left behind — of the underclasses in this country and in the motherland as well. Later, in his sermon, Chester Baker, a young visiting minister, will address this attempt at spiritual linkage with, and obligation toward, Africa. He tells the congregation, numbering more than 750: "These people who are oppressed in Africa *are our people*. And those who don't see this unity lack ancestral integrity. They are our people. For if you think of yourself as white, then you are going to treat our people like the racists treated us."

Yet how much the congregation knows of Africa is worthy of contemplation. More than likely, the thinking would go something like this: There are oppressed, poverty-stricken people over there; they are black and we are black; they have been oppressed and so have we. Wherever the black man is in the world, he is catching hell. We came from Africa; therefore, we must help them. And it is in this sense that the black man here identifies with the heartaches over there.

Many Chicago Poles have relatives in Warsaw, and many who live here speak Polish; there is a Polish-American newspaper in Chicago. Mayor Daley was only two generations removed from Ireland; and the Jews have myriad ties to Israel—language, direct Biblical linkage, and physical presence there. Black Americans can share little of this kind of linkage with their motherland.

But before Reverend Baker turns to this issue, he takes a good look at the congregation and apparently decides that he has a lot to say about what he sees now and about what he has seen on the streets. He denounces unisex fashions as a craze, claiming, "We are trapped in a gender twilight zone, somewhere between male and female." Given the growing role of gays in choirs at many black churches, one wonders whether someone should warn this young preacher to exercise some restraint. But Reverend Baker is witty, and the idea of castigating the congregation for giving in to wayward influences has an ancient heritage.

"You can stand on the el platform and see women wearing hats like Indiana Jones," he shouts. "You see men wearing pants so tight you can almost see the label of their underwear." (This unleashes much lighthearted laughter from the membership.)

"Christmas is not the time for us to parade under some illusion that we are a part of the cast of *Dynasty*." (How well this sits with the beauties here who are bathed in finery *à la* Joan Collins or Diahann Carroll can only be left to speculation.) The minister warns the flock: "If Jesus had wanted us to celebrate his birth, he would have told us so. We need an internal confirmation that we don't get from outside the church. We need to be asking ourselves what can we do to be saved."

The choir of 100 voices at Liberty is one of the more impressive on the South Side. The members follow closely the Biblical edict "Make a joyful noise unto the Lord." Their first song for the service—"Jesus Is the Light of the World"—was at one time the signature song of the famous First Church of Deliverance, at 4301 South Wabash Avenue. One of the most profoundly influential institutions on black church tradition in Chicago, it was not Baptist, but rather nondenominational.

In the old days, if you were out driving on the South Side on a Sunday night, you might set your radio dial for the 11 P.M. services emanating from the First Church of Deliverance to hear its monumental choir commence the evening to God with a heaven-ascending version of "The Lord's Prayer" and then lead into a driving, stomping rendition of "Jesus Is the Light of the World." The choir toured the world, and it was celebrated for the range of its magnificent voices.

Equally well known for his way of weaving the Word in and out of the flesh, in and out of this world, was the Reverend Clarence H. Cobbs, the church's preacher from the late 1920s until his death in the late 1970s. His style in the pulpit was in sharp contrast with that of the huge, high-spirited choir. Yet they complemented each other to form a path-breaking service. Reverend Cobbs's delivery was low-key, urbane, naughty, and layered with pithy insights. Intimate as a ballad sung by Nat King Cole, his conversational sermons were constantly punctuated, accented, and underscored by the church organist. The large, romping rumble of the organ actually took on the role of the chorus. Cobbs's singing voice was a sweet and sassy high tenor, sometimes swooping to an alto register akin to that of the Ink Spots' lead singer, Bill Kenney. His normal speaking voice recalled Cole's or Sam Cooke's or perhaps, in our time, Marvin Gaye's.

Reverend Cobbs spun his sermons out of vignettes from life and from the Bible, out of epiphanies from spiritual witness, out of coined aphorisms and stories of people who called on him for advice (often prisoners wrote to him). Cobbs was in the tradition of the stand-up monologist who spoke off the cuff and from the heart during the frontier makings of this country. His delivery was that of an intimate friend you might call in the still of the night when your woman left you, when your younger brother got stabbed in a South Side bar, or when you couldn't make groceries. He would save a bit of hyperbole for a key moment, and like the great entertainers of the American stage, he knew that timing was everything.

Like the best of James Baldwin's rambling essays, Reverend Cobbs's sermons seemed to be running notes to man and God; they had the structure of a crazy quilt, and yet they worked beautifully. Indeed, his sermons were rendered up in a street-corner rapping voice; listening to them was like opening up a telephone booth on, say, 39th Street and King Drive and falling in on an envoy from God whose feet hurt and who was telling his best friend's story to the Maker. There was no slaughterhouse oratory in his sessions. He was something of a brother-confidant, as opposed to the preacher as father over his flock.

Not only did Cobbs's style of preaching and the expanded role that he allowed the choir influence other churches but he also was one of the first church leaders in the Negro community to use a regular radio broadcast as a major religious voice. Cobbs knew that many people wouldn't be caught dead in church but that they still found moments of ecstasy in spirituals and gospel music. When you listened in on the radio, you didn't have to pay to pray. . . .

The service at Christian Tabernacle, a Baptist church at 4712 South Prairie Avenue, reflects the influence of First Church; and the Reverend Maceo Woods is very much in the tradition of Cobbs. . . .

The role of the choir at Christian Tabernacle is even more expansive than that at Cobbs's church in the old days. They back Woods and two organists, a drummer, and a tambourine player. In this church, the music seems to set the stage for the performance in the pulpit, and Reverend Woods cunningly blends into the fabric of the moment. This freedom from domination by the personality of the minister makes Christian Tabernacle, a former theatre, a popular place to worship. It draws young people with a feel for music, as well as those who need to act out, or jam with joy, for Jesus.

The choir here is professional and solemn in the beginning, and then all holy hell breaks loose. On this Sunday, tenor Melvin Smothers leads in a voice of power and fire heading toward furor. The song is "He Walks with Me," and when Smothers disengages himself from the body of the choir — "Got a new walk . . . got a new talk" — and begins to speak in a witness-bearing, singsong voice, I'm reminded that theatre emerged from religion.

It is the force of the music — the obsessive and repetitive rhythm — tied to lyrics suggesting a reordering out of chaos that leads one from a state of self-possession to a momentary state of blessed assurance, when you "take hold of your life through Jesus Christ." The singer — as caught-up spiritual performer — is in control and then loosens control over his spirit. When he appears to be on the verge of losing control, he is actually opening himself up to be taken over by the Holy Spirit. And that is why Melvin Smothers and the others can "get happy."

Just now two young men become so enraptured that they can't break the spell. Nurses move quickly to the rescue, but the lads are starting into a holy jumping, stomping dance to Jesus, and they are babbling in tongues. During these seizures, the anklebone and the hipbone, the hipbone and the backbone seem almost disconnected, so violent is the shock of the rhythm. One can only wonder about the polyrhythms of the blood flow to the chambers of the heart during these fitful flurries. And one can't help but reflect on how these holy dances have influenced popular dance patterns. For under the cover of the church and in the name of God, you might act out dance steps that you would not show at home, nor even think to attempt. But here the creative juices are up; you are encouraged to let the mind and spirit romp, roam, and reinvent. And if you are high in your ecstasy for Jesus, who knows what the body might tell the soul to reveal? So much of James Brown's act came out of the church, particularly those moments of ecstasy, seizure, death, and rebirth that he brings to his stage performances.

At every stage of the service at the Antioch Missionary Baptist Church, at 6248 South Stewart Avenue, the Reverend Wilbur N. Daniel is a mighty presence — and he is an awesome anchor for his people.

Every Sunday the church has a responsive Scripture reading; and because we are two weeks from Christmas, Reverend Daniel's selection is taken from Matthew 2:1 – 11, which covers the birth of Jesus in Bethlehem; the troubling of the evil King Herod over the star — implying his downfall — so luminous in the East, with the miraculous shock of the Savior in its fierce light; Herod's calling of the wise men to inquire when the star appeared; his command that they go search for the infant and report back to him, "so that I may come and worship him also." Reverend Daniel's dramatic rendering—coupled with his radio announcer's voice and his romance with language—turns this story into a kind of mini-sermon, as well as a call-and-response recitation for pastor and congregation.

A powerful singer, Reverend Daniel now leads the congregation and the choir in one rousing chorus of "O Come, All Ye Faithful," immediately followed by a sober performance of "The Lord's Prayer." Then Reverend Daniel breaks that mood, as if suddenly caught up in the scale-ripping spirit of the pianist. He announces:

"Jesus didn't come to bring sadness into the world. If you are gonna be sad, don't put out any Christmas tree, don't wrap any presents. There is nothing about Christmas that is designed for sadness." He proceeds to do a parody of "O Come, All Ye Faithful":

"Oh come, all ye doubters, sad and defeated. Oh come ye to Mississippi. . . . Oh come and behold him from skid row. Oh come let us weep and mourn for Joe, the drunkard." Reverend Daniel warns his congregation, "The Lord was not born for you to be sad. You may not get all you want for Christmas, but you can have all the joy you want." He says that he's so happy with spiritual joy that he might even fly: "How would you folks in the balcony feel if on this Sunday I would fly into the balcony? Would that frighten you? . . . The kind of joy I'm talking about doesn't depend on what you have, because if you don't have joy with that rabbit coat, you won't have any with that mink."

In calling for the benevolent offering, however, Reverend Daniel is all seriousness. A young deacon, his head bowed, gives the prayer over the collection. Much of what he has to say is predictable; yet what gets the attention of the membership—the "Amens" and the "Yes, Lords"—are the stock phrases, some from the Bible, others with an oracular cast that speaks to the group ethos:

"We know You [Lord] love a cheerful giver. We stand in need of Thy divine blessing, Father. We want to thank You for waking us up this morning. For when we awakened we found that You had left watch angels to guard us while we slept. We thank You for touching us this morning with love, so that our eyes flew open and we beheld a sunlight and a day that's been coming since creation. . . ."

Then, sounding like a blues singer, the deacon cries forth: "We need You . . . can't get along without You. Hold our hands while we run this race." One of the elder deacons rises, and he and Reverend Daniel do a variation on a call and response in which a member, usually a deacon, "lines the pastor out": The deacon provides the pastor with lines from the Bible that he either repeats or uses as the basis for improvisation. After he has absorbed the lining out and repeated it or exhausted his improvisation of the Word, the pastor will usually say, "Line me out some more"; and the deacon will provide him with more text.

After the collection has been blessed and prayed over, Reverend Daniel announces that the choir will sing "Move Mountain." The lead singer, Paula Williams, gives such a surging rendition of the song that I can't help but think she might well do battle with and win out over those two divas at Mount Pisgah. The choir here at Antioch is better than average, and this young woman — with an angel's wing touched to the harp of her throat bone — can move mountains. You can hear the influences of Mahalia Jackson, Rosetta Tharpe, and Clara Ward in Paula Williams's voice. But her interpretation of the song puts power behind the phrases, that celebrate the will of the individual — not only those that honor spiritual fiber but also the lines rooted in the secular ruggedness of grit and guts. Now I know what the old folks meant when they told me that to make it in life you needed "grit, shit, and mother wit." And I am now one with the congregation as we all unleash a thunderous shout when Paula Williams flies us to the mythical mountain. . . .

Later, in a calmer mood on this Sunday so close to the birth of the Redeemer, I feel a renewal of faith and intellect as I reflect upon Williams's anchoring interpretation for all of us who must stand alone before that mountain of ascendancy.

# Michael Anania
## (b. 1939)

*Born in Omaha, Nebraska,* MICHAEL ANANIA *worked in the State University of New York system before coming to the Chicago area in 1965 to teach at Northwestern and the University of Illinois at Chicago. Starting as an instructor at UIC, he went on to become chair of the Program for Writers, where he has been a pivotal figure in the careers of several fine Chicago writers, including Tina De Rosa, whom he helped as she wrote her early versions of what would become her novel* Paper Fish.

*He has been poetry editor for Chicago's Swallow Press and has written or edited several volumes of poetry, including* New Poetry Anthology I *(1969),* The Color of Dust *(1970),* Set/Sorts *(1974),* Riversongs *(1978),* Constructions/Variations *(1985), and* Selected Poems *(1994). He is also author of* The Red Menace *(1984), a book about American culture in the 1950s. Perhaps some lines from the following poems best sum up the experience of reading Anania: "new explosions contend/with old salvage," or, if not explosions, always something else — "like/the lyric that stammers/inside the songs" — trying to break through, trying for a chance to speak and "show you what I mean."*

◆ ◆ ◆

NEWS NOTES, 1970
  *for John Matthias*

                    i

and the bottles    rocks flew
Grant Park    the yachts still
lolling their slow dance of
masts and flying bridges
tear gas    a few gunshots
evening papers tally the costs
in police cars    fashionable windows
several injured    none dead
fear a new alliance beginning

"the brothers and the longhairs"
"mellow," one said    surprised

                ii

music from a flat guitar
its neck angled across
his crotch like a gunbelt
right arm almost straight
music like the stone extended
reports through the microcircuit
concussion registers rock
against a head just turned
the tallied windows    cars
overturned and burning
a mellow swirl of bodies
breaks over the ear like music
fades out with evening
echoes only in newscasts
prolongs a traffic jam

                iii

if we could name each part
pick through every archipelago
the city's wash contains
species that waddle
history through the streets
islands brush past us
their clatter gathers
volume    then subsides
the landscape dips and curves
notes for a full catalog
curl in the fire
new explosions contend
with old salvage    sludge
the air we crouch in
expecting martial music
beating through the drone

                iv

for two weeks studying
a handspan of spruce

extrapolating glaciers
the silt this limestone
still imitates   breaking
into flat shelves   lines
the receding waters left
trees rooted in their faults
pine pitch fills the air
a cardinal flares in the brush
moving against its greenery
as water moves against stone
closing off this valley's
tumbling progress with
repeating crest   break-over
ebb   and sounding fall
as ice moved a millennium
as the earth moved   extruding
silt compacted into stone
as we move now   compacted
shouldering buildings into
place   hefting post and lintel
shouldering it all down
cities   valleys   plains
the intricate dance of greenery
we presumed the world at rest
tread into a widening slag

## VARIATIONS FOR A SUMMER EVENING

*I have heard what the talkers were talking . . .*

### 1

"Thank you and goodbye,"
and now she turns, hair
asway, skirt furling,
the peonies, each one
of them a pink tangle,
sunlit quartz sidewalk.
*Lester leaps in.*

### 2

Flowering Cheyenne,
ladyfingers, white

blossoms, bees
and butterflies,
the skyline, pure
Chicago, this paper
cut-out of itself,
watertown solitaries,
a deuce-and-a-quarter
listing by.

3

The voice I hear
under the locust tree
in the courtyard,
so definite, the rush
of the El, box elder,
poplars stirring.
"All I want," she says,
"or anyone, for that
matter, is a chance
to show you what I mean."

4

Haze after haze,
the city and evening:
music seems implicit
in conditions perfected
years ago, gaiety,
the Venetian glass swirl
of warm gin over ice.
Dear saxophone, the breathy
instant before the sound
comes on like anything.

5

America, it's hardly worth
mentioning. These happy
accidents occur as they
occur, something the horn
ribbons out into moist
air and indigo. "To show

you what I mean," like
the lyric that stammers
inside the songs. *Embraceable*
*You*, never quite uttered,
assumed, like Max Roach,
an insistence that
sometimes comes to call.

6

Elm crowns above the scattered
rooflines, *my sweet*, the Smoke King,
so close you could hear him
fingering the keys, *embraceable*
valve pads opening and closing,
riding above the notes
and darkened leaves, breath flared
like steam against lacquered brass.
Sometimes this sadness is intolerable.

7

"All I want," the narrow leaves
like fossils stamped in anthracite,
"or anyone," ice cubes hissing
their breath away, an insistence
turning just where the light furls
round their sadness. "Thank you
and goodbye," *my sweet embraceable*
night air and its thickening
apprehension, "for that matter,
is a chance to show you what
I mean," *my sweet embraceable you.*

# Sterling Plumpp
## (b. 1940)

*Voices of rural Mississippi, where he was born, always haunt* STERLING PLUMPP'S
*poetry, even when the subject is urban life and urban people. Since the early 1970s he
has taught at the University of Illinois at Chicago and produced books of poetry including* Clinton *(1976) — winner of an Illinois Arts Council Literary Award —* The
Mojo Hands Call, I Must Go *(1982) — winner of a Sandburg Poetry Prize — and
the very highly regarded* Blues: The Story Always Untold *(1989).*

*From the beginning Plumpp has been praised for his ability to render the complex
musicality of black speech and song forms with a powerful style distinct from the more
aggressive street lingo so popular in the black arts movement of the late 1960s. Dudley
Randall has called him "more of a poet's poet," though Plumpp's prose works like*
Black Rituals *(1972) directly confront the psychology of oppression running through
the black community, and his involvements in various black cultural institutions speak
loudly of his social and political commitment. Finally his poems, as they trace, in his
words, "the survival lines of my people in the many ways they did things," result in as
viable a social and political outcome as poems that speak more directly to those issues.*

*Reading his poems one is reminded of Ralph Ellison's statement that "blues are
not primarily concerned with civil rights or obvious political protest; they are an art
form and thus a transcendence of those conditions created within the Negro community by the denial of social justice. As such they are one of the techniques through
which Negroes have survived and kept their courage during the long period when
many whites assumed, as some still assume, they were afraid." His most recent work
is* Ornate with Smoke *(1997), poems reflecting jazz.*

✦ ✦ ✦

## BLUES FOR LEON FORREST

I got the blues of a fallen
teardrop. Prostrate on the mercy
bosom/pushed down, way down/a long
ways from home of the spirit. Way

back home/in a corner where big foots
of indifference/steps on my patented
leather hopes. Deep down near
wayfaring roots and Lucifer socked
conspiracy in scars of wayside dwelling
children/living in the Bucket of Blood
of despair. I got the real/unbaptized
blues. Bone dust of lost souls blues.
I got the Invisible Man cellar blues.
That's why I be so bad I hire
a metaphysical wheelbarrow to haul
my scrambled soul around. Got the bone
dust blues/testified before a sky.
Dripping with blood of my folks.
The fallen teardrop blues. Water
rinsed red in polluted eyelids
of clouds/acid alienness of hate
and oppression. The apocalypse blues
of falling eyewater/drifting down
unabridged cracks in concern. Falling
slowly down blues. The soundless
disappearances of dreams in a teardrop.
I got the blues/a long ways from Satchmo
and the mask of my humanity. I got
the long ways from home blues/got
the fallen teardrop blues

## WIND

(*for Daniel Clardy*)

The blues walks in slow/
dancing.
A woman holds her man's
pain in her steps.
The man
closets his concern in
sacred masculinity.
Lifts
his fist. To mask
all
the love he can

not admit.
The music
walks in/yesterday's
speech. Rolls timbres of
affirmation. Years done
pushed
down with images.
The old
country walking
and talking back
woods clod
hopper. No teeth,
big
feet and colors/loud
enough to challenge
an A-bomb. Telling
his troubles. His
woman/tallow perfuming
her hair. Rips
the proverbial head
rag from her spirit/stands
prophetic: with her pride
waving in air like corn
silk.
The
blues takes this story/puts
it
in the face of immortality.
Shakes
its head/lets
its ancestral bone
slip. Tacks declarations
on confinement.
Mates
its words over the bonding pond of
drought.
And the music/rolls.
Rolls.
Rolls.

## KOKO TAYLOR

She
holds her mojo out
to a bar.
Tender. Who.
Was my father.
Who was my mother's brother.
Was my longings.
Puts a
wang
dang
doodle loop
round retired dreams.
Pitches a
cannon
ball on toes of
stillness.
Calls
apron-wearing nannies
back from big houses.
Calls
uncle-toming butlers
from pockets of myth.
Holds
her mojo out
to a bar.
Tender. Who.
Was celebration.
All
night/long.
All
night/long.
Puts
great specks of time
on folks. And they
slay stillness.
Follow
a wang
dang
doodle loop.

All
night/long.
All
night/long.

# Philip Caputo

## (b. 1941)

PHILIP CAPUTO *grew up on the South Side of Chicago and spent eight years as a* Chicago Tribune *staffer, first as a local reporter, then a foreign correspondent in Rome, Beirut, Moscow, and Saigon. His reporting stint in Saigon, coupled with his military service in Vietnam as a lieutenant in the Marine Corps in the mid-1960s, has led him to focus much of his writing on war — the horrors of war, of course, and its social, physical, and psychological aftermath, but also on how war is itself a condition of knowledge and how it is known and represented in reporting, memoir, and fiction. This latter concern has led him to a blending of traditional writing genres that has put Caputo in the forefront of what is currently known as creative nonfiction.*

*His books include the memoirs* A Rumor of War *(1977) and* Means of Escape *(1991), and the novels* Horn of Africa *(1980),* DelCorso's Gallery *(1983), and* Indian Country *(1987). Writing in the* Los Angeles Times Book Review, *William Broyles noted that Caputo's journey "is far more than one man's journey into the dark regions of our times; it is, through him, an American journey from abundance and promise, through defeat and disillusionment, to a kind of peace."*

*Chicago is one of the great centers of the mystery novel, and, strangely, the following article, which appeared in the May 1997 issue of* Esquire *on the death of crime novelist Eugene Izzi in December 1996, traces a similar journey. (Izzi's last book,* The Criminalist, *was published in September 1998 to mostly good reviews.) But what are the conditions of knowledge and the kinds of peace that can come from what Caputo says may be the first "postmodern" suicide?*

✦ ✦ ✦

## Dangling Man

Eugene Izzi, a Chicago crime novelist of modest fame, tried to get away with murder — his own.

He was a powerfully built man, six feet tall and two hundred pounds, with thick, dark hair, a prominent nose, piercing eyes, and an intensity that electrified some people and intimidated others. On December 7, 1996, he committed suicide in a spectacular fashion, after leaving a trail of clues designed to lead the police and the public to conclude that he'd been murdered by an Indiana militia group. For a while, his colleagues in the midwestern chapter of the Mystery Writers of America — novelists whose minds run in winding channels of plots and conspiracies — bought into his fiction. Within hours after he'd been found hanging out the window of his fourteenth-floor office in Chicago's Loop, they began issuing statements that Izzi, who had a reputation for taking risks to gather material for his novels, could not have died by his own hand. The ever-competitive Chicago media printed and broadcast these pronouncements, and soon Izzi's death had become a whodunit, with all the melodramatic elements of the potboilers he wrote.

Even Izzi's closest friend, a man he called his brother, inadvertently fed the wild speculation: "There is no question that Guy [as Izzi's friends called him] was in the midst of investigating certain individuals at the time of his death — that's beyond dispute," Andrew Vachss, a New York lawyer and a crime novelist in his own right, told the *Chicago Sun-Times.* "You don't wrap yourself in a Kevlar vest and carry a handgun if you're relaxed about the environment around you. He was completely sane and dedicated to his craft, which happened to mean digging up dirt."

Izzi was wearing a bulletproof vest when he died and had been carrying a .38-caliber revolver for weeks. The fully loaded gun was found on his office floor when Chicago police and firemen recovered his body. They also discovered other items in his trouser pockets and in the pockets of his blue winter overcoat: brass knuckles, a can of Mace, three computer diskettes, a couple of threatening notes containing the words *danger* and *beware*, and the transcript of a phone call that had been left on his voice mail. In the days before his death, Izzi had played the message for anyone whose ear he could grab. At least half a dozen people had heard the halting female voice say that Izzi's infiltration of the Indiana militia had been discovered; he'd been tried by a kangaroo court and sentenced to die by "a flaming rope."

In early November, claiming that he feared for his family's safety, he moved his wife, Theresa, and their two sons into a downtown hotel from their apartment on Printer's Row, a district of renovated printshops and binderies south of the Loop.

The plot was all set up. At some point in the early hours of last December 7, Izzi opened the north window in the spartan ten-by-twelve cell where he wrote his books, Room 1418 at 6 North Michigan Avenue. He methodically tied one end of a coarse hemp rope to a leg of his desk with a slipknot, wrapped the other end around his neck four times, and secured it with another slipknot. He straddled the windowsill, tightly and for some time. Izzi was afraid of heights. The Cook County medical examiner later found deep bruises on his inner thighs. He sat there, mustering the nerve to jump. Finally, he did.

Or did he? His body was found with the feet dangling just below the window of the room one story beneath his office, a distance of some eight to ten feet. That could have been just enough to break the neck of a man his weight, but his neck wasn't broken. He died of asphyxiation. Izzi's body hung there long enough for rigor mortis and the frosty air to turn it hard as concrete. It wasn't spotted until 11:30 A.M., when a doctor glanced out his window while he was treating a patient in his office in an adjacent building at 30 North Michigan Avenue.

Chicago firemen, who arrived first on the scene after the doctor's 911 call, forced open the bare wooden door to Room 1418, which was locked from the inside, and hauled the body back up through the window. Detectives Michael D'Alessandro, Gregory Baiocchi, and Michael Gerhardstein of the Area 4 homicide squad arrived shortly afterward and took notes on details great and small — the blue steel revolver lying on the floor just west of the window; the desk jerked one and a half feet from its original position by the weight of Izzi's body; the length, thickness, and type of rope. They collected the contents of Izzi's pockets, identified him from his driver's license, and classified the case as a "death investigation." That meant they weren't sure whether it was suicide, homicide, or some kind of freak accident. It is indicative of Izzi's limited reputation as a crime novelist that these real-life cops had never heard of him.

The next day, some of Izzi's friends and fellow writers reported that he had feared for his life and had shown no signs of being depressed, much less suicidal. Izzi had every reason to live. His marriage was happy; his sons, Gino and Nick, were doing well in school. Only the year before, he'd signed a major contract with Avon Books for a sum his publisher wouldn't disclose but one big enough to rule out financial problems as a motive for suicide. The press leaped on the story. This was hot stuff for TV tabloids like *Hard Copy* and *Inside Edition* but also for the sober national media — *The New York Times, The Washington Post.* Soon, the verdict was in: Izzi must have been murdered.

The trio of detectives, meanwhile, strongly suspected that they were dealing with an elaborate ruse. During the first week of December, Izzi had been acting out of character. Often taciturn and even surly toward strangers or people he knew casually, he had been passing out Christmas presents to the janitor and others on the staff of his office building. He had seemed unusually jovial. The cops were not psychiatrists, but they were savvy, and Izzi's yuletide cheer looked to them like an attempt to make amends. Perhaps he wanted to leave people with pleasant memories of him. Either that, or he was trying to reinforce the illusion that he was too happy to kill himself.

The detectives learned that Izzi was under psychiatric care for clinical depression and had been taking Zoloft, an antidepressant drug. There were other pieces of evidence pointing to suicide: the office door that was locked from the inside and the absence of any signs of the ferocious struggle that presumably would have occurred when the heavily armed Izzi — who lifted weights, worked out on punching bags, and sometimes sparred with a karate black belt — confronted his attackers.

Chicago police technicians were able to trace the threatening message on Izzi's voice mail: The call had come not from Indiana but from a pay phone around the corner from Izzi's office. The more the detectives listened to the woman's halting delivery, the more certain they became that she was reading from a script — one probably authored by Izzi himself. They couldn't identify the woman but surmised that she had been paid by Izzi or was doing him a favor.

The police traced another phone call, the last one Izzi ever made. It came from Room 1418 at 6 North Michigan Avenue late on the night of December 6. Izzi spoke to one of his sons, saying that he'd forgotten the keys to his office and asking whether the boy could bring them to the lobby of their hotel. Izzi met the boy in the lobby, hugged him, and said, "No matter what happens, I want you to know that I love you."

In late December, after computer experts cracked the password to the three diskettes found in Izzi's pocket, police made a startling discovery: The documents they contained were segments of a novel, a long one, eight hundred pages. The hero was a Chicago crime novelist who resembled Izzi in all ways but name. Details of the fictional writer's life matched the real-life writer's almost point for point. Then came this remarkable scene: Members of an Indiana paramilitary group, after discovering that the novelist has infiltrated their ranks, break into his office at night while he's working. He's wearing a bulletproof vest and is armed with Mace, brass knuckles, and a .38-caliber revolver. Nevertheless, the militiamen overpower him and hang him out of his fourteenth-floor window, tying one end of the rope to a leg of his desk. The passage is identical in every respect to Izzi's hanging, with the exception that the make-believe hero hoists himself back up into his office and overcomes his assailants.

It was a hall of mirrors, a fiction within a fiction within a fiction, but as far as the Chicago police were concerned, the case was no longer a homicide. Perhaps, then, Izzi was the victim of a weird mishap. A stickler for verisimilitude, he had once lived as a homeless man for a week in order to write an article on homelessness for the *Chicago Tribune*'s Sunday magazine. Had he slipped while rehearsing the scene from his novel?

Some of Izzi's fans and acquaintances latched on to the accident theory as the only plausible explanation. Others were, shall we say, far more skeptical. As one veteran newsman told me, in a comment that was pure Chicago in its fusion of midwestern pragmatism and big-city cynicism: "If he was practicing, he should have done it on the first floor."

On January 15, the Cook County medical examiner's office ruled Izzi's death a suicide. But when I went to Chicago in January to look into his suicide, surely the most bizarre in American literature, I still found people clinging to the homicide and accident theories. I suppose they found a conspiracy or a mishap a more palatable explanation for what had happened. Consciousness of death is the curse of being human, and our dread of nonexistence is the mother of all our dreads. Yet the capacity for suicide is another power unique to human beings. Believers have blamed the act of self-murder on Satan, who lures sinners into despair, the gravest sin. Psychologists have sought answers in metaphorical devils that spring from childhood sexual abuse or war or the sudden loss of loved ones. Biopsychiatrists look to the brain's chemistry: Malfunctions in neurotransmitters deprive the sufferer of all ability to experience joy or hope, inflicting a mental anguish so acute that death seems the only way to end it.

Whatever its causes, suicide is more frequent in certain professions than in others. Policemen kill themselves more often than, say, gardeners, for obvious reasons. So do writers, for reasons that may not be so obvious. Hemingway remains America's most famous literary suicide, with poets Sylvia Plath and Anne Sexton close seconds. William Styron's *Darkness Visible*, a frightening but beautiful account of his danse macabre with his self-destructive monsters, has practically become a textbook on the link between creative fire and suicidal impulses.

As an artist, Izzi had nowhere near Styron's or Hemingway's stature. Nor did he aspire to literary greatness. He wrote pulp fiction, albeit a variety of that genre that might be called "high pulp." But as a suicide, Izzi is in a class all his own. The way he scripted and choreographed his death might well turn out to be his greatest creative achievement. The question is why he did what he did. That he was under treatment for depression barely explains things. Lots of people who are treated for depression don't kill themselves. What, then, had driven him to such an extreme?

When I read about Izzi's death in *The New York Times*, I was reminded of something Anne Sexton said when she heard that Sylvia Plath had sealed herself in the kitchen and turned on the oven gas: "That death was mine." Not that I could imagine a death like Izzi's as being mine; and yet I could not help but identify with him. I am a writer, born in Chicago into an Italian American family of modest means; my career, like Izzi's has had its peaks and valleys, valleys in which I felt the cold wings of depression fold around my soul. I've never gotten so low that I've seriously thought about suicide as the only way out, but I've been low enough to understand how it could become an option for some people. I have awakened at 2:00 A.M. —Napoleon's test of the bravest soldier's valor—with my heart shrouded in dread and the taste of ashes in my mouth and my insides filled with the awful suspicion that everything I've done in life has been pointless.

Did Izzi feel something like that on the night he straddled the window ledge, fourteen floors above Michigan Avenue? I wondered.

"The only reason you're interested in him is because of the way he died," Andrew Vachss said to me when I phoned him at his New York law office. Fair enough. I hadn't heard of Izzi, mostly because I read very little crime fiction. But Vachss's comment raised a question: Was Izzi seeking in the manner of his death a recognition he hadn't achieved in life? I didn't like myself for that thought, but it was impossible to ignore.

Born on March 23, 1953, Izzi grew up in Hegewisch, a blue-collar neighborhood on Chicago's southeast side, next to the Indiana state line, under the perpetual pall of smoke and grit spewing from the stacks of giant steel mills— U. S. Steel, Wisconsin Steel, and Republic. Poles, Serbs, Croats, Italians, and Irish, big men with muscular arms and sooty faces, worked in those mills, or in nearby foundries, or in the oil refineries in Whiting, Indiana, where gas towers blazed like enormous torches day and night and the air pollution created sunsets of tropical brilliance.

Hegewisch is about eighteen miles from downtown Chicago. Most of the mills are shut down now, but when I visited the neighborhood, six weeks after Izzi's death, I had the feeling that I had traveled back in time, to the Chicago of the late 1940s and early 1950s. The seemingly endless plain of smokestacks, the industrial canals lined by coal yards and freight yards and warehouses, the frozen Calumet River, with its icebound barges, winding toward Lake Michigan under the steel geometry of drawbridge elevators, seemed light-years away from the glittering office towers downtown, from the busy mine galleries of the LaSalle Street financial district and the whole digitized, computerized world of the information age. Even the neighborhood saloon, an all-but-extinct institution elsewhere in the city, was thriving. There was one on almost every corner, places with Old Style signs hanging over the streets and simple, direct names like Steve's or East Side Tavern. Hegewisch is a last remnant of Nelson Algren's and Mike Royko's Chicago, Carl Sandburg's Chicago, grimy and rough, "laughing even as an ignorant fighter laughs who's never lost a battle."

Of course, this part of Chicago has taken a few hits by now. Guy Izzi lived here, in a two-story bungalow at Brainard and Burnham avenues. He went to St. Columba's grammar school, at the corner of 134th Street and Avenue O, and for two years to Washington High School. Hegewisch was the setting for most of Izzi's novels, and critics said he was best when writing about it. The neighborhood isn't the concrete jungle he sometimes made it out to be, but it can be tough. Toughness was central to Izzi's image, and he fostered it sometimes. Other times, he tried to back away from it, disturbed by the way journalists depicted him as an urban primitive. But the roots of Izzi's suicide won't be found in anything that happened to him on the streets.

They're to be found in what happened to him under the roof of the bungalow at Brainard and Burnham. Saying Izzi's family was dysfunctional would be like calling the Karamazovs unhappy. Izzi's father, Eugene Sr., had a reputation as a small-time mafioso who got his start as a knee cracker for mob loan sharks. Between 1967 and 1978, he was convicted four times, on charges ranging from interstate racketeering to drug trafficking, and spent most of those years in jail.

Izzi once described what happened when his father wasn't behind bars: "My earliest memories of my childhood are of my father beating my mother. . . . His wild, drunken brutality, and the terror it instilled, is never far from my memory." Izzi recalled "the bull-like expulsions of air that exploded from my father's nostrils as he tried to choke my mother with his belt or as he beat her with his fists."

Later, Izzi continued, he felt those hot, furious expulsions in his face as his father challenged him to be a man and fight him. Eugene Sr.'s spells in jail brought no relief from cruelty. In a 1994 article in the *Chicago Reader*, Izzi's older sister, Fabian Fisher, said her brother was a "human punching bag, a very battered child, physically and emotionally. My grandmother hated him because he looked like my father, and we lived with her when our dad was in jail. She would use any excuse to beat Guy up or call him the most disgusting names."

When he wasn't being smacked by his grandmother, he was dodging swats from his mother, who Izzi said drank a lot. Once, Fabian recalled, Izzi stood up to her and hit her back. He was banished to the basement to await the arrival of an uncle who had vowed to "spill his blood all over the walls" if he misbehaved. Izzi escaped through a window and hid out on the streets or in friends' houses for the next two days.

He found another way to flee the violence of his household.

"I turned to books for escape," he wrote to a fan years later. "They took me away and transported me to a place that was safe and without pain. The first book I read that did this for me was *The Deep Blue Good-by*, by John D. MacDonald. I was ten years old." Izzi had also begun to write. He won an essay contest when he was in third grade, a triumph so rare in his dreadful childhood that he recalled it thirty years later, in an interview with *Chicago Tribune* writer John Blades.

It was during his adolescence that Izzi began to forge his tough-guy persona. John Smierciak, today a forty-five-year-old photographer, recalls riding the Chicago Transit Authority bus to school with him.

"Guy smoked a lot, and he'd sit on the bench seat in back, his legs out in the aisle, talking real loud and tough, you know, trying to act like a mob wiseguy because he was Italian. He'd brag about his father. He'd say he idolized him, wanted to be just like him. Once, I asked him where his old man was, and he said he was in Marion — the federal pen in Illinois — and Guy acted like he was proud of that."

Izzi dropped out of high school when he was sixteen and joined the Army the next year. Most of Hegewisch's sons were shipped to Vietnam, but Izzi was sent to Germany. He earned his high-school-equivalency diploma and began to write fiction, knocking out what he would later call "Mickey Spillane clones" on an army-issue typewriter. Home on leave, he had a final confrontation with his father, who was between prison sentences. Eugene Sr. once again bellowed a challenge to his son, who accepted it. No frightened adolescent now but a trained soldier, Izzi beat his father senseless, and that was that. So far as is known, the two men spoke to each other only once in the next twenty-odd years. It wasn't much of a conversation. Izzi's father, angry about something his son had written, called him and said, "Change your fucking name!" and then slammed down the phone.

Izzi was discharged as a sergeant in 1972. Returning to Hegewisch, he followed the well-worn path into the steel mills. His first job was with U. S. Steel, which was already beginning to scale back production as Japanese manufacturers took over the market. Hired, laid off, and rehired, Izzi began to drink heavily and to snort or smoke whatever drug he could get his hands on. He fell in with a crowd of petty mobsters, rogue cops, and B-girls — characters that would later populate his novels. But he wasn't gathering material; he was living the life, living it to the point that he acquired an identification-record number with the Chicago Police Department: 0266-268. Things might have gone very badly for him if it had not been for his passion for writing. Between steel-mill jobs, he pounded on his typewriter with the feverishness that other young men from bad backgrounds bring to boxing gyms, and for the same reason. Writing was to be his ticket out of a dead-end life.

The legacy of his background is more complicated than that. Izzi was uncommonly compassionate and generous toward the abused, the dispossessed, and the outcast. Even when his fortunes were at a low ebb, he gave money to shelters for abused children and battered women. Once, he bought thirty-six pairs of new basketball shoes for a South Side home for troubled youths. Another time, he pulled a homeless drug addict and alcoholic off the streets, bought him food and clothes, and guided him through a three-month detox program. He gave of himself to his few close friends. One of them, who asked to remain anonymous, recalls, "You could call Guy at 2:00 A.M. if you were having a problem. He could be secretive and needy but very generous. I'll never forget that he was the first person to see me after my son was born. He held the kid so tight I was jealous. Worst thing you can do, he told me, is to mistreat a child."

Izzi's compassion, and his sense of social justice and moral outrage, burned through his writing. Those are qualities sadly lacking in a lot of literary writers today. They're on English-department faculties now, competing for tenure and foundation grants; they band into groups and give one another awards; they whore after celebrity. Izzi might have been a pulp writer, but he was in some ways a throwback to the likes of John Steinbeck and Algren and James T. Farrell. In 1990, he wrote a touching article about a sexually abused four-year-old girl for the *Chicago Tribune*'s Sunday magazine. His story on the homeless for the same publication was graphic and powerful. Some perceptive reviewers have noted a serious moral vision beneath the terse crime-story prose and melodramatic events in Izzi's fiction.

So angels were born in the same hatchery as Izzi's devils; and if the devils won in the end, their triumph did not diminish the angels' brightness. But it's to the demons that we must return. A childhood like his carves a terrible, indelible message into the child's mind: He is worthless and entitled to nothing but punishment and failure. At the same time, it instills, at least in some individuals, a contradictory and overpowering greed for success, applause, recognition, adoration. The world is called upon to give him the approval he cannot give himself and to validate his existence. The world's respect becomes a sign of absolution for sins both real and imagined. But if he gains those rewards, he never truly feels he deserves them and secretly thinks himself a fraud. From deep down, a voice censures him for his presumption, and he becomes caught in a psychological trap: He craves and demands more success, more recognition, to silence the voice, but the more he gets, the louder the voice becomes.

"Considering what he came from, it's a fucking miracle that Guy published one book, let alone twelve," a close friend of Izzi's told me. "But he felt like an impostor a lot of times. We had conversations about that. That he didn't belong where he was, that he was going to be found out."

In the mid-seventies, Izzi married a woman he'd met in a south-suburban restaurant where she was a waitress and where he stopped for coffee when he went to the track. He and Theresa had a son, Gino, in 1977. Nick was born four years later. But the marriage was a disaster. Izzi discovered that the Beast from outside had become the Beast within. While the family lived in a shabby two-room flat, Izzi worked on-again, off-again at U. S. Steel and blew his money in bars. When Theresa reminded him of his responsibilities as husband and father, he hit her. The last time he struck her was around 9:00 A.M. on August 15, 1981 — he would remember the hour and date the rest of his life. Drunk again, Izzi gave her a shot to the stomach as he stumbled toward the bathroom, where he passed out. When he woke up, Theresa and the boys were gone.

Two weeks later, evicted from his flat, Izzi found himself living in the back of a Hegewisch barbershop. He drank all day and slept in the shop's bathroom, on an exercise mat. One night, his bottle empty, he sat in one of the swivel chairs and considered killing himself.

"I would stare, longingly, at the stropped razor blades on the back shelf, nestled there between the electric equipment and the combs, the brushes," he wrote in a magazine article years later. "Their sharpness appealed to me; the light glinting off them was my salvation. It would be fast, painless. . . ."

Three months later, Theresa forgave him and took him back. Izzi vowed never to touch another drink and never to raise a hand to her again. He kept those promises. So salvation came to Izzi not in the beckoning glint of honed blades but in a woman's love and in the one talent he had. He read Elmore Leonard, Ed McBain, and other masters of the pulp-fiction trade while writing six novels in as many years. Not one was published. Every night, he prayed for something good to happen, something that would pull him out of the mills (what was left of them) and his family out of the stifling confines of Hegewisch. All his life, he would say later, he had been an outsider looking in, and he imagined that everyone inside the mansion called success was "warm and happy and having a helluva good time." He was going to take his place at the table, and if he wasn't invited in, then he'd kick the goddamned door down.

In 1987, he sold his first novel, *The Take*, to St. Martin's Press and signed a contract to write three more for $20,000. That isn't a big advance for four books, but it was more money than Izzi had ever seen outside a betting parlor. *The Take*, a story about a heist, and its successors, *Bad Guys*, *The Eighth Victim*, and *The Booster*, sold well. *The Take* was also made into a TV movie, and Izzi wrote three screenplays, one of which was commissioned by director William Friedkin.

A few years later, Izzi left St. Martin's for Bantam Books, the giant commercial house and flagship of the Bantam Doubleday Dell publishing fleet. He published several novels with Bantam, including *Prowlers*, *Invasions*, *King of the Hustlers*, *The Prime Roll*, and *Tony's Justice*.

His reviews were good. One critic hailed him as Chicago's new Algren; another compared his 1990 novel, *Invasions*, to no less a literary masterpiece than Robert Stone's prizewinning *Dog Soldiers*. A little closer to earth, most comparisons were made to Izzi's hero Elmore Leonard, though some reviewers noted that Izzi's work lacked Leonard's polish, nuance, and streamlined plots. Izzi could take such slaps on the wrist. By the early nineties, a million copies of his books were in print, and he'd said goodbye to Hegewisch. He and his family had bought two houses in Park Forest, an upper-middle-class suburb. One house was to live in, the second an office for Izzi to work in. He was driving a new Lincoln instead of a secondhand clunker. On book tours or trips to Hollywood to meet movie producers, he flew first-class and was met at the airport by drivers in stretch limousines.

But all that was not enough. "In order to function as a human being, Izzi needed success, recognition, and esteem the way other people need oxygen," said Stuart Applebaum, a top executive at Bantam. According to Applebaum and Esther Newberg, Izzi's former literary agent, Izzi dreamed of national recognition but felt that he wasn't getting it. None of his books stood out among the dozens of good crime novels published in the previous decade. His name was only one in a crowded genre. Izzi loved boxing, and if he'd been a fighter instead of a writer, we'd have to say he was a ninth- or tenth-ranked contender. He didn't like being there.

Izzi may also have felt a need to break out of the two ghettos he found himself in: genre and place. Although two of his books had been nominated for the Edgar, the Mystery Writers of America's top award, Izzi did not consider himself a mystery writer, and in some ways he was right. He also was a Chicago writer, as opposed to a writer from Chicago. Chicago writers have a sense of place and a loyalty to their city as fierce, bitter, and ambivalent as southern novelists have to their region. They also have something of an inferiority complex, for they're aware that the capital of American letters lies eight hundred miles to the east. Izzi once called New York "enemy territory," but in a letter to a fan he also said that he wanted respect, "and you don't get respect in New York without sales."

In 1992, Bantam presented itself as the genie that would grant Izzi's wishes. "Bantam was supposed to turn his life around," Newberg told me. He was going to get it all—the respect, the sales, the national fame—with the publication of his new novel, *Tribal Secrets*.

For professional and psychological reasons, Bantam and Izzi could not have chosen a worse candidate than *Tribal Secrets*.

The psychological reasons first. The novel was Izzi's most autobiographical—too autobiographical. You can't help but conclude that the novel's success would have been a validation of Izzi's life, would have given meaning to the indignities and brutality he had suffered. Its failure would have been a repudiation, a sign that the world would not grant him the respect and redemption he hungered for.

And yet, the book itself suggests that Izzi feared and despised the very thing he wanted. Part of the story turns on the relationship of its hero, Babe

Hill, to Edna Rose, an evil woman who stalks him. She is the bitch goddess—"a metaphor for success," as Izzi confirmed to a reporter writing a profile of him. Hill escaped Edna's clutches with the help of his wife, and that, Izzi said, "took courage."

The professional reasons next. In *Tribal Secrets*, Izzi's strengths—his passion, intensity, and moral vision—are far outweighed by his flaws. He could be a raw, undisciplined writer, with a weakness for cliché and melodrama; moreover, he did not like to rewrite. When he was on, he didn't need to, but when he was off, "he needed a strong editor to work with him on his writing," said Sheldon McArthur, owner of the Mysterious Bookshop West, a prominent crime-fiction store in Los Angeles.

"The trouble with Bantam was that they published whatever he sent them. I was astounded that they chose *Tribal Secrets* as his big breakout book. No one could understand why they did that. It was the worst book he'd ever written," McArthur continued.

If people at Bantam were aware of the novel's flaws, they apparently hoped a powerful marketing campaign would compensate. Izzi was flown to New York to attend meetings on promotion strategies for his novel. He saw storyboards for TV commercials, mock-ups for print ads. In the spring of 1992, Bantam brought him to the American Booksellers Association's convention, held that year in Anaheim, California. When a publisher brings an author to the ABA, it is telling the industry that he or she is an in-house star, and there was Izzi, the gangster's son, the ex-steel worker, at the center of attention.

"The Friday night before the convention started, Bantam threw a big party for its West Coast writers, but Izzi was the feature attraction," remembered McArthur. "He made it an A-list party that booksellers wanted to go to. Izzi was even dressed in a suit, which he almost never wore—he always played the tough guy, wearing leather jackets over T-shirts, but there he was in a suit, meeting and greeting booksellers and salesmen, holding court, smoking a big cigar. Before the party was over, he must have been seen by three or four hundred people."

Izzi also signed some of the ten thousand advance copies Bantam had given away to grease the bandwagon's wheels. He was told that he would be going on a thirty-city tour, with appearances on network talk shows, when *Tribal Secrets* came out in September.

It never happened, thanks to those ten thousand free copies. Through the summer, the comments coming back from booksellers were dreadful. Advance reviews were disastrous. *Tribal Secrets* was sloppily written, they said, probably Izzi's worst book.

Bantam's reaction was swift and ruthless. The TV commercials and print ads were pulled; the talk-show dates and book tour were canceled. The novel was discounted from \$22.95 to \$14.95. Izzi said he wasn't told about any of this until the last hardcover copy was shipped.

When he found out, he phoned Bantam, called his publishers "dishonorable liars," and severed his relationship with the house. That brought legal problems because Izzi had taken advance money for several more novels he was to write for Bantam.

"They wanted him to repay the advance, which is standard practice when a writer leaves a house," Newberg explained.

But Izzi could not repay it; he was the breadwinner in his family, and they needed the money. The dispute was resolved when Bantam waived repayment on the condition that Izzi not publish another book under his own name for three years.

It isn't difficult to imagine his rage, his sense of betrayal, and his fear. Writing was his only source of income; he had tried to bring dignity to the name his father had disgraced, and now he couldn't even use it. But I can also imagine that voice calling to Izzi, "This is what you deserve."

He continued to write, but neither he nor his agent would find a publisher willing to sign an author who couldn't write under his real name for three years. He sold the two houses in Park Forest and the Lincoln and moved his family back into the city. His new office, in a dingy warehouse district on Wabash Avenue, was a grim, steam-heated cubbyhole that looked like the lair of a film-noir private eye. He signed on with Simon & Schuster to write three novels under a pen name, Nick Gaitano. Working midnight to dawn, he produced *Mr. X, Special Victims,* and *Jaded.* He was back in print, albeit in disguise.

His friends said that Izzi's idiosyncrasies — his secretiveness, his wariness of strangers — began to curdle into pathologies during this period. The mailbox in his apartment building bore no name, as if he was wallowing in his return to obscurity. He kept changing his unlisted phone numbers and the Mail Boxes Etc. outlets where he received his mail. He remained generous toward those close to him, gave to worthy causes despite his financial problems, but became increasingly distant from others. Some friends and family members said they thought he was going out of his way to alienate people. He was also becoming more paranoid. He pinned an obscene, threatening letter to his office wall. It came, he said, from a skinhead he'd interviewed for a new book he was working on, *Bulletin from the Streets.* There was something odd about this message, which was signed, cryptically, "Romantic Violence." Izzi claimed he had sent a copy of the manuscript to the skinhead. The pages contained a fictional but very unflattering portrait of the young man. Why, I wonder, would Izzi have done such a stupid thing? How did the neo-Nazi thug find out the secretive Izzi's address? Finally, did he really exist, or was he a creature of

Izzi's increasingly addled imagination? Printed in block letters, the note calls Izzi a "nigger-loving queer," among even more vulgar descriptions, and then comes this prophetic warning: "You will swing from your neck from a light post afire!"

Real, fictional, or in between, was this the genesis of the eight-hundred-page novel found on Izzi's body?

There were other dark signs. In 1994, he told the *Chicago Reader:* "I'm a walking heart attack. It's the way I choose to live. I flat-out refuse to be eighty years old and need somebody to feed me and change my diapers. I'd rather go out early."

Izzi tried to give the impression that he was content to accept something less than the respect and recognition he'd strived for. He'd kicked the door down and swaggered inside, and then, he said, "I took one look around and skulked right back out. It wasn't warm and happy in there. It was cold and phony and it stank. That's not the life I want. That's so shallow, so phony, so self-centered that it makes me sick to remember wanting it."

Who knows — maybe Izzi really believed this. Maybe it was that ancient voice from childhood telling him he should feel sick about wanting what he couldn't, shouldn't, have. Maybe he was relieved, now that the pressure to be a star was off.

But Edna Rose, the bitch goddess, came calling again. She arrived in early 1995, alluringly dressed as a five-book contract with Avon. Izzi and Lou Aronica, Avon's publisher, began discussing the first book of the series, a suspense novel that would begin with a drive-by shooting and a race riot in Chicago. It was to be an epic-size novel, a genre breaker told from multiple points of view. It would be called *A Matter of Honor: A Novel of Chicago.* If Izzi met his deadline, it would be the first book to appear under his name in almost five years. April 1997 was set as the publication date.

"Guy told me I was giving him the chance to write the kind of books he wanted to write. He was very excited," Aronica said.

No one knew, of course, about the Zoloft flowing through his veins, or knew that Izzi's monsters hadn't been slain, only tranquilized. His suspicious, furtive ways continued. Moving from his Wabash Avenue lair to the barren Michigan Avenue cell from whose window he would hang himself, he did not leave a forwarding address. Without a name or number, the wooden door to Izzi's new office looked like the door to the janitor's closet. And the janitor could not have a key to Room 1418. Nor the cleaning lady. Not even Jerry, the white-bearded building superintendent, could have one. All the keys had to be in Izzi's possession. Never know — somebody could bust in and *steal* one of his manuscripts. Jerry laconically cracked that he wouldn't know what a manuscript looked like, so how could he steal one?

Izzi pounded out *A Matter of Honor* with his usual speed. (Newberg said he could finish a novel in three months.) No one knew that he was writing another novel at the same time. No one would find out about that book until its publication date.

In early December, Izzi received the bound galleys of *A Matter of Honor.* He called Aronica. "He was so excited. He couldn't wait to see his name in print again. We talked over the outline he'd written for his next one, a novel set in Las Vegas," Aronica told me. "He was incredibly optimistic."

A week later, he was a frozen corpse, swinging from a rope against a sooty brick wall.

Only a suicide can tell us the reasons why, and even he may not be sure. And so we are left free, within certain limits, to ponder and draw our own conclusions. Some who knew Izzi still cannot accept that he killed himself.

"It wasn't in his nature, wasn't his style," Esther Newberg told me recently. "He loved his family, and he had a new book coming out that people were saying was his best. And why would he hang himself when he had a loaded gun right there? It just doesn't make sense."

And it doesn't, if one assumes that a person committing suicide is rational.

I think Izzi was terrified. He was terrified because his hopes were up again and his fear that he would suffer another failure became greater than his fear of death. I think he was even more terrified of succeeding. Success carries weight and responsibilities: Keeping it is twice as hard as getting it. That old voice was whispering to him again, then shouting — the voice that would not allow him to respect or forgive himself. Finally, I think he was overwhelmed by the terror of his boyhood, which had become an abstract, free-floating dread without object or reason. He could endure living with it no longer.

"I think Guy was murdered," says his good friend. "His father killed him, only it took him forty years to do it."

Three years ago, at a conference exploring the links between literary creativity and suicide, psychiatry professor Robert Jay Lifton said, "There is the quest for a future in suicide, the desire to make a statement in a way that the person could not in life." It's hard to know what statement Izzi was trying to make, if any; hard to envision what future he sought as he lowered himself down into the chill, black, unforgiving night.

# Daniel Pinkwater

## (b. 1941)

DANIEL PINKWATER *was born in Memphis, but grew up in Chicago, which is the setting of a number of his essays. He is the author of more than fifty books, most of them for children and many as both writer and illustrator under the name Manus Pinkwater. Among these books are* Lizard Music *(1976),* The Hoboken Chicken Emergency *(1977; made into a PBS television movie in 1984), and* The Snarkout Boys and the Avocado of Death *(1982). As these titles might suggest, Pinkwater is known not just for the fantasy of his children's writing but for the way the absurd and surreal continuously erupt into everyday life. He has admitted that he actually looks for a book to get out of hand, but at least one reviewer has criticized him for a "continual weirdness" that drains the patience. Despite this weirdness, Pinkwater exhibits a high seriousness about the importance of writing for children, who he feels are "more receptive to art than adults," and about the role art plays for everyone in making sense of an increasingly complex world. Since 1987 Pinkwater has also been a regular commentator for National Public Radio's* All Things Considered, *collecting many of his radio pieces in two books:* Fish Whistle: Commentaries, Uncommentaries, and Vulgar Excesses *(1990), from which the following essay comes; and* Chicago Days, Hoboken Nights *(1991). A* Washington Post *review of the latter calls Pinkwater ". . . a superb writer and social critic, one of America's very best humorists."*

✦ ✦ ✦

## *Where Is the Grease of Yesteryear?*

*from* FISH WHISTLE

When I was fourteen, my family left Los Angeles, where we'd lived for five or six years, and moved back to Chicago. Naturally, I was glad to leave L.A., but I was miserable and lonely in Chicago.

I didn't know anybody. The high school I transferred to was a hotbed of early Elvis-worshippers and thugs. My parents rented an ugly apartment in a brand-new, shoddily built high-rise—a place I hated from the first day. And I was entering the state of adolescent crisis that lasted until I was thirty-two years old.

I spent my time wandering the streets. I liked walking through city streets, especially at night—and do so to this day. It was about this time that I began an earnest pursuit of the other activity which has characterized and shaped my life—gluttony.

My funds were limited, but I was able to sample many truly frightening varieties of 1950s junk food. When I hear experts inveigh against the fast food of today, which, if a little light in nutritional content, is at least fairly sanitary and made mostly of things you can eat, I remember such haunts of mine as Fred's Red Hots.

Fred's Red Hots was not far from the apartment building. It was in one of those triangular buildings you see where two streets converge diagonally. There were never a lot of customers at Fred's. Just Fred. Angry face. Big nose. Grease-soaked apron. White paper cup. Mumbling.

Grease was the motif at Fred's. Instantly I would enter the place, a fine mist of grease suspended in the air would adhere to my eyeglasses—diffracting the light—so I always remember Fred's as a pointillist painting.

A monster fan over the door blasted grease-laden air out into the street, and made a roaring sound.

The red-hots I regarded more as objects of art than something to eat. Bright red, they tended to snap and squirt hot fat when you bit into them, and left a strange chemical taste in the mouth for days. Even I knew they were deadly, and left them alone.

I was a cheeseburger customer. Fred dispensed the cheapest cheeseburgers in Chicago. They came as singles, doubles, triples and quadruples. This referred to the number of patties of semiliquid fat and gristle. I believe a quadruple was under a dollar with a heap of dripping French fries, nearly raw in the middle, a limp quarter-pickle, and a bun with one last redundant gleam of schmaltz on top.

To make a balanced meal of a Fredburger, one could spoon on ketchup and scary bright-green pickle relish from bowls on the counter, thus adding vital trace minerals.

A quadruple contained more cholesterol than the average Copper Eskimo gets in a month. And indeed, most of my memories of Fred's are also of wild blizzards and eyeball-freezing February Chicago nights.

Not only did I thaw out at Fred's, and fortify myself for further wandering through the whiteout—Fred himself was, for the first few months I lived in Chicago, the only person I knew to speak to. I would tell Fred of my life, my suffering, my hopes and dreams.

"Yeh? So what?" Fred would ask, and give me a free limp, warm pickle spear.

It was good to know someone who listened.

Even after I began to make friends with various other misfits and delinquents, and have places to go and things to do, I would stop in at Fred's for a double or triple to fill the gap between the end of school and suppertime — or late at night, on my way home from committing an act of vandalism, I might drop by for one last infusion of lipids to help me sleep.

Probably the last time I visited Fred's was about the time I defied the predictions of guidance counselors and juvenile officers and left for college.

Seventeen or eighteen years later I was in Chicago with my wife. I drove Jill around the old neighborhood, and told her stories of my youth, which was at the very least misguided.

There was Fred's. Unchanged. I was charmed and filled with nostalgia.

"Let's go in," Jill said.

"Let's," I said. "But don't eat anything."

"Don't?"

"If you value your life."

We entered. I felt the grease-cloud envelop me. It was all exactly the same. Fred was exactly the same. It smelled exactly the same. The little greasy dust icicles hung from the transom exactly the same. Four or five Chicago cavemen sat at the counter, gnawing cheeseburgers.

"It's like stepping back in time," I whispered.

Jill, overcome with nostalgia on my behalf, ordered a red-hot.

"No!"

"It's fine," she said. "Just like the Bronx."

There is no arguing with Jill. She does as she pleases. Fred handed her the red-hot. Later she would pay the price of her arrogance.

"Do you recognize this man?" Jill asked Fred.

Fred eyed me.

"My husband used to come in here all the time, twenty years ago. He always talks about you. He says you were his only friend."

"Yeh? So what?" Fred replied.

It's not that you can't go home again. It's that most people know better.

# Stuart Dybek

## (b. 1942)

*Currently a professor at Western Michigan University in Kalamazoo,* STUART DYBEK *was born and raised on Chicago's South Side and worked for a time for the Cook County Department of Public Aid. Though his first book,* Brass Knuckles *(1979), was a volume of poetry, he is primarily known for his short fiction collected in volumes such as* Childhood and Other Neighborhoods *(1980) and* The Coast of Chicago *(1990), which has been compared with James Joyce's* Dubliners *and Sherwood Anderson's* Winesburg, Ohio. *Besides a visiting professorship at Princeton, these stories have brought him such honors as the Ernest Hemingway Foundation Award, the Cliff Dwellers Award, an O. Henry prize, the Whiting Award, and a Guggenheim fellowship.*

*Many of Dybek's stories unfold in Chicago's working-class neighborhoods, and they balance a deep fondness for sense of community against creeping urban decay, both physical and social. As John B. Breslin noted in the* Washington Post Book World, *Dybek's characters are often "young men . . . whose imaginations are their only defense against urban reality."*

*At times Dybek's prose is so lyrical it threatens to undermine the often gritty nature of his subject matter. "Pet Milk," the final story in* The Coast of Chicago, *shows the author at his most precise and most evocative, managing to imply not only an entire relationship, but an entire world, in a few thousand words.*

◆ ◆ ◆

## Pet Milk

### *from* THE COAST OF CHICAGO

Today I've been drinking instant coffee and Pet milk, and watching it snow. It's not that I enjoy the taste especially, but I like the way Pet milk swirls in the coffee. Actually, my favorite thing about Pet milk is what the can opener does to the top of the can. The can is unmistakable — compact, seamless looking, its very shape suggesting that it could condense milk without any trouble. The can opener bites in neatly, and the thick liquid spills from the triangular gouge with a different look and viscosity than milk. Pet milk isn't *real* milk. The color's off, to start with. There's almost something of the past about it, like old ivory. My grandmother always drank it in her coffee. When friends dropped over and sat around the kitchen table, my grandma would ask, "Do you take cream and sugar?" Pet milk was the cream.

There was a yellow plastic radio on her kitchen table, usually tuned to the polka station, though sometimes she'd miss it by half a notch and get the Greek station instead, or the Spanish, or the Ukrainian. In Chicago, where we lived, all the incompatible states of Europe were pressed together down at the staticky right end of the dial. She didn't seem to notice, as long as she wasn't hearing English. The radio, turned low, played constantly. Its top was warped and turning amber on the side where the tubes were. I remember the sound of it on winter afternoons after school, as I sat by her table watching the Pet milk swirl and cloud in the steaming coffee, and noticing, outside her window, the sky doing the same thing above the railroad yard across the street.

And I remember, much later, seeing the same swirling sky in tiny liqueur glasses containing a drink called a King Alphonse: the crème de cacao rising like smoke in repeated explosions, blooming in kaleidoscopic clouds through the layer of heavy cream. This was in the Pilsen, a little Czech restaurant where my girlfriend, Kate, and I would go sometimes in the evening. It was the first year out of college for both of us, and we had astonished ourselves by finding real jobs — no more waitressing or pumping gas, the way we'd done in school. I was investigating credit references at a bank, and she was doing something slightly above the rank of typist for Hornblower & Weeks, the investment firm. My bank showed training films that emphasized the importance of suitable dress, good grooming, and personal neatness, even for employees like me, who worked at the switchboard in the basement. Her firm issued directives on appropriate attire — skirts, for instance, should cover the knees. She had lovely knees.

Kate and I would sometimes meet after work at the Pilsen, dressed in our proper business clothes and still feeling both a little self-conscious and glamorous, as if we were impostors wearing disguises. The place had small, round oak tables, and we'd sit in a corner under a painting called "The Street Musicians of Prague" and trade future plans as if they were escape routes. She talked of going to grad school in Europe; I wanted to apply to the Peace Corps. Our plans for the future made us laugh and feel close, but those same plans somehow made anything more than temporary between us seem impossible. It was the first time I'd ever had the feeling of missing someone I was still with.

The waiters in the Pilsen wore short black jackets over long white aprons. They were old men from the old country. We went there often enough to have our own special waiter, Rudi, a name he pronounced with a rolled *R*. Rudi boned our trout and seasoned our salads, and at the end of the meal he'd bring the bottle of crème de cacao from the bar, along with two little glasses and a small pitcher of heavy cream, and make us each a King Alphonse right at our table. We'd watch as he'd fill the glasses halfway up with the syrupy brown liqueur, then carefully attempt to float a layer of cream on top. If he failed to float the cream, we'd get that one free.

"Who was King Alphonse anyway, Rudi?" I sometimes asked, trying to break his concentration, and if that didn't work I nudged the table with my foot so the glass would jiggle imperceptibly just as he was floating the cream. We'd usually get one on the house. Rudi knew what I was doing. In fact, serving the King Alphonses had been his idea, and he had also suggested the trick of jarring the table. I think it pleased him, though he seemed concerned about the way I'd stare into the liqueur glass, watching the patterns.

"It's not a microscope," he'd say. "Drink."

He liked us, and we tipped extra. It felt good to be there and to be able to pay for a meal.

Kate and I met at the Pilsen for supper on my twenty-second birthday. It was May, and unseasonably hot. I'd opened my tie. Even before looking at the dinner menu, we ordered a bottle of Mumm's and a dozen oysters apiece. Rudi made a sly remark when he brought the oysters on platters of ice. They were freshly opened and smelled of the sea. I'd heard people joke about oysters being aphrodisiac but never considered it anything but a myth — the kind of idea they still had in the old country.

We squeezed on lemon, added dabs of horseradish, slid the oysters into our mouths, and then rinsed the shells with champagne and drank the salty, cold juice. There was a beefy-looking couple eating schnitzel at the next table, and they stared at us with the repugnance that public oyster-eaters in the Midwest often encounter. We laughed and grandly sipped it all down. I was already half tipsy from drinking too fast, and starting to feel filled with a euphoric, aching energy. Kate raised a brimming oyster shell to me in a toast: "To the Peace Corps!"

"To Europe!" I replied, and we clunked shells.

She touched her wineglass to mine and whispered, "Happy birthday," and then suddenly leaned across the table and kissed me.

When she sat down again, she was flushed. I caught the reflection of her face in the glass-covered "The Street Musicians of Prague" above our table. I always loved seeing her in mirrors and windows. The reflections of her beauty startled me. I had told her that once, and she seemed to fend off the compliment, saying, "That's because you've learned what to look for," as if it were a secret I'd stumbled upon. But, this time, seeing her reflection hovering ghost-like upon an imaginary Prague was like seeing a future from which she had vanished. I knew I'd never meet anyone more beautiful to me.

We killed the champagne and sat twining fingers across the table. I was sweating. I could feel the warmth of her through her skirt under the table and I touched her leg. We still hadn't ordered dinner. I left money on the table and we steered each other out a little unsteadily.

"Rudi will understand," I said.

The street was blindingly bright. A reddish sun angled just above the rims of the tallest buildings. I took my suit coat off and flipped it over my shoulder. We stopped in the doorway of a shoe store to kiss.

"Let's go somewhere," she said.

My roommate would already be home at my place, which was closer. Kate lived up north, in Evanston. It seemed a long way away.

We cut down a side street, past a fire station, to a small park, but its gate was locked. I pressed close to her against the tall iron fence. We could smell the lilacs from a bush just inside the fence, and when I jumped for an overhanging branch my shirt sleeve hooked on a fence spike and tore, and petals rained down on us as the sprig sprang from my hand.

We walked to the subway. The evening rush was winding down; we must have caught the last express heading toward Evanston. Once the train climbed from the tunnel to the elevated tracks, it wouldn't stop until the end of the line, on Howard. There weren't any seats together, so we stood swaying at the front of the car, beside the empty conductor's compartment. We wedged inside, and I clicked the door shut.

The train rocked and jounced, clattering north. We were kissing, trying to catch the rhythm of the ride with our bodies. The sun bronzed the windows on our side of the train. I lifted her skirt over her knees, hiked it higher so the sun shone off her thighs, and bunched it around her waist. She wouldn't stop kissing. She was moving her hips to pin us to each jolt of the train.

We were speeding past scorched brick walls, gray windows, back porches outlined in sun, roofs, and treetops — the landscape of the El I'd memorized from subway windows over a lifetime of rides: the podiatrist's foot sign past Fullerton; the bright pennants of Wrigley Field, at Addison; ancient hotels with TRANSIENTS WELCOME signs on their flaking back walls; peeling and graffiti-smudged billboards; the old cemetery just before Wilson Avenue. Even without looking, I knew almost exactly where we were. Within the compartment, the sound of our quick breathing was louder than the clatter of tracks.

I was trying to slow down, to make it all last, and when she covered my mouth with her hand I turned my face to the window and looked out.

The train was braking a little from express speed, as it did each time it passed a local station. I could see blurred faces on the long wooden platform watching us pass — businessmen glancing up from folded newspapers, women clutching purses and shopping bags. I could see the expression on each face, momentarily arrested, as we flashed by. A high school kid in shirt sleeves, maybe sixteen, with books tucked under one arm and a cigarette in his mouth, caught sight of us, and in the instant before he disappeared he grinned and started to wave. Then he was gone, and I turned from the window, back to Kate, forgetting everything — the passing stations, the glowing late sky, even the sense of missing her — but that arrested wave stayed with me. It was as if I were standing on that platform, with my schoolbooks and a smoke, on one of those endlessly accumulated afternoons after school when I stood almost outside of time simply waiting for a train, and I thought how much I'd have loved seeing someone like us streaming by.

# Roger Ebert
## (b. 1942)

ROGER EBERT *won the Pulitzer Prize for distinguished criticism in 1975 for re-*
*views and essays published in the* Chicago Sun-Times. *He is still the only film critic*
*ever to be so honored, a fact often obscured by the celebrity status he has achieved as*
*co-host of such nationally syndicated television shows as* Sneak Previews, At the
Movies, *and* Siskel and Ebert, *the latest incarnation of his famed partnership with*
*another Chicago columnist, Gene Siskel. Besides writing for the* Sun-Times *and de-*
*claring himself a newspaperman first and foremost, Roger Ebert writes for maga-*
*zines such as* Esquire *and* Rolling Stone *and has written the screenplay* Beyond
the Valley of the Dolls *(1970). His books include* A Kiss Is Still a Kiss *(1984),*
Two Weeks in the Midday Sun: A Cannes Notebook *(1987), and the extremely*
*popular collections of his movie reviews, first issued as* Roger Ebert's Movie Home
Companion. *These were updated annually from 1985 to 1993, and are now issued,*
*with periodic updates, as* Roger Ebert's Video Companion. *Most recently he has*
*edited* Roger Ebert's Book on Film *(1997), a collection of his favorite writings on*
*the cinema. He has been hailed as America's wisest and wittiest film critic, a writer of*
*unerringly good taste who has a knack for choosing the telling detail that captures the*
*essence of an entire film. The excerpt below comes from* A Kiss Is Still a Kiss *and*
*captures the humanity and excesses of John Belushi.*

◆ ◆ ◆

*from* A Kiss Is Still a Kiss

*The Spin Cycle*
*Chicago, 1983*

> *Death is the slamming of the door in your face, and the sound of bolting on the inside.*
> — C. S. Lewis

It was just a year ago, on March 5, that John Belushi went to his last party. According to the fragmented reconstructions of his last night on earth, it began
as pretty much a routine evening, for Belushi, of drinking and rock clubs and

cruising the Sunset Strip and, at some point in the evening, making a drug connection that would be blamed as the cause of death.

The images from a year ago still are fresh in the memories of those who loved Belushi: the faded Hollywood glory of the Chateau Marmont residential hotel, where his body was found; the pasty-faced "unidentified woman" being led away in handcuffs by police; his best friend, Dan Aykroyd, dressed in a Chicago cop uniform, leading the funeral procession on a motorcycle. Soon the flowers of a second spring will bloom near John Belushi's grave.

Hardly a week goes by without a reminder of John's death. He's there on the TV every weekend, on the reruns of "Saturday Night Live." A poster from his movie *Continental Divide* hangs in my office. That was the one where he played a Chicago newspaper columnist, and on the poster, he's poker-faced and maybe a little sad, with a copy of the *Sun-Times* jammed under his arm. Every once in a while somebody will be talking about some comedian, and they'll say he does something "like Belushi used to do," and then I think that Belushi would have been only thirty-four years old if he still were alive today. And then I think, damn it all, John, why did you slam that door so soon?

I think I know the answer. The answer is not that John slammed the door and bolted it shut from the inside. The answer is that the door slammed shut on him. The kid from Wheaton whom I met in the early 1970s, who drank in the bars of Old Town and went to New York and became a star, and who came back to Chicago and opened his own private saloon, where he could drink all day and all night, was one of the most talented comic actors of his time, but he drank too much and drugged too much and it killed him. That's pretty much what happened.

Belushi liked to party, but there were a lot of bartenders in his old Chicago neighborhoods who were not overjoyed when they saw him coming. Some places were thrilled to have a guy like Belushi in the house, especially after he got famous. Other places asked him not to come back again.

When you are in your late twenties and making hundreds of thousands of dollars a year, there is an answer to a problem like that: Open your own bar. Belushi and Aykroyd took over a place near the corner of North and Wells that used to be named the Sneak Joynt, and they renamed it the Blues Bar. In the right circles in Chicago, the word spread quickly when John was in town, and his friends, or those who thought of themselves as friends, dropped in to have a drink with John.

He loved to play host. For some reason, he seemed driven to be there, to be available for hours on end—in case somebody else might turn up or another crowd might come in. I think, in a way, he saw it as paying his dues. Although he probably never consciously put it into words, he basically was saying that even though he was a millionaire, he still was one of the guys and still ready to party all night with his old friends — or his newfound friends, as it often turned out. One night I saw him chugging from a bottle of Jack Daniel's and then plunging his face into the tub of ice behind the bar. Here's an irony: I was in pretty bad shape myself that night, and the question I asked myself was not *why* does he do it, but *how?*

That would have been during the time he was shooting *The Blues Brothers* in Chicago. It was common knowledge around town that a lot of cocaine found its way onto the set of that movie, as it found its way onto the sets of other movies Belushi made. The theory was that you couldn't get physically addicted to cocaine, but as George Carlin once explained, "The way cocaine makes you feel is like having some more cocaine."

Belushi sometimes thought he knew the answer to that dilemma. He thought the answer was control, also known as not partying too late when you gotta work the next day. I remember one Saturday afternoon during *Blues Brothers* when he came over to my house with his wife, Judy, and ate a microwave pizza and drank 7-Up and was, as he put it, "in training." In the hierarchy of the Belushi legend, Aykroyd was his "best friend" and Judy was his "wife," but the way I read it, Judy was John's best friend in the life-and-death things, and maybe it was no accident that he seemed to get into more trouble when she wasn't around. That afternoon he talked about a movie he wanted to make about a Chicago newspaperman — a guy something like [the late columnist] Mike Royko, who had been a friend of his family since before he was born.

The filming schedule of *The Blues Brothers* ran into a lot of delays because of problems with "talent," as they call the people who appear in front of the cameras. John was trying to go full-speed twenty-four hours a day. It cannot be done, but let it be said that he gave it a better shot than most people. He had such talent and such energy, and such a natural rapport with Aykroyd, that, problems or no problems, they made a big, funny, aggressive, entertaining movie.

After *Animal House* and *Blues Brothers*, both big winners at the box office, John could have continued to make the same kinds of movies indefinitely. But he turned down the various proposals for *Animal House* sequels and went ahead with plans for the newspaper movie, *Continental Divide*. After it was finished, he and Aykroyd committed themselves to a very strange project called *Neighbors*, which was like nothing they'd done before and which they changed even more by "switching roles," so that Aykroyd played the weirdo guy in the movie, and Belushi, the weirdo expert, played the middle-class homeowner.

Belushi shot scenes from *Continental Divide* here in the *Sun-Times* features department, where I ran into him one Saturday afternoon. He looked great. He was thinner, he seemed bouncier, his eyes were clear and he was in a good mood. I told him he looked in pretty good shape. "Yeah," he said. "I'm in training. No more booze." I told him I'd stopped drinking, too. "Great," he said.

"Way to go. My system is, no booze, no drugs, watch what I eat and work out a little. This is the new me." That would have been a year or so before he died.

When *Continental Divide* was released, it got so-so notices and did disappointing business at the box office. *Neighbors*, which was released for Christmas, 1981, got a more complicated reception. During a lackluster holiday season, it was one of the top grossers in early returns, maybe because Belushi and Aykroyd fans expected a rerun of their "Saturday Night Live" and Blues Brothers relationship. Then the movie dropped off; its eccentric charms were lost on the Belushi fans who cheered when he mashed beer cans against his head in *Animal House*.

Three months later, he was dead. He had stayed fairly straight after Christmas, his friends said, but when he went out West, away from Judy and Dan, to talk to Paramount about a script, he fell in with the Hollywood version of his Chicago friends, with the druggies and groupies and drunks and punks. After Belushi's death, Aykroyd said in an interview that John called his partying periods "the spin cycle" — that after getting off the booze and other stuff while making a movie, he was inclined to reward himself afterward. When he hit Hollywood that last time, he also was depressed because of the relative failure of his two attempts to break out of his *Animal House* image, and because Paramount hadn't liked his screenplay.

What actually happened on the last night of Belushi's life still is a matter of controversy. The last woman to see him alive told her story on television, and as I watched her I felt mostly pity, because it was clear from her voice, her manner and her bearing that she was not a villainess but just another victim, a person who met John while they were on the same merry-go-round. Some people blamed that sad woman for Belushi's death, but, watching her, I couldn't believe she made him do anything. She was just part of a system that enabled him to do drugs that last night, if he had the money and the inclination.

If it is true that nobody can really make anybody else take drugs, let it be said that another thing also is true: After a certain point, the drinker and drug user is no longer really free to make a decision about his own usage. By that I don't mean that John was so stoned on his last night that he didn't know what he was doing when he popped his last balloon. I mean that he was completely helpless in the face of the *first* drink or the *first* drug, because he had become trapped in a vicious circle: "in training" and "the spin cycle."

People tried to help him. From everything I've heard, his wife did her best. Aykroyd said he had talked to Belushi a few days before his death, had sensed an unhappiness and perhaps even sensed the approaching tragedy, and told him he needed some time to get away, be alone, be quiet, get the stuff out of his system. Aykroyd was planning to get together with Belushi and try to help him do that when the news of his death came.

John Belushi was a talented man who gave so generously of his talent that now, a year later, people still remember that he made them happy and resent the fact that the door slammed shut on him. What could have saved him? Who can say. A lot of movie stars have serious drug and booze problems. They say drug addiction and alcoholism are progressive diseases — that they always get worse, never better, that "moderation" is a joke and that the only answer is to get off the stuff and stay off the stuff.

A lot of stars have been able to do that; *Rolling Stone* seems to be featuring the Recovering Alcoholic of the Month on its covers these days. A lot of others, however, have not stopped, and sooner or later, many of them have died.

There was that macabre "Saturday Night Live" sketch where John Belushi went to visit the graveyard of dead SNL veterans and danced on their graves. After John himself was found dead, some TV stations used ironic excerpts from the sketch in their obituaries. Was that in bad taste? I don't know. Think about it. The message in the sketch was one of victory — the victory the living always have over the dead, the victory Belushi had over Jim Morrison, Janis Joplin, Elvis, Jimi Hendrix and the others who lived as if they were immortal. "They may be dead," the deeper symbolism went, "but I, John Belushi, still party, am still alive, still get away with it, still survive." It was the same careless shout of victory that all of those dead legends carried with them to the grave.

# Haki R. Madhubuti
# (Don L. Lee)
## (b. 1942)

*Although known mostly as one of the leading poets to emerge from the black arts movement of the 1960s,* HAKI MADHUBUTI *is also an influential critic, the publisher and editor of Chicago's Third World Press, and director of the Institute of Positive Education. Through these and many other projects he has become not only "a lion of a poet," as David Llorens has hailed him, but also one of the most respected, fiercest champions of independent black institutions and the cultural unity of black people in America and throughout the world.*

*His many nonfiction works include* Think Black *(1967), the highly influential* Dynamite Voices I: Black Poets of the 1960s *(1971),* Enemies: The Clash of Races *(1978),* Black Men: Obsolete, Single, Dangerous? *(1990), and* African Centered Education: Its Value, Importance and Necessity in the Development of Black Children *(1994). His many volumes of poetry include* Don't Cry, Scream *(1969),* Directionscore: Selected and New Poems *(1971),* Killing Memory, Seeking Ancestors *(1987), and* Groundwork: New and Selected Poems of Don L. Lee/Haki R. Madhubuti, 1966–1996. *Even without the help of a major national distributor, Madhubuti's books have sold more than one million copies. Though his poetry has often been criticized for being overly political and protest-oriented, Madhubuti's daring voice, his inventive phrasing, his ability to capture the rhythms and sardonic moods of black speech have made him one of the two or three most imitated black poets in America.*

*An associate professor of English at Chicago State University since 1984, and the director of the Gwendolyn Brooks Center there, he has also edited* To Gwen with Love *(1971) and collected his own poetry and prose in* Say That the River Turns: The Impact of Gwendolyn Brooks *(1987).*

✦ ✦ ✦

## Wake-Up Niggers

(you ain't part Indian)

were
don eagle & gorgeous george
sisters
or did they just
                    act that way —
in the ring,
in alleys,
in bedrooms of the future.
                    (continuing to take yr / money)
have you ever
heard tonto say:
                    "I'm part negro?"
                    (in yr / moma's dreams)
the only time
tonto was hip
was when he said:
                    "what you mean WE,
                    gettum up scout"
& left
that mask man
burning on a stake
                    crying for satchal page
to throw his
balls
back.

&
you followed him niggers —
all of you —
                    yes you did,
                         I saw ya.
on yr/tip toes
with roller skates
on yr/knees
                    following Him
down the road,
                    not up
following Him

that whi
te man with
that
cross on his back.


## One Sided Shoot-out

*(for brothers fred hampton & mark clark, murdered 12/4/69 by chicago police at 4:30 AM while they slept)*

only a few will really understand:
it won't be yr/mommas or yr/brothers & sisters or even me,
we all think that we do     but we don't.
it's not *new*     and
under all the rhetoric the seriousness is still not serious.
the national rap deliberately continues, "wipe them niggers
     out."
(no talk do it, no talk do it, no talk do it, notalk notalknotalk
     do it)

& we.
running circleround getting caught in our own cobwebs,
in the same old clothes, same old words, just new adjectives.
we will order new buttons & posters with: "remember fred"
     & "rite-on mark."
& yr/pictures will be beautiful & manly with the deeplook/
     the accusing look
to remind us
to remind us that suicide is not black.

the questions will be asked & the answers will be the new
     clichés.
but maybe,
just maybe we'll finally realize that "revolution" to the real
     world
is international 24hours a day and that 4: 30AM is like
     12:00 noon,
it's just darker.
but the evil can be seen if u look in the right direction.

were the street lights out?
did they darken their faces in combat?

did they remove their shoes to *creep* softer?
could u not see the whi-te of their eyes,
the whi-te of their deathfaces?
didn't yr/look-out man see them coming,   coming,   coming?
or did they turn into ghostdust and join the night's fog?

it was mean.
& we continue to call them "pigs" and "muthafuckas"
      forgetting what all
black children learn very early: "sticks & stones may break
                        my bones but names can
                        never hurt me."
it was murder.
& we meet to hear the speeches/the same, the duplicators.
they say that which is expected of them.
to be instructive or constructive is to be unpopular (like: the
      leaders only
sleep when there is a watchingeye )
but they say the right things at the right time, it's like a
      stageshow:
only the entertainers have changed.
we remember bobby hutton.   the same,   the duplicators.

the seeing eye should always see.
the night doesn't stop the stars
& our enemies scope the ways of blackness in three bad
      shifts a day.
in the AM their music becomes deadlier.
this is a game of dirt.

only blackpeople play it fair.


## GWENDOLYN BROOKS: DISTINCTIVE AND PROUD AT 77

how do we greet significant people among us,
what is the area code that glues them to us,
who lights the sun burning in their hearts,
where stands their truths in these days of MTV
      and ethnic cleansing,
what language is the language of Blacks?

she has a map in her. she always returns home. we are not
open prairie, we are rural concrete written out of history. she
reminds us of what we can become, not political correctness
or social commentators and not excuse makers for Big people. always a credit-giver for ideas originated in the quiet of
her many contemplations. a big thinker is she. sleeps with
paper and dictionary by her bed, sleeps with children in her
head. her first and second drafts are pen on paper. her husband thinks he underestimates her. she thinks we all have
possibilities. nothing is simplified or simply given. she wears
her love in her language. if you do not listen, you will miss her
secrets. we do not occupy the margins of her heart, we are
the blood, soul, Black richness, spirit and water-source pumping the music she speaks. uncluttered by people worship, she
lives always on the edge of significant discovery. her instruction is "rise to the occasion," her religion is "kindness," her
work is sharing and making words matter. she gives to the
people everybody takes from.
she is grounded-seeker. cultured-boned.
she is Black sunset and at 77 is no amateur.
rooted willingly and firmly in dark soil, she is last of the great
oaks.
name her poet.
as it does us, her language needs to blanket the earth.


## A Calling

*(for Rev. Frank Madison Reid III*
*on the occasion of 25 years of service in the ministry)*

we are short memory people,
too willing to settle for artless resumes of
rapid life    brief prayers    cappuccino.


our young adapt to contemporary clothing without question,
as we fail to acknowledge brilliance among us
displaying a hesitancy to tell this preacherman, this good
     brother
how his journey has become our journey.
in him is ordered-calm, deep thought, quality-love, a probing
     mind.

are pastors inspired to read Baldwin, Morrison, Diop,
Chomsky, Said and Brooks? are their ears prepared for
Monk, Aretha, Trane, Chuck D and music screaming for the
tongues of hypocrites? can a serious minister be known for
anything other than knowing God's name, being clean, loving
his family and saying double yes to fried chicken dinners?
cultural essentiality?

we are short memory people,
you have been planted among us
artfully seeded in Black earth to illuminate the texts,
shepherd our prayers, spiritualize our commitments and
help us seal the holes in our souls.

some arrogantly shout that this is your job,
in kind smiles and rather meditatively, others voice
we don't remember you ever filling out an
        employment application.

# Carolyn Rodgers
## (b. 1945)

During the 1960s the Chicago Organization of Black American Culture was one of
the most vital centers of literary activity in the city, and Chicago-born poet CAROLYN
RODGERS was one of its brightest stars. Author of ten books or broadsides of poetry —
including Paper Soul (1968), The Heart as Evergreen (1978), and Finite Forms
(1985) — as well as a novel and short stories, Rodgers went on to win such honors as
the Society of Midland Authors 1970 Poet Laureate Award, and a nomination for
the National Book Award (1975) for her collection of poetry how i got ovah.

Bettye J. Parker-Smith has referred to "two distinct and clear baptisms" reflected
in Rodgers's work. The first baptism, represented here by "how i got ovah," is an im-
mersion in what Parker-Smith calls a "rough-hewn, folk-spirited" ethos. The second
baptism, represented by "how i got ovah II/It Is Deep II," is an extraordinary revisit-
ing of the first poem. Besides her celebrations of black community and her exploration
of the social crises and tensions within, she has gained recognition for her concern over
feminist themes, some of which revolve around mother-daughter issues. This second
poem represents a more sophisticated striving to "understand the mysteries/of mystical life the 'intellectual'/purity of mystical light." It represents a re-embrace of the
mother and of religion, a sense that the outer, sometimes revolutionary concerns of her
earlier poems must be joined to a deeper sense of how some of the things we used to flee
can become resources for an inner life, strong and resilient enough to meet the demands of an outer revolution we never suspected would take so long.

◆ ◆ ◆

## how i got ovah

i can tell you
about them
i have shaken rivers
out of my eyes
i have waded eyelash deep
have crossed rivers

have shaken the water weed out
of my lungs
have swam for strength
pulled by strength
through waterfalls with electric beats
i have bore the shocks
of water deep deep
waterlogs are my bones
i have shaken the water free of my hair
have kneeled on the banks
and kissed my ancestors of the dirt
whose rich dark root fingers rose up reached out
grabbed and pulled me rocked me cupped me
gentle strong and firm
carried me
made me swim for strength
cross rivers
though i shivered
was wet was cold
and wanted to sink down
and float as water, yea —
i can tell you.
i have shaken rivers
out of my eyes.


## how i got ovah II/It Is Deep II

*(for Evangelist Richard D. Henton)*

just when i thought i had gotten away
my mother
called me on the phone
and did not ask,
but commanded me
to come to church with her.

and because i knew so much
and had "escaped"
i thought it a harmless enough act.

i was not prepared for the Holy Ghost.
i was not prepared to be covered by the
blood of Jesus.

i was not ready to be dipped in
                    the water. . . .

i could not drink the water turned wine.

and so i went back another day
trying to understand the mysteries
of mystical life the "intellectual"
purity of mystical light.
and that Sunday evening while i was
sitting there and the holy gospel choir
was singing
        "oh oh oh oh somebody touched me"
somebody touched me.
                    and when i turned around to
see what it was whoever touched me wanted
my mother leaned over and whispered in my ear
        "musta been the hand of the Lord"

# Carol Anshaw
## (b. 1946)

CAROL ANSHAW *teaches at the School of the Art Institute of Chicago and has written two highly acclaimed novels,* Aquamarine *(1992) and* Seven Moves *(1996). The trademarks of her style are biting, jazzy humor and sparkling dialogue, but most of all what one critic described as "a touching reverence for the power of loss." The excerpt below from* Seven Moves *characterizes the relationship of Christine Snow, a Chicago therapist, and her lover, Taylor, who seems to Christine to be always "slipping through her fingers, like spilled mercury." In fact, shortly after the scenes sketched here, Taylor does disappear, mysteriously. Her disappearance sets Christine on a long journey of attempted recovery and discovery. She discovers, for example, that her faith in Taylor has probably been misplaced, and this leads not only to a loss of that relationship, and through that the loss of a major marker of her identity, but also a loss in the confidence of her own powers of perception — something leading to, as one reviewer put it, "a therapist's worst fear — she hardly knows her own mind."*

✦ ✦ ✦

## *from* SEVEN MOVES

Chris is just out of an appointment with her chiropractor, Eileen, whose approach is becoming disconcertingly mystical. She has been spending more and more of their sessions with her hands hovering in the air above Chris's back, adjusting energy fields. Today she asked if Chris has been eating a lot of nightshade. Chris would like to keep these ministrations limited to cartilage crunching, which is what Eileen used to do to her. She thinks she might give Taylor's chiropractor a try. This woman is supposedly a hulking gum chewer. Darla. All business. Snap. Crackle. Pop.

Chris shifts around in the driver's seat, her lower back crabbing again, her energy fields, she supposes, slipping once again out of alignment. It is taking her forever to get home today. Traffic up and down Lincoln is glued to itself on account of this first, goofball, way-out-of-sync day of spring, an afternoon that has shot into the seventies. Everyone in the city has come out to contribute to the gridlock. Cars, of course. Rollerbladers and runners. Fat girls in halter tops. Swift bicycle thieves. The homeless, who were already out, but now with élan, and plenty of company. The sidewalk in front of Betty's Resale, a junkyard just south of Addison, is filled with milling customers, as though avocado-colored stoves and dressers covered in contact paper have suddenly soared in value on some secret stock exchange.

Finally, she passes the giant, comic head of Abe fronting the Lincoln Restaurant, and turns onto her street. She pulls up in front of her house and taps the last of a bag of M&Ms into her palm as she listens to Norman Greenbaum pumping out "Spirit in the Sky" on the oldies station. It's an unleavable song and so she sits a moment longer, rocking and rolling a little in her Corolla, contemplating her real estate, this small, shambly frame house with salt-and-pepper asphalt siding and buckling wooden steps.

The neighborhood is changing, upscaling but in an ungainly way. That is, while several houses on their block have been renovated by new owners — Board of Traders, young dentists, and the like — who quickly ensconce themselves behind tasteful, Italianate dark green wrought-iron fences, the tenured residents of the block are people who work in factories and grocery stores and on job sites. So any one of the yuppified houses, for all its landscaping and ADT alarming, might well sit squarely across the street from a two-flat with a rooster in a cage in the front yard.

Chris and Taylor hope to eventually join the ranks of the renovators, but have had the house only a few months and so far have been able to afford only the most meager and necessary improvements. This is the first house either of them has ever owned, and it makes them feel as though they've moved to America. After years of apartments with stairwells full of peculiar cooking odors, ceilings throbbing with other people's stereos, discouraging connections with the flooding bathrooms and stray roaches of strangers, they are now blessed with autonomy and silent nights, and a backyard for grilling and letting the dog out in the morning, for planning a garden. They no longer have to lug everything long blocks from parking spaces in their former, high-density neighborhood.

They have a washer and dryer in the basement, Stone Age machines left behind by the previous owners. The first time Chris ran the dryer it made a huge, chainsaw-massacre noise that rattled the walls and drove the dog up to the attic. She shut off the machine and stood appraising it in ignorance. She tried to guess how old it was. Realistically, thirty years. "Now that I look more closely," she came upstairs and told Taylor, as though she had come to the crux of the matter, "it's not even a Kenmore, it's a *Lady* Kenmore."

"Might be tricky to get that fixed," Taylor said. "I think there's a regulation. I think the repair guy has to bring a female attendant along."

The problem turned out to be nothing. A nail fallen into a baffle. Neither of them knew what a baffle was; they just wrote the check for the service call and went along merrily until the next appliance revealed its failings. First it was the oven, which didn't ignite; then the freezer, which did freeze, but also alternately defrosted at whim.

Chris is aware of the house clearly being, more than walls and ceilings around them, mortar and mortising between them. She and Taylor never speak of these weights and adhesions directly, only natter about the small charms of the place, its value as a sound investment, the dog's kingly happiness here. Sometimes Chris thinks it's kind of sweet how careful they are with each other. Other times she wonders what they are being so careful about.

Having bought the house, they have both become ambivalent about it, although they would never admit their hesitations to each other. Instead, they offset their praise with small complaints about drafts or the cramped clawfoot tub in the upstairs bathroom. In this way, the house has become a rich metaphor for the unspoken, inarticulable nettles they have with each other, about what is happening, or not happening, between them.

Chris is fairly certain that with Taylor's previous lover, it was in some measure the property they held together that freaked Taylor out of the relationship. Taylor once said she felt as though a plastic dry-cleaners bag was being pulled over her head. Chris worries the house is forcing them to replicate that situation.

The concertedly domestic arrangements of most couples of their acquaintance have a sameness, a smugly settled quality that she and Taylor used to make fun of. In the beginning they talked a bit about resisting the subliminal pull toward turning into what Taylor calls the "boring lesbian personality casserole." But in spite of this skittishness, Taylor eventually began lobbying for a house, needing, like most people, to press a thumb down on her particular psychic bruise. In her case, longing to have her affections tucked into the folds of a recognized relationship, even though her heart continues to prowl the night like a werewolf.

And so she scanned ads in six months' worth of Sunday *Tribune*s until she came up with this house and its eager sellers, the Herbsts, who were eager due to Mr. Herbst's imminent transfer to Tulsa, making the house at the price an incredible deal, but one which had to be seized within the next five minutes. This catch left Chris and Taylor no time for long discussions searching the soul of their relationship, plumbing their issues of intimacy and domestic partnership. They only had time to leap, and now, having regained consciousness, they find themselves on the other side, in this place where Chris needs to keep a sharp eye out to try to determine if Taylor is beginning to turn blue inside the bag.

Although she is sympathetic to Taylor's restlessness, Chris quickly winds up feeling worse for herself, having to share a bed with someone who is always tossing and turning, punching at the pillow.

On the surface of things, at the level that would show up on the home videos, Taylor is, aside from her penchant for flirtation, a dream lover — attentive and considerate, surprising. She brings fresh mozzarella home from the Italian grocery, massages Chris's hands with almond oil. Everything truly troublesome about her is buried cable, subterranean trunk line. The closest Chris can get to Taylor's true identity is feeling the vibration of this secret information as it rushes deep beneath the ground the two of them stand on, facing each other with pleasant expressions, good will, and smooth, practiced approximations of intimacy. It's a little like being married to a spy.

She mostly finds this fascinating, and thinks herself quite lucky to have found a partner whose depths are so seemingly bottomless. There are moments, though, when she imagines an alternate life with a person she thinks of as Patti. A homebody who, a little ways into their long, calm, predictable relationship, starts getting her hair cut the way Chris does, then signs them up for ceramics classes together. Someone from whose feet both shoes have already dropped.

Chris pauses a moment on the front porch and tries to call up what they are supposed to be doing tonight. Someone is coming for dinner. Taylor's friend Leigh and her new girlfriend.

She sees that the back door off the kitchen is open and goes out onto the tiny deck that precedes the short flight of steps to ground level. Taylor is out there at the back of the yard, breaking ground for a garden they've planned, prying out one of a pair of generic bushes, legacies from the Herbsts.

Taylor relishes difficult projects. She once hauled a file cabinet up three flights by propping it on the front of her thighs. When she cooks, the recipes she takes on are daunting even on the page, projects starting with unhusked coconuts or raw squid, or requiring pastry tubes and springform pans, mortars and pestles, ignition with cognac and match. In the same studied, painstaking way, she is determined to make something pretty out of this rectangle of patchy grass and dusty ruts worn by the Herbsts' anxious German shepherd, Lassie. (All the dogs in this as-yet-untrendy neighborhood are named Lassie or Princess or Rex. Several are offspring of various large females and one busy basset hound. The results are German shepherds and Labradors with six-inch legs.)

On the other side of the fence is the yard of their neighbors Cy and Dolores, whose last name they don't yet know. The yard, in one small plot of ground, manages to contain a pedestaled, sapphire-blue mirror ball, a Virgin in a grotto, a porch rail dripping with wind chimes, and a plastic duck family eternally toddling toward a strip of dirt that Taylor is pretty sure is going to reveal itself as a patch of sunflowers.

"The wind chimes are going to have to go," Taylor told her this morning. "I'm going to have to have a little talk with Cy. Maybe with Dolores."

"I think most people wouldn't find wind chimes a problem," Chris told her. "I myself find them rather charming."

"I myself," Taylor countered, "find they make me want to shoot somebody."

This digging today is a first step in Taylor's opposition to Cy and Dolores's antic backyard, creating on their side of the privacy fence a traditional English garden. She has already hacked the bush down to a stump, and now, with a pitchfork sunk in at its base, tines tangled in the roots, is prying it up and out. She is wearing long, baggy shorts, her legs dark from having been in the desert, her hair restrained by a bandanna. She is tall, taller even than Chris, with much of her length in her legs. Chris is still a little in love with the way Taylor looks, still grateful for a beautiful lover. It's like having been born in Sorrento, having the rest of life like everyone else, but always also this.

Taylor's struggle with the bush has become fierce. The bush doesn't care that it is offensively Middle-American in the yard of hip urban dykes intent on recasting this landscape with what, in their better moments, they realize are their own pretensions. The bush has tenure here and is not relinquishing its presence easily. Bud sits nearby and watches closely, as though his presence is crucial to the task being accomplished.

"I'll help," Chris shouts, startling Bud, and possibly Taylor, although she would resist showing that. Instead she turns and smiles against the lowering sun. Chris can't see her eyes behind her shades.

"It's okay, I've almost got it," Taylor says. "Besides, you have company."

Only then does she notice that Taylor is not alone in the yard, that Chris's father is sitting at the wobbly redwood table (another legacy from the Herbsts), a glass of iced tea sweating in front of him as he deals hands for a poker game with invisible opponents. His showing up unannounced like this means he needs money.

Chris looks to Taylor for help and in return gets a jaunty little salute. He's not *her* father. Chris goes down the steps.

"Take a seat," he says, gesturing with the hand not holding the deck of cards.

"We're having company for dinner," she tells him. "Girls, but not your kind of girls. I'll have to start cooking soon."

"How about some tea?" Taylor asks Chris, and lopes up the stairs and into the house, calling back down to ask Tom Snow if he wants a refill.

"Mmm," he says, having heard something, but not specifically what anyone has said, then, when Taylor is inside, out of earshot, he prompts Chris. "Pick up your hand. Tell me what you've got."

"Not bad," she says, tapping the side of her nose, pushing her shades up a bit as she studies her cards for a few seconds, then lays down a straight to the jack.

"That's the beauty of this one." He fans a flush on the table to beat her. "You give the other fellow something to bid up, a piece of hope."

"Nice," Chris says with admiration, in spite of herself. "Low-key. Where are you working this?"

"Country club. Golf is great, you know. All those wads of cash folded inside clips, flapping around in all those baggy pants pockets. Money that really, when you think about it, means so very little to them."

She hates when he starts again with cards, leaving behind the small magic shows — for children, for sweet sixteen parties — that make him impatient, there being too little money or risk in honest sleight of hand. Even though he is a first-rate sharp, there's always a good chance he'll get caught out. People — especially men — don't like to think they're bad at cards. They'd rather think they're being cheated. Which puts her father under an unfortunate spotlight because he is indeed usually cheating them. He has been beaten up several times, once gravely, and has been to prison twice, but he is pretty much uncontrite as both stints turned out to be quite lucrative. "The incarcerated," he points out, "are among the few who really have the time and inclination for cards."

Chris takes the deck from him, shuffles, puts it down, and taps it for him to cut. Then she proceeds to deal him a handful of garbage, herself three aces and a pair of kings. When they lay down their hands, fanning out their cards on the splintery wood of the tabletop with soft, feathery clicks and rustles, like sounds from an African dialect, conveying meaning without words, he smiles slowly, swelling up with parental pride.

During Chris's summers and spring breaks and Christmas vacations from boarding school, Tom Snow taught his daughter about cards, and they began working together. Poolside venues. Cruises. He taught Chris everything he knew, and then she shot past him. They didn't know she'd have such a talent for it.

Even if she hadn't been so good, she would have had an advantage simply on account of her age. For their nights out, she dressed like a murderess with a good lawyer, not only in a way that emphasized her youth, but a more innocent girlishness of several decades before her own. Middy blouses, cardigan sweaters with little chain clasps at the neck. The persona they set up for her was slightly petulant, bored on vacation, nagging Daddy to take her horseback riding, sailing, whatever. He would persuade her to stay for just a few hands — why didn't she play? Here he'd even stake her, write out a little crib sheet laying out flushes and straights. And then she'd lose for a little while, befuddled and adorable, then win for just long enough. She would offer to give the money back. "You mean it isn't play money?!" But, of course, no one would ever take her up on the offer. Meanwhile, with Chris serving as a distraction, her father would also be winning in a less conspicuous way, steadily through the night.

The money allowed them, for a while at least, to play at the lifestyle of the men Tom had gone to public school with back in England when he was a scholarship boy. They drove a BMW, shopped at Brooks Brothers and Tiffany, ordered shrimp cocktails and prime rib from leather banquettes and stayed in four-star hotels, able to be their true selves — thieves among thieves — only when they were alone together in the early-morning hours in their paneled cabin or suite, counting up their winnings over large white plates of eggs and bacon, tomatoes and fruit, the food itself arrayed like winnings.

It was her share of their take that got her through school, with a nest egg left over that she never touches, has told no one about. Not her father, who probably assumes it's all been long spent. Not even Taylor knows. Chris has never been able to bring herself to tell her about the money or the sharping, her part in it. It has never felt far enough behind her to work into anecdote. Nor is her reconstructed life of good works and upstanding behavior quite enough of a shield. There is still hardly a day when it doesn't cross her mind that she could get on a plane to Vegas, check into a small suite at the Four Queens, go downstairs to the poker tables, and, in a couple of hours, before she attracted too much attention, leave with more money than she makes in a year of private practice. It is an extremely peculiar power to hold, unused.

Today her father has come to ask for start-up cash, membership dues for the club. When he sees the reluctance in her expression, he says, "Tell yourself I'm taking up golf. It'll be good for my health." He has been idly shuffling the deck and begins turning over jacks and queens in alternation.

"Show-off," Chris says. Then, "How much?"

"Eleven hundred?" It is always an odd amount, to imply the seriousness, the direct applicability of the money requested. She looks at her father from a greater distance than she actually sits from him. Bud's chin is on his thigh. The dog selects his own friends from among their visitors. In mulling over her father's request, Chris silently runs through a series of calculations, not all of which have to do with money.

"We're a little house-poor at the moment," Taylor jumps in, back with glasses and a pitcher of iced tea, which she sets on the table. Tom tamps, and then pockets, his deck of cards.

"Ah, a bit pinched, eh?" he says. He's English by birth and milks this. In his line of work a dash of class helps. Chris's mother met him on a cruise ship. She was traveling with her parents, was young and deeply naive. Their affair was as silly and inconsequential as an Astaire-Rogers movie; it should have had lyrics rather than dialogue. But pregnancies come out of far less, and there they were, under-acquainted, ill-suited, and about to be parents. Which is how, nearly forty years later, Chris comes to sit across from this childish man, bound up with him in ways that make her feel, irrationally she knows, that Taylor is at the moment interfering, rather than only trying to help.

She notices that his hair — reddish with faded dye — has thinned out a bit since she last saw him; his scalp looks pink and exposed between the comb marks raked along the sides. His throat has caved in so deeply that an egg could fit inside the hollow. The buttoned collar of his sport shirt loosely circles his ropy neck. Because he has always been overly fastidious, she takes this lack of fit as a sign of decline. One of her most indelible memories of the time she spent with him, when they worked as a team, is the waiting for him to be ready. Hours at a stretch on the sofa with teen magazines, itchy on the crushed velvet upholstery of the sofa in this hotel room, that stateroom, waiting as the ritual moved toward its eventual completion — waiting for the shower steam to evaporate and the minted scents of shave cream and toothpaste to recede as the air from the bathroom began to deliver the bracing cologne that signaled he was done. It was like being the child of a great diva preparing to walk out onto a stage filled with elephants and extras, to sing *Aïda*. When in fact all her father was primping for was another evening of cards.

Now his glory days are quite a ways behind him, and he seems so terribly diminished to Chris, reduced to waiting for her to decide if she's going to give him a bit of money. She's not interested in holding this cheap power, and so she goes inside for her checkbook.

Chris stands back, Bud's tail swishing against her leg, as she watches Taylor under the tree overhanging their parkway, the sunlight thin and watery on her as she shuts the door of Tom's car (a fairly new Bonneville won in a long night in Miami Beach) and leans through the open window to graze his cheek with her lips. She is courtly with him, as though he is their most valued visitor. As they watch him drive off at about fifteen miles per hour, though, she says, "We could have used that eleven hundred. To replace the worst of the rotting windows, for one thing."

"I know," Chris says, and prepares herself for the hard words they're going to have about her misplaced generosity. Which will doubtless lead into a lecture on how much more Chris could contribute, not to mention how much better off she'd be financially, if she weren't such a soft touch for the deadbeats among her clients.

But the lecture doesn't come. Instead, Taylor runs a hand through Chris's hair and smiles, which is worse somehow. Usually money is a great opportunity for an argument between them — their lack of it at any given moment, the different uses to which they each think it should be put. Chris's spendthrift bent in opposition to Taylor's skinflintiness. It's dispiriting, Taylor taking a pass on a fight when she has Chris dead to rights.

Chris tries another test of Taylor's mood. She watches as Taylor pulls a bunch of carrots out of the vegetable bin in the refrigerator and takes them over to the sink, starts running water, finds the peeler in the drawer. Then Chris comes up behind her, reaches inside her shirt, traces fingers around her waist, then up to her nipples.

She feels Taylor tense beneath her touch. This is much worse than a worded rejection, worse still for not being the first time. Through most of their relationship, they've accommodated each other's impulses, moods, open to stopping on a dime in the middle of a day or a project and finding their way to the bed or sofa, or just down onto the floor they're standing on, which is what Chris is negotiating at the moment.

It is just lately that she has been apprehensive about making passes, fearful they will, as in this moment, get snagged on Taylor's unspoken reluctance. There's been more of this since she got back from Morocco, and Chris is too afraid to ask about the connection. It would be pointless anyway. Taylor would just lie, Chris knows it. Of all the feelings Taylor can engender in Chris, the one she hates the most is feeling a door being ever so gently and kindly, but firmly, shut in her face.

After so many thousands of hours spent listening to the misery of clients at the hands of troublemakers, Chris knows certain warning signals. Unfortunately, her own lover came with a full complement. From the first, red flags fluttered through the air around Taylor. If one of Chris's clients had fallen in love with this woman and brought in a detailed description, she knows she would have put up a licked finger to discern the sharp, tricky winds ahead.

Leigh and her new girlfriend (the women who are not dating material for Chris's father) are due to arrive soon. All of Leigh's girlfriends are short-term. She attracts them easily by her charms, and by her mild celebrity status as a reporter for the Channel 5 news. She likes to bring them by for Chris and Taylor's approval, an exercise that seems particularly pointless to Chris, in that by the next time they have dinner with Leigh she will be with a new date.

"Tish?" Chris says, mincing an onion, trying to remember the name of this latest one.

"Tiff."

"What can that be about?"

"Short for Tiffany, I think."

"Tiffany's the name of Myra's bird. A cockatiel."

"Well, it's also the name of this girl we're going to be very nice to tonight." This is another sign. There is too often lately a color to Taylor's tone, some verdigris of irritation or weariness, covered quickly, softened and brightened with the next sentence, but still.

"She's going to be terrible," Chris says.

"Maybe she'll be okay," is all Taylor says, purely out of devotion to Leigh. They were involved with each other for a short time a million years ago. Lesbians, even in a place as large as Chicago, draw their friends and lovers from the same pool, which often leads to some confusion at the start of things and some awkwardness in the aftermath, but also to friendships like Leigh and Taylor's — fine, sturdy houses built on some nearly forgotten rubble of romance.

Tiff stands in the middle of the living room, her hands flattened against an imaginary pane of glass between herself and her audience, which is composed of Chris and Taylor and a rapt Leigh. Tiff's face is a child's twist of consternation. The only sound in the room is the sticky creaking of her leather jeans.

"She's trying to break through the fourth wall," Leigh finally explains, as though to a meeting of the Dunderhead Society. "Her pieces are self-conscious; they're about the failure of performance to obtain meaning." This line sounds suspiciously to Chris like a sentence cribbed from an art magazine Leigh picked off a coffee table. A lot of Leigh's conversation has this air, as though she has been, five minutes earlier, briefed on the subject by a researcher, given a digest report while she's jogging.

Tiff falls onto the sofa, dramatically exhausted, and nuzzles her girlfriend.

"Hasn't mime kind of fallen into eclipse?" Chris asks, unable at the moment to address Tiff's performance directly.

"Everybody just thinks that," Tiff says.

"Tiff's work is different," Leigh says. "She's interested in stretching the boundaries of the form." She locks eyes with Tiff as she pleads her case to the cultural philistines.

In the kitchen, Chris and Taylor rev up the cappuccino maker.

"What can the attraction be?" Chris says as Taylor opens up with a stagy flourish an imaginary bag of coffee beans and measures them into the grinder with an imaginary scoop.

"Come on, she's hot, don't you think?" Taylor gets the real coffee out of the freezer. "Skinny blond girls in black leather, come on."

"But you'd have to talk with her afterward."

"From what Leigh says, afterward doesn't come for a long time, or very often. And she brings along a product, some unguent or poultice or something that takes away the marks from the thumb cuffs."

"What are thumb cuffs?"

"Think you could shout that a little louder? There might be a small chance they didn't hear you."

Chris grabs Taylor's arm, presses her mouth against a shoulder to blot her laughter. "Tell me. I need details. Diagrams. Greasy Polaroids."

"I'm not telling you anything. Especially not about the prison scenes. You're indiscreet. You're very unreliable."

"Please."

"No way," Taylor teases. "Besides, cappuccino's ready. We don't have time for idle gossip."

When they are done in the kitchen, she tightropes down the hall with grave concentration, carefully balancing two cups, which nonetheless slosh milky foam onto their saucers.

And so Chris thinks things are back to being easy between them, that Tiff is a joke she and Taylor share, until late into the evening when she has come downstairs from the bathroom and passes Leigh, who is at the wall phone in the kitchen, having been beeped by the station.

"Train wreck in Indiana," she says to Chris, who nods soberly at this distant tragedy. Then, in search of a mislaid corkscrew, Chris comes upon a smaller, domestic, misadventure: Taylor in the living room, by the bookshelves, pushing aside with her hand the great wave of pale blond hair that falls over Tiff's left eye. For her part in this vignette, Tiff is playfully biting the base of Taylor's thumb.

"Please," Taylor says later, when they are alone, gathering up glasses and dessert plates. "Let's not get into some big scene about something that was nothing." The standard response Taylor gives whenever she is found out. Like the night Chris belatedly decided to go with her to walk Bud and caught up at the 7-Eleven, where she was hunched over the mouthpiece of an outdoor pay phone. Or the time she found a small, folded piece of heavy gray notepaper in the back pocket of a pair of Taylor's jeans, which she was throwing in the wash, and written inside (in a studied, squared-off script Chris didn't recognize) was "Madly."

"I'm assuming it was nothing," Chris says. "I'm not accusing you of getting matching tattoos and asking her to have your children. I just want you to see that you've made me feel extremely lousy in this particular moment. Which is not nothing."

Chris is furious at having her nose rubbed in all of Taylor's pathetic subterfuges and diversions, the very sort of insignificant liaisons she thought they had both given up. She herself has not so much as made a flirtatious remark to anyone else in these nearly four years. To be honest, she hasn't had the impulse. So the discrepancy doesn't seem unfair, only sad. They're both white mice in this test cage of commitment. Chris sits content, though, while Taylor still hunches over the bar, pressing. She still needs girl pellets.

"You knew this part of me from the start," Taylor says in weak defense. "If I hadn't flirted with you at that party, we wouldn't be here tonight."

"Yes, but I wasn't looking to be the next person who'd lose you."

"I didn't really love Diane. You know that. You knew it that night. And you know I do love you."

"That's not quite what I'm looking for at the moment. I'm hoping for something more along the lines of an apology, some promise of reform, even if it's a lie. Giving me nothing backs me against the wall, do you see that?"

Taylor shakes her head. "You think you love me, but you don't even know me. You don't have a fucking clue."

They lie together but apart, facing the outer edges of the bed. Chris evens out her breathing so Taylor will think she's asleep, although she worries Taylor's own even breathing probably means she simply *is* asleep.

After a rubbery length of time during which Chris shuttles between sleep and a kind of racy mulling, Taylor slides out of bed.

"I'm just restless," she says, clearly lying, when Chris turns over and lifts herself a little off the bed inquisitively. "I'm afraid of keeping you up."

"It's okay."

"No." She's taking the extra quilt off the armchair in the corner. "I'll just go downstairs for a while. Read a little, maybe."

"Hey," Chris says, not sure what she's going to follow with. But Taylor is already on the stairs, Bud's toenails clattering after her down the wooden steps.

Near dawn, Chris finally falls into a profound, dreamless sleep after a couple of hours tuned in to the sounds of Taylor's limbs pulling the quilt on and kicking it off, the creaking in the springs of the sofa. The faint signs that she is there, even if "there" is becoming an increasingly tricky place to define.

# Paul Hoover
## (b. 1946)

*An assistant editor's job at the University of Illinois Press brought* PAUL HOOVER *to Illinois in 1973 from his birthplace in Harrisonburg, Virginia. In 1974 he married the writer Maxine Chernoff and began a professorship at Columbia College, which continues to this day, though he and Chernoff live most of the year in California. Among his volumes of poetry are* Letter to Einstein Beginning Dear Albert *(1979),* Somebody Talks a Lot *(1983), and* Nervous Songs *(1986). He has also edited the influential anthology* Postmodern American Poetry *(1993) for Norton. The excerpt presented here is from his novel* Saigon, Illinois *(1988). The plot of the novel is based in part on the author's experience as a conscientious objector on the staff of a Chicago hospital during the Vietnam War.* Saigon, Illinois *exhibits a bemused irony shading into contempt at the various strategies we use to evade social and political reality, including intellectualism (pseudo or real), various degrees of what we may call love, and even Chicago baseball. Such bemused irony runs through much of Hoover's work.*

◆ ◆ ◆

*from* SAIGON, ILLINOIS

Metropolitan Hospital is located on Chicago's Gold Coast, a few blocks from Lake Michigan. It has 900 beds, 18 floors, and seen from above, looks like the letter *H*. Associated with a major university, it's a teaching institution for both nurses and doctors — just the sort of place where hospital melodramas are set. There would be legions of tough nurses with big hearts, eager but overworked interns, arrogant resident physicians, conniving administrators, and frightened, often victimized patients. My first interview was with Mr. Bolger, an officer in Personnel. He was impeccably preppy, wearing a blue blazer, school tie, and shiny penny loafers. This was also, more or less, how I dressed at the time; we sat there, older and younger versions of an ageless archetype. When we first shook hands, I thought we might melt into each other, like water into water. But his talk was all Texas, and he could crease your clothes with his gaze.

"Says here you need a CO job. We're always glad to have your kind," he said with comfortable ambiguity. "At least with you COs we know you'll stay around for a couple years. Believe it or not, COs also tend to make good employees."

"That's nice."

"But let me tell you something," he said, leaning over the desk. "This is a nonunion hospital. The first word we hear of your organizing the staff, or of any political activity whatever, and we report it to the draft board. Understand?"

I nodded yes, but my eyes were narrow.

"We had this kid in the laundry room — thin white kid from Indiana, just like you, who started organizing the black employees. This we could not take."

"So you fired him?"

"Only been here a few weeks, and already he's organizing. Unbelievable!"

I assured him that he didn't have to worry about me. When he smiled, I found myself staring at his teeth, which leaned against each other like a shelf of old books.

"It gets hot down there, you know."

"Excuse me?"

"In the laundry. It gets to about a hundred and twenty degrees on a summer day, and there's no air conditioning or windows for ventilation, just these fans that move the hot air around so you think you're going to choke. Over in the corner, under the laundry chute, there's a pile of sheets higher than your head with shit and blood and pus all over them. The smell is just unbelievable!"

Did he want me to work in the laundry, or was this his way of issuing a friendly warning? If I didn't behave, would I find myself assigned to the shit chute? He gave me a confiding look and patted the back of my hand, which rested on the edge of his desk. It was obvious there was a reason for the organizing of employees. It was also clear that most of the workers there were black. If they had put the other CO in the laundry, would they put me there too? On the other hand, I had the right to refuse an assignment. It was up to me to find any means of employment at a certified institution, just like any citizen. The job didn't have to be demeaning, but they tried to make it so, out of patriotism. Why should the boys in Vietnam have to suffer and COs get off with easy tasks? In spite of my own beliefs, this made perfect sense. I was prepared for whatever miserable task they offered, but first I wanted to see what was available.

Bolger sent me on three interviews, none in the laundry. The first was in the Gastro-Intestinal Center, in the Radiology Department. Ahmad, a small black man in a stained lab coat, took me into a dark room containing X-ray equipment. He explained that my job would be to stay in this room eight hours a day, with an hour off for lunch and breaks, sticking tubes down people's throats. The tubes, some of which were big enough to choke a catfish, were used to introduce a radioactive dye into the stomach, which was then repeatedly X-rayed as I manipulated the tube for different effects. The main problem, he said, was that people gagged a lot and threw up on the table. Most of them were very sick in the first place, usually with cancer. I had a vision of jaundiced, skeletal patients, like survivors of Auschwitz, struggling in my grasp. In order to keep them quiet, said Ahmad, you had to strap them down. He pointed to four large leather straps that hung from one end of the table. I leaned over the table as he instructed me in their use, eyeing the gleaming grommets and hefty buckles. He stroked one of the straps with the finger and thumb of one hand.

"This is my idea," he said. "I used to work up in Psych, and ain't nobody gonna get out of 'em." There was a small flash of light near his chest, then a bright V in the air. A religious medal had fallen from his shirt as he leaned over and now it dangled in the air on its silver chain. On it was a writhing Jesus Christ, with eyes closed in an attitude of suffering. Ahmad quickly tucked it back into his shirt. His reaction left the impression the room was used for more than professional purposes. As we left the room, he looked back fondly at the table, now shiny in the hall light, the way some people eye a new car. He was completely in love with the object. Late at night, after everyone but the janitor had gone home, he probably returned to the room, strapped himself or a friend onto the table, and did those things only mirror and chrome understand.

I decided against the GI Center, as it was called. Bolger pretended he was miffed, but in the corner of his eyes there was amusement.

Next was the research wing, located on the fourth floor behind two metal doors, completely separate from the patient-care areas of the hospital. Its smell explained why. Halfway down the hall I entered an olfactory fire storm of alcohol, rubber, urine, rotting meat, dust, fur, and something like tapioca on a hot day. This experience was multiplied upon entering the research area itself. Agonized howling of many large dogs. Cages clanking and rattling. Inside one room several lemurs sat quietly in a cage, wearing helmets to which a halo of screws was attached. In another, a frog was crucified on a metal frame, all four limbs stretched to the limit. Each leg had an electrode attached, as if to measure the amount of muscle quiver. Surely somebody named Igor would step into the hallway, holding a candle.

Instead, it was Dr. Perez, a Filipino researcher with a round angelic face and a continental suaveness you see only in old movies. I had no idea how he'd gotten there; he'd simply appeared, as if he'd stepped through a wall. His handshake was smooth as smoke. Wordlessly we entered a laboratory to the left. An entire wall was filled with bloodhounds in cages, the great sad hounds of Basil Rathbone movies. The noise was monstrous and rare, but Dr. Perez silenced them with a wave of his hand.

"What do you use them for?" I asked.

"Oh, these," he said with a disdainful wave of the hand. "These are not mine. Dr. Sarnisi uses them for his heart research."

"You mean . . . ?"

"The heart of the bloodhound is the same size as that of man," he said. With a magisterial gesture he indicated the shelves around us. I saw for the first time that they contained pale dog hearts in solution.

I failed to mention that I'm tall and thin. When I'm not wearing a shirt, you can see the ribs rising and falling with each breath. My face is long and thin, like a dog's. I could feel my heart blowing around in my chest like a piece of tissue paper. The room began to stagger, and someone in it gave a low howl of disbelief.

It was me, but the doctor didn't seem to notice. He slipped into his office around the corner and offered me a chair. He sat on the edge of the desk, one hand in the other, like a basketball coach preparing to have a serious talk with one of his players. There was only one attempt at decoration, a large pastel drawing of a mouse, the kind people buy for their kids at Lincoln Park Zoo. It wasn't as cute as it should have been. Standing on its hind legs with sharp claws sticking out, looking as if it had just eaten something, it glared at me knowingly over Perez's shoulder.

"I see you admire my picture."

"Oh, yes. Very nice."

"Mice are wonderful animals," he said dreamily.

"I imagine so," I said.

"We find them very useful in our experimental projects. They're small and easy to manage, and moreover they are cheap."

"What is it, exactly, I'd be doing here?"

"I have a grant of three million dollars from the National Science Foundation for the study of semipermeable membranes. We take a specimen of tissue and place it in various solutions, like water, alcohol, and so on, to see how fast — and in what volume — the liquid is absorbed. Your job is mainly to kill the mice, about ten of them each morning. You then remove a section of intestine and make a small balloon from the tissue that surrounds it, much as one makes sausage. These you will place in the solutions, and after a controlled period of time you record the data gathered."

"I have to kill ten mice."

"That is correct.

"So that's about two hundred mice a month, not counting those with thirty-one days. In two years, I'll have killed maybe five thousand mice."

"That is sufficient for our studies."

"And five thousand mice into three million dollars is about . . . "

"It is six hundred dollars per animal," he said with pride. "That is what the grant allows for." He leaned forward, as if awaiting my decision — to be, or not, the Eichmann of mice. The mouse on the wall seemed to move, as if wind had blown through its fur. Ursa Major, light-years away, moved slightly on its axis. Cars streamed down Lake Shore Drive, taking their occupants off to jobs, shopping sprees, and love affairs. Fish in the lake were rising, gasping for air. The city worked like a woman in labor. What did I do? I told Dr. Perez I'd be back in touch, shook his hand, went straight to a bar, drank six beers and three shots of bourbon, danced with the waitress, kissed the bartender on top of his head, and went home to bed. When I woke up, there was woman in bed with me. Thank God, I thought, for this.

Her name was Vicki Cepak. We'd known each other since college, but as far as I could remember, this was the first time we'd slept together. Then I remembered another time, dozens of times, but I couldn't remember last night. She was watching the Cubs game on the ancient black-and-white television. Randy Hundley, the Cubs catcher, wobbled in a dream toward the bunt Lou Brock of St. Louis had just laid down. He got out of his crouch the way your father gets out of his chair after a big dinner. Hundley overthrew first base and Brock cruised into third. Vicki smoked a cigarette and leaned against the wall at the head of the bed.

"About time you woke up," she said.

"What time is it?"

"Third inning." If you lived in Chicago, you knew what she meant. On summer afternoons, you didn't tell time by the clock. The game started at one thirty, so it had to be around two thirty.

"How did the interview go?"

"I can either stick tubes down people's throats or make balloons of mice intestines."

"Charming," she said, like Lauren Bacall. So that's who she was today. Yesterday it was Ethel Mertz. She could be cute and flirty or cranky and wise, but she was always trying to be somebody else — that's how you knew it was Vicki. Today, she was whiskey-voiced and sexy, letting her red wavy hair hang over her shoulders, but mostly she was a girl from Wisconsin who'd learned to smoke last year. I thought maybe we liked each other for all the faults we shared, but I couldn't say if it was love. One thing was for sure. Her period was ten days late, and she'd come down from Richland Center to get a pregnancy test. She'd gone to the clinic yesterday to give a urine sample, and they said to call back in about two days.

I took a drag on her cigarette and developed an erection. It wasn't something you could hang your hat on, but it was sure there. One thing about living in the sixties was, you didn't have to worry about how much noise you made. We did it head-on, sideways, and upside down. We did it loud, soft, and moderato. Right at the end, Vicki got very soprano, like a small locomotive straining uphill, finding its plateau, and coasting down the other side with happy shrieks. We were sweating a lot by now. My head was butting the wall where Rose the Poet had painted a muddy Christ figure. Applause could be heard from the kitchen, just outside the bedroom door.

Right now, Vicki looked like she was fifteen years old. She had small soft features and thin bones. When she was happy, she was pretty, and when she was angry, she looked kind of mousy. Lately, she had been incredibly happy, a Pre-Raphaelite madonna with half-closed eyes.

"Hey, what's the score in there?" It was Rose the Poet, one of the roommates, and he didn't mean the game.

"Tied!" shouted Vicki, already going back to sleep.

I gave her a kiss, put on some jeans, and went into the kitchen to greet David Rosenstone, whom we called Rose the Poet, sitting in front of a bowl of brown rice. He ate it often, with a sixteen-ounce Coca-Cola. The rice was supposed to clean the system and make you a better person. Everything he did had some philosophical purpose, but the more rice he ate, the weirder he became. Or maybe it wasn't the rice, but all the drugs he'd taken. He'd recently resigned his job writing the *Playboy* Advisor column and was living on his profit sharing, which would give him about a year of free time. One day he just got tired of writing articles on the joys of mutual masturbation, rose from his desk, and never returned. The first day of his "retirement," he took some speed, wrote thirty poems in two hours, all containing the words *pink* and *electric* in capital letters, and had a nervous breakdown. Often, in the middle of the night, we'd find him testing the door to see if it was locked. He would stand in front of it for hours, opening and closing it, a look of doubt on his face. He also liked to walk around in the nude, and sometimes he answered the door that way. Once this caught the landlady by surprise, and she plunged back down the dark stairwell, mumbling an apology, as if *she* had committed the indiscretion. There was so much residual lysergic acid in Rose's system you could start a car with it if you could get him hooked up to the jumper cables. At least that's what the Selective Service psychologist said when he declared Rose emotionally unfit for the army.

"You look well rested," he said, staring into the rice he'd warmed up from yesterday. The congealed leftovers were still in a pot by the stove, next to some remaining shallots and a bottle of Tamari.

"Looks good," I said, "but maybe I'll eat some wallpaper instead."

"Was that the game on in there?"

"Yeah. Cubs and St. Louis. You want to check it out?"

"All right!" he said, with more enthusiasm than expected. He wasn't much of a sports fan, but we'd gone to Wrigley Field a couple of times out of what Rose called "sheer sensibility." He also spoke eloquently of the "pastoral aestheticism" of the game, but I suspected he'd read the phrase somewhere. He said he didn't believe in competition, though he was an intrepid competitor, giving the impression on the tennis court of an explosion in a bell-bottom factory. Neither of us played very well. The real players in their perfect whites stared at us with contempt. We always played in jeans and T-shirts. Once Rose even went onto the court in street shoes, which drove a middle-aged man on the next court into a rage.

We decided to go to the game. I kissed Vicki, who wanted to sleep, and threw on some clothes. We were halfway out the door when the phone rang. It was Bolger. He had another interview for me and I'd better be there first thing in the morning. If it all went all right, he said, I could be a unit manager on the evening shift, for twice the money the other positions offered. There was something in his voice between a growl and a purr, which I took to mean, "I like you, kid, but don't fuck around."

I said I'd be there, and off we went in my car. Rose broke out his grass, and we got so slowed down and high that everything rose up in front of us like a billboard or monument. A bag lady crossed the street in front of us and showed us happy teeth. I couldn't tell whether the car was moving or standing still.

Looking in the rearview mirror, I realized we couldn't have appeared any more different from each other. He had long black hair parted in the middle and wore farmer jeans and basketball shoes. I had on beige stay-pressed chinos, a blue oxford cloth shirt, and brown penny loafers. My blond hair was neatly combed.

About three years later we arrived at Wrigley Field. I parked the car illegally in front of the Sports Corner bar at Addison and Sheffield, then we bought general admission tickets and headed up the zigzag ramp leading to the upper deck. Half-way up, we stopped and looked back at the street, where a fat cop, his foot on the front fender, was giving my car a ticket. There were already fifteen or so forming a warped bouquet on top of the dashboard. He looked at them in irritation. We laughed and climbed the last ramp, which suspends you over the general admission seats.

On the upper deck we were almost overwhelmed by the pointillist fervor, the bloom and buzz, of the crowd. They chatted, dozed, ordered beer, and rose suddenly to cheer the double tying the game: it was like watching a human flag wave in the breeze. We watched with pleasure as cheering rolled out of the park and down Waveland Avenue to the lake, then over the park like a great balloon, swelling up Sheffield, past old couples on lawn chairs, and entering Graceland Cemetery, where Louis Sullivan, Potter Palmer, and other famous Chicagoans lie beneath beautiful stones.

The color of the grass was amazing, as if painted, and on it players moved like threads of neon. For no apparent reason, a beer vendor handed us two beers and said they were on the house. For the rest of the game we strolled the concrete walkway separating the box seats from the general admission, watching the game, taking in the crowd, and goofing around with the Andy Frain ushers, who looked like they'd just escaped from a marching band. Rose loved the white gloves they wore, which reminded him of Mickey Mouse, and we listened to the swish of fabric as a beautiful young usher walked by, a stern look on her face. Then someone hit a fly ball that hung in the air so long it was evening before it landed. We stood with our jaws open, staring at the sky and getting older.

That night Vicki and I sat on the couch, and Rose sat on the floor next to the television set with a quart of beer. As usual, the news was all about Vietnam. In the field, a camera jaggedly took pictures of some mud and weeds, machine-gun fire rattling softly in the background. The cameraman had gotten caught in a cross fire and fallen in a ditch. The legs of soldiers flickered by on the road above, and you could see a couple of abandoned trucks in the distance. If the GIs couldn't see the enemy to shoot them, how could cameras catch their quick shadows? Then Walter Cronkite reported that fifty-three U.S. soldiers had died in the war that day. It seemed like a lot.

One of them was Terry Grubbs of Tin Cup, Indiana, who'd lived in the same dorm as me at Rhineland College and become one of my best friends. I couldn't believe it. They had prepared a special story about the small town he was from, and how everyone had known him. There were pictures of him from different times of life — Terry in the fifth grade with a silly-looking crew cut, Terry on the basketball team. They interviewed one of his high school teachers, who wore a flowered dress and looked very mean, like she was trying not to cry. Then there was a film clip of metal caskets being unloaded at an air force base in Delaware while an honor guard stood by. It was the same film they had shown yesterday and the day before, taken from a file. Terry had stepped on a mine, the reporter said, and the body inside the metal casket was terribly broken. Vicki had known Terry, too, and she cried and held me tight.

Terry had lived just down the hall from me in college. He was a phys. ed. major and president of the roller skating club, which had about four members. He also used to play Mantovani and Johnny Mathis records when everyone else was interested in rock and roll. He even thought he could sing like Mathis, but his voice was terrible. From the beginning of the war, he talked about wanting to fight in it, but he worried about being too tall. He was 6'6" and

250 pounds, and he feared they wouldn't take him when he enlisted after graduation. He got his local congressman to send a letter to the draft board on his behalf, indicating his value to the army. He did push-ups and sit-ups and ran in place. He cursed the television when there were scenes of draft resistance. I thought he was one of the stupidest people on earth about politics, but we were still friends.

Suddenly I was on my feet, punching a hole in the wall by the TV set. Rose scrambled for cover, plaster dust in his hair, and Vicki held her hands over her mouth. There was blood and plaster dust on my knuckles. I walked to the door, went downstairs into the street, threw up in some bushes, and headed toward the park.

Terry had always owned a gun, even when we were in college. One day he called me into his room, locked the door, and took down a dictionary from the shelf. Inside, where he had cut out the pages, there was a very real, cold, and heavy pistol.

"It's for protection," he whispered, looking furtively at the door. He was big enough to throw me out the window, and he needed a gun for protection? The college was located in a little town in the middle of cornfields. There weren't too many criminals around.

"It's just in case," he said. "Dad gave it to me for my birthday. He said I would probably need it up at the college, what with all the draft dodgers and all." He looked at me with no special significance. His paranoia had a certain sweetness, and in some ways he was a true innocent. It was his father who'd made him think these things. He took to such opinions the way other kids make model airplanes.

His father, Russell, was a furious crypto-fascist who lived for illicit arms, survivalism, and antisemitic tracts on cheap paper. He ran an insurance agency for a living but didn't do too well, so he sold Knapp shoes door to door, meaning farm to farm, for extra money. There was always a copy of *Soldier of Fortune* or *Plain Truth* in his truck, bleached by the sun. The world was coming to an end anyway, and Russell Grubbs wanted to be there when it happened. He wasn't about to lose the final battle — he'd already lost all the others. The real desolation angels weren't motorcycle outlaws and suburban beatniks; they were ordinary grocery clerks, mechanics, band presidents, and housewives who believed in the inevitability, therefore the beauty, of the first nuclear dawn. . . .

Rose the Poet was testing the front door in his underwear when I got home. He seemed unconcerned with what had happened earlier that evening. He said hello with a grunt and wave of the hand and returned to his consuming task like someone studying a movement in chess.

Vicki was reading *The Floating Opera* in bed when I climbed in beside her.

It was still early in the evening, but when she was visiting we stayed in the bedroom because of the roommates.

"Are you all right?" she wanted to know. I breathed in the affirmative and stared at the ceiling. You could hear the building settle, the way old wood does on summer evenings. It sounded like someone was climbing the stairs.

"I'm sorry," she said, putting her head on my shoulder. "Maybe it wasn't him. Maybe it was another Terry."

"It was him, all right. There are only eight houses in Tin Cup, Indiana, and only one Terry Grubbs."

"It isn't fair!" she said, kicking the book off the bed.

"If I know Terry, he was probably relieved it happened," I said. "I mean, if you die at least something important has happened to you."

She leaned on her elbow. "That sounds kind of cold, you know. Who knows what will happen with any of us?"

"The way I see it, Terry's mission in life was to die as soon as possible. He'd drive his car like crazy and take all sorts of chances. Once he threw himself out of his dorm window on a dare and broke both arms. He even asked some guys to tie him to the railroad tracks one night, but the train didn't come through as scheduled, and he only caught a cold."

A car moved down Halsted Street, throwing a wedge of light across the ceiling. We lay there for a while, deciding if we really liked each other. I got out of bed and stood beside it, agitated.

"What's the matter with you?"

"I've got to call Terry's parents," I said, knowing it was a dumb thing to do even as I said it. "I've got to do something — I was his friend."

Standing in the dark of the hall, I called information and listened as the exchanges clicked in, working their way into central Indiana. The operator had a southern accent, which surprised me. Maybe I had one, too, and didn't know it. I dialed the number. There was a long pause and it began to ring: lonesome rasps like you hear only on country phones. After six rings, Mr. Grubbs picked up. He didn't say hello, so I didn't either. He just breathed into the phone with a masculine patience that meant, "Yes, my son has died, you contemptible weakling. What are you going to do about it?" It also meant he would never forgive Terry for beating him to the punch. He was supposed to be the bloody hero, going down in a firefight with the state police. Now survival was all that was left, and the fun had gone out of it. He had probably been sitting there most of the day with a pistol in his hand, wearing his commando gear and eating from rations cans. Now we breathed at each other over the phone, a kind of conversation.

In this way, we mourned Terry together.

# David Mamet
## (b. 1947)

*Director, playwright, screenwriter, essayist, and fiction writer,* DAVID ALAN MAMET
*was born in Chicago in 1947. Although he has found success in both New York and
Hollywood, he frequently returns to his hometown for inspiration. A prolific writer,
especially of short plays, Mamet's important full-length dramatic works include*
Sexual Perversity in Chicago *(1974), which was made into a 1986 film entitled*
About Last Night *and featured Rob Lowe, Demi Moore, and Jim Belushi;* American Buffalo *(1976);* Glengarry Glen Ross *(1983), winner of the Pulitzer Prize
for Drama and later a movie starring Al Pacino and Jack Lemmon;* Speed-the-
Plow *(1987); and* The Cryptogram *(1994), winner of an Obie Award for Best
Play. Among his original screenplays are* The Untouchables *(1986),* House of
Games *(1987),* Things Change *(1988, with Shel Silverstein),* We're No Angels
*(1989), and* Hoffa *(1992). In addition, Mamet has published a novella,* Passover
*(1995), and collections of nonfiction prose, including* Writing in Restaurants
*(1986),* The Cabin *(1992), and* A Whore's Profession *(1994).*

*Mamet is deservedly renowned for his harsh, elliptical, and often very funny di-
alogue.* Newsweek *noted that "the synthesis he appears to be making, [employs]
voices as diverse as Beckett, Pinter and Hemingway." That synthesis is evident in the
selections below from* The Blue Hour: City Sketches *(1979). The people who in-
habit Mamet's world never seem quite capable of saying what they want to, yet their
attempts to communicate can be as heart-wrenching as they are frustrating.*

◆ ◆ ◆

## PROLOGUE: AMERICAN TWILIGHT

MAN: In great American cities at *l'heure bleu* airborne dust particles cause
buildings to appear lightly outlined in black. The people hurry home.
They take a taxi or they walk or crush into the elevated trains or subways;
or they go into the library where it is open and sit down and read a magazine and wait a bit so that the crush of travelers will dissipate.

This is the Blue Hour.

The sky is blue and people feel blue.

When they look up they will see a light or "powder" blue is in the Western sky where, meanwhile, in the East the sky is midnight blue; and this shade creeps up to the zenith and beyond, and changes powder blue to midnight and, eventually, to black, whereat the buildings lose their outlines and become as stageflats in the glow of incandescent lamps. This is the Blue Hour — the American twilight as it falls today in the cities.


## BUSINESSMEN

*On an airplane.*

GREY: . . . Yes yes. We *had* eaten there!

BLACK: How did you find it?

GREY: Well . . .

BLACK: What did you have?

GREY: We had the fish.

BLACK: We never had the fish.

GREY: It wasn't good. (*Pause.*)

BLACK: No?

GREY: No. Not at all.

BLACK: We never had the fish.

GREY: It was not good.

BLACK: No?

GREY: No. (*Pause.*) It could have been that night.

BLACK: Uh-huh.

GREY: I don't know. (*Pause.*)

BLACK: Well, we always enjoyed it greatly.

GREY: I'm sure. I am sure. No. (*Pause.*) The atmosphere was *fine*. The *wine*, the *wine* was good . . .

BLACK: Uh-huh.

GREY: The *service* . . .

BLACK: Uh-huh.

GREY: No. (*Pause.*) No, we should go back again.

BLACK: You should.

GREY: No. I think that we should.

BLACK: It probably was that night.

GREY: Yes. (*Pause.*) It very, very well could *have* been. (*Pause.*)

BLACK: What was it?

GREY: Sole.

BLACK: Mm. With sauce?

GREY: Yes. With some white wine sauce.

BLACK: Uh-huh . . .

GREY: *You* know, with a . . . *yellow* sauce.

BLACK: Uh-huh.

GREY: No, I'm sure that it was the fish. (*Nods.*) Fresh fish . . . (*Shakes head.*)
You never know. (*Pause.*) No. When I was in the army we had one whole
company down sick one week.

BLACK: From fish?

GREY: Uh-huh.

BLACK: Yes?

GREY: Fish soup.

BLACK: Uh-huh. I don't doubt it.

GREY: Sick as dogs.

BLACK: Where was this?

GREY: Fort Sheridan.

BLACK: Uh-huh.

GREY: Outside Chicago.

BLACK: Uh-huh. (*Pause.*)

GREY: Sick as dogs. (*Pause.*)

BLACK: And this was your company?

GREY: No. No, thank God.

BLACK: Uh-huh. (*Pause.*)

GREY: No. Got out of that one. (*Pause.*)

BLACK: Mmm. (*Pause.*)

GREY: I missed that one somehow.

BLACK: Uh-huh.

GREY: I think that that's about the only *one* I missed.

BLACK: Uh-huh.

GREY: You in the army?

BLACK: No.

GREY: Armed services?

BLACK: No. (*Pause.*)

GREY: Uh-huh. Uh-huh. (*Pause.*) Yep. (*Pause.*) Used to go down into *Chicago*
weekends.

BLACK: Uh-huh.

GREY: Raise all *kind* of hell down there.

BLACK: Down in Chicago.

GREY: Well, yeah. The base is just about an hour bus ride from *town*, eh? Fort
*Sheridan.*

BLACK: Uh-huh.

GREY: (*Meditatively*): Yep. (*Pause.*) There used to be this *chili* parlor on the, just across, just kitty-corner from the bus, on, on the *corner* . . . the *corner* of Clark and Lake Streets. Underneath the Elevated. (*Pause.*)

BLACK: Uh-huh.

GREY: *Good* chili. (*Pause.*) Good chili. (*Pause.*) Good coffee. (*Pause.*) My *God* that tasted good, out in the cold. (*Pause.*) In those cold winters. (*Pause.*) I can still taste it. We would sit, we would sit in the window, steamy. Smoking *cigarettes.* (*Pause.*) Looking out the window. Underneath the El . . . (*Pause.*) Steamy . . . (*Pause.*) Well, I'd better get some *work* done here. (*Takes out pad and pencil.*)

BLACK: Yes, I best had, too.

GREY: You going home?

BLACK: No, going to work. (*Pause.*) You?

GREY: Going home.

BLACK: Good for you.


## COLD

*A man, A, waiting for a subway; another man, B, comes down into the subway and looks up and down the track.*

A: Everybody always looks both ways. Although they always know which way the train is coming from. Did you ever notice that?

B: Yes. I did. (*Pause.*)

A: You going home?

B: Yes. (*Pause.*)

A: I'm going home, too . . . Did you ever notice sometimes when it's cold you feel *wet?* (*Pause.*)

B: Yes. (*Pause. A looks up.*)

A: (*Of grating overhead*): They make those things to let in air. (*Pause.*)

B: Uh-huh.

A: From outside. Listen: Listen. . . . (*Pause.*) Where are you going now?

B: Home.

A: Do you live near here?

B: No.

A: Where do you live? (*Pause.*)

B: Downtown.

A: Where?

B: Downtown.

A: Where, though? (*Pause.*)

B: In Soho.

A: Is it nice there?

B: Yes.

A (*Pause*): Is it warm?

B: Yes. (*Pause.*) Sometimes it's not so warm.

A: When wind gets in, right? When the wind gets in?

B: Right.

A: So what do you do then? (*Pause.*) What do you do then?

B: You . . . stop it up.

A: Uh-huh. (*Pause.*)

B: *Or* . . . you can put covers on the windows.

A: Covers.

B: Yes. Storm covers. (*Pause.*)

A: Storm covers.

B: To keep out the draft.

A: And does that keep the draft out?

B: Yes.

A: Have you been waiting long?

B: No. (*Pause.*)

A: *How* long? (*Pause.*)

B: Several minutes. (*Pause.*)

A: Are you going home now?

B: Yes. (*Looks at sound of subway in the distance.*)

A: That's the other track. (*They watch the train passing.*) Do you live alone?

B: No. (*Pause.*)

A: You live with someone?

B: Yes.

A: Are you happy? (*Pause.*)

B: Yes.

A: Are they there now?

B (*Pause*): I think so. (*Pause.*)

A: What are they called?

B: Hey, look, what business is it of yours what they're called. (*Pause.*) You understand? (*Pause.*)


## EPILOGUE

MAN: I love the way the sun goes down. One moment it is dark, the next, light.

# Albert Goldbarth

## (b. 1948)

ALBERT GOLDBARTH *was born in Chicago in 1948. His father, Irving, was an insurance underwriter, and some of Goldbarth's most poignant poems recount the elder Goldbarth's earnest but poorly paid, on-the-job struggles. Goldbarth himself has spent most of his life as an academic. He graduated from the University of Illinois at Chicago in 1969 and received an M.F.A. from the University of Iowa Writers Workshop in 1971. He taught for a year at Elgin Community College in the northwest suburbs and worked for a time as coordinator of the Traveling Writers Workshop for Chicago-area public schools. Goldbarth was a professor at the University of Texas from 1977 until 1987, when he joined the English department at Wichita State University in Kansas as Distinguished Professor of Humanities.*

*Albert Goldbarth is certainly among the most prolific poets in American history. His first volume,* Under Cover *(1973), published by a small press in Nebraska, has been followed by almost two dozen others; among these are* Jan. 31 *(1974),* Different Fleshes *(1979),* Original Light: New & Selected Poems *(1983),* Arts and Sciences *(1986),* The Gods *(1993), and* Adventures in Egypt *(1996).* Popular Culture *(1990) was winner of the Ohio State University Press Award for 1989, and* Heaven and Earth: A Cosmology *(1991) won the National Book Critics Circle Award for Poetry. Goldbarth has also written two collections of eclectic essays,* A Sympathy of Souls *(1990) and* Great Topics of the World *(1994).*

*It would be impossible to represent the entire range of Goldbarth's work in the limited space available. The editors have, therefore, chosen one of Goldbarth's own favorite poems about Chicago. "Letter Back to Oregon," originally published in 1972, is typical of Goldbarth's work inasmuch as it frequently moves backward and forward in time, incorporates several different voices, and alludes both to the very contemporary—"you can walk into the Central Y"—and the very esoteric—"the ancient Sumerians ate onions/as we eat apples."*

❖ ❖ ❖

# LETTER BACK TO OREGON

1.

"Hello! Good luck: the trip out west blew our hair free of the city knots, and
we arrived in Eugene on a sunny day. Now we are bouncing along route 5
south from Eugene to Wheatfield, California. We have 20 isosceles triangles
in the bus, components of a sundome to put up over a swimming pool. This
is a new direction for us."

With nothing but such a sky to reflect,
no wonder the human brain is gray.
As birds migrate far to the south
of our dreams, other thoughts
pass through our heads like bullets.
Birds here are doorstops, or stuffed in the cracks.
Ira, Chicago prepares for winter.
The Midwest hugs September and November
on either side, armed guards.

The garotte may differ
but not the cold. In some suburbs
mink collars tighten
surreptitiously against the wind.
In my neighborhood, a man could die
for want of hugging; a woman's arm
is all there ever is between my neck
and weather. It's worst at night.
Ira, Chicago prepares for winter.
We slide for love on the icy line
that separates scarves from strangulation.

We look to sparrows for how to survive.
What could I say that a sparrow hasn't
told the world with a single shrill crack
in the language of milkbottles
left on the stoop? My breath
is already white with that word.
It clatters in the pan.
We look to sparrows, to the alley-dogs.
We bury the best bones
deep in our flesh. How huge must we be

for the lake to freeze,
but the heart in the fish-ribs
keep warm at bottom? Where
to cache that one wet drop?
Ira, we walked on the lakeshore last night
and though she held my hand, the thighbones
chattered in our thighs.
It is Chicago winter; and, too cold
to swallow or even part the lips, our teeth
turn against us,
still needing meat.

The time of my life reflects the times:
the arms of women accept me
permanently no more
than turnstyles; I tell time
by departures. The time of the land
is on our wrists, is pressing
the pulse, is a watch
making circles: assassination
hasn't changed much,
some loving man crucified
on the cross-hairs. The time of the land
is divided by mountains,
is three hours long from coast to coast,
is grotesque. One midnight, clock
hand pointing up like an arrow
too late to stop the birds' migration, Ira,
we'll be in different years.

The Midwest exists under too much pressure.
Tremors, by the time they rattle
households here, exaggerate
the trembling crib, the huddling bed,
the sharp and shivering kitchen-knives.
All year, the coasts press
Lake Michigan in; and in winter,
ice even under our nails,
the lake closes in upon itself.
We look to sparrows for how to survive.
If soot is their blanket, we look to soot.

Theirs is the stationary virtue.
But tropic birds, the flamboyant, the leaders
of flocks, tell time
in their hollow bones: what enables flight,
what tells them when the time is up.
And the clock hands open
to let them rise, Ira

how are things
at the edge of the nation?
Give my regards.
Wish you were here.

2.

"We are looking soon to buy land. I remembered the Indians and eastern
concept of cycles. To push our belief in symbolism through — to live
roundly. So we sought out dome builders. Domes are strong, inexpensive
and spiritual dwellings; we're working on the sundome now."

The concept "bond" encompasses
the fact of separation. What
is a link, if not a distance
leading from one person to another?
Even on the wedding night,
the ring keeps one band of his flesh
from hers. Even after the suicide,
the hanged man is a communication.
This is only to speak of hope,
to say that there is never loss
between Eugene and Illinois
that isn't balanced at both ends
when you exhale
and Chicago breathes in.
Where else do we find the tie that binds
if not at the end of our rope?

Where I work now, a one-armed man
serves as office receptionist,
the switchboard headphones tapping
each coast into one of his ears,
New York or Frisco, his one hand

*Driving from*
*Mt. Rushmore,*
*a white mt. goat*
*ran in front*
*of us. We stopped,*
*just looked*
*at each other*
*a while.*
*Strange*
*creatures*
*we were*
*to each other.*
*Spent 3*
*nights*
*with Ann*
*and Bob*
*Nett: friends*
*of Mary-Alice's;*
*they've*
*a shack,*
*patchwork*
*barn, and 5*

flying among the lights and wires
so fast it's a blur, the other
flown so fast, no one can see it.
He is the man who connects us
with each other. Any day of the week
you can walk into Central Y and find him
with one arm connecting our chorus,
and one arm rummaging the hole
in the air where nothing seems to matter.
There is a progression implied by lack.
There is something symbolic in his loss
that we talk through him
faster than by letter.

*acres. Bob*
*showed me*
*Domebook* II.
*Ann collects*
*eggs on a*
*chicken ranch*
*for 4 hours*
*a day, 6 days*
*a week.*
*During those*
*4 hours*
*she picks*
*about*
*14,500*

*hammer, wheel, cheek, seed, typewriter keys, book,* *eggs*
words still warm
with the touch of your palms.
By the object we know the ownership.
By the fingerprint we know the finger.
Ira, by your written words I could read
your pressing on the page, I could roll
those unravelled lines back up
and lead myself to Eugene; and find you
cuddling Mary-Alice.
Alone, in the terrible Midwest dark, hands
like mine have been known to quiver.
Each of my knuckles have battered like dice
in a tin cup. I have dipped them in that cup.
I have dropped in the cup of a handicapped man.
I have given to him, and in my fingers
weakened, as if their joints were wounds
broken into the bone. Maybe
yours too? Ira, when two friends are that scared
together, the fooled world calls it
*shaking hands*, a mutual quaking,
a sign of love,
a strength to channel up to the shoulders.

There is a progression implied by lack.
What any receiving end of a headset hears
as the word "newcomer,"

the point of origin, the giving end, recognizes
clearly as "ambassador" or "pioneer." Thus I look to you,
your winter still three hours away,
to tell me something incomprehensible,
some translation, what gulls recite.
I look to the coast for its view
past all boundary:
the sound
the dog hears;
the touch
at the villi;
the blue waves
washing against the visible spectrum;
the feeling of ocean
for beach;
something
of what the amputee knows,
his left arm
already in heaven.

3.

"Yeah! We did it. It's 30' in diameter and 18' high covered with 9 gauge
vinyl. We didn't have a scaffold, only a 12' ladder so the roof components
were raised on long pipe lengths and Mike stood on the ladder to fold them,
looking like an acrobat. Eugene is a good location for optimists."

*We begin losing brain cells*
*at age eighteen.* Each day a word
sloughs off, I can feel it
by the chill thread of wind in my head.
I can feel the brain
stitched like an amnesiac's.
What weight I carry,
what small vocabulary I know best,
I say for you
with the mouth of a smokestack
where sparrows have nested
and sparrows have hatched. They're words
I stammer on your behalf.
Sometimes they fly into women's mouths
for warmth; but mostly

they shrug against frost; mostly
they hoard their Chicago themesong.
Ira, the weight you carry for me
between pines to the Pacific:
are you truly my representative?
Do you still remember the one word for blood-
binds-us-as-brothers-the-way-ocean-
nourished-bathed-and-linked-
our-primal-ancestors? A word
like *air* or *pain*, something shared.

That burden we sometimes feel, I think
we are all the legs of the same huge animal.
Everybody, branded alike.
Neither the fakir,
the junkie, nor the drunken sailor
feels the needle.
I think we are all one animal.
The fakir sleeps on his bed of nails,
the junkie dreams,
and the sailor wakes: with butterflies,
battleships, vipers, and showgirls
tattooed on his back.
And somewhere, what
I dreamt, what shapes the painful stabs
in my back were transformed into,
appear in the rashes and hickeys
this animal bears
on its skin,
on its transcontinental flexing.
We carry nothing so heavy as flesh.
The tightest yoke
is a neck;
the world's most foolproof shackles
are wrists.
Now the fakir without a license,
the junkie trapped in his tunneled arm,
and the sailor breaching some debutante's peace
are less closely bondaged
to their captors than to that one beast
for which they sleep, and dream, and wake;

for which their wrists are a secret chain gang.
Such handcuffs bind us
inevitably to whatever
pulse is synchronous with our own.
Whose kiss,
what fangs, which pummeling
wings whistle
one night between your shoulderblades?
Look, I think
how we each cut the x there.

The ancient Sumerians ate onions
as we eat apples; lovers breathed sweet
onionscent on lovers. Because we weren't there,
never in its entire history
did Sumerian breath stink. Ira,
the word is: *air*. Despite what you think
or write to me of the foetid skyline
entering through Chicago doors like mustard-gas
into the nostrils of doughboys, despite that
mouth in my city hall
defending an unjust war with the oxygen
your plants, green spider-plant and avocado,
leave in Chicago as a sign of your stay:
breathe deep with me. Lay down the apples
and kneel before the small green flags
on their stems; and think, when you pant
hard above Mary-Alice, close upon her like topsoil
spreading down roots, that love,
it is but one of many ways
two hearts can be congruent.

Everybody remembers a summer
spent leaping over creeks,
almost a flying, our bodies the constellations
fish imagined, our shadows
the fish's night. But this is winter
in the Midwest. The creek is the silver
glut of ice naked hands could freeze to.
Ira, although I must return to them,
I remove the woman's hands from mine.

My gloves go off. My blue veins glisten.
Ira and Mary-Alice Brown,
I open the pores on the palms of my hands
and breathe with my hands into Illinois;
and exhale these words with the cells of my brain:
air is what there is between us.
By distance you could not deny it.
By factories you could not pollute it.
By calling it fart you could not degrade it.
By apples and onions we keep it alive.
And now we know how fruits are sundomes,
and vegetables sundomes,
and animals sundomes
admitting light through their clearest parts.
And now the effects of sun on ice,
how I'm coming to you, through this hemisphere, already,
alright, how my hands are dissolving.

# Tony Ardizzone
## (b. 1949)

*Born in Chicago and educated at the University of Illinois at Chicago and Bowling Green State University,* TONY ARDIZZONE *has been an instructor and professor of English at several institutions; currently he teaches at Indiana University, Bloomington. He is the author of the novels* In the Name of the Father *(1978), a classic of Italian American life, and* Heart of the Order *(1986). His short story collection* The Evening News *(1986) won the Flannery O'Connor Award for Short Fiction, and his collection* Larabi's Ox: Stories of Morocco *(1993) won the Milkweed National Fiction Prize, the Chicago Foundation for Literature fiction award, and a Pushcart Prize. Praised by Paul Hoover for the command he has over a range of styles, from urban realism to the experimental, and for his "thrilling use of point of view," Ardizzone is also known for the evident affection he has for his characters. "Yet," as Stuart Dybek says, "his great affection . . . never blinds him to the tough realities and inequalities of life on American streets." The story below, from* Taking It Home *(1996), cleverly blends three fevers — religious, scarlet, and baseball — two of which the protagonist overcomes. It seems classically Chicagoan in its focus on neighborhoods — the subtitle of the book being, after all,* Stories from the Neighborhood.

◆ ◆ ◆

## Baseball Fever

*from* TAKING IT HOME

Because just as the game has its men in black who call the balls and strikes, the fairs and fouls, the safes and outs, so my life has its crew of women dressed in black hoods, floor-length black robes cinched by beads, and oversized white bow ties. The Sisters of Christian Charity, to whom I was delivered at age six by my well-meaning parents for instruction and the salvation of my eternal soul. Imagine the toughest Marlboro cowboy driving the naive calf from its mother's shadow and then roping it, tying off its hooves, drawing out from the Pentecostal flames of the campfire the red-hot brands of Guilt and Fear, and then burning the calf's hide while it writhes and squeals like one of the Three Little Piggies being devoured by the Big Bad Wolf and you have a fairly accurate picture of my life's early religious education.

I believed them when they said that what they were doing was for our own good. I believed them when they collected our monthly tuition envelopes and said it was our parents' highest duty, the very least our folks could do.

I believed them when they taught us that Protestants were misguided (led by a doubting lunatic, they refused to worship the Virgin or believe in confession, the nuns would hiss), that Jews were worldly (they were looking for a material king, Heaven on earth), that all atheists and agnostics were eternally damned (their downfall was their senseless egotism). After we were introduced to world geography I learned there were Muslims, Hindus, Buddhists, pagans, naked backward heathens — a myriad of wrong-minded religions and ways — popping off the inflated plastic globe with souls as starving for God's True Word as the broom-thin children with their hands out pictured in the ads for CARE.

My parents told me only to do as I was told. To learn, to obey, not to waste all the advantages I had. After all, they continually reminded me, I was the first of both of their families to be born in this great country. I carried the weight of expectation of all the Bacigalupos, all the Paradisos. So I'd better not screw up.

My mother took me with her to Mass every Sunday. She was partial to rear, side-aisle pews, where she'd kneel and say several rosaries, ignoring everything else that went on except Holy Communion, which she'd receive with so much reverence and humility that I'd worry she'd levitate and never return to her normal self. After each Mass we'd light a candle beneath the statue of the sad-eyed Madonna. "For special intentions," my ma would always say, then pat her always-pregnant stomach.

My father hit the pews with us on Christmas Eve and Easter Sunday, the only times other than weddings or funerals he ever wore a tie. He'd watch everyone and everything, turning like a top, now and then sucking his teeth, and didn't seem to know when to kneel or stand or cross himself. He never said any of the Latin responses. He never cracked a hymnbook and sang. He never stood and followed my mother in the line for Holy Communion. "I eat my own bread," he'd whisper as she'd try to pull him after her into the aisle. Then he'd add loudly, "Lucia, don't argue."

I didn't argue either. I concluded I'd eat my own bread too when I was old enough. In the meantime I'd be a good kid and not waste their hard-earned tuition money and learn and try to please my ma.

So I learned. Not that the earth is flat or that the four humours govern physical size and personality, but that way up in the sky is Heaven, a supposedly wonderful place full of clouds thick enough to stand on, saucers of light behind everyone's head, God's magnificent throne, and twenty-four-hour-a-day genuflecting.

I could think of several places I'd rather spend eternity (Wrigley Field, Lincoln Park Zoo, Riverview, any playground with monkey bars and unbroken swings, even the old sofa in front of Aunt Lena's black-and-white TV), but the Sisters told us our choices were Heaven, Hell, or Purgatory — no substitutions. Hell and Purgatory were made up of fires so hot you got a headache just thinking about them. The heat was worse than a glowing waffle iron, the nuns reminded us every week, so intense that the flames boiled and bubbled the miserable marrow inside your bones. In Hell even the nails of your two little fingers screamed with agony. And you'd have to stay there with nothing to do but suffer for longer than any teacher was able to count. For more years than there are grains of sand on all of the world's shores and beaches, and that wouldn't even be the first hundredth of the first second of time, which would never end because it was eternal.

During some of these "Exactly How Bad Is Hell?" lectures, my little classmates actually peed their uniform skirts or regulation navy-blue parish pants, prompting Sister to put the gory details on hold and call for the janitor and his broom and pan and bucket of sawdust.

Thanks for cluing me in, I'd think as the janitor muttered to me how I should be ashamed, how I was a big second grader. "Daniel," Sister told me, "try and sit still and perhaps your clothing will be dry by lunchtime." I nodded, then stared at my desk top. See, I was grateful. God punished bad people whether they knew about Hell or not, and Sister was giving me a lifetime of advanced warning. I'd grow up and be a very good person, I promised God. I figured you had to be really evil to end up in Hell. Hell was for people like Adolf Hitler.

But then the good Sisters pulled the old hidden-ball trick on us, and all of us smug little snotnoses were caught flat-footed, a mile off base. Because, the nuns informed us, even though we were barely able to cross Clark Street with the aid of a green light and two patrol boys, all of us had *already earned* Hell's hottest flames, all because of two people we hadn't even met.

Let's pencil in Adam and Eve, the moronic apple eaters. They had a fantastic thing going (the Garden of Eden, tons better than Heaven by the way the nuns described it), but then couldn't resist listening to the talking snake. They had to go and nibble the forbidden fruit, in the process blowing the game for the rest of us.

So God punished not only dumb Eve and Adam but everyone else who came from their apple seeds. Which meant *everybody*, from the Chinese with their chopsticks to the Eskimos in their igloos to the Australians with their crazy boomerangs. The sin boomeranged throughout the ages. Which meant we were all brothers and sisters (momentary confusion and panic: then who will I be able to marry when I grow up?), damned to the neverending broiler, furnace, blazing hibachi of Hell.

It didn't seem fair to me. I thought hey, hold your horses, *I* wasn't there to resist the temptation. *I* didn't get to choose. If only I'd have been there — man alive — that apple would've rotted on the tree! I might have *looked* at it once or twice, maybe nodded to the snake, thrown him a dead alley rat so I could watch him eat. I might have touched the apple with my fingertips, given it a little sniff. Maybe even put my lips, my tongue, my teeth . . .

I'd have eaten it too.

I realized then that I was one of the lucky souls. I knew the truth. Plus I had a bona fide Catholic baptism stamped on my forehead. For at least a week I did my chores around the house without my ma having to tell me twice.

She was right, I concluded. You should eat God's bread. Kneeling next to her in church, I'd think of little pagans exactly my age all over the world who'd never even heard of original sin. How, when they died, their tiny heathen hands and screaming fingernails would crackle like slices of bacon in my ma's cast-iron frying pan. I'll travel all over the world when I grow up, I thought. I'll carry a hundred canteens of holy water and baptize every pagan I meet, even if I have to wrestle them first down to the ground. "It's good for you, honest, no fooling," I'd tell them. They'd be grateful to me later on. They'd shake my hand and thank me when they saw me again up in Heaven.

The missionary life was extremely attractive to me. As long as you watched out for cannibals and Communists, and didn't step on or listen to talking snakes, going around sprinkling water on heathen foreheads seemed just about the surest way to keep your buns out of the incinerator.

The nuns cushioned the Fall of humanity with another story, the Fall of the angels. It seems that trillions of years before Paradise some of God's finest archangels and seraphim were disobedient too. The good Lord was on them in a millisecond. Also he had several legions of good archangels (my first lesson in the concept of a deep bench) waiting with drawn swords behind him. The defeated lay at his ankles, gasping. God unplugged their halos, plucked their feathers, stripped them of their mighty wings. Then he stepped on a giant pedal that opened a yawning trapdoor in the clouds and all of the militant angels tumbled down from the blue sky.

In that moment of eternity's early timelessness, it rained angels — it rained devils — and they plummeted through space with a moan: like falling meteors, comets, Skylabs, Cosmos 1402s, twisting in an everlasting sizzle as the eager tongues of Hell's waiting fires leapt past their cloven feet to their devil mouths and French-kissed them.

This was the creation of Hell. Wowee! we all thought.

Indirectly these stories also taught us a lot about this strange being we called God. For one, he wasn't a father who took much sass. Also he didn't seem to give second chances. (We didn't get to the New Testament until third grade.) God was all-powerful and knew and saw everything, everywhere, always; and to top it off he was invisible. Ogres in the Brothers Grimm seemed more benign.

What choice did we have? We could hardly raise our trembling hands and ask Sister to tell us a different fairy tale. This, the stern women in black were teaching us, was for real. Each year for eight years the well-meaning Sisters of Christian Charity trotted out these horror stories, and each year for eight years I listened with increasing fear.

We were told that, as Adam swallowed, the lump of apple caught in his throat and remained there, a constant reminder of our sinful, evil nature. We were told that the talking serpent still slithers through the world in the form of creeping communism. All we had to do was ask our fathers to read us the newspaper; President Ike was combating it every day. One of the statues in our classroom showed Mary stepping on the writhing serpent. "See?" the nun would say. It was all the proof we needed. Evil was in our throats, in our world, even under the foot of the Blessed Virgin. Evil was everywhere. After the flames kissed them, the evil angels escaped from Hell and worked their way up to the earth, where they walk our streets and alleys, always in disguise, always looking like normal people, always there behind a streetlight pole or the open door of a strange car, hoping to lead us into the darkness of despair, into temptation, occasions of sin, eternal everlasting damnation.

I should tell you that my number is 13, so you'll recognize me down on the field. Every team from high school on gladly allowed me to wear it. No one else wanted 13 but me. Because when baseball collided with Mickey's death and I was forced to abandon my dreams of becoming a missionary, I felt it was only right and proper that the rest of my playing days be spent in sheer defiance of misfortune.

Because the first of our line of Paradisos and Bacigalupos to be born into the nation of baseball earned his birthright and stepped right out of Paradise into the foul mouth of the wolf.

Because I believed the good Sisters when they said that at seven you tag the age of reason, that from the moment the candles on your birthday cake go out everything you do goes into the record book. Because at age eight I was involved in a very extraordinary, extremely tragic play. I wish I could say it was a bit part in a grammar-school production of *Macbeth* or *Hamlet*. It wasn't. It was purple-faced, bulging-eyes real.

I didn't want to be evil and re-earn Hell, but if you've got the genes of a natural-born ballplayer it's not easy to pass up a fat pitch.

So I went with the pitch that began my life as a ballplayer.

On the city's North Side, on a street named Olive, in the middle of a solid neighborhood of working-class Irish and Germans and Poles, with a few Italian families like mine sprinkled here and there, like basil, for flavor. Everyone lived in gray or red brick two-flats. Upstairs lived the tenants, preferably old people who didn't smell and who treaded the hallway quietly. The front of every house had a porch that faced a tree. Everybody except the old people and the Meenans and the Jankowskis had a new baby every year or so. At first we babies stumbled around our tiny backyards, eating grass and twigs and pebbles too large to stick in our nostrils and crunchy paint chips from the wooden garages that opened into the *stay away from there, do you hear me!* alley, touching fingers through the tilted square gaps in our chain-link fences that separated us, careful not to trample our fathers' tomato plants. Then we were promoted to the front yards, where we were yelled at by everyone. Because the new open space turned us into a herd of stampeding buffalo, and everyone had just planted marigolds or snapdragons or new grass seed. Perhaps because they were trained to be dainty, the girls at once obeyed. But we boys had no control over our shoes. So we fled and graduated ourselves to the alley.

The girls stayed in the front yards because they said the alley wasn't clean. Really they were afraid of the rats you would see sometimes munching on the day's garbage that spilled out of the big oil drums each house kept alongside its alley gate. Humorless men from the rodent-control section of the city's board of health marched through every spring stapling signs to the telephone poles:

WARNING!
THIS BLOCK HAS BEEN BAITED
WITH RED SQUILL AND WARFARIN

So we called ourselves the Rat Squill Warfarins and armed ourselves with fifth-grader Joey Petrovich's baseball bat, and the alley became our kingdom, our playground, our limestone-and-asphalt Garden of Eden.

We explored every inch of it, naming every garbage can (Blue Streak, Rusty, Triple Dent), garage door (Big Ben, Lucky Green, Smasharoo), backyard gate (Squeaky, Busted Man, Fort Comanche). In the front yards our sisters stepped around the nodding petunias and drew squares on the ratless sidewalk with pieces of colored chalk. They began wearing dresses, barrettes, and red rubber bands to hold back their long hair. From our knees in the alley we could hear them sing.

"I live on Ol-live!"

Over and over and over, until we thought we'd go mad.

"Ay lives on Ol-live!
Ee lives on Ol-live!
I live on Ol-live!
Oh lives on Ol-live!
Do you live on Ol-live?"

And they always sang *see wye see oh?* (can you come out?) when they called from the backyards to one another to come out to play. I'd hear my sisters Rosaria and Tina. I'd listen, tempted to open my mouth and sing *en wye* (not yet) or *eye ay ell double you* (in a little while). But we were Rat Squill Warfarins; our rules said you couldn't sing. Our voices might scare away the rats that we hunted with rocks and Joey's baseball bat.

Whenever it rained or when one of our fathers would unroll his green garden hose and soap down his car, the potholes in our alley would brim deliciously with water and our playground would become the Chain of Great Lakes. We would play Dams and Beavers, on our hands and knees, using stones and sticks and pieces of broken glass. We'd see which one of us had the biggest beaver's buck teeth. Then Joey Petrovich's dark eyes would twinkle and he'd play Dive Bomber and smash our dams with his bat.

HOMES, Frankie Biermann taught us. Huron, Ontario, Michigan, Erie, Superior. Frankie had blond hair and polio and a brace on one leg. When you asked him if he had polio he said, "Yeah, that's how come my middle leg's so short." Skeeter Egan, who always wore his hair in a flattop and who could run faster than Old Lady Misiak's alley cat, and whose twin sister Deirdre was the most beautiful girl in the world, said Superior was the best.

Then for a while it didn't rain, and everyone's father's car was clean, and everything had a name, and the rats had made themselves so scarce that we forgot all about them. Then Lenny Sakowicz, whose arm muscles were as hard as cue balls, got a baseball and a genuine autographed mitt, and we all begged our parents for mitts. After my father told me no, "Don't be stupid, Danilo, I'll slap you, don't even ask," I got the scissors from the pantry and cut out all the pictures of baseball gloves in the Sears and Montgomery Wards catalogues my mother kept in a drawer in the china cabinet, and every night I'd stick one with my spit to the bathroom mirror, where he'd see it the next morning when he shaved. Each morning when I woke to go to school I'd find my mitt floating in the toilet bowl. Dive bomber, I'd think as I'd sink the bit of paper with my pee.

But enough of the other kids got gloves. Then Joey and Lenny created the Olive Street Alley League, and Frankie got a pencil and wrote all of the rules down.

*Hitters gitters* was the first commandment. That included even the backyards of childless old people who owned fierce dogs. *Ricochets are fair in play* was commandment number two. Off a garage roof was foul. Off telephone wires, fair. Pitcher's hands, you're out of there. Break somebody's window and everybody runs, with the hitter responsible for picking up the bat. Joey and the big guys foresaw most, but not all, of the possibilities.

"This here's a league of line-drive sluggers," the big guys said.

"Line-drive sluggos," echoed all of us little guys, even Frankie Biermann, whose leg brace made it awful hard for him to run.

Mickey Meenan was a very quiet kid, and most of the time he was around you didn't even notice he was there. He was tall for a third grader, gawky, spotted everywhere you could see with freckles, and he'd pick his earwax with his little finger or a stick and then stare at it for so long he made you ask him what was he going to do with it. "I dunno," he'd always say, and then he'd always eat it or wipe it on his pants leg and then start working on his other ear. All the kids thought he was spoiled because he was an only child. Really, we were jealous. Mickey had a hundred toys, none of them broken; a thousand comic books, not one page torn.

Other than Grace Jankowski, in our neighborhood of mostly Catholic families Mickey was the only only child. Even though he was Catholic, his parents sent him to the public school on Bryn Mawr. So he was doubly strange.

Mickey's father had a job with the city, sleeping in trucks parked along the street where they had big potholes or busted water pipes, and he'd let us gather inside his garage as he'd boast that his CAUTION MEN WORKING signs sweated more in summer than he did. He was a big man and always smoked a fat cigar, and he'd tell us how great it was to go up to Wisconsin to shoot birds, really blast them out of the sky, or blow little squirrels or bunny rabbits to smithereens, and then he'd take out his shotgun and put a finger to his lips and say, "Shhh, be vewy vewy quiet. I'm hunting wabbits." We'd clap our hands with glee. Then he'd tell us how he'd once been a professional boxer, though he quit before he got cauliflower ears. He'd let us look at his ears, and we'd beg him to do Elmer Fudd again, and he'd say he was pleased as punch we played with his kid, and then he'd grab Mickey and rub his head real hard with his knuckles. Mickey would say nothing, except his face got fire-truck red as he squirmed.

Sometimes we'd tease Mickey about eating earwax and being spoiled, until he invited all of us over to his house. Mrs. Meenan made a hundred oatmeal cookies and ten gallons of Wyler's lemonade, and Joey and Lenny swiped a bunch of comics, and Frankie fell on a couple of toys and broke them all to pieces, and Mr. Meenan laughed and laughed and stunk up the house with his cigar, and everybody but poor Mickey had a wonderful time.

It was an accident, and it happened before I could even drop the bat and run.

Winky Winkler danced on second base. Mickey was playing the garage door just behind first. It was a Saturday in early April and we had planned a triple-header, and we were getting good because several of us had our timing down.

Because it was a league of line-drive sluggos.

The ball cracked off the bat and I started to drop it as I ran toward first base, but I heard a hollow squish and Mickey stood there by Lucky Green staring right at me with no expression on his face. Then the world stopped as his bulbs went dim and he fell to his knees. For half a second I thought it was just a joke; I thought that Mickey had suddenly been struck by a sense of humor, that he'd begin to pray in pig Latin or sing "I live on Ol-live!" or crawl like a turtle toward the ball. I wanted him to pick the ball up because I knew I could beat his throw. I wanted him to stand. I wanted him to say *something*.

Because suddenly I was terribly afraid.

By the time we got to him he had fallen to his face. Then Lenny and Joey and the rest of the guys rolled him over. His face and neck were turning blue. His throat was trying to pronounce the letter *K*. His eyes looked backward into his head.

"You're all right, Meenan," everybody said.

"Right off his Adam's apple! Didja see it?"

"Wake him up."

"Get the smelling salts."

"You shoulda seen it! It looked like he was trying to eat the ball!"

"You're OK, Meenan."

"Get up, sluggo."

"You killed him, 'Galupo. Honest to Jesus!"

"He ain't even breathing."

We got him under his armpits and tried to make him walk. "You're all right, Meenan." His feet dragged like a Raggedy Andy doll. "Honest, Danny, I bet you killed him." Some of the guys laughed, scared and nervous. Little Frankie Biermann looked like he was going to cry. Then somebody took off down the alley toward Mickey's house. "Take deep breaths, Meenan, you're OK, you're OK." He wasn't very heavy. His skin still felt warm. His head rolled on his chest like Mr. Sakowicz's on Friday nights when the men from the foundry walked him home drunk.

Mrs. Meenan bawled over Mickey as she knelt on her front-yard grass. We waited for the ambulance. I thought I could hear the trees above me whisper their name. "Meenan," the leaves in the wind whispered. Then somebody shouted, "Hey Danny, better make yourself scarce."

There are times when events overload your circuits, and inside you blow a fuse. Your head suddenly goes dark. Dad says, "Lucy, where the hell did I

put that goddamn flashlight?" You help him as he walks down into the basement, thinking maybe you'll get lucky and see a rat, hearing the sudden roar of
the furnace as it kicks in. The sound frightens you but you're with your dad.
Yet he says nothing as he shines his flashlight, the only light in the world, on
the gray fuse box.

"Say something to him, Francis."

"Get me a clean shirt. I have to shave."

"Again?"

"I can't go over there wearing a filthy shirt."

Supper, some soup and noodles, and nobody talked until Louie started to
sniffle, then cry. Mamma held Francis Junior and said, "Eat." Only the baby
ate, one hand raised and wrapped in Ma's dark curly hair, the other holding her
breast so she wouldn't pull it away. The rest of us sat around the table, not eating. Louie wiped his tears with the fist that held his spoon. Dominic poked his
noodles with his fingertips. Gino stared up at the ceiling, making stupid sounds
with his tongue, and Tina held her rubber doll just like Mamma held Francis
Junior. Rosaria's hands hid her face. I looked at their dark heads, then down at
my soup, then at the little piece of bloodstained toilet paper Dad had clinging
to his chin, then at the dish towel he wore over his immaculate white shirt.

Mamma thought I was asleep when they came back from their visit to the
Meenans that night. Everybody was in bed. She kissed the others, then touched
my forehead with her hand, pressing the coolness of her palm against me for
several moments. Now I realize that she most likely said a prayer, that she
meant the touch to be comforting, reassuring. But it confused me then. I
couldn't understand why she didn't bend down to kiss me until the middle of
the night, when sound-asleep Louie woke me by peeing out his misery against
my leg.

She didn't kiss me, I thought, because my forehead now had the mark of
Cain, and even in the darkness my own mother could see it.

I'll run away, I thought. I imagined myself as a hobo with a burnt-cork
Halloween beard, a stick over my shoulder, and all my belongings inside a red
bandanna, riding the rails to the Wild West's unknown frontiers, my leg eternally wet with my brother's pee.

The next day I escaped, just before I could be taken to church. Ma was
busy changing Francis Junior's diapers. Dad shaved in the bathroom. I scooted
out the back door and ran to the Bryn Mawr El station, slipping under the
turnstile and jumping on the first passing train, which happened to be going
south. I was terrified when the cars dipped into the dark tunnel just beyond
Fullerton. I thought the El was always elevated. I feared that God was sending
me down to Hell. But then the ride leveled off. I rode that train until I was the

only white person on board, then got off, somewhere on the South Side. I took the next train that stopped at the platform, riding north to Howard Street, the end of the line.

Then I went back south, plunging deeper, no longer afraid of the tunnel or of being the only white. People were friendly to me. "Where you going, boy?" they asked. "Say, you lost?" I pretended that I couldn't speak, pointing to my mouth and shaking my head no. "You must be one of them deaf-mutes." I nodded yes and smiled. An old woman gave me a stick of peppermint gum.

I rode back and forth most of that Sunday. I don't know why I finally went home. No one said a word to me about my absence. At my place at the kitchen table there was an empty plate, a fork, a spoon. My ma looked like she wanted to ask me where I'd been all day, but my father's silence made the house too heavy for her or anyone to talk.

And then I became so sick that the doctor had to quarantine the house. I didn't fall sick with scarlet fever because I'd murdered Mickey Meenan, though at the time I was convinced that was why. I fell ill because I inhaled streptococci in one of those El cars, and a legion of homeless scarlet-fever bees built a hive inside my heart. Then the bees' bubbling honey leaked into my bloodstream and fried my cheeks, my legs, my bones. My guts flamed. Everywhere I was aching hot. Thrashing on the sweat-soaked sheets of my parents' double bed, I boiled like a lobster inside the steaming pot of my skin.

The parish priest wouldn't come to the house to bless me because of the quarantine. My mother rinsed my forehead and chest with holy water she pilfered from the vestibule. She filled the bedroom with a hundred red votive candles that flickered everywhere I could see, and then the room grew dozens of stand-by-themselves crucifixes, and three times each day my brothers and sisters knelt outside my closed door and recited the rosary and the Litany for the Dead. *Oh Lord, deliver them. We beseech thee, hear us.* I ate ice cubes made of water and red wine. When I could I peed into a soup pot. My ma brought every vigil candle on the North Side into that room, and after each rosary and litany she cracked the door open and tiptoed in and had me kiss the feet, hands, side, and head of each of the crucifixes that stood behind the tiers of bouncing candles and hung on my sickroom's four walls.

You'd think I would have lain on my damp sheets praying for the eternal salvation of my wretched soul and for eternal rest for the dearly departed Mickey Meenan. You'd think the words *I'm so sorry, dearest God* would have been starters in the lineup on my lips. They weren't even on the team. My mind and soul sang a different cha-cha.

"My little sister Tina could've gotten out of the way of that liner, dear God. You know I ain't lying. So why couldn't you have let the spaz catch it? Or at least made him duck? A dog would have known enough to duck. You make the pigeons fly away when the ball goes near them. So how come it didn't work with Meenan? You can do *anything*, remember? You could have let it ricochet off his forehead. Given the kid a shiner. Busted his nose. Knocked out his two front teeth. Why'd you have to let me kill him? Our Father, who art in Heaven, what you let happen couldn't have been worse! All right, so maybe you really needed him up there in Heaven for some strange and mysterious reason. In school Sister's all the time telling us that's the way you like to operate. But you could have killed him a million other ways! You could have let him catch rabies from one of the alley rats! Why me? What did I ever do? *What did I ever do?*"

While my family knelt in the hallway outside my door, respectfully slurring *the Lord is with thee* and *blessed is the fruit of thy womb.*

I thought a lot about Hell. I'd let my fever work itself up until I felt I was made of fire, and then I'd squint at the endless rows of candles. The flames would shimmy in their little cups and I'd see a dancing sea of red. I'd pretend it was a glimpse of Hell, and I was just outside, in one of Hell's waiting rooms, about to receive my punishment. I'd try to imagine eternity and begin to multiply two times two times two times two until the numbers melted in my brain. Sometimes I'd pull myself to the bed's edge and reach out and stick my little finger into one of the flames. I'd try to hold my finger there, the multiplication tables hovering on my lips, but my arm always pulled my hand back. Then I'd feel my forehead for my mark of Cain and lie back on my pillow, exhausted.

I'd play a game with the crucifixes. If I lay perfectly still there was always at least one Jesus whose hollow cheeks reflected the flames in a way that made his head move. I'd stare at that Jesus and ask him questions.

"Are you happy hanging on your cross?"

No, his head would shake.

"Is Meenan still alive?"

Again, no.

"Will I be well in time to make my First Holy Communion?"

No.

"Does anybody love me?"

No.

"When I die, will I go to Heaven?"

Always no, no, no.

"Then stay on your old cross," I'd whisper, then feel terrible and cry until my tears made little puddles in my ears.

I'd think of baseballs, endlessly arcing in on me, my hands gripping the bat, my wrists snapping the sweet part against the lazy ball. I played more games in my head than convents have black shoes and stockings. In every one I always hit safe line drives that were at least fifty feet over every fielder's head, that sailed like kite strings through the air, touching nothing, nothing, ever. Never old Adam's forbidden apple stuck in an innocent freckled kid's throat. No, my balls would always land with a magnificent splash in the middle of Lakes Huron, Ontario, Michigan, Erie, and Superior.

Only when the fat doctor came to probe me with his instruments would the room fill with blinding light. I imagined him as Satan's chief inspector trying to decide which boiler room I'd be sentenced to and how high to set the thermostat. "His fever hasn't broken yet," he'd say. "Let's give it some more time." Then he'd turn with a belch or a fart, and my ma would sigh and turn off the terrible light, then replace the spent candles, then call the little disciples to the hallway for the evening's rosary and litany, which was followed by another round of sacred wound kissing.

Meanwhile my former classmates shuffled through practice and then real confession en route to their first-Sunday-in-May march up to the Eternal Bread Line. "So what if I miss making First Holy Spumoni?" I hissed at the flickering flames. I was sick of being sick and so jealous I wouldn't be with them that I wished none of them would have any fun. I prayed the monsignor would screw up and none of the Sacred Snacks would get consecrated. "No, no, no," said the Jesus with the moving head.

I pictured the church, glowing more greenly than kryptonite, as the priest topped each communicant's virgin tongue. I imagined their sin-free souls gleaming like my feet in the X-ray machine at Maury's Bargain Shoe Store. I saw the ribboned pews and kneelers. All the kids filling their chipmunk cheeks with Christ. Everyone afterward posing on the church steps for adorable snapshots. Then they'd all tumble like socks in a dryer into a hundred just-washed Fords and Chevies, happily driving home to hamburgers on the grill, reheated roast beef, pineapple-covered ham, white First Communion cake. And all of them knowing why I, the little murderer nailed to the cross of scarlet fever, wasn't there.

By then I was able to sit up and not feel woozy, and that afternoon I held the wall and slid my feet to the window, then pushed apart the dusty drapes and pulled up one narrow yellow slat of the venetian blinds. I was able to gaze out on a sunny sliver of Olive Street, so I stayed there, dizzily holding on to the drapes, until Mr. Egan's pine-green Plymouth scraped its whitewalls against the curb and Skeeter bounded out of the backseat in his white suit and bow tie. Sanctifying grace beamed all over his face. He twirled his thick Communion candle like a baton. Then Deirdre slid from the car like an angel on Christmas morning. I cried then, if my body had enough liquid left in it to cry. I began knocking down the rows of crucifixes and blowing out the thousand candles. It felt like a cruel birthday party I hadn't been invited to, and since I couldn't blow out all the candles with one breath, I realized that I wouldn't get my wish.

Which wasn't that the liner had never left my bat or if it had that it hadn't struck Mickey or that Mickey could be resurrected. I was more selfish than that. My wish was that I could be *normal* again.

Because I'd seen what happened to the kids who weren't. The others ganged up on them like a school of pet-store piranhas. They took chunks out of you until you were barely alive. They tripped you whenever you tried to walk down their row. They stuck KICK ME I'M AN ASSHOLE signs on your back with chewing gum. They snotted out gobs of boogers on your seat, then hooted like hyenas when you sat in it. They hid Tootsie Rolls of dog shit in your desk. No one would sit with you in the lunch room, mess around with you on the playground, stand next to you when you waited in line.

So I blew out every one of the damn candles and kicked over the soup pot and then got up on a chair so I could take all the crucifixes down from the walls when my ma came in and screamed, "Francis, Gino, Dominic, Rosaria, Tina, Louie, Francis Junior! Thank God! Our prayers are answered! Danny's well!"

And, in a way, I was.

# Barry Silesky

## (b. 1949)

BARRY SILESKY *was born in Minneapolis in 1949 and moved to the Chicago area in 1967 to attend Northwestern University. After receiving a B.A. in English in 1971, he taught junior high on the South Side and later drove a cab. He received an M.A. from the Writing Program at the University of Illinois at Chicago in 1976, then moved to rural northwestern Wisconsin where he and his (now ex-) wife built their home by hand. In 1980 he returned to the North Side, where he has lived ever since.*

*Silesky began working as an editor for the influential* Another Chicago Magazine *in 1983, and he has been the principal editor and publisher since 1990. His books include the poetry collection* The New Tenants *(1991) and a volume of prose poetry,* One Thing That Can Save Us *(1994). He has also published a biography of Lawrence Ferlinghetti,* Ferlinghetti: The Artist in His Time *(1990) and is currently at work on a biography of John Gardner. The three pieces here showcase Silesky's fertile imagination and sharp wit, offering us the compassionate yet trenchant poet as postmodern man.*

✦ ✦ ✦

## THE KINGDOM

Gold and whores a thousand years announced that
heaven: another feast, wine, music. So the Pope
slept with the daughter, who slept with her brothers.
So the king beheaded another wife. Let's torture
the infidel, march to the border.

But that was another century. Everyone says
this Cardinal's "a regular guy." His house has rooms
we can't guess, old, square chimneys on top,
Mercedes in the drive. It's the only yard
at the end of the block. Blood and gold

leaves stir the sky, the park across the street,
the museum of history on the corner. There's no sound
inside the house, then muffled chimes, and the back door
opens. Plain as her white habit, the nun takes
my letter: his message reaches us all: I'm a Jew,

I want to tell his story. They say he'll write back
thanks, but there's no time to talk, nothing
new to say. The child walking to school
is shot in the back, a car wraps the bridge's frame,
the father is gone. Face twisted with the loss, the throat

shuts, but we can't look away. Every day there's more
pain. Don't we love this death, the wild blue water,
the trees' fire? Hold this hand. We're alive.
So the Indians watched the geese circle these banks
as the buffalo swept the prairie, huddled

for the invaders' guns, dove off cliffs. So the priest
drinks with the mayor as they toast the re-election.
Steel and glass blink in the sun, and it's Halloween, winter,
spring again. But the basement of this house has a hole
I've got to fix, an upstairs window that needs a new frame.

The Cardinal leads another prayer. Everyone knows
he's dying, and we can't resist the details:
he's thanking the priests, blessing the schools,
writing to the Supreme Court. He's trying to breathe.
The river that emptied into the lake flows the other way.

His letter never comes. Now, he says, he's free.


## TREE OF HEAVEN

When I first came back to the city I wanted
to bring the chain saw. The scar
above my left knee, cut when a young oak fell
the wrong way in the woods I left was fresh,

and I can still see the torn
jeans, the gap the chain

opened as it leapt by into the snow.
I stared at the wound, breath

gone smoke as blood spilled over the space.
But I was afraid I might use it, set the engine
roaring against garbage trucks, el trains
screeching past the porch, drunks

splattering bottles in the alley. I swore
this was no place to live. Then every June
catalpa's white flowers, October
berries of mountain ash, gaudy reds and golds

of all those immigrant plants painting
buildings, parks, lakeshore remind us
we do. And there's more. The latest storm blows
out over the lake. Leaves turn, fall, come back.

Years later I brought the saw here to trim
mulberry and chinese elm in my new front yard.
The engine needed work, the chain sharpening,
it woke the babies, the neighbors stared.

But I loved the country it brought me, power
filling hands, arms, skin, blotting
airplanes, traffic, rock 'n roll
screaming from the apartment across the street.

Now let that scum who snuck in our yard
to steal my bike show his face, the one who clipped
our tulips in their finest bloom a night last May.
The one who beat the old woman down the block.

They grow like weeds, these ailanthus, these
"trees of heaven" that stink and spread everywhere,
their shade patches that won't cool
in some paradise no one believes. Roots thicken

under us, invisible ring by ring
until concrete and asphalt swell, buckle;

streets, walks, foundation walls lean and
break open. We've got to cut out those trees

before they do their damage. The one on the edge
of the walk scraped our window all winter, split
the short wall holding back the neighbors' yard.
I want room for a flowering crab, its obscene flush

painting a week so delicious I can almost
taste flesh, flower, spring; or cherry, magnolia,
no matter what diseases those foreigners
might bring. Such May days feel

half the reason we live, and this year I'm going to
clear the junk, lose those extra pounds,
get to work. But I gave the saw away.
No time to keep the engine tuned, chain sharp

for the one day a year it might be used.
I took a bow saw up the ladder, balanced
in the first crotch, roped the bough to pull it
and cut the notch in front so it would fall

in our yard when I made the back cut.
Almost through, I stepped on the ladder, leaned
and held the other branch, sawed down.
And it worked: the familiar sweat and crack

as the bough broke off. Now the window's quiet
in the wind, but more than half that tree's
left, leaning over the deck next door.
The lower trunk's flush against the fence;

if I had the chain saw I could cut a notch,
work the tip into the back. I'd have to be
careful, fell it against its lean.
But that machine's long gone.

With only the bow saw, a ladder too short,
a little rope, I can't figure how

I'll get the rest of it down.
Last week someone sprayed a gang sign

on my back door. It looks like a fetus, blown up and
twisted beyond anything we can name.
This is my neighborhood, and I'm going to paint it
over, though I know they could be back any night.

They're everywhere. It looks like some version
of my initial. That scar on my knee's almost
gone now, but a month later a dozen new twigs
break from the old trunk. No saw can stop it.

## ONE CHANCE

We know they don't come back, despite what they say. Sorry to see you go, so
young and frightened — or is that only imagination? The room was huge and
there was so much more. Light pools over the table, dissolves, and a new crowd
rushes in the minute my head turns away. I'm staring out the window while the
basement door's pried open, the lock falls and the merchandise is stolen. I was
right there and I never heard a thing; believe me, that's exactly what happened.
I *am* interested in all that you say, drawn to the scent, the skin, pores standing
open. The outside looks so pretty, though it's cold and cluttered with scraps
of foliage, books and papers and color, then all these people milling between
us — too much to see clearly. Best to stay right here. Soon it'll be time to
close, and they'll take away all these tables. There goes my favorite armchair.
Nothing's nailed down. It's only the place we live.

# Marc Smith

## (b. 1949)

MARC KELLY SMITH *was born and raised on the Southeast Side of Chicago, near the South Chicago Steel Works, which employed both his grandfather and, briefly, his father. Smith attended but did not finish college, then married (he was later divorced) and fathered three children; he worked in construction to support his family and wrote poetry on the side.*

*Smith's life changed in 1987, when he began the "poetry slam," which he is generally credited with both inventing and popularizing. Working out of the Green Mill Tavern on the North Side, Smith saw the slam as a way to recapture poetry from the elite and return it to the people, where he believes it belongs. He later created and developed a number of poetry organizations and ensembles like Pong Unit One, Neutral Turf's Chicago Poetry Festival, and the Poetic Theatre Project. A dynamic performer of his own work, Smith has appeared at readings and festivals around the country. His poems are collected in* Crowdpleaser *(1996).*

*The three pieces we've selected display Smith's colloquial diction and populist sympathies at their most engaging. Smith claims that Carl Sandburg "jump-upstarted" him, and one sees the older poet's belief that poetry shouldn't be afraid to get its nose dirty, let its feelings show, and occasionally even have a laugh in not only "Sandburg to Smith, Smith to Sandburg" but in the other two poems as well.*

*As of this writing, Smith continues to be considered the Grand Master of Chicago's slam poetry, and the Uptown Poetry Slam on Sunday nights at the Green Mill remains a fixture of the city's cultural life more than a decade after it began.*

✦ ✦ ✦

## SANDBURG TO SMITH, SMITH TO SANDBURG

Once you were the Hog Butcher for the world.

Elmo from Dakota stuck those pigs
Because it was a job nobody wanted

And he had to take it.
The blood came over his heels
And the pigs squealed.
And every time a street car turned a corner
Those squeals came back to him.
Bloodthirsty men.
Hogs to kill.

Once the tools were made here.
Are they now?
Buy 'em at Sears.
Buy everything at Sears.
Buy the whole god damn world
And cram it all into a thirty foot lot.

Renovate it. Rejuvenate it.
Hire a Polish immigrant to point the bricks.
A Czech to polish the floors.
Make the tools with Japanese steel.

"Stacker of Wheat" he called you.
Well, it must move through here somewhere.
Piled onto a boxcar.
Piped down into a ship's hold.
Stored in a concrete silo.
But where?

Louie Gomez quit school at sixteen to shovel grain off the slip docks
of the Calumet Harbor. It was hard fuckin' work, but he had to take it. Now,
a Champaign Biz-Grad, who builds his body with free weights and cleans his
Caribbean suntan at the health club sauna, trades stacks of wheat we never
see making Louie's wages at sixteen (times) sixteen (times) the years of infla-
tion (times) the tick tick seconds of a Market that closes at midafternoon
when and where Louis, now forty, sweeps the floor.

Player with railroads, eh? Handler of freight.

There is no more romance to handle there now. No pride. Just sleepy-
eyed union stooges who walk the yards killing time; pressing a button now
and then. Robots, both mechanical and in the flesh.

Half hour coffee at ten.
Gin mill at 12:15.
Timetable says:
 a smoke at 2:20
 punch the day's end ticket at a quarter to four
 go home
 eat the dinner
 watch the TV
 bawl at the kids
 wake up
 do it all again.

City of Big Business Ventures
 (like riverboat gambling)
And routine subsistence
 (like changing the sheets
 in the big hotels).
 They told him you were wicked, hooked pin. He saw painted women
under the glass lamps luring the farm boys. I see hot crack tricks prowling,
almost naked on Dearborn, pulling North Shore football heroes upstairs
into fifty buck rooms for thirty buck wipes of their runny noses.

 And they said to him:
 "You are crooked."
 And CROOKED STILL YOU ARE!

 Crooked at the top. Crooked in the middle. Crooked at the bottom —
where maybe you should be crooked. Where maybe there's an excuse
for being crooked. Where gunmen still kill and go free to kill again for
those at the crooked top. For those at the crooked middle, too moral
to pull the triggers themselves.

 Brutal? You bet, you're brutal.
 On the faces of women and children I've seen the worn mask of
brutality. And I've asked myself what's the use. What's the use in turning
to these old pages of pride and optimism. What's the use in throwing
back the sneer saying:

**Come and show me another city with lifted head**
 **singing so proud to be**
 **alive and coarse and strong and cunning.**

Flinging magnetic curses amid the toil of piling
     job on job.
Here is a tall bold slugger set vivid against
          the little soft cities;
     Fierce as a dog lapping for action,
Cunning as a savage pitted against the wilderness;
          Bareheaded,
          Shoveling,
            Wrecking,
             Planning,
     Building, breaking, rebuilding,
Under the smoke, dust all over its mouth,
          laughing with white teeth,
Under the terrible burden of destiny laughing,
          as a young man laughs,
Laughing even as an ignorant fighter laughs
     who has never lost a battle,
Bragging and laughing
     that under his wrist is the pulse,
     and under his ribs the heart of the people,
          Laughing!
Laughing the stormy, husky, brawling laughter of Youth,
     half-naked, sweating, proud to be . . . proud to be

. . . proud to be . . .

        What's the use in being so proud
        when the things that change shouldn't
        and the things that should stay fixed
        in the blind imbalance of Liberty
        that Hamlin . . . Masters . . .
        and Sandburg saw so long ago?

Come show me now Hog Butcher, Tool Maker, Stacker of Wheat,
     Player with Railroads and Freight Handler to the Nation.
Show me where we're going now. Show me our proud new destiny.


THE GOOD SAMARITAN

Taking the angry poet home
On a rainy night after the Slam

Is not a driving experience
Recommended by the Chicago Motor Club.

No, it's more like
Paddling upstream in a wind storm
On a planet other than your own
In a dream that loops endlessly around
The relentlessly boring question of:
"What is, or what is not, *real* poetry?"

And it doesn't help
That this would-be captain of words,
With whom you have chosen to set sail
Subcompactly in your nearly paid-off car,
Has seen fit to balance precariously
On the dashboard
Two wounded sailors
From a crew of bottled blond boys
He massacred only moments ago
At the mass of the mahogany rail.

He takes a gulp from each
Then blows out his puffy disputation:
"THAT'S NOT POETRY!"

By-and-by, navigation proceeds
Through the seamy, rain-soaked Uptown streets
In accordance with abrupt directions
Belched out by this stylized Columbus of verse
As he gasps for air between diatribes against
The most malicious, malignant, malodorous,

Malpracticing poet leech
He has ever, ever seen or heard.

Which is, of course, *you!*
Who is driving him home
So that he doesn't stumble into the gutter
And perhaps die of drowning.
Or worse, for him, acquire lockjaw and tetanus,
Which would certainly kill him quicker —

Not to be able to speak his mind freely
Unencumbered by sense or sensitivity.

And as you approach a destination
You pray
Will be a spot he recognizes as his own,
You, all of a sudden, notice
A finger in the air
Punctuating phantom exclamation points
Which hover ghostly near your nose.

You are busy maneuvering down congested Broadway.
Headlights. Traffic signals. Pedestrians.
You mention
That it might be more conducive
To your common well-being
If the finger pointing would STOP!

This transforms his finger into a fist
Which he pounds against the dashboard
Shaking the bottles, making your eyes
Jump from the road to the bottles to the fist
To the face of this *angry    alienated    poet.*

And for a moment, you see yourself
(How many years ago?) frothing at the mouth,
Assailing some other older poet you did not really know,
Reproving him for proving himself false in your eyes,
For not living up to your standards of *real* poetry.

Your muscles relax.
Your heartbeat slows.
There's a breeze in your soul
About to waft out of your throat
With words of peace and understanding.

When suddenly, a hand hits the horn.
The horn on the steering wheel in front of you.
It's not one of your hands.
Your hands are responsibly guiding the vehicle.
It's *his* hand!

Slamming down hard on the horn honking:
"HOW CAN YOU CONDONE THAT BULLSHIT!
THAT'S NOT POETRY!
NOT ONE WORD I HEARD ALL EVENING WAS REAL POETRY!
YOU DON'T EVEN KNOW WHAT A REAL POEM IS!
YOU WOULDN'T KNOW A REAL POEM IF IT
    **HIT YOU IN THE FACE!**"

No, taking the angry poet home
On a rainy night after the Slam
Is not a driving experience
Recommended by the Chicago Motor Club.

## MY FATHER'S COAT

I'm wearing my father's coat.
He has died. I didn't like him,
But I wear the coat.

I'm wearing the coat of my father,
Who is dead. I didn't like him,
But I wear the coat just the same.

A younger man, stopping me on the street,
Has asked,
"Where did you get a coat like that?"

I answer that it was my father's,
Who is now gone, passed away.
The younger man shuts up.

It's not that I'm trying now
    to be proud of my father.
I didn't like him.
He was a narrow man.

There was more of everything he should have done,
More of what he should have tried to understand.

    The coat fit him well.
    It fits me now.
    I didn't love him,
    But I wear the coat.

Most of us show off to one another
Fashions of who we are.
Sometimes buttoned to the neck.
Sometimes overpriced.
Sometimes surprising even ourselves
In garments we would have never dreamed of wearing.

    I wear my father's coat.
    And it seems to me
    That this is the way the most of us
    Make each other's acquaintance —
    In coats we have taken
    To be our own.

# Angela Jackson

## (b. 1951)

ANGELA JACKSON *was born in Greenville, Mississippi, raised on Chicago's South Side, and educated at Northwestern University and the University of Chicago. She won the National Book Award in 1985 for* Solo in the Boxcar Third Floor E *and has received a National Endowment for the Arts Creative Writing Fellowship. Her 1993 volume* Dark Legs and Silk Kisses: The Beatitudes of the Spinners *won the 1993 Chicago Sun-Times* Book of the Year Award *in poetry and the 1994 Carl Sandburg poetry prize. From the apocalyptic vision of "Transformable Prophecy," to the celebration of a public figure to the heart carried aloft by love, the following poems from* Dark Legs and Silk Kisses *show some of the wonderfully wide range of ways Jackson employs the metaphor of spiders and their silk.*

✦ ✦ ✦

### TRANSFORMABLE PROPHECY

When the world ends
a great spider will rise like a gray cloud
above it.
She will rise and swell, rise and swell
until she covers green earth, brown rock,
and blue water.
She will seize Creation inside herself
when the world ends
in the last days between the fire and the cold
the ones left will gather tins to beat into shelter
and weeds to eat with decaying mouths
like women in South African bantustans.
They will love what they have gathered among ghosts
and heaped into a place.
The coffee can over smouldering ashes
will hold stone soup.

A thousand species of decay will be born
when the Great Spider squats Creation
back down. A thousand demispecies of spiders
will flourish like flowers walking through
the burning ash, the hot, hot dust.
Crickets will break out of their cages
and tremble down the sky like rain,
twitching on the ground, while the sky turns cold.
The ones left will gather sick skin around bones,
sit in fires that smolder in the earth.
Myriad-legged creatures will scramble through
scorching dust,
legs on fire writing writing prayers God knew
when earth first smoldered, squalled
and begged to be born.

## Totem: African-American Woman Guild

*Artists for Harold Washington*

In the middle of the day, the world
alive in the house.
A spider
bobbing delicately down from kitchen ceiling
on a lean single
thread — a sign
Mama said
of a guest coming,
someone you haven't seen
in a long time.

You,
dangling from cornerless sky
out of nowhere,
what surprise visitor
is on the way
we haven't seen for a mighty
long time?
Coming down the road singing
victory
in harmony
with us.

Creature of faith,
who climbs down and
up on a single breath
line, who trusts the thread
unbreaking —

I believe I hear someone
coming down the road
singing victory
home at last
among us.

## THE TRICK IS NOT TO THINK: ON THE ART OF BALLOONING

*for DFaye*

The trick is not to *think*.
It's in the body (some light you let go —
then ride).

The trick is not to think.
Could it be the heart can breathe and drag you on its breath
as far as love can go?
Could it be the heart can breathe?
Don't think.

Could it be you could hold the heart's breath?
Don't think.
Could it be you could let the heart's breath go —
then follow? Oh! grabbing, grabbing hold. Whatever is
traveling,
surging away!

Could it be you could cast off in blue sky
over blue water
and come upon a ship far at sea
you are at sea
but you be anyway?

Could it be you arrive far afield. Gleefully.
        In a cradle.

In your own backyard.
Could it be life took you for a ride?

Could it be you let your conscience be
                         your guide?

Or not. (Just the heart.)
And wind up where you are.
The trick is not to think up scenes you've left behind.
Not to hold what stays
down.
Just leap out on a dream, an air of savoir faire
that leaps from inside you
and carries you, wondrous, bouyant,
to the place you are you    anew, oh! traveler,
traveling magic show
let go all old sorrow
away, away we go!

# James McManus
## (b. 1951)

*A* Los Angeles Times *review of* JAMES McMANUS'*s novel* Chin Music *(1985) called him "the most exuberant, imaginative, poetic writer since Joyce." Born in New York City, McManus has taught at the School of the Art Institute of Chicago since the early 1980s. He is author of a collection of prose poems and stories,* Antonio Salazar Is Dead *(1979), the story collection* Curtains *(1985), the long poem* Great America *(1993), and, in addition to* Chin Music, *the novels* Out of the Blue *(1984),* Ghost Waves *(1988), and* Going to the Sun *(1996), which won the Sandburg Prize for fiction.*

*For McManus the vision of impending nuclear holocaust at the center of* Chin Music *combines with his sense of the on-the-edge quality of everyday, personal life to produce a style that one reviewer likened to a crossbreed between "rock 'n' roll's gut immediacy with the cool articulation of a Bach fugue." At the heart of "Finalogy" is the story of ordinary life spinning out of control as a son goes down the roads of depression and drug abuse. What holds father and son together is their mutual love of basketball and the Chicago Bulls. Sports seems to provide McManus another outlet, another way of understanding his own supercharged sense of the confluence of coolness and edginess in everyday life. As does Dante. McManus loves Dante's sense of finality, his "millennial fever." In the end, however, he does not heed the advice to "Abandon hope, all ye who enter here." Others have to abandon hope: the Bulls conquer, and in doing so somehow help father and son pull through their own personal hell.*

◆ ◆ ◆

## Finalogy

In the fall of 1992 my son, James, scored 17 points in a six-minute quarter: five of six threes and a breakaway layup after a steal. A hundred and thirty-six points and eight steals, I silently projected, in a regulation NBA game. James was playing for the seventh-grade travelling all-stars from Washburne School in Winnetka. He was 13 years old, five feet tall, and weighed about 85 pounds.

There were players in the league who weighed twice that, who had hair on their forearms and calves, who shaved on a regular basis. But James could hang in with these guys. More than hang in. He usually had three or four steals, and was often the game's high scorer.

The all-stars played two or three 4:15 games a week after school, games I wouldn't have missed for anything but which often conflicted with the 1–4 lit classes I taught at The School of the Art Institute. To make it from the Loop to Winnetka in time, I had to catch the 3:35 Metra train, which required me to cancel the twenty-minute break we usually took at 2:30 and wrap the class up by 3:10. My factual but duplicitous excuse tended to be "a family situation." I apologize now to those students.

When I wasn't at school, or during the evening, James and I played c-l-a-n-k or b-u-l-l-s-h-e-e-t or g-n-u in the driveway, or went one-on-one. That tide was already turning. He was two steps quicker than me, a more proficient ballhandler, a deadlier shot. I tended to rely on lazy jumpers during which my toes never left the asphalt, as a videotape makes all too clear. When I wanted to win very badly, I could usually score by backing him down, pushing up baby half-hooks, getting second-chance points off rebounds. But James was still beating me three out of five, reversing our longstanding ratio.

When it was too cold or dark out we used the plastic rim and backboard screwed to the door of his room, shooting a quarter-sized foam-rubber ball patched with gray tape. Long after it was time for dinner or homework or bed, James procrastinated with a series of one-last-shots, providing his own play-by-play in his still squeaky alto: "Michael pulls up near the top of the key, Ehlo with a hand in his face," "Scottie with a steal and the easy run-out," "Paxson for three at the buzzer!"

We also watched Bulls games together. We followed the New Trier varsity, the state highschool championships in Urbana, shared a ten-dollar sheet with his stepmother, Jennifer, in her office's NCAA tournament pool. But the Bulls were our team. Three nights a week on TV, on the car radio when we had to be driving somewhere during those sacrosanct two-and-a-half-hour slots, once a month or so when I was lucky enough to procure tickets (from a colleague or scalper) and we went to the Stadium. We tried to get there early enough to see the players, or more likely their cars, arriving outside Gate 3½: G MAN 54 or NEWS or FEAR 33 from the Land of Lincoln, M AIR J from North Carolina . . .

Because of James's size (and his father duplicity), we sometimes got in on one ticket. Following my instructions, James lagged a few places behind me in line, then scrambled ahead when he got to the turnstile while I hollered peremptorily to the Andy Frain teenager that she'd already torn both our tickets. Not one time did this stunt not work, although I continued to buy two tickets whenever two were available, and I apologize now to those ushers. To

Jerry Reinsdorf I say, as Jack Lemmon and Ed Harris and Al Pacino and Alec Baldwin have already testily reuttered for TNT's unintentionally hilarious, bowdlerized cut of *Glengarry Glen Ross:* Forget you. Not that Mr. Reinsdorf is selling me parcels of Florida swampland, but still. If he wants to discuss it, I'll be at the Como Inn, trying to scrounge two good tickets.

Once we sat down or found decent standing room, James and I made a point of ignoring the paroxysms of hoopla attending the actual game: cheering to goose the Fan-O-Meter when the ball was in play, or during timeouts applauding the various mascots and Bulls Brothers and chip races and dizzy fans trying to dribble. It made me proud that James seemed to understand that the entire point of being there was to see, in person, the best basketball player who ever was, and maybe the best team as well.

We watched the second game of the 1991 Finals against the Lakers from alongside NBC's first-balcony camera: a stone bargain at three hundred dollars a seat. A lot of people remember this as the game in which Sam Perkins forced Michael to change his shot from a righthanded tomahawk dunk to a lefthanded scoop, basking in the certainty that the Bulls won that series 4 – 1, handily sweeping the last three games at the Forum to claim their first championship. But until it was over Game 2 felt like a perilous, must-win predicament: every basket and every stop counted. At that point the Bulls had never won a championship, never even reached the Finals before, whereas the Lakers had been world champions five of the previous eleven years and, worse, had just won Game 1 at the Stadium when Michael's 19-foot jumper rimmed out with a couple of ticks left on the clock.

The key issue was who would guard Magic. At 6-2 and poky by NBA standards, Paxson wasn't the answer. This left it to Michael to defend against Magic, and chasing and trying to outmuscle a 6-10 Hall of Fame point guard cost him two early fouls as well as significant energy, leaving him with that much less juice for offense.

After conferring with Michael and Scottie, Phil Jackson put Scottie on Magic. In June of 1991, Scottie was still an unknown quantity. Many basketball fans were convinced that one of the main reasons the Bulls had been stopped by the Pistons during the previous three playoffs was Scottie's failure to stand up to the physical (and often illegal) tactics of Dennis Rodman, John Salley, James Edwards and their Bad Boy cohorts. But now, as James and I bellowed our encouragement, Scottie stepped up. In possession after possession, he either denied Magic the ball or bodied him the length of the floor, forcing the Lakers to begin their half-court sets with their point guard's back to the basket. When Magic gave up the ball and went into the post, Scottie matched him with quickness and muscle. By halftime the Bulls were up 48 – 43, and they never looked back from this point — not until May of 1994, when

Hue Hollins' obscenely amateurhour late whistle on Scottie bailed out the Knicks for a couple of weeks before the Rockets took over.

It was Michael's spectacular dunk-to-layup maneuver that made the high-light tapes, but it was Scottie's execution of the switched defensive assignments that changed the momentum, and James and I both took great pleasure in knowing this. Whenever those highlights came on, we shared a moment of serene, irreplaceable friendship — or was it camaraderie? Partnership? Love? I don't know. But we knew how the Bulls had won that key game. We had been there.

It felt like we'd be there forever.

During the fall of 1993, as James entered his last year of junior highschool, he began to gradually — then suddenly — spiral down into an inferno of rage, depression, and cold, quiet, passive-aggressive defiance. His mother and I had separated in 1988, divorced in 1990, and she had remarried and had a child al-most immediately. Our daughter, Bridget, four years older than James, "acted out" or "up" from the beginning, while James's reaction got delayed for some reason until he, too, reached adolescence. It didn't help either of them that their mom and I hated each other.

James quit even pretending to do schoolwork and seemed to take pleasure in an across-the-board refusal, especially of any idea remotely associated with his father. In October he shocked not only me but his coaches and teammates by declining to try out for the eighth-grade travelling team. How come? we all wanted to know. "I just wanna play my guitar." Or sometimes: "For no particular reason." He expressed zero interest in what he'd be doing even one or two days in the future. Most of his time he spent holed up in one of his rooms — he had two, about five blocks apart — with his CD's and Stratocaster, which I had bought for him but which Dan, his new stepfather, had taught him to play. Another hard rivet to swallow.

James's first band consisted of jocks who were also musicians. They covered Hendrix, the Stones, Led Zeppelin and Nirvana with startling fidelity, but nothing much else seemed to come of it. Band members quit, changed schools, got replaced; the only necessary constant was a drummer with parents who were either deaf or preternaturally tolerant. After one sequence of baffling (to me) permutations, James wound up with four guys he referred to as "serious musicians," though from what I could tell their most serious pre-occupations were smoking cigarettes and marijuana, taking acid, and drinking whatever alcohol they could boost from their parents. Actual rehearsals or jam sessions, which required five eighth-grade boys to sync up their sched-ules, were irregular in any number of ways.

Since sports were no longer an option, and I didn't play a musical instru-ment, I had to scramble for ways to spend time with my son — not that he seemed to want me to all that badly. A few of my former students were in bands that played in north side clubs like Lounge Ax or Phyllis's, but you had to be twenty-one to get into these places. On the rare occasion I was able to persuade the manager that James was there for the music and would only drink Coke, I still had to be prepared to stand in a packed ashtray of a room until 2:12 A.M. in order to see a full set. We had some good nights together, though, seeing Souled American and Shrimp Boat and Lake Effect, the Pogues and the Popes, Liz Phair and Mint Aundry and The Sea and Cake. We also played pool, a game which James picked up with his customary precociousness. Yet both the quality and quantity of our "quality time" was becoming more and more sporadic. And besides: rock joints and pool halls do not the best father-son habitats make. By the time John Paxson hit The Shot (with a nervous assist from Horace) to clinch the 1993 Finals against Phoenix, James and I were seldom in the same room together. I don't even think he was watching.

But not watching sports was the least of it. By the first semester of his freshman year at New Trier, he had quit going to class altogether. His mother and I enrolled him in the Chicago Academy for the Arts, hoping that the school's emphasis on music would help James snap out of it — whatever *it* happened to be. (As Stuart Dybek's death-haunted Frank Marzek proposes in "Sauerkraut Soup": "Like all *its*, it swam in the subconscious, that flooded sewer pipe phosphorescent with jellyfish.") In any event, changing schools didn't work. Zoloft and Elavil didn't work. Tough love didn't work. New guitars didn't work. It later turned out that he'd smashed both the instruments I'd gotten him as birthday and Christmas presents. He mistrusted no one in the world more than he mistrusted me. When he did deign to speak to me, what came out of his mouth was a scratchy baritone mumble of contempt or despair. Where was "the old James"? I had no idea, but I missed him.

Other parents — especially, I couldn't help noticing, the ones who were also divorced — lamented the reckless adolescent hijinks and experimentation, the slovenly hygiene, the low self-esteem their daughters and sons were exhibiting. I listened but had no real sympathy. Whatever James was suffering from went far far beyond teenage antics or angst. Other parents' children had posters of Hendrix, Kurt Cobain, or Keith Richards on the walls of their rooms, but James took these guys at their word:

> I'll meet y'all in the next world
> and don't be late. Don't be late.
>
> I like it, I'm not gonna crack
> I miss you, I'm not gonna crack
> I love you, I'm not gonna crack
> I kill you, I'm not gonna crack

> Can't you see, Sister Morphine,
> I'm tryin' to score?

The hardcore posturing of "Voodoo Child" and *Sticky Fingers* that I'd perfunctorily employed twenty-five years earlier was suddenly a code my son lived by. Which meant, if I understood things correctly, and in the absence of zero evidence to the contrary, that he was ready to die for it. I never saw him livelier during this period than when we were slogging through two inches of beer and piss on the floor of the balcony of the Aragon Ballroom to get better views of old Keith. I myself had always been a Stones guy, as opposed to a Beatles guy. Even as an adult, the writer in me recognized that Keith's unbridalled buccaneer's abandon was at least artistically viable, even if he required crack teams of attorneys and doctors and fresh supplies of clean blood to keep himself operative. Now that my son had adopted such an M.O., it seemed vicious, insane and contemptible.

As James spiralled downward through circle after circle of Hell, a number of psychiatrists became involved. There were also police orders, trips to emergency rooms up and down the North Shore, a psychotic 29-year-old girlfriend, hastily assembled conferences with social workers. His mother and sister and I — not to mention aunts, uncles, friends — tried every way we could imagine to connect with him. The nature of his depression, however, was that he was determined to maintain it *by any means necessary.* His most potent weapons system was deft psychological judo: the harder we pressed to reach him, the harder we landed, angry and expensively bruised, on the canvas.

What probably scared me the most was that James wasn't really there behind his eyes any more, and whoever was in there was altogether capable of killing my son. As our friend David Breskin put it in his poem, "A Small Boy, Your Son":

> . . . Gifts
> you gave came hurtling back, broken but unused:
>
> the electric guitar that could care less,
> jumpless Air Jordans and wasted tickets
> to the Bulls, Hendrix boxed sets, sundae treats,
> explanations of divorce. He's weighed all
> this and plowed it under. He knows how new
>
> becomes old, how rust rots the teeth of marriage,
> how the ground shakes beneath your feet. He knows
> the appeal of the approaching train. Now,
> on a drug beginning with the letter

Z, offspring of a certain compound P,
the doctors with their dosage plans can build

him back to being, but can't erase the scenes:
snarly sirens of police, I.V. drips
like grinding clocks, his squint against the morning's
sullen light, a machinery of shrinks
stoking the bright furnace of hospital.

Put more prosaically, my role in James's life had become the desperate, shaky, humiliated wreck who filled out insurance forms at emergency rooms, had murderous disputes with claims supervisors, made appointments with psychiatrists and phoned in prescriptions, or reported his son's pairs of addresses and phone numbers to police officers young enough to be my son, too.

Only because neither of us had been raised by people who used violence to solve problems, we came to blows only once. It didn't last more than ten seconds, but the outcome was harrowing: while I pinned his arms to his sides in a bearhug, he slammed his head as hard as he could against the wall a dozen times — more? — before I managed to drag him down onto his bed.

By January 1995 he was in the psychiatric ward of Highland Park Hospital. Now when I left a class early (or canceled it) it was to drive up through blizzards to make urgent meetings with one or another M.D. Whatever filaments still connected me to my son had been pretty much lacerated. There was blood, there was love, there were legal and fiduciary responsibilities, but these were abstractions that only seemed to make things get worse.

One of our very few palpable links were the Bulls. We could still, albeit rarely, sit in front of a television and curse referees, or even touch fists when Cliff Levingston got an offensive rebound or Craig Hodges hit a key three. We may have been sitting across from each other in the visitors' lounge of a psych ward, watching the Jordanless Bulls struggle to stay in playoff contention; what few remarks we did make may have been widely separated by sullen silence on James's part, rage and anxiety on mine; yet other than brief exchanges on who might get credit for a steal, or what the Bulls' (or Bears') chances would be in the post-season, there was nothing much else we had to say to each other.

While I didn't appreciate this at the time, I now see how precious and necessary it was to have a common subject for our frayed and smoldering attentions. If we communicated only peripherally, talking more at the TV, addressing our remarks to whom it may concern, at least we were in the same room, facing in approximately the same direction. I also believe that if those ricocheted afterthoughts and lateral, nonverbal regard hadn't been bouncing between us, we may have lost one another forever.

Eventually, around his seventeenth birthday, James began to come out of it. While in fact it was an excruciatingly gradual process involving scores of friends and family members and professionals, over two years of in- and out-patient therapy, trial runs with four different anti-depressants, and ongoing therapy with a miracle-worker of a psychologist named Peggy LeMire, the reversal James has made seems to me almost as sudden as the one that overtook him three years ago.

He now takes the same dose of Prozac that I and his stepfather take. Though the hair on his head has been shaved, he has hair on his calves and his face, and has callouses again on his fingertips. His girlfriend is sixteen years old, listens to gangsta rap, and wears the same too-long bellbottoms torn and frayed at the heels that the girls I hung out with had on when I was seventeen. Although she claims to find sports "so like annoying," she will tolerate James shooting hoops with their friends for an evening, provided that smoking is legal while dribbling.

James has not returned to school, but he has registered to take the GED and is planning to sit in on a music history class next fall at SAIC. Since his girlfriend's mother's house is three blocks from mine, James and I eat dinner together more often, although his time at the table invariably gets interrupted by flurries of phone calls and last-minute changes of plans.

We watched parts of about a dozen of the Bulls' 72 regular-season wins, and we've already seen two early-round playoff games together. This evening we have plans to watch Game 5 of the Knicks series, though we both understand that a band practice may run late, a search committee dinner may get rescheduled, or James's girlfriend may finish her homework a half hour early. But these days I'm a bit more relaxed about that. So is James.

Pax is now one of the coaches, but the combination of Ron Harper and Steve Kerr seems a reasonable on-court facsimile. James disagrees. Kerr's regular-season three-point shooting percentage may be higher than Pax's was, he notes, but the line is now two feet nearer the rim, and Kerr runs away from his shot in the clutch — or, when he does take it, misses. So Kerr as the New Pax or the Anti-Pax is something we argue about. Also: Would Rodman or Horace help win more championships, given that placing Horace back on the Bulls subtracts him from the lineup of their toughest opponent? Is Big Penny at 22 better than Money at 33? Discussions like these sometimes lead to discussions of other things — girls, college, jazz, Dostoevsky — during which James is less automatically skeptical of what may come out of my mouth. We even joke about things, especially while watching a game: Robert Parrish's pot habit, how we've always liked Rodman, Red Kerr's flatulent babbling. After an eternity of mostly hostile silence, these edgy little exchanges feel holy and strange and quite soothing.

Just the other morning, when James didn't know I was home, I even heard him singing.

I'm teaching a course in Dante's *Inferno* in Florence this spring, from the last week of May through the third week of June. I've been doing this poem at SAIC off and on for three years, mainly because the bad place I was trudging through with James made Virgil and Dante's bad place make even more sense to me. I'm particularly fascinated, of course, by Ulysses and Telemachus, the affection and dread felt by Guido Cavalcante's father, Ugolino's ghastly fate with his sons and grandsons. I'm also in love with what I call Dante's finalogy: his millennial fever, setting his poem in 1300, in the middle of what he presumed would be the seventy-year journey of his life (especially pungent as I turned 45); the scrupulous interlocking of his end rhymes; the overwhelming spirit of finality in his vast infernal analogy for human corruption and pain. Some things end season by season, some things don't end, some things end once and forever. It's never not curtains for someone. The best students eat this stuff up.

The only problem is that The Inferno in Florence overlaps with the culmination of The Season of the Black Shoes — and, now, Socks. The Eastern Conference Finals, and then the real Finals. To have the Bulls in a Game 5, 6, or 7 against the Magic, or the Sonics or the Jazz, and not to be watching, or to scan a box score two days later — is this not laughably unacceptable? Yet to be able to offer to art students *The Inferno* under any circumstances, let alone during the late spring in Florence — the city of Dante's birth, the city he never stopped loving or writing about, the city that sentenced him and his sons to be burned at the stake — is the sort of scarce privilege that cancels the anguish of missing your own city's basketball team play for its fourth and what may well be its final world championship. Isn't it?

James is coming over to stay with Jennifer and me in an apartment on the Via de Tornabuoni. He's bringing his latest guitar, on loan from Dan, as well as both of his pairs of pants and both T-shirts. There's a TV in the apartment, though it's still not clear whether the playoffs will be broadcast live by NBC, in Italian at four in the morning, in Italian after eight-hour delays, or indeed will be broadcast at all.

In the meantime Bulls fans from Fengzhen to Fiesole, and Chicagoans in particular, feel fairly good about now. Newspapers are thicker, hotels and restaurants and vendors of T-shirts are busier, Scottie Pippen's Dodge Store will move a few dozen more Dodges, and my son has come back to me. The Stadium and its unprofitable density of combativeness is very long gone, the west side remains a catastrophe while the owners and sponsors get richer, but my son has come back to me. When you arrive at O'Hare, along with the huge glossy photos of the Water Tower, the Art Institute lions, and the neon gum-ball lunacy on the floor of the Board of Trade, there is old MJ, our *David*, elevating tongue-sideways above our opponents, a blown-up stained-plastic savior illuminating our hoariest twenty-first-century duomo, welcoming folks to our town with his impossible majesty, but warning them too: ABANDON ALL HOPE, OPPONENTS WHO ENTER HERE. Because our baddest guys — our hired guns and contract killers, in wars fought by soldiers in camouflage or, better, by surrogate warriors in eyecatching uniforms — have conquered every other towns' baddest guys. We feel pretty proud of ourselves.

The Bulls have helped us all to pull through, in huge ways and small, so long may they reign.

I'm already missing them terribly.

# Neil Tesser
## (b. 1951)

*Although* The Playboy Guide to Jazz *(1998) is* NEIL TESSER'*s first book, he has written and done broadcast commentaries on jazz for more than twenty-five years. He has served as jazz critic for the* Chicago Daily News *(1975–77) and* USA Today *(1984–89), and his articles and criticism have appeared in the* New York Times Book Review, *the* Los Angeles Times, *and* Rolling Stone. *He has written more than two hundred liner essays for jazz recordings, one of which, his essay for* Stan Getz: The Girl from Ipanema: The Bossa Nova Years *(1985), earned him a Grammy nomination for writing. He has hosted talk shows and jazz shows for several Chicago stations, done broadcast commentaries for National Public Radio's* Future Forward *series, and written several radio scripts for NPR's award-winning* Jazz from Lincoln Center. *In the early 1990s Tesser also wrote for the short-lived* Chicago Times Magazine, *where he was able to indulge another of his passions— baseball. He is the self-appointed commissioner of the fantasy-baseball Bourbon League of Amateur Club Owners, and his baseball writings include the following piece on old Comiskey Park all buttoned up for the winter.*

♦ ♦ ♦

## *Out of Season*

In the first week of January it squats and sprawls, next to the expressway, cold, stark, and colorless. The stadium structure seems out of place, but not because of its architectural surroundings: Comiskey Park, the oldest ball yard in the major leagues, has belonged to and in fact *defined* its surroundings for seventy-nine years. Rather, the park seems out of place with the dry snap of the frozen air and the unmelted snow on the nearby bungalow roofs and the ice patches in the parking lot. The incongruity is not between the ball park and the neighborhood, but between the ball park and winter. A ball park has no place in winter.

Still it can't simply fade from existence for the season (the way it fades from our thoughts), and so it lies there, dormant. Like a mammoth crocus bulb it waits, through the months with long names, for the days to lengthen so it can bloom again.

Inside the stadium, one of those little tractors used to work the field rests awkwardly in the walkway in front of a boarded-up entrance to the right-field bleachers. Out behind the visiting-team bullpen, a lone squirrel sprints cheerlessly along a gun-metal security fence. In the upper deck, a workman wearing heavy clothes sprays blue-gray paint on the undersides of several rows of seats. Out on the field, two wooden signs, propped up like road-work warnings, flank the pitcher's mound, and they read "KEEP OFF GRASS." In early January, this would seem to be a minor worry, because to get *on* the grass you'd have to shovel about seven inches of snow. The snow blankets the diamond and the outfield, the concrete steps and the tops of the dugouts; the warning track, which rings the playing field, is a skating rink.

The snow doesn't bother Roger Bossard, the head groundskeeper at Comiskey Park; the winter has done what it's supposed to do, and so has Bossard. While the ball park hasn't been used since September 28, when the Sox won their home finale against the Texas Rangers, and even though his thirteen-man crew has scattered for the winter, Bossard explains that his "season" actually extends to December 1, at least. He has spent the end of 1988 rebuilding the dirt portion of the infield, adding clay to the spots that have been worn down by sliding ballplayers and Rototilling the rest to add body to the soil; maintaining the drainage system that prevents the field from flooding in even a heavy rain; and adding fertilizer not once but twice, in October and November, to ensure that the grass will "green up" fast in April. "Like any good farmer," he points out, adding, "I couldn't plan on doing all this in March; the weather's too iffy."

By mid-January, Bossard will have put in his orders for most of the non-farm implements specific to his job. Among them: crushed limestone, used to mark the foul lines and the batter's box before each game; four sets of bases (three per set) and a supply of home plates; and two-and-a-half tons of quartzite, which the grounds crew will spread on the warning track. (On reaching the track, a speeding outfielder with his eyes on a just-pummeled baseball can feel the different surface under his feet and slow down before splattering himself against the outfield wall.) Most major-league ball clubs use crushed brick or cinders in the track; Bossard uses quartzite, which must be trucked in from the Black Hills of South Dakota, because he likes the way its deep, ruddy red contrasts with the color of grass.

This off-season has been busier than most for Bossard. He usually fills the autumn and winter months with speaking engagements and with his consultation work: He advises five other major-league ball clubs, as well as the Chicago Bears (now that real grass has replaced synthetic turf at Soldier Field), about their playing surfaces. But this year, he has also been building a brand-new field at the White Sox's spring-training facility in Sarasota, Florida, and that project has required weekly trips to the Sunshine State. Come February, he'll head there for his annual six-week stay, manicuring and maintaining the training grounds so they'll be as similar as possible to those at Comiskey; that way (so the reasoning goes), when the Sox settle in at home, they won't have to adapt to different field conditions.

Bossard strolls back to the grounds crew's equipment area, where he has spent much of the day cleaning and checking equipment, and past Comiskey Park's main reception desk, the visible part of the stadium operations department. "This desk is always open," says Jim Kucera, the assistant director, whom everyone calls Duke. "There's someone here twenty-four hours a day, 365 days a year." During the baseball season, this desk is popping, awash in details of stadium maintenance and security, fielding everything from complaints of dissatisfied customers to stadium maintenance to on-field security to requests from prospective skybox leasers. But now, this spot offers the repose you'd expect from a ball park in winter.

"The biggest request we get at this desk?" repeats Duke. "*Now?* It's when someone comes in from the outside and points to the parking lot and asks, 'What are all those cars doing out there?' It's like they don't expect us to be working."

If people are surprised to find the lights on and somebody home at a ball yard in winter, it's a testament to what goes on there in the summer. A baseball stadium on a game day might be the liveliest place in the world. The sense of anticipation combines with the warm weather, the peanut vendors and the pennant sellers, the El trains spewing customers, and the dress-rehearsal atmosphere of batting practice; there's a tangible vibrancy to the scene that would be rich enough for Whitman. Against this picture, the quiet winter emptiness stands in such marked contrast that it's no wonder people assume the place is in cold storage.

"Actually, this is my busiest time," says Tim Buzard, the White Sox's vice president in charge of finance. The organization's fiscal year ends October 31, and the auditors need to be finished checking the books by December 12, which gives Buzard and his department very little time to deal with what he calls "the hard technical stuff": the compiling and translating of figures to conform to the ubiquitous "generally accepted accounting principles." At roughly the same time, beginning in September, Buzard's office is working with the corporation's other departments to compile the 1989 budget—a particularly demanding process, since the highly decentralized budget structure includes more than one thousand separate accounts. From December through March 15, they're at work on the forms for the team's 1988 taxes.

"And then I gotta worry about Opening Day," he says. "Once that's past, I can relax a little. I take all my vacations during the season."

Buzard is in his midthirties, applecheeked, and middle-American: His office contains a wood-framed family photo (wife, daughter, and dog) and, behind his desk, a Tiffany-style lighted sign bearing the White Sox logo. He was also a ball player — at the University of Illinois, from where he would drive up to Chicago each year for Opening Day at Comiskey Park — and, after school, a CPA at Ernst & Whinney. When the White Sox controller's job opened up in 1981, he applied and held his breath:

"My dream was to work in the financial department of a major league team — but I wouldn't work for the Cubs, being a diehard Sox fan, and I didn't want to move from Chicago." Buzard admits that some of the fan in him has departed, and that "I can't tell you I ever get used to" cutting those biweekly checks of $30,000 to $40,000 for the higher-salaried ballplayers; but he also admits that "I'm still pinching myself to see if all this is true."

Tim Buzard further admits that he's glad to see the new year. It's easy to understand; after all, the Chicago White Sox was an organization under siege for most of 1988. The team's public and messy threatened relocation (can we go to the suburbs? should we go to Florida?); the city/state/neighborhood haggling over a new stadium; the potentially fatal collapse and seizure of the team's first baseman (Greg Walker); and the general malaise of supporting a lousy team during a losing season, in a city that ranks them second among baseball teams, took quite a toll on the morale of the people who come to work all year long. But now Buzard sees a close-knittedness, a new camaraderie among his colleagues.

That spirit is in full flower at lunch, which is served cafeteria style (but without charge) each day at noon in the Bard's Room. This wood-paneled dining area, famous in baseball circles, is a pregame watering-hole for journalists during the spring and summer; all year long, though, it belongs to the staff, a Comiskey compensation for the fact that 35th and Shields is not exactly State and Madison when it comes to nearby restaurants. As the mostly youthful staff convenes, it resembles a dormitory lunchroom. But there's something of a bunker atmosphere, too. One supposed that T-shirts reading "I survived the summer of '88" might do a brisk business in the Bard's Room.

Don Esposito's office at Comiskey Park has a slightly tawdry flatness about it, sort of what you'd expect if you wandered in behind the colored lights at a carnival midway. Littering his desk and spilling onto a nearby tabletop are an assortment of inexpensive "prizes," including three sunshades, a couple of Yo-Yos, some painter's caps, a miniature baseball bat made of wood, a vinyl seat cushion, a tote bag, a set of plastic cups, two tank-top shirts, some baseballs, a complete series of small enameled collector's pins, and a variety of other marginally useful products under consideration as White Sox party favors for the summer of '89.

"We start immediately after one season to prepare for the new season," says Esposito, who receives this stuff from manufacturers hoping for the chance to supply fifteen thousand or thirty thousand units — bearing the Sox logo and the name of the sponsoring company — for, say, MCI Corduroy Cap Day (celebrated last year). The marketing department lines up the various promotions, and Esposito locates the appropriate items.

Esposito runs the purchasing department for the White Sox. And while the purchasing department runs all year, it runs fastest during the winter. "From December to Opening Day, that's the peak of the purchasing year," says Esposito, who is a rarity in baseball. Most major-league teams don't have a separate purchasing department; instead, each branch of the operation places its own orders for supplies and services, a system that's inefficient and usually expensive. But the White Sox have Esposito, who is charged with seeking the best deal, and then placing the order, for just about everything a major-league ball club might have to buy. (According to Tim Buzard, Esposito's department saves the White Sox perhaps $250,000 each year.)

Right now, Esposito is busy ordering print runs — first for the tickets, wallet-size schedules, and calendars, which have to be printed before mid-February, and then for the preseason media guide, followed by the White Sox yearbooks, and then the programs for Opening Day. He's laying in the janitorial supplies, from the expected (mops and solvents) to the exotic (vomit absorbent), and in early January, he signed the contract for some repair work on the Comiskey Park roof. Also in January, Esposito puts in a call to the Rawlings Sporting Goods Company in St. Louis, ordering one hundred twenty uniforms for the 1989 White Sox, enough to outfit thirty players, each receiving two home and two road uniforms. (The fittings will take place in Sarasota.)

Esposito buys the players' bats and jockstraps and the plants that line the patio areas. He buys the umbrellas that shade the picnic tables in the left- and right-field corners. He buys Roger Bossard's quartzite from the Black Hills. In past years he bought the costumes worn by the White Sox's late and unlamented mascots, Ribbie and Roobarb. He buys the small rockets that depart the Comiskey Park scoreboard after home-team home runs, and he buys the full-scale fireworks displays that keep the crowd in their seats after Saturday night games. If the umpires use up the league-supplied amount of mud with which they rub the gloss off new baseballs before each game, Don Esposito buys more mud.

And of course, Esposito buys the baseballs, for which scouting out the best price is futile. You can't save a cent on baseballs: they're available only from

Rawlings, they're all manufactured in Haiti, and they cost $38.50 per dozen, no *handling* permitted. This is a shame, since the White Sox buy eighteen hundred dozen baseballs each year. The first three hundred dozen are sent to Sarasota for spring training, the next three hundred dozen arrive at Comiskey Park in late March, and then another two hundred dozen are delivered to the ball park the first of each month from April through September. "And we usually have to order more," says Esposito.

(If, during the season, the White Sox discover a sudden shortage in their baseball supply, Esposito will dispatch an assistant to borrow ten or eleven dozen from the nearest available source — Milwaukee, where the Brewers play. The Cubs, a National League team, would be of no help, since the White Sox must use official American League baseballs — the only difference being that these bear the signature of the American League president.)

To top things off, Esposito will spend part of this January asking for bids, checking the prices, and finally putting in his order for a bridge. The White Sox have decided that they need a prefabricated, ready-to-use steel walkway leading from the front of the stadium, above 35th Street, to Parking Lot B, and Don Esposito will make the deal. "*That's* the most unusual purchase I've ever made," he says. "I never thought I'd have to buy a bridge."

Out on the field, the scoreboard clock is functioning, but it's an hour fast: Daylight Saving Time, as opposed to the Standard Time we're on in early January. Which makes perfect sense. In late October, when the clocks were set back an hour, the baseball season was over; and Standard Time will return the first Sunday in April, about thirty-five hours before Opening Day. So, come baseball season, the scoreboard time will again be right.

There's never any need for a ball-field clock to fall back or spring ahead. It's a summer clock.

As I'm walking around inside the stadium, a cat picks me up: a stray shorthair, prowling around the deserted refreshment stands, as out of place in a ball park as a ball park is in winter. I let him out into the stands with me, and he hops on my lap as I settle into a field-level box seat, aisle 121: terrific view, great angle on first base and the batter's box, somewhat spoiled by the twenty-four-degree temperature. The cat is almost all black, except for white paws (you expected pinstripes?), and I decide his name is Minnie, after Orestes Minoso, the very first black cat to wear White Sox.

The memory of Minnie Minoso is welded to the Comiskey Park girders, which have seen more than their share of baseball history. Part of the reason is that the ball yard is so old, but part of it has to do with the propensity of unique events to occur at Comiskey, events that belong to the lore of not just the White Sox but all baseball. The sport's biggest scandal happened at Comiskey, in 1919, when the Sox took a dive in the World Series; sixty years later, they threw a "Disco Demolition" bash that almost destroyed the field. The first All-Star Game was held there, in 1933; on the fiftieth anniversary of that game, also at Comiskey, came the first (and thus far only) All-Star grand slam homer.

The event that spurs this reminiscing is the impending demolition of the stadium itself, with work beginning this spring on the *new* Comiskey Park (right next to the current site). It's a project that has sparked controversy, charges of concealment and dissembling against White Sox management, and complaints from taxpayers, legislators, and nearby residents — the kind of talk that an already beleaguered baseball operation can best do without. The kind of talk that Paul Reis attempts to counter all year long.

Reis, who is boyishly handsome with a tall forehead, laughing eyes, and a well-shaped smile, is the White Sox's manager of community relations. He works at one of the five desks crammed into a thirty-by-thirty-foot room that houses the public relations staff. In one corner sits a control panel that governs the huge message board facing I-94 from the stadium's east facade ("UNITED AIRLINES/THE OFFICIAL AIRLINE/OF THE WHITE SOX/COCA-COLA/THE OF-FICIAL SOFT DRINK/OF THE WHITE SOX/DAN RYAN DRIVERS/BUCKLE UP!/ BUCKLE UP!")

During the season, Reis coordinates the pregame presentations; he over-sees the distribution of the one hundred tickets per game set aside by the White Sox for nonprofit organizations (primarily kids and senior citizens); and he acts as a liaison between the front office and the players, right down to scheduling the public service announcements they tape for radio and TV. He also continues to handle the flood of mail — one hundred letters a week, all year long — from charitable groups requesting game ducats to raffle and other items (bats, uniforms, anything) to auction.

But from the end of September through the new year, Reis spends most of his time on the White Sox Caravan, the two-pronged early-January attack launched upon baseball complacency in the outlying regions. The caravan comprises two groups of players, augmented by broadcasters and Sox manager Jeff Torborg, who visit two cities per day for a series of press conferences, din-ners, autograph sessions, and the like. Apart from baseball's winter meetings and any major player-trades, the caravan — a promotional tool used by most teams — is the biggest news a ball club makes between the World Series and spring training.

The idea, he explains, is "to get outside the immediate Chicago area, to go to people who normally don't get to be close to baseball — at a time when no one's *thinking* about baseball — and get them involved in that way." The hope is that this personal touch will help expand and solidify the team's fan base, and that these folks, in Merrillville and Lafayette (Indiana) and Galesburg and

Kankakee and LaSalle and Sycamore (Illinois), will sooner come see the Sox play in August for having seen them gladhand in January.

That same objective — getting people into the ball park — drives Dan Fabian, the team's broadcast coordinator. Fabian treads some of the same territory as Reis: While his daily routine involves servicing the White Sox radio network (which in past years was operated by a subcontractor), his real quest is the expansion of that network, bringing the Sox into more and more homes throughout the Midwest.

As quests go, this one is only slightly less challenging than the Crusades. The White Sox are not just the second team in Chicago, but the *third* team in Illinois. "There's a lot of resistance to carrying White Sox games," Fabian admits, "in the northern part of the state due to the Cubs, and downstate due to the Cardinals," whose St. Louis home is more alluring than Chicago to the populace of southern Illinois. (When White Sox officials went to lobby the state legislature regarding financial aid for the new stadium, several downstate lawmakers arrived wearing Cardinals baseball caps.) The Cubs's radio network numbers eighty or so stations, and the Cardinals are heard on one hundred ten; by comparison, the White Sox network comprises twenty-seven outlets in Illinois, Indiana, and Iowa.

But Fabian — whose father is the general manager of WGN Radio, the Cub's flagship station — hopes to reach forty stations this summer. He's determined to "get Sox games to areas where there haven't been Sox fans before" — places like Peoria and the Quad-Cities and Terre Haute. "Baseball on the radio is part of the whole fabric of the Midwest," he says, picturing kids staying up too late, craning to hear their nearly voiceless radios squirreled under the bed sheets. "It's just as important that fans in Anna, Illinois, have the same chance to listen as fans in Rockford."

Fabian's job will get much easier when the Sox get better, and Chuck Bizzell — the White Sox's new minor league administrator — is in a position to help. When the Sox hired Larry Himes as general manager, in 1987, they got a man with a known distaste for baseball's version of the "quick fix." Himes treats highpriced free agents like they were muggers and has made only one major trade in two years; his prescription for recovery revolves around the rebuilding of the Sox's farm system, so that it will continually pump new talent into Comiskey Park.

Chuck Bizzell makes sure this farm system runs smoothly, which keeps him "as busy, if not busier," in the winter than the summer. He pays the bills for the spring-training facility in Sarasota, but he also administers all the expenses for players on the six minor-league teams affiliated with the White Sox.

So Bizzell gets the checks out to about one hundred fifty players, shepherds the immigration papers for incoming Latin American prospects, and handles the paper trail for worker's compensation to injured players. That means he also administers the insurance policies taken by the Sox to protect their investment in their eighteen- and nineteen-year-old franchise savers. In fact, the injuries and insurance take up a surprising amount of Bizzell's time — and space. In his tiny office, the top surface of the big filing cabinet sprouts a bumper crop of binders that contain injury reports; the cabinet's wall blooms with squares of paper showing emergency numbers for insurance agents in minor-league towns across America. It reads like an atlas of the boondocks.

"Other than scouting players — and deciding who should *be* a scout or a player — everything else in the minor-league operation falls to me," says Bizzell, one of two blacks in the Sox front office of forty-five and the only black minor-league administrator in baseball. He's a former athlete — a catcher — and now, in his midthirties, he looks like he could still suit up and do the job. He played high-school ball at New Trier, college ball at Illinois State, and then a year in the low minors — "but I could see I wasn't going to make it to the majors, so I decided to get a real job." He sold insurance for six years, spent three years as a golf pro, and then landed with the White Sox a couple years ago.

On top on the ongoing clutter of details that defines his job, Bizzell's winter crowds in with all the tasks that can't be attended to in the summer. In the winter, he arranges the less urgent medical operations that have been put off until the season ends; he works with the team's director of player development, who stays in Florida, to realign the coaching staffs for the new season; he has already spent two weeks at the winter meetings, to participate in the draft of minor-league players; and now, in early January, he's starting to read and remember and file the scouting reports on high-school players that arrive from around the country.

None of this can be done during the summer, when baseball reigns and the multiple details of the minor-league season cloud the air. It's almost as if playing the game interferes with running the shop.

"Opening day to a groundskeeper is the biggest day of the year," Roger Bossard is saying. "You want to have the grass as green as possible and everything looking perfect. So I have some tricks I use."

The words "Bossard" and "tricks" go hand in glove. Both Roger and his father, Gene, who tended the Comiskey greensward before him, have attained baseball legend with their creative pursuit of the "home field advantage." But when Roger Bossard refers to his Opening Day "tricks," he's talking about an entirely different subject:

"In March, I use overhead heating to help get the grass green quicker. I spread canvas over the grass during the day, for about four-and-a-half hours of sunlight. This raises the normal daylight temperature of forty degrees to fifty-six degrees, which helps bring the grass plants out of dormancy a little earlier. I also aerify the soil, which allows for greater soil heating, and when I do the final fertilization, I use a mixture that's seventeen percent ammonia nitrate, which contains lots of iron; that helps green it up."

But perhaps the most important step is the one Bossard *doesn't* take, back when the old ball yard seems packed and sealed for the fall. "The conventional wisdom is to cut the grass for the last time in mid-November," he explains. "But I don't cut it then; I leave it a little long. You see, during the winter, when the grass grows dormant, the top three-quarters of the plant goes brown. But because I've left it a little longer, when I then cut it in the spring, the green part is a little higher [and consequently more visible].

"It goes against the book on agronomy — but then, the book on agronomy doesn't need green on April 4."

# Maxine Chernoff
## (b. 1952)

*A most-of-the-year resident of California,* MAXINE CHERNOFF *was born in Chicago and regularly returns to teach at Columbia College. Chernoff has published five volumes of poetry:* A Vegetable Emergency *(1977),* Utopia TV Store *(1979),* New Faces of 1952 *(1985) — winner in 1986 of the Chicago Public Library Award —* Japan *(1988), and* Leap Year Day: New and Selected Poems *(1990). Her collection of stories,* Bop *(1987), was hailed in the* New York Times Book Review *for its "marvelous deflationary humor," and though she admits to being an experimentalist in poetry and a traditionalist in fiction, this "marvelous deflationary humor," coupled with a compassion for the difficulty of adapting to life's unexpected turnings, best describes her style and vision in both poetry and prose. "Bop" amply illustrates this tendency. Lloyd Sachs, writing in the* Chicago Sun-Times, *describes Chernoff as a writer "who packs a minimalist attention to detail into a maximalist's soul." She has written three other works of fiction:* Plain Grief *(1991),* Signs of Devotion *(1993), and most recently the novel* American Heaven *(1996).*

✦ ✦ ✦

## *Bop*

*from* BOP

The machine would not cooperate. It photographed his original, but when Oleg looked in the metal pan, the duplicate was zebra-striped and wordless. Three more times he inserted the grocery ad. He got back stripes leaning toward each other and crossing in the middle like insane skate blades.

"Please, if you will."

It was obvious that the woman wasn't interested in her job. You could tell by the way she handled the paper. Her nails tore the pleasant green wrapping that reminded him of larger American money. Her eyes never met the machine that perhaps needed ink, fluid, straightening, or encouragement. Her behavior wouldn't be tolerated if he ran the place.

"Can I ask you something?" she said.

"It is free country. One may ask what one wishes."

"You come here every day with something different. I know I'm not supposed to look, but here you are again Xeroxing garbage and your machine is acting up. Why do you make me so busy?"

"Please, I will tell you. The duplication of materials is of great interest to me. Since I came to this country, for three years now, I make copies of everything. If I could, I would copy my hair, my clothing, my food, and my bowels."

She had walked away. He left the office carrying the perfect finished copies of the grocery ads. These went into the large books stamped *Souvenirs* purchased from Woolworth's. He had filled fourteen already.

Now he was back in his small apartment, whose attitude toward America was one of total acceptance. Plastic-molded coral and gold-flecked seats blended with torn leather. A portrait of a sailboat edged up to a Degas dancer. A Cubs schedule followed. Family photos marched along in the parade. A wall clock resembling an owl's face kept the beat. And leading the line was a caricature that a street artist had done at a fair. Since he already thought he resembled a red-haired Pinocchio, the artist didn't need to use much imagination. His eyes were blue points, his mouth a slit, his ears question marks, and his nose pointed aggressively, like a blind man's white cane. His hair was unruly. He was never going to get on a beauty pageant, but maybe his odd array of features would not be discouraged on the quiz shows he loved to watch.

"Please," he'd say to the check-out girl, "what city has the highest ratio of pets to people?" If she didn't know it was Los Angeles, he'd tell her right out. But he wouldn't embarrass her. He'd say it gently, as if he were providing her with a blessing. One check-out woman, whose badge read *Marta*, seemed especially eager to see him on market days. "There's Mr. Know-It-All," she told her bag boy. They both laughed. Americans were very pleasant.

Upstairs the jesters were at it again. That's not what they were called, but he could never remember the name for what they were. How could two men practicing the art of silence make so much noise? Was it the rope pull or the human washing machine they were doing? Were they sizzling down to the floor like angry bacon, or were they sentimental clowns on an invisible tightrope? He hated what they did. It reminded him of loneliness, of which he already had enough evidence. He had taken to tapping the ceiling with a broom lately. The jesters had taken to giving him free tickets to their performances.

He went to the kitchen, poured lukewarm tea into a *Star Wars* glass, and went back to the letter he'd left that morning. "I am sorry to say," he continued, "that there is proliferation of bad ideas here. It reminds one, if you please, of the duplication industry. For a nickel, which is very small, a man can copy anything, including his ears. However, who is it that needs four ears? The same with ideas. Everyone in America has the opinions. I read a paper and there is opinion on where dogs should leave their excrement, there is opinion on homosexuals adopting infants, there is opinion on facial hair and robins. There is opinion on cooking cabbage without odor. A child even has opinions. He thinks the governor is fat. Here is large black cat in ad choosing one cat food. If you please, why is every goddamned thing discussed in America?"

He would leave the "goddamned" out when he sent it to the "Personal View" column of the paper. If it was printed, which it wouldn't be with cursing, he'd receive five hundred dollars. But for now it exhilarated him to curse. He pounded the table for emphasis. The red Formica was unresponsive.

He worked every night from nine until five in the morning. His job was to sit at a switchboard that was hooked into store alarms. If an alarm rang, his switchboard would wail, and he would call the police, giving them a code, and call the store owner with the news. In his eleven months of employment, there'd been only twenty-seven alarms, and most of those were due to faulty wiring. He was able to spend most of his time sleeping, just as Mr. Kaplan had suggested upon hiring him. Mr. Kaplan had been insanely happy to give him a job. Just sixty years ago, Mr. Kaplan's own father had come over here, untrained, illiterate, and if weren't for a *landsman*, he would have perished. Mr. Kaplan got very emotional then and swiped at his eyes with a big hanky and hugged Oleg Lum stiffly and told him, "Welcome, brother." Oleg thought Kaplan might burst into an American spiritual song. Although his job paid minimum wage, he had his days free to do as he wished. Usually he wished to go to the library.

The influx of Russian immigrants to the Rogers Park area had altered its environment. Russian shoemakers hung shingles on every block. Several Russian delicatessens displayed gleaming samovars next to pickled fish in windows, and the library had begun to carry a good amount of Russian-language books but mostly the classics. He had already read those books in Russian, which he had once taught. Now he wanted to read American books rich in history: Sacco and Vanzetti, Sally Rand, Nat Turner, and Howard Hughes. And when he flashed his neat green library card at the girl, who even in summer required a sweater, she always smiled at him. Maybe she, like Mr. Kaplan, assumed he was uneducated, a pretender to the American shelves. She never spoke, but once when he'd asked for a book on the process of photocopying, she had looked worried, as if her patron might be a spy.

He liked sitting at the blond wooden tables with the other patrons. Though protocol barred speech, there was good spirit to share in silent reading. He liked watching the old men who moved their lips as they read. Maybe their false teeth read words differently, trying to trick them. And children, he noticed, read in the same way. For the last week he'd observed a girl about eleven years old who had been sitting across from him. She always used encyclopedias and took notes. She was plump and had hair that wouldn't cooperate. It deserted its braids and bristled in front like cactus. Maybe even American plants had opinions, he suddenly thought.

"Have a pen? Mine's out of ink."

"Please, for you to keep." He handed a ball-point to the girl. Americans were generous, and so he wished to practice in small ways. He kept pens and paper clips and rubber bands and note paper in his pockets for such occasions.

"Thanks," she said and began copying again.

He was rereading the part in *The Grapes of Wrath* in which the turtle slowly, slowly crosses the road. The passage is marked by adversity, he'd have told a classroom of students. At one point the turtle is intentionally hit by a sadistic driver, yet it survives. In fact, the driver speeds the turtle across the road with the force of his cruelty. Oleg had arrived in America in the same way: the crueler his government had become, the more reason he had to leave. He would write an article entitled "The Cruel Kick," as soon as he had a chance.

"What's you name?" she was asking.

"I am Oleg Lum."

"Nice to meet you, Mr. Glum. I'm Carrie Remm. Where're you from?"

The other people at the table were eyeing them. He suggested with a nod that they move outside. Taking her spiral, she followed.

"I am from Moscow," he said, once outside. "And you?"

"Chicago. I'm ten years old, and my parents are divorced. My mother always looks sad because she had an operation. Now she can't have children, but since she's divorced, I'm not sure it matters that she can't have children. I just think the operation was the last straw. Anyway, I like to get out of the house. She makes me nervous."

"Please, what means *last straw?*"

"It means *curtains, cut, that's it, I've had it.*"

"And your mother is alone then all the time?"

"Oh, she calls her friends. But she never goes out. When my dad comes to pick me up on Sundays, she looks a little better."

Cars whizzed by, as Lum smoked a cigarette. He liked the bold bull's-eye of Lucky Strikes.

"You would like a cigarette?" He kept an extra pack at all times for his generosity training.

"No thanks. Kids don't smoke here."

"You would like maybe ice cream?"

They walked silently to the Thirty-One Flavors, took a corner booth, and talked all afternoon.

They decided on dinner for Saturday night, his night off. On Saturday night Mr. Kaplan's son Denny answered the phones for time and a half. Once when Denny had had a tooth extracted, Oleg had taken his place.

He was worried about Mrs. Remm's grief. Losing one's reproductive ability, he imagined, was tragic for a thirty-four year old woman. He might buy her a get-well card, but he didn't know that she was really ill. Maybe a sympathy card was in order, and flowers, but they'd have to wait for Saturday.

"Please, if you may help," he asked a small wizened woman who looked like a lemur he'd seen at Brookfield Zoo. When one got old, hair and face turned gray together, and fine down started growing everywhere. The woman's cheeks, chin, and ears were furry. She looked as if someone had spun a web over her.

"Yes?"

"If you please, a dozen flowers."

"We have roses, carnations, combos, mixed in-season, zinnias, peonies, Hawaiian, birds-of-paradise, honeymoon bouquets, orchids, the woodsy spray, and dried. Can you be more specific?"

"The woman has lost her reproductive abilities. I wish to supply her with flowers."

"How about roses?"

They cost him fourteen dollars and ninety-five cents, and accompanying them was a card with etched blue hands folded in prayer. Inside, the card read, "With *extreme* sympathy upon your loss." He signed it Oleg, hoping for the intimacy of first names. No one called him Oleg anymore, except an old friend from Moscow he saw now and then at The Washing Well. Sometimes it was hard to remember that Oleg was his name. "In *extreme* sympathy," he repeated, liking especially how the word *extreme* looked in italics. They were a marvelous invention. He hoped for an entire evening of wavy italic emotion. When he caught his reflection in shop windows, his nose appeared optimistically upturned, and the bouquet he held, wrapped in paper depicting a trellis of ivy and roses, waved like a banner.

"Get the door," he heard through the wood after he'd been buzzed into Claire Remm's apartment-building hallway. Claire was a lovely name. It reminded him of water.

When Carrie opened the door, she appeared cross. "You're on time. I thought you were the pizza. I was hoping it'd come first."

"I am not pizza. However, it is good to be here." He hoped she wouldn't assume the flowers were for her. He hid them behind his back. Since she didn't ask what he was holding, he knew she understood.

"Mom, it's Mr. Glum."

"Who?" She sounded confused, but her voice was melodic, a song, a tribute. "My friend, Mr. Glum."

Never, he thought, had so much natural beauty been wasted on such a negligent caretaker. Not on the American side of Niagara Falls, not in those Tennessee caves where stalagmites and stalactites are overwhelmed by tepees and imitation Indian blankets. Claire Remm had blue eyes, shiny black hair one usually saw on Japanese women, and a complexion somewhere in the range of infant pink. She wore furry slippers, blue jeans, a sweat shirt that said SPEED WAGON, and no make-up. Her hair wasn't combed but stuck over one ear as if it had been glued there. Her eyes looked dried up, like African drinking holes.

"For you, Mrs. Remm, with thanks." Oleg extended the flowers in a shaky hand.

"Who are you?" she asked, peering over the flowers. She had the look of someone who doesn't care she's being observed, a look he'd seen on sleepers and drunks.

"I am Oleg Lum, friend of Carrie."

"I thought . . . Well, I'm sorry, Mr. Lum. I thought Carrie had invited a child."

"It is no problem. I eat very little. Like a child." He smiled so hard he thought his face might crumble.

"You don't understand, Mr. Lum. I've ordered a pizza. I assumed you two would eat and watch TV while I read a book." Her thin neck wobbled.

"The plans can exist. And may I ask, what book is engaging you?"

"*Pride and Prejudice.* I haven't read it since college."

"Is tale of civil-right movement or of women's movement?"

Claire laughed and called Carrie. "Why didn't you explain, Care?" Carrie shrugged her shoulders and left the room again.

He pointed the flowers in Claire's direction, and she finally took them. "Please," he said, "if problem, I can exit."

"No, Mr. Lum. The pizza should arrive soon. Would you like a beer?" She had put the flowers on a silver radiator.

"May we plant the flowers?" Oleg asked.

"Oh," she said and told Carrie to get a vase and water. Lum wasn't certain, but he thought maybe she was smiling ever so slightly like someone who is trying not to laugh at a joke.

While Carrie and Claire sat on the couch, Lum sat in an oversized tan corduroy chair that made him feel fat. He assumed that the chair was Mr. Remm's and that Mr. Remm was a large man with bristly hair like Carrie's. He wondered if it made Carrie sad that he was sitting in her father's chair. He would have asked, but Claire and Carrie were watching *Dance Fever.* They concentrated on it like scholars at the Moscow Institute of Technology.

"Is good for fashion education."

"You bet," Carrie assured him. Claire watched the television and absentmindedly dissected the pizza, which sat in the middle of the floor. Carrie had placed the roses next to the pizza in a green vase that hid their stems. He wondered whether Claire might reach for pizza and come up with a rose. The room appeared freshly painted, meaning that everything had been taken down and the walls whitewashed. No decorations had been rehung where picture hooks and curtain rods waited. It looked as if a civilization had perished there. The place made him feel foolish. It was not the first American home he'd visited. Mrs. Kaplan's was, with its plastic-covered everything and miniature dog statues and candelabra. But hers could have been the aberration. Suppose Americans were more like Danes in character than he'd imagined: melancholic, spare, and joyless.

During a commercial he spoke. "Mrs. Remm, your daughter is a very clever girl and hard worker at library. She tells me about you. She is sorry for you."

"She is?" The voice was shrill, a verbal grimace.

"She is sad that you are not able, may I say, to reproduce."

"Carrie, why did you tell him *that?*" The entire room vibrated with new energy. He imagined lamps crashing to the floor. Carrie shrugged her nonchalant shoulders.

"I am sorry, Mrs. Remm, to cause this trouble. She is loving you and wanting to be of help."

Now Claire was smiling and Carrie exhaling. It couldn't have been his explanation. Some signals, he imagined, like those third-base coaches use to coax on their runners, must have been exchanged in the blink of an eye. The blink must have been invented for such a purpose. What had happened in the invisible moment was a détente. Finally Carrie spoke. "Mom, he's okay to tell things to. Who do you think he knows?"

Lum smiled. He knew he'd been insulted, but the insult was harmless. Besides, it had made Claire smile again.

"Mr. Lum," she began, "I expected a little Russian boy. You know. Pointy ears. Fat cheeks. Shorts. Sandals. Instead, you walk in knowing everything about me, bringing me flowers. I guess I must be very glum!"

They all laughed. It was a moment of joy, one he'd recall along with his first erection and leaving Russia. A triptych of pleasure. Claire kept laughing even after he and Carrie had finished. Quacking and quacking like a beautiful blue-eyed duck until she said, "I haven't read the card. Let's read the card." She opened it with high drama and stared at Lum's hopeful smile. More signals were exchanged with Carrie, who, after reading the card aloud, stared at Lum too. Mother and daughter then slapped hands palm to palm, and Claire suggested that they all take a walk.

"Better yet," Oleg said, "a trick is up the sleeve. I have procured tickets for an event of pantomime to begin in twenty minutes. We should begin our arrival now."

Claire excused herself. He and Carrie stood in the doorway at nervous attention. He could look beyond Carrie and see down the hallway to the roses opening in the vase next to the pizza cardboard. "Let's go," Claire was saying as she joined them, "or we'll be late." She was dressed as an Indian princess.

Dear Readers of Chicago:

It strikes me as new American that much is made of largeness in your country. Examine, if you please, the Mount Rushmore. Here are the great stone faces of the profound leaders of men. But here is a man also. He is cleaning the stone faces. Up the nostril of Abraham Lincoln, freer of slaves, the cleaner climbs, as a fly, without notice. Or, let us say, a family on vacation takes his photo. There is the great stone Lincoln. There is the tiny man with huge brush for nostril cleaning. Thus is humor because the size of man is made small by large design of beauty.

In America I hear many jokes. Some are about women whose husbands cannot meet their desires, which are too large. In others, several members of Polish nation are trying to accomplish small goal, the removing of light bulb. Their effort is too large for smallness of task.

On a certain Sunday I was driving with American acquaintance down the Madison Street. My American said, "You'll never believe what we waste our money on here," and it is true that in Soviet Union largeness is always minor premise of grandeur. There are large monuments to workers, huge squares to fill with people cheering for politics, heads of Lenin the size of cathedrals, and many women with large breasts, who are called stately by the Russian men. Now on American Sunday I look to right, and there stands a huge bat of metal. It stands, perhaps, fifty feet tall like apartment building. I say to my friend, "The baseball is grand American entertainment. The baseball is your Lenin." "No," says American friend, "the bat is joke about wasting money. It has nothing to do with baseball."

The bat is then humorous. I believe words of my friend, who is businessman. In poor or undemocratic countries there is no humorous public art. History is the only public art. The huge stone pyramids are not meant as joke. In America the bat of abundance is cynic's joke. Same cynic points at huge genitals of corpse. He makes public monument to frozen bat. The lover of art points to the living genitals or makes the beautiful statue like Michelangelo's *David*.

As the huge Gulliver was tied down by the little citizens for possible harm done, so the public shows the disdain for size, even with its power. Thus is opposite, humor from largeness. The bully is, yes, strong, but he is also fool. He is laborer digging in dirt. His brain is mushroom producing no truths. Largeness is victory and also defeat. To largeness we prostrate ourselves and then up our sleeves die laughing.

Thank you,
Oleg Lum

Since it was Sunday and Carrie would be away, he thought of calling Claire and arranging a private visit. The evening before had been a success, the pantomimists having done a version of *Antony and Cleopatra* in which the larger, bearded Cleopatra swooned into the compact Antony's arms. Carrie quacked like her mother. Claire cried when she was happy. Both mother and daughter had walked him home, kissed him good night, and said they'd treat him to lunch on Monday.

If he called her now, the spell might be broken. She'd infer the obscene length of his nose in his altered phone voice. She'd laugh at his misuse of articles. He'd not flirt with ruin. The beach beckoned with its Sunday collage of summer bodies.

"What is your name, little boy?" Lum asked the child who sat next to his towel squeezing sand between his toes. He wore a seersucker sunsuit and a bulging diaper. His cheeks were fat, but he was not tan. In fact, he was pale and resembled Nikita Khrushchev with his spikes of just emerging white-blond hair. He was no older than a year and a half, though Lum might be wrong, having had no experience with babies.

"Do you know your name?" Lum asked again. The sun was behind them, and he felt his skin radiating heat. He'd fallen asleep in the afternoon, and, judging by the sun's angle, he'd slept two or three hours. It was evening. People were beginning to pack up for the day. The lifeguard, who had made a white triangle of cream on his nose, looked bored. Not enough people were swimming, Lum observed, much less drowning, to give his life definition.

Lum offered the child a piece of banana, which he greedily accepted. He mashed it in his hand and pressed pieces slowly into his mouth.

"Bop," said the boy.

"Pleased to meet you. I am Oleg Lum." The child looked at Lum's extended hand.

"Of course, babies do not understand the handshake," he explained. "Tell me, little Bop, is your mama here?"

Bop stood on tiptoe in the sand, wobbled, and tumbled to Lum's towel. A cascade of sand followed him.

Lum pointed at a young couple loading cans of Coke into a cooler. "Do you know these people, little Bop?"

Bop ignored all questions, sharing Lum's blanket, kicking his feet in the air, and humming, "Gee-dah, Gee-dah."

After an hour of Bop's company, Lum thought of asking the lifeguard about a lost-and-found service. He was afraid, though, that the lifeguard would call the police and scare the boy, who looked at Lum with such peaceful eyes, who joyously accepted crackers, and who laughed at the seagulls' W-shaped assaults, at bugs he found in the sand, and at Lum cooing, "little Bop, little Bop."

Bop had fallen asleep at the edge of Lum's towel, sucking the corner he held in his fist. Lum folded another triangle over his back to protect it from the waning sun.

When the lifeguard was tying up his boat and the sun had changed to a forgiving twilight, in which couples twisted together on blankets or faced each other with their legs folded Indian-style to share a joint, Lum realized there were no families left to step forward and claim Bop. It was clear in this instant that he would either have to call the authorities, men whose hands shot lead at robbers, who poked sticks into kidneys, or keep the child with him. The law would not recommend that decision, he was sure, but parents who'd forgotten a child at the beach, in the way he might leave an umbrella on a bench, weren't worthy of a search.

He'd carry the child home with him. In the morning he'd read the paper, hoping for news. And if news didn't materialize, there was Claire waiting, arms open, bereft of the ability to reproduce. She had said the night before, admiring Carrie's impressions of the mimes, that she'd have liked to have had one more child, a son. Then she'd wrinkled her nose, frowned, smiled, looked away, asked for a cigarette, and shrugged. Every emotion could be observed as it changed direction like a sailboat wobbling to shore in cross winds. She'd thank him for the child. It was clear the police weren't needed.

The lifeguard had left the beach, surrendering the safety of its inhabitants to Lum. He'd not disappoint the lifeguard. He put his book and wallet and keys in his back pockets, slid into his sandals, gathered the child up in his towel, and began walking, Bop snoring soundly in his arms.

He'd never thought of having a child himself. He had spent his years getting out of Russia, while other men searched for lovers or wives. Now, diapering the boy with the clean supplies he had bought at midnight last night when the need presented itself, it seemed he had never done anything more natural. Lum soothed Bop's rash with Vaseline, powdered his plump half-moons, and watched in awe as Bop cooed and pulled his pink penis, doubling over it, snail-like, and curling around his softer part. At least the parents had fed the poor child and not in any way hurt him. He was mottled pink, plump, and clean in all places but the creases, which were easy to overlook even if one was diligent.

The seersucker sunsuit was drying in the washroom. The child had eaten crackers, cheese, a peach, and milk already. Bop pronounced "milk," "shoe," "dog," and "bird." Lum pronounced, "Little Bop is very clever." Bop pointed at Lum, wordless. The morning passed quickly.

Walking to Claire's, he hoped that Bop would not soil himself on Lum's new shirt. He had even given Bop a bath for the occasion and combed his sparse hair so it stood in neat little rows, like toy farm crops. He wanted to meet Claire upstairs with the child rather than on the street, where her reaction might be too private for display. Suppose she thanked him with tears or fell into his arms, a crest of emotion filling her chest. Suppose she suggested marriage on the spot, Oleg Lum the father of little Bop, she the mother, Carrie the big sister, a home on a quiet street, maybe a dog, lots of American television to cool his rapid-fire brain. He carried Bop, who mostly smiled. Lum smiled too. It might be his wedding day.

"Just a minute," he heard through the door. As he'd hoped, Claire answered. But she didn't meet him with sobs or whispers of praise.

"What, Oleg!"

"Is boy I found at beach. Is he not handsome?"

"You found him at the beach? Didn't he have parents?"

"Parents could not be located. I wait until beach closes and only drug takers remain. Then I take him home."

"He spent the night with you? You didn't call the police?"

"I do not want government thug with stick in belt to take child and frighten him. I want you to take him."

"Me, Oleg?"

Lum looked hopeful. Bop offered Claire a sucked-on cracker.

"Oleg, let's sit down." They walked into the front room. Carrie was not home. Bop sat on the floor and busied himself by dismembering a magazine. "I know you mean well, Oleg, but laws are strict. If a child is lost, he must be given to the authorities. They'll find his parents."

"Parents dump child on beach like trash. They leave him there. Why should such parents have themselves found?"

"It's true, Oleg, but there are laws. I wouldn't be surprised if his damned Easter picture weren't being flashed on every newscast."

"Is no damned flashing. I watch last night and news today."

"Oleg," Claire continued, "you could be considered a criminal."

"Is no crime to help little Bop and to hope that you will also help."

"How do you know his name?"

"I ask him, 'Baby, what is you name?' He says, 'Bop.'"

"Oleg, Bop isn't an American name. Bop isn't any kind of name. Babies make sounds."

"Bop is not name. Parents are not caring. Police are not called. What should I do? Take baby back to beach? Leave him in rowboat like Moses?"

"No, Oleg. I'll call the police. They'll come for him and find his parents or relatives. You were very kind to care for him. Bop is lucky to have found you, Oleg." She kissed the crown of his head.

"Please, before police, let us sit together and watch Bop."

Claire sat down next to him, and he took her hand. Bop was pretending to water some violets with an empty watering can. Then he sat down opposite Oleg and insisted, plainly, on milk. Claire got a small glass and offered it to Bop.

"He is needing help," Oleg suggested and held the glass for him.

They sat hand in hand for an hour, Oleg enjoying the most mundane fantasy. They were at an American pediatrician's, taking their child for a checkup. She was the bride he'd met in college, and she still wore her modest wedding ring, though he'd have liked to have been more extravagant. She didn't have to talk, his wife of many years, just sit and admire their little son.

"Police are not needing to be called."

"I'll call them now, Oleg. I'll explain. You go home, and I'll phone you after they've left."

Lum felt large tears forming under his lids. He watched Bop shredding the interior-design magazine. The blurry room lost its sofa, its draperies, its rug. Everything was in pieces. This was not to be his wedding day.

> Dear Personal View:
> Everything in America gets lost, sometimes stolen. I lose my umbrella on el train. It is never returned. Meanwhile, baby is left on beach to weather, danger, criminals, drug takers, God knows. Parents come to police. Say they are sorry, so baby is returned. Why in America is easier to find lost baby than umbrella costing nine dollars? But I worry most for sandy American baby who is found on beach like walking rubbish heap called Bop. He is dirty, hungry little immigrant. I give him new life visa, which police revoke.

The switchboard was howling. An alarm had gone off at Cusper Motors, but Lum closed his eyes and listened as the howling continued. He was not going to call the police. Let the thieves do as they wished to Cusper's Fords. The police were worse than criminals. They were blind men, liars, fools. Lum disconnected the phone, and in the sudden silence, he willed his eyes closed and tried to fall asleep. He would sleep until his shift ended, until all Mr. Cusper's Fords were taken, until the police were running over the whole city in search of car thieves and drug takers and lost babies.

# Ana Castillo
## (b. 1953)

ANA CASTILLO *has returned from stays in the West and Southwest to Chicago, where she was born and raised. With a passionate and original writing style shaped by a heritage of Mexican storytelling and the magical realism of South American writers like Isabel Allende and Gabríel Garcia Márquez, she often focuses on the Chicana experience and its sociopolitical implications. She has been praised for her ability to render and explore not only the loneliness and sadness of women, but, as Patricia De La Fuente has said, "the unfairness of female existence in a world designed by men primarily for men."*

*Castillo has written several volumes of poetry, including* Zero Makes Me Hungry *(1975),* Women Are Not Roses *(1984), and* My Father Was a Toltec *(1988). Her first novel,* The Mixquiahuala Letters *(1986), an examination of the changing role of Hispanic women in the U.S. and Mexico, won the American Book Award. Her second novel,* So Far From God *(1993), won the Carl Sandburg Fiction Prize. The following selection, the title piece from her short story collection* Loverboys *(1996), explores the struggle of the physical and metaphysical in human relationships.*

✦ ✦ ✦

## *Loverboys*

### *from* LOVERBOYS

Two boys are making out in the booth across from me. I ain't got nothing else to do, so I watch them. I drink the not-so-aged house brandy and I watch two boys make out. It's more like they're in the throes of passion, as they say. And they're not boys, really. I think I've seen them around before, somewhere on campus maybe. Not making out though.

One gets up, to get them each another drink I guess, and he and I check each other out briefly as he passes me up on his way to the bar. He's a white boy wearing a T-shirt with a graphic of Malcolm X on it.

This is the way my life is these days or maybe it's a sign of the nineties: a white boy with a picture of Malcolm X on his T-shirt and me, sitting here in a gay bar trying to forget a man.

Well, okay. He must not have been just any man and I'm sure not just any woman. Before him there were only women. Puras mujeres (¡sino mujeres puras)! A cast of thousands. Women's music festivals, feminist symposiums, women of color retreats and camp-outs, women's healing rituals under a full moon, ceremonies of union and not-so-ceremonious reunions, women-only panels and caucuses at conferences, en fin, women ad infinitum.

And then one day a boy — not much older than either of these two loving it up in front of me, nor the half-dozen other clientele here on a dead Monday night for that matter — comes into my store asking for a copy of *The Rebel*. I point in the direction of Albert — whom once I was so fond of we were on a first-name basis — and he, the boy in my store, kind of casually goes over to check out what we got on the shelf. We're always stocked up on the existentialists, so I didn't bother to offer assistance.

My partner — who used to be my partner in all senses of the word and whom I bought out a year ago — and I opened up the store about ten years ago. We thought about making it a woman's bookstore, a lesbian bookstore, a gay and lesbian bookstore, a "Third World" bookstore, or even an exclusively Latina bookstore. Heaven knows, any town could use at least one of each of those kind of bookshops — stocked up on alternative-press publications that inform you about what's going on with the majority of the population when you sure don't hear it from the mass media. You know? But no, spirituality won out — since all roads eventually lead to one place, we reasoned.

So along with Camus, Sartre, and Kierkegaard, we . . . I carry almost anything you can imagine that comes out of the East and Native imaginations and ancient practices.

I sat back and picked up the book I was reading. I let the boy browse. I saw him leafing through some other things and, finally, he came over with a copy of *The Stranger.*

"Didn't you see *The Rebel* up on the shelf?" I asked, not really looking at him, just taking the book and ringing it up.

"Yeah. But I don't think I'm ready for it," he answered. "I read this in high school. I think I'll read it again . . . I really like this translation anyway," he said, referring to the edition he had chosen.

I rang it up. But he didn't pick up his package right away. Just kept looking at me. I looked back and smiled, a little cockily. I'm a mirror that way. You look at me a certain way and I respond in kind. Just like with this white guy here who just passed me by again with two Coronas. He looks. He doesn't smile. He just looks like I don't belong here. *I* don't belong here? I helped start this joint about twelve years ago when you couldn't find a gay bar within ten miles of this town.

Me and Rosie and her compadre, who's over there tending bar — the big guy with the Pancho Villa charm and beer belly. He looks like someone's father, right? Not the kind of bartender you would expect to find in a gay bar. Well, just for the record, he *is* somebody's father. His oldest son enlisted in the air force — overcompensating for his dad's dubious machismo or patriotism, if you ask me. He just got shipped off to the Middle East last week. His daughter, Belinda, Rosie's godchild, got married last summer.

That's the way it goes.

Yeah. His wife knows he owns this bar. And she knows all the rest, too. But she's pretty religious and would never have thought to divorce him. Besides, Rosie told me that his wife really doesn't find the men in her husband's life a threat to her marriage. He's got it pretty good, huh?

Anyway, I say to this young man with Indian smooth skin like glazed clay, and the offhanded manner of a chile alegre if I ever saw one, after he's been staring at me for a good minute or so without saying anything, "Is there anything else I can help you with?"

His dark face got darker when he blushed, and he laughed a little, "Naw, naw . . . ," he said, shaking his head. "Actually, I *did* wanna get that one of his, too, but I can't afford it till payday," he admitted, referring to *The Rebel*.

Liking his white, uneven teeth, although I'm not very good with quotes, except to massacre them usually, I said, "'I was placed halfway between poverty and the sun.'" With that he got this expression like I had just done a wondrous thing by quoting Albert spontaneously. I was ready to part the sea if I could continue to elicit that gaze of a devotee from those obsidian eyes, so I dared to continue quoting: "'Poverty kept me from thinking all was well under the sun and in history; the sun taught me that history was not everything . . .'"

He laughed out loud. He laughed like he had just discovered he was in the presence of Camus himself and he slapped his thigh, as if to say, "What a kick!" He stared at me some more and then he left, still laughing.

After that it was all out of our hands. He came back a few more times that week and finally one evening just before I closed. He wasn't buying anything, just browsing and talking with me when I had a minute between customers. By this time we were old chums — talking about all kinds of things, literature mostly. He likes poetry. He writes poetry. Well, at least he says he does. He never showed me anything. But who am I to question or to judge?

So we went to get a taco down the street at my favorite taco joint. I'm really a creature of habit, no doubt about it. There's only one place where I go for tacos and only one place where I go to get loaded. And there's my store. In between is home and sleep.

Anyway, then we came here, as you might have guessed, to have a drink. I used to come just on weekends but since about the time when we stopped hanging out I am here just about every night of the week, it seems.

That night we got pretty "hammered," his favorite word for what we used to do very well together — besides make love. We made love anytime, anyplace, as often as we could — like a happy pair of rabbits — with the one big difference that I don't reproduce — never did when I could and now I never will.

He's really gonna hate me for telling you all this (and I don't doubt that he'll find out someday that I have, since it was the very fact that I'm kind of a public person that scared him off), but little by little, his PMS started to get the better of him. You know, his "Pure Macho Shit." Maybe it's not fair to call what he started to feel towards me that, but I don't know what else it was. I can't explain none of it. I don't know why he's gone, why I'm here worrying about it . . . why *you're* here, for that matter . . .

Except to drink. And we know how far that will get you. It's just like that Mexican joke with the two drunks just barely hanging on to their bar stools. "Well, why do *you* drink?" one asks the other. "I drink to forget," the other guy replies. "And what's it you're trying to forget?" the first guy asks. The other looks up, kind of thinking for a bit, then says, "I dunno. I forgot."

Well, it's a lot funnier in Spanish. Or maybe you have to be Mexican. But for sure, you have to be a drunk to get it . . . or maybe just drunk.

I went over to the pay phone when I first got here and tried to call him. Although I promised myself never to look for him again, I broke down finally — because between books and drinks, there's only him in my head, like one of those melodies where you only know half the words. I called him without thinking about it, like I had done so many times before, and him always on the other end, and pretty soon, he would be with me.

I called the gas station where he *used* to work 'cause I can't call his house, but apparently he's not gigging there anymore. The guy that answered couldn't tell me anything. High turnover in those places is all the consolation he could give me.

Where do you think my boy went? Fired, most likely. Left town, maybe? I doubt it. He's not ready for that kind of wandering, the kind of wandering his soul takes when he's alone and the kind of wandering loving me gave his imagination. Unless I really underestimated him.

Well, see, in the beginning he seemed very cool about my life. The fact that I had not been with a man since college, just women . . . one woman mostly. Considering himself a sensitive progressive politically conscious self-defined young male of color — *of course* he was cool about my life, he said. How could he not be, he insisted.

But that didn't stop him from jumping on top of me the first night we were alone, did it? — when he came over to my place with the excuse to drop off a copy of Neruda's *Veinte poemas de amor y una canción desesperada* that he bought in Mexico where he lived for a semester as an exchange student.

A bright young man, he was. Is. A bright splendid ray in my life. But like Picasso said, "When you come right down to it, all you have is your self. Your self is a sun with a thousand rays in your belly. The rest is nothing." But for a while, he was all mine. Mio. Mio. Mio.

Then his brothers started ragging him about running around with a lesbian — or worse, a bisexual, nothing more shady or untrustworthy (except for a liberal) — who plays soccer and who knows how to do her own tune-ups and oil change. And his mother, about me being a woman with a past. And his father, about me being an independent businesswoman, and what could he teach an older woman?

As if my loverboy were not tormenting himself well enough on his own day and night over all this as it was. Once he was reading a book by a male psychologist that talked about the history of goddess worship and said that in early times the pig and cow represented the female and were considered powerful deities. So one night we were sleeping and his body gave a great jerk and we both woke up. He told me, "I was dreaming that I was at home in the kitchen and I was telling my brothers that a pig was after me . . . and suddenly this huge pig leaped right through the window at me . . . and I jumped!"

Well, of course it didn't take a genius to figure out who the pig was but I was pretty impressed by his metaphorical interpretation of what I was in his life. He was cool about us for a while, as I said, although he did spend the first months doing some hard drinking over it. Then he sobered up so that he could sort it all out with a clear head, he said.

And then he left.

I went on with my business without missing a beat. You know, I got the store to run. And I spoke at a pro-choice rally last weekend. I started dating a woman I met some time back who had asked me to go out with her before, but I was too busy being in love with an existentialist Catholic pseudo-poet manito fifteen years younger than me to have noticed even Queen Nefertiti herself gliding by on the shoulders of two eunuchs. ¡Jijola! Was I cruisin' for a bruisin' — ¿o que?

I stopped drinking too. You know? For about a week. I couldn't take the hangovers, I told my new friend, who was already frowning pretty seriously on the extent of my alcohol consumption. "You drink too much," she told me at the end of our first date as she walked me to my door. Then she turned around and left me standing there feeling bare-assed with my drunkenness showing and my broken heart, which I would not admit to no matter what. Like everybody, she comes from a dysfunctional family and all that brings up too much stuff for her, she said.

But the funny thing was that when I stopped drinking, I didn't feel any better about him, but I did feel worse about *her*. I just took a good, hard, sober look at her one day and thought, who wants someone around who's gonna be telling you about yourself all the time? Especially when you haven't asked her for her opinion in the first place.

So I told her last Sunday that we were gonna have to be just friends and we talked about it for a while on the phone (I didn't have it in me to tell her to her face) and she said, "Fine, I understand."

Yeah, yeah, yeah. After we hung up I went out. I came here, naturally, and around closing time I made it back home, seeing cross-eyed and hardly able to find the keyhole to get my key in the door when I jumped back and would have screamed like a banshee except that nothing came out of my mouth I was so scared by something moving suddenly out of the darkness coming right at me. And there she was. She had been sitting on the front porch all night waiting for me.

Now, I ask you: Is there justice to this life at all? Or maybe the question should be: Is life even supposed to make sense? Or maybe we shouldn't bother trying to figure it out, just go about our business tripping over it like that crack in the sidewalk that sends you flying in an embarrassing way and when you look back to see what tripped you, and everybody's looking at you, there's nothing there.

I mean, I have been half out of my mind since I said goodbye to my lover-boy and I ain't heard nor seen hide nor hair of him since; and meanwhile this woman, whom I forgot the moment I hung up the phone saying goodbye, is convinced that God has put her on this planet for the sole purpose of rescuing me from myself!

Yeah, you heard right just now. I know I said earlier that he left me. But it was me who suggested we not see each other anymore. I mean, it was just a suggestion, right? A damn good one I thought at the time, driven by my self-respect as I am, since he had just told me that he was gonna take a trip and travel around South America with a college friend of his, and didn't know exactly when we'd see each other again. So I decided to give him a head start on feeling what it was to not see me anymore and said I was gonna be pretty busy myself and as of that moment didn't know when *I* could see *him*.

Well, let me tell you how it was with us. We had done all the hokey things people in love do. We stayed up in bed for hours after making love, just talking, confessing all our childhood traumas to each other; we cried together about a lot of things. We went to the zoo, the movies; we took walks and had picnics.

We even kissed in the rain, making out in the downpour like nobody's business.

Which of course, it wasn't. He said to me once, "You are the kind of woman who deserves to be kissed in front of everybody."

We had only one fight in all those months. I don't remember what stupid thing started it, but the next thing I know I threw a cushion at him that must've been tearing already because it hardly had an impact and there was fluff all over the place like it was snowing in the room. Well then, he throws a cushion at me. And before you know it, we're laughing and pounding each other with almohadas destripas, a flurry of feathers and fluff all over the room.

That's the way it was with us. A lot of laughs. A lot of good times. It's real hard to find someone to laugh with, you know?

Like, you see those two guys still sitting there in the dark? Now they're not smooching anymore. In fact, it looks like they're a little pissed off at each other. Who knows why? I was sitting here since before they came in and never once did those two laugh with each other. They came in, sat down without a word, and as soon as the one got the other a drink, they started making out. Now, they're mad at each other.

But those two will probably grow old together because they really know how to be mad at each other, while me and my loverboy who didn't have a bad moment together have already gone up in smoke — with the force of burning copal and all the professed tragedy of La Noche Triste — succumbing to our destiny. Between the sun and poverty there was us for a little while.

Well, someone had to take my lunch away. I don't mind admitting it. I hurt Rosie pretty bad after being with her all our adult lives, practically. I just fell out of love with her and even out of like, since we fought so much toward the end. Actually, I know by then that she was seeing that woman who she ran off to Las Cruces with. But she would never admit to that. I couldn't prove it, but I knew it in my heart — the little emaciated excuse for a heart I had left when she took off. But I can't say I blame her for leaving since it wasn't happening with us anymore.

Anyway, I don't really know why I'm telling you about Rosie. That's all over with. But it's like the one who matters is too hard to talk about. I can't talk about it without thinking I look ridiculous — like the classic jilted older woman. Of course it wasn't going to work out. *I* knew that. *He* knew that. And his family didn't help it any either. But even so. Somewhere in the middle of all its fatality, *we*, me, him, even his mother, who was busy having Masses said for her son's salvation — and I'm not putting down his mother either, in case you ever run into him and tell him any of this — *she* knew that what we had was indelible.

I'm gonna stop drinking. This time not because someone is shaming me out of it. And not because I can stand to go to bed at night thinking of him or waking up alone remembering waking up with him. But because it doesn't help anymore.

I'm gonna stop torturing myself in all the ways that I've been doing; I'll even stop playing all those Agustín Lara records he brought over — for us to make love to. And we did, over and over again.

I saw Agustín Lara perform in Mexico City when I was a kid. Did you know that? He was gaunt and very elegant. My mother was swooning. I was just a little kid, so I was just there. But when I mentioned it to my loverboy, he gave me the sign of la bendición — implying that I was among the blessed to have laid eyes on the late, great, inimitable saint of Mexican music:

Santa, santa mía, mujer que brilla en mi existencia . . . His saint he called me, his saint and his treasure. His first and only love.

I've been thinking about renting the storefront next to my bookstore and extending my business to include a café. You know, café latte, avocado-and-sprout croissant sandwiches, and natural fruit drinks. I think this town is ready for a place like that. Maybe I'll exhibit local artists there, not that there are too many good ones around. But there are a few who are going places — I'll get them to show in my establishment before they do . . .

I think he already split town with his friend; he's probably somewhere in Veracruz at Carnival at this very moment — having a great old time. Well, at least for his sake, I hope so.

You think that maybe he misses me a little bit?

Probably the saddest boy in Mexico right now, you say?

I hope so.

Let me tell el compadre over there to send those two unhappy lovers a couple of beers, on me. There's something insupportable about being pissed with the one person on this planet that sends your adrenaline flowing to remind you that you're alive. It's almost like we're mad because we've been shocked out of our usual comatose state of being by feeling something for someone, for ourselves, for just a moment.

He made me feel alive, cliché or not. Drunk or sober. If he ever finds out I told you all this, he'll really be furious. I guess he felt like he was living in a glass bowl with me. Not that I'm not discreet, but everyone in town seems to know me, or at least think they do. But I like my privacy, too, you know? Mis cosas son mis cosas. I just had to talk to somebody about it. Been carrying it around inside me like a sin, a crime, like that guy in *Crime and Punishment*. And it wasn't like that at all — far from it.

Anyway, I haven't used any names, in case you didn't notice, not even yours — even though people'll figure it out soon enough. And everybody already knows who I am. I run the only bookstore in town that deals with the question of the soul. All roads sooner or later will lead you there.

# Carlos Cumpian
## (b. 1953)

CARLOS CUMPIAN *has published three books of poetry,* Coyote Sun *(1990),* Latino
Rainbow *(1994, a children's collection on U.S. Latino heroes), and* Armadillo
Charm *(1996). He has also been represented in numerous journals and anthologies.
An active promoter of poetry, he founded the La Palabra reading series at Randolph
Street Gallery, serves as editor-in-chief of* MARCH*/Abrazo Press, and conducts
poetry workshops with the Guild Complex. He teaches in the Chicago public schools and
at Columbia College and has been awarded two Community Arts Assistance Grants
from the City of Chicago's Department of Cultural Affairs. His poetry combines the
lyricism of Latino-American culture with street toughness and a near-apocalyptic vision
concerning issues of humanity and justice.*

✦ ✦ ✦

### WHEN JESUS WALKED

"You don't wanna die like Crow McDonald, do ya?"
My cousin just shook his dark bushy hair,
took another beer and tossed his jean jacket on a chair.

I was talking 'bout Crow, a tall hook-nose peddler
in a black leather cabretta and jeans, who flew face first
into a soda delivery truck outside of Ragos food shop,
the truck's red and white logo branding his
beer-soaked brain.

Crow's casket was draped with biker colors while
ganja laughter closed the lid on that cold day,
six-feet under, after a Chicago Outlaw's funeral.

Weeks later on a sleepy Sunday afternoon
I struggled to stay awake, and asked in a daze,

"Cuz, you used ta be an altar boy.
Think there's something in the incense that makes
people slower before dinner and Disney?"
"I wouldn't know, I haven't been to church in years,"
he replied. Then I drifted off and dreamt of Crow's
bony arms all folded up like wings as he said,
"Caw caw, I'm doing fine," and disappeared into the egg of darkness.

Waking up I sing, "We got to get up off this couch
        and find someone with a car.
See ya later Mom, I'll be back around eight."

Then who pulls up in his daddy's white Cadillac — Italian Tony,
with music pulsating the plush-padded interior,
we hop in and take a quick spin,
seven guys filling front and back seats,
it's so crowded we had no need for restraints, with our bony
shoulders pinned against each other, we bobbed ridiculously
to each tune, until fuzzy-haired Charlie Olsen squeaked,
"Let me out at 111th and the Ave,
I want to get somethin' to eat . . ."
Bye to the guy whose cremated parents
were kept at home in two rice-colored jars.

We drove on to find something
to smoke at Finchum's West Pullman pad,
after ten minutes of knocking, we agreed,
nothing could rouse Finchum from his lair,
if he was inside, he must've been out cold.
"Nah, I called him yesterday," Larry claimed,
"Said he's been wide awake for days on speed
reading books, *The Idiot* and *The Stranger.*
Weird, I can hear some mumbling, but there's no answer."

Under late September's autumnal rays
car windows rolled up, I clapped to full-throated
rock gospel on the car's radio,
"O happy days, when Jesus walked, O, when He walked."
In contrast my companions sat, stoned grass-eyed mystics.

Pausing at a four corner stop in a residential block,
normally as uneventful as changing a channel,
we philosophers at leisure missed
the pale blue transparent flashes
that grew bigger as it bounced
off a parked car's window,
too late,
we rolled out
to be struck broadside
by speeding Chicago cops,
Tony's daddy's caddy wavered,
then flipped onto its side,
as the song echoed the chorus.

Each shaggy head emerged from that tycoon's chariot
with the grave spoor of fear
mixed with the hashish breath
that greeted the huckleberries
as they peered in and asked,
"You ladies alright?" Hell, they changed their tunes
as soon as they saw Blackie's and Tom's mustaches,
while the rest of us held the unblinking golden
stare of the zig-zag rolling papers man,
before we heard,
"You're all under arrest, climb out
and assume the position,"
mixed with the radio's blissful,
"O, when Jesus walked, He took my pains away."

## SOON IT'S ROBOTS

Smokers huddle at a thousand doors,
withdrawing 12 minutes every day
from the new-world mirage,
no one inhales the same any more,
as mosquito-mean bosses look for blood in
every dollar, expecting us to laugh to forget our stress.
Ya don't call in "sick" or expect a raise, so fragile are
job guarantees these days, that pink slips
are sent without a two-week notice or regrets
for your IDs and keys.

It's about to rain fiscal ill-will when auditors
show up in green rubber boots and umbrellas,
they'll purge the place for pro-bono fame,
to contribute to the mayor's re-election bid,
fully expecting his guano-covered ship to win.

Every Christmas your debts throb hangover hard,
followed by numb New Year reruns, waking to dark
cold coffee, back to shuffling papers and
leaving three phones unanswered.
Pete, another colleague, has gone seeking
precarious temp employment
somewhere up the street.

What don't you believe? That you'll be sacrificed
by greedy priests serving the one-eyed money moloch?
If you're smart, you won't light another match,
even if it's the white man's most ingenious planetary gift,
you see, the company is watching,
checking conversations, wastebaskets, and computer screens,
I'd say you're better off eating that damn cigarette
when your file is so thick.

Over in a glass building reflecting like a highway patrolman's
mirrored shades, manicured applause flutter
across a board room, followed by discriminating cigars
and brandy poured into crystal goblets, they close with pithy
toasts in celebration of profits after reduction in personnel.

We haven't moved a muscle but we're ripped,
hopes down-sized, and for our loyalty we're shown
the bottom line, and soon it's robots and our exit time,
to look for that phosphorus head of luminous
full-time commitment, amid crushed butts
and ashes at our feet.

# Sandra Cisneros
## (b. 1954)

SANDRA CISNEROS *has worked as a poet-in-the-schools, a teacher of high school dropouts, a college recruiter, and an arts administrator. Winner of a MacArthur "genius grant" and two National Endowment for the Arts fellowships, she has published several volumes of poetry, including* Bad Boys *(1980),* The Rodrigo Poems *(1985), and* Loose Woman *(1996), and two highly praised short story collections,* The House on Mango Street *(1983) and* Woman Hollering Creek *(1991).*

*Born and raised in the Chicago area, Cisneros currently resides in Texas, closer geographically to the border that forms the thematic center of much of her work. Yet as real as the U.S.-Mexican border is for Cisneros, it also stands symbolically for many other borders — the border between rich and poor, men and women, the broken heart and soaring heart, commitment and abandonment — her tough yet lyrical explorations of which have put her in the forefront of contemporary American writing. The following story, "Barbie-Q," from* Woman Hollering Creek, *like her widely anthologized story "The House on Mango Street," examines, among other things, the relationship between pride and poverty.*

◆ ◆ ◆

## *Barbie-Q*

### *from* WOMAN HOLLERING CREEK
#### *for Licha*

Yours is the one with mean eyes and a ponytail. Striped swimsuit, stilettos, sunglasses, and gold hoop earrings. Mine is the one with bubble hair. Red swimsuit, stilettos, pearl earrings, and a wire stand. But that's all we can afford, besides one extra outfit apiece. Yours, "Red Flair," sophisticated A-line coat-dress with a Jackie Kennedy pillbox hat, white gloves, handbag, and heels included. Mine, "Solo in the Spotlight," evening elegance in black glitter strapless gown with a puffy skirt at the bottom like a mermaid tail, formal-length gloves, pink chiffon scarf, and mike included. From so much dressing and undressing, the black glitter wears off where her titties stick out. This and a dress invented from an old sock when we cut holes here and here and here, the cuff rolled over for the glamorous, fancy-free, off-the-shoulder look.

Every time the same story. Your Barbie is roommates with my Barbie, and my Barbie's boyfriend comes over and your Barbie steals him, okay? Kiss kiss kiss. Then the two Barbies fight. You dumbbell! He's mine. Oh no he's not, you stinky! Only Ken's invisible, right? Because we don't have money for a stupid-looking boy doll when we'd both rather ask for a new Barbie outfit next Christmas. We have to make do with your mean-eyed Barbie and my bubble-head Barbie and our one outfit apiece not including the sock dress.

Until next Sunday when we are walking through the flea market on Maxwell Street and *there!* Lying on the street next to some tool bits, and platform shoes with the heels all squashed, and a fluorescent green wicker wastebasket, and aluminum foil, and hubcaps, and a pink shag rug, and windshield wiper blades, and dusty mason jars, and a coffee can full of rusty nails. *There!* Where? Two Mattel boxes. One with the "Career Gal" ensemble, snappy black-and-white business suit, three-quarter-length sleeve jacket with kick-pleat skirt, red sleeveless shell, gloves, pumps, and matching hat included. The other, "Sweet Dreams," dreamy pink-and-white plaid nightgown and matching robe, lace-trimmed slippers, hairbrush and hand mirror included. How much? Please, please, please, please, please, please, please, until they say okay.

On the outside you and me skipping and humming but inside we are doing loopity-loops and pirouetting. Until at the next vendor's stand, next to boxed pies, and bright orange toilet brushes, and rubber gloves, and wrench sets, and bouquets of feather flowers, and glass towel racks, and steel wool, and Alvin and the Chipmunks records, *there!* And *there!* And *there!* And *there!* and *there!* and *there!* and *there!* Bendable Legs Barbie with her new page-boy hairdo. Midge, Barbie's best friend. Ken, Barbie's boyfriend. Skipper, Barbie's little sister. Tutti and Todd, Barbie and Skipper's tiny twin sister and brother. Skipper's friends, Scooter and Ricky. Alan, Ken's buddy. And Francie, Barbie's MOD'ern cousin.

Everybody today selling toys, all of them damaged with water and smelling of smoke. Because a big toy warehouse on Halsted Street burned down yesterday — see there? — the smoke still rising and drifting across the Dan Ryan expressway. And now there is a big fire sale at Maxwell Street, today only.

So what if we didn't get our new Bendable Legs Barbie and Midge and Ken and Skipper and Tutti and Todd and Scooter and Ricky and Alan and Francie in nice clean boxes and had to buy them on Maxwell Street, all water-soaked and sooty. So what if our Barbies smell like smoke when you hold them up to your nose even after you wash and wash and wash them. And if the prettiest doll, Barbie's MOD'ern cousin Francie with real eyelashes, eyelash brush included, has a left foot that's melted a little — so? If you dress her in her new "Prom Pinks" outfit, satin splendor with matching coat, gold belt, clutch, and hair bow included, so long as you don't lift her dress, right? — who's to know.

# Li-Young Lee
## (b. 1957)

*Born in Jakarta, Indonesia, to Chinese parents,* LI-YOUNG LEE'*s family settled in the U.S., first in Pennsylvania, then in Chicago. The stormy and fascinating saga of these moves, having partly to do with his father's incarceration as a political prisoner in Sukarno's jails, is recounted in Lee's memoir,* The Winged Seed *(1995), which was recently adapted for the stage by David Mura. In part because of these early experiences of flight, Lee's poetry, even while it seeks to find images strong enough to rest on, seems always to convey the feeling of a continual searching, especially for the father, that extends into the past, permeates the present, and marks out an uncertain road into the future. The poem "Furious Versions" printed below embodies this feeling, and one is often shocked when searching of the past turns into an actual encounter with a living ghost of that past, as it does here on the streets of Chicago. One of the featured poets on Bill Moyers's* Power of the Word *series, and one of thirty-four poets celebrated by Moyers in his* The Language of Life, *Li-Young Lee has become one of the preeminent poets of his generation. His first book,* Rose *(1986), won the 1987 Delmore Schwartz Memorial Poetry Award. His second book,* The City in Which I Love You *(1990), won the Lamont Prize from the Academy of Poets.*

◆ ◆ ◆

## FURIOUS VERSIONS

### I.

These days I waken in the used light
of someone's spent life, to discover
the birds have stripped my various names of meaning entire:
the sparrow by quarrel,
the dove by grievance.
I lie
dismantled. I feel
the hours. Do they veer
to dusk? Or dawn?

Will I rise and go
out into an American city?
Or walk down to the wilderness sea?
I might run with wife and children to the docks
to bribe an officer for our lives
and perilous passage.
Then I'd answer
in an oceanic tongue
to *Professor, Capitalist, Husband, Father.*
Or I might have one more
hour of sleep before my father
comes to take me
to his snowbound church
where I dust the pews and he sets candles
out the color of teeth.
That means I was born in Bandung, 1958;
on my father's back, in borrowed clothes,
I came to America.

And I wonder
if I imagined those wintry mornings
in a dim nave, since
I'm the only one
who's lived to tell it,
and I confuse
the details; was it my father's skin
which shone like teeth?
Was it his heart that lay snowbound?
But if I waken to a jailer
rousting me to meet my wife and son,
come to see me in my cell
where I eat chocolate
and smoke the cigarettes they smuggle,
what name do I answer to?
And did I stand
on the train from Chicago to Pittsburgh
so my fevered son could sleep? Or did I
open my eyes
and see my father's closed face
rocking above me?

Memory revises me.
Even now a letter
comes from a place
I don't know, from someone
with my name
and postmarked years ago,
while I await
injunctions from the light
or the dark;
I wait for shapeliness
limned, or dissolution.
Is paradise due or narrowly missed
until another thousand years?

I wait
in a blue hour
and faraway noise of hammering,
and on a page a poem begun, something
about to be dispersed,
something about to come into being.

2.

I wake to black
and one sound—
neither a heart
approaching nor one shoe
coming, but something
less measured, never
arriving. I wander
a house I thought I knew;
I walk the halls as if the halls
of that other
mansion, my father's heart.
I follow the sound
past a black window
where a bird sits like a blacker
question, *To where? To where? To where?*
Past my mother's room where her
knees creak, *Meaning. Meaning.*
While a rose
rattles at my ear, *Where*

*is your father?*
And the silent house
booms, *Gone. Long gone.*

A door jumps
out from shadows,
then jumps away. This
is what I've come to find:
the back door, unlatched.
Tooled by an insular wind, it
slams and slams
without meaning
to and without meaning.

3.

Moonlight and high wind.
Dark poplars toss, insinuate the sea.
The yard heaves, perplexed
with shadows massed
and with shadows falling away.
Before me a tree, distinct
in its terrible
aspects, emerges, reels, sinks,
and is lost.
At my feet, shapes
tear free, separate darknesses
mingle, then crawl to the common
dark, lost.
At the brink
of my own now-here now-gone
shadow stand three flowers,
or two flowers,
and one's shade.
Impatiens? Alyssum?
Something forbids me to speak
of them in this
upheaval of forms and
voices — there are voices
now, plaintive, anxious.
I hear
interrogation in vague tongues.

I hear ocean sounds and a history of rain.
Somewhere a streetlamp,
and my brother never coming.
Somewhere a handful of hair and a lost box of letters.
And everywhere, fire,
corridors of fire, brick and barbed wire.

Soldiers sweep the streets
for my father. My mother
hides him, haggard,
in the closet.
The booted ones herd us
to the sea.
Waves furl, boats
and bodies drift out, farther out.
My father holds my hand, he says,
*Don't forget any of this.*
A short, bony-faced corporal
asks politely, deferring to class,
*What color suit, Professor, would you like*
*to be buried in? Brown or blue?*
A pistol butt turns my father's spit to blood.

It was a tropical night.
It was a half a year of sweat and fatal memory.
It was one year of fire
out of the world's diary of fires,
flesh-laced, mid-century fire,
teeth and hair infested,
napalm-dressed and skull-hung fire,
and imminent fire, an elected
fire come to rob me
of my own death, my damp bed
in the noisy earth,
my rocking toward a hymn-like night.

How, then, may I
speak of flowers
here, where
a world of forms convulses,
here, amidst

drafts—yet
these are not drafts
toward a future form, but
furious versions
of the here and now. . . .

Here, now, one
should say nothing
of three flowers,
only enter with them
in silence, fear, and hope,
into the next nervous one hundred human years.

4.

But I see these flowers, and they seize
my mind, and I
can no more un-see
them than I can un-dream
this, no more than
the mind can stop
its wandering over the things
of the world, snagged on the world
as it is.
The mind is
a flowering
cut into time,
a rose,

the wandering rose
that scaled the red brick
of my father's house in Pennsylvania.
What was its name?
Each bloom, unsheathed
in my mind, urges, *Remember!*
*The Paul's Scarlet!*
Paul, who promised the coming
of the perfect and the departing of the imperfect,
*Else why stand we in jeopardy every hour?*

I thought of Paul
the morning I stepped out my door

and into an explosion of wings,
thudding and flapping, heavenly blows.
Blinded, I knew the day
of fierce judgement and rapture
had come. I thought
even the dooryard rose,
touched by wind, trembling
in anticipation
of first petal-fall,
announcement of death's commencement,
would take back
its flowering, claim glory.
So the rose and I
stood, terrified, at the beginning
of a new and beloved era.

It was pigeons, only pigeons
I'd startled from the porch rafters.
But the dread and hope
I carry with me
like lead and wings
let me believe otherwise.

True, none of this
has to do with heaven, since the sight
of those heavy birds flying away
reminded me
not so much of what's to come
as of what passes
away: birds,
hours, words, gestures, persons,
a drowned guitar in spring,
smell of lacquered wood
and wax when I prayed as a boy,
a pale cheek cut
by a green leaf,
the taste of blood
in a kiss,
someone whispering into someone's ear,
someone crying behind a door,
a clock dead at noon.

My father's hand
cupping my chin, weighing
tenderness between us,
pressing my mother's hip, weighing desire,
and cleaving a book open.
On the right of his hand, the words:
*The Song of Songs, which is Solomon's.*
*Let him kiss me with the kisses of his mouth.*
On the left of his hand the words:
*For God shall bring every work*
*into judgement with every secret thing,*
*whether it be good,*
*or whether it be evil.*
Outside his window, his rose,
aphid-eaten, bad-weather-wracked,
stem and thorn,
crook and bramble groping,
gripping brick, each sickly
bloom uttering, *I shall not die!*
before it's dispersed.

5.

My father wandered,
me beside him, human,
erect, unlike
roses. And, unlike
Paul, we had no mission,
though he loved Paul, read him continually
as, republic to republic,
oligarchy to anarchy to democracy, we arrived.

Once, while I walked
with my father, a man
reached out, touched his arm, said, *Kuo Yuan?*
The way he stared and spoke my father's name,
I thought he meant to ask, *Are you a dream?*
Here was the sadness of ten thousand miles,
of an abandoned house in Nan Jing,
where my father helped a blind man
wash his wife's newly dead body,
then bury it, while bombs

fell, and trees raised
charred arms and burned.
Here was a man who remembered
the sound of another's footfalls
so well as to call to him
after twenty years
on a sidewalk in America.

America, where, in Chicago, Little Chinatown,
who should I see
on the corner of Argyle and Broadway
but Li Bai and Du Fu, those two
poets of the wanderer's heart.
Folding paper boats,
they sent them swirling
down little rivers of gutter water.
Gold-toothed, cigarettes rolled in their sleeves,
they noted my dumb surprise:
*What did you expect? Where else should we be?*

6.

It goes on and it goes on,
the ceaseless invention, incessant
constructions and deconstructions
of shadows over black grass,
while, overhead, poplars
rock and nod,
wrestle *No* and *Yes*, contend
moon, no moon.
To think of the sea
is to hear in the sound of trees
the sound of the sea's work,
the wave's labor to change
the shore, not for the shore's sake, nor the wave's,
certainly not for me,
hundreds of miles from sea,
unless you count
my memory, my traverse
of sea one way to here.
I'm like my landlocked poplars: far
from water, I'm full of the sound of water.

But sea-sound differs from the sound of trees:
it owns a rhythm, almost
a meaning, but
no human story,
and so is like
the sound of trees,
tirelessly building
as wind builds, rising
as wind rises, steadily gathering
to nothing, quiet, and
the wind rising again.
The night grows
miscellaneous in the sound of trees.

But I own a human story,
whose very telling
remarks loss.
The characters survive through the telling,
the teller survives
by his telling; by his voice
brinking silence does he survive.
But, no one
can tell without cease
our human
story, and so we
lose, lose.

Yet, behind the sound
of trees is another
sound. Sometimes, lying
awake, or standing
like this in the yard, I hear it. It
ties our human telling
to its course
by momentum, and ours
is merely part
of its unbroken
stream, the human
and otherwise simultaneously
told. The past
doesn't fall away, the past

joins the greater
telling, and is.
At times its theme seems
murky, other times clear. Always,
death is a phrase, but just
a phrase, since nothing is ever
lost, and lives
are fulfilled by subsequence.
Listen, you can hear it: indescribable,
neither grief nor joy, neither mine nor yours. . . .

But I'll not widow the world.
I'll tell my human
tale, tell it against
the current of that vaster, that
inhuman telling.
I'll measure time by losses and destructions.
Because the world
is so rich in detail, all of it so frail;
because all I love is imperfect;
because my memory's flaw
isn't in retention but organization;
because no one asked.

I'll tell once and for all
how someone lived.
Born on an island ruled by a petty soldier,
he was wrapped in bright cloth
and bound to his mother's hip,
where he rode until he could walk.
He did not utter a sound in his first three years,
and his parents frowned.
Then, on the first night of their first exile,
he spoke out in complete sentences,
a Malaysian so lovely it was true song.

But when he spoke again
it was plain, artless, and twenty years later.
He wore a stranger's clothes,
he married a woman who tasted of iron and milk.
They had two sons, the namesakes

of a great emperor and a good-hearted bandit.
And always he stood erect to praise or grieve,
and knelt to live a while
at the level of his son's eyes.

7.

Tonight, someone, unable
to see in one darkness,
has shut his eyes
to see into another.
Among the sleepers, he is one
who doesn't sleep.
Know him by his noise.
Hear the nervous
scratching of his pencil,
sound of a rasping
file, a small
restless percussion, a soul's
minute chewing,
the old poem
birthing itself
into the new
and murderous century.

# Mark Turcotte
## (b. 1958)

*Mixed-blood Chippewa poet* MARK TURCOTTE *spent his earliest years on North Dakota's Turtle Mountain reservation and in several migrant camps in the western United States. Drawn to Chicago in 1993, partly because of the city's thriving poetry scene, he has worked at the Chicago Historical Society while establishing himself as a unique voice among Chicago poets. He is the author of two books of poems, the children's book* Songs of Our Ancestors *and* The Feathered Heart, *both published in 1995, the same year he was chosen as a Significant Illinois Writer. The poems below come from* The Feathered Heart *and illustrate Turcotte's unusual blending in both theme and language of Native American culture with the notion of whiteness (in "Horse and Cradle," his most popular poem) and with urban landscapes (in "Song for the Endless Others").*

♦ ♦ ♦

## HORSE AND CRADLE
### *for Dorothea Marie*

she white woman fell
in love with the
black wave
of his hair with
the way his
voice rose up out
of him from the earth the way
his flirtatious hands
fell over
the strings of his guitar

she fell white woman
in love with
the points

of his eyes the soft
circles they cut
through her shoulders
the way he
came to her bed dressed
in savage feathers
her bed
where she climbed upon his
copperbrown
horse of a back
where she
carried the arrow in
her heart she
became my mother
the gently ever gently
rocking cradle

of my soul.

## Song for the Endless Others

mornings at my kitchen table
drinking coffee
while the city rumbles low
i see the endless others
who live within the walls
as they linger
in the doorways
sit upon the window sills
spin blade to blade
fan to fan across the ceiling
and flutter to the floor

where my woman curls up tight
upon the bed
against her breast our drowsy son
i see the endless others
who between the blankets run
as they wrap
and as they weave
these two sleepers that i love

within soft dreams
that spread to wings and into wings
sweeping out across the floor

nights when i move about the city
smoking Luckys
shaking off the autumn chill
i see the endless others
sparkling blue beneath the El
as they laugh
and as they dance
across the station walls
train to train
out into the streets to tangle
up the taxis in their hair

the endless others
watch my nights
give straightness
to my crooked hands
give me voice and give me voice
chant and chant
within my bones

the endless others
guide my days
medicine the scars
that fill my throat
give me voice and give me voice
chant and chant
within my feathered heart.

# Campbell McGrath
## (b. 1962)

CAMPBELL McGRATH *is the recipient of the Kingsley Tufts Poetry Award (1997) — the largest poetry prize ($50,000) in the United States — for* Spring Comes to Chicago *(1996), which has been characterized as a work "that combines comic ebullience and reflective intelligence in a bravura display of contrasting poetic styles." Born in Chicago, McGrath grew up in Washington, D.C. He attended the University of Chicago and Columbia University, has taught at the University of Chicago and Northwestern University, and now teaches in the Creative Writing Program at Florida International University. He has also received a Pushcart Prize and the Academy of American Poets Prize, and has published two other books of poems,* Capitalism *(1990) and* American Noise *(1993).*

*McGrath calls himself a "fragmented epic poet, wedded to larger social and cultural concerns," and though the two selections below only imply the scope of such connections his other work embraces, they do illustrate another important facet of his style — a burning, near-apocalyptic vision always on the verge of lifting a veil. Poet Garret Hongo has described McGrath's poetry as "ironic romanticism." McGrath is currently working on a series of prose poems about travel.*

◆ ◆ ◆

## WHEATFIELD UNDER CLOUDED SKY

Suppose Gauguin had never seen Tahiti. Suppose the *bêche-de-mer* and
    sandalwood trade had not materialized
and the Polynesian gods held fast in the fruit of Nuku Hiva and the milk-
    and-honey waters of Eiao.
Suppose that Europe during whichever century of its rise toward science
    had not lost faith in the soul.
Suppose the need for conquest had turned inward, as a hunger after
    clarity, a siege of the hidden fortress.
Suppose Gauguin had come instead to America. Suppose he left New
    York and traveled west by train

527

to the silver fields around Carson City where the water-shaped, salt- and
  heart-colored rocks
appeased the painter's sensibility and the ghost-veined filaments called
  his banker's soul to roost.
Suppose he died there, in the collapse of his hand-tunneled mine shaft,
  buried beneath the rubble of desire.
Suppose we take Van Gogh as our model. Suppose we imagine him alone
  in the Dakotas,
subsisting on bulbs and tubers, sketching wildflowers and the sod huts of
  immigrants as he wanders,
an itinerant prairie mystic, like Johnny Appleseed. Suppose what
  consumes him is nothing so obvious as crows
or starlight, steeples, cypresses, pigment, absinthe, epilepsy, reapers or
  sowers or gleaners,
but is, like color, as absolute and bodiless as the far horizon, the journey
  toward purity of vision.
Suppose the pattern of wind in the grass could signify a deeper
  restlessness or the cries of land-locked gulls bespoke the democratic
  nature of our solitude.
Suppose the troubled clouds themselves were harbingers. Suppose the
  veil could be lifted.


## SMOKESTACKS, CHICAGO

To burn, to smolder with the jeweled incendiary coal
of wanting, to move and never
stop, to seize, to use,
to shape, grasp, glut, these united
states of transition, that's
it, that is it,
our greatness, right
there. Dig down the ranges, carve out
rivers and handguns and dumps, trash it,
raze it, torch
the whole stuck-pig of it. Why
the fuck not? Immediately I am flying
past some probably
pickup truck with undeniable motor
boat in tow, a caravan
of fishermen no less, bass and bronze eucalyptus scars,
red teeth of erosion click-clacking

their bitterness. And
the sports fans
coming home through a rain
of tattered pompoms. And the restless
guns of suburban hunters shooting
skeet along the lake. Desire is
the name of every vessel out there, but
I think the wind that drives them
is darker. I think I see
the tiny sails are full of hate
and I am
strangely glad. Don't stop,
hate and learn to love your hatred,
learn to kill and love the killing of what you hate,
keep moving,
rage, burn, immolate. Let the one
great hunger flower
among the honeysuckle skulls
and spent shells
of the city. Let longing
fuel the avenues of bowling alleys and flamingo
tattoos. Let sorrow glean the shards
of the soul's bright jars
and abandoned
congregations. Harvest moon
above the petrified
forest of smokestacks.

# Afterword

It has become a cliché for anthologists to lament all the work they have had to leave out, but anyone who has ever assembled an anthology knows that such a complaint is inevitably sincere. We knew even before we began putting *Smoke-stacks and Skyscrapers* together that we would need to reserve a section in which we could mention a few of the many works we could not include because of limitations of time, space, and money. Rather than apologize for each omission, we offer the following afterword as a suggested reading list for those whose curiosity about Chicago literature has not been sated by the current anthology. There are, however, a few omissions we regret so much that we almost feel that an apology is due. The works of the following were actually typed and biographies written before last-minute exigencies forced us to exclude them:

> **Tina De Rosa.** We had planned to include an excerpt from *Paper Fish*, a gorgeously lyrical novel that many feel is destined to become a classic of Italian-American life.
> **David Mura.** An excerpt from *Where the Body Meets Memory*, set in the Chicago suburbs, explores the relationship between race and sexuality.
> **Achy Obejas.** We intended to use chapter 3 of *Memory Mambo*, a novel about Cuban Americans in Chicago.
> **John Powers.** "Swank" is chapter 16 of Powers's classic of American Catholic life, *The Last Catholic in America*. In the words of reviewer Martin Levin, Powers shows clearly not only that you can't go home again but also "why you shouldn't want to."

Before discussing the primary works, we should credit some of the many careful readers of Chicago literature who came before us. Especially useful for students of this subject are Lennox Grey's unpublished dissertation *Chicago and the "Great American Novel"* (1935), Bernard Duffey's *The Chicago Renaissance in American Letters* (1954), Kenny Jackson Williams's *In the City of Men: Another Story of Chicago* (1974) and *Prairie Voices: A Literary History of Chicago from the Frontier to 1893* (1980), Thomas Kilpatrick and Patsy-Rose Hoshiko's *Illinois! Illinois! An Annotated Bibliography of Fiction* (1979), Clarence A. Andrews's *Chicago in Story: A Literary History* (1982), and Carl S. Smith's *Chicago and the American Literary Imagination, 1880–1920* (1984). The Illinois

State Library in Springfield has also published *A Reader's Guide to Illinois Literature* (1985), edited by Robert Bray, which is available free to Illinois residents. The most complete anthology of Chicago literature prior to *Smokestacks and Skyscrapers* is Albert Halper's *This Is Chicago* (1952). Other collections of primary texts include *Illinois Literature in the Nineteenth-Century* (1986), *Chicago Stories* (1993), and "Chicago," a special issue of *TriQuarterly* (No. 60, Spring/Summer 1984). This latter included a roundtable discussion on Chicago literature from which comments by Fred Shafer, Stuart Dybek, Reginald Gibbons, Saul Bellow, and Cyrus Colter used in the introduction to this anthology were taken.

## pre-1900

As our selection from Juliette Kinzie makes plain, Chicago was still a Wild West prairie town well into the 1830s. The city's most important early event, the Fort Dearborn Massacre of 1812, resulted in dozens of accounts by (mostly white) survivors that we felt were more of historical interest than of literary significance. The first volume of poetry published in Chicago was William Asbury Kenyon's *Miscellaneous Poems* (1845). And Major John Richardson's *Hardscrabble; or, The Fall of Chicago* (1850), which takes the Fort Dearborn Massacre as its chief subject, is generally considered the first Chicago novel. Two of the great orators of the nineteenth century, Abraham Lincoln and Stephen Douglas, were residents of Illinois, but neither can really be called a "Chicago writer." There is, of course, an entire body of "fire literature," created within days of the 1871 catastrophe and for years afterwards, but most of it is by nonprofessional writers and, again, we felt that the work was primarily of historical rather than literary interest. Readers interested in the subject might look at Sophia B. Olsen's *The Fall of Chicago* (1871), Edward Roe's *Barriers Burned Away* (1872), Thomas Clarke's *The Burning of Chicago: A Poem* (1872), and Martha Joan Lamb's *Spicy, A Novel* (1873).

Horatio Alger set three novels in Chicago: *Luke Walton, or the Chicago Newsboy* (1867), *The Train Boy* (1883), and *Walter Sherwood's Probation* (1897). One of the first of the hundreds of mysteries set in Chicago is Robert H. Cowdrey's *Foiled by a Lawyer, A Story of Chicago* (1885). Steele MacKaye's *Paul Kovar, or Anarchy* (1887) is an interesting play based on the Haymarket Affair of May 1886. Although he is virtually forgotten today, Joseph Kirkland, who served briefly as literary editor of the *Chicago Tribune*, had a sterling reputation as a realist in the final fifteen years of the century; his major novel is *Zury: The Meanest Man in Spring County* (1887).

By the time one moves to the 1890s, when Chicago writing truly began to deserve the name "literature," an editor's choices become more abundant.

We included the work of Edith Wyatt, for instance, but left out the equally popular Clara Louise Burnham, whose *Sweet Clover: A Romance of the White City* (1894) is set during the World's Columbian Exposition of 1893. Harriet Monroe's "Columbian Ode" is the most famous Chicago poem of the time, although Daniel Oscar Loy's *Poems of the White City* (1893) are of passing interest to the specialist. And many readers will recall that one of the key chapters in *The Education of Henry Adams* (1907) centers on Adams's visit to the fair, a visit which leads him to formulate his famous contrast between the Dynamo and the Virgin.

Also excluded from *Smokestacks and Skyscrapers* because of lack of space are what critic Lennox Grey called the "social service novels," which followed in the wake of the founding of Hull-House in 1889: Lillian Sommers' *Jerome Leaster* (1890), Katherine Donelson's *Roger Latimer's Mistake* (1891), Preserved Wheeler's *From Side Streets to Boulevards* (1893), and Mary Alice French's *The Heart of Toil* (1898) (the latter two books are actually collections of stories). Opie Read's *The Colossus* (1894), by contrast, is more concerned with the business than the working class. Many other forgettable novels and nonfiction works were published during the 1890s, though we feel obliged to call attention to one of the most popular Chicago books ever published, William T. Stead's tract *If Christ Came to Chicago! A Plea for the Union of All Who Love in the Service of All Who Suffer* (1894).

## 1900 to 1930

Frank Norris's *The Pit: A Story of Chicago* (1903) was an extraordinarily popular book, which eventually became not only a play and a silent film but also a Parker Brothers card game. Had our anthology not become so swollen, we would certainly have included an excerpt depicting the frenetic, cutthroat world of the Chicago Board of Trade. Other works of fiction from this time period may or may not be of more than historical interest. Journalist Will Payne wrote a number of books (both novels and story collections) that examine the intricacies of Chicago business. Among these are *The Money Captain* (1898), *On Fortune's Road* (1902), *Mr. Salt* (1903), and *The Automatic Capitalists* (1909). Other novels that may be worth a glance are George Barr McCutcheon's *Jane Cable* (1906), Frank Harris's *The Bomb* (1909), and Howard O'Brien's *New Men for Old* (1914). Edgar Rice Burroughs, the creator of Tarzan, is from Chicago; his novel *The Mucker* (1921) gives a gritty portrait of life on the West Side. Myrtle Reed's historical novel *The Shadow of Victory: A Romance of Fort Dearborn* (1903) returns to the city's roots for its setting, and Clarence Darrow's *An Eye for an Eye* (1905) inaugurates a tradition of lawyerly fiction which Scott Turow would revisit decades later.

The Little Theater movement, which thrived in Chicago, did not, unfortunately, engender a vigorous tradition of original dramatic writing in the city, although interested readers will want to glance at Cloyd Head's *Grotesques* and Alice Gerstenberg's *The Unseen*. In the literary magazine arena, Margaret Anderson's *The Little Review* for a time rivaled Harriet Monroe's *Poetry* as an intellectual outlet for writers from the city and elsewhere.

Despite the encouragement offered by these journals, prose remained Chicago's genre of choice, both in terms of quantity and quality. A few of the minor poets worth remarking are William Vaughn Moody, who taught at the University of Chicago from 1895 to 1907, and Yvor Winters, who was a student there later. Moreover, several African American poets, such as Fenton Johnson, produced interesting work. Johnson's books include *Visions of Dusk* (1915) and *Songs of the Soil* (1916). Dorothy Dow is the author of *Black Babylon* (1924) and *Will-O-the-Wisp* (1926).

Women writers continued to flourish in Chicago in the early decades of the twentieth century. Susan Glaspell, a major American writer, set her first two novels in Chicago: *The Glory of the Conquered* (1909) and *The Visioning* (1911). Also notable are Clara Laughlin's *The Penny Philanthropist* (1912), Maude Radford Warren's *The Main Road* (1913), and Mary Hasting Bradley's *The Wine of Astonishment* (1919). Each features intelligent, inquisitive female protagonists.

During the 1920s, Chicago's gang wars caught the nation's attention. Two of the better novels with gangster themes are Albert Bein's *Love in Chicago* (1929) and W. R. Burnett's *Little Caesar* (1929). Chicago also has a long tradition of journalists as novelists. Among the novels by newspapermen published in this period are Henry Justin Smith's *Josslyn* (1924) and John Gunther's *The Red Pavilion* (1926).

## 1930 to 1960

Despite the Great Depression and the onset of World War II, a great deal of literature was written during this period in Chicago, and it becomes increasingly difficult to separate books that are of passing interest from those that truly deserve to be remembered. Writers such as Frank London Brown, Leonard Dubkin, Janet Ayer Fairbanks, Arthur Meeker, Sam Ross, Marion Strobel, and Mary Jane Ward are all competent, sometimes inspired craftspersons, yet their names will be unfamiliar to most readers. Margaret Ayer Barnes (younger sister of Fairbanks) won the Pulitzer Prize for her *Years of Grace* (1930), yet we found it difficult to get very excited about this chronicle of three generations of a Chicago family.

Others who deserve at least some notice include the first Chicagoan to win a Pulitzer Prize in poetry, George Dillion, an editor with *Poetry* magazine;

*The Flowering Stone* (1931) was the 1932 winner. Peter DeVries, who set much of his fiction in Chicago, is the author of many humorous novels, including *But Who Wakes the Bugler?* (1940), *Angels Can't Do Better* (1944), *The Vale of Laughter* (1967), and *The Glory of the Hummingbird* (1974). Numerous Chicago mystery writers were also working at midcentury; Harvey Stephen Keeler, Mignon G. Eberthart, Clyde B. Clason, and Thomas Blanchard Dewey are only a few.

Several African American writers anticipated the breakthrough made by Richard Wright. Jean Toomer, one of the leaders of the Harlem Literary Renaissance, lived in the city on and off. He is best known for his novel *Cane* (1923), which is set in Georgia, but Chicago appears in *Nellie Bloom and Other Stories* (1929) and *Guardian Angel and Other Stories* (1932). Like Toomer, Langston Hughes is more closely affiliated with New York than Illinois, although *Not Without Laughter* (1930) is set in Chicago. And Waters E. Turpin's *O, Canaan!*, which examines the African American migration from the South to Chicago, was published in 1939 to wide acclaim.

## 1960 to present

Reading through every work of Chicago literature published over the past forty or so years is both an exhausting and, frankly, impossible task. All we can really hope to do is suggest a few works worth the readers' attention, and suggest that they, like the editors, keep their eyes open as the many new Chicago writers worth reading continue to emerge.

In fiction, a few among the many intriguing books are Paul Crump's *Burn, Killer, Burn* (1962); Ronald Fair's *Hog Butcher* (1966) and *We Can't Breathe* (1972); Sam Siegel's *Hey, Jewboy* (1967); William Brashler's *City Dogs* (1976); Edith Freund's *Chicago Girls* (1985); Norman Maclean's *A River Runs Through It* (1976); and Larry Heinemann's *Close Quarters* (1982), *Paco's Story* (1987), and *Cooler by the Lake* (1992). Other fiction writers of note include Charles Dickinson, Jack Fuller, and James Park Sloan.

One of the most notable literary phenomena has been the astonishing explosion of detective and mystery novels set in Chicago. The profusion of fictional sleuths, both professional and amateur, working the Chicago area beat include Andrew M. Greeley's Blackie Ryan, Stuart Kaminsky's Abe Lieberman, Barbara D'Amato's Cat Marsala, Hugh Holton's Larry Cole, Monica Quill's Sister Mary Teresa, Michael Raleigh's Paul Whelan, and, most famous of all, Sara Paretsky's V. I. Warshawski.

Chicago poetry during this period has changed dramatically. University of Chicago professor Elder Olson's *Collected Poems* (1963) is formal, erudite, and often dry. Published only seven years later, Clarence Major's *Swallow the Lake,* winner of the National Council of the Arts Award, is radically different in both tone and subject matter. *15 Chicago Poets* (1976), edited by Richard Friedman, Peter Kostakis, and Darlene Pearlstein, shows the influence of earlier poets such as the late Paul Carroll, editor of the magazine *Big Table*, and indicates that the Chicago poetry scene of the time was one in which street smarts and experimentation were both highly valued.

Building on that street sense, Chicago poetry of the last ten to fifteen years has been heavily influenced by Marc Smith and his Uptown Poetry Slam; we've included Smith's work, but there are dozens of other "slam" poets we could have also featured. Another important influence on the Chicago poetry scene has been Luis Rodriguez's Tia Chucha Press, which has published many of the city's up-and-coming writers of color. Patricia Smith's *Life According to Motown* (1991) and *Big Towns, Big Talk* (1992) are only two of the many interesting collections brought out by Tia Chucha.

Lack of space forced us to exclude several fine poets currently teaching at area universities, including Mary Kinzie and Susan Hahn, editor of *Tri-Quarterly* at Northwestern University; Reginald Shepard at Northern Illinois University; and Elizabeth Alexander at the University of Chicago. Another Chicago-area poet, German-born Lisel Mueller, won the Carl Sandburg Award in 1990 for her poetry collection *Waving from Shore* and in 1997 was awarded the Pulitzer Prize for *Alive Together: New and Selected Poems*.

As this very incomplete list should suggest, no anthology of Chicago literature will ever be truly complete. Not only is the amount of work written in and about the city overwhelming, new material is being created all the time. If the editors have one wish, it is that it does not take forty-eight years for the next comprehensive anthology of Chicago literature to appear.

# Permissions

*Every effort has been made to contact copyright holders. The editors would welcome information concerning any inadvertent errors or omissions.*

Excerpt from *Chicago: City on the Make* by Nelson Algren. Reprinted by permission of Donadio & Ashworth, Inc. Copyright © 1951, Nelson Algren.

"News Notes, 1970" and "Variations for a Summer Evening" from *Selected Poems* by Michael Anania, published by Asphodel Press, Kymbolde Way, Wakefield, RI 02879. Used by permission.

"For What?" by Sherwood Anderson. Used by permission of Four Walls Eight Windows.

Excerpt from *Seven Moves* by Carol Anshaw. Copyright © 1996 by Carol Anshaw. Reprinted by permission of Houghton Mifflin Company. All rights reserved.

"Baseball Fever" from *Taking It Home* by Tony Ardizzone. Copyright © 1996 by Tony Ardizzone. Used with the permission of the author and the University of Illinois Press.

Excerpt from *Humboldt's Gift* by Saul Bellow. Copyright © 1973, 1974, 1975 by Saul Bellow. Used by permission of Viking Penguin, a division of Penguin Books USA, Inc.

"A Bronzeville Mother Loiters in Mississippi . . . ," "The Last Quatrain of the Ballad of Emmett Till," "The Chicago *Defender* Sends a Man to Little Rock," "The Chicago Picasso," "Uncle Seagram," and "White Girls Are Peculiar People" by Gwendolyn Brooks. Used by permission of the author.

"Dangling Man" by Philip Caputo. Used with permission of the author.

"Loverboys" from *Loverboys* by Ana Castillo. Copyright © 1996 by Ana Castillo. Reprinted by permission of W. W. Norton & Company, Inc.

"Bop" from *Bop* by Maxine Chernoff. Used by permission of the author.

"Barbie-Q" from *Woman Hollering Creek* by Sandra Cisneros. Copyright © 1991 by Sandra Cisneros. Published by Vintage Books, a division of Random House, Inc., New York, and originally in hardcover by Random House, Inc. Reprinted by permission of Susan Bergholz Literary Services, New York. All rights reserved.

"The Beach Umbrella" from *The Beach Umbrella* by Cyrus Colter. Used by permission of the author.

"Pet Milk" from *The Coast of Chicago* by Stuart Dybek. Copyright © 1990 by Stuart Dybek. Reprinted by permission of Alfred A. Knopf, Inc.

Excerpt from *A Kiss Is Still a Kiss* by Roger Ebert. Copyright © 1984 by Roger Ebert. Reprinted with permission of Andrews and McMeel Publishing. All rights reserved.

"The Evergreen" from *Selected Poems* by John Frederick Nims. Reprinted with permission of the University of Chicago Press. "Poetry Workshop (First Semester)" by John Frederick Nims. Used by permission of the author.

"The Journal of a Wife Beater" by Harry Mark Petrakis. Used by permission of the author.

"Where Is the Grease of Yesteryear?" by Daniel Pinkwater. Used by permission of the author.

"Blues for Leon Forrest," "Wind," and "Koko Taylor" by Sterling Plumpp. Used by permission of the author.

"The Striders," "Epitaph on a Street Dog," "Take Care," "Chicago Zen," and "The Black Hen" from *Ramanujan: Collected Poems* by A. K. Ramanujan. Reprinted by permission of Oxford University Press, New Delhi.

"how i got ovah" and "how i got ovah II/It Is Deep II" from *how i got ovah* by Carolyn M. Rodgers. Copyright © 1968, 1969, 1970, 1971, 1972, 1973, 1975 by Carolyn M. Rodgers. Used by permission of Doubleday, a division of Bantam Doubleday Dell Publishing Group, Inc.

Excerpt from *Boss: Richard J. Daley of Chicago* by Mike Royko. Copyright © 1971 by Mike Royko. Used by permission of Dutton Signet, a division of Penguin Books USA, Inc.

"The Fly," "The Conscientious Objector," "The First Time," and "Homewreck" by Karl Shapiro. Copyright © 1942, 1987 by Karl Shapiro by arrangement with Wieser & Wieser, Inc., New York. Used by permission.

"The Kingdom," "Tree of Heaven," and "One Chance" by Barry Silesky. Used by permission of the author.

"Sandburg to Smith, Smith to Sandburg," "The Good Samaritan," and "My Father's Coat" by Marc Smith. Reprinted with permission from *Crowdpleaser* by Marc Smith, Collage Press, P.O. Box 1904, Chicago, IL 60690-1904.

Excerpt from *Born in a Bookshop: Chapters from the Chicago Renascence* by Vincent Starrett. Used by permission of University of Oklahoma Press.

"Packages" by Richard Stern. Used by permission of the author.

Excerpt from *Division Street* by Studs Terkel. Reprinted by permission of Donadio & Ashworth, Inc. Copyright © 1967 by Studs Terkel.

"Out of Season" by Neil Tesser. Used by permission of the author.

"Horse and Cradle" and "Song for the Endless Others" from *The Feathered Heart* by Mark Turcotte. Used by permission of Michigan State University Press.

Excerpt from *An Autobiography* by Frank Lloyd Wright. Copyright © 1943, 1992 the Frank Lloyd Wright Foundation, Scottsdale, AZ. Used by permission.

Excerpt from *Native Son* by Richard Wright. Copyright © 1940 by Richard Wright. Copyright © renewed 1968 by Ellen Wright. Reprinted by permission of Harper Collins Publishers, Inc.